MAKING HISTORY/MAKING BLINTZES

# MAKING HISTORY/MAKING BLINTZES

How Two Red Diaper Babies
Found Each Other and
Discovered America

MICKEY FLACKS AND DICK FLACKS

RUTGERS UNIVERSITY PRESS
New Brunswick, Camden, and Newark, New Jersey, and London

Library of Congress Cataloging-in-Publication Data

Names: Flacks, Miriam Hartman, author. | Flacks, Richard, author.
Title: Making history/making blintzes : how two Red Diaper babies found each
    other and discovered America / by Mickey Flacks and Dick Flacks.
Description: New Brunswick : Rutgers University Press, [2018] | Includes
    bibliographical references and index.
Identifiers: LCCN 2017059112| ISBN 9780813589220 (cloth : alk. paper) |
    ISBN 9780813589251 (web pdf)
Subjects: LCSH: Flacks, Miriam Hartman. | Flacks, Richard. | Political
    activists—United States—Biography. | Jews—United States—Biography. |
    United States—Social conditions—1945– | United States—Politics and
    government—1945–1989.
Classification: LCC E184.37 .A1348 2018 | DDC 305.892/4073—dc23
LC record available at https://lccn.loc.gov/2017059112

A British Cataloging-in-Publication record for this book is available from the
British Library.

www.rutgersuniversitypress.org

Manufactured in the United States of America

We did this, first of all, for our children and grandchildren:
Charles Wright (Chuck) and Marc Ajay; Mo and
Olivia Klatch; Alison, Marlena, David and Samuel Flacks;
... and for our comrades and friends and their offspring;
... and in appreciation of our own parents, Sonia and
Charles (Yekhiel) Hartman and Mildred and David Flacks;
... and to all those who have, over generations, been
struggling to make America become America at last.

# CONTENTS

# PREFACE

It wasn't our idea to write a shared memoir. The suggestion came initially from friends who believed we had a distinctive experience of the sixties as young marrieds who were involved in the making of the new left while making a family.

Our particular "take" on this era—both as we were living it, and in writing about it—is to try to communicate how we made both history and life. Once we got started on the writing (about a decade ago) we realized that the story we had to tell had to begin with our parents. We're both "red diaper babies"—a sixties-era label for the sizable number of children of communists, socialists, and other radicals. Our lives have been fundamentally shaped by that parentage and we wanted to explore how.

So, the story we tell here begins more than a century ago, with our mothers' births (in very different circumstances) and with their struggles before we were born. They were participants, in those years, in the making of a richly layered world; by the late thirties, especially in New York, many people's lives were embedded in institutions and cultural practices shaped by the Left. We try to convey something of that world as we experienced it growing up, and what happened to that world and to us—when the Red Scare of the fifties defined it all as alien and as Khruschev confessed the crimes of Stalinism.

We discovered each other on the eve of the sixties, and started married life at the very beginning of that decade. Together, we experienced a political rebirth when black students started to openly defy segregation and small bands of college students started to protest the Bomb.

We seized the chance to help define and organize a new left. And over the next half century, we've been learning how to balance intense activism with the needs of marriage, children and family life, and eventually how to "think globally and act locally," how to live in a small city in California, helping to make a progressive community. We sought to live both fulfilling and useful lives within our particular left, secular, Jewish tradition, and transmit those values to our kids as best we could. At Port Huron, Michigan, in June 1962, we helped launch Students for a Democratic Society (SDS) as a national

organization for the new left. We came to understand that the left subculture we were raised within was part of a larger left tradition whose unifying
theme was the struggle to make society and its institutions authentically
democratic—arranged so that its members could participate in the decisions that affect them in the course of their daily lives. As community activists in our region we've worked to make something of that vision come into
being. We hope that something of what we learned will be of interest and
use to others.

It should be noted that this book was written by two separate people who
have shared much of the events described. Sometimes, there are separate
descriptions of those same events. Who wrote what is indicated in the text.

The blintzes referred to in the title are a part of our Jewish tradition,
shared, in fact, by most Ashkenazic Jews. We believe that just about every
culture has some sort of fried dough delicacy, and this is our version. We
have used the term "blintzes" as a stand-in for "everyday life," as suggested
by our good friend (and excellent titler) Harvey Molotch. But our blintzes
are the best, of course (they *have* to be, since they must stand in for all of
Left Jewish secular culture) and our recipe (inherited from Sonia Hartman,
Mickey's mother) follows:

## BLINTZES
*(Yield = about 1 doz.)*

### Batter for crepes:
2 eggs
1 cup flour
1 cup water (more if needed)

### Filling:
½ lb. FARMER cheese (<u>NOT</u> farmer's)
½ lb. pot cheese ("pot style" cottage cheese, or well drained cottage
    cheese)*
2 eggs
Sugar and salt to taste

*Both cheeses are generally available only in neighborhoods with many
Jewish residents; sometimes, these cheeses may be found in, as they say,
"well-stocked supermarkets." We have occasionally (in desperation) made
"multicultural" blintzes, substituting ricotta cheese packed in a strainer/
container for the (hard-to-find) farmer cheese.

For the crepes, beat the eggs well; then beat in flour and water. Batter should be liquid, but not runny—sort of like thin syrup; add water, if needed, a little at a time. Place approximately 2 tablespoons (¼ to ⅓ cup) batter in one corner of a very lightly greased, heated, 6 inch frying pan; tip the pan back and forth so batter thinly covers the bottom. After 30–45 seconds at moderate heat, invert the pan over a clean dish towel lying on a flat surface, and bang it on the table; crepe should fall out with cooked side up. Repeat until all the batter is used, lightly greasing the pan as needed—not after every crepe. Allow the crepes to cool and dry; stack them up and wrap and refrigerate until next day, if desired, or fill and fry immediately.

Beat the eggs for the filling, and add to the cheeses—all mixed together. Add a pinch of salt, and sugar to taste, 1 tablespoon at a time. We like them mildly sweet, not cloyingly. Place 1 heaping tablespoon of the filling at one end of the cooked side of crepe; fold the sides over, and roll it up like an egg roll. Continue until all are filled.

Generously grease a large frying pan (or two) with Crisco-type shortening. When shortening is melted and hot, add the blintzes to fit the pan(s). Fry (not deep fry) until tan/brown on one side, then flip and brown other side. Remove each blintz as it is done and let cool. Serve warm or cold, with sour cream and/or cherry preserves (or whatever you like).

We usually double the recipe, and make the crepes in advance, filling and frying them the next day. They can also be frozen (after frying) in a single layer, and stored in a plastic bag. Thaw and warm in a 350-degree oven. Usual serving is 2–3 (or more!) blintzes per person. Enjoy!

# 1 ▸ SONIA HARTMAN

MICKEY:

This chapter is about my mother. I do not vouch for its absolute veracity—in the words of my parents, "I vasn't dere, Cholly" (apparently a vaudeville trope from the 1920s), nor have I done exhaustive historical research. I tell my mother's story as she told it to me—and that's what it is: her story.

In Sergei Eisenstein's 1925 film *Battleship Potemkin*, there is a title card that reads "July Days." It is presented to indicate the period after the sailors have taken over the czar's ship in July 1905. On July 10, Sonia Hartman, my mother, née Miller (alternatively, Granek), was born in a cellar in Odessa, where her mother had taken refuge from the impending battle between the insurgent sailors and the czar's troops onshore. She was thus born directly into the cauldron of revolution, and it was to inform her entire life.

Sonia was born the youngest girl in a family of two boys and three girls. Another brother was born five years later. The father, Solomon, an observant Jew, occasionally served as a cantor in the synagogue, but worked mostly as a bookkeeper. He also wrote letters to America for those who had relatives in the Golden Land but could not write well enough to manage their own correspondence. Though he was born Shlomo Granek, his surname was Miller because as a boy, amid a family of boys, he had had himself adopted by a family of that name who had no sons of their own; this was a common practice to foil the czar's military conscription, which exempted "only" sons— even if created by adoption. He reclaimed his family name, Granek, when he made his way to America before World War I. My grandmother, Chaya (Ida) Miller (actually née Granek—she and her husband were second cousins), was a quiet, retiring woman, who deferred to her husband and to her wealthy brother, who lived in a nearby rural area. She bore nine children, of whom six survived.

Sonia grew up in the relatively modern, sophisticated milieu of Russia's most Westernized city, in the heady days following the 1905 reforms. She received a standard, Russian education, eventually attending gymnasium. Her Russian (rather than Jewish) development was reflected even in her name— Sonia, the Russian form of the Jewish Sarah—and she grew up answering her parents' Yiddish with her Russian. At family seders, bored with the Hebrew droning, she would often bury her head in a Russian novel. "Get that *chometzdik* [non-kosher for Passover] book away from the Passover table," her father would chide. She did love to accompany her father to synagogue services, however, especially if he would be singing the liturgy. After her menarche, of course, she could no longer stand with her little brother near her father, but was made to sit on the other side of the *mekhitza*, the curtain separating the men and boys from the women and adolescent girls. This was her first experience with the sexism of Orthodox Judaism, and her girlish indignation flourished into full-scale hatred of Orthodoxy and religion in general.

Early in 1914, Solomon emigrated to America, taking his eldest unmarried daughter, Rokhl (Rachel, later becoming Rose), with him. His eldest children—two sons and his daughter Roza (actually Rose, a name that was a constant source of confusion in my childhood)—were married and living in Odessa. He also left behind his wife and the youngest children—Sarah (Sonia) and Yankl (later Jack)—who were to join him when he was settled and earning enough for their passage and support. Chaya (Ida) moved with her children to her brother's "estate" in the village of Anchikrak outside Odessa, with Sonia continuing her education. The outbreak of the First World War laid waste to their emigration plans, and the 1917 revolution changed everything. Sonia was, along with Jewish youth in Odessa generally, swept into the revolutionary spirit of the day. Although a child of twelve in 1917, she identified with the Bolsheviks in the October Revolution and developed her commitments and associations with the Reds in the years of civil war that ravaged Ukraine. Years later she would tell of a troop of Red Army men who approached her uncle's estate ready to eradicate the "bourgeois elements" to be found within and were welcome to all the provisions they could carry, but that she was a Young Pioneer and the family was not really bourgeois. Sonia was acquainted with the commander from her gymnasium days, and her presence convinced him to simply raid the granary but leave the inhabitants unmolested—and even leave some food behind for the family.

Conditions were barely tolerable in Anchikrak during the six-year civil war: starvation was imminent, typhus and cholera were rampant, and chaos was everywhere. Sonia cared for those around her, nursing her mother through a bout of typhus and acting as surrogate mother to her little brother—while simultaneously identifying with the Reds who were defending the Bolshevik revolution and continually arguing with her petit bourgeois relatives. In 1922 it was determined that the Miller family would be reunited in America, and passage was arranged for Chaya (Ida), twelve-year-old Yankl, and seventeen-year-old Sarah (Sonia). Of course, Sonia had no desire to leave now that the revolution appeared to be secure. She was involved with other young Bolsheviks in preparing for the bright future they saw for the Soviet Union. Her plan was to accompany her mother and brother to America, leave them with her father, and return "by the next boat." Tearful good-byes were said to her comrades, who gave her a pocket watch with all their names inscribed on the back, and Sarah-Sonia set off for America. They had no proper visas for the various borders to be crossed before they reached Cherbourg, France, their embarkation point, so they had to be smuggled across borders. In Romania, they were caught and detained by border guards. Sarah-Sonia was briefly imprisoned along with other "undocumented" Russians. On the boat, while her mother lay seasick below, Sarah-Sonia found a group of Russian young people and spent the days at sea with them.

The family group arrived at Ellis Island on the eve of Rosh Hashanah. When they were asked, "Does anyone speak English?" the word "speak" sounded like "spies," and Chaya (Ida), aware of Sarah-Sonia's politics, exclaimed in Yiddish: "Oy, they have already recognized her!" By this time, the Hebrew Immigrant Aid Society was virtually administering Jewish immigration at Ellis Island, and all processing was halted for the two-day Jewish New Year holiday. Sonia and her family were detained and housed in the infirmary, where Sonia again seethed with indignation at the injustice visited upon her by the forces of Jewish religion. She later told of idly reaching up to the top bunk of the double-decker in which she lay and finding a Russian book that some other immigrant had left behind. She claimed that it was that book that allowed her to survive the days on Ellis Island—which grew to a week because Solomon Miller, who was supposed to be their sponsor, could not be found. As it turned out, the man Sonia's little family was looking for had taken back his "real" name, Granek, when he arrived in free America.

Eventually, Solomon Granek did appear and took them off the island—however, he couldn't take them home, because he was living behind a laundry, as was known from his letters, but he was also living with the laundress, which they hadn't known. The older sister Rachel (now Rose) had already married, and Sarah-Sonia was left as head of the household consisting of herself, her mother, and her young brother.

Moving to Amboy Street in the Brownsville section of Brooklyn, New York, Sonia found employment through family friends. She began working in a shoe factory, and her meager paycheck was the basic support of her now decimated family. Her little brother, Yankl—now Jack—was left to grow up in the mean streets of Brownsville, soon falling into the ways of the street gangs of the 1920s. Sonia later reported that she was so lonely for the culture she had left behind that when she saw anyone on the subway reading a Russian newspaper—even the rightist newspaper, even if the reader was an old drunken Cossack—she felt like embracing him or her. The shop where she worked and the streets of Brownsville were alive with Yiddish, spoken by thousands of workers, many of whom were members of trade unions (garment workers' unions or the nascent shoe workers' and fur/leather workers' unions), and some were members of the various socialist groupings or of the pro-Bolshevik Communist Party USA. Naturally, Sonia gravitated toward the latter and soon joined the Young Workers' Club, which grew into the Young Communist League. She also helped organize the shoe workers' union, using the shoe factory's fire escapes (while pregnant with her first child) to distribute leaflets to the workers within when the main entrances were barricaded against union organizers. Eventually, she was blacklisted by the shop owners from working in the industry.

At one of the many street-corner rallies often in progress on Pitkin Avenue in Brownsville, a speaker was haranguing the crowd on some subject or other. A young man in the throng (Sonia later reported) asked some "intelligent questions" of the speaker. He caught her eye, and they soon began a romance. The young man was Yekhiel (Charles) Hartman, and after some months of courtship they decided to live together. Yekhiel said that he would marry Sonia in any fashion she chose, if she wished; Chaya (Ida) very much wanted them to get married, and he was willing. Sonia, arguing with her mother, agreed to any civil ceremony—anything but a huppah (traditional Jewish wedding canopy)—which she adamantly and categorically rejected. Ida rejoined that if it wasn't a huppah, then it wasn't a wedding anyway, so it wasn't necessary. "So we don't need anything," said Sonia, and thus began the common-law marriage (later "legitimated") that was to produce two children and last until Yekhiel's death thirty-five years later. They, like many radicals of the 1920s, did not believe that their commitment to each other required the sanction of either church or state.

Yekhiel, who was thirteen years older than Sonia, had come to America in 1912 from Warsaw, Poland. He did not speak Russian; he barely spoke Polish. His language was Yiddish, and, by the time they met, Sonia's life was also conducted primarily in Yiddish (learned on the streets of Brownsville, in Brooklyn)—with a little English on the side. Yekhiel was nicknamed "Khiel" by his family (resulting in "Charles," bestowed by a clerk of the steamship company that brought him) and was thus known as Khiel to his kin. In the garment shop where he worked as a machine operator he was generally called Hartman, and in the Communist Party he was known as Comrade Hartman. For Sonia, the word *Khiel* sounded akin to a Russian obscenity, so she always (and forever) called him Hartman. Sonia was soon taught by her husband to read and write Yiddish and became a reader and supporter of the *Morgn Freiheit* (Morning Freedom), the daily Yiddish newspaper within the communist orbit. Their lives revolved in that sphere: in the shop, they had been members of David Dubinsky's International Ladies' Garment Workers' Union (ILGWU), but it was the Communist Party's dual unionism that they were soon involved with—trying to create a parallel Communist-led union to rival the ILGWU. In their friendship circles, it was fellow Party members who met together for social interaction; in their cultural lives, it was studying Marxism with activist and publisher Alexander Trachtenberg or going to movie or book discussion groups—all in Yiddish, all within the Jewish community. Sonia later boasted that the leaders of both factions of the Communist Party USA, William Z. Foster and Jay Lovestone, had been in her home. (She seemed to have had "an eye" for Lovestone, but eventually became a Fosterite—while Lovestone went on to an anti-communist career eventually in alliance with the Central Intelligence Agency [CIA].)

Sonia and Hartman had an "egalitarian" marriage: both worked and both cared for the home and family obligations (and Hartman, a quiet sort, was, much to his chagrin, often called "Comrade Miller"). They seemed to have an (unspoken) philosophy that life demanded a certain amount of crap and that if a couple was sharing a life, they had to "share the shit" as well: if only one member worked for money, the other worked at home; if both worked out-side, the housework, too, was done by both. (I grew up within this approach.) When their son was born at the end of 1929, they named him Hirsh Naftali (Harold Anatol, called Hershl), in honor of two martyrs of the "cause": Hirsh Lekert, an 1880s would-be assassin of the czarist governor of Vilna (Lithua-nia), and Naftali Botwin, a Polish Jew who was executed in Poland, in 1927, for killing a police informer.

In 1931 Sonia Miller (as she was then known) and her (common-law) hus-band and young son fulfilled her dream and returned to the Soviet Union, planning to live in the Union of Soviet Socialist Republics (USSR) and help build the world's first socialist state. They were among a number of American Communists—some, like them, former immigrants and some, like Eugene Dennis (later general secretary of the American Communist Party), native-born Americans—who saw their personal and political destiny in Russia. Hartman was trained as a welder, given work laying railroad tracks, and dis-patched over much of the country. Sonia was assigned as a translator, working with American engineers sent by Henry Ford. Sonia and Hartman did not find a socialist paradise—but they weren't necessarily looking for one. Sonia was home, and she was secure and comfortable in her own language and culture. Hartman, however, was more of a foreigner than he had been in New York, and he was treated simply as a pair of hands and eventually sent to work back in the garment shop—which he hated. Sonia, too, had prob-lems: she later told of working with a group of Soviet and American engi-neers who were having trouble with a recalcitrant truck. The Russians stood around stroking their beards, developing hypotheses about the possible cause of the difficulty and complaining about poor workmanship; the Ameri-can engineers soon rolled up their sleeves and crawled under the machinery to fix it. Sonia, admiring the American engineers, realized that she might have become an acculturated American. She was not shy about complaining to various bureaucrats at various agencies about promises not kept, accommo-dations and services not provided, and a general "who cares?" attitude that soon became synonymous with the state socialism of the USSR. Moreover, times were hard, and there was barely enough food for the family. Though they weren't truly disillusioned with the socialist dream, they did decide to return to the United States—probably thereby preventing their destruction by Joseph Stalin or Adolf Hitler. (Sonia's two older brothers eventually served in the Red Army during World War II and were killed at the front, along with two of their sons. Sonia's elder sister Reyza, who during the war was evacuated to Tbilisi, in the Caucasus Mountains, returned to her old apartment in Odessa in 1944 and eventually immigrated to the United States in the 1970s.) Sonia, never shy about protesting injustices, would undoubtedly not have fared well during the purges of the 1930s and 1940s; some of her closest friends were imprisoned in that period.

Sonia had traveled on her old Russian passport; in order to return to the United States, she needed to marry Hartman, who was an American citizen. They went to some sort of bureau and were married by a Soviet official. Their three-year-old son, Hershl, witnessed the event. The official looked from Hershl to Hartman to Sonia, a perplexed expression on his face. "Sometimes," said Hartman, "it happens that way."

Sonia and her family returned to a United States mired in the Great Depression. They threw themselves into union organizing and Party work, moving to a new apartment every year to take advantage of the offered rent concessions—nine months' rent for a year's lease. They helped organize "rent parties" to pay the rent of their even poorer neighbors; they carried the furniture off the street back into the apartments of evicted tenants; and they organized and joined rallies of the unemployed, with Hartman having his nose broken by a police officer's billy club at a city hall demonstration. They joined in the general spirit of labor's demanding its share of the American pie; they worked politically as Communists, helping to elect Communists Ben Davis and Pete Cacchione to the New York City Council; they marched for the Loyalists in Spain (Hershl and Hartman also picking up discarded cigarette packets to send the tinfoil for making Loyalist bullets for Spain)—and they also helped build the Jewish Left.

The Yiddish secular socialist movement in America had its roots in the political formations of late nineteenth-century Russia. In October 1897, thirteen workers—artisans and intellectuals of several cities representing socialist circles and trade groups and the two illegal Yiddish periodicals— met in Vilna to establish the Jewish Labor Bund of Russia and Poland. It sought to propagandize Jewish workers in their own language and to defend their civil and political rights—all within the overall sphere of the Russian revolutionary socialist movement. At first, the Bund (which means "union")

FIGURE 1.1. The Hartman family upon return from the Soviet Union, circa 1933
(*from left to right*: Sonia, Hershl, Ida [Sonia's mother], and Yekhiel [Hartman])

considered itself solely an organization of Jewish workers in Poland and
Russia. In 1898 it played an important role in the founding of the Russian
Social Democratic Party, which it joined as an autonomous unit.[1]

As the Jewish labor movement developed in the United States, and as it
played a critical role in the development of overall American labor and progressive movements, it was possible to be a significant actor on the stage of

the American Left in the first half of the twentieth century as part of the Yiddish secular movement—even while speaking Yiddish.

In 1930 the International Workers Order (IWO) was created by former members of the Workmen's Circle, a basically social democratic/socialist, mutual self-help, Jewish organization. A majority of the Workmen's Circle membership saw themselves as closer to the Communist Party USA, and an internal struggle for the soul of the organization began in the late 1920s, centering on differing views of Soviet Russia and on how militant the Workmen's Circle should be in the labor struggles of the period. Members of the Left group were readers and supporters of the *Morgn Freiheit*. The Left faction had also organized secular Jewish schools within the Workmen's Circle—after public *shules*, which taught Yiddish language and literature ("Poppa in shop" was the first sentence of the primer); Jewish biblical and modern history (from a distinctly materialist and anthropological, rather than a faith-based, perspective); and cultural activities, such as singing, dancing, and dramatics. By 1929 these *shules* numbered eighty-three, across the United States and Canada. In March 1930, five thousand Left (essentially pro-Soviet) members of the Workmen's Circle were expelled from the social democratic organization; they became the base for the IWO, consisting of 157 "branches." In the next few years, they were joined by four thousand members of the Hungarian Workers' Educational and Benevolent Society and another four thousand from the Slovak Workers' Society and were affiliated with the Russian National Mutual Aid Society. The IWO, in contrast to the Workmen's Circle, had a truly internationalist perspective. In July 1933, the Jewish Section was officially established; it was renamed the Jewish People's Fraternal Order (JPFO; known as the *ordn* in Yiddish) in the 1940s.

The IWO became a means of organizing immigrant workers into the Communist Party orbit, recognizing the workers' needs for social, political, and cultural expression in their own language(s). Many self-help organizations existed in immigrant communities—among Jews, they were called *landsmanshaftn*—which provided burial benefits, mutual aid of all kinds, and a sense of belonging for these aliens in a strange land, but these often had no political dimension. The JPFO developed a myriad of institutions including choruses (*gezangs fareins*), summer camps for children and adults, publications (in Yiddish and English), cemeteries, an educational bureau overseeing the system of children's *shules* teaching Yiddish language and secularism, and social/cultural "branches"—clubs that were usually organized by neighborhood (or trade) and met weekly. In addition, a low-cost medical, dental, and life insurance system was created (a health maintenance organization [HMO] precursor) and plans were made for an old-age home. In short, the various functions of fraternal organizations were combined with some functions of educational institutions to create an organization for a number of immigrant groups—each with its own language—and all within the highly universalist politics of the Communist Party USA. At its height, after World War II, the IWO had almost two hundred thousand members.[2]

Sonia Hartman, American worker and Communist, and her family lived a life within the movement that Chaim Zhitlovsky, the philosopher of Jewish secularism, helped create.[3] The framework was the JPFO—especially since the Sonia and Hartman's garment workers' union, the ILGWU, was firmly in the hands of the "right-wing Social Fascist David Dubinsky and his crowd" and union activity became less possible for Communist workers. (Even the ILGWU saw the necessity of relating to its members as Jews or Italians— not simply as garment workers: the union's publication, *Justice*, appeared in at least three languages—Yiddish, Italian, and Spanish.) Hershl went to *shule* (with English as his third language, after Yiddish and Russian) and to Camp Kinderland, and Sonia sang in the *gezangs fareyn*, the Jewish People's Philharmonic Chorus (where director Jacob Schaefer arranged folk music for mixed chorus, wrote operettas and oratorios with librettos by Yiddish poets, and taught unschooled immigrant garment workers who had never seen a musical score to sing in eight-part harmony and present concerts to a packed Carnegie Hall). Yekhiel Hartman never missed an IWO branch meeting, read the *Morgn Freiheit* on the subway to and from the shop, and pored over the Yiddish literature of Sholem Aleichem, the proletarian poets of the sweatshops, the Soviet Yiddish writers, and, above all, I. L. Peretz, in much the same way as his forefathers had studied the Talmud: reading and rereading, constantly gleaning new meaning and new pleasure from the process. Their cultural and political and social and family and, ultimately, human identity was shaped by and lived out within the JPFO-IWO.

Zhitlovsky had argued, "*Vos mer mentch, altz mer yid; vos mer yid, altz mer mentch*" (The more a Jew was a *mensch*, the more he was a Jew; the more he was a Jew, the more he was a *mensch*). The Hartman family lived that maxim.

The Depression hit the Hartman family hard, with both Sonia and Hartman mostly unemployed. Their political commitments continued unabated with a new sense of self-sacrifice. Once, when a collection basket was passed to help sustain the *Morgn Freiheit*, Sonia had no money to put in. With a sob, she deposited the watch given to her by her friends when she left Russia. In later years, she presented this action as an example of the level of "sekrrifice" (her pronunciation) necessary for a serious, valid social movement and was dismissive of anything less as armchair posturing. It is interesting to note that the "sekrrifice" she valued was not necessarily "putting one's body on the line," not necessarily a supreme sacrifice to save another's life, but the giving of one's all for a newspaper, a Yiddish newspaper! Clearly she saw that newspaper (and the culture it represented) as her social, even revolutionary, movement. (She was, however, always a bit skeptical of movement functionaries, who were paid by contributions that Sonia and her comrades made and who lived on a higher economic level than the workers who paid them.)

In January 1940, after Sonia had been blinded in one eye by a retinal detachment and after numerous abortions (because the family could not afford to grow during the 1930s), she gave birth to me, Miriam Sally Hartman. My parents named me Miriam (for Sonia's girlhood friend Mira, who had died in an accident) and Sally (for Ida's sister, Shayneh-Layeh). The shift from Mira to Miriam was done deliberately in the face of developing Hitlerism. "A biblically Jewish name *oyf tzelukhes* [for spite]," said Sonia. The birth was by Cesarean section because Sonia was recovering from a failed surgical attempt to reattach her retina. She later told of having her long hair parted on the pillow, with sandbags placed on either side to prevent her from moving her head—for days at a time. It was in this condition that she gave birth. Her recovery period was, therefore, quite long, and Hartman and ten-year-old Hershl, at home by themselves, came to visit her with visible signs of malnutrition. My layette and baby furniture were sent from Macy's by a family friend. Times were, indeed, hard.

I (as Hershl before me) was raised speaking Yiddish, learning English only shortly before I was enrolled in public school in the Bronx.

# 2 ▸ A RED DIAPER BABY

## Mickey's Story

I WAS BROUGHT up in two seemingly contradictory contexts: a sense of alienation (from the larger society) and a profound sense of belonging (to a vitally important and sustaining subgroup). I spoke only Yiddish until shortly before I entered kindergarten at five years old. My parents were as different from the "American family" as one could imagine: immigrant, Yiddish-accented-English-speaking, working-class, late middle-aged, Bolshevik-style Communists. We lived in a lower-middle-class neighborhood where the wave of wartime (World War II) prosperity left us with a largish apartment and a boarder in one room to help pay the rent. Except for the accents, our neighbors and the parents of the kids I went to school and grew up with did not resemble my parents. I was taught that we were different from our neighbors—we had a "higher" consciousness, we were "political," we took responsibility for improving the world around us. The prevailing society and culture (I was taught) were capitalistic and corrupt, racist, anti-Semitic (or, if Jewish, self-hating), lowbrow, anti-intellectual, and generally and profoundly evil. (One could quickly be contaminated with this evil if one so much as picked up a *New York Daily News* or brought into the home a newspaper published by William Randolph Hearst.)

For a child to be brought up with this overwhelming sense of separation and alienation from the prevailing surround can lead to a strong sense of isolation and, often, a bitterness toward the world or the parents—or both. It may be that some of the "red diaper babies" who now earn their bread among the neo-conservatives are victims of that bitterness. In my case, however, I was provided with an alternative culture, which offered a vibrant, creative, fulfilling life outside the rather "blah" mainstream: namely, the world of left-wing Jewish secularism. From the age of seven, most kids in my neighborhood went to some sort of additional, after-school program: the Jews to Hebrew school, the Catholics to catechism classes (I don't think there were any "WASPs"). I went to the Chaim Zhitlovsky Shul 23 of the Jewish People's Fraternal Order (JPFO) of the International Workers Order (IWO). There, every afternoon after school, I learned to read and write Yiddish and was taught biblical Jewish history—from a secular perspective— emphasizing the prophets and their demands for social justice, Yiddish songs and dances, and English "little songs on big subjects" (like "You Can Get Good Milk from a Brown-Skin Cow" or "It Could Be a Wonderful World"). After four years, I graduated to the Bronx Jewish *mittleshul* (high school—one of three in New York at the time), where I continued my studies, adding modern Jewish history (from a Marxist perspective), Yiddish literature, Hebrew (as the modern language of Israel), and "current events" (from a Jewish/communist perspective). *Mittleshul* met on Friday evenings and all day Saturday. After *mittleshul*, on Saturday nights, we students socialized like other New York teenagers, but in largish groups, not coupled off in dates. My closest friends were drawn from the kids at *mittleshul*, not from my neighborhood or high school. I even had different names: Miriam at school, Mickey at *shul* and among my friends.

In the summers, beginning at age twelve, I went to Camp Kinderland— an IWO-JPFO-affiliated camp—along with many of my *shul* friends. Camp was a continuation of *shul*, though not as "academic." (The saying was "From *shul* to camp, from camp to *shul*.") We played softball and went swimming and had cookouts and sleep-outs, but we also sang Yiddish songs and rehearsed to perform songs, dances, and plays for the parents and other adults at Camp Lakeland, an adjoining resort. (Those of us who showed

FIGURE 2.1. The Hartman Family, circa 1941 (*from right to left*: Hartman, Miriam, Hershl, and Sonia)

some talent and were comfortable onstage had a great time; I'm not so sure about the others.) These summer camps of the Left have sometimes (ignorantly) been characterized as "training camps," with an implication of dark, conspiratorial, paramilitary goings-on. It was not revolution that was taught, however, but more benign progressive notions like the "dignity of labor" ("Don't forget to bus your tables, and don't leave a mess for the kitchen workers"); the "sharing of work" (artfully contrived rotations for cleaning

FIGURE 2.2. Graduating class, JPFO Shul 23, circa 1951 (teacher Zalman Yachness seated in center, music teacher Hal Colter standing behind; Mickey seated at right end)

the cabins); the injustice of segregation and discrimination against America's Negroes, with a great deal of attention to African American history and music; and "peaceful co-existence" (an international Olympics at the end of the summer, rather than a color war). Above all, in Camp Kinderland, we were taught the central importance of secular, progressive, Yiddish culture in all its forms. These forms have changed, of course, over the nearly ninety-five years of Camp Kinderland's existence, from, for instance, a primarily Yiddish-speaking milieu to one that treats Yiddish as a part of bygone days but reiterates the values it contained. (As we have seen, the very codification of Yiddish as a formal, written language was part of what can only be called "premature post-modernism"—like the "premature anti-fascism" of the 1930s. Just as modern Hebrew later became an integral part of Zionism, so sophisticated, literary Yiddish developed with the revolutionary movements of the period.)

All in all, the progressive, secular Jewish movement provided for parents, children, and youth an almost total social, cultural, political milieu, where they could feel completely unalienated as they immersed themselves in their own unique culture—cognizant always of the values it shared with the cultures of other oppressed minority groups, especially Negroes. In my neighborhood in the northeast Bronx, there was even a massive physical manifestation of our "special" milieu: a cooperative housing project, built by the Communist Party in the late 1920s, consisting of four five-story, vine-covered buildings around a landscaped courtyard, aligned on two blocks facing Bronx Park. (The United Workers Housing Cooperatives, as they were called, were designated a National Landmark by the U.S. Congress in 1986.) The hundreds of people who lived in the "Coops" created an ambience, for about one square mile, of a proletarian, progressive, politically aware and involved universe (especially for a child). The local candy store sold ten *Daily Workers* or *Morgn Freiheits* (the newspaper of and for Yiddish-speaking Communists) for every one *New York Daily News*; the graffiti on the walls of the playground handball court read "All out May 1st!"; the record store would play Paul Robeson albums on its public address system, blaring into the street; the sidewalks, which were originally poured in the 1920s, had hammers and sickles carved into them instead of initials; the benches surrounding the playground were filled with people talking politics (making them eminently unsuitable for clandestine necking—as I later found out); the basements of the Coops buildings were arranged into meeting rooms and libraries, and one was the site of my *mittleshul*.

This sense of belonging to a large community outside the standard, visible, conventional society was nourishing and sustaining for most of us. It reinforced a sense of specialness, encompassing a feeling of responsibility toward both the "inside" and "outside" communities.

Even when that "special responsibility" was not so much fun for me, I would exercise it because it was clearly a part of who I was. For instance, Sonia had organized the fifty-four families who lived in our apartment building into a tenants' union (affiliated with a citywide union). About once a month, it was my chore to deliver a flyer to each apartment door in our building; I rang the bell and announced "Important message from the tenants' union" and also collected dues from any families who weren't paid up. I really hated doing this: it was time-consuming, embarrassing (especially when I had to ask for a dues payment), and offered no rewards whatsoever— nobody ever thanked me for coming to their door. But I strongly remember a sense of obligation to do it, coming, not simply from my mother, but from an inner feeling permeating my nine- or ten-year-old self; it was what one did if one was the person I was. In short, the culture that we were immersed in and the community it created helped develop an identity that made our lives meaningful and our politics possible.

I remember asking my big brother, Hershl, about what a gearshift was on a car, what it meant (I must have been about six or seven). To explain it he said: "Do you know the American Labor Party symbol [two clasped hands, one black and one white, bordered by a round gear]?" "That's a gear," he told me. I was able to imagine both the logo's wheel and the concept of inter-locking gears from that simple definition. I venture to say that nobody else learned about cars that way!

Sometimes that culture helped shape our lives in unusual ways. I began smoking cigarettes experimentally at age ten. By the time I was twelve, I was a full-fledged, habitual smoker. That summer, I went to Camp Kinderland for the first time; I was in a group with other eleven- and twelve-year-olds, and smoking was, of course, unthinkable. I was quite mature—physically and otherwise—and spent much of my time hanging out with my counselors, who were smokers. They soon became aware of my problem and gave me cigarettes on the condition that I smoke only outside the presence of my fel-low campers. The camp's co-director, a wise New York teacher named Morris Saltz, of course became aware of what was going on, and he invited me to join him for a little walk and chat. I freely admitted smoking, and he made the fol-lowing argument: "We know that your smoking is just a habit that you picked up, but you want to help organize other young people for the *shul*s or the Labor Youth League or whatever—right? Well, what would the parents of those kids think if they knew that you smoked? Probably, that you were some kind of hoodlum or otherwise disreputable, and they wouldn't let their kids join your organization." Here was an argument that made sense (and made me quit—for a short while, anyway). I began to understand what Sonia had meant by "sekrrificing for the movement," and it made eminent sense!

It was also important for a child to be secure in knowing that member-ship in this deviant subculture did not cut one off completely from the "real" world out there. We listened to the same radio shows (or, later, watched the same TV programs) as the other kids, we played on the block with whoever was around, we had friends in school. When our two worlds conflicted, we needed resolution—preferably, in favor of the deviant world. At Passover, for instance, the Jewish kids, who formed the majority in my school, brought their lunch sandwiches made with matzo. My secular bread sandwiches provoked much derision from my schoolmates. Sensing that my Jewish (*shul*) education was of more significance to me than their sporadic religious training was to them, I countered: "Oh yeah?" (the New York kid's primary and immediate response). "So how come you're supposed to eat matzo at Passover? What's the meaning of it? Bet you don't know." And they didn't, because they had heard the Exodus story only in unintelligible Hebrew at a grandparent's house at a Passover seder, whereas we had discussed it in Yiddish and English in *shul* and at home. The wife of the Orthodox rabbi who lived in our apartment building apparently hadn't heard of my Passover exploits. She once berated my mother for not giving me a "proper" Jewish education (i.e., in the Talmud Torah she ran). My mother immediately challenged her to test me and any eight-year-old of her choosing from the ranks of the Talmud Torah students, on our respective knowledge of Jewish religion, customs, and mores. She never set up the contest, but my mother's confidence in me as expressed by her challenge was a significant "victory for our side" for an eight-year-old, teaching me that our "deviance" could stand up to their "real" world, any day. I was taught to "stand up" literally, as well. When I was about six or seven, I came up from playing in the street, crying that "Donald," a neighbor boy, a year or two older than I, "hit me." My mother would not comfort me, but ordered me back to the street, to "hit him back!" I took that lesson very much to heart and rarely felt threatened in the streets again—believing that I was not a helpless victim. (Hillary Clinton told a similar story about herself at the 2016 Democratic National Convention. Does that mean that I can run for president?!)

We were all severely tested with the coming of the postwar Red Scare. The spirit of the times resulted in many of our "straight" neighbors depositing their wartime Red Army Chorus and Paul Robeson records along with various "lefty" books on the floor of the apartment building's incinerator vestibule (where, since World War II, they were accustomed to placing newspapers for recycling by the building "super"). They probably couldn't bring themselves to actually throw them down the incinerator chute. (Burning books? No way.) Our apartment was next to the vestibule, and my father promptly added to our book and record collections by monitoring the neighbors' fear-generated discards and bringing them all into our home—which still sported a bas-relief bust of Vladimir Lenin and a picture of Joseph Stalin in the entry hall. My parents viewed the fear and caution that the McCarthyist hysteria produced as a sign, not only of betrayal to previously deeply held beliefs and values, but of the most craven kind of surrender, akin to collaborationist acts in the recent world war. They sensed that people hadn't really changed what they thought but were only acting out of fear. At the beginning of the month, Sonia would greet her elderly neighbors who often sat on folding chairs in large clumps on the sidewalk in front of the building, clutching the Social Security checks the mailman had just delivered, with the taunt: "Those are Communist checks you have!" To their astonished questioning looks, she would reply: "It was we Communists who fought for Social Security, and that's why you have the checks!" Her response to the hysteria was a proud, public renewal of her politics and identity. I learned from this that part of being a responsible Communist (or leftist or activist) was to proudly "own" who you were, not hide or try to deny it. Had I been an adult during the McCarthyist anti-communist hysteria, I think I would have advocated such a policy to all my comrades.

When my high school civics teacher was assigning different students to read and report on the eight or so daily newspapers then being published in New York, I volunteered to read the *Daily Worker* and reported on it honestly. Later, in college, when many of my friends were "closed" Labor Youth League (LYL) members, that is, known only to fellow members, I became chair of the Marxist Discussion Club and was interviewed as such by the *New York Times*, and my parents were proud—of my being interviewed in the *New York Times*, as well as forthrightly representing the Marxist Discussion Club, in 1957 at the City College of New York (CCNY)! It should be said that Sonia, as an immigrant Jewish mother, was very much concerned about her children's future and was worried that left-wing politics might negatively affect it. When Hershl dropped out of CCNY in his sophomore year to work full-time for the *Morgn Freiheit* (the only American-born writer on the staff of any Yiddish-language newspaper—writing in Yiddish), Sonia was not thrilled and developed an ulcer. When I was ready to apply to college and had won a New York State Regents Scholarship that would have paid my tuition at Syracuse University, Sonia urged me to go. I responded: "CCNY is where I want to go, Ma, and I can use the scholarship for expenses. Why should I go to Syracuse?" "Because if you go to CCNY, you'll be branded forever as a Red," she chided (in 1955). (By 1957, Sonia seemed to have forgotten about how she counseled that I should attend Syracuse University, rather than CCNY.)

The strong sense of Jewish/political identity helped us weather the repression of the fifties. When the New York City Board of Education evicted the IWO, which had been renting space in school buildings, we accused them of anti-Semitism—even though it was Rabbi Benjamin Schultz (an extreme rightist, later one of Richard Nixon's defenders) who had brought the matter to the board. In fact, the Catholic Church–dominated Board of Education was quite anti-Semitic: the vast majority of the teachers it subsequently fired for violating the Feinberg Law (which required teacher cooperation with any legislative investigating committee and subjected to dismissal any teacher who invoked the Fifth Amendment) were Jewish, and Jewish schoolteachers had been subject to special speech tests and other harassments for years. We looked to the ancient Jewish tradition and its hatred of the "informer" to vent our fury at the host of informers who paraded daily before the various investigating committees. We were sure, even more than Pastor Martin Niemöller or Jean-Paul Sartre, that attacks on "Reds" and attacks on Jews came together and that we had to defend ourselves as both.

The McCarran-Walter Act targeted immigrants, allowing Communists to be stripped of naturalized citizenship. We understood that all our parents could be targets and, again, saw our Jewish identity and politics intermingled. The newly revitalized American Committee for Protection of Foreign Born (originally founded in the 1920s), along with the Emma Lazarus clubs (an IWO-affiliated Jewish women's organization, designed as a sort of left alternative to Hadassah), sponsored annual trips to the Statue of Liberty— putting us among the rare New Yorkers who had actually visited the statue. We also knew the words on the base by heart, thanks, in part, to learning them as lyrics to the Irving Berlin song: "Give me your tired, your poor, / Your huddled masses yearning to breathe free."

But for us, the most terrifying moments of the fifties came with the arrest, trial, and subsequent execution of Julius and Ethel Rosenberg. Although the Rosenbergs were not themselves immigrants, they were of our parents' generation, and we easily identified with Michael and Robbie, their two young sons. For us, there was no doubt of Julius and Ethel's innocence: we knew our parents weren't spies. We knew from our own World War II experience and from listening to and learning pieces like the "Ballad for Americans" that American patriotism, ethnic identity and pride ("I'm just an Irish, Negro, Jewish, Italian, French and English, Spanish, Russian, Chinese, Polish, Scotch, Hungarian, Litvak, Swedish, Finnish, Canadian, Greek and Turk, and Czech and double-check American," sang Paul Robeson), left politics, and sympathy and loyalty for a foreign nation—be it Russia (for us) or Israel (for many of our neighbors)—could all go hand in hand and presented no paradoxes or conflicts. We knew that the government had cynically assigned Jewish prosecutors and judges in the Rosenberg case to mask an essential anti-Semitism, and we felt betrayed by a Communist Party that sought, publicly, at least, to distance itself from the Rosenbergs.

I was about eleven years old when the campaign to save the Rosenbergs began, led mainly by the *National Guardian*—a non-communist left-wing weekly. The local headquarters of the campaign were at 683 Allerton Avenue, a second-floor loft a few blocks from the Coops, which housed, at various times or simultaneously, JPFO Branch No. 127, the neighborhood headquarters of the American Labor Party and the food gathering center for the Russian War Relief (during World War II), and food donations for striking coal miners in 1946. Especially as their execution date approached, I spent every afternoon in that loft, stuffing envelopes, putting up posters, learning to run a mimeograph machine—any tasks that could be entrusted to a precocious eleven- or twelve-year-old. During that year, large "Save the Rosenbergs" rallies were held at sites like the Randall's Island Stadium, and our *mittleshul* gang would attend as a group of young teenagers, sometimes performing songs or dances as part of a cultural program. For that period, our cultural, social, political, and spiritual lives revolved around Ethel and Julius Rosenberg and the international campaign to save their lives. On the eve of their execution, a Friday (the government's final cynical act was, in the face of protest that the execution date fell on the Jewish Sabbath, to move it up by a few hours to an hour before sunset on the preceding Friday), Sonia would not let me attend a massive rally and vigil at Union Square because she feared there would be violence—by either protesters or police. She stayed with me while my father went downtown, and we listened to the broadcast of the execution with tears flowing freely. The next day was the previously scheduled *mittleshul* boat-ride excursion up the Hudson River to Bear Mountain. Since it was all already arranged and paid for, we all went—but with enormously heavy hearts. We must have been quite a strange sight: a few hundred teenagers on a special excursion, sitting somberly on the boat and then quietly dipping in the swimming pool at the recreation site. I got severely sunburned and had a temperature of 101 degrees the next day, so I couldn't go with my parents to the Rosenbergs' funeral. Again, I stayed home (with Ida, my *bubbeh* [grandmother]) and wept. It wasn't ideology in my weeping; it was the emotional response of a teenager who could see her own parents being taken, who identified with two young orphans—and who was learning about political defeat. One had to understand that defeat and overcome it; one had to continue in the struggle whether one triumphed or not; I came to believe that growing up meant learning how to do that (a skill that has come in quite handy over the years).

I learned other "skills" around this time. The main leadership of the Communist Party USA had been convicted under the Smith Act of "conspiring to teach and advocate the overthrow of the government by force and violence" and had been sentenced to five years in prison. Fascism did indeed appear to be around the corner (or so we imagined). Taking a page from the heroic book of the Communist Party of Spain, which had maintained itself as an important organization all during Francisco Franco's dictatorship, the Communist Party USA decided to have some of its leaders jump bail and go underground to provide the leadership necessary to maintain the Party during the dark times ahead. I later learned that the plan involved using non-leadership cadre, who would disappear from their usual lives and maintain an underground network to harbor and support the bail-jumping fugitives. My brother, Hershl, and his wife, May, were among those chosen for this task, selected to help harbor Gil Green, a Party leader from Chicago. I was fifteen at the time and was given only a vague explanation of what Hershl and May were doing. I was told they were in Denver (they never actually went farther than New Jersey), doing important and secret Party work. My story to anybody who asked was that they went to Denver for good jobs. Anybody who asked, however, was not to include Federal Bureau of Investigation (FBI) agents. I was explicitly instructed never to speak to anyone from the FBI or ever let them into our home. When two "Feebies" inevitably appeared at our apartment door one afternoon, I told them that my parents weren't home and I knew nothing about anything. When they asked to come in to "make a phone call," I directed them to the pay phone at the candy store down the block and firmly closed and locked the door. These experiences did not seem frightening or alien to me: they were simply part of what people like us did. And I knew that WE were the patriots, not Judge Irving Kaufman or Roy Cohn or Joe McCarthy or the FBI agents! WE believed in peaceful co-existence with the Soviet Union, in democracy, and in "liberty and justice for all" (even though WE no longer recited the Pledge of Allegiance at school, since the words "under God" had been inserted, we thought, as part of the "Christianization of America" in the battle of the Cold War; I didn't say "under God" for years and have recently foresworn saying the pledge at all—why do Americans have to keep reaffirming their loyalty to "the flag"?)

A few of the escaped communist leaders were caught; the rest turned themselves in when it seemed probable that fascism had been delayed. Hershl and May came home in August 1956, had a baby, and continued with life, influenced, however, by their first experiences outside the orbit we had all grown up in, coping on a daily basis with ordinary jobs among ordinary folks interacting with "real Americans."

At Camp Kinderland in 1953, when I was thirteen, I learned some new lessons. Our young teenage group had been organized as a "Kindercity," with an elected mayor and city council and a daily (one- or two-page) newspaper, which I edited. We wrote about group activities, and I was encouraged to write editorials urging enthusiastic camper participation in activities and also a weekly column in Yiddish (for parent, rather than child, edification, I now realize). On the weekend marking the one-month anniversary of the Rosenbergs' execution, we planned a special Rosenberg memorial issue for general, camp-wide distribution. As we were mimeographing the last copies in the office, the camp's directorate entered and told us that we could not distribute the issue. "It's too dangerous," they said. "Don't you know that the American Legion has threatened to burn us down and that we have to patrol the camp's perimeter at night? If this newspaper got out, who knows what would happen!" "Shades of collaborationism again," I remember thinking (or some version of that), and I promptly replied that we would not move from the office until the newspapers were distributed as planned— we knew all about sit-down strikes. Here was our first opportunity to show up our elders, to point out their hypocrisy and apparent cowardice. Here we could take all the principles and the history they had taught us and fling it in their faces, affirming our own adolescent identities formed in the very molds our parents had provided and now seemed to be betraying! We sang "We Shall Not Be Moved" and stayed in the office until late in the evening, when a compromise was agreed to: we would distribute the newspapers only in Camp Kinderland, not in adjoining Camp Lakeland, where many parents came to spend weekends and where copies could more easily "fall into the wrong hands." This incident also held lessons for me: your elders could not always be trusted to do as they advocated; people could betray their principles, but that did not sully the principles themselves. The official "Left" that we knew and its leadership did not necessarily have all the answers or always do the right thing. These lessons stood me in very good stead in the years and decades to follow. Perhaps the grown-ups were simply exercising reasonable caution, but it felt to us that they were overreacting and giving in to anti-communist hysteria, and we kids felt like the brave and virtuous ones.

By 1953, Camp Kinderland itself—along with the rest of the IWO and its institutions—were under governmental, not just American Legion, attack. The New York State Department of Insurance, which had regulatory authority over the IWO because of its health and life insurance programs, decided to investigate communist subversion in New York State. During that summer, a number of Kinderland counselors were called to testify before a state committee, and, in 1955, the IWO was dissolved and its assets were seized by the state. (Camp Kinderland survived as an independent entity, however, and does so until this day, in a new site, with something of a new outlook, but still very much Camp Kinderland.) Some of the *shul*s and the branches continued—the branches now called clubs or societies—and other former JPFO activities continued in new guises. The youth organization—the Jewish Young Fraternalists—had existed parallel to the Communist Party's LYL, to provide an organizational framework for progressive, secular Jewish youth, from which they could interact with their Zionist or other mainstream counterparts. They had helped form the Jewish Young Folksingers, a chorus (like the *gezangs farein* of Sonia's generation), open to all, developing the musical ability of its members and of its various conductors and arrangers—some of whom went on to notable careers in the folk music revival of the sixties. (Robert De Cormier, for instance, the late magnificent choral director, became the arranger and conductor for Harry Belafonte and mentor for Peter, Paul and Mary—I knew Mary as the late Mary Travers, with whom I had sung in the alto section of the Jewish Young Folksingers. She wasn't actually Jewish, but had followed De Cormier, her music teacher at Elisabeth Irwin High School, to the Jewish Young Folksingers chorus.) A severe blow came in 1952, when—again at the urging of the Rabbi Schultz types in the larger Jewish community—the Jewish Young Fraternalists was kicked out of the National Jewish Youth Conference, the large Jewish umbrella youth organization. But the chorus continued and prospered, meeting and performing in Jewish community centers as well as in concert halls around the city.From 1952 to 1956 I was a high school kid. I was a precocious reader and something of a "wise guy," which meant that I did well on IQ-type exams. I had skipped first grade entirely (reading well above grade level) and was already one-half year ahead because my birthday was in January (Don't ask—it was the notorious elimination of the "B" classes [1B, 2B, etc.]), and I was given (along with most sixth graders) an IQ-type test to see whether I qualified for the "rapid advance" program (seventh, eighth, and ninth grades in two years of junior high). My score was such that I was to go into the program. With the other rapid advances, I would have graduated from high school at fifteen and a half. My mother (who handled such things) put her foot down, and I finished eighth grade at my neighborhood K–8 school, Public School 76. In the eighth grade, however, my teachers encouraged me to take the exams for New York's "special" high schools, Bronx High School of Science and Hunter College High School. (Those were the only ones open to girls, with a strict quota system at Bronx Science, allowing no more than one-third of the freshman class to be girls.) For eighth-grade science at Public School 76, I had had one of the only male teachers at the school—a young, handsome fellow, just home from the Korean War. He encouraged my interest in science, and I took the test. I was soon admitted—actually before the Hunter test was even given. The day of the test for Hunter High (affiliated with and on the campus of Hunter College, one of New York's famed, free colleges—at that time, open only to women), we were making cream puffs in my cooking class, and I knew I didn't want to go to an all-girls school anyway, so I opted for Bronx Science (and stayed to make and eat the cream puffs; food was always a high priority for me!).

Bronx Science was truly a special place and excellent for a troublemaker like me. The prevailing attitude was that Bronx Science kids were so smart and "special," that they could do no wrong—even when they blatantly broke the rules. In my first year, I cut school for two weeks (to be with a friend of mine who was having problems) and was caught (of course). My mother was terrific about it: "You know that I don't like that kind of thing, but I believe that it is something that should be between us, in the family, and the school shouldn't be the policeman. If you like, I will tell them that you had my permission to cut." Wow! Here I learned that we believed in the "separation of morality and state." I thanked her but chose to tell the school disciplinary folks that I simply had cut school, and when they didn't punish me, but offered all sorts of counseling and hoped that I "was all right" and would let them know if I wasn't, I realized that Bronx Science was indeed special. A few years later, we all were at a special Arista assembly, to witness the induction into the honor society of seniors who had maintained a high average. I found the ceremony bizarre, in that this bastion of rationality chose to have people in robes, lighting candles, and being generally medieval. When I was subsequently invited to join Arista, I politely refused and asked if I could instead explain at the Arista assembly why I had refused. "Aren't

FIGURE 2.3. Bunk 19, Camp Kinderland (Mickey seated in chair, at left end)

we special enough? Must we continually seek to separate ourselves from the rest of our generation?" I asked (or something like that). I was upset by the elitism constantly being practiced by the school and was guilty for being a part of it.

I did, in fact, practice a different kind of separation: my school friends and my *shule*/camp friends. I lived, really, in two different worlds—though sometimes they overlapped. I had been involved with an after-school club called Forum, a current events and politics discussion group, which often had outside speakers. In the 1954–55 school year, Martin Peretz (later publisher of the *New Republic*) was president of the Forum. At the end of my junior year, elections were held for the following year's officers. I ran for president, and a younger student whom I knew from camp was among those who counted the secret ballots. I was opposed by a fellow handpicked (by Peretz), and it was a close election. When I was announced the winner, my camp friend winked at me, as if to say, "We did it! I helped in the count." I never did ask him if that's what he meant.

I had some teachers at Bronx Science who deeply affected my life. One, Herbert Falkenstein, taught "social studies." He was an enigmatic sort, and rumors abounded that he had been an Office of Strategic Services spy during World War II. He taught what I now recognize as critical thinking in

approaching social studies—quite different from the somewhat uncriti-
cal didacticism I was used to—from both school classes and *shul* classes.
A few years later, his classes included Bob Ross (a founder of Students
for a Democratic Society [SDS]) and Stokely Carmichael—who, I
believe, were influenced by his quiet way of helping students get to the
truth.

I had one somewhat unpleasant experience at Bronx Science in those
McCarthyist years. In junior-year English, my teacher (whose name I really
don't remember) assigned a "research term paper." She taught us something
about using reference materials in the library, but gave little instruction
otherwise on how to write a research paper. I must admit that I procrasti-
nated and found myself writing at midnight the night before the paper was
due. My topic was "three hundred years of Jewish settlement in the United
States" (it was 1954, the tercentenary of that first settlement), and I really
hadn't done much research. I relied on what I had learned from Morris
Schappes, editor of *Jewish Life*, a magazine of the communist-leaning Jewish
Left. I didn't plagiarize—I cited him extensively, but I essentially rewrote
his articles. My teacher questioned my source and gave me a C-plus on the
paper, which reduced my grade in the class from an A to a B. That meant
that I was no longer eligible for the senior-year English elective, creative
writing (taught by my teacher's sister). It turned out to be a blessing in dis-
guise, leading to (1) my publishing a story in the school's literary magazine
(an anti-war story, selected by student editors) and (2) my being invited to
take public speaking as my elective, taught by Abraham Tauber. He and
I immediately hit it off, and I learned a great deal about public speaking—
which has been and continues to be one of my strongest, most usable qualities. Talk about sweet revenge!

I was so happy in Mr. Tauber's class, that on Senior Day (when we were
encouraged to be creative) I impersonated him in front of our class, wearing
my father's tweed jacket and even my father's shoes (which had the same
crepe soles as Mr. Tauber's). I know that he firmly believed in imitation
being the highest form of flattery and that he was quite pleased—as was I.

I began a lifelong practice at Bronx Science of never hiding my politics—
following in my parents' footsteps. Asked in a freshman civics class to volunteer to report weekly on one newspaper from among New York's rich
array, I raised my hand for the *Daily Worker*. I scrawled *peace* (then a slightly
subversive concept) wherever I could, and, hanging out with a group of
kids who were getting into the folk revival, I sang: "The banks are made of

marble, with a guard at every door, / And the vaults are stuffed with silver that the workers sweated for." And my school friends joined in gleefully. I was in fact something of a celebrity, because I knew all the words to "those" songs!

All in all, my experience at Bronx Science not only gave me a great high school education, which helped prepare me for a career in science, but also gave me an appreciation of the wider world of American young people. I am grateful.

## NEW LEFT BEGINNINGS

In 1956 the world of the Communist Party–oriented American and Jewish American Left was dealt the blow that McCarthyism could never really fully deliver. Soviet premier Nikita Khrushchev, addressing the Twentieth Congress of the Communist Party of the Soviet Union, detailed the crimes of Stalinism and began the process of de-legitimization of the Soviet Union, Soviet-style socialism, and the world's Soviet-oriented Communist parties. In the Communist Party USA, and especially in the pages of the *Daily Worker*, thousands of American Communists began to express their own critiques of the Party and sometimes their hope for the Party's reconstruction, liberated from a slavish adherence to Soviet (and U.S. Party) orthodoxy and culminating with the departure of many thousands from the organization. A sense of a non-communist (but not anti-communist) Left began to develop among many of these members and "fellow travelers," looking to American experience and language for its ideology. Initially, its roots were deep in the Communist Party USA, but later a New Left would emerge, truly free of the rhetoric and orthodoxy of the past.

That summer, while waiting to enter CCNY in the fall, I worked at Macy's on Herald Square in New York. It was great being a grown-up! Once a week or so, after work, I met with some friends from the teenage section of the LYL, of which I had been a member since I was thirteen. We continued among ourselves the "whither (or wither) communism and the Party?" discussions that were raging in the pages of the *Daily Worker*. We felt allied to the "John Gates faction" of the Communist Party leadership, which advocated, essentially, for a left movement that was truly part of the American working class and that spoke in an American vernacular, not in the Germanic or Russified Marxist cadences that typified the Party's publications or speeches. At around that time, a West Coast woman named Decca Treuhaft—also known as Jessica Mitford, later the author of *The American Way of Death*—produced a sort of comic book, *Life Itselfmanship*—mocking that Communist Party style. I remember a drawing of a steam shovel, on which a stout young fellow was suspended, labeled "Raising the broad masses." That little booklet seemed to summarize what we were feeling at that time—in a style and language we could eagerly relate to. We believed that the LYL was an impediment to relating to American youth and planned to organize in the fall to disband the teenage league. Members of the main body of the LYL, college students, were similarly planning to disband the entire organization.

We didn't know it quite yet, but, for us, the New Left was being born.

## ENTER DICK

One Friday late afternoon in May 1957, my friend Judee Rosenbaum and I went up to the Camp Kinderland office on Union Square in New York. We were both going to be working as youth group counselors that summer, and we had some business to discuss with the camp's director, Elsie Suller. A tall, young man was there, whom I had never met. Judee introduced him as Richard (Dick) Flacks, who was going to be a group leader at camp that summer. He was not exactly Adonis-like (nor was I anywhere near a 10), but despite his glasses and braces, he seemed to me better looking than most of the guys in our usual crowd. Maybe it was his blondish curly hair, blue eyes, and six-foot height.

We all chatted, and I asked Judee about her trip to the doctor earlier that day. "He said I had vernal catarrh," she replied. Dick said, "That sounds like a song!" Whereupon I grabbed an "air guitar" and burst out with "Oh vernal, vernal catarrh, I love my vernal catarrh" (to the tune of "Johnny Guitar"). Nobody else in the room had understood Dick's joke, and he and I felt an immediate kinship—one that has lasted through nearly sixty years of marriage. It was born of the fact, I think, that we each felt a wee bit alienated from our hitherto nourishing milieu and were beginning to imagine politics and life not tied to the red diaper baby experience. Dick was entering his senior year at Brooklyn College and was thinking about graduate school for the following year. At that point, very few of the people I knew were contemplating graduate school; a college education was expected of all of us, but then we were going to teach school or do some other lower-level professional job. I was majoring in biology at CCNY, after having been introduced to the wonders of science while attending Bronx Science, and I could see myself as a lab technician in a medical facility or, at best, doing research in a drug company lab somewhere in New Jersey.

I was exposed at CCNY to one of the best teachers I've ever seen. I took an animal behavior course in the psychology department. It was taught by Daniel S. Lehrman, a CCNY alumnus who was a professor at Rutgers University. He taught only the one course, at a graduate level, to (mostly) New York City schoolteachers earning credits toward a master's degree. The course was given in the evening, from six to ten, for the benefit of those teachers. Lehrman was such a dynamic lecturer that the class often refused to take a break midway, opting to have him continue teaching us about the fallacies of "instinct theory" in explaining behavior and exposing us to the ideas of T. C. Schneirla, curator at the American Museum of Natural History, who emphasized the role of learning in animal, as well as human, behavior. I began to dream of going to graduate school at Rutgers, to study with Lehrman.

In camp that summer, we were part of the leadership group, planning the summer's cultural program. With (American-born) Elsie Suller (a former Camp Wo-Chi-Ca group leader), we were trying to bring the camp into the second half of the twentieth century, replacing Yiddish classes with swimming classes and developing an outdoor camping program. (We could hear our parents' generation's voices saying, "Did I send my child away from a New York tenement so he could sleep on the ground?!," and understood that we had a big job to do.) We spent our weekly days off that summer (and the next) visiting other "institutional" (i.e., nonprofit, non-private) camps in the area to see what we could learn from their programs. We learned that it was possible for kids to plan their own programs (with the guidance of a counselor, of course), that there didn't have to be "top-down" direction for everything, and that kids liked sleeping on the ground. At the same time, we learned that our Kinderland kids had a certain sense of history and tradition that was not so common at other camps. My recollection of one girl in my group the following summer perhaps illustrates it best: I was a counselor in the Senior Work Camp, for fourteen- to sixteen-year-olds who were to do various work projects as part of their summer program. A major project was to paint the outsides of our own "bunks" (a corruption of *bungalows*, which is what we called our cabins). The girls in this group, many of whom had been in camp for years, were known to be difficult—preferring to lie around mooning over boys, rather than participating in the camp's programs. To motivate them, I made a big deal of learning how to paint, to do some skilled physical labor that would make less abstract the notion of "worker." This worked especially well for one of the girls, a leader in the bunk, whose father had died a few years before. He had been a housepainter (one of the many Jewish immigrant trades in New York), and she saw her painting the bunk as continuing his tradition, creating a bond between her and her father and her father's co-workers in the painters' union. All of the camp's programs took on new meaning for her—and for the other girls in the bunk. I realized that these kids (unlike the kids in the other camps we visited) could understand and appreciate their heritage if it was presented to them in a way that related to their lives. But the "red diaper baby milieu" that we were suffused with needed some freshening, some "real American" wind blowing through it.

Dick and I (and another group-leader friend) spent that summer and the next trying to bring some of the American summer camp experience to Camp Kinderland, to overlay its left secular Jewish/Yiddish traditions with Woody Guthrie songs, sleep-outs, trips to nearby cultural events, and other products of the second half of the century. By the summer of 1959, after Dick had graduated from Brooklyn College, we "abandoned" our camp to work at Camp Wel-Met, a social work–style camp, run by the New York Jewish Welfare Board (a program of the Jewish Federation). This camp was founded by social workers and was originally intended for "underprivileged children." By 1959, the kids came not from the Lower East Side slums but from Roslyn and Flushing, Long Island, and the counselors came for their week of training sporting purses and high-heeled shoes. The program was called "bunk-centered," meaning that it was the bunk's counselor, with the kids, who decided on the daily program (within the larger group program). It was a lesson in cooperation and democratic participation.

During that summer, Dick and I were planning our marriage for after I had graduated from CCNY the following June. Away from our old Kinderland friends, we became very close that summer, and (of course) I became pregnant. I was nineteen years old, in my senior year of college, and it was thirteen years before *Roe v. Wade*. I called my sister-in-law, May Hartman, and she took me to her gynecologist, Dr. Alexander (Allie) Katz, who was, in fact, a friend of Dick's parents and a physician in the old IWO health plan. (Although May lived in the Bronx, she traveled to Dr. Katz in Brooklyn for gynecological and obstetric care—again, the culture of the secular Jewish Left.) At that time, I had never even had a gynecological examination. I told

May to tell Dr. Katz that I thought I was pregnant and that if I was, "I didn't wanna be." After examining me, he lectured me: "I would expect this from an uneducated poor girl, but YOU!" He did something quite painful to me, and I started bleeding. I felt that he was punishing me. "Go to Brooklyn Jewish Hospital," he said. "Tell them anything you want, but be sure to tell them you were bleeding before you came to my office. I'll meet you there in a half hour. And don't tell your friends about this; I'm not looking to be in the business."

May took me to the hospital, where the intern who interviewed me was very suspicious of my account. When he heard who my doctor was, he shrugged and admitted me for a "D&C" (dilation and curettage), which Dr. Katz did in a little while. They told me that I would stay overnight, and they wouldn't discharge me unless someone picked me up. What to do? It was a weekday and everyone I knew was working. Finally, we called Hank Aron (an associate of Hershl and May's from the underground), who worked nights at a hotel, and he came by to put me in a cab the next day. (I had called my parents to tell them I was staying over at a friend's house, "to study.") The surgery and hospital stay cost us all the money we had earned that summer.

Mine was not a typical abortion for the times. Although I did feel like a criminal, and was careful not to endanger Dr. Katz, my experience was very different from that of my friends—who went to Puerto Rico or to some mysterious place in Pennsylvania. I felt very fortunate, and I forged a new bond with my mother, who had had two or three illegal abortions between the births of my brother and me—because she and Hartman could not afford a child. (Her doctor refused to abort me because he feared for her health.) The legalization of abortion had profound effects on young women—which, I'm afraid, today's young women do not understand. The threat of an unwanted pregnancy hung over all of us, and effective contraception was not easy to come by—and was illegal in some states. True "women's liberation" did not exist before January 22, 1972.

My mother later found out about the abortion and demanded to see Dick, who had come to New York from Ann Arbor, Michigan, to be with me after the ordeal. The secret was still to be kept from my father—who had had a heart attack and was to be shielded from all stress—so Dick came to our apartment in the dead of night, while my father was asleep. She kissed him on both cheeks and then slapped him. "If you're going to do this kind of business, why don't you get married right away, instead of waiting for June?"

she shouted at him (in a very loud whisper, at which my mother was adept). This was from a woman who had herself felt no need for marriage.

And so we did—all in secret from my father. Everyone else in the family (including Dick's parents) knew, but the shield for my father held. I had been planning to go visit Dick during the Thanksgiving break, so we decided that I should arrive a week earlier. Hershl took me to the airport and gave me a bottle of champagne, to take for celebration. That Friday before Thanksgiving, November 20, 1959, Dick and I (me in a fancy white and gold dress I had bought at Klein's in New York), along with two friends as witnesses, stood before a justice of the peace, Orville Kapp, on Nixon Road (off Joy Road), in Ann Arbor, and spoke marriage vows. (Mr. Kapp winked, "Do your parents know about this?," and he apologized to the "university folk" for reading a psalm as part of the "ceremony.") We kissed the traditional chaste wedding kiss and went to the A&P in town to buy steaks to go with Hershl's champagne, which we ate and drank at Dick's apartment (having evicted his roommate for the week). The rest is (certainly) history.

# 3 ▸ MILDRED FLACKS

DICK:

My mother went to teach at Junior High School 35 in the Bedford-Stuyvesant neighborhood of Brooklyn at age twenty-one. Bedford-Stuyvesant, even in those days, had become one of the largest—perhaps the largest—urban black ghettos in America, and the school she taught at, as she described it to me when I was growing up, was a ramshackle wooden building with ancient plumbing, terrible facilities, and overcrowded class-rooms. Almost all of the students were African American. Mildred was a first-grade teacher (and remained one for the rest of her teaching life).

Mildred was raised in an immigrant family, the Weitzes. Her father, my *zayda* (grandfather), never spoke English in all of his decades of life. He was a butcher in Williamsburg, Brooklyn, and owned a kosher butcher shop on Bedford Avenue, and I remember the store as a dingy and dimly lit place. The family lived in the upstairs loft, which was equally dingy. We went to visit my mother's parents fairly often when I was very young. Zayda was a pious man, and he looked like a rabbi. We have a picture of him hanging on our dining room wall. It's a colorized image clipped from a New York news-paper and shows him blowing the shofar on Rosh Hashanah. After my *bub-beh* (grandmother) died, Zayda went to live in a Lower East Side home for

FIGURE 3.1. The Weitz Family, circa 1915. Mildred is the young girl at the center (*standing left to right*: sisters Rebecca, Sarah and Rose; *seated on left*: sister Kitty, mother Molly, father Samuel)

the aged, spending most of the day davening (praying) in the *shul* (synagogue). One of my cousins recently told me that Zayda was actually the illegitimate son of a Polish count and that he got in trouble for possible violation of rationing rules during World War II. But he maintained a *shul* in back of the butcher shop, and, for his grandchildren, he represented the essence of pious purity.

Mildred was determined to break completely with her parents' cultural and religious worlds. She had four sisters, all older than she and all born in Europe; she was quite a bit younger and was the only one born in America. She remembered being horrified and disgusted by some of her very pious father's practices—for example, the *kaporos* ritual of Yom Kippur, which involved the whirling of a dead chicken around her head. Young Mildred (she was called Minnie by her sisters) was something of a tomboy, and she soon was playing tennis in McCarren Park, not far from the family's house on

FIGURE 3.2. Samuel Weitz (my *zayde*) late in life, blowing the shofar for the congregation at his lower east side nursing home in New York, circa 1951

Bedford Avenue; instead of going to Talmud Torah, she sneaked away to a sister's apartment, where her tennis gear was stored. She took a lot of pride in the fact that she became the junior girl tennis champion of the park at age thirteen. Tennis came before communism as her pathway into America.

Like a lot of Jewish youth in post–World War I New York, she decided to go into teaching. She got her teaching degree at Jamaica Training School for Teachers. In those days the teacher training schools were, for young women, an alternative to getting a full-fledged bachelor's degree (a practice later done away with in New York City).

When she made the decision to go into the schools of Bedford-Stuyvesant in 1931, it was the depths of the Depression. She and my father, Dave, were married on August 31; she started teaching at Junior High School 35 less than a month after they were married, both young teachers in the New York public schools in the depths of the depression.

Recalling this decision of hers, I find myself amazed by her pluck. Maybe teacher openings were scarce at that time—maybe Bedford-Stuyvesant was one of the few places where she could get a job. But certainly her decision to

FIGURE 3.3. Dave Flacks and Mildred Weitz, courting, circa 1930

teach in these conditions had something to do with a budding moral commitment.

My parents never seemed to regard those Depression years as a time of hardship for them. They often said that, although teachers weren't paid much, they had jobs and therefore the means to buy a car, take vacations, and see the country together. Mildred taught Dave to play tennis; they eagerly looked forward to their free summers when they could go away to the country. Tennis was a primary feature of their vacations.

They did a lot of traveling before I was born: in 1936 they took a cross-country road trip with another couple, and they always recalled how bold a thing it had been to drive all the way to California and then down to Mexico. It was their last fling before having the kids they had postponed because of the Depression.

By 1938, both Dave and Mildred had become quite active not only in their local schools but also in the New York Teachers Union. Teachers, along with most public employees in America at that time, had no collective bargaining rights—had no right to union representation in contract negotiations with their school boards—but all across the country clusters of teachers in big cities were, in the early thirties, forming unions affiliated with the American Federation of Teachers.

Many of those union pioneers in New York and other cities were Communist Party members. The mid-thirties were the peak moment in what later was called the "Red Decade"—a period when the communist movement was a powerful magnet for young people eager to find ways to do something significant about the Depression and the looming threat of fascism in Europe. The Party was training young workers and middle-class youth to take leadership in creating a labor movement; it was the only national association consciously promoting racial justice and trying to be interracial in its own organizational world; it was allied to the Soviet Union, which was then seen as a great experiment in social transformation. The Party seemed to be attracting support from many of the leading writers and artists, and it helped recruit hundreds of young people to travel underground to Spain to join the armed resistance to Franco.

I'm not sure when my parents first identified with the communist movement. Perhaps it was in the late twenties when my father was a student at CCNY; he had, after all, grown up in a socialistic family (his father had been a charter member of the Jewish socialist Arbeiter Ring, also known as the Workmen's Circle), and certainly the college was a site of radical activism when he went there. Whatever the starting point of their identity, by the mid-thirties they were constructing their lives in relation to political commitment.

My mother, while passionately involved in teaching her first-grade kids in Bedford-Stuyvesant, was also dedicating herself to building community-based organizations. She was one of the few white members of the Bedford-Stuyvesant Neighborhood Council and was elected as its vice president. She helped form and then led the Schools Council of Bedford-Stuyvesant. Here was a woman in her twenties, who was not in fact a very assertive, out-spoken person in public, nevertheless elected to leadership positions in an overwhelmingly black community—a leadership involved in struggles spurred by the desperate community need for major change, especially in her work, the need for decent schools that were physically habitable and that might make a difference for the children and families there.

My father was teaching in the Brownsville section of Brooklyn, at PS 174. It was then a predominantly Jewish working-class neighborhood, so he was not up against the same kind of race and class challenges that Mildred had to struggle with. Dave taught sixth-grade classes in a school whose princi-pal, Garibaldi Lapolla, was a noted practitioner of progressive education methods. He flourished in that environment, by his own account—doing a lot with music and theater and sports along with his classroom efforts.

Dave became active in the leadership of the Teachers Union, served on its executive board, and was one of the people who helped produce its weekly newspaper, *Teacher News*, a widely distributed publication in the city's schools. The Teachers Union in its heyday counted about six thousand members from a total teaching staff of perhaps forty thousand. At the time, it far outstripped its union competitor, the New York Teachers Guild. Both unions arose from a split of the original local of the American Federation of Teachers. The Teachers Guild remained affiliated with the old-line Ameri-can Federation of Labor (AFL). True to its craft union tradition, the guild organized only those teachers with permanent positions—and such jobs were rarely available in the Depression years. Thousands of newly minted teachers who worked as "substitutes" were excluded from its ranks, even if they were assigned to long-term slots.

The Teachers Union in New York split from the American Federation of Teachers and affiliated with the dynamic new Congress of Industrial Organ-izations (CIO), embracing the "industrial" union spirit it represented. The Teachers Union actively organized the thousands of young teachers who couldn't obtain permanent licenses. Underlying these cleavages was a deeper ideological divide. The Teachers Guild leadership was conservative and fiercely anti-communist. The Teachers Union leaders were allied with, if not all members of, the Communist Party.

My mother was not as active as Dave was in the citywide union. But her leadership in Bedford-Stuyvesant community life was rooted in the small group of fellow union members working in that neighborhood. The union provided a framework of support for these teachers—and their counterparts in Harlem—young, predominantly Jewish, predominantly women, for whom teacher unionism meant, above all, a commitment to community struggle for equality.

So I grew up taking for granted that my parents were people working hard to make the world a better place. I had no reason to resist them as role models. I don't recall resenting the time they took for meetings or the time I spent in nursery school. Years later, I learned that I was in fact a "latch-key kid," coming home from school to an empty house. I thought at the time that this was a positive and "modern" situation—that both parents were working and doing important things in the world was better, I believed, than if my mother was just a housewife. I have no recollection of any hunger for more of their attention. Indeed, my after-school time was spent hanging out with excellent close friends in the free space of our neighborhood streets.

## DAVE FLACKS'S STORY

At the turn of the century, Dave's father, Grandpa Jake, was an early member of the Workmen's Circle, a Jewish socialist organization. We restored and framed a picture taken of a Workmen's Circle picnic crowd. It was taken in Allentown, Pennsylvania, where Jake and his wife, Mary, and baby Dave had moved so that Jake could take a job in a bed-spring factory. Mary is seen proudly holding up the Workmen's Circle banner. According to her, Eugene V. Debs was among the socialist leaders who came to Allentown, and she claimed that the tall Gene Debs hoisted baby Dave on his shoulder. She recalled hearing the famous socialist professor Scott Nearing as well. So, without knowing much detail, I always assumed that Dave was raised to be a socialist—even though Mary often complained about Jake's failure as a provider, most particularly because he had the habit of giving kids free candy when Mary briefly tried to operate a candy store in Brooklyn.

FIGURE 3.4. Workmen's Circle picnic circa 1906, Allentown, PA; Grandma Mary, hand on hip in top row, holding the Workmen's Circle pennant

Mary arrived in the United States, from Hungary, at age thirteen and started working in a cigar factory. She was so small that a union organizer chose her to crawl under the tables where the workers were stationed and furtively hand out leaflets. She often told me this story and about how she got caught and lost her job. For her, it was a cautionary tale about the risks of being politically outspoken. She often warned me against sticking your neck out, but what I absorbed was her courage and her willingness to take those kinds of risks. I think of that picture, hanging on our dining room wall, of the Workman's Circle picnic in Allentown where she's holding up the banner—she must have been a striking figure, with flaming red hair and her shoulders thrown back.

My father went to CCNY in the 1920s, which by then was pretty famously a hotbed of radicalism. I can't remember asking him much about the political scene there, but it seems quite obvious that it was in the college's cafeteria that some of his allegiances and perspectives were formed. His own college reminiscences focused on endless bridge playing (some with partners who later became professionals in the game), but it's pretty clear to me that alongside the card games was some semblance of Marxism.

## THE RED SCARE COMES HOME

In 1951 a special investigating committee appointed by the New York City Board of Education summoned my mother to ask her about her membership in the Communist Party.[1] She was one of a few dozen New York teachers who were called in the first wave of targets of that inquiry. The board had appointed a special investigating staff under the terms of the Feinberg Law, which banned Communists from teaching in New York State public schools. Mildred and her colleagues decided not to answer questions about their Communist Party affiliation on the grounds that those questions violated their First Amendment right of political expression.

From the point of view of the Board of Education and the school system's leadership, the Communist Party was not a political organization but a vast conspiracy to destroy American institutions; therefore, schools had the right to know whether teachers were affiliated with this operation, and the Feinberg Law created the legal framework for such an inquiry.

The New York schools anti-communist investigation was a major local version of the national congressional apparatus established by the House Un-American Activities Committee (HUAC) in partnership with the FBI. But the purge of New York teachers began before World War II when an inquisitorial project was initiated by a state legislative committee. The Rapp-Coudert Committee went after Communists in New York City's colleges. And the New York Teachers Union by the late thirties had become a focus of investigation and attack in the right-wing media. The Feinberg Law and the New York City investigations in the early fifties were the culmination of more than a decade of effort by right-wing and Catholic anti-communists.

My mother was one of eight teachers who were publicly suspended pending trial because they refused to answer the questions about their Party affiliation. The suspension of that group of eight was preceded by the dismissal of an initial group of Teacher Union leaders. All of them had refused to cooperate with the board's investigation, defining their action as a principled defense of the First Amendment. They also feared that denial of membership could lead to perjury charges (whether or not they had actually been Party members), while an affirmative answer would open the door to a chain of questions to compel them to inform on others and to extensive further and illegitimate questions about their political

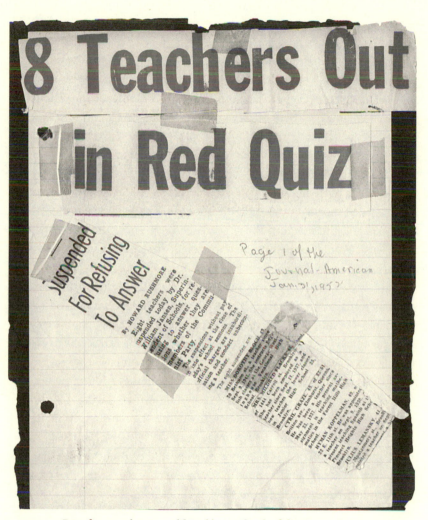

FIGURE 3.5. Page from twelve-year-old Dick's scrapbook of clippings

ideas and activity. My mother was among the first of several hundred people eventually forced out of the public schools as a result of the board's witch hunt.

I recently came across a scrapbook that I'd begun to keep at age twelve when my mother's case became public. The firing of the "red" teachers was front-page news in all the New York dailies. A very large red banner headline ran in the *New York Journal-American* (the Hearst newspaper):

"8 Teachers Out in Red Quiz." The story of the purge appeared on the front page of all the dailies, and I'd clipped most of them.

Mildred asked that her hearing before the Board of Education be postponed until after my bar mitzvah in 1951, and this request was granted. Of course, when she did appear, she refused to respond to questions about her political affiliation, particularly her membership in the Communist Party.

To the day of their death, neither of my parents, Dave or Mildred, ever said to me that they had been Party members. Their refusal to answer those questions in governmental settings somehow led them to refuse to answer the question ever, to anybody. I thought that it was hardly an appropriate stance. But given that the public raising of the question eventually cost both of them their jobs and their dignity, their insistence on keeping the matter private made sense. From their point of view, you could never tell when an admission of Party membership might be held against you and your loved ones.

The story of the American Communist Party from the thirties on was very much shaped by the fact that most members kept secret their affiliation in order to function in wider institutional, social, and occupational ways. It was generally believed by Party people, even before the McCarthy days, that if you wanted acceptance for purposes personal or political, it would be better to keep secret the fact that you were a Party member. Once the inquisitions by congressional committees and by bodies like the New York City school system began, refusal to answer the question became a matter of principle. My parents and their comrades came to justify their secrecy on the grounds that privacy is guaranteed by the Bill of Rights—and that this protection would be undermined if they were to answer the interrogators' questions. In addition, since the New York teachers' inquisition was initiated by the Feinberg Law, which barred Communists from teaching in the public schools, any admission of Party membership would be followed by demands to renounce the Party and to prove loyalty by naming other members. That law, and other government efforts aimed at outlawing the Party, put the final seal on Party members' lips.

When my mother came to her inquisition, she knew that her job was in danger. The threat occurred despite her twenty years of working in the Bedford-Stuyvesant neighborhood as a dedicated teacher of disadvantaged students, who tried to keep in tune with educational and pedagogical innovation and who reflected deeply about how to be as effective as possible in her role as teacher. Conscientiousness was central to her personality. Moreover, because of her contributions to the community, when she was suspended and charges were brought up against her, many leaders in that community expressed alarm, concern, and support.

After her suspension on charges of "conduct unbecoming a teacher" for refusing to answer the Question, there was a public hearing presided over by a subcommittee of the Board of Education. One subcommittee member in Mildred's case was Reverend J. M. Coleman, a well-known minister from Bedford-Stuyvesant, who was the first black member of the board. Mildred's lawyer was the prominent labor and civil liberties attorney Royal W. France. France tried to establish incontestably that Mildred was an exemplary and valuable teacher. First, he cross-examined the superintendent of schools for Bedford-Stuyvesant and the principal of her school, inquiring about Mildred's record as a teacher. To the district superintendent Samuel Levinson, he asked: "What is your impression of her character?" Levinson replied: "She had a nice character." (I'm quoting from a typed summary of this proceeding that was in my scrapbook.)

When asked, "Have you changed your opinion?," Levinson said, "No." The notes continue: "Her lawyer asked the superintendent about the conditions of schools in Bedford-Stuyvesant and brought out that Mrs. Flacks had worked hard and continuously to improve these conditions with some success. [Levinson replied:] 'I organized the Board of Human Relations for better amity in the neighborhood and I put Mrs. Flacks on as one of three teachers out of 1400 teachers in my district. I chose her because she was a very fine teacher and there were 15 members on the board.'"

Her lawyer inquired: "Have you received any evidence, any information that she's indoctrinated anybody in the classroom?" "No," said the superintendent.

The note taker records: "Parents of pupils all agreed to the highest report on Mrs. Flacks' character. . . . Sample comments: She helped interpret the program of the schools to the parents, very impressed with her splendid work; excellent reputation in the community; dealt very well with difficult children, surpassed by none—were statements made under oath in this hearing." The notes continue: "The principal was asked was her suspension unfair and he said[:] I feel she must be suspended for her refusal to answer but the schools lost the services of an excellent teacher."

Before the hearing, my father had the idea that Reverend Coleman himself be called to the stand since he knew Mildred from the neighborhood. He testified in a similar vein. She was an outstanding teacher—in fact, he recalled that one of his daughters had been a pupil of hers (something

Mildred hadn't realized, apparently). He testified that she was an impressive leader of the community and her dismissal would be a loss to the schools.

All of this evidence of the impact of her work, of course, made me, now fourteen years old, super proud of my mother. I'd heard all these things from her own accounts, but that these were the opinions of even those sitting in negative judgment over her because of her political views stirred me deeply—and still does.

That such a rare and valuable person would be purged because she refused to discuss her membership in the Communist Party with a government inquisitorial body was quite characteristic of the McCarthy time The board, including Reverend Coleman, voted to suspend her and seven other teachers, all of whom had similar exemplary records, many of them in disadvantaged neighborhoods.

My father lost his job a couple of years later under somewhat different circumstances. He and my mother were among a number of people called to testify at a hearing held in 1954 in New York by HUAC, the notorious witch-hunting congressional committee. HUAC had first gained notoriety in 1947 for its Hollywood investigations, featuring accusers and accused film industry figures—hearings that caused the Hollywood blacklisting of those who refused to "clear" themselves of communist affiliation, hearings that promoted the careers of young committee member Richard Nixon and Screen Actors Guild president Ronald Reagan, hearings that led to the jailing of ten directors and screenwriters who refused to answer the committee's questions.

In the years after the Hollywood events, HUAC traveled the country, holding hearings in city after city, subpoenaing hundreds of people named as Communists by informers. To avoid the charges of contempt of Congress that had led to the jailing of the Hollywood Ten, "unfriendly" witnesses relied on Fifth Amendment protections against self-incrimination as a basis for refusing to answer questions.

My parents accordingly "took the Fifth." But my father, with much heat, said that he was refusing to answer on the grounds of the First, Fourth, Fifth, Ninth, and Tenth Amendments. He wanted, I think, to indicate that his grounds for noncooperation had to do much more with defending the Constitution and the Bill of Rights than in protecting his own skin (which taking the Fifth implied).

The New York hearings, like many others HUAC held, were widely publicized and excerpted on the TV news. So, on the evening of my parents' appearance, we were able to watch my father berating the committee and insisting on his constitutional rights. These hearings received a lot of publicity, in large part because the committee subpoenaed as witnesses people who were well known in show business or were otherwise in the celebrity spotlight. For example, on the very day that my parents testified in the morning, the great jazz clarinetist Artie Shaw appeared that afternoon. Shaw (whose celebrity included the number and fame of his wives) testified that he was ashamed that he had been attracted to the Communist Party, saying that he had been a dupe, a jerk, and a schmo for having done so. He never recovered from his rather desperate performance on the stand and soon after emigrated to Spain.

Mildred and Dave were identified before the committee as members of the Communist Party by an African American woman named Dorothy Funn, who had taught in Bedford-Stuyvesant in the thirties and became a leader in the Party-oriented national civil rights organizations. Funn seems to have left the Party in the late forties and by 1950 was espousing the view that the Communists' support for civil rights was a smoke screen for their pro-Soviet agenda. She told the New York school authorities that the Teachers Union was controlled by the Communist Party and named many union actives as Communists (including my parents). In her public testimony before HUAC, Funn named about 150 people. My mother was deeply shocked by Funn's betrayal, based on their earlier friendship. Funn's public turn came on the heels of a denunciation of the Party and the Teachers Union by Bella Dodd, a former Hunter College professor, who had been a beloved leader of the union and then a visible and respected spokesperson for the Party in New York.

My parents and their friends tended to express pity for these two women, thinking that they must have gone through some kind of personal turmoil, though believing, too, that Funn must have made some personal gain from her appearance as an informer. Recently, I've come to hypothesize that part of what triggered such conversion was the likelihood that both of these people, having taken roles as functionaries of the Communist Party, became alienated from the Party by the obtuse and bullying behavior of top Party leaders struggling to toe the Party line emanating from Stalin's Moscow—especially at the end of World War II.

In 1944 the Communist Party, under its leader Earl Browder, undertook a major transformation. The Party changed its name to the Communist Political Association and announced that it was ready for permanent participation in coalition with liberals, because the wartime alliance between the United States and the USSR signified that class war was now obsolete and peaceful social evolution was now possible. Browder believed that this ideological shift reflected Stalin's own views, and Party discipline led most to express support for this startling new line. In a few months, however, the international Party leadership (embodied by the head of the French Communist Party) denounced Browderism and declared that, in the postwar world, the class struggle would certainly revive.

Browder had clearly misread what Stalin's wishes were. He was expelled, and the Party leadership, not for the first time, swung 180 degrees overnight—to the hard-line Stalinism espoused by Browder's opponent and replacement, venerable labor leader William Z. Foster. In the U.S. Party, rational discussion of policy was overshadowed by brutal and sudden doctrinal shifts of this kind coupled with sharp attacks on those who had deviated. I am guessing that people like Dodd and Funn may well have been quite disgusted by the slavish mentality they came to see in their fellow Party bureaucrats. Both became apparently willing partners of the FBI and HUAC and therefore, of course, were totally shunned, not only by former comrades but by liberals in general. Ironically, perhaps, it's hard to find in the public testimonies of these women, much evidence of evil practice by Party members. What they testified was that the Party's support of worthy issues masked a treacherous devotion to the Soviet cause.

I have the sense that my parents, and their friends and comrades, paid little attention to the inner-Party maneuverings; rather than involvement in Party internal affairs, their own political commitment was expressed through the union and the community. For them, the Party was in fact the equivalent of a church: your faith nourished your commitment, but you were neither qualified nor that interested in assessing the theology and the inner workings of the priesthood.

After the HUAC hearing, my father was immediately dismissed from his job in the New York City school system. The city code of New York had a provision that said that refusal to cooperate with a congressional investigation by a city official was grounds for dismissal. The charter provision used to fire Dave and his colleagues was adopted originally when congressional committees were investigating corruption in New York City government, but its main use was against those refusing cooperation with HUAC. My father, unlike my mother, did not even have the benefit of a hearing.

Both of my parents were thus purged from the public schools during my early teen years. Readers may be assuming that there was a lot of emotional trauma for me and my eight year old sister into this story.

Both of our parents lost their jobs—but both were eventually able to get teaching jobs (at lower pay) in good private schools. There was negative publicity about them, but, for the most part, the teachers we had in school were supportive and some went out of their way to express sympathy or solidarity. In the neighborhood, there was very little, if any, negative response that I can recall.

Still, it's not a pleasant experience to be children whose parents are on the front pages of the newspapers because of their notoriety as Commies. I remember feeling fairly constant anxiety about who knew what and how we were perceived. Like most red diaper babies, we learned that there was a secret part of our family identity and that some kind of persecution or danger was always a possibility, and so the family secret needed to be protected. Telltale material, like the *Daily Worker*, was not to be left lying around. Our parents' message was, be proud of the rightness of our faith, but be very careful how much of it you reveal to others.

When Mildred lost her job in the public schools, she was able to find employment rather quickly at a private progressive school in New York called the Downtown Community School, where she taught for another twenty years. The Downtown Community School was founded in the thirties by Norman Studer, a very distinguished exponent of progressive education. He also founded and directed a children's camp called Woodland, notable not only for its left-wing orientation but also for its deep immersion in the dying folk culture of the Catskill Mountains. The "Catskills" have always been seen in the popular imagination as the borscht belt—where New York City Jews vacationed at big resorts and were entertained by rising comedians and entertainers, ate enormously, and played a lot of pinochle and mah-jongg. But this version of the Catskills overshadows the fact that these mountains were a settlement, in earlier centuries, like those in Appalachia and other southern regions. As in the South, the mountaineers in the Catskills created a rich body of folklore—song, story, crafts. Studer collected these materials and the surviving practitioners of the local folk culture to create a foundation for camp programming. Woodland was one of the places that Pete Seeger frequented during the summers as he toured around the

FIGURE 3.6. Rally in support of eight suspended teachers, 1952; Mildred Flacks second from right

FIGURE 3.7. Schoolchildren picketing in support of David Flacks at his dismissal hearing before the New York City Board of Education, Brooklyn, 1954

children's camps of the East, and he helped create and present annual Catskill music festivals at Woodland.

Studer's work at the camp, his passion for folk culture and its preservation, suggests his creativity as an activist intellectual leader. He was happy to acquire the services of a number of those who had been politically purged from New York schools. These were, after all, outstanding teachers, and Mildred and her friends who got jobs at the Downtown Community School and at other private progressive schools were important assets. The schools benefited from their dedication and experience, and the teachers were able to continue their calling (but at salaries and with pension benefits much lower than they would have received had they been able to stay in the public school system).

At the Downtown Community School, Mildred's pupils were no longer overwhelmingly poor and black. Still, she devoted her energy to mastery of the teaching of reading and other elementary skills, avidly engaging with the debates then raging about children's learning and the teaching of basic skills. She delighted in making use of new ideas about pedagogy, but she also liked to say that a serious practitioner like herself had a lot more wisdom than credentialed experts in pedagogy who spent their time in the schools of education.

Dave Flacks, for some reason, thought at first that losing his teaching job was going to be an opportunity to have a different career. He always claimed that his real interests were in some kind of business. His major venture was to partner with a couple of other guys to buy and operate a family summer resort in the Poconos.

Dave and Mildred had for years worked summers as social directors at such resorts—getting family summer vacations, rather than cash salaries, as their compensation. So partnering in operating Barrow Lodge seemed like a logical use of their ten years of experience in this sort of work. Morton and Ruth Barrow were experienced hotel managers and lived at the Pocono mountain lodge year-round as full-time managers. A shop-teacher friend, Ookie, was the third partner and was in charge of the physical maintenance of the place.

Dave persuaded some of the wealthier relatives to invest in the resort. Our family was involved with Barrow Lodge for about six years (from 1948 to 1954). All concerned lost money in what was, after all, a declining sort of enterprise.

The resorts Dave and Mildred worked at were the opposite of Catskill hotels. They were rustic places with very modest accommodations (shared bathrooms, bare-bones rooms, and modest dining facilities). My parents chief requirement was an excellent tennis court. Barrow Lodge had a nice pool fed by icy mountain springs. It also had a great kids' day camp. Evenings were organized by Dave and Mildred and featured campfires, charades, 16 mm classic movies, and occasional guest performers. It was a simple and enjoyable opportunity for nice summer vacations—but by the late fifties its modest rustic amenities couldn't compete in the expanding tourist industry.

Despite this business failure, Dave decided to try other commercial opportunities. He relied for a while on various brothers-in-law to help him find work in their business worlds. I recall in particular that he was a sales representative for a while and dealt with New York–area gas stations. It didn't take long for him to learn that such jobs were not all that lucrative or psychically rewarding. So after a couple of years, he returned to teaching, finding positions at various private schools, and in his last years as a teacher he coached tennis and taught science.

My parents were among some two hundred teachers called before the New York City Board of Education's investigative inquisition. About twice as many others left the school system rather than face the risk of public exposure. Like my parents and their friends, a great many of these hundreds were no doubt deeply dedicated, skilled, and valuable teachers.

In the Red Scare era, the purging of Communists seemed, to the powers that be, somehow a benefit that outweighed the loss of such valuable talent. And maybe the generalized fear of the Reds actually motivated those who undertook the purge. But as Clarence Taylor in his recent history of the Teachers Union tells, deep conflict between the board and the Teachers Union dated back to the thirties and had much to do with the union's chal- lenges to the policies and practices of the education bureaucracy.[2] And behind those conflicts were others. For example, most of the Teachers Union's membership—and the newest wave of teachers entering the system—were Jewish, and their arrival certainly was threatening to the rather entrenched domination of teaching jobs by and outlooks of Catholic teachers. The Catholic Church in New York—and particularly in Brooklyn—was exceed- ingly right-wing, having, for example, endorsed the Franco forces in the Spanish Civil War. So the Church's deep hostility to the Teachers Union, combined with rank-and-file Catholic anxieties about the rise of young

Jewish teachers, may help explain the deep emotional underpinnings of the teacher purge in the fifties.

Teachers did not have collective bargaining rights in New York until the 1960s. The union my parents helped to create focused its energies not so much on the contractual interests of teachers (although it did work hard for the rights of thousands of substitute teachers unable to get regular positions during the Depression years of budgetary austerity) as on a broader set of struggles that I would summarize as an effort to democratize the schools. It was the Teachers Union in New York that helped popularize the idea of what was then called Negro History Week (later African American History Month); it put out a great deal of material to aid classroom observance of Negro history. It was a pioneering effort, a precursor to what eventually became the full-blown academic discipline of black studies. The Teachers Union exposed cases of classroom racism and anti-Semitism, helping make such taken-for-granted behavior unacceptable. The union published major studies of textbook bias that were powerfully effective in raising public sensitivity to racial stereotyping and the everyday ways that racism was perpetuated. It was, to my mind, remarkably ahead of its time in these matters—and I can't help but feel that the purge (which eventually destroyed the Teachers Union) wasn't simply a civil liberties issue but was also a disaster for the quality and potential of public education in America. An organized force that mobilized teachers for the cause of universal, democratic, quality education was destroyed. A union that understood its role to be the advancement of education and justice for all—as well as for the rights and needs of teachers—was liquidated.

That destruction was systematic. The New York City Board of Education in the fifties denied the Teachers Union any right to use public school facilities and refused to deal with it as a legitimate agency of representation (even though its membership included about 15 percent of the teaching staff).

Eventually, teachers won collective bargaining rights in New York and around the country, and the attitude of teachers toward unionization was transformed. The Teachers Union was the pioneer union in New York, but it was its smaller rival, the Teachers Guild, that, refashioned as the New York Federation of Teachers, became the sole teachers union in the city's schools. Ever since, teacher unionists have struggled to define the mission and character of their unions. But it's disturbing to me (as it was to Mildred Flacks) that these days it's conventional wisdom to think that the teachers unions are a barrier to educational reform rather than in the vanguard of it.

# 4 ▸ THE HOUSE I LIVED IN

## Dick's Story

## BROOKLYN

In the late 1930s and 1940s, Brooklyn was teeming with left-wing expression. The political commitments expressed by my parents were shared by a wide circle of their friends, many of them also schoolteachers. My red background meant that I had plenty of political arguments with my close school friends (mostly about religion and Russia), but everyone was at least liberal.

An indicator of the political complexion that prevailed in Brooklyn was the fact that the lead vote-getter for the New York City Council from Brooklyn after World War II was the nominee of the Communist Party, Pete Cacchione. I remember large campaign picnics for "Pete." On the city council at the time were a couple of Communist Party members (including Ben Davis, representing Harlem) and several more from the Party-supported American Labor Party. These electoral successes were a measure of the political strength that the Party-oriented Left had in the city when I was growing up. They were made possible by the fact that council elections were organized in terms of proportional representation (a European parliamentary approach

FIGURE 4.1. Mildred and Dick Flacks, Brooklyn, 1939

that allocated council seats according to the proportional strength of a party at the ballot box). The major parties succeeded in eliminating proportional representation as the Red Scare gathered force in the late forties—and that was an important sign that the brief and fragile legitimacy of the Communist Party in New York public life was not going to last.

The cultural world created by the 1930s Left had more social and political meaning than its electoral forays did. From the nineteenth century on,

American radicals of every stripe had constructed an array of institutions that encouraged participants to develop socialistic values, attitudes, and perspectives while sustaining and enriching their everyday lives. The Communist Party in the United States emerged out of the Socialist Party and the Industrial Workers of the World and a variety of left-wing immigrant forms of organization after the Soviet revolution in 1917. Early in the formation of the Communist Party (1920–22), there was intense struggle to create or seize control of cultural institutions, especially in the New York area, but across the country as well. This institution building was a response to the need for community and for various kinds of material and cultural support among those large numbers of American leftists of immigrant background. From this need arose mutual aid and insurance programs for health care and funeral services as well as all kinds of cultural activity—language schools, theater groups, choruses, newspapers, magazines, book publishers, speakers' bureaus, and, most important for a child like myself, children's summer camps.

There were the annual May Day parades in Union Square in New York; there were huge political picnics (at least huge in the eyes of an eight-year-old kid); there were concerts and festivals. All of this I took for granted as the kind of thing families do, as American as apple pie. Later, of course, I came to realize how distinctive this left-wing counterculture was.

If you were a red diaper baby in those years, your days had a soundtrack and much of it consisted of the very popular recordings made by Paul Robeson, the great African American singer and actor, who was a huge celebrity in the late thirties and early forties. Robeson was famous for his concertizing of Negro spirituals beginning in the twenties and for his stage performances in *Show Boat* and *Othello*. During the Second World War he released a hit album called *Songs of Free Men*, which featured songs of the Spanish Civil War and of Red Army resistance to Nazism and pieces that celebrated the struggles of the common man. Along with these was his recording of the "Ballad for Americans"—a ten-minute pop cantata that fused American history and its symbols with a strong emphasis on justice and equality. America, the song says, was built by the "'nobodies who are everybody." The "somebodies" disdained those values, according to the narrative embodied in the ballad. It was the "nobodies who are everybody" who kept the American faith.

Another song that Robeson sang was "The House I Live In," which was written near the end of World War II and became famous because Frank Sinatra performed it in an Academy Award–winning movie short. The song begins with the question "What is America to me?" and answers: "A name, a map, the flag I see, a certain word—democracy, that is America to me." The song continues with a litany of everyday and historical items that it then goes on to inventory in many scenes and experiences that one might have as an American, with an emphasis on populist imagery and on racial integration: "All races or religions. That's America to me."

The song's lyrics were written by Abel Meeropol and published under his pen name, Lewis Allen. Meeropol was a teacher and, like my parents, a New York Teachers Union member. His most important song was "Strange Fruit." Billie Holiday recorded the song and made it her own, and it came to be one of the songs of the century and continues to be a key anthem of black suffering and struggle. It was first printed in the *Teacher News*, the Teachers Union's weekly newspaper that my father helped edit.

In 1953 Meeropol and his wife, Anne, adopted the children of Ethel and Julius Rosenberg, the convicted atomic spies who were electrocuted in June of that year. The juxtaposition of these two facts—that Meeropol wrote one of the most stirring and effective patriotic songs of the World War II period and that he was the adoptive father of the Rosenberg children—says something about what I'm trying to suggest in my own experiences as a red diaper baby.

The music to "The House I Live In" and for "Ballad for Americans" was composed by Earl Robinson. Earl was known by every red New Yorker in my childhood. He lived in Brooklyn (and was a central figure in a Brooklyn left-wing cultural/family/social network that included doctors, lawyers, and folksinger Woody Guthrie). He is most famous for having written the song "Joe Hill" for a campfire program at a communist camp, where he worked as a cultural director. Like others in the left-wing cultural front of the New Deal era, Robinson was deeply engaged with political/cultural projects and, at the same time, had a good deal of success in the commercial mainstream. His music was a big part of my childhood soundtrack. It was music that intentionally tried to fuse the struggle for social justice and the American experience itself. This fusion—the quest to make it a valid way to understand the American past and to make a path for the future—is at the heart of what it means to me to be a red diaper baby.

Any Americans who were children during World War II no doubt remember it as a time of patriotic display and shared sacrifice. In school we bought savings stamps and war bonds. We collected scrap metal to help the war effort. I proudly wore a little soldier suit that my parents got me. I remember marching as a family in a patriotic, pro-war parade, probably sponsored by a left-wing coalition. I have a vivid memory from when I was five: my father was drafted into the navy, and I remember him with his duffel bag packed, when suddenly in the news came word that the upper age limit for draftees had been reduced to thirty-five, and so he had just escaped serving (he was thirty-six at the time). His brother, my uncle Joey, did serve in the army; one of my earliest memories was of his wedding to Aunt Rose, with Joey in his private's uniform. What Joey did in the war, we never knew; since he was stationed in England, I always assumed his silence about his service was rooted in embarrassment that it had been mundane and uneventful. Just last year, however, the family learned that he was one of the American GIs assigned to Bletchley Park in the effort to break the Nazis' codes. All of those guys had been sworn to silence for life regarding that assignment.

At the end of the war, Joey spent some time in Germany. He came back with many souvenirs; for some reason, he gave me a German officer's dress sword. I imagined that he'd captured it somehow on the battlefield, and I hung it over my bed. As a red diaper baby, I was an enthusiastic member of the war effort.

The fusion of communism and patriotism in my childhood experience had its political origin in the embrace, by the communist movement, of the Popular Front during the Depression. A far-reaching political project, it redefined the essential nature of that movement, away from the sense that it was a foreign-born and foreign-bred, alien force and toward an effort to ally politically with democratic, pro-labor, "progressive" movements and organizations. The Popular Front was a coalition against fascism (and its domestic manifestations), and the fascist threat certainly made such an alliance desperately urgent. But for many of those swept up in the political project, like my own parents and their friends, it was, even more, an opportunity for discovering and acting on emotional, cultural, and even spiritual connections to the American mainstream.

Obviously, for a lot of Communists, Hitler's invasion of the USSR was a final powerful incentive for supporting the war effort and for coalescing with all who were part of it. But my own experience tells me that the pro-war spirit of the Left wasn't simply or even mainly about defending the Soviet Union. It was about trying to fulfill the Party slogan "Communism is twentieth-century Americanism," a phrase often used to mock the American Communists of that period. But it contained the kernel of a promise about how communism as well as America might change.

My experience as a red diaper baby has made me come to understand that being "left" in the United States is not primarily about particular ideology, organization, or specific political belief. More than any of these, being "left" means identifying with a tradition and adopting an identity.

My family is part of that tradition and retelling its history helps in understanding my own political identity. My mother's evolution was more difficult to trace to the kind of roots that my father had. Mildred came from a very orthodox, traditional family. She certainly didn't get her attitudes from her parents. Indeed, from her own accounts she was rebellious at an early age—with her escapes on *shabbes* (the Sabbath) to the McCarren Park tennis courts symbolizing such rebellion. Tennis, like bridge for Dave, was one of the means through which these young people coming out of the Jewish immigrant world became Americans. And for them, the cultural world of Depression-era communism seemed a natural part of that evolution. It was so natural that neither Mildred nor Dave ever tried to explain to me or my sister how they became involved.

For me, 1947 was a formative year. April 26 was my ninth birthday. A couple of weeks earlier, at the start of the baseball season, Jackie Robinson came to play for the Brooklyn Dodgers. We lived about ten blocks from Ebbets Field, so the Dodgers were very much a part of who we were. But apart from the neighborhood bond, the fact that the Dodgers acquired Robinson became a very significant experience for red diaper babies of my generation. The *Daily Worker*, the communist newspaper, had for years crusaded for an end to the color bar in major league baseball. The role of *Daily Worker* sports writer Lester Rodney in helping spark a crusade to integrate the game has become celebrated in recent years. Although the part he played was largely ignored in the Cold War years, his constant effort to publicize the exploits of the star players in the Negro League and the attempts by black leaders to challenge Jim Crow in baseball forced public acknowledgment that brilliant players were being excluded because of their race.

Robinson's advance to the Dodgers was a victory for a campaign that the Communist Party had helped to spark. But as a kid, what was exciting for me was the possibility of an authentic hero, not only as a player on the field but as a human being. So, of course, one of the things that I did for that birthday in 1947 was to go with my father to my first major league game. My best birthday present was a little Brownie camera, and I was fascinated with it. The first pictures I took with it were at that game. I still have those tiny, almost indecipherable snapshots, whose significance only I can know.

Five days after that memorable game, my father took me to my first May Day parade in Union Square. There I was, with my Brownie camera; a couple of my snapshots from that day have also survived. The parade featured signs expressing worry about the threatening Red Scare. President Harry Truman had just announced a loyalty program that authorized the investigation of thousands of government employees about their alleged communist affiliation. Truman was trying to pre-empt the Republican effort to label the New Deal as a communist-tainted operation and to counter the fact that Republicans had taken over control of Congress in the 1946 elections. The new Congress passed the Taft-Hartley Law in 1947, aimed at curbing labor union power. It banned communist leadership in unions as part of a broad array of debilitating regulations of the labor movement. Taft-Harley had passed over Truman's veto.

So the May Day parade that year was held under the shadow of an emerging hysteria about the communist threat, but as a nine-year-old, these dark forebodings were not mine. For me, that birthday week was like a coming-of-age—my first Dodger game, my first May Day parade, my new camera!

## WO-CHI-CA

The summer of 1947 was also my first time away at children's camp—another big marker of exciting growth. The camp I went to was called Wo-Chi-Ca, in New Jersey. The name sounds like a Native American word, but it actually was a contraction of Workers Children's Camp. Wo-Chi-Ca was created under the auspices of the International Workers Order (or IWO—the Communist Party–oriented split-off of the Workmen's Circle). The camp's creation was a departure from the ethnically based cultural projects of the IWO (including the establishment of Camp Kinderland, the left-wing Yiddish camp, founded in 1923, where Mickey and I later fell in love). In contrast, it was, intentionally and systematically, designed as an interracial camp, with staff chosen to be racially mixed and campers brought not only from middle-class Jewish neighborhoods like mine but from all parts of the New York region. The camp's fees were cheap, and a good deal of subsidy was available to enable poorer minority kids to come. Its primary thematic purpose was to give kids the opportunity to have a terrific time together outdoors in the country, getting to know and be close to people of "all races and religions." But alongside the intention to create a kind of interracial oasis were other moral concerns that shaped the program and the experience. For example, there was a kind of "camper democracy" in which each bunk elected a representative to a camper council that was responsible for convening camp-wide town meetings, and there was a good deal of camper participation in planning group activities. These practices of democracy were largely symbolic. Still, as a camper, I was absorbing the idea that this was the way the world should be organized.

We kids took such learning to heart. During my first summer at camp, a bunch of us nine-year-olds undertook a picket of the group director's tent. I don't recall what the issue was, but we went on strike for a whole afternoon. I'm not sure whether the camp authorities were pleased that the kids had learned that particular form of expression. That was my first direct experience with a picket line and strike, but it seemed to fit in with the songs and the discourse that I had been raised from birth to hear and that were celebrated every day at camp. I ended up going to Wo-Chi-Ca for the next four years, and I think of those years as having had a very profound impact on shaping who I am.

Music was crucial in the camp. Some of the counselors were highly spirited musicians in the Pete Seeger vein. Fred Hellerman and Ronnie Gilbert, who joined Seeger and Lee Hays to form the Weavers, got their start as counselors at Wo-Chi-Ca, as did other folk performers of note, such as Ernie Lieberman and Bob Carey. Seeger (oddly) never came to Wo-Chi-Ca, but we had a young counselor named Dave Sear whose banjo and voice were identical to Seeger's when you closed your eyes. In 1948 we came to camp to discover an astonishing-looking new building, with a big sign that read: Paul Robeson Playhouse. It was a recycled Quonset hut from World War II, and it seemed huge to a little kid—the size of a full-scale gym. It served as a very effective auditorium, and its acoustics were such that when a group of kids were singing, the sound was just overwhelming, at least to my young ears. In that hall, our group singing became an enrapturing daily experience.

One of my best childhood friends was someone I met at Camp Wo-Chi-Ca. His name was Bobby Williamson. He was the son of John Williamson, who had been labor secretary of the Communist Party. John was one of a dozen or so Party leaders who in 1948, under the Smith Act, were put on trial for conspiring to teach and advocate the overthrow of the United States government. Bobby was one of my bunk mates in 1948. The opportunity to get to know him as a friend and to visit his family once we returned to the city put me in the midst of the postwar Red Scare as it was beginning. Bobby and the other kids and relatives of the "Smith Act victims," as they were called, formed an organization and I was a part of it. It was called something like Friends of Smith Act Victims. I have no memory of anything specific that we did as an organization, but what I do recall is a series of gatherings with these children and pretty intense conversations with some of the defendants in the Smith Act case and their spouses about the trial in particular and about what was then being imagined by the Party as the looming threat of fascism. I guess that was my first experience in a serious political scene, and, as a result, I became avidly interested in the civil liberties question.

Bobby had brought to camp a loose-leaf binder filled with the lyrics of political songs. He had done an exhaustive job of compiling anthems and protest songs from around the world (and had typed a lot of those lyrics himself). In the front of the binder he had typed the quotation "Beware a movement that sings," a line much favored by the Wobblies (members of the Industrial Workers of the World). He and I would sit on the steps of the bunk, just learning the songs. These songs symbolized our political fealties in those dark days of threat; Bobby and I would fantasize that someday these songs would be sung by everyone.[1]

There were other features of the camp program that had a memorable effect on my development. In 1950 I had a group leader who was remarkably talented, named Joanie. She had the creative capacity to engage a group of twelve-year-olds in an experience of writing a musical theater piece literally from scratch. One of the plays that we developed, which took about two weeks from creative beginning to production, was a story about the boys refusing to play softball with the girls and, as a result, the bats, balls, and gloves going on strike until the boys understand that they need to play with the girls. Once that plot outline developed, a lot of creative activity resulted. Joanie was able to get kids to write songs in a magical sort of group process. Kids would shout out a line and then she'd shape it up; we'd shout out another line, and pretty soon we were writing lyrics; then she'd say, "Well, how does that line sound, musically?," and some kid would sing out the line, which she'd play on the piano and eventually note down. The songs that resulted were terrific. Another group of kids were engaged in choreographing the music. There was also costuming and set making. For us, the theater became the center that summer for a wide range of creative activities involving a lot of learning of skills and crafts. At the same time, of course, the theme of the show was pretty profound.

It was 1950. "Male chauvinism" was then a very live issue in Camp Wo-Chi-Ca, decades before the women's movement re-emerged. Gender integration of the ball field was not just a theme for theatrics. It was central to the way softball and other sports were played every day in camp. There were no skill distinctions during athletics—in fact, in order for everyone to have a chance to play, the typical ball game might have had twelve or thirteen kids on each team. This style of play was comfortable for me—since I was painfully self-conscious about my lack of athleticism at that age—and reducing the competitiveness of the game greatly relieved my embarrassment. One needn't think, however, that the camp was consistently puritanical about sports competition; we'd all turn out to watch very fierce basketball played by the staff and work campers. Indeed, unlike later New Age communalism, Wo-Chi-Ca wasn't rigid about behavioral prescriptions—except when it came to racism and sexism.

One summer, some of the bunks got caught up in discussing racial stereotyping in comic books and children's games. A kid had brought a Little Black Sambo board game to camp. After much camp-wide discussion, the bunk wrote a letter to the Milton Bradley Company, calling attention to the crude stereotypes portrayed in the game. The company responded to the letter and eventually tried to transform the game to eliminate the stereotypes. The comic book discussions were aimed at sensitizing kids to racist images—not only of blacks but also of Asians, Mexicans, and other sorts of caricature. Indeed, the discussion spilled over to a more general cultural criticism. Somehow, in the midst of swimming, sports of all kinds, theater, singing, and crafts, alongside endless lights-out dirty-joke telling and talk about girls and coupling—there was a lot of pretty serious discussion about Reds and red-baiting, capitalism and socialism, and race.

Fun and games and intense talk just at the point in our young lives when we were determining who we were and who we should be were paramount matters. The camp's regular programs and routines provided the space and the structure for all of that—but there was even more. Wo-Chi-Ca somehow had become a significant haven for embattled cultural workers. Particularly important, I think, was that for some of the great African American artists who were on the camp's staff, it provided a little livelihood and relaxed time. They included Pearl Primus, a major figure in the dance world, and artists Charles White, Elizabeth Catlett, Jacob Lawrence, and Ernest Crichlow. Each week, the camp's town meetings or other assemblies featured fascinating guests. Among them were people who had been blacklisted, including harmonica master Larry Adler, dancer Paul Draper, novelist Howard Fast, poet Aaron Kramer, and basso Kenneth Spencer. A legend in camp was Ella Reeve "Mother" Bloor—the Communist Party's own Mother Jones—and Aunt Molly Jackson, an old-time veteran of the class war. But, of course, the leading guest was Paul Robeson. In the late thirties, Robeson had been a key figure in raising money and support for the camp, attracted strongly by the project of making an interracial children's paradise. I was at camp when Robeson visited in 1948. My group took the softball field, and he somehow was on the field with us (and I am certain that I got a Robeson tickle in the ribs).

His visit that year was an especially big deal, because it was on that occasion that the Robeson Playhouse was dedicated. Robeson's voice filled the hall as he talked and sang about his vision of a world music. A number of other dignitaries of the IWO were onstage as well, including the famed graphic artist Rockwell Kent, who was honorary president of the organization. We were accordingly immersed in the cultural world of the communist movement (including a surfeit of Soviet movies, mixed with Charlie Chaplin shorts on the weekly movie nights).

That a communist-run camp was an indoctrination program for inducting young minds and bodies into the dogmas and disciplines of the Party is probably taken for granted. The story I'm telling is different, and it had a surprising outcome, for me at least. It's the story of an intensely moral project whose aim was to inculcate, not doctrine and party loyalty, but radical democratic and egalitarian values. About a fourth of the staff were African American, and one out of five children who attended were black—so the lived experience of the camp, combined with the content of its program, surely had significance when it came to the racial attitudes of those who went there. Along with this was the lived experience of camper democracy, of cultural criticism, and of valuing American cultural traditions (embodied in folk music and square dancing, in reading the works of John Steinbeck and Carl Sandburg, and in much else that came to us in those years following the era of the Popular Front and the New Deal).

For me, the experience at camp had a lot to do with how I came to be a conscious, identified, and committed lefty, fusing that leftism with a powerful conviction about the necessity of democracy in the fullest sense. That conviction was important a few years later in enabling me and others like me who had been at Wo-Chi-Ca to question and then reject the Communist Party's authority and legitimacy, because the Party in the United States as well as in the Soviet Union departed so totally from the democratic principles that we had imbibed in our time at camp. Incidentally, I was appalled to read a piece by David Horowitz some years ago in which he invents the idea that "politically incorrect" comic books were ritually burned in bonfires at Wo-Chi-Ca. Horowitz was a camper there, too—and for some time in the sixties and seventies, he was a creative left-wing intellectual. He's one of the few from my generation who broke with his communist childhood to end up on the Far Right. When some former Wo-Chi-Cans challenged his tale of comic book burning, Horowitz admitted that he'd never witnessed such a thing but had relied on someone else's (very distorted!) memory of a story in the annual Wo-Chi-Ca yearbook. The camp that I recall encouraged us to read and debate rather than burn even racist comics.[2]

My primary political preoccupation at age twelve or so was how what we called the communist witch hunt was contradicting and undermining the democracy I'd learned to value. Defending democracy at that time meant becoming aware of and resistant to the Red Scare and the attempt to purge the Left from American life. My experience with Bobby Williamson and his family and the others (many of whose children were fellow campers) who had been indicted under the Smith Act and related government prosecutions was my first personal encounter with that emerging climate.

At home, I was beginning to sense the dangers. My parents became more wary of having evidence of left-wing affiliation lying around, exposed. So, although we subscribed to the *Daily Worker*, copies were hidden away, whatever company was coming. And like many other red diaper babies, I remember an occasion when there was a housecleaning to remove a lot of pamphlets and other incriminating materials and to store them away in secret hiding holes in the house.

A very traumatic episode in that process revolved around Camp Wo-Chi-Ca in the last year I was there. Local hooligans were threatening the camp—carloads of local youth drove into camp, demanding that the sign with Robeson's name be removed and threatening to burndown the playhouse. By the end of that summer, we later learned, some staff were patrolling the camp's grounds with arms because of threats to poison the water supply.

That was in 1950, in the aftermath of the Peekskill riots. These were the violent episodes in which Paul Robeson concerts, planned for outdoors, near Peekskill, New York, were attacked by mobs. White youth recruited by veterans groups beat people while police stood by. It was that experience in the late summer of 1949 that probably crystallized the view in Party circles that there was a fascist threat in the United States.

For fifteen years prior to the rioting, Robeson had been popular on a global scale. He was probably the highest-paid black performer in the world and was certainly one of the best-known and most recognizable human beings on the planet. His stage and film performances were celebrated, his recordings sold widely, and his concerts in the United States and Europe sold out. But Robeson had been to the USSR and in the late thirties had turned articulately to the left, speaking out on race issues in the United States and against the Cold War and favorably on the Soviet Union after World War II.

After Peekskill, Robeson was totally banned from making public appearances, on the grounds that his presence would invoke violence. His commercial record contracts were terminated. His passport was revoked. Camp Wo-Chi-Ca, as one of Robeson's projects, had become a target of hatred locally and consequently faced multiple dangers to its survival.

So, in the summer of 1951, a new camp was opened on its site, Camp Wyandot. Wyandot was, innocuously, an actual Native American tribal name. The renaming and the transfer of the camp's operation to a new group was a deliberate effort to cleanse its public face a bit. All noticeable symbols of political affiliation on the camp's grounds were removed. These included plaques on several water fountains and other monuments to camp staff members who were killed in the Spanish Civil War. When campers arrived in 1951, there was a new leadership in place, insistent on the need to protect the camp by depoliticizing at least its public image. I was in the group for thirteen-year-olds, and the most disturbing thing that the new directors decided to do was to prevent one of our friends, Danny Green, from coming to camp (actually turning him away when he tried to board the bus to camp at the start of the season). Danny's father, Gil Green, had been convicted under the Smith Act, and along with several other younger convicted Party leaders he had decided to go underground rather than to jail. We campers— Bobby Williamson, myself, and others—were infuriated that the camp sent Danny back home to Chicago. The camp directors argued, with some justice, that it was the only way to keep the place safe, not only from hooliganism, but from FBI penetration. I doubt very much that they were able to prevent the latter, but at least they thought that the overall security and safety of the camp required the actions that they took.

Wyandot functioned for one year at that location and then moved to New York State—far away from the clearly dangerous New Jersey site.


## BAR MITZVAH

My mother was originally called for her hearing before the New York City Board of Education in April 1951, a week before my bar mitzvah, but the board agreed to postpone the interrogation until after the ceremony.

That I had a bar mitzvah was itself strange. My parents were totally secular. Unlike Mickey's family, which was immersed in the Jewish socialist Yiddish world, my parents had little interest even with that tradition. My father's father, Jake, had no use for the practices and rituals of tradition, although Yiddish was his everyday language and he followed the Yiddish press. Mary, my paternal grandmother, insisted on ritual observance—*bentching licht* (lighting candles) on *shabbes* before a regular Friday night family dinner, going to *shul* on High Holy Days, and keeping kosher—more or less. It wasn't hard for my father, Dave, to break away from traditional versions of Jewish identity, especially given the thoroughly ritualized practices of his mother coupled with his father's disdain. As they became politically conscious, my parents were much more interested in assimilating, and although they both spoke some Yiddish, they used it only to speak to their parents. Mary was a Yiddish speaker. But she had gone to adult education classes and worked hard to rid herself of any obvious accent. Still, she faithfully made *shabbes* dinners for her two sons and their families—dinners that always featured chicken soup, boiled chicken, and, for dessert, her legendary *rugelach* (pastry).

I've already made mention of my mother's much more orthodox rearing by her very pious and unassimilated father and her deliberate self-emancipation on the tennis courts of Williamsburg, in Brooklyn.

Two of my best friends were kids who were not from the kind of left background that I came from, but their parents, of course, like most everyone in the neighborhood, were quite liberal. Both friends, Bernard Goldstein and Paul Kushner, were highly engaged with their own Jewish identity and quite naturally defined it in largely religious terms. Paul was one of my best friends at Public School 221. He later became a rabbi, and his brother, Harold Kushner, became one of the most well-known rabbis in the United States because of his best-selling books on Jewish spirituality. My other friend, Bernard, became a noted authority on medieval science and religion, specializing in Hebrew and Arabic texts. What they became as adults was foreshadowed by who they were when we were entering puberty. We were a highly intellectual trio, debating everything from the nature of the cosmos to religion, politics, and baseball. Paul and Bernard insisted that I needed to have a bar mitzvah, even though my parents didn't have an interest in or even a positive feeling about it. The three of us had decided to take Hebrew in junior high school. In the late forties, as we were entering junior high, Hebrew was introduced as a language elective in the New York schools. That was just after the founding of the state of Israel was announced—an event as celebrated by the Left as it was by the rest of the Jewish world. It seemed to me, as well as Bernard, that taking Hebrew in school would be a great thing to do. I had already learned to read the Hebrew alphabet, from attending Yiddish class at the IWO *kindershul,* and taking Hebrew in the public school meant that I could, without going to religious school, learn the prayers appropriate for the bar mitzvah ceremony.

Paul persuaded me that, without a bar mitzvah, I had no right to call myself a Jew, and my parents had no coherent answer to that. My father, against his will, went to the nearby Reform temple to arrange for my cere- mony. Paul was able to instruct me in the chanting of the necessary prayers (which, it turned out, was good practice for his subsequent rabbinical voca- tion), and the rabbi gave me the Torah portion and advised me on the other necessary preparations for the ceremony.

I've never regretted that bar mitzvah, even though it was, in some sense, consenting to a religious definition of my Jewish coming-of-age. I liked then, and still do, that I was able to participate in one of the defining rituals of Jewish tradition. And, unlike the other boy who celebrated his bar mitz- vah along with me that day, I could actually read the Hebrew.

It wasn't until I met Mickey Hartman at Camp Kinderland that I began to understand at some deeper level what the secular Yiddish socialist- humanist tradition provides in the way of ritual and substance. At that point I began to see how Jewish identity could be proudly and coher- ently expressed in a strictly nonreligious way. This understanding has been an important part of who we are in our life together, ever since we first met in 1957.

## WHAT AMERICA WAS TO ME

In school in the fifties, we learned that one of the darkest features of life in the Soviet Union was the fact that children were induced to turn in their parents for speaking against the government. It seemed to me then that many of the things said about repression in the Soviet Union could be on the horizon in American society. As the McCarthy period continued, as the purges and inquisitions went on, the felt need to mask one's political identity intensified, and the masking came to be normal. For a politically conscious kid, that hidden identity was made still more problematic because of the inescapable sense that the truth about the Soviet Union was something much darker than what we'd been raised to believe.

FIGURE 4.2. Dick, Mildred, and sister Nancy Flacks, summer in the late forties

FIGURE 4.3. Dick Flacks, circa 1949, in a favorite location

Despite such dark feelings, my main emotional response to those days was not one of fear and distress. Instead, I proudly identified very strongly with the stance that my parents took, defining it as a heroic defense of the best aspects of the American Constitution and the American political tradition. They were defending the right of free speech, the right of political association, the right not to be interrogated by the state about your politics. They exemplified to me the free exercise of dissent.

I was greatly aided in that interpretation by attending events sponsored by the Teachers Union in defense of my parents and other teachers who were being purged. These included public rallies in places such as Carnegie Hall where I got to hear heroes of the progressive tradition, like W. E. B. DuBois, the great educational reformer Alexander Meiklejohn, and Harold Taylor, the young president of Sarah Lawrence College. These are some of the people I remember seeing in the flesh, lucidly and passionately speaking about civil liberties. One person who made a vivid impact on me was a philosopher named Barrows Dunham. Dunham had been politically purged at Temple University. His work is completely forgotten now, but he was a wonderful writer and one of the few in the communist orbit who could translate Marxism into elegant philosophical and literary language. I recall being deeply inspired by a speech he delivered about the primacy of the right of the citizen versus the state—the democratic state is supposed to serve its citizens, not the other way around.

In the fifties, to be on the left came to be much less about economic justice, government planning, and state direction of the economy than about individual freedom, nonconformity, and dissent as a right and a duty. I was developing in that time a strong identification with the traditions of defiance and dissent in American history, with Thomas Jefferson and Thomas Paine as articulators of a distinctively American stance vis-à-vis government. Avidly and hungrily, I was reading as much as I could in this vein, listening as much as I could to those who articulated such ideas.

It wasn't just that I wanted to see my parents as courageous and heroic. It was that their stance helped me to think about broader issues, not only regarding McCarthyism, but also with respect to the good society as such. These ideas connected quite well with what I had already glimpsed as a result of my experiences in the town-meeting democracy of Wo-Chi-Ca. To be on the left meant to be for radical definitions of freedom of speech and expression—an understanding that came to be impossible to reconcile with the realities of either the Soviet Union or, I soon learned, the American Communist Party.

# 5 ▸ COMING OF AGE
IN THE FIFTIES

DICK:

Mickey and I are really children of the fifties rather than the sixties. I started high school in the early 1950s and therefore was inevitably shaped by the youth culture of that decade. But to be a red diaper baby at that moment was to lead a double life as a teenager. On one hand, in the ever-present world of school, there was the pop music and the subcultures defined by dress and class and race. On the other hand, in the margins, there were spaces that nurtured and enriched the political and cultural identity I'd been born into.

I was a student at Erasmus Hall High School, in Brooklyn—a venerable institution, founded back in the eighteenth century by Alexander Hamilton. When I went there it was an imposing Gothic-style quadrangle surrounding a restoration of the original Erasmus Hall Academy that Hamilton had created. In the fifties, the student body was predominantly Jewish—a mix of kids from the somewhat posh surrounding Flatbush area and more working-class and lower-middle-class kids from the Crown Heights and East New York neighborhoods to the north. It was a time when pop music created specifically for teens was coming into its own, and I was an avid listener of Martin Block and his afternoon radio show called *Make Believe Ballroom*. His Saturday morning show pioneered the Top 40 format, but Block gave us kids something of an education in pop history as we tuned him in every afternoon as a soundtrack for math homework, presenting a well-chosen mix of music from the recently past heyday of swing, alongside what was then current. The hit parade of my high school years featured the sugary pop music defined by singers such as Eddie Fisher, Joni James, and Patti Page. Social acceptance of course depended on being up on the hits, even though, it turned out, lots of kids were hungry for richer fare.

I think the fifties were the moment when dress became an absolutely crucial way to express teenage identity. In my Erasmus years, the elite boys wore charcoal gray slacks with the belt buckle in the back, white bucks, and crew cuts. And then there were the working-class kids who dressed in outlandish, shocking pink and fuchsia attire. I'm not sure what names we gave to these different crowds. But like all periods in teenage life, these factional differences were very marked and reflected fairly defined class differences. Like a lot of the more nerdy guys, I couldn't bring myself to become any of the popular types—though I did have a crew cut and wore charcoal grays.

But I led a double life, as most red diaper babies did during that period. In addition to the school youth cultures, we red diaper babies were creating an alternative. Those of us who went to the left summer camps had our own music. It was folk music, and our Elvis was Pete Seeger. The music, as often happens, helped create social scenes: for instance, in the mid-fifties, a lot of red diaper baby–type kids came from New York City's outer boroughs and suburbs to Washington Square Park in the Greenwich Village neighbor-hood of Lower Manhattan on Sundays with their guitars and banjos to swap songs and to hang out and make out.

Every couple of months, on a Saturday night, hootenannies were held in large ramshackle auditoriums in the city. The performers were a heady mix of troubadours in the Seeger vein, singing politically oriented songs, together with a considerable range of traditional performers of many cultural back-grounds. You could see blues legends like Brownie McGhee, accompanied by Sonny Terry on harmonica; all manner of Southern mountain, bluegrass, and country performers; and always a sprinkling of the international. Hoo-tenannies were not supposed to be conventional concerts. The atmosphere was informal, and there was a great deal of audience participation in the singing. After the program ended, lots of schmoozing and socializing followed—with clots of us ending up in a nearby cafeteria.

The folk music subculture that emerged in the fifties was one of several in New York and other big cities that were created by and for the many young who, for whatever reason, felt alienated from the mainstream. The folk music, folk dancing, and modern jazz venues that developed in the city in the early to mid-fifties were seedbeds for what later became the counterculture—a full-blown bohemian subculture that, for a time, challenged the hegemony of mainstream commercialized youth culture. But in the fifties, we thought that we were taking part in a more or less private and, to some extent, secret social possession of our own. Indeed, some of the key performers and cultural leaders of those scenes were blacklisted in the mainstream entertainment world.

If you were coming of age in a world that largely despised and profoundly contradicted the identity and the values with which you were raised, it was exhilarating to have such a private social world and to feel sort of brave for being in it. But if you were "political," you had much reason to question the desirability of such insulation from the mainstream and to worry quite a lot about being so isolated that you might be unable to make a difference in the world. Red diaper babies couldn't very well be satisfied simply by having some space to be ourselves.

Seeger and the Weavers had achieved huge mainstream popularity in the early fifties, and it looked for a moment as if some elements of our particular cultural perspective were going to break through into the mainstream. But the Weavers were soon blacklisted. They were denied recording contracts and concert and nightclub appearances. Their silencing seemed a sure sign that the cultural mainstream was going to be thoroughly homogenized.

But in 1955, at Christmastime, one of the memorable experiences that many red diaper babies of my generation shared was the Weavers comeback concert. Their brilliant manager, Harold Leventhal, had persuaded the quartet to reunite after a couple of years of inactivity due to the blacklist, and he persuaded Carnegie Hall to rent the space for such an event in defiance of the prevailing acceptance of the blacklist in the entertainment business. The concert was a huge success financially; in fact, a second concert had to be scheduled to accommodate the demand for tickets. Attending the concert, we thought, was itself defiance of McCarthyism. And even though the content of what the Weavers performed that night had very little overt political substance, that they were performing in the face of the blacklist and that we were all there was a liberating experience, signifying perhaps that the McCarthy cloud might be blown away.

I graduated from Erasmus in 1954, and a number of my friends went on to Columbia and other private colleges. I was just sixteen when I graduated from high school, and still pretty immature physically, so it was just as well that I continued to live at home, rather than try to deal with the social strains of dormitory life with kids who would be two years older than I. Brooklyn College, one of the campuses of what became the City University of New York (CUNY), was a completely free commuter school. I actually made some money by going there, since I had won a New York State Regents Scholarship and the award of several hundred dollars a year could be used for books and other expenses. Indeed, I was by that time pretty self-sufficient financially, taking odd jobs as a stock and delivery boy in a local drug store and babysitting for Uncle Joey and Aunt Rose's two kids, cousins Hank and Andy. I liked babysitting for them in large part because it gave me a chance to acquire a taste for jazz—listening to Benny Goodman records and the other good 78s that Joey had collected.

In the summer of 1954, I went to Camp Wyandot. I'd been going there since the camp had moved in 1951 from its New Jersey site, where it had been located after it replaced Camp Wo-Chi-Ca. The new site was at Mount Tremper, New York, not far from Woodstock. It had been the site of an old religious school or camp, and it was dominated by an imposing stone building with a large embedded cross. This dining and social hall was at the foot of a steep hill, with a very hard clay soil that turned to slippery mud when it rained. The soil posed real problems for the sewage system. Wyandot's director, a former Teamsters Union organizer, seemed to think that we soft middle-class teens needed the discipline of extremely hard labor. When the sewer system failed, my teen work group was given the task of digging trenches in very inhospitable soil conditions in the hope of restoring the leaching field. That was the hardest labor I'd ever experienced, until one day we piled into dump trucks to try to transport to the camp dozens of exceedingly heavy abandoned railroad ties (donated for no clear purpose that we knew of). I'm not sure that these experiences instilled in us a deeper appreciation for the dignity of labor (we campers, among ourselves, would make joking reference to slave labor being our fate). We did show off our blistered hands— and maybe did feel some pride that we survived these ordeals.

Those in charge of the new camp made a valiant effort to sustain it, against great odds. The political climate of the McCarthy years certainly reduced the camp's clientele, and the physical difficulties of the new camp site were serious challenges. But the biggest threat came in 1953, the year of a huge and traumatic international polio epidemic. Wyandot was especially hard-hit: eventually, six campers and staff were diagnosed with the then-dread disease, and one camper, Marian Cuca, died. The camp closed midway through the summer, and we all received a very painful regimen of gamma globulin injections (the vaccine that Jonas Salk developed wasn't available until two years later).

In 1954 the camp re-opened, with a much reduced number of kids. I went off to Wyandot, ostensibly to again participate in the teenage youth group, but as soon as I arrived, I was called to the office and offered a job as a counselor (to replace someone who hadn't showed up for the position). The offer was startling because I was considerably younger than the rest of the staff. I took it as a sort of tribute to my maturity and leadership potential that they thought that, as a sixteen-year-old, I could do the job.

That turned out to be an excellent opportunity for me, developmentally speaking. There were four of us counselors who shared a room located in between two bunks of ten-year-old boys, and we were co-counselors, each pair of us, for one of the bunks. Wyandot, perhaps even more than Wo-Chi-Ca, had been able to recruit an interracial staff, so my bunk mates included a young guy from Harlem. Phil introduced us to a new musical sound: rhythm and blues. He had a great collection of 45s he'd brought to camp, and that summer was a boom year for the music. I was, by then, a jazz fanatic, and I remember avidly reading a lot about the history of jazz and the blues in my free time. Another bunk mate was Hank Wortis. Hank was the son of a famous left-wing psychiatrist, Joseph Wortis, who that very year had published a memoir of his experience as an analysand of Sigmund Freud and later became a Marxist critic of psychoanalysis. The Wortis clan was a large, rather elite, circle of lefties in Brooklyn whose members included Alan Arkin, Earl Robinson, and other cultural figures of some note.

Hank was already a student at the University of Wisconsin, in Madison. He was president of the only chapter of the Labor Youth League (LYL), the Communist Party youth organization, allowed to function on an American college campus. It was a pretty large club at the time and, in the fifties, was one of the few visible expressions of the Left on American campuses. Hank was someone I certainly looked up to. The opportunity to work and bunk with these guys was a major growth experience for me, as was the opportunity to be in charge of a group of kids—a job that, I assume, I did pretty well despite my inexperience. I guess it was that summer that helped me crystallize my lifelong interests in working with young people, in understanding the dynamics of small groups, and in music. And it was a moment that enhanced my then-shaky self-confidence.

It was a wonderful summer for me, but not for Camp Wyandot. The polio epidemic in the previous year depleted the number of families willing to send their kids there—and by the last weeks the camp was no longer sustainable because of a falloff in registration. The summer's end marked the end of the Wo-Chi-Ca/Wyandot project.[1]

## BROOKLYN COLLEGE

I started at College in the fall of 1954 and declared myself a biology major. I was drawn to science as a practical career framework. What I really wanted to do was become a constitutional lawyer and a civil liberties champion. I had asked some lawyer friends of my parents about how I might pursue that dream. What I heard from them was an extreme disdain for the possibility that one could fulfill one's ideals as a lawyer. "Basically," they said, "you'll become an ambulance chaser. You will be consigned to a life of dealing with matters that are of little significance. Hardly anyone gets to be a constitutional lawyer—don't get trapped." I rather stupidly accepted this advice without further investigation. Ever since, I've advised students searching for their calling to thoroughly investigate the possibilities. I'd been too casual about searching for mine. To this day, I believe I could have been a very good lawyer.

Another path that I was attracted to but ruled out was journalism. By the time I got to college I knew I could write, and I was an avid consumer of the journalism of the day. But I couldn't imagine how I would make a living that way given my political convictions. There was only one genuinely left national publication that I could imagine working for—the weekly *National Guardian*—but I knew it was very unlikely that one could survive doing that. One big way the world has changed since that time has been the emergence of alternative media, providing all manner of vocation for young people seeking space and opportunity to work outside of the dominant corporate media. The opening up, since the sixties, of manifold avenues for vocations oriented to cultural and political opposition is an important achievement I strongly feel—even as I join in the chorus of complaint about concentrated corporate control of the mainstream media.

My experiencing the intellectual and cultural world as largely inhospitable to whatever talent I might have had led me to believe that at least in the sciences one might find a career where brains counted—and, I realized, in pursuing one's studies in science, one would never be faced with the threat of the draft. That threat was real for me; even though the Korean War was over by the time I got to college, the peacetime draft remained and its looming shaped my life choices. In the fifties, it seemed as if science was the one professional direction that was relatively apolitical, potentially fulfilling, and safe from the possibility of military conscription.

Fortunately for my future happiness, such considerations were unable to outweigh the tedium of freshman biology and chemistry. I saw almost immediately that my passions were instead stirred by the social science, literature, philosophy, and history courses that I was taking.

I ended up deciding to major in psychology. Sociology and other social sciences, I imagined, were evidently inhospitable to my Marxian faith. Moreover, in those years, psychology was a prime arena of fascination for young intellectual types like me. Psychoanalysis and other psychologies were big topics of conversation, both on campus and in the wider intellectual world; the chance to probe these theories was most intriguing, as was the sense that maybe I'd find ways to understand my own personal conflicts and anxieties. So I avidly took classes in social psychology, experimental psychology, and personality and read books by great psychological theorists, getting immersed in Freud, Alfred Adler, et al.

One of my jobs in college was to babysit the two-year-old son of a psychiatrist friend of my parents. Her name was Helen, and she lived in a residential hotel in Brooklyn Heights. I would come by after class in the late afternoon to look after the child, while his mother received patients in another wing of the apartment. The hotel lifestyle itself was new for me. For example, the child knew how to call for room service for his supper, ordering the delivery of "a burger and fries and a chocolate milk" on the house phone. I would arrive at mid-afternoon, take the kid out to the playground, and play with him until dinner. The apartment fridge was well stocked with exotic takeout dinners from the several food specialty shops that lined Montague Street near the hotel. In the evening, after a stab at my homework, I'd prowl through Helen's extensive library of psychotherapeutic and psychological literature. I remember first coming across Simone de Beauvoir's *Second Sex* on her shelves. My presence two or three afternoons and evenings a week allowed her to meet clients but also enabled her to go out on dates in the evening. She'd come home fairly tipsy sometimes, and it wasn't until years later that I realized that her occasional offers to me to spend the night might have been expressing more than maternal concern about sending a seventeen-year-old kid out at 2 A.M. to brave the New York City subway.

By the time I got to Brooklyn College it had become well known in the academic world for its repression of dissident and left-wing student activism. In the thirties and forties, Brooklyn was known as a red hotbed—though the City College of New York (CCNY) certainly exceeded Brooklyn College as an activist center. In Brooklyn, in those years, the Catholic Church was a powerful force, and the church was dominated by an extreme right-wing politics. That was the diocese that supported Franco in the Spanish Civil War as well as a variety of right-wing causes. The newspaper of the diocese, called the *Brooklyn Tablet*, was a prime mover behind the witch hunts in the New York City schools that led to the purge of my parents and the destruction of the Teachers Union. One of the achievements that Brooklyn Catholic leadership seemed to be proud of was cleansing red influence out of Brooklyn College.

I remember that a major Catholic clergyman gave a speech when I was a student there. He spoke proudly of the church's role in bringing Harry Gideonse to the presidency of the college in 1939. Gideonse was famous as a staunch anti-communist. Beginning in the late 1940s, Gideonse certainly did clean house. He abolished student government. He banned from the campus several student groups and expelled a number of left-wing activists. These things happened a few years before I arrived in 1954. So by the time I was at Brooklyn College, it was quite depoliticized. There was an unelected student government, the student paper was subject to administration control and censorship, and the extant political organizations on campus had a combined membership of maybe fifty people in a student body of around twenty thousand. In addition, several leading members of the faculty had been purged in the McCarthy period, including literature professor turned psychoanalyst Harry Slochower, the beloved literature professor Frederic Ewen, and famed classics scholar Meyer Reinhold. In short, a decided atmosphere of intimidation pervaded the place in my time there.

Soon after arriving at college, I joined the LYL. As the youth wing of the Communist Party, the LYL was banned from official recognition at the city colleges in New York and, indeed, at most colleges around the United States, but we had a chapter that met regularly off-campus in people's apartments. One of our activities was to study Marxism, and the Party intellectuals who came to our meetings to instruct us presented it as an arcane discipline, mastery of which required deep study. I learned later on that this kind of mystification of Marxism was characteristic of a Stalinist approach to Marx. It was a way of creating a "Marxist-Leninist" secular religion whose secrets (encapsulated by the phrase "dialectical materialism") were best understood only by a select few. Later, in the intellectual climate of the post-sixties, I again tried to immerse myself in Marx's work, no longer as sacred text but as a social theory open to test, revision, and deep debate—which, I learned, was how Marx himself wanted his work to be treated.

The discourse of the communist-oriented intellectual community I was part of then was very narrow, but the same might be said of the discourse within the walls of the college. Being in both worlds compelled me to think more deeply about big issues than I would have had I simply lived in one or the other.

For some years, a thriving educational institution, the Jefferson School of Social Science, had been operating under the aegis of the Communist Party. The Jefferson School, which occupied a building just off Union Square, offered many classes of many kinds and had a pretty distinguished part-time faculty, whose members included those forced out of academia in the McCarthy purges, as well as left-wing celebrity writers and artists who identified with the Party. I remember going to a series of lectures on film noir by Dashiell Hammett, the legendary mystery writer. The Jefferson School went out of business in the 1950s, but it was replaced by a number of informal Marxist studies forums and classes toward the end of the decade. So even in the darkest days of Cold War repression, an intellectual life connected with Marxist theory and philosophy could be found in New York City. Like the folk music scene, this Marxist intellectual niche helped define a distinctive shared identity, and taking part in it seemed as well to be a moral act—to keep alive an intellectual flame that the powers that be were determined to extinguish.

We in the LYL chapter were interested in action as well. It was hard to figure out in the mid-fifties how we could undertake public activity in our own name given all the dangers and fears associated with bearing the red label. Indeed, at that time there were no models of public, "open" expression and action by the Communist Party that we could look to. The way we could be effective, we thought, was for interested chapter members to join existing political groups on campus. This was called "mass org(anizational) work." I joined and became active in the campus Young Democrats. My closest LYL friend, Richard, similarly joined Students for Democratic Action, the student arm of Americans for Democratic Action. We both were elected president of our respective campus chapters.

At first glance, one might say that we were "infiltrating" these groups with insidious communist purpose. But in our own minds, our intent was to revitalize these organizations—to make them actively fulfill their stated goals. Given the profound apathy of the student body, we believed—and, among ourselves, discussed—that our goal was to get students engaged.

When I joined the Young Democrats and became chapter president, the organization was simply a channel for recruiting students to do basic campaign work for the local political machine during elections. I remember going with a group of Young Dems to the local Democratic Party headquarters near the college and being greeted by a guy who could've been drawn by Thomas Nast. He was a big, fat-bellied guy sporting a vest with a watch chain, smoking a cigar, and sitting behind a very large desk. I couldn't quite believe my eyes. It was 1956, during Adlai Stevenson's campaign for president, and Stevenson, of course, was someone who a lot of us student Democrats were pretty excited by. But the party boss sitting behind the desk said: "Look, kids, you gotta get why the only thing that we can elect that means anything is the judges. So forget about campaigning for Stevenson (who'll lose anyway). We need turnout for the judges." Of course, if you were part of a corrupt machine, it was very important to have the judges. Such was the everyday politics of the Brooklyn Democratic machine.

My own view as both a Young Democrat and an LYLer was that the Young Democrats should be more engaged in the issues of the day and in particular the increasingly urgent civil rights cause. In 1955 a young woman named Autherine Lucy broke the color barrier to gain court-ordered admission to the University of Alabama. Riots by violent mobs caused the university to suspend her after three days. I suggested that the Young Democrats work to get our student government to voice its support for Lucy—which we succeeded in doing. Then I proposed that we set up a table near the school cafeteria to get signatures in support of anti–poll tax legislation that was being introduced in Congress. Staffing that table for a few days gave me a sense of what the students at Brooklyn College were thinking about politically. Very typically, kids would come to the table, read our material, and then say:

"Well, my mother said when I got to college I should never sign anything of a political character because I would be in trouble later in life. So I better not sign this." That memory stands out for me as characteristic of the damage that the McCarthy period had been doing to democratic possibility in the country.

Still, only a few years later, there was a noticeable increase in student interest in the state of the world. After all, it was in those years that the bus boycott in Montgomery, Alabama, took place, and it was a very stirring experience. By 1958, several thousand New York students were mobilized by Bayard Rustin (a lieutenant of Martin Luther King Jr.) for the Youth March for Integrated Schools in Washington, D.C.

My leadership helped a bit in getting the local chapter to work to fulfill the agenda of the liberal wing of the Democratic Party. I participated in city-wide meetings of the emergent college-based reform Democrats. The reform movement seemed then to have a lot of potential, not only for overturning the stale machine domination of the party but for advancing a progressive policy agenda. A memorable occasion was a Young Democrats citywide meeting to which Eleanor Roosevelt came to talk. It wasn't a large event, so we had a chance to see Ms. Roosevelt up close. She gave a pep talk to those assembled, encouraging us to support the developing reform movement in the Democratic Party in New York City.

My friend and comrade in the LYL, Richard, played a similar role as head of the Students for Democratic Action (SDA). SDA, like other liberal organizations in the postwar period, had a specific clause in its constitution barring Communists from membership. Richard, nevertheless, became chairman of that chapter and operated, as I did with the Young Democrats, as a rejuvenating force for that group. We didn't accept the legitimacy of such blanket exclusionary rules in liberal organizations—rules that categorized and prejudged people like us. As the fifties went on, red diaper babies across the country, who wanted to participate in liberal organizations, were coming up against this problem. We very much wanted to work against the nuclear arms race and to support the civil rights struggle—and yet the organizations championing these causes would have excluded us if they had known about our inherited political sympathies. For a few years in the late fifties, I and my "red" compatriots practiced deceit so that we could be sincere members of those organizations. As we'll later see, the issue of membership exclusion was central in the founding moments of Students for a Democratic Society in the sixties.

At any rate, the two leading liberal organizations on campus—the Young Democrats and Students for Democratic Action—were thus headed by two secret members of the LYL. We didn't receive any direction from the LYL leadership but were guided by our own instincts and impulses for our "mass org work." In fact, my engagement with mainstream politics helped in my decision to support the abolition of the LYL in the aftermath of the Khrushchev revelations. I was beginning to see the need for a politics that was free of the moral and political failings of both the communist and anti-communist versions of the left.

Our band of LYLers was not the only grouplet of self-identified Marxists in my time at Brooklyn College. There was a chapter of the Young Socialist League (YSL) on campus. I'm not sure what they did politically as a group, but I got to know several of their members because the handful of campus politicos routinely schmoozed in the cafeteria. All of the half dozen YSLers were extremely bright and extremely articulate, and I certainly felt an affinity to their radicalism. I'd never really known, before encountering these folks, that one could be staunchly Marxist and vituperatively anti-communist at the same time. Since they knew me politically only as chair of the Young Democrats, I'm sure that my politics, a Democrat who was professedly socialist, confused them, too.

The YSL group was more overtly bohemian and stylistically radical than was typical of the red diaper babies who were my friends. But unlike most bohemian kids of that time, they had become highly politicized. The leader of the International Socialist League (ISL), the parent organization of the YSL, was Max Shachtman, who was a close follower of Leon Trotsky but who broke with the main Trotskyist formation in a big fight about the nature of the USSR. Shachtman argued that Stalinism was not producing a "deformed workers' state" as Trotsky and the Socialist Workers Party believed, but was instead a totalitarian society dominated by a bureaucratic ruling class. Shachtman's position, represented by his tiny but talented band of followers in the ISL, led many of them eventually to back the United States in the Cold War.

Michael Harrington was the chair of the ISL in its heyday. I had a chance to see Mike Harrington in person when the YSL group invited him to speak at Brooklyn College after the Hungarian revolution of 1956 was suppressed by the Soviet army. Mike, then in his early thirties, was a stirring speaker; he was one of the best political speakers I'd seen in the 1950s. I was bemused to realize that he could combine a fierce and bitter anti-Soviet perspective with a very open, articulate advocacy of socialism and Marxism. After all, the LYL and the Communists I knew were not advocating socialism or Marxism in public, but Mike was. My political evolution was certainly fostered by the fact that he was a bitter enemy of the politics that I identified with, while, at the same time, he was expressing eloquently the social vision that politics was supposed to be advancing.

Mike Harrington was able to speak at the city colleges in New York, but Communist Party leaders were not allowed to do so. The colleges had a rule that anyone who had been convicted of a felony was banned from appearing on campus, and the top Party leaders had served jail time under the Smith Act (for allegedly "conspiring to teach and advocate the overthrow of the United States government"). The speakers ban became an issue in 1956, when many of those leaders began to openly and deeply criticize the Soviet Union and the Communist Party's mode of operation. John Gates, who was the editor of the *Daily Worker* and a leader of the effort to transform the Communist Party, was not allowed to speak on campus simply because he had been convicted under the Smith Act.

That convulsion in the Communist Party was precipitated by the speech Nikita Khrushchev delivered at the Twentieth Congress of the Communist Party of the Soviet Union in 1956. In that speech, which was printed in the *New York Times* and then in the *Daily Worker*, Khrushchev made a fierce and stunning denunciation of Stalin, providing a detailed litany of crimes that Stalin committed against the Communist Party and its leadership, as well as against the Soviet people. Khrushchev's speech, which was intended to initiate a process of de-Stalinization of the Party, was a tremendous blow to those remnants of the Communist Party who were still trying to maintain the organization. They had publicly denied the whole history that Khrushchev was now declaring to be valid. In addition to the liquidation of most of the leadership of the Bolshevik revolution, Khrushchev confessed to the false accusations against much of that leadership in the famous purge trials of the 1930s—trials that the American Party had strained hard to justify. He confessed to the creation of labor camps in which millions of people had been incarcerated—thereby validating much of the case against Stalin and the Soviet Union that Communists had always denounced as capitalist propaganda.

Most Party veterans were of course devastated by these revelations, even if a few believed that the speech was a CIA fabrication. But I think for many in the communist orbit, the speech was liberating. I was eighteen years old and had been avidly political for at least five years. In those years, I'd come to believe that there was a tremendous disjunction between what the Party claimed the Soviet Union to be and its reality. After all, it was hard to deny events such as the suppression of the East German workers revolt in the early fifties, among other glaring instances of repression. Khrushchev's speech gave a license for the U.S. Party to launch a critical examination of its entire history and mode of operation. It was to the credit of Gates and other staff of the *Daily Worker* that they opened its pages to an unprecedented free discussion of all those issues. For months after that announcement, the newspaper was filled with debate, astonishing for its fierceness. The Party had always operated under the principle of so-called democratic centralism, under which discussion was supposed to be allowed prior to a decision (but certainly not in public view) until Party policy was set by the leadership, after which criticism was forbidden. Such public debate within the Party hadn't happened for decades.

The debate raging in the Party newspaper spilled over to the LYL. I was not only a member of our local club in Brooklyn but went to meetings city-wide for representatives of college chapters. In the aftermath of the Khrushchev speech, those meetings became fascinating forums in which dissident members of the LYL leadership and other Party people came to talk to us about what was happening. We were drawn into an organized effort to repair fundamental flaws in the operation of these organizations and to suggest that new directions were needed. For me, this moment was tremendously exciting and creative. It meant that you could denounce much of the practice of the Communist Party in order to restore a radical quest for social change and engage in a freewheeling search for strategy and modes of action that might bring such change. The opening up of this discussion made this search more valid and more available to ordinary members.

One of the Communist Party's great delusions was that its top leaders had more wisdom than anybody else, and Party discipline required fealty to the Party line as defined by the central committee. Apart from the inherently authoritarian mode of operation that deeply conflicted with the Party's claim to be the leading force for human emancipation, it was a model that was doomed to failure. For to be in the leadership of the Communist Party of the United States was to be inevitably separate from much of the reality of ordinary working people—while simultaneously claiming to be their Vanguard. On the other hand, ordinary Party members, like my parents, were experienced in the daily realities of life in their workplaces and their neighborhoods. They, accordingly, had knowledge gleaned from their direct efforts in organizing and living everyday life. Given the structure of the Party, however, that knowledge, that wisdom, that experience, was not able to percolate to the top of the Party. Moreover, of course, Party policies were set in accordance with the Soviet Party's demands and decisions. Time and again, the U.S. Party line was changed to fit what the its leadership claimed was conformity with the defense of the Soviet Union and of international communist unity. The Party line was set by leaders whose lives revolved around maintaining this organization and retaining their control of it, not by people who were engaged in the day-to-day processes of organizing and communicating, of living and working with the "masses." Some Party leaders had excellent experience and achievement as organizers, but most of these had long since lost connections of that kind. Most of them rarely even spoke to wider publics, since, in the McCarthy years, they were denied that opportunity.

The most well-known Party leader in the 1930s was probably Earl Browder, who ran for U.S. president and who, in those years, had regular contact with mainstream labor leadership. He was by no means a great man, but at least he was an authentic leader with some following and some connection to mainstream reality. Browder was expelled from the Communist Party in 1945 after trying to initiate a reformation of the Party to make it possible for it to participate in a progressive coalition in America, rather than have it continue to claim to be a vanguard organization in the revolutionary Leninist sense. Browder seemed to think that his direction was getting Stalin's approval, but, it turned out, the international communist leadership decided to denounce "Browderism." So Browder and whoever was following him left the Party after World War II; the Communist Party was, as a result, much more subject to the control of those determined to maintain the orthodox ideological framework and a slavish adherence to the Soviet line.

All this history and practice became subject to debate—at least for a few months after Khruschev's speech—in the LYL and the Party world. I experienced this moment as a time of great romance. It enabled someone like me, who had been reared within the framework of communist ideology and culture, to learn about a wider variety of ways of being on the left—a wider appreciation of possibility—than that given by Party policy, and to formulate an articulate basis for rejecting the validity of the Party as a vehicle for political hope.

## CAMP KINDERLAND

Because Camp Wyandot folded after the disastrous summer of 1954, I decided in 1955 to work as a counselor at Camp Kinderland, the oldest of the communist-initiated children's camps in the United States. It was founded in 1923 by Jewish Marxists—the same group that had founded the first Marxist-Leninist newspaper in America, the Yiddish *Morgn Freiheit*. Camp Kinderland was established not only to instill socialist values in the children but to nurture instruction in Yiddish culture and language. It was built on Sylvan Lake, not far from Poughkeepsie, New York, and it was paired with an adult resort called Lakeland—a flourishing institution for many years, serving as a cheap vacation destination for Jewish working-class people of several generations. A number of us refugees from the Wo-Chi-Ca/Wyandot circle gravitated to Kinderland, although we tended to be critical of its perspective, imbued as we were with the idea that a summer camp should be an interracial, multicultural experience rather than be focused, as Kinderland was, on a more particular ethnic identity and tradition. Once at Kinderland, I came to realize that there was a long-standing tension in the communist Left in the United States between an emphasis on ethnic identity and a perspective that was multicultural and interracial. Class consciousness in the United States has always been expressed through ethnic solidarity; ethnically identified Marxists in the United States sought to build a left political culture using the languages, histories, and values of their particular ethnic communities. Kinderland (still operating after ninety-five years) exemplifies that path. Wo-Chi-Ca, which opened at the height of the Popular Front in the 1930s was an experiment that fostered anti-racism and anti-sexism, multicultural learning; it was a utopia of brotherhood and sisterhood.

Both Kinderland and Wo-Chi-Ca were owned by the International Workers Order (IWO). The IWO had split off from the Workmen's Circle in the 1920s as a result of a bitter internal struggle in the aftermath of the Bolshevik revolution. The old guard members of the Workmen's Circle were, for various reasons, strongly opposed to the possibility that it might express support for that revolution, and eventually, after a battle over the soul of the organization, the Left split off to establish the IWO. The IWO, accordingly, began as a Jewish working-class socialist organization designed to provide cultural activity and services to Jewish workers, just as the Workmen's Circle did. Kinderland was founded before the split and remained in the embrace of the Left. After the split, the Workmen's Circle created a rival camp across Sylvan Lake, called Kinder Ring. These were two parallel and hostile Yiddish socialist universes for decades, living testaments to what seemed an interminable war within the Left and the labor movement.

Unlike the Workmen's Circle, however, the IWO became a federation of diverse ethnic groups. There was a Russian federation, a Finnish federation, and a variety of other ethnic groupings with semi-autonomous organizations, choruses, funeral societies, and publications—a host of cultural activities and self-help arrangements. In the thirties, the IWO membership was at least double that of the Workmen's Circle. Much of its appeal had to do with the fact that it provided health and life insurance benefits, which were simply unavailable or unaffordable for many of its members in the wider society. The IWO insured miners, who were otherwise uninsurable, and blacks, for example. In its heyday, it was one of the most important organizational achievements of the communist movement. In the mid-fifties, the IWO came under ultimately fatal attack by New York State insurance authorities, who claimed that its political character jeopardized its insurance capabilities. But Kinderland/Lakeland survived the attack.

Somehow, the decision to go to Kinderland became a Flacks family affair. My father, always looking for a chance to work in a summer resort, was hired as assistant manager of Lakeland. I'm not sure what his job description included, but I assume that he had to deal with all kinds of issues, from plant maintenance and the functioning of the dining room and the hotel facilities to overseeing the social and cultural activity available to the guests. There was a considerable offering of such activity: each week, there were featured name performers, folk dance callers, drama and choral groups, and daily political lectures and discussions.

As they had managed in most previous summers, my parents got a free summer stay in a nice resort, with a beautiful lake and, of course, a tennis court. I'm not sure if Dave made additional money as well. My sister spent the summer as a camper in Kinderland. It was a family arrangement that lasted for a couple of years after that.

In 1955, at age seventeen, I was the counselor for a bunk of ten-year olds, in subsequent years I was promoted to group leader, eventually playing a very active role for a couple of summers in the core directorate of the camp. These summers were crucial in my personal development. Just taking charge of a group of pre-adolescent kids and learning on a daily basis how to encourage their collective spirit, while attending to their individual troubles, certainly enabled me to grow. It was also a role in which I had to acquire some useful skills—camping, sports instruction, leading group games and activities, and learning a lot about "nature." We did some theatrical activities with the kids that I was very proud of, especially putting on a production of *The Diary of Anne Frank*, which I directed.

Camp is also an opportunity for forming deep personal connection. And in that time, in the mid-fifties, such connection was lifesaving. We staff were all red diaper babies, all in our formative years, all looking for political and vocational direction. Many of the people I encountered when I arrived already knew each other. They were longtime Kinderlanders and typically grew up together in the city, in the IWO *kindershuls*. Coming to Kinderland meant that I was breaking into a new and cohesive social world, making close friendships that I've sustained ever since.

Of course, the most important thing that happened to me in the Kinderland years was meeting Mickey Hartman, who came in the summer of 1957 as a camp counselor. We bonded pretty quickly and have remained bonded ever since. That bond and how we lived it is, of course, the heart of the story this book is telling.

I think, right from the start, we knew that we were meant for each other—as friends and lovers. But the time in camp was exceedingly demanding on time and energy. I was now a group leader, supervising three bunks—while still counselor for one of them. At the same time, we were intensely interested in the way the camp was functioning. Mickey and I and another couple, also in leadership roles, decided to spend our days off traveling to other nonprofit camps, Jewish and otherwise, to see how they operated. Many of us younger staff had come to believe that Kinderland was not reaching its potential as a fulfilling children's camp. There was too much emphasis on Yiddish pedagogy and on practices that, rather than child-oriented, seemed instead to implement a script defined by venerable "cultural commissars," as we called the long-standing elders and leaders of the Yiddishist Left. There was not enough sheer fun, nor was there sufficient thought given to camper interests and needs. With respect to Yiddish language and culture, camp felt like a school, and, accordingly, most of the children were alienated from the formal camp program. We wanted to reform Kinderland—to make it more truly a children's camp, to make it more open to practices and cultural expression that went beyond the boundaries that had been set in its own particular tradition. Traveling to many of the thriving camps in the region was eye-opening for us—and inspiring. There were a number of other Yiddish camps still operating that we visited. There were camps run by various settlement houses and Jewish Federation camps that were governed by professional social work principles. Seeing these other camps, and having our own discussions that summer, led us in the following summer, 1958, to work to redo the camp program—to modernize it, if you will.

That effort was part of a more general project that I was now committed to. Could we help modernize and transform the Left that we had been born into, to make it more truly fulfilling of its stated objectives? I had come to believe strongly that the Left had reached not only a dead end but a moral abyss. My junior and senior years in college were really formative ones for me. Personally, I now had a relationship that was fulfilling on every level. And in those years, my intellectual perspective began to crystallize.

I took courses in social psychology and became passionate about a field that, until then, I'd never heard of. My first feeling of passion for social psychology was inspired by a textbook called *Social Psychology* by Solomon Asch. Asch's book is one of the most creative works in the field I've ever read. He was the experimenter who conducted the famous study in which individuals were asked to make visual judgments comparing the length of lines in the presence of a group of people. The "naive" subjects in the Asch experiments were unaware that the others participating with them were the experimenter's accomplices, who deliberately gave false responses to the task. Asch's question was whether people who were presented with data that they could see with their own eyes but that was contradicted by data provided by the claims of other people would submit to those group claims or would maintain their own perceptions. It was a striking study in its own terms, particularly in the context of the climate of conformity in the 1950s. That one could take urgent social questions and make them subject to controlled experiment was really intriguing to me.

But the book provided further challenge and fascination. Asch strove for a brilliant synthesis of Gestalt psychology (in more contemporary terms, a kind of cognitive psychology) with an implicit Marxism. He presented a strong critique of both behavioral and Freudian psychologies—the then-dominant paradigms. If there's any single intellectual experience that inspired me to become a social psychologist, it was reading Asch's book. I was, incidentally, further pleased to learn that he had been teaching at Brooklyn College in the 1940s but had left to avoid the witch hunt.

Harold Proshansky, as a classroom teacher and as a mentor, helped inspire me to see social psychology as a field directly connected to social reality and encouraged me to think that I might have some aptitude for it. Proshansky did influential work in what came to be called environmental psychology, but his main achievement was to rise to the presidency of the CUNY Graduate Center soon after it was established. He was a formative figure in the creation and development of the CUNY Graduate Program, which he presided over for nearly twenty years, becoming something of a legendary figure in the making of the City University. I credit him with setting me on my career path at the very start of his own.

Proshansky encouraged me to apply to graduate school at the University of Michigan, which at the time had the pre-eminent graduate social psychology program.. Two other classmates of mine also applied to the university, and the three of us Brooklyn boys were accepted. As a group, we went to Ann Arbor in June 1958 to scout around for a place to live and to see the lay of the land. We three—Alan Guskin, Doug Robbins, and myself—like many of our provincial Brooklyn peers—had never lived anywhere but Brooklyn; never even flown in a plane before. So that was a memorable trip in itself. It was, it turned out, the beginning of my journey not only out of Brooklyn but into America.

MICKEY:

I joyfully began at CCNY, the first of the New York city colleges, which were established to be free of charge, to educate a generation of immigrants' children to be the teachers of immigrants' children and grandchildren. (The one thing I KNEW I didn't want to be was a teacher of children, but I DID want to go to CCNY). My parents couldn't really afford the expenses of the college—books, lab fees, and so on—and even though I lived at home and commuted to college, I was otherwise financially independent and had been since my first summer job at age fourteen. Also, as a recipient of the New York State Regents Scholarship, I received $1,400 for four years, and that more than covered all my college expenses. I continued to work at various jobs all through college, which gave me cigarette and "spending money" but sometimes interfered with my college work.

My time at the Bronx High School of Science had convinced me that I wanted a job in science—biology seemed to be a choice that would all but guarantee my being employed anytime, anywhere. That was, in fact, true—but my 4.0 average in liberal arts courses (especially English) combined with my 2.5 average in all the required science courses (3.5 in the elective courses) yielded a respectable B average upon graduation. I spent a good deal of my college career in left-wing political activity, mainly in the Marxist Discussion Club (as its chair) and the like (hanging out in the famous CCNY cafeteria, discussing the nuances of left-wing thought), and not leaving really enough time to learn organic chemistry—nor did I have the inclination to learn it.

I remember a few great teachers at CCNY: Mr. Rosenberg, who used the Socratic method to teach us about democracy in Government 101, helped me shed my totalitarian tendencies (learned, I think, at my mother's knee: I used to say that I could understand the ills of the USSR if I imagined my mother in charge of it). Professor Root, who taught biology, allowed me to organize a course in comparative physiology, which had not been taught in decades—he then taught the course within the context of the laws of thermodynamics, particularly the law of entropy. I fondly remember wonderful student discussions after class about what we had just been studying—a rare experience.

But the best college teacher imaginable was, as I noted in an earlier chapter, Daniel S. Lehrman, a professor of psychology at Rutgers University, who was a CCNY alumnus and continued to teach in the college's evening session. In a course I took, Lerman introduced us to the concepts of "reductionism" in science, which sought to understand animal (and, ultimately, human) behavior by reducing it to its lowest forms. He had been a student of T. C. Schneirla, who was a pioneer in debunking the simplistic, reductionist concepts of many of the psychologists of the fifties. Lehrman studied ring doves, and it was a joy to watch his 250-pound self waddle around in imitation of the doves' mating behavior. I have never seen a more compelling teacher.

Both Lehrman and Schneirla died tragically too young, and both biology and psychology, for a while, fell into the hands of racist "thinkers." I urge any reader who is interested in the debate surrounding "nature or nurture" to look at the writings of Schneirla and Lehrman.

I also had a wonderful teacher in an elective philosophy course—but more on that in a later chapter.

## TEEN LOVERS IN THE RED CITY

DICK:

Mickey and I returned from camp at the end of summer 1957 more or less committed to each other. We dated and did the usual things that a young couple might want to do in New York in the fall in the fifties. Our first date was a big jazz concert in Central Park featuring Dizzy Gillespie, Lionel Hampton, and other stars; Mickey was willing but not eager to listen to jazz—so from then on we planned our dates to maximize our shared interests. We got season tickets to the New York City Center Opera, which that year featured some recent American operas. In those years it was affordable to sit in the far balcony at Broadway shows, and we went to several. We saw Richard Burton in *Look Back in Anger* and Anthony Perkins in *Look Homeward, Angel*. The first musical we saw together was the initial production of *West Side Story*. And, of course, there were the hootenannies and the Pete Seeger concerts. One thing we loved to do was get "twofer" coupons to eat at one of Arthur Maisel's restaurants in Manhattan. You could get two moderately priced steak dinners (including martinis) for the price of one, with a coupon, distributed for free at the Grand Central subway station. As a result, we typically went to the shows rather stoned on those martinis. Mickey was under the legal age of eighteen—but she always managed to avoid being carded.

Fundamental to our bonding was, of course, our shared identity as red diaper babies and our shared, growing questioning of the communist movement; so some of what we did together was a bit unusual for a young couple in love. At that moment a series of what were called "socialist forums" were being organized in the city by someone we were not familiar with at the time, A. J. Muste, who invited an array of leaders of the various warring socialist sects to appear together to debate the future of socialism. It was probably the first time that people like Eugene Dennis, head of the Communist Party, appeared on the same stage as Norman Thomas, head of the Socialist Party, and Trotskyist leaders as well. We found these events intriguing and very much to our liking. Muste seemed to understand the need to transcend the age-old profound conflicts of the radical Left.

Those forums were glimmers of hope in our quest for paths toward a transformed Left. I had been reading in school the works of C. Wright Mills, and he became, quickly, one of my heroes. His great work *The Power Elite* had just been published, and this book pointed, both in theory and in analysis, to ideas and modes of thought that the Old Left had not yet understood—about changes in the class system and about the problems of advanced capitalist society, including nuclear war, bureaucracy and the state, and corporate domination.

One experience we both remember quite well was going to a meeting of young communist-oriented students and youth, under the auspices of the Communist Party. We went in order to provoke questioning on the part of the people who were there; some of those present were much more ortho-dox and traditional Party-oriented people than we had become. We brought with us a copy of Lenin's *Left-Wing Communism, an Infantile Disorder* (in a Little Lenin Library edition), which we prominently displayed as one way to provoke. Some aging leaders of the Party addressed the group in terms that I found incredibly irrelevant. I recall Gus Hall instructing the youth that the best way to reach the masses was to join volleyball teams and attract recruits through that kind of sport. In any event, I found myself standing up in front of the group and saying that it seemed to me no longer possible for the Communist Party to serve in any way as an authority for us, given its total failure of moral leadership and its total subservience to the Soviet line.

By this time, the Gates faction of the Party had pretty much been elimi-nated, the Party was back in the control of its slavishly Party-line leaders, and a number of our elders whom Mickey and I were close to and who had been active in the Party quit after their failure to reform it. So we were, in certain ways, bitter, yet at that time in 1957 we were sure that the future of the Left in the United States wasn't going to be found in the precincts of the past. During that year, as participants in the LYL, we had helped to disman-tle that organization in the hope that something new might emerge.

However, my decision to go to graduate school in social psychology upon graduating from Brooklyn College expressed my own belief that political possibilities were not that evident. I thought that I should pursue my intel-lectual passion and an academic career, not knowing when we might have new opportunities for honest political engagement. In the fall of 1958, I embarked for Ann Arbor along with my other Brooklyn College buddies and thus started an entirely new chapter in my life.

Mickey was then a sophomore at CCNY, but we vowed that we would continue "going steady"—though we were not yet ready to think about marriage.

Moving out of Brooklyn and out of New York and into the Midwest was transforming. I'd never been west of the Hudson River, and our Brooklyn trio had never had to enter a world that was not predominantly Jewish and that was Republican to boot. Yet it didn't take long to realize that our New York–bred sophistication was itself a kind of provincialism—that New Yorkers were cut off from cultural and political stirrings beginning to ferment in the rest of America.

My physical move to Ann Arbor and the Midwest was simultaneous with my political move away from the Old Left and my emotional move away from my parents' world. It was decidedly a new chapter.

# 6 ▸ STARTING OUT IN THE SIXTIES

DICK:

In the fall of 1958 we three social psychology students, Alan Guskin, Doug Robbins, and I, were joined by Richard Frucht, an anthropology student who also had just graduated from Brooklyn College. We settled in a ramshackle old house near campus—four guys in a two-bedroom shabbily furnished apartment. I think our shared monthly rent was probably around $150 for the apartment, and we each chipped in about $5 a week for the food budget. We made most of our meals at home; a typical supper was a huge bowl of macaroni, cottage cheese, and ketchup. We soon learned to make oven-fried chicken, spaghetti and meatballs, and burgers—all possible within our weekly $20 food budget.. All of us were fully financed by our graduate departments. In 1958, prices were low and federal support for graduate education was high.

The two years I lived with roommates were the most carefree time in my life. I hadn't had the experience of going away to college, so it was only now that I was living on my own. The idea that my entire day was under my own control was quite liberating. Surprisingly, graduate school turned out to be freer than college. There were fewer classes to take, and although we had research and teaching assistant jobs, much of our day had no fixed schedule. In the graduate school environment you are continuously being judged by your professors and your peers. Such judgments are of course quite fateful—your performance on exams, your brilliance in seminars, and in informal interaction, determined your standing in the eyes of professors and peers and your career opportunities beyond.

Despite these ostensible pressures, I marveled at my feelings of freedom. As someone who was academically quite adept, the competitive demands were not ones I found onerous. In fact, I reveled in the opportunity to be totally immersed intellectually and to be on my way to becoming a professional scholar.

The pleasure of that experience in Ann Arbor at that time had much to do with the particular nature of the social psychology graduate program at the University of Michigan. Social psychologists in the 1940s had demonstrated for the war effort the utility of survey research, laboratory experiments in group process, and other systematic methodologies for studying social behavior and attitudes. The social research entrepreneurs who converged on Ann Arbor after the war were able to obtain substantial government funding to build the research and training programs they ambitiously envisioned. They had both the connections and the track record to secure the needed grants—and to persuade federal decision makers that big postwar investment in social research was a good thing.

This pioneering group, which included my mentors Theodore (Ted) Newcomb and Daniel Katz, established the first PhD program in social psychology, envisioning it as a new discipline born out of a fusion between psychology and sociology. Ann Arbor became the national center of empirical social research, housed in the Institute for Social Research, featuring ambitious survey research projects and innovative labs for experimental study of small group dynamics.

We arrived at the peak of the Ann Arbor social psychology empire. By the 1960s, more than one-third of all the research ever published in the field of social psychology had been done by faculty and graduates of the University of Michigan program (which was then only ten years old).

My primary mentor was Newcomb (whose first greeting for new students was, famously, "Call me Ted!"). In the 1950s, Newcomb had become one of the pre-eminent figures in American social psychology. He had published widely read textbooks and research compendiums and had done very significant pioneering research in the field. He was a powerful academic figure, but he let me know, after a while, that he had been active in supporting organizers of the Congress of Industrial Organizations (CIO) as a young teacher starting out at Bennington College, in Vermont, and considered himself most definitely to have been quite radical back in the 1930s. My other mentor was Katz, who, like Newcomb, was a pre-eminent figure in social psychology. Katz, it turned out, had left Brooklyn College, where he taught right after World War II, partly to escape the impending Red Scare purges there.

It was not an accident that the leading figures in Michigan's social psychology program had this background in the Left. The field itself had roots in left-wing theoretical and political impulses. Social psychology was shaped by an urgent need to try to understand attitudes that, from the point of view of the researchers, needed to change—especially, of course, racism and anti-Semitism. Émigré German social scientists led the way because of their impassioned effort to understand the popular bases for Nazism. Formative in the development of social psychology were the famous studies of the "authoritarian personality" led largely by German émigré scholars who had relocated to the United States, to the University of California, Berkeley. These escapees from Nazism were obsessed with trying to figure out the roots of anti-Semitism and fascism. Their effort to investigate these matters led to methodological innovations in research as well as theoretical developments that helped define social psychology as a whole.

Also quite significant in the Michigan scene was the work of Kurt Lewin, an émigré German social psychologist. His laboratory experiments, which aimed at discovering social arrangements in small groups that could foster democratic participation and democratic attitudes, were the foundation for the field of group dynamics. Lewin and his followers, based largely in Ann Arbor, helped create the field of experimental social research and were also important in developing forms of group therapy that became enormously popular after the war.

My mentors, Newcomb and Katz, who, in the 1930s, considered themselves part of the rising labor-led liberal movement, did not consider themselves to be at odds with the American government, despite their left-wing political identification. The government they experienced initiated the New Deal; in that era, these young social science researchers took for granted that the science they were creating could help inform the policy and practice of a reform-minded American leadership. They came to believe that those in government and even those in some corporate management positions were interested in a more rational, more humane mode of management—and that social psychological research could be the key to making that possible.

The war against fascism reinforced such perspectives. That war, in which the fate of civilization was at stake, was led by an American government both deserving of active support by progressives and needing the research and skills that social scientists could offer. Leading social scientists persuaded military and other government officials that sponsorship of social research would enable a more effective war effort. The results included a massive study of the morale and conditions of the life of the American soldier and a large-scale program of analysis of Hitler's uses of propaganda and ways that the American message could be better purveyed. Such projects helped advance the methodology of survey research. Scientific sampling of large populations, sophisticated statistical approaches to handling survey data, techniques for formulating survey questions and objective interviewing—all were advanced by the enlistment of social scientists in the war effort.

There was a dark side to the development of social psychology during the war and in the postwar period. Many of the leading figures in social psychology who worked for the Department of War, the Office of War Information, and the Office of Strategic Services were serving as precursors to the Cold War efforts by the CIA and other agencies to create a social science that was wedded to the national security state as an imperial rather than an anti-fascist vehicle. My own mentors may have been troubled by the ways that their initiatives had evolved politically, but it wasn't until later in the 1960s that the social role and responsibility of social science became topics for critical discussion.

The result of our teachers' alliance with the military and civilian government agencies was, for us, a research empire that could employ all of the graduate students in the program (and in sociology and political science), and a number of federally funded fellowships as well. Everyone in the doctoral program in social psychology in my day was fully supported during the time it took to complete their degree—which for some took many years.

One might think that the social science empire at Michigan would generate a corporate mode of operation internally. That wasn't my experience, however. The half dozen faculty members who officially ran the program adopted a decidedly humanistic perspective toward the forty or so graduate students they had recruited. There was an attitude among the faculty that if you were admitted, you were undoubtedly well qualified to get the PhD, so rather than try to weed out laggards and reward the most competitive, their model tilted toward nurturance and support.

The attitude and the research of the social psychology faculty was rooted in their progressive values. Katz, for example, had done quite a bit of research demonstrating that participation of employees in management promoted productivity. It was not a stretch for him to encourage the idea that the students should be participants in the governance of the graduate program. That was in the 1950s—before the 1960s wave of student demand for participation. So we elected a graduate student council that had an active voice in shaping the program and its policies: this certainly fostered a sense of collegiality among the students and faculty. Competition is endemic in the very nature of graduate and professional training, but in our program at that time there was a collaborative culture of mutual respect. We studied collectively for exams, sharing reading notes that had been passed on to us by previous generations of students. I remember all-night sessions of deep discussion of what we were reading, enriched by the benefit of our predecessors' reflections. For me, those prepping sessions were a kind of intellectual heaven, despite the underlying pressure of the looming exams.

The social psychology doctoral program was our eventual home, but to be formally accepted into it, one had to get the equivalent of a master's in either psychology or sociology. We three Brooklyn College kids had entered the program through psychology, and so much of the first two years in Ann Arbor involved deep immersion in Michigan Psychology. The Michigan psychology department in the late 1950s was nationally pre-eminent. Our first year was largely taken up with an intensive course in general psychology, in which the department's leading figures presented their current and often cutting-edge research. I learned a lot about physiological psychology and neuropsychology, experimental psychologies of many different kinds, scaling and measurement, and theories of learning and personality. On Friday afternoons, the department colloquium, which was attended by all the students and faculty, featured some of the greatest names in the history of psychology. We got to experience in the flesh legends such as B. F. Skinner, James Olds, Harry Harlow, Donald Hebb, and Edward Tolman.

It was the heyday of psychology then, and Michigan was at the center of discovery.

## TED NEWCOMB

DICK:

One of the classic studies in social psychology was done by Ted Newcomb when he was a teacher at Bennington College in the mid-1930s. He observed that this small, newly established women's college had a transforming effect on its students. Newcomb arrived at Bennington in its very early days as an experimental progressive college. Its students were women from rich families, who were in some sense rebelling against their parents, or otherwise "difficult." Most came from fairly conservative homes, yet Newcomb observed that many became quite liberal, quite quickly.

Newcomb realized that Bennington might serve as a natural laboratory for understanding how attitudes change in a social setting. He found, through an imaginative research design, that one's social standing in the Bennington student world was related to one's embrace of liberal attitudes. Women who remained conservative were socially marginalized. Following the three hundred students through their years at the college, he showed that in general they became more liberal over time. This study, published in 1943, became a classic in social psychology, for its depiction of the relationship between social life and mental processes.

I learned, in 1959, that Newcomb wanted to replicate the Bennington study. He was planning to go back to Bennington to see what had happened there, given that the political engagement of the 1930s had given way, by the 1950s, to a climate of political disaffiliation. In addition to undertaking a new four-year survey study of the Bennington student body to parallel the original study, Newcomb intended to locate his research subjects from the 1930s and see what had happened to their political outlooks in the twenty-five years since he had encountered them at the college.

Intrigued, I went to see him and asked whether I could join his project; he most enthusiastically hired me, and so for the next several years I was part of a team of three graduate students who served as the research staff for the new Bennington study. One of our number, Katherine Koenig, was assigned the work of interviewing the Bennington alumnae. She traveled the country to undertake extensive face-to-face interviews with as many of the original women as could be located. Don Warwick was the other team member, and he and I were primarily responsible for collecting and analyzing survey data from the current students at Bennington; each year, between 1960 and 1962, our team would spend a couple of weeks at Bennington collecting the data from questionnaires that we distributed to the Bennington students. During these visits, the three of us did depth interviews of a sample of students and otherwise tried to get a feel for the life of the college. Bennington is nestled in the Vermont mountains, quite insulated from the larger world. As soon as you arrive there, you can understand how particularly affecting, in many ways, this social cocoon must be for its inhabitants.

That was my formative research experience as a social psychologist, and it was a very rich one. It was my great good fortune to be able to work with a founding figure in the field and on a project that was so intrinsically fascinating. One consequence was that I developed a lifelong interest in understanding student cultures and their impact on members' identities and attitudes. A good deal of my subsequent work revolved around this theme.

We studied Bennington College prior to the explosion of student activism in the 1960s. When we were there the most popular students at Bennington were not the political activists (as they had been twenty-five years earlier) but the modern dancers. Bennington had become famous as one of the centers for modern dance, and it was those dancers who set the tone for the college as a whole. These were the students whose look, style, and outlook were what typified the "Bennington girl" in those years. A "bohemian" perspective set the norm in the late 1950s and early 1960s (much the way liberal politics had done in the 1930s). In the late 1950s and early 1960s, our data didn't give any clue that a new wave of student political activism was in the offing.

## BECOMING A GROWN-UP

DICK:

The four Brooklyn boys who shared a house in that first year in Ann Arbor shared a sense of discovery—including what it meant to be in the Midwest in a non-Jewish world, intensely immersed in a scientific discipline, learning to be professional academics, and teaching students (who were almost our age).

All of us had girlfriends, and the first Thanksgiving in Ann Arbor was highlighted by their arrival for the weekend. By then, Mickey and I were quite bonded. One night that weekend we all went to an engagement party for a fellow graduate student. I drank a lot. And by the end of the evening, inspired by the occasion, I proposed to Mickey that we get engaged. She said, "We'll see what you remember in the morning!" I did remember, in fact, and accordingly reaffirmed the proposal. Our plan was to marry when Mickey graduated from CCNY in June 1960.

We spent the summer of 1959 working in a new camp. We'd decided to leave Kinderland, despite our deep loyalty to the place, to explore the wider world of progressive children's camping. I applied for a supervisory position at Camp Wel-Met, and Mickey got a position as a staff member in the camp's office. Wel-Met was a huge institution in Narrowsburg, New York, run by the Jewish Federation of New York. Some fifteen hundred children were enrolled at any given time during the summer, and therefore the camp was organized in a very systematic fashion. What particularly intrigued me was that the camp operated according to professional social work methodologies. As a twenty-one-year-old supervisor of a group of eight college-aged bunk counselors, I had the opportunity to learn and practice some professional procedures for the supervision and training of camp counselors. I was one of a team of supervisors who met regularly for staff meetings and seminars, and each of us had our own supervisor to whom we were accountable. We learned how to run training sessions for our staffs and to work with individual members—not only to ensure that they were doing their jobs effectively, but also with an underlying goal of aiding their personal development. True to social work professionalism, we were expected to write detailed reports on the daily functioning of our bunks, the well-being of individual children, and the work effectiveness of staff members.

The Wel-Met experience deepened my interest in children's camping as a framework for socialization and cultural enrichment. Wel-Met's practice made it clear that our criticisms of Kinderland were well founded. In the few years that we were in leadership roles at Kinderland, I think we helped make Kinderland people more aware of the need to be child-centered rather than didactic and to develop a program that tried to meet children's needs rather than one driven by institutional ideology.

Yet Wel-Met's practices, I noticed, seemed to have a philosophical connection with classic socialist thinking. Like Camp Wo-Chi-Ca, Wel-Met encouraged democratic participation by the campers and put a lot of emphasis on the collective. These similarities, it turned out, weren't coincidental. Some of the leading figures in the creation and administration of Wel-Met had gotten their start as staff at Wo-Chi-Ca and other left-wing camps. I came to realize that the whole field of social work in New York was populated by onetime activists and organizers of the 1930s Left who'd gone on to become professional social workers and, in fact, leaders in that field. Indeed, one important impetus for the development of the "helping professions" after World War II may well have been the vocational quest by the younger generation of old leftists, looking for ways to live their values after the loss of their ideological faith in the throes of the Red Scare.

Working with kids that summer meshed beautifully with my graduate work in social psychology. There's no better place than a children's bunk to observe how the power of peer groups shapes personality and selfhood, to see firsthand the ways that personal growth could be enhanced through active social engagement. That was true not only for the children whom I worked with but for myself as well. My self-esteem rose a lot as I experienced the respect of a large bunch of kids and young staffers and found that I had some talent at leadership. All in all, that summer had a sort of idyllic quality, not least because Mickey and I deepened our romantic relationship there. I went back to graduate school in the fall of 1959 (just a little over twenty-one years old, incidentally) a happy camper indeed.

Early that fall a bunch of us graduate students had a game of touch football, during which somebody slammed his arm on my upraised right hand and broke my second finger. I had to have it set in traction to try to restore the finger to full use. After getting back from the hospital that afternoon, the phone rang. It was Mickey, calling to tell me that she was pregnant. That was stunning news, to be sure, and I quickly arranged to fly back to be with her in New York; before I arrived, she was able to have an abortion performed by an obstetrician who was a friend of the family. These were, of course, the days when abortion was illegal, and most of the people we knew had to make all kinds of arcane arrangements to travel to places like Puerto Rico, for an underground abortion. So we were extraordinarily lucky that Mickey was able to have the procedure done in a New York hospital, due to the special favors of a sympathetic gynecologist. By the time I got to the Bronx, we felt relieved—if somewhat traumatized.

Although Mickey had tried to keep knowledge of the pregnancy from her parents, her mother, Sonia, had no trouble figuring out that something was up. By the time I arrived, Sonia was determined that we get married right away rather than wait several more months as we had originally planned. Mickey and I liked this idea, in fact, because there had been a good deal of tension between our families about what kind of wedding celebration we would have. Mickey and I envisioned a big party, nothing fancy, but a joyful celebration with family and friends. Unfortunately, Mickey's parents couldn't afford even a simple version of such an event and had anticipated the Flacks family's financial participation. My mother, Mildred, was horrified, I think, by her image of such an affair, presupposing that her sisters (whose tastes and aspirations were decidedly bourgeois) would be disdainful of it. Mildred proposed that we have a small family dinner at Tavern on the Green (the fanciest New York restaurant that she could think of). The prospect of that was in no way appealing to us.

So Mickey flew to Ann Arbor the week before Thanksgiving. We arranged to be married by a local justice of the peace, with two of my Brooklyn College roommates as witnesses. On November 20, 1959, we all drove out to the farmhouse where the justice of the peace, Orville Kapp, resided. It was located on Nixon Road, just off Joy Road (a source of much amusement given what Richard Nixon signified then as well as forever after). We were greeted by a large woman in bib overalls, who turned out to be Mrs. Kapp. Mr. Kapp was a much smaller gentlemen, dressed in a shiny blue serge suit. He read the required language, asked permission to read a Bible passage, and pronounced us husband and wife. Observing how young we were, he asked, after the ceremony was over, whether we had our parents' consent to marry. We assured him that we did.

Our friends drove us back to town on Joy Road and dropped us at the A&P, where we bought filet mignon for the occasion, to be shared with a bottle of champagne that Mickey's brother had given her when she boarded the plane in New York—and that was our wedding dinner. Strangely, the next day I had to get up early to take the GRE (Graduate Record Examination) to qualify for a National Science Foundation fellowship that I had applied for. But after that interruption, we spent the week together in my apartment. On Thursday, we were alone and went out in the blustery, icy streets of Ann Arbor to find a restaurant that served a Thanksgiving dinner. All we could afford was a meal at the Thompson Diner, where we had the usual slice of turkey breast and mashed potatoes drowned in brown gravy. The place, of course, was populated by all the lonely people in Ann Arbor. But we were not among them, reveling in our marital bliss and sharing the strange experience of being two New York Jewish kids loving each other in the midst of an alien midwestern wintry town.

For the rest of that academic year, we lived apart, since Mickey had to go back to New York to finish college. I've often said that the stability of our marriage can be accounted for by the fact that we were able to skip the first

FIGURE 6.1. Mickey and Dick wedding photo, 1959 (Summer Studio, Ninth Avenue, New York City)

year. Of course, we visited back and forth. Most importantly, I went back to New York for the Christmas break, and there we were the beneficiaries of four different wedding celebrations. Each set of parents made parties in their apartments for family and friends. Our friends made a bash just for friends of ours, and Mickey's brother and sister-in-law also made a party for us. So, ironically, we had a far more extensive communal celebration of our marriage than we would have had we followed our initial plan. We had a nice haul of wedding presents as well!

When the school year ended, I went back to New York for Mickey's graduation from CCNY. We then packed the car with all of the wedding presents and left for Ann Arbor, spending a night at Niagara Falls en route. The moment we arrived in Ann Arbor, Mickey made a call to her parents and heard the news that her father had died, the very day after we departed. We immediately went back to New York for the funeral and to help Sonia adapt to the new situation that she faced.

MICKEY:

Sonia never really did adapt. The death of my father, Hartman, was something of a shock to us all, and it left Sonia bereft of companionship (and help, which she sometimes needed) as well as economically impoverished—since his rather meager pension was reduced when he died. She was forced to find some sort of employment. For a while she worked (as her mother had done) as a "nurse," for invalids. After one of her "patients" died in her arms, she found continuing the work to be psychologically impossible.

It turns out that the state of New York provides training for blind people (and the initial inventory) to run a rent-free newsstand. So in her sixties, with less than 10 percent normal vision, my mother became one of those folks who staff the little stands at subway stations (or el stations), wear canvas aprons with pockets for change (my mother's aprons were, of course, snowy white and meticulously ironed), and sell newspapers. Her stand was at a local stop in upper Manhattan and was not very busy or lucrative. She derived some enjoyment from the work (I think it made her feel part of the proletariat again), but she was very resentful of her needing to do this rather difficult (and, in the winter, chilling) work just to survive. When she had earned enough to pay the required Social Security taxes and reached sixty-two years of age, she retired, and she spent her time cleaning for and socializing with an old friend who was her "boarder."

DICK:

Mickey and I moved into our new apartment on South Fourth Street in Ann Arbor when we got back to town, and I remember feeling at the time that we had all we needed, materially, for a comfortable and enjoyable life. Both of us were working: I as a research assistant on the Bennington project, she as a lab assistant in the campus Mental Health Research Institute (MHRI).

FIGURE 6.2. Our first home, 536 South Fourth Avenue, Ann Arbor, Michigan, 1960–64 (photo taken in 1989 during an Ann Arbor Women for Peace reunion; Jean Converse, a leader of the group, is in the foreground)

I think our total income was probably around $5,000, but with the help of the wedding gifts that we received and the 1954 Chevy that my father gave us, we were able to feel fully equipped for comfortable well-being. We had bought a wonderful Blaupunkt FM radio and had a nice turntable we could plug into it. We had a growing collection of folk music and jazz LPs. We had been given a portable TV set and all the kitchen appliances we might need. In the summertime we could drive after work to a nearby lake on hot days, have a picnic supper, and go swimming. We could enjoy the classic film programs put on each weekend night by the University Film Society or take in the new movies at the local theaters. Mickey and I thus started a habit we have maintained for the past half century—going out to the movies at least once every week.

Ann Arbor, of course, was not a conventional small town and the moment of our settling there, right at the start of the 1960s, marked the early days of a burgeoning avant-garde in the community. Ann Arbor became the site of an underground film festival, an alternative music festival, and many other such cultural offerings led by local artists. Folksingers and poets performed in the beatnik-style coffeehouse. Bob Marshall's bookstore flourished as the place to get cutting-edge paperbacks and literary journals and to schmooze over coffee in front of the fireplace.

The cultural avant-garde was flourishing by the 1950s in most university towns, where rent was low and where communities of support were richly available. A number of our friends were budding writers, artists, and musicians who were active in such scenes in Ann Arbor. We came to feel that the cultural environment there was more venturesome, more interesting, than that in Greenwich Village at the time. Not only were we adapting to Ann Arbor and the Midwest; we believed that we had grown away from New York, which, at the start of the 1960s, seemed to us provincially oblivious to the creativity we were seeing in the rest of America.

## THE SIXTIES BEGIN

DICK:

On February 1, 1960, four black students went to the lunch counter at the Woolworth's store in Greensboro, North Carolina, and ordered coffee. That single action sparked the youth-based civil rights movement of the 1960s and signified the emergence of a new era in American history. In the immediate aftermath of the Greensboro sit-in, literally dozens of other communities in the South were the sites of similar protest. Many of them were spontaneous reactions to what students in Greensboro had done, and some, as in Nashville, Tennessee, were larger-scale mobilizations that had been contemplated and planned, for which Greensboro provided the needed propulsion.

These days, we think that, because of the Internet and other new means of technology-based communication, such mobilizations are readily facilitated. "Occupy" protests supposedly occurred in at least one thousand U.S. cities (and in many places around the globe). The scope of these were certainly aided by the Internet and social media. More than sixty years ago, an action by four black students in a particular Southern town provided the spark for a similar wave of nonviolent civil disobedience that eventually brought down the entire edifice of legal segregation in a few years. Advanced technologies of those days helped as well; it was TV news reports and telephone networking that then served the mobilization.

The lunch counter sit-ins at five-and-dime stores quickly spread to cities in the North. In Ann Arbor, as in many other college towns that spring, people were called to picket the local Woolworth's in support of students in the South; the picketers were telling people to boycott Woolworth's until segregation ended in their Southern stores.

Most of the one hundred of us who showed up for the first couple of weeks of picketing had not met beforehand. For many, it was their first public display of political conviction. For a red diaper baby like me, the sit-in explosion was a striking contradiction to my assumption that political apathy would dominate the American political scene. Overnight, hundreds of students were getting together to try to make a difference. Taking a public stand seemed suddenly both possible and effective.

The picket line was a social space within which people of like political mind could meet one another and, as a result, contemplate the possibility of ongoing action. It was clear that the case of Woolworth's was not going to be an isolated occurrence. The battle against segregation in the South would have many unfolding dramas for us to take part in.

So, by the summer of 1960, as Mickey and I were setting up our household in Ann Arbor, a new political scene had begun to take shape there. Among the signs was the founding of a campus political party—VOICE—through which undergraduate liberal-minded students could mobilize to compete in elections for student government. And there was an emerging liberal Democratic Party network that sought to revitalize the electoral scene in Ann Arbor. Parallel developments were beginning to stir in many other parts of the country.

One of the interesting initiatives was the creation of a "peace center" aimed at advancing a pacifist anti-war perspective in the community. The establishment of an anti-war activist center in Ann Arbor was surprising and intriguing to me. Although ban the bomb protests had been spreading from England to the United States by the late 1950s, I hadn't expected to find anti–arms race consciousness in a small midwestern town. I didn't think of myself as a pacifist, having never committed to a position of conscientious objection or to a personal pledge of nonviolence. But I'd already begun to see, in the sit-ins and mass protests led by Martin Luther King Jr., the political potential of nonviolent direct action. I think by that time I was reading *Liberation* magazine and following the ideas and efforts of A. J. Muste, the venerable father figure of what he called "revolutionary pacifism." But until our settling in Ann Arbor, I'd been unaware of the ways in which Quakers and other religious liberals had sustained activist communities for generations in towns like this one.

The Ann Arbor Friends provided a lot of leadership in the early 1960s for civil rights and peace education and action. Mickey learned of an initiative called Women Strike for Peace (WSP), which was organizing women to protest the arms race and to figure out activity that would engage the community in such a movement. She was embraced by a circle of women (many somewhat older than she) who were engaging in a collective political project that seemed remarkably fresh and promising.

My parallel involvement in the Ann Arbor Peace Center turned out to be a less positive experience. The project was led by a couple of young pacifists who were enamored of the idea that Cold War anti-communism could be sustained through nonviolent rather than militaristic approaches. They wanted to work to end the nuclear arms race—but were part of a particular pacifist tendency that asserted opposition to communism to be a primary goal.

In the aftermath of the 1930s, some left intellectuals and activists had coalesced around the idea of creating a Left that would be staunchly opposed to the Soviet Union and to the American communist movement. There were a number of variations and factions in what came to be called the Democratic Left; it was, after all, constituted by a fractious collection of ex-Communists, Trotskyists, old-line Socialists, and Social Democrats. Whatever their internal differences, there was strong adherence to a policy of refusing to ally with Communists and communist sympathizers and to exclude "Stalinists" and "Stalinoids" from their organizations and campaigns.

I had only a dim awareness of this sort of political practice, until the Peace Center leadership made it clear that they wanted those who participated to make a declaration of their opposition to communism. Although I wanted to participate actively in the Peace Center, I found that their use of a kind of loyalty oath was repugnant. I tried to argue for a different perspective on these issues—that you could oppose the Communist Party without excluding individual Communists or the children of Communists or those who were sympathetic to some Communist Party–sponsored causes or "fronts." I argued that we needed a Left that could be inclusive of people who shared common goals, not one that borrowed McCarthy-like tendencies to engage in guilt by association. I was surprised by the dogmatic insistence of the Peace Center's pacifist leaders on these matters and left the group before they finally decided how to respond to me.

That particular local story, I later learned, reflected a wider national tension within student peace organizations. The student wing of the Committee for a Sane Nuclear Policy (or SANE, the national liberal anti-nuclear organization) was going through a serious internal upheaval over the issue of excluding Communist Party members' children, many of whom were eager to participate. Just at the moment when it was possible to build a grassroots young people's movement against the nuclear arms race and the Cold War, these factional battles were threatening its development. It seemed most unreasonable—and even immoral—that individuals, despite agreeing with an organization's aims, could be purged or excluded from it simply because of some suspicion about their associations or because of their principled unwillingness to take the anti-communist oath. These experiences, which occurred as an upsurge of student activism was beginning in the late 1950s and early 1960s, were important in shaping what became the American New Left in the years to come.

By 1960–62, Mickey and I were getting increasingly active in the Ann Arbor political scene. In that period, support activity for the Student Nonviolent Coordinating Committee (SNCC) was attracting the interest of growing numbers of students and others in the community. There was much interest in the Cuban revolution and anger at the Kennedy administration's effort to overthrow Fidel Castro's regime, most notably at the time of the Bay of Pigs invasion. And a group of University of Michigan faculty members were organizing to promote "peace research"—that is, research on topics such as conflict resolution, military policy, and disarmament and a wide range of related matters. We were inspired to believe that the climate of fear and apathy that prevailed in the 1950s was being replaced by increasingly intense and innovative political debate and initiative.

Meanwhile, our New York circle of red diaper babies was also in ferment. Some of our old friends gravitated to the Progressive Labor Party, a new Maoist-oriented splinter from the Communist Party. In the late 1950s and early 1960s, the Progressive Labor Party was articulating a militant and refreshingly critical perspective, even as it maintained the doctrinaire sect-like character of the Communist Party itself. The Communist Party was trying to build a new youth wing, called the Progressive Youth Organizing Committee (PYOC). Mickey and I were no longer part of that New York political scene, but we did go to a Communist Party–sponsored youth meeting (described in chapter 5), where we publicly denounced the Party leadership as having nothing more to say to the American people given leaders' moral compromises. By then the Party leadership was constituted almost entirely by those who had defeated the movement for internal reform, and opposed the rise of "Euro communism" in Italy and other European Communist parties—Parties now critical of the Soviet Union and independent of it.

Mickey and I felt quite righteous in denouncing the Party at that meeting—though a couple of the young folk in the room denounced us in return. From a personal point of view, that meeting (which must have taken place in 1960 or 1961) is worth recalling simply because it was a moment where both of us made public our renunciation of the politics associated with our upbringing.

## SDS

DICK:

One of the four Brooklyn College guys with whom I roomed in that first year in graduate school, Alan (Al) Guskin, had also become intensely politically active in the early years of the 1960s in Ann Arbor. Al was one of the thousands of us who had gathered during the presidential campaign of 1960 at the steps of the University of Michigan student union, where, at 2:00 A.M., John F. Kennedy, running for president, talked about the idea for a form of national service that, he seemed to say, would be an alternative to the military. Al was galvanized and immediately reached out to others to form a group of students whose goal initially was to promote this idea and encourage Kennedy's commitment to it. They went as a delegation to visit candidate Kennedy with a petition signed by thousands of Michigan students. Al and the others are credited, in the history of the Peace Corps, for having picked up on what may have been a more or less casual comment by JFK and helping to make it a reality.

In the course of his activity, Al got to know quite a number of student leaders, most particularly, Tom Hayden, who was editor of the *Michigan Daily*, the student-run newspaper on campus. The *Daily* was an exceptionally good college newspaper. In fact, it served as a source of news coverage for the entire town; to be its editor was a particularly distinguished achievement for a student journalist. Al was very impressed with the eloquence and intensity of this new editor.

One day while walking on campus, I ran into Al and Tom, and we were introduced. I don't remember anything in particular about that encounter, but it led me to follow Tom's writing for the *Daily*—an extraordinary series of long articles announcing and documenting the emergence of a new student movement. In the previous months, Tom had been to Berkeley, where he witnessed the rise of a radical student party and saw the students participating in the emerging farmworkers' organizing efforts and in a campaign against capital punishment in California. Tom soon became acquainted with many of the leaders of the Berkeley student Left. He went South and covered some of the emerging developments there for the student newspaper. I commented to Al that Tom's articles might themselves conjure up a student movement—they were constructing an image of something that was not yet real.

In the fall of 1961, I heard about an effort by Tom and others in Ann Arbor to try to found a new national student organization, which they were calling Students for a Democratic Society (SDS). A meeting of a number of these people occurred in Ann Arbor in November—a meeting that I heard about after the fact. But I soon was able to get hold of some mimeographed copies of the memos that Tom was writing and that others were discussing, where he talked about many of the principles on which such a new organization would be based.

The nascent SDS group decided to convene a national convention for June 1962. Its location was to be in Port Huron, Michigan, at a retreat center operated by the United Auto Workers (UAW). I was very excited by the ideas and even the language that I saw in the pre-convention materials, yet my experience with the Ann Arbor Peace Center had me worried that my background as a red diaper baby would make me unwelcome as a participant. But I began to feel less worried the more I read of what they were saying about this particular matter.

Al Haber (who may be said to have been SDS's founding father) advocated explicitly for an organization that would be a home for red diaper babies as well as people of other political backgrounds. Accordingly, the kinds of anti-communist oath taking and rigidities that were then typical of the Student Peace Union, the Young People's Socialist League (YPSL), and Student SANE should not characterize SDS.

I decided to go to Port Huron, but because I had no delegate status and did not belong to SDS, I suggested to the organizers that I attend as a correspondent covering the meeting for the *National Guardian*. The *Guardian* was a well-known left-wing weekly with long-standing sympathies with the communist side of the Left but was independent of the Party. Mickey and

I had done some local representation for the *Guardian* in the preceding months. We had invited several *Guardian* staff members to speak in Ann Arbor and tried to promote the newspaper in town. We were friends with some of the *Guardian* staff, most particularly Joanne Grant, who had become famous in the civil rights world for her weekly coverage of SNCC for the paper. I persuaded the *Guardian* editors to let me claim credentials at the Port Huron meeting as a *Guardian* reporter.

I went there with a carload of others from Ann Arbor. Mickey remained behind because she was working, but she was able to take some time off and so arrived in Port Huron later with our car. We were delegated to drive back to the Detroit airport early in the week-long meeting, to pick up Michael Harrington and another member of his circle, named Don Slaiman, a staff member of the American Federation of Labor (AFL). Both Harrington and Slaiman were among several notables invited to speak at the start of the conference.

Despite the reassuring language of some of the pre-convention documents, we continued to have anxiety about how we'd be regarded at Port Huron. SDS was, after all, the student wing of the League for Industrial Democracy (LID), an old-line anti-communist, right-wing social democratic organization. LID's history went back to 1905, when it was founded as the Intercollegiate Socialist Society by an illustrious band of young intellectuals, including people like Jack London and Upton Sinclair. Its name was changed in the 1920s, I suppose, because the founders were no longer "collegiate." By 1960, of course, LID's name sounded terribly archaic. In 1960, Al Haber became a key leader, and what was by then the Student League for Industrial Democracy (SLID) changed its name to Students for a Democratic Society (SDS), while remaining as the student arm of the LID. The LID board included a number of labor leaders and social democratic intellectuals, some of whom Mickey and I thought of as dishonorable. They included some who had engaged in bitter internecine warfare within their unions and other liberal organizations with communist-oriented factions. Our own parents had been involved in struggles with some of these very people. Most immediately troubling to us was that SDS, before Port Huron, had a membership card on which appeared an oath declaring that one was not a member of a "totalitarian organization."

Driving Harrington and Slaiman from the Detroit airport to Port Huron reinforced our anxieties about this political world we were entering. Their conversation was filled with barbs about the Left that we identified with, including nasty comments about Cheddi Jagan, who had recently been elected leader of British Guiana and was a darling of the Marxist Left internationally. Mickey and I both knew quite a bit about Harrington, having heard him speak at our respective campuses in the fifties. One couldn't help but respect his eloquence and his evident Marxian consciousness, but his vitriolic anti-communism made him someone we feared. Slaiman was hardly as impressive, and his style and formulations were those of a bully. During the car ride, he ranted against labor intellectuals who dared criticize racism in the labor movement.

If these were guests and allies of SDS, we had reason to worry.

One of our first observations at Port Huron, however, was seeing Steve Max, whom we had known from the New York red diaper world. Steve's father had been an editor of the communist *Daily Worker*, and Steve was well known in the young left circles of New York. We viewed him as a compatriot, and his presence was reassuring.

We were impressed by the diversity of those who attended the Port Huron meeting. There were about sixty people, many of them student leaders from the major campuses of states including Texas, Illinois, Wisconsin, and Michigan and a variety of Southern schools. A lot of them weren't Jewish, which startled us, because our whole experience in the Left in New York was that its character was overwhelmingly Jewish. We already knew that Tom Hayden came from a Catholic background (in fact, his parish priest was the notorious Father Charles Coughlin, who in the thirties was well known as a far-right-wing anti-Semite). Tom had recently married a beautiful blonde Southern woman named Sandra Cason, better known as Casey. Casey Hayden was a striking figure at Port Huron (and has been ever since), not only because of her physical beauty but because of her bearing and her moral intensity. She had been raised in a Southern segregationist environment, but her strong Christian values made her feel at odds with Southern mores early in her life. She was one of a group of young Southern white people at Port Huron, who had already had a baptism of fire in the Southern movement. They included Robb Burlage, who was editor of the University of Texas student newspaper, and Bob Zellner, who had already spent time in several jail cells for civil disobedience activities in relation to the anti-segregation campaign. Some of the African American leaders of SNCC were present, including President Chuck McDew. One of the people we met early at the meeting was Mary Varela, a young Catholic activist, who had been involved in civil rights activity herself (and later became a legendary community organizer in rural Latino agricultural villages in New Mexico). So almost everyone we got to know as the days went on had a history that was inspiring and surprising to us New York provincials. The very makeup of those Port Huron participants suggested that a new kind of leftism was beginning to emerge.

A key moment in our relationship with SDS came at the start of the meeting when there was a question about the seating of a young man named Jim Hawley, who represented the Communist Party's PYOC. He was there not as a voting participant but as an observer. The YPSL members in attendance argued that there was no place in the meeting for a Stalinist—even as an observer. The great majority of people there did not have a history with the anti-communist Left and thought that the argument was silly. That the body voted to seat Hawley as an observer became a key episode in the defining of SDS in relation to the Old Left. Ironically, Hawley left the meeting right at the start—he never actually used that opportunity to break the historic barrier that the so-called Democratic Left had put up against those who came from communist roots. (Hawley later renounced his affiliation with the PYOC and the DuBois Clubs and joined SDS because of the comparative attractiveness of the New Left.)

The question of seating a PYOC observer was soon followed by an issue about the membership restrictions in SDS; a motion was made and carried to eliminate specific language in the SDS charter that could be read as a kind of loyalty oath. We took the vote, correctly, to mean that we were in fact welcome in this new organization in a full and wholehearted way.

Port Huron was a remarkably rich experience without parallel in my long history of going to conventions and conferences. The meeting lasted six days. Some of those days were spent in educational discussions. Al Haber, Tom Hayden, and the other organizers had invited some older left intellectuals and activists to talk with us, and our exposure to them was itself instructive.

We had a special, memorable session with Harrington in which he tore apart Tom's draft of the proposed manifesto. He was particularly concerned about two aspects of the draft. One was that the document was going to be critical of the leadership of the American labor movement for its lack of militancy, its lack of political independence, and its willingness to support the Cold War rather than challenge the status quo. Harrington and Slaiman argued vociferously that it was not the place of a left organization to "wash the dirty linen of the labor movement in public" (as they put it) and that by doing so we would be cutting ourselves off from possible alliance with and support from unions.

The second point mightily upsetting to Harrington was that Tom's draft contained a very strong condemnation of anti-communism. It argued that anti-communism had become an ideology in itself that was destructive to the possibilities for progressive coalition and creative discourse among liberals and Socialists. The ongoing hunt for Communists within the Left had superseded struggle for social change, Tom wrote. There was no trace of sympathy for the Soviet Union or the communist movement in the draft, but it was decidedly anti-anti-communist.

In any event, Harrington was furious and made it clear that the draft would not be acceptable to the LID if its tone with respect to these issues remained. He didn't stay for the main act of the conference, which was a series of day and night sessions to debate and rewrite the draft. Although Harrington's manner and words were the source of much anger among the SDS organizers, the meeting debated quite freely the matters he raised. Harrington was led to believe, by some YPSL members, that the meeting ignored his advice, even though major rewriting to take account of it actually occurred.

Another speaker at Port Huron was Arnold Kaufman, a young University of Michigan philosophy professor who had been a teacher of several Ann Arbor SDSers, including Tom Hayden and Bob Ross. Kaufman was a remarkable academic at that time because of his intense political engagement. It was Kaufman who had invented the phrase *participatory democracy* to define a vision for a social alternative not burdened by the heavy weight of "socialism" in American political culture. Tom's use of *participatory democracy* as a term and as a vision is the most distinctive contribution of the Port Huron Statement to the thinking and language of the American, and indeed the world, Left.

Kaufman was given an evening to read to the assembled students excerpts from a manuscript that he had been working on. It was a strange moment in a political convention to have a professor reading an academically oriented piece of writing, with several dozen young folk literally at his feet. Even though the sixties generation engaged in a battle against all forms of authority, there was a strong tendency to want to find gurus in academia who seemed to have some capacity for touching meanings and core values that would help us live and act. Kaufman had played that role for the SDS founders in his classes at Michigan.

At Port Huron, Kaufman was, as I recall it, trying to define for us ways to fulfill the role of a fully democratic citizen. The most memorable thing he did, as far as I was concerned, was to declare that we make a big mistake in political action when we "role-play the president," tailoring our demands on the president by empathizing with the dilemmas that the president faces in trying to respond to those demands. Instead, we need to articulate the demands that we define as ours, that are in accord with our values—and it's the president's job to figure out how to respond. It's the citizen's job, not to anticipate the president's trouble, but to create pressures that the president must take into account.

There were other invited speakers of note at Port Huron. Among them was Harold Taylor, past president of Sarah Lawrence College in its formative days. Taylor was a very well-known liberal advocate of reform in higher education, and his presence helped validate the adventure that we were trying to undertake.

What was that adventure? The announced purpose of the meeting was to launch a new student organization on the left that would link together the separate single-issue campaigns for civil rights, disarmament, civil liberties, and university reform that were already frameworks of student activism. The new organization was to be a home for students who derived their activism from diverse issues but who saw the value of finding a common ground for mutual support and discussion. The people who came to Port Huron encompassed rather well the range of interests and perspectives needed to fulfill that claim.

This organizational goal was coupled to a more far-reaching ideological ambition. In drafting the Port Huron Statement and in the preparation for the conference, Tom Hayden and Al Haber and some of the others had been reading material from England, possibly introduced to them by Arnold Kaufman, by a group of remarkably eloquent intellectuals calling themselves the New Left. Many, writing for newly founded journals like *New Left Review*, had quit the Communist Party, after the invasion of Hungary and the anti-Stalin speech Khrushchev delivered in 1956 at the Twentieth Congress of the Communist Party of the Soviet Union. The British ex-Communists had abandoned the Party but not the struggle for socialism. They were joined by other intellectuals who did not share that specific history but who agreed that a New Left was needed, not only in England but in Europe as a whole. And the "new" for them included not only overthrowing the morally debased communist legacy but also overcoming the political compromises of the Labour Party and other social democratic organizations in Western Europe.

So the term *New Left* was very much in Tom Hayden's consciousness; I overheard him remarking at Port Huron to Al Haber: "I'm sure that the editors of the *New Left Review* will be quite happy with what we are accomplishing here."

There were exponents of a similar attitude in the United States who did not necessarily adopt the label "New Left" at the outset. One who did was C. Wright Mills, the Columbia University sociologist whose many writings (*The Power Elite, The Causes of World War Three,* and *The Sociological Imagination,* in addition to many articles) were powerfully influential for Tom as well as others of us who'd come to Port Huron.

Mills had written "Letter to the New Left," endorsing the British project and presumably extending its possibility to the United States. Before Port Huron, Tom had written an essay modeled after the Mills piece, "Letter to the New (Young) Left," advocating many of the ideas that were embodied in the Port Huron Statement itself.

There were other intellectuals in the fifties whose work was pointing in the same direction. Most important, I thought, was Paul Goodman, the anarchist essayist, poet, and novelist. His book *Growing Up Absurd* was a major best seller on college campuses. Goodman added something to the socialist-oriented discourse that was dominant in the British New Left and in the work of people like Mills. He added an emphasis on decentralization, on democracy from the bottom up. His anarchist project asserted the necessity and possibility of creating the new world in the midst of the old, of institution building, of taking matters into your own hands.

Goodman's anarchism converged with revolutionary pacifism, conveyed to us not only by SNCC and King but also by the writing of A. J. Muste, Dave Dellinger, David McReynolds, and others in the pages of *Liberation.* At Port Huron, we were searching for the common thread at the heart of all of the ideologies and parties of the Left. We wanted to revive the Left but not on the terms on which it had been established in previous generations. We didn't want a party that would be organized in the fashion of the old Communist Party, with its highly authoritarian internal structure, or of the old Socialist Party, whose internal democracy was expressed mostly through endless and futile doctrinaire dispute. We were repelled by the ideological grandiosity characteristic of tiny Trotskyist sects striving to establish their revolutionary credentials against other groups with similar claims. All of that we wanted to throw into the dustbin of history. We imagined new forms of organization, new ways of communicating, new vocabulary to replace what we defined as worn-out Marxism. Forms of organization, rooted in anarchist and pacifist and Quaker experiments, were emerging in the civil rights and peace movements—and these were inspiring our own efforts.

C. Wright Mills and some other left intellectuals, by 1962, had come to challenge the fundamental Marxian assumption that the fate of society depended on the emergence of an increasingly powerful labor movement, representing a radicalizing working class. For us, it was the civil rights movement and the issue of race, not class struggle, that were igniting change. The Cold War and the war economy were our preoccupations—not capitalism as such. Indeed, state bureaucracy, exemplified by the Pentagon, but also evident in our experience in the university, needed to be resisted and challenged—and these were matters to which Marxism seemed blind—as the anarchists had always claimed.

There was something else that was in our minds and in our discourse, and that was an effort to make the academic world connect to the critical analysis and collective action that was emerging. Most of those at Port Huron had been active in campus leadership roles—several student government presidents and campus editors were in attendance—and had been recruited to Port Huron at national gatherings of the National Student Association, an arena where Tom Hayden, Al Haber, Bob Ross, and Paul Potter were highly visible players. A deeply questioning attitude toward the institutional practices of the university was shared by all of these campus leaders, and so there was much interest in what we then called "university reform." This meant that rules that restricted freedom of expression on the campus had to change. It meant that students should have a more direct voice in campus rule making. It meant most of all an engagement on the part of faculty and students in the issues and movements of the day.

The Port Huron Statement rather prophetically argued that in the new advanced economy that was emerging the university had a strategic role in the operation of society. The ivory tower was no longer an appropriate metaphor for defining the nature of the university. On the one hand, the academy's traditional claims to autonomy were increasingly endangered. On the other hand, the statement saw the university as a strategic resource for finding levers for social change. The freedom for debate it made available, the knowledge it housed, and the moral climate it fostered, the statement declared, opened new possibilities for social action.

These were among the ideas that animated Tom in the drafting of the document. At Port Huron, we set up situations where we could talk about, debate, and modify that draft. These included small group meetings that intensely examined various sections of the draft and formulated proposed changes for the plenary sessions to vote on.

The most contested part of the Port Huron draft was the section that Tom had written about communism and anti-communism. He had been appalled in previous months by Harrington's readiness to condemn some stalwart civil rights activists, because of their alleged associations with "Stalinist" politics. He was very upset by attacks on Anne and Carl Braden, two Southern white progressives with a long history of resistance to racism in the South. The Bradens were highly respected by SNCC folk, who were in turn beginning to be labeled as pro-Communists and therefore beyond the pale, because of their willingness to ally with supporters regarded as politically tainted by those in the anti-communist Left. Experiences like that led Tom to write, in the draft, his critique of left-wing anti-communism as an ideological buttress to the status quo and to raise serious questions about the depiction of the USSR as expansionist. More than fifty years later, the language of that section of the draft is strikingly thoughtful and hardly an apologetic for the Soviet Union. But Harrington came to Port Huron in order to make a strong attack on what Tom had written.

After Harrington had delivered his condemnations and departed the meeting, I decided that I would volunteer for the work group assigned to discuss and rework the "Communism and Anti-Communism" section of the draft. I thought that the draft did in fact suffer from a lack of clarity in its condemnation of Soviet communism, and so I offered to redraft that part. As one of the resident red diaper babies at the conference, I wanted to restate SDS's position on the communist movement. I thought that it was important for the statement to clearly differentiate the New Left from "communism" as well as from right-wing social democracy and other old left traditions. So, after some discussion in the breakout group, I stayed up much of the night, banging away at the typewriter, redrafting the statement's section on these matters. Tom decided to try to sleep on the floor, waking occasionally to check on my progress; he fell asleep in the doorway so that if people started to come in for breakfast he'd be awakened. The section in the final document on communism closely resembles what we worked on that night.

Most of the other changes in the Port Huron Statement were made in a marathon plenary session that took place for most of the final twenty-four hours of the conference. Rather than try to redraft specific language, Paul Booth (a young delegate from Swarthmore who was elected SDS vice president at Port Huron) suggested that proposed changes be voted on in the form of what he called "bones"; smaller, less contentious changes were called "widgets." In this way, fifty or so folks were able to discuss and vote on dozens of general points and therefore avoid frustrating debate about specific verbiage. The body was willing to trust a final draft committee led by Tom to fulfill the spirit of what had been decided in this fashion.

As a footnote, it might be mentioned that at Port Huron we operated according to parliamentary procedure and majority rule. I make this point because, in some writing of the history of SDS, much has been made of the procedural ways in which the organization eventually made use of participatory democracy. In the years after its founding, SDS increasingly used models of consensus decision making rather than majority rule. We did that in large part under the influence of Quaker traditions passed on to us by some of the pacifist activists with whom we were interacting. Similar consensus rules were adopted by SNCC and by WSP, the anti-war organization that Mickey was active in during the early 1960s. This way of making decisions in social movement organizations and collectives has been passed down and refined—becoming one of the defining features of Occupy Wall Street and the initiatives that followed. Indeed, there's a considerable social science literature on participatory democracy in face-to-face groupings. But at Port Huron, when we talked about participatory democracy, we weren't thinking much about internal group process. We meant the term to apply to the society at large and its major institutions.

Still, participatory democracy is inherently a framework for critical scrutiny of all forms of social interaction: To what extent, here, in this place, do members have a voice in decisions that affect them? How must we be organized to provide that voice? It was inevitable that SDSers would ask those questions about their own practices as well as those of established institutions.

We finished our work as the sun was rising over Lake Huron, and as we came outside to view it, we took that sunrise as a very positive omen. The most detailed account of the conference appears in Jim Miller's book *Democracy Is in the Streets*, and it is well worth reading to get the full flavor of the tenor and the context of it all. He quotes the recollections of many of us, twenty-five years after, about that final moment. As Sharon Jeffrey recalled, "It felt like the dawn of a new age."[1]

In retrospect, it's pretty remarkable to me how we folks—in our late teens and early twenties—felt that we were making history on the shores of Lake Huron that week. The very idea that a group of young people could claim the wisdom and insight to rewrite the framework of the American Left, to aim to develop a new vocabulary and a new synthesis of the ideological strands of the Left—all these claims, made by people so young, seem astonishing. And yet it seemed natural to us at the time.

There were reasons for our *chutzpah*. The early sixties were a moment in which young people could see that the main perspectives that dominated the political and cultural worlds were played out. It seemed natural and even necessary that new ways of thinking depended on a new generation. That notion got a lot of support from some of our elders. C. Wright Mills, for example, made these kinds of points repeatedly in his essays of the late 1950s and early 1960s.

Indeed, the idea that a new generation of leadership was needed for the United States was strongly reflected in the 1960 presidential campaign. JFK boasted that he was the first presidential candidate born in the twentieth century and that he would succeed Dwight Eisenhower, who, at the time, had been the oldest person ever to be president. We were severe critics of Kennedy, but his trumpeting of the arrival of a new generation of leadership certainly affected our own understanding of what was possible as well as necessary.

More inspiring to us was SNCC. The lunch counter sit-ins, the freedom rides, and the other brave and bold actions and dedicated organizing in the face of oppression that young activists were engaged in challenged the working assumptions and organizational structures of established liberalism. There was no question that it was youth who were leading the Southern struggle—and succeeding, often against the advice of their elders.

The regenerative capacity of youth was evident in popular culture. Bob Dylan, aged twenty-two, represented a musical counterpart to ourselves—and his songs in those years powerfully spoke to us and for us. Dylan was one of a set of young troubadours who, synthesizing folk music and political expression, were inspired by and inspiring to the rising movements. Some years later, anthropologist Margaret Mead wrote a book in which she argued that in the post-modern world the young would teach the old, reversing traditional cultural patterns in which, of course, wisdom resided in the elders and even reversing the modern experience in which generational difference was not seen to be important in the transmission of knowledge and wisdom. Mead took the youth rebellion of the sixties not as a passing moment but as a sign of what the future would be like. In retrospect, such romanticizing of the youth revolt of the sixties seems quaint. But as the sun rose over Lake Huron, we all felt the romance.[2]

MICKEY:

In June 1960, I graduated from CCNY, with a bachelor of science degree in biology. Graduation ceremonies were on a Thursday, and on Friday Dick and I left for Ann Arbor with a car full of household goods that we had bought with wedding gift money in the discount stores of New York—pots and pans and dishes and a vacuum cleaner (which Dick didn't believe we really needed) and a Blaupunkt shortwave radio and a television set (which he most certainly needed). We set a route through Canada and had a one-day honeymoon in Niagara Falls on that Friday night. By Saturday evening, we were in Ann Arbor. I called my folks to tell them of our safe arrival, and a neighbor answered the phone. She informed me that my father had died of a heart attack earlier that day. By Sunday, we were flying back to New York.

My mother later reported that all day Friday he had wandered around the apartment looking at my empty closets and dressers. He was like the father in a Yiddish song, "Dray tekhter" (Three Daughters):

THREE DAUGHTERS
When—with luck and health and life—
We will marry off our eldest daughter,
I will dance—hup, hup!
A burden I have given up!
Play, musicians, play with verve,
We've married off our eldest daughter today!
We're left with only two more,
I wish we were at their weddings already!
Play musicians—tune your instruments!
Let the whole world celebrate with us,
Our joy is known only to God,
And to he who has daughters.
When I will already see the second daughter

Wearing a white wedding dress—
I will drink and be joyous
A stone removed from my heart.
Play musicians today, begin fiddling!
We've married off our second daughter with great joy,
Only the youngest is left—
Oh, how I wish we were dealing with her.
Play musicians for all the in-laws,
Let poor people also have some joy sometime—
To marry off a child! And a daughter yet!
When at the youngest's wedding I'll hear music,
I will somehow stand and think—
The last little daughter now also gone,
What is left now? What goal?
Play musicians, welcome the bride,
All my children have been taken.
As hard as it was to raise three daughters,
Oy, it's harder still without them.
Play musicians, make us cry,
The last little bed will be vacant tonight,
The whole house, her closet,
Oy vey, how bare and lonely.

His funeral was in the tradition of our movement, with a chorus singing labor songs and the Yiddish song to a fallen revolutionary: "You have fallen in the heroic struggle of the class war . . ." My tears fell only at that singing—otherwise, I was in a kind of shock. At the gravesite, a man who had been renting a room in my folks' apartment (thereby paying half the apartment's rent) wanted to say kaddish (the traditional prayer for the dead). "No!" I screamed, remembering how my father had hated the hypocrisy of secular comrades who had bar mitzvahs for their children or had a rabbi perform a wedding or funeral service. My brother had better sense than I and said that the kaddish would be not for my father's sake but to express the feelings of our boarder, and it was not our place to forbid it. He was right.

After a brief stay with my mother, Dick and I returned to Ann Arbor to pick up our new life. It must be stated that New Yorkers are (or were) the most provincial people in the United States. "There's nothing worth seeing west of the Hudson" is an apt phrase to describe the attitudes of many native

New Yorkers. My neighbors in the Bronx couldn't understand how I managed to marry a boy from Brooklyn! I thought I was more sophisticated than that, but I found that Ann Arbor (and the Midwest in general) provided a culture shock: people spoke differently, had different words for things (groceries in a "sack," like potatoes, not in a grocery bag), ate white bread (even in the Chinese restaurant), thought a restaurant called "McDonald's" was a big treat, and were altogether too nice! We displaced New Yorkers would gather on Sunday mornings at a local bookstore, where bagels and the Sunday *New York Times* were imported from Detroit. I felt a little like one of the immigrant hordes experiencing America for the first time!

We spent that summer living on Dick's fellowship money and cashing in the wartime bonds that my grandmother had left me, buying furniture and fixing up our apartment. Both of us were intent on not living like students but living like adults—with a couch and two chairs, lamps, a TV, and a rug. (For a coffee table, Dick draped over a steamer trunk a serape that my mother had given me.) I bought supermarket magazines for recipes and had a collection from my mother—which I had laboriously made her dictate to me before I left home—and began having dinner parties and making good food an important part of our lives. It wasn't long before that food and carpet and TV set became a significant part of New Left student life in Ann Arbor.

In September, I began a job at the University of Michigan's Mental Health Research Institute (MHRI), working as a lab technician for a project in brain biochemistry. The institute was steeped in a "systems theory" approach that held that the laws of systems could be applied "from the cell to society." We who worked on cells (first rat and then pig brain cells) were, of course, in the basement, while seminars discussing issues in social psychology and sociology were on the top floor. I have always enjoyed lab work, and the ethos of MHRI could almost convince one that isolating a phosphatase enzyme from animal brains would help elucidate rules that would apply "from the cell to society." The brains had to be fresh: at first, I cut the heads off living rats with a tin snips and pried their brains out, dropping the bodies in an industrial garbage disposal; when I objected to this gory procedure, I found a slaughterhouse in town that could provide fresh pig brains. Twice a week, after going home for lunch, we would stop at the slaughterhouse, where the workers, too, were eating lunch—just off the killing floor, with their high rubber boots covered in blood. I would bring a bucket of crushed ice from the lab, and the guys would be absolutely overjoyed to carefully place the still steaming pig brains on the ice. They, too, believed that they were somehow part of the advancement of science. The research was quite organic: the substrate was cholesterol, a phosphorous compound that we extracted from a dozen fresh egg yolks (the whites went home for angel food cakes); freshly ground-up carrots provided a necessary co-enzyme, and the brains could be made to produce an enzyme that split the cholesterol molecule. The supermarket was our chemical supply house.

It was a regular eight-to-five job, and I began to be just a wee bit jealous of my husband's graduate student flexibility. After about a year, I left MHRI and started working where Dick did, at the Survey Research Center of the Institute for Social Research at Michigan. I learned some coding and other social science research techniques—and, more importantly, was able to participate in discussions among the graduate students working there. We talked about the work, about the nature of social science, about politics—in short, all the things that were never discussed in the basement of MHRI. This was the beginning of my becoming what I would later call myself—an "osmotic sociologist"—learning by osmosis. (Also, I was working part-time, and the hours were more flexible.)

Our friends at this time were mostly graduate students and their partners. Some of the wives were involved in a nascent group that had had its first national meeting in Ann Arbor, in December 1961—Women Strike for Peace (WSP). As part of our anti–Cold War heritage, we had been participants in anti-nuclear rallies, Easter marches, Stockholm Peace Petition campaigns, and the like, for many years. In our youth, the word *peace* was subversive; I used to graffiti it wherever I could in New York. In fact, in my freshman year at the Bronx High School of Science, when my art teacher, Bernard Kassoy, gave us the assignment "say something about yourself in art," I (who had zero artistic ability) decided to letter the word *peace* in about fifteen languages (*paz, pace, mir,* etc.), embedding the letters in swirls of color and abstract design. Mr. Kassoy (who, it turned out, was the cartoonist for the Teachers Union newspaper) put it up in the hallway! So I was no newcomer to the anti-nuclear war movement.

WSP was founded by a few Washington, D.C., and New York women, calling for an end to nuclear testing. They spoke as women and mothers on behalf of the world's children, who were endangered by the fallout from the above-ground atmospheric testing being conducted by the United States and the USSR on a regular basis at that time. I have come to believe that these were, in fact, the first stirrings of both the New Left (in that WSP was anti-anti-communist) and the reborn women's movement (in that the

women were speaking as women and were finding new voices and empowerment). In Ann Arbor, a group of women whom I vastly respected (including Elise Boulding, wife of Kenneth Boulding, an economist at Michigan,
both of them active Quakers) had begun a WSP "chapter" (there was very
little organizational structure—another harbinger of things to come), calling itself (in a mild midwestern manner) Women for Peace (WfP). We met
regularly in one another's houses—mostly faculty and graduate student
wives—and planned activities that would help spread the anti-testing message to the larger community of women. It was here that Torry Harburg,
wife of social psychology student Ernie Harburg, introduced the concept of
"peanut butter ladies," which I made some use of in later years and have
always tried to maintain and apply as an organizing principle.

Torry was an early "organic freak" and used to travel to a neighboring town
to a farm store to buy organic peanut butter to feed to her three kids. There
she met other moms doing the same thing. Their concern for their children's
well-being, and mistrust of the "establishment" in their refusal to buy Skippy,
suggested to Torry that these women would be concerned about nuclear
testing as well. Her point was that to convince people of the rightness of
your issues, you had to talk to them about their concerns. No matter how
many facts and figures you had at your disposal (and some WSPers became
experts in the area of nuclear testing and, later, arms control), you would be
convincing only if you started where they were—peanut butter. This was in
some contrast to my early days, where WE had the truth and our job was "to
raise the level of the broad masses." . . . I was learning.

Although we shied away from the personal in our meetings, WfP sessions were somewhat like the later consciousness-raising of the women's
movement. Here were married women (mostly), meeting weekly and more,
without their husbands, and self-consciously creating new forms of thought
and action. We were not afraid of the "Red" label, we discussed international policy with due respect to the USSR as a major player (not necessarily an enemy), and we sought ways to engage the "peanut butter ladies" (and
all in our community) in the campaign to end nuclear testing and war. The
Quaker influence (of Elise Boulding and others in the group) was most profoundly expressed in our decision to run our meetings not by parliamentary
procedure, with motions and votes, but by consensus. *Consensus* had a very
special meaning in our lexicon: it meant that we had to discuss controversial
things very thoroughly, and then people who still had not convinced others
of their position had to decide if they could live with the apparent group

consensus, even if it was not exactly what they wanted. This process was distinctly different from simple compromise. It required that people listen very carefully to one another, to try to tease out where the common ground lay.

For me, that was entirely new. I was used to arguing until I was blue in the face, convinced in the rightness of my position, and reluctantly giving in only when I saw that the votes were against me. Here I had to seriously try to meet the objections of someone who disagreed, understand her position, and often re-examine my own. I actually found it exhilarating. Both Dick and I learned from this experience and have tried to maintain this way of functioning in groups—even when they don't operate by consensus. (For many in our WfP group, this was new and exciting also. One woman said, "Until now, I couldn't even spell *consensus!*") In later years, as the New Left began to disintegrate into various factions, we were especially alienated because we saw that this way of thinking and behaving had become entirely absent. I think that those of us who never joined any faction were still imbued with this Quaker spirit.

I also learned something about the power of nonviolence from Elise Boulding, a "founding mother" of Ann Arbor's peace activist movement and a member of the Quaker Meeting. During the Cuban missile crisis, in October 1962, the campus peace community—students and others—responded quickly with a demonstration on the "Diag" (originally known at the Diagonal Green)—the central point on campus. After a few speeches, the group decided to march to the Washtenaw County Courthouse on Main Street— about five blocks from campus, in the "townie" part of town. (I believe that decision was due to the large participation of WfP in the demonstration.) As we began to march on one of the paths leading off campus, we found ourselves facing a gauntlet of fraternity boys, waving American flags and calling us names. Some of them tried to rip our signs out of our hands, and it was very ugly and threatening—although no overt violence took place. As we left campus, they followed us to the courthouse and continued to scream invectives and insults; it seemed as if violence might break out soon. We were simply standing in front of the building, when Elise Boulding shouted, "Everybody sit down!," which we promptly did. The fraternity boys, faced with ladies in proper ladylike attire (stockings and all) led by white-haired Elise, audibly and visibly gasped, fell back, and slowly drifted away. I had never had quite that experience, and my Bronx street-fighting smarts quickly and forever took a backseat to this demonstration of the power of nonviolence.

The very best demonstration I ever participated in (in terms of positive reaction from people on the street, as well as FUN!) was a 1963 WfP project on Hiroshima Day (August 6). There was a legend about a young girl named Sadako, who survived Hiroshima (or Nagasaki) and was dying of radiation-induced leukemia. Japanese folklore held that if a person could origami-fold one thousand paper cranes, he or she would never die. All over the world, people began folding paper cranes for Sadako. In Ann Arbor, we learned to fold them, and our meetings for a few weeks were taken up with folding hundreds of cranes. On August 6, we bought hundreds of balloons and attached the cranes—along with a printed ribbon of paper telling Sadako's story and urging people to oppose nuclear testing. For the first time in my experience of handing out leaflets and other "propaganda materials," people on the streets of Ann Arbor lined up to accept our balloon-crane-ribbon. I learned again: respect where and who people are, and seek to relate to them, not simply "inform" them.

Another project—this one national—was created by Barry Commoner, an epidemiologist at Washington University in St. Louis, Missouri. One fear from testing was the release into the atmosphere of strontium-90, a radioactive isotope created in a nuclear explosion. This isotope was known to be very dangerous to humans, particularly children, because their growing bones would take up the isotope rather than calcium. There was controversy about whether this uptake was indeed happening, and, epidemiologically, it was necessary to have thousands of samples to see whether children were indeed being affected and whether there were geographical indicators corresponding to the drift of nuclear test fallout. Commoner had demonstrated that the strontium-90 content of children's teeth was an indicator of what was happening to their bones. He and WSP began a nationwide campaign to collect thousands of baby teeth that had fallen out in the natural course of childhood development and accumulate a sufficient sample size to draw conclusions about strontium-90 uptake. WSP created "I gave my tooth to science" buttons to pin on children, and the campaign was enthusiastically received all over the country by both moms and kids. Tens of thousands of teeth were collected and analyzed, and the hypothesis that nuclear fallout was being picked up by kids' bodies in direct relationship to where they were located with respect to the fallout cloud was unequivocally confirmed.

In addition to the "I gave my tooth to science" button, we promised the kids whose teeth were donated an invitation to a special event at the end of the campaign. We arranged a concert at the high school auditorium, including a magician, a puppet show, and other fun kids' stuff. Leading off the afternoon was a "folk group," consisting of Paul Potter on harmonica, Rennie Davis (a key SDS organizer) on banjo, Dick on guitar, and me on mandolin. None of us could play very well, but our theme song was the chorale from Beethoven's Ninth Symphony. We called our group Greenslime (as in Bluegrass), and a fun time was had by all!

WSP was now a group on the national scene. The House Un-American Activities Committee (HUAC) took note of WSP and, in 1962, scheduled a hearing on its activities and issued subpoenas to some of its spokeswomen. After all, wasn't WSP preaching that the USSR was to be negotiated with, not terrorized? And hadn't we sent delegates to the Soviet Union to attend an international conference against atomic and hydrogen bombs? Of course, HUAC took note!

Midwestern women from Champaign-Urbana, Illinois, and Ann Arbor decided to go to Washington, D.C., to attend the hearing. (A generous benefactor on the West Coast chartered a plane to bring the active California women to Washington.) There were three of us in the Ann Arbor WfP who decided to carpool with three women from Champaign. We drove to an agreed-on spot on the Ohio Turnpike, left our car in a Howard Johnson's parking lot, and were picked up by the women from Illinois. There was an air of apprehension among the carload of women, who remembered the grim days of McCarthyism; I must admit that, given my personal history, I sat in the hearing room quite uneasily, almost fearing that I would be next.

The hearing, to my mind, put the final nail in the coffin of HUAC specifically and in acceptable McCarthyism in general. The *Vancouver (B.C.) Sun* reported: "When the first woman headed to the witness table, the crowd rose silently to its feet. The irritated Chairman Clyde Doyle of California outlawed standing. They applauded the next witness and Doyle outlawed clapping. Then they took to running out to kiss the witness. Finally, each woman as she was called was met and handed a huge bouquet. By then Doyle was a beaten man. By the third day the crowd was giving standing ovations to the heroines with impunity." The committee subpoenaed Dagmar Wilson, whose call had first created WSP. When Dagmar took the witness chair, she was greeted by women from the packed audience with armloads of flowers, which she continued to hold while testifying. In response to questions, she explained how she sent a call out, first via her Christmas card list, asking women to join her in a silent vigil outside the White House—and suggesting that they invite others. Thousands of women came to stand on the sidewalk one cold December day. "So are you the leader?" asked HUAC's counsel. "We are ALL leaders," Dagmar answered, rather demurely. One reporter described her as lecturing the committee as a patient third-grade teacher would talk to her pupils, trying to get them to understand what WSP was about. "What if Russian women wanted to join your group?" they asked, snidely. "Oh," gushed Dagmar, "if only they would! We could work together for peace!"—the committee was flabbergasted. Dagmar continued: "Differences of politics, economics, or social belief disappear when we recognize man's [sic] common peril. We do not ask an oath of loyalty to any set of beliefs. Instead we ask loyalty to the race of man. The time is long past when a small group of censors can silence the voice of peace." All through the hearing, the audience of WSPers laughed at what was going on, to the chair's consternation, while their children squealed and squirmed, to more consternation. There was no fear, no apology, no big speeches among the women who testified, only a straightforward account of what WSP was trying to do—and the implication that it would continue to do so, the committee be damned! The press was enormously sympathetic throughout the three days of the hearing. The *Vancouver (B.C.) Sun* concluded: "The dreaded House Un-American Activities Committee met its Waterloo this week. It tangled with 500 irate women. They laughed at it. Kleig lights glared. Television cameras whirred, and fifty reporters scribbled notes while babies cried and cooed during the fantastic inquisition." Waterloo, indeed!

By now, in addition to our graduate student and faculty friends, Dick and I were beginning to be aware of political stirrings among the undergraduates on the University of Michigan campus. The student newspaper, the *Michigan Daily*, was edited by Tom Hayden, who wrote two-page editorials about student issues. These were the days of in loco parentis, where the university believed that it had the right to control students' lives (in the place of their parents, as the Latin has it)—which was a big reason that I had decided to go to CCNY and not subject myself to that regimentation at some out-of-town college. Tom wrote endlessly, criticizing these practices, and exposed the university's dean of women, who had contacted a co-ed's parents, because she was dating a "Negro." Students had organized weekly picketing of the local Woolworth's five-and-dime, as part of a nationwide boycott of stores that segregated their lunch counters in the South, and they had a "political party," VOICE, to participate in student government.

The local city political scene was dominated by Republicans—elected by a combination of Ann Arbor's small business owners and the faculty at the University of Michigan's various professional schools (doctors, lawyers, engineers, et al.). One ward of the city, where many black folk lived, had elected a Democrat to the city council, Eunice Burns. She had sponsored a bill that would prohibit discrimination in housing in Ann Arbor—where it was well known that all minority groups had difficulty buying or renting. The hearing on the bill was held to a packed audience, organized by the more progressive churches in town, WfP, and students from VOICE. We had planned to not leave the building unless the ordinance was passed—which, of course, it wasn't.

We remained after the building closed, and several hundred of us were arrested for "trespassing"—but not until after the chief of police lectured us that this arrest could be a felony (because we had "conspired to commit the misdemeanor of trespass"), would go on our "permanent record," and could affect our future ability to be lawyers, doctors, or other professionals. We were then segregated by gender and held in locked rooms for a few hours (where the women sang and carried on as if we were in Mississippi) and were then released on our own recognizance. It was agreed with the city attorney that in lieu of a trial for the several hundred of us, we would each agree to plead nolo contendere in exchange for a fine of $10 or thirty days in jail. There was some talk of "filling" the jails, but no one was quite prepared to put his or her life on hold for a month—except Ruth Zweifler (a WfP member and the wife of my future boss). She had five children, all under ten years of age, and her action made headlines in the local press and gave our protest and the issue of fair housing both greater currency and import than it would have otherwise had. It was my only arrest, and, more importantly, was another lesson learned.

There was also a chapter on campus of the national Student Peace Union, and Dick got involved with it, planning a national picketing of the White House to demand a nuclear test ban treaty. One snowy day in February 1962, we were off to picket the White House. A few hundred students (plus a number of Washington WSPers, who had co-sponsored the picket) circled in the sleet, snow, and slush that covered the street. After a while, the White House gates opened, and a liveried (black) butler appeared, with urns of hot coffee. "From President Kennedy," he explained. Of course, a great debate ensued about whether or not it would be "selling out" to drink the coffee, but the sleet and snow and cold prevailed, and we all staved off pneumonia with JFK's coffee. A group of students from Harvard University, leaders of an organization there called Tocsin, left our picket line to meet, we were told, with a group of foreign policy experts at the State Department, in Washington's Foggy Bottom neighborhood. There was no meeting of the minds (these were, after all, "the best and the brightest"—on both sides), but I was very impressed at how seriously all these kids were being taken by the "establishment." It really felt as if we were on to something important.

Sometime during 1961 or early 1962, Dick and I were visited by Kumar Goshal, a correspondent for the *National Guardian*, a non-communist left-wing weekly. He came to give a talk on campus, I think, and we invited him for dinner. I knew nothing about him, but his name sounded Indian or Pakistani—something from the days of the Raj. I had an old-fashioned cookbook that I had picked up from somewhere, and it had a recipe for roast beef and Yorkshire pudding—just the thing, I thought, for Goshal. I don't think I had ever made it (and my mother had taught me never to experiment on "company"—but I figured, when else would I make new things?), but recipes are actually like biochemistry formulas, and I could handle that. It came out great—and Goshal said it was the best Yorkshire pudding he had ever eaten. (Maybe it was the only Yorkshire pudding he had ever had foisted on him, but I didn't care.) It became a staple of my early repertoire, and I continued to consider myself something of a cook.

In June 1962, I was working again in biology, as a research technician in the Hypertension Unit of the Kresge Medical Research Center of the University of Michigan Hospitals. (Why did all these places have such long, highfalutin names? It was something to do with the funding, I think.) This time, I was not cutting heads off rats, but working with patients or research subjects on peripheral blood flow in normal subjects, patients with high blood pressure, or patients with Raynaud's disease. I didn't cut their heads off, but indirectly measured their blood flow into hands and feet under different circumstances. I didn't terribly like sticking peoples' hands into ice water until blood flow ceased to their fingers and then waiting to see how long it took their blood vessels to recover. But the patients thought that what I was doing was therapeutic (this was long before the days of informed consent)—and the table in my apparatus was more comfortable than their hospital beds, many of them told me—and the subject students were eighteen-to-twenty-two-year-old healthy males who were being paid to have their hands made cold—so I didn't feel too bad. In our spare time, I and the other technicians figured out how to use my apparatus as a lie detector, recording vasoconstriction when any of us lied in answer to a question. One of my bosses was Andrew Zweifler, whose wife I had accompanied to Washington for the WSP HUAC hearing and who had gone to jail during the fair housing ordinance protest. It was great working for someone I could be friends with, but I didn't want to unfairly exploit our friendship. So when something called Students for a Democratic Society (SDS) was having a convention in nearby Port Huron, Dick was going to go without me because I didn't want to take time off from work.

After he left, I became quite upset/angry/jealous that I couldn't go, too. He, with his graduate student's flexibility could take off at the end of the semester, while I, the family breadwinner (I made slightly more than what his fellowship paid), had to continue to work. I suddenly felt a burning sensation in my throat and esophagus (really), something I had never experienced before. The doctors in my unit examined me and sent me for a barium X-ray of my upper gastrointestinal tract, which revealed a slight "hiatal hernia" (the stomach bulging up through the diaphragm)—heartburn. Now I had a fancy-sounding diagnosis, so I took the bottle of medicine they prescribed and used my sick leave to go to Port Huron. (I really did continue to have periodic bouts of this condition and continued to use the medicine—so I wasn't really lying.)

Recalling that time, reminds me of an old Jewish joke: A young man gets married and leaves his mother's house to live (and eat) with his wife. After a few weeks, he goes in anguish to his doctor. "What's your problem?" asks the doctor. "Doctor, doctor, I'm dying!" he says, pointing to his chest. "The fire went out!"

We had read a draft of the SDS statement of principles earlier that year and were extremely impressed. In a new language of the Left, it made a cogent critique of American society—calling it "corporate liberalism"—and pointed to a New Left movement of American students (its rumblings had already begun in the United Kingdom). We were particularly struck by the section that criticized the adult peace movement and the old socialist Left (SDS was, at that point, an incarnation of SLID) for its rabid anticommunism and pledged to remove the clause on SDS's membership card that swore that the holder was not a Communist (or something like that). It seemed to be making a point of welcoming old red diaper babies to join it, without fear of red-baiting.

Fifty years later (!) I was invited to participate in a conference on Port Huron at the University of California, Santa Barbara. I believe that I was asked to participate in that conference as an "affirmative action appointment"—which was fine with me. Affirmative action is a useful tool to ensure women's participation, and as former chair of the Santa Barbara County Affirmative Action Commission, I was happy to accept the invitation. Some of the following was included in my presentation at that conference.

At Port Huron, I was not a student but was working as a research technician at the University of Michigan and had to feign illness in order to take time off from my job; as a result, I came a few days late and missed the opening events, which included addresses by various old Socialists and labor leaders—not a big loss.

When I arrived at the convention site, located at a UAW camp, I was struck by a few things:

- The young people there were neatly dressed—not in the jeans and T-shirts of my New York left-wing student days; they weren't scruffy.
- They were incredibly articulate and smart—everyone who spoke knew how to be eloquent as well as to the point.
- They spoke a language that was not redolent of the Germanic phrases of classical Marxism but was more like the cadences of the United States Constitution and had been honed by their participation in student governments at their campuses and leadership in the National Student Association, the organization of student government leaders.
- They were masters of parliamentary procedure, using it to promote, not stifle, debate—which is what I was used to from my leftist student days—and ensuring a truly democratic expression of varying points of view.

I saw a group of Southern white students, people whose existence I had imagined, but whom I had never seen. These folks—including Robb and Dorothy Burlage and Casey Hayden (Tom's new wife)—were, to my mind, sensational: I thought Robb would make a great president of the United States. They spoke articulately, but with the soft accents of their native Texas, making their words seem softer, yet more insistent, more important. Casey in particular seemed the queen of Port Huron: she was quite beautiful and had a regal presence, somehow, that would cause all eyes to turn to her when she entered a room, all ears to tune to whatever she had to say. I was mightily impressed and somewhat intimidated.

I met Michael Vester, an exchange student from Germany and leader of the German SDS. He was the first German I had ever seen who didn't call Nazism to my mind; I was prejudiced, I admit (being a left-wing Jewish girl from New York), but his presence made me confront my prejudice and grow in understanding.

I was stunned to see Steve Max, whom I knew from my days in the teenage section of the Communist Party's Labor Youth League (LYL) and had last seen when we spent the summer of 1956 (post Khrushchev's speech and, for us, post high school) plotting the dismantling of the teen-age section of the LYL. As I thought about it, I realized that his—like mine—was a natural progression from those days to these, from the Old to the New Left. He was an organizer for SDS, still in New York City and still resistant to some of the far-out-seeming ideas that occasionally floated up. He was hardheaded and practical and represented, to me, a breath of "home." (At one point he joked, "We'll have them singing the 'World Youth Song' yet!"—the song of the Soviet-led World Federation of Democratic Youth, with which we had been raised in the post–World War II era. And, also in jest, we sang it before the meeting ended!)[3]

Both Steve and I were red diaper babies and had accepted a Communist Party USA perspective with our mothers' milk. The events of the mid-1950s drove us from the Communist Party orbit—but left us a bit high and dry, politically. Many socialist or liberal organizations required their members to sign a non-communist oath—and we certainly did not feel welcomed in any of them. We were non-Communists, but we weren't ready to be anti-Communists. We believed that led to what later became known as neo-conservativism, and we wanted no part of it or of any organization that insisted on its members' signing an oath. Although SDS, when it was essentially SLID, had had such an oath, part of Port Huron's task was to eliminate it and to define SDS's anti-anti-communism. Only SDS and WSP had dared to articulate such a position. A leader of the DuBois Clubs, the LYL's successor youth organization, was also at Port Huron, asking to be seated as an observer. Many student delegates rushed to get a look at him: they had never seen a Communist before! Over the objections of some of the socialist and labor leaders, he was granted such status (and promptly left; he later quit the DuBois Clubs and joined an SDS chapter in New York). I believe that this rejection of defining non-communist as anti-communist was one of the most enduring legacies of the Port Huron Statement and the organization it spawned—making it possible, for instance, to later oppose the United States in the Vietnam War without supporting the Vietcong—but allowing those who liked to wave Vietcong flags to participate in SDS-led demonstrations and marches. Port Huron was about inclusion, not exclusion. When the Du Bois Club member was granted "observer" status, I had my first real taste of ANTI-anti-communism!

Nevertheless, I felt a bit like an outside observer myself, mainly because I wasn't a student. I don't remember speaking at Port Huron, because I do remember feeling "outclassed"—in every sense of the word. I think I was a bit intimidated by the acumen of all those folks, and the "star status" of some of them—especially Tom and Casey Hayden and various National Student Association past presidents and officials. I also remember worrying about embarrassing Dick if I spoke: I was afraid that my contribution would not match that of those brilliant folks. Such may be the legacy (in 1962) of a working-class woman from CCNY in the company of suburban kids from the Ivy League or major universities.

Besides Tom and Casey, we were the only other married couple there. That was true for many succeeding years, where we slept blissfully in the double bed provided for us at various meeting sites, while everyone else played musical beds. I later learned that there was a good deal of admiration of our seemingly unshakable, faithfully married state, though at the time, I felt like something of a dork.

The Texans and other Southerners were truly special. They were white folks involved in the burgeoning civil rights movement—and they all talked in what I thought was a redneck accent. I was absolutely in awe of them— and of the delegation from the Student Nonviolent Coordinating Committee (SNCC), most of whom were black. Here were people truly on the front lines. The queen of all those folks (in my mind) was Casey Hayden. During the sometimes rancorous debates of that week, she spoke in her soft Mississippi/Texas accent, and quiet voice, with an authority born of her years-long participation in the civil rights struggle. She was quite beautiful and had a kind of regal presence. She would have been at home at a cotillion (or so it seemed to me), and here she was in SDS!

The final work on the statement was done at an all-night session on the last day. In the morning, a group of us, bleary-eyed, stood outside as the sun rose over Lake Huron. I was reminded of the story of Benjamin Franklin at the Constitutional Convention in Philadelphia in 1787, observing the sunburst design on the chairs in the hall. "I have been staring at that sun," he said, "trying to decide whether it is a rising or a setting sun. I now think that it is a rising one." The sun at Port Huron was definitely rising, and while it might not have signaled the birth of the nation, it did portend a new era in American social movements and left a legacy of a politics that, as the PHS stated, "seeks to maximize the participation of people in the decisions that affect their lives."[4]

DICK:

We left Port Huron exhilarated. We accomplished what we had set out to accomplish—to make the new organization, SDS, a reality. At the same time, we who were together for that week had forged pretty deep bonds of friendship and even love. Most of the people there shared the experience of being in communion with people of different backgrounds but of remarkably like mind, who now shared a mission and perhaps a destiny. Such deep bonding of like-minded peers, according to Erik Erikson, who invented the idea of youthful identity formation, can be a profound moment in the making of identity and history. At Port Huron, in addition to experiencing a political birth, we found ourselves.

Mickey and I returned to Ann Arbor, and almost immediately we set out on a summer trip that took us to the East Coast. It was one of the more eventful journeys we had ever taken, colored as it was by our Port Huron experience.

As I recall it, the first destination was the home of Harold Taylor, the past president of Sarah Lawrence College, who had spoken at Port Huron and who was a special friend of the early SDS leaders, especially Tom Hayden. Taylor, like Arnold Kaufman (and C. Wright Mills), was a disciple of John Dewey, and at Sarah Lawrence he had presided over the most "progressive" college in the country. He was a strong advocate of student participation in college governance. Not incidentally, he was a member of the board of LID.

On our drive to Boston and Martha's Vineyard, we stopped at Taylor's country house in New Hampshire, because Tom was there and had suggested that we show up for a discussion with Taylor about how he could help us with fund-raising and other support.

Taylor was an intellectual celebrity in those days. He had stepped down at Sarah Lawrence but was active in a number of cultural arenas in New York. A few months after the visit in New Hampshire, a couple of us SDSers had an appointment to meet with him at his Greenwich Village town house.

We were in one room; in another, Taylor was meeting with a group of supporters of the American Ballet Theatre (with whom he was then playing a
leadership role). And I think in another room there were some people
seeking his support for some political fund-raising effort. Taylor was a
glamorous-looking guy, with a flowing gray mane and a ready smile. He was
a host on one of those Sunday morning TV cultural programs and a sought-
after public speaker. And, memorably, the Taylors had a parrot, whose
screeching voice woke us in the morning, calling out "Harold!" in tones
strikingly similar to those of his then wife. This visit opened up a world that
neither Mickey nor I had had any prior contact with—the world of the liberal, sophisticated, and privileged intellectual class.

We had never been to Boston—or, indeed, New England—before that
trip, and after visiting with Taylor, we headed for old friends of ours who
were spending the summer in Boston. Alan (Mac) and Ricky McGowan were
people we had known in our New York days. Ricky and I worked together as
counselors at Camp Kinderland, and she was a fellow student at Brooklyn
College. We became close friends at camp and in our little political world at
Brooklyn. She then married Mac, who had come from Boston to join up
with the New York red diaper crowd that we were all involved in. Mac and
Mickey had much in common, since he, too, was a scientist, and so the
McGowans were one of a number of couples that we bonded with in the
early days of our married life. We did a touristic couple of days in Boston on
our own and with Ricky and Mac, and then they took us on a drive to Cape
Cod, ending up in Provincetown.

Not only was that a nice experience for Mickey and me in terms of seeing
this region, which we found enormously attractive, but it gave us a chance
to try out our SDS line with these old red diaper friends. I am not sure that
I remember their reaction, but I know that it was a chance for us to rehearse
our new political lingo.

Another couple that we had formed a close bond with was Ernie and
Torry Harburg. Ernie and I shared an office at the Institute for Social
Research; he was also a student in the social psychology doctoral program—a
couple of years ahead of me. Torry was active with Mickey in WSP. I soon
learned that Ernie was the son of E. Y. (Yip) Harburg, the renowned Broadway and Hollywood lyricist. He was famous for having written the songs for
*The Wizard of Oz*, including "Somewhere over the Rainbow." He had written classic songs such as "Brother, Can You Spare a Dime" and "Paper Moon."
But what made him special for Mickey and me was that he was the creator

of the Broadway show *Finian's Rainbow*. A long-running popular musical comedy, it had been produced soon after World War II. Its plot included a pathbreaking interracial theme relating to the struggle of black and white sharecroppers in the South, and its songs were both widely popular and remarkably political.

In our first summer together at Camp Kinderland, one of the first times that Mickey and I made out, we were listening to the LP recording of the Broadway production of *Finian's Rainbow*. We both much loved the delightful and socially significant songs, and the circumstances of our shared listening to it meant that it had a special place in our relationship. So Yip Harburg meant a lot to us. When I told Ernie all of this, he was astounded that people our age would be that knowledgeable about his father's work. Our appreciation of Yip helped cement a friendship with Torry and Ernie. The Harburgs were older than we were—Ernie was about ten years older than I. He had been a World War II veteran, in fact, and came back to graduate school after his time in the army. The Harburgs were our first friends with children. They had three boisterous sons, who, when we met, were all under six or seven years old. We spent much time with them, in the work space, the political space, and many enjoyable social occasions.

Yip had a house on Martha's Vineyard, and, in 1962, the Harburg family was staying nearby for the summer, so when they learned that we were en route to Cape Cod, they invited us to come over to the Vineyard and visit. We were most happy to accept that invitation!

Yip was very interested to learn about what had happened at Port Huron. He was politically very engaged and had been for a long time; indeed, he considered his songwriting to be a serious kind of political contribution. He was blacklisted in Hollywood, having refused to follow the script laid out by the witch hunters of confessing and repenting his political past and informing on compatriots who shared his political allegiances. He was, nevertheless, able to work on Broadway productions, where the blacklist had not become pervasive.

One of the perhaps dirty secrets of the Old Left is the numbers of Marxists who owned property in nice (and even posh) resort locations. The Harburg place was nestled in a veritable nest of Marxists, or so it seemed to us. In particular, Yip's neighbors included the editors of the *Monthly Review*, Leo Huberman and Paul Sweezy; almost as soon as we arrived, Yip was eager to have us meet Huberman. He took us to Huberman's abode, where we found the venerable working-class intellectual stretched out on a chaise longue. Yip excitedly said to him: "Leo, you gotta hear what these kids have been up to! They're founding a new left-wing student movement." Huberman turned out to be skeptical. "Are you Socialists?" he asked. "If not, what's the point?" I asked him to define *socialism*. "A planned economy under government control," was the definition he gave. I wondered if that was a vision American young people could find attractive.

Huberman responded: Wasn't it more important to defend Castro's revolution than to take on the impossible task of changing America? And, he said, what he really wanted was to make sure that Cheddi Jagan had the guns to defend his government in British Guiana. "Anyway, the world is likely to be blown up in the next decade." Yip grew increasingly impatient and declared himself to be on the side of imagination and fresh thinking. For me, Huberman's sour response reinforced the need for a New Left (but also suggested that at least some of the older generation, à la Yip, might be on our wavelength).

Later, Yip took me on a walk down to the nearby yacht-filled Menemsha harbor. Pointing to these, he said: "You guys might get a lot of recruits from the children of these people. They see the emptiness of owning things." It was a most perceptive observation, I thought, since there were, at Port Huron, a surprising number of children of elite parents, expressing considerable guilt at the privilege they'd experienced growing up. And then Yip said something like, "I like what you're trying to do, trying to help people see that rainbow." A most revealing comment, it made clear to me that the work he was doing as a writer of popular songs was, for him, genuinely political—and radical. The "rainbow"—that was his primary symbol for personal and social possibility.

Yip wrote a number of "rainbow" lyrics over the years. One of the great songs in *Finian's* is "Look to the Rainbow": "Look, look, look to the rainbow. / Follow the fellow who follows a dream." And if you juxtapose from "Over the Rainbow" the lines "Somewhere over the rainbow, skies are blue. / And the dreams that you dare to dream really do come true," you can see how he was striving to expand social consciousness in ways that were embedded in deeply pleasurable popular songs. That he was more on our wavelength than Huberman somehow meant a lot to Mickey and me—even though Huberman was so much more the political authority in the room.

When we got back to Ann Arbor after that trip, SDS found itself in trouble. Our parent organization, LID, had launched an effort to kill this baby in the crib. Al Haber, Tom Hayden, and Steve Max, who were paid staff of the organization, were terminated; an effort was made to change the locks on the doors of SDS's office. The members of the new SDS National Council quickly convened in New York to deal with the emergency, and Mickey and I both flew to the city.

Tom and Al had been called before a kind of ad hoc tribunal that included Michael Harrington and Vera Rony, who was the LID's director. They charged that SDS had been taken over by the pro-Soviet, or "Stalinoid," mentality and that this was unacceptable for the LID itself and violated the entire tradition of what they called the Democratic Left.

The national council members gathered in Steve's Riverside Drive apartment and listened to a recording of the hearing that led to the reprisals against SDS. It was hard to believe our ears because of the bizarre nature of the allegations. One quite memorable charge was that Al was communicating with a Japanese organization called the Campaign Against A- and H-Bombs. "Didn't you know," Harrington demanded, "that this was a communist front—that they criticized American nuclear testing, but not Soviet nuclear testing? How dare you be in communication with them!"

Al replied on the tape, "But what do you think we communicated?" "It's irrelevant" said Harrington. "The whole tradition since 1940 is that we have nothing to do with these groups." Al said, "Well, what we communicated after they had invited us to their international conference was that we could not attend because of their one-sided position on the nuclear test issue!" Harrington persisted, however, insisting how illegitimate it was even to send a letter. There was a long list of allegations about what was in the Port Huron Statement. But these were based on Tom's draft, not on what had been rewritten and actually decided at the Port Huron meeting. We later learned that Harrington had been informed by the YPSL members present at Port Huron that when he spoke at the conference the convention did not listen to his demands for changes. That report was false, but it was one basis for the draconian action that the LID took against SDS. At one point in the Riverside Drive meeting, Tom turned to Tom Kahn, who was a member of the SDS National Council and a leader of YPSL, and angrily declared: "You, Kahn, will be our worst enemy. You are much worse than HUAC. You will be the kind of people that we will be fighting in the coming years."

It was quite a shocking outburst and yet a prophetic one—Kahn, indeed, became a vocal foe of the New Left, as an intellectual adviser to George Meany, who was head of the AFL, and as an advocate for conservative perspectives within the civil rights and the labor movements.

Kahn was a somewhat mysterious figure to me and, I think, to the Left in general. I had been acquainted with him at Brooklyn College back in the 1950s. While there, he was recruited to the Young Socialist League (YSL), whose leader was a then young Michael Harrington. Kahn went on to Howard University, the predominantly black university in Washington, D.C., where he befriended people like Stokely Carmichael and others who went on to found SNCC. Kahn's incisive Marxian analysis was influential in that young, emerging activist world, but he, even perhaps more than Harrington, became imbued with anti-communist ideological fervor.

Kahn went on to work with and become the lover of Bayard Rustin, and both of them took a direction quite opposed to the more militant and nationalist turns of the black liberation movement in the late 1960s. In retrospect, it was not that their emphasis on electoral politics, coalition strategies, and economic issues was wrong but that it was aired in ways that fueled conservative hostility to the movement, while having little chance of being heard within it. Kahn ended up in the AFL headquarters as Meany's adviser, a speechwriter for Senator Henry Jackson, and an ally of the most rightwing elements in the labor movement. Somehow, Tom Hayden had accurately predicted the trajectory that Kahn's political life followed. Kahn, it seems, was revered by his close political partners, especially Rachelle Horovitz, who was another participant at Port Huron and a fellow alumna of Brooklyn College and also a member of the AFL inner circle. It remains mysterious to me that Kahn felt more at home with the George Meanys and Henry Jacksons, than with his first mentor, Harrington, and others in the Socialist Party world who eventually opposed the Vietnam War and who tried to maintain linkages with the movements of the 1960s. Kahn died, of AIDS, at age fifty-three.

The meeting at Steve Max's apartment developed a strategy for defending SDS. Steve reported that he had anticipated the changes on the locks, and so he had managed to remove from the SDS office our address files and key documents before the locks could be changed. We decided at that meeting to draw up an inventory of the charges made against Al Haber and Tom Hayden and respond to those charges in detail in a memorandum to LID's board of directors.

Much of the LID board had not heard about or played a role in the decision to suppress SDS, and so this memorandum was able to challenge the "Harrington definition" of SDS. Soon after we met, an LID board meeting was convened and the decisions of Harrington and Rony were overruled.

One of those most vocal on behalf of SDS was Harold Taylor. Norman Thomas was also a member of that board, and in a dialogue with SDS leaders some time later he said: "I have seen many manifestos in my day. Yours is no worse and no better than most of them. I thought the better part of wisdom would be for us to give you enough rope to either hang or prove yourselves." In the months after that, the LID took a more tempered approach and tried to reinvigorate itself with a younger leadership— Harrington became board president and Kahn took Rony's place as executive director.

SDS's battle with the LID strongly validated our shared conviction that a New Left was needed and that it was our mission to bring it into being. We learned how to differentiate within the Old Left those who grasped that a New Left was necessary, if there was to be any Left at all, from those who reflexively moved to protect their habits and positions.

Meanwhile, Mickey and I had our own learning experience with our old pro-Soviet Left. I'd gone to Port Huron as an accredited reporter for the *National Guardian,* and so when the convention ended, I dutifully wrote a story on the convention and an opinion piece as well. Neither was published, and instead there were a couple of lines declaring that a new student organization had been created in June as a youth wing of the LID. Not only was my report omitted, but I got no explanation from the *Guardian* editors. So, during the trip to New York for the emergency SDS council meeting, we made a side journey to the *National Guardian* office. There we met with Jim Aronson and Russ Nixon, the editors of the newspaper. Both said that they could not trust my report because they did not trust the LID, which they correctly characterized as violently anti-communist. They pointed out that nobody the *Guardian* respected had been invited to speak at Port Huron. So they decided that my romantic view of the SDS potential was something they couldn't print, and they predicted that the organization would not last the year.

In the course of that conversation, Nixon explained to me that he personally had battled communist leadership when he was an organizer for the great left-wing union, the United Electrical Workers. He was, as editor of the newspaper, constantly having to deal with readers who thought the publication was not sufficiently sympathetic to the Soviet bloc and China. I argued that the newspaper's credibility depended on its moving in a more independent and critical direction, rather than continuing to either avoid or misrepresent conditions in the communist world. Aronson and Nixon argued that in order for the newspaper to survive, it had to avoid offending its readership and donor base.

We were disappointed, to say the least. We had admired the *Guardian* as a courageous outlet during the McCarthy era, and, unlike the *Daily Worker* and other Communist Party organs, it was a genuinely journalistic endeavor. In fact, Aronson had been with the *New York Times* early in his career, and the full-time reporting staff (several of whom we had gotten to know) were highly competent reporters and writers.

Our experience with the *Guardian* editors paralleled our conversation with Leo Huberman. We admired these people's refusal to join the anti-communist crusade, but we came to realize that they were not ready to embrace the New Left vision of a reconstituted Left and might not even be ready to engage in free discussion of its prospects. So, like the experience with the LID, this encounter at the *National Guardian* greatly reinforced our determination to go ahead with the New Left project, without waiting for support from what we had started to call the "Old Left."

The SDS effort to persuade the LID board to support rather than strangle the new organization was successful in averting disaster. Accommodations were reached and agreements signed in the summer of 1962. A national council meeting at the end of the summer in Bloomington, Indiana, featured the appearances of Norman Thomas and Michael Harrington, who came (Thomas was pushing eighty) to make some peace between the LID leaders and SDS. At that meeting, Thomas told us of his advice to the LID to "give us more rope." Harrington was irritated by the fact that we had won the battle to stay within the good graces of the LID; he thought that we were still off on the wrong track, but he kept quiet about it at that meeting, though he grumbled to Mickey when she drove him to the airport afterward.

That fall, Ann Arbor became the center of SDS leadership. The national office of SDS remained in New York, but Tom Hayden, who was the newly elected president, joined SDS founders like Bob Ross and Sharon Jeffrey as well as a large group of other committed folk living in Ann Arbor.

Tom and Casey Hayden rented a house on Arch Street in Ann Arbor. The house featured a nice apartment on the first floor and a finished basement, which we all agreed would be a good place to have the headquarters for the Ann Arbor leadership. Tom and other SDS leaders were well respected by liberal faculty in Ann Arbor, and some of them gave considerable support for helping set up a functioning office in the Arch Street

basement. Most notable was a donation of a mimeograph machine by Kenneth Boulding, the well-known economist and political theorist and Quaker
peace activist, and his wife, Elise. In those days if you had a mimeograph,
you were in business as an organization—and now we had a spanking new
one. The Arch Street basement became a meeting place for regular weekly
discussions and a space where SDS leaders worked on finishing the Port
Huron Statement and publishing other new material that would advance
the perspectives of the organization. At the same time, local anti-war and
other political groups found it helpful to make use of the mimeograph
machine and other office items that we had there.

It did not turn out, however, to be very helpful to Tom and Casey's marriage that this hive of activity was carried on in their basement, but we didn't
immediately notice that impact. I was active at the center of this activity,
doing some pamphlet writing and helping to lead the weekly discussions
where we tried to develop our analysis and prepare our ideas for wider consumption. We never thought that the Port Huron Statement was the end-
point of what we had to say about America. We prided ourselves, as young
intellectuals, on being very capable of injecting a fresh perspective on the
state of the world. We thought that we could contribute to the emerging
movements some kind of insightful analysis, vision, and program. And we
were hungry to bring our academic training to bear in these ways.

MICKEY:
In the fall of 1963, the young SDS leadership would meet regularly and often
in Tom and Casey's finished basement on Arch Street in Ann Arbor. Saturday mornings were scheduled for weekly seminars and discussion groups,
with the meetings often drifting on until well into the afternoon. On those
Saturday afternoons, less than a mile away, the University of Michigan stadium was filled with football fans cheering on the Wolverines. During previous autumns in Ann Arbor, Dick and I had discovered midwestern football
and found that we really enjoyed the experience, and we were among that
101,001 capacity crowd at the stadium.

One October Saturday at noon, Dick was still at Arch Street, even though
it was time to go to the game. With great trepidation, but with even greater
determination and sense of purpose, I marched into the ongoing meeting to
tell Dick that it was time to leave if we were going to make the kickoff. Dick
rose and a little sheepishly, it seemed to me, began to leave. To incredulous

cries of "Where are you going? We haven't finished yet," I replied: "We go to the football games on Saturdays," and we did.

That moment has always remained with me as a symbol of our determination to keep the movement in perspective with respect to our "everyday lives," of the primacy of our marriage and its needs over whatever the political needs of the moment, and of our willingness to assert those principles even in the face of possible derision from our peers and leaders. In later years, when "self-sacrifice," guilt over "white-skin privilege," and put-downs of "middle-class morality" became the watchwords, I remembered that moment in Ann Arbor as an early clarification for ourselves of how we would continue to "make life" while we were "making history." It may well be that those who are not clear on the dialectical relationship between the two often find themselves in the wasteland of burnout or cynicism or "crazy" unstrategic political activism. Perhaps remembering that politics and activism are, first and foremost, in the interest of improving everyday life is critical to a successful and meaningful political movement—and life.

DICK:

The tension between heavy discussion and football afternoons was a good example of how Mickey and I worked on the balance in our relationship between the political and the personal. We believed that the intense, nearly totalistic, commitment that Tom, for example, tried to practice was not only bad for his personal relationships but was actually dangerous politically. We came to see that the more you were single-mindedly engaged in intense political activity, the more cut off you could be from the everyday experience of the people on whose behalf you claimed to be trying to remake the world.

By the end of 1962, the Tom-Casey relationship was really badly frayed. Mickey and I should have foreseen how having a buzzing crowd of people in the basement of their house had added to other tensions in their marriage. Neither Tom nor Casey was clear at that time what the marriage meant in their lives, and both had a lot of trouble reconciling conventional marriage norms with their intense political dedication and their shared desire to break away from traditional culture.

We were taking a very different path in that respect. We had grown up in families where political activism was taken for granted as part of life. In our experience, family was not marginalized or neglected in favor of the movement. Yet our parents were quite active and sacrificed a good deal for their political engagement. Moreover, until it became necessary for Sonia's re-admittance to the United States, Mickey's parents deliberately refused to get a legal marriage as an expression of their exuberant youthful rejection of the "bourgeois." Still, we were raised by people who cared about us as their first priority and cared about each other as well. Both sets of parents struggled through life to balance and integrate the necessities and joys of everyday family and work with the demands and dangers of activist engagement.

At least, that's how we understood our growing-up experience, and it is that experience that led us to see the intertwined personal and political value of our commitment to each other. Of course, ironically, as Tom argued, social movements may need a critical mass of single-minded activists in order to happen at all. There's a need for some to be able to take high risks because they are not burdened by the responsibilities of family, children, and a regular job. There's a necessity for organizers and leaders who can deploy their time and energy and way of life in ways dictated by movement, rather than personal, imperatives.

MICKEY:
That may be an irreconcilable contradiction of social movements that future generations may have to resolve.

DICK:
So, in that first year of SDS in Ann Arbor, we learned that there was a difference between Tom's "lifestyle" and what we were trying to make for ourselves. It was a difference that he tended to honor and appreciate, even if he himself was refusing to become more domesticated. In fact, the SDS crowd seemed to appreciate our more settled domesticity. Our apartment became a haven for many of the Ann Arbor SDSers, a space that offered some peace and comfort, TV and records—and even an occasional home-cooked meal.

## CUBAN MISSILE CRISIS

DICK:
In our Arch Street discussions, one of the central questions for us was how to relate to the Kennedy administration. We already had a good deal of anger because of the Bay of Pigs invasion, which seemed to have been

launched out of a combination of delusion about the potential for bringing down Castro and a caving-in by Kennedy to the demands of the CIA. We were even more disturbed by the Kennedy administration's resistance to enforcing the Constitution in the South, allowing continuing brutality and unconstitutional violation of rights without effective intervention by the federal government. Yet the emerging student activist movement believed it had the lines of communication to the White House and the national administration. For example, during the February 1962 White House picketing in support of a nuclear test ban treaty, the Harvard students who helped organize the protest had arranged for a delegation from the demonstration to visit inside the White House with some of Kennedy's advisers. (Indeed, as Mickey noted above, big coffee urns emerged from the White House, transported by liveried, white-gloved servers as a gesture to the demonstrators. The political meaning of accepting the coffee was debated, but in the end many of us compromised ourselves to ward off the February chill.) The belief was fairly widespread that there were people listening to us inside the administration and that we should not cut off the potential for such communication.

A similar dynamic was at work in the civil rights movement, where, despite the dismay with Kennedy's refusal to really enforce the Constitution, activist leaders in the civil rights movement were able, and felt the need, to continue to interact with the White House and the Justice Department in order to get whatever resources and support could be obtained. The relationship between the White House and the movements was complex, contradictory, and fascinating.

The question—whether the Kennedy administration was to be a target of pressure or opposition—came to a head in October 1962 when JFK announced that the Soviet Union had put missiles that could reach U.S. soil into Cuba and that this move was totally unacceptable. That announcement created the threat of a nuclear confrontation, and we, in the basement of Arch Street, became convinced that the threat of nuclear war was real. We debated, even in the midst of fearful crisis, how to analyze what was going on: Was this a militaristic move by Kennedy, or had there been some kind of military coup that forced his hand? We could not quite believe that John and Robert (Bobby) Kennedy would put the world at risk to challenge the Soviet missiles.

We reached out across the country to student and other anti-war leadership, trying to figure out how to respond in this crisis and feeling quite powerless in the face of the looming danger. A bunch of us ended up going to Washington on Saturday of that week, to once again picket the White House, joining an impromptu mobilization of East Coast peaceniks. The peak of our hysteria over the prospects for nuclear war came that Saturday afternoon when we and everyone else on the picket line convened at a church in Washington to figure out what to do. One of the speakers was I. F. Stone, one of the most beloved and respected left-wing journalists in the United States, and we eagerly hoped he'd clarify the situation. Stone declared that he thought human history might possibly be coming to an end—that nuclear war seemed to him, at that moment, inevitable. There were screams in the audience. One man shouted that he had no right to be so dark in his prediction, while others wept. Immediately after, various groups convened to try to figure out what to do in the face of such a threat. Ruth Zweifler, an Ann Arbor WSP member, wife of the doctor whom Mickey worked with, and mother of four children, said she was ready to risk everything by lying down on Pennsylvania Avenue in front of the White House. Others in the WSP group thought they could reach Albert Schweitzer or even Pope John and have them bodily insert themselves onto the missile pads in Cuba to prevent the United States from bombing. As we left the church, totally perplexed and desperate, a young man, likely a member of a Trotskyist party, was standing on the steps. He loudly asserted that the only possible hope was to rouse the working class to exercise their power to stop the threatened holocaust. That was the atmosphere that afternoon in Washington in the midst of the Cuban missile crisis.

We—Mickey, me, Tom Hayden, and Bart Meyers (one of my graduate student buddies)—did not know what do with ourselves after the hysterical scene in the church. We ran into Robb Burlage and some other SDS comrades—and we all confessed that we were starving. Was it appropriate to go have a meal while expecting the world to literally crash? That's what we did, in any case. No one in the cafeteria seemed to share our agitation, and, to this day, I am not sure whether it was we, or the folks going about their everyday lives, who were more rational.

We knew that a group of compatriots was to meet soon at Arthur Waskow's house in Georgetown to discuss what to do next, so we made plans to go over there. Waskow was one of several somewhat older friends and advisors to SDSers, a congressional aide, and very interested in finding a new political direction for the country. As we all drove in a couple of cars over to that meeting, we heard on the radio the news that the crisis seemed to have been averted—the Soviet ships carrying missiles were turning around and some kind of agreement had been reached. We stopped the cars in the middle of traffic and jumped out screaming and hugging one another. The world was not coming to an end that day. We had really believed that it might.

That evening, we gathered with other anti-war young people and with Waskow and other left-wing congressional aides to talk about what was next. The climate in the room was that this crisis compelled us to renew our commitment to a movement to end the Cold War and the arms race rather than rely on the supposed rationality of the Kennedy administration. The next morning, we drove home to Ann Arbor in what seemed like unusually brilliant fall sunshine.

MICKEY:

It was so beautiful that I cried on the Pennsylvania Turnpike. How could such beauty be destroyed by the actions of some willful old men? I had the same feelings years later on a lovely fall afternoon on September 11. This world was too precious to disappear in a nuclear holocaust or meaningless acts of terrorism!

DICK:

By that time, Ann Arbor had become a center in the growing national peace movement. Key members of the University of Michigan faculty, including Kenneth Boulding, Anatol Rapoport, and other social scientists, had established the Center for Research on Conflict Resolution, which was publishing a journal dealing with issues ranging from arms control policy to small group dynamics. Many of these scholars were politically active, particularly in helping a congressional contender in the 1962 elections become a "peace candidate." An electoral peace campaign had gathered force across the country in the early 1960s—seeking to elect to Congress (or at least to enter congressional races) candidates willing to take positions on disarmament and U.S.-Soviet relations, opposing the arms buildup and Cold War rhetoric that characterized the first years of the Kennedy administration. Our local candidate, an auto dealer named Tom Payne, was willing to have his campaign shaped by the peace issue (he had nothing to lose given the Republican domination of the district).

Such peace politics, we thought, could be paralleled by direct action and protest and fueled by sophisticated policy analysis, research, and innovation—all aimed at challenging prevailing assumptions and policies about national security, the Cold War, and the war economy. The October missile crisis was instructive, however. For it heightened our sense of urgency about the possibilities for nuclear war (in later years, even Bobby Kennedy revealed that he had been deeply frightened in the war room, realizing that, in the days of the crisis, he had been participating in planning a possible nuclear holocaust).

And the crisis forced us to realize how war fears could quite easily stifle dissent and debate. Payne told us, as soon as the crisis was under way, that he could no longer continue as an advocate of disarmament.

# 7 ▸ OUR SIXTIES

## Blowin' in the Wind

DICK:

The SDS National Council met during Christmas week, 1962, in Ann Arbor. It was a moment when we began to define our way of operating, how to conduct ourselves together.

One way the Old Left, particularly the old Socialist Party, had driven itself into a ditch was its practice of trying to pass resolutions on every topic on the planet. The result was endless splitting and hairsplitting. So at the Ann Arbor national council meeting, when some people wanted to adopt resolutions about certain international happenings, we declared a policy that we should take stands only on issues where we could actually take action that might make a difference. It was a way of bracketing potential differences that might arise if we tried to debate situations over which we had little control or direct experience. And in particular we were deliberately keeping the organization from destructive debates then typical in the Old Left about situations in communist and Third World societies.

SDS was going to be pragmatic in its approach to such matters. It was going to focus on its own programs and its own potential agenda. We were not to be a party that represented itself as having stands on every conceivable issue.

As the meetings went on, Casey Hayden took initiative in questioning the character of the discussion. She famously declared at one point, in her soft Southern accent: "Why can't we be kind?" She blurted this out in the midst of some intense contention and argumentation, and her assertion compelled everyone in the room to pause for some pretty deep reflection. She was, without knowing it then, making a feminist challenge to a bunch of young white men, vying for alpha position based on their intellectual brilliance and eloquence. She was, at a gut level, irritated by this display—and went on to point out that women in the room were not talking very much.

This tension came to a head on New Year's Eve when the council persisted in meeting even up to the point where partying, by all normal standards, should have begun. Casey led other women, including Mickey, to disrupt the meeting so that the party could get going.

MICKEY:

We women left the meeting early. Reluctantly and somewhat shamefacedly, we went upstairs to prepare the food and drink that we—the women—had planned for the New Year's Eve party. We were, after all, young people who could reasonably be expected to celebrate the new year's arrival with gaiety and booze. . . . As midnight approached, it was clear that the men were not finishing the meeting, but were preparing to ignore the new year completely. Casey had had enough: she led us downstairs to the Arch Street house's basement, where the men were meeting, and we excoriated them for ignoring New Year's Eve—and us!—still talking "business."

DICK:

Those moments in Ann Arbor in 1962 prefigured the role that Casey would play in coming years in SNCC and SDS. She is inscribed in histories of second-wave feminism as one of the pioneers within the New Left in raising feminist issues. She wasn't being a feminist in a fully conscious way in 1962 on New Year's Eve (because feminist language hadn't yet been invented!), but the initiative that she took, and that the other women joined, made an important impact on those assembled and on the nature of the organization. We needed to pay attention to our process and not just to the content of our

ideas. We needed to be aware of the ways that the interpersonal relationships around a meeting table could affect the very politics in which we were
engaged. We needed to be aware of the inequalities in the room that under-
cut our claims to be a participatory democracy. We hadn't yet adopted consensus modes of decision making, but sensitivity to those who were silent
or to the position taken by those in the minority became more present in
our way of operating.

One of the things we started at that meeting was to create a series of
"projects" to advance particular programmatic activities on behalf of the
organization. I took the lead, for example, in establishing a program called
the Peace Research and Education Project. Steve Max and others started
the Political Education Project. Each of the "projects" was understood as an
*experiment in strategic direction*. Rather than debate for and against directions, or foster factions pushing against each other for support, why not see
what the proposals that had significant support and interest could accomplish? No one, we thought, could rightfully claim to know the "correct path"
for the organization or for the Left as a whole. If a significant group of
people had an idea, they ought to be given some resources and support to
create an experimental project about it. Steve, for example, who led a group
that was a minority on the national council, urged that SDS emphasize progressive electoral politics as its central goal. Most of us were not enthusiastic
about that particular strategy—a perennial source of fierce debate in the
American Left. Instead of voting to defeat Steve, the council supported the
development of an experimental project that would try to engage and educate students for electoral action.

The Peace Research and Education Project, as a group of us conceived it,
focused on articulating a perspective that we wanted to advance in the peace
movement at large. That perspective grew out of our efforts, in our Arch
Street discussions after the Cuban missile crisis, to find an integrated understanding of how American society operated. We felt we had some fresh
insight to offer.

We were impressed with the fact that the Kennedy administration was
moving toward a nuclear test ban and agreement with the Soviet Union on
nuclear arms control. These moves, expressed in JFK's famous speech at
American University, in Washington, D.C., in June 1963, were real victories
for the peace movement and seemed to mark a considerable reversal of
Cold War policy. But several of us, in Ann Arbor, had the chance to participate in a University of Michigan–sponsored national conference on arms

control, which featured, among other speakers, a few top policy thinkers from the Pentagon. What we heard administration figures say was that there was an interest in détente with the USSR, not so much on behalf of peace, but as a way to free the United States to intervene in local non-nuclear wars. We learned that the administration was most worried about civil war and revolutionary upsurge in the Third World—and that it felt militarily hamstrung because intervention in small local conflict could readily escalate toward big power confrontation and nuclear danger. Détente with the Soviet Union might allow more freedom of action to militarily suppress local revolts. We believed, accordingly, that the major peace organizations needed to focus on the threats of war arising out of "Third World" conflicts as well as on the nuclear arms race.

We also argued that one way to challenge the arms race and the power of the military-industrial complex was to emphasize the domestic economic demands of working people and the poor. We saw the civil rights movement not only as a struggle for rights but as a transformative movement that was challenging the priorities of the nation as a whole. We expected and advocated that the civil rights movement be understood as a spearhead for achieving not only constitutional rights for Southern blacks but economic equality and justice. To end poverty in America, we argued, required a scaling back of the military budget and the global ambitions of the American state.

So the SDS peace project was an attempt to influence the peace movement, on the one hand, to recognize that the nuclear issue was not the only issue bearing on the possibilities for war and peace—that conventional warfare aimed at suppressing Third World revolutions might come to the fore. On the other hand, we wanted the peace movement to ally itself with the civil rights movement and the emerging struggle for justice in the United States, not only because that was a morally correct stance, but because, in fact, raising the internal pressures on the power elite could change American global policy as well as domestic priorities.

Tom Hayden and I were able to get a small grant from a peace foundation in Canada to write a document that we called "The New Possibilities for Peace," which embodied this perspective. We succeeded in disseminating this document to leaders in the peace movement in the months that followed. The grant helped in supporting Tom's full-time engagement as a leader of SDS and in his efforts to speak and organize across the country. He traveled indefatigably, a veritable Johnny Appleseed for a New Left, attracting recruits to SDS and to our ideas, on campuses and in communities.

Our writing and discussions during winter and spring of 1963 helped lay the foundation for drafting a new manifesto or program statement for debate at the SDS convention to be held in June 1963. I was delegated to do a lot of the drafting for that. I started to work on the draft that winter and spring—along with my dissertation and a load of teaching that I was also doing. When we look back to those years, we're amazed to realize how much we were able to accomplish and how much energy we had. I was a full-time graduate student with full research and teaching agendas and, at the same time, was taking a leadership role in SDS. Meanwhile, Mickey was working full-time in a biology research lab while also being active, especially on the community level.

DICK:

The SDS convention in June 1963 was held in a children's camp in Pine Hill, New York. It was a much bigger affair than Port Huron; clearly, our reach across the country had grown. Steve Max had spent the months prior to the convention as a field organizer for SDS, and many new chapters were created in the wake of his visits (especially, we joked, at the small women's colleges he seemed to favor). The work at Pine Hill was to be focused on the draft document that we in Ann Arbor had prepared, eventually titled "America and the New Era."

We were wrestling with issues of *strategy* for a resurgent Left. Port Huron laid out a statement of vision and values and provided a critical analysis of the gap between those hopes and societal reality. At Port Huron, we had framed the strategic question in terms of the long-standing battle within the Left about whether a new party independent of the two old parties should be created or whether we should work within the Democratic Party for what we called its "realignment." The realignment perspective, of which Michael Harrington was a major proponent, saw that, for the most part, the labor and civil rights movements and other liberal forces operated within the Democratic Party but were far from controlling its direction. That direction was dominated by an alliance between extremely conservative, white supremacist Southern Democrats and machine Democrats of cities in the North, like Chicago and New York. The realignment strategy argued that the party should be remade. Authoritarian and corrupt machines were being challenged by rising reform movements in many cities and states. A new politics in the South could force the Dixiecrats into the Republican Party, where they ideologically belonged. It imagined that a coalition of labor and other liberal forces with the civil rights movement could take leadership in the remaking of the party—and could then win support from the majority of the electorate.

In those early days of the sixties, there was some evidence that this kind of strategy might work. Indeed, in Michigan, the realignment of the Democratic Party had begun after World War II, with the United Auto Workers (UAW) playing a big role in creating what was essentially a new and much more dynamic Democratic Party in that state. Labor people who had led that political drive were among SDS's key financial supporters—some of them were even parents of SDS founders.

One of the primary leaders of that Michigan effort, Neil Staebler, lived in Ann Arbor. We had the chance to have lunch with Staebler sometime in early 1963. He seemed happy to meet us, but he had some observations that bothered us immensely. He talked about how he had been a Socialist at our age and abandoned the Socialist Party during the years of Franklin D. Roosevelt, supporting Roosevelt in 1936. Staebler learned, he said, that we needed to "take off our red ties and enter into the mainstream politics." That was a point we had sympathy with, but then he went on to say: "Now we have achieved all of the goals we have set out to achieve." We found that observation appalling—it was made at the height of the turmoil in the South, when battles in Selma and Birmingham, Alabama, and in Mississippi were ongoing. His New Deal–era feeling that the progressive agenda had been already achieved seemed to us another of many illustrations of the dead end that the Old Left, in all of its diverse expressions, represented.

That encounter, like many others at that time, helped us see that the point we needed to figure out was not whether to work within or outside of the Democratic Party. We understood (or most of us did) that third-party politics was itself a dead end. The political structure of the United States at many levels depended on a two-party model, and unlike prevailing European parliamentary models, third parties could not have electoral success, but could instead hinder the possibility for more progressive outcomes. Third-party candidacies could defeat what third-party advocates called the "lesser evil," but those "lesser evils" in power could provide space for social movement victory (as seemed to be happening in the Kennedy years). A new party was needed in the United States—but it would, we thought, have to come through a struggle within the Democratic Party—a struggle that was in fact happening.

At the same time, we were skeptical that a realignment of the Democratic Party was going to fulfill its promise if led by the then-dominant labor leadership and liberal politicians. In the first place, we doubted that they would take that initiative. And even if they did make a serious effort to win control of the Democratic Party, we doubted that they had the will to achieve it.

"America and the New Era" found inspiration in what we called "new insurgencies"—efforts on a community, city, and state level to undertake new political coalitions that might operate within the Democratic Party but that were able to set their own agendas and define their own strategies and tactics. We saw this happening in places like Texas, where a new liberal-labor coalition had won considerable electoral success on the state level as well as in some localities. In California, the California Democratic Clubs and related formations were transforming the Democratic Party in that state. We saw it in reform politics in New York City and in nascent reform movements in Chicago and other urban centers. We saw it in the congressional peace campaigns of the early 1960s that were raising issues about the United States' global role and, in some cases, electing people to Congress on peace agendas. We saw in some university towns the possibility of a new politics emerging, as seemed to be happening in Madison, Wisconsin, and Cambridge, Massachusetts, as well as in Ann Arbor. It was on these diverse local insurgencies that we based our strategic arguments—hoping to transcend the interminable debate about "working within or without." Our pragmatist, experimental way of thinking led us to see locally based initiative as most promising for creating a new politics.

Of course, undergirding and overriding all of the above was the civil rights movement, which was in the streets throughout the South but was also engaged in an increasingly intense voter mobilization effort in places like Mississippi and Alabama, where blacks were never before allowed to vote. Voter registration efforts in the South were getting support from the Kennedy administration and its political allies, who were hoping to divert the movement from the dramatic street protests and civil disobedience that, broadcast around the planet, were enormously embarrassing to the Kennedys and destabilizing to the status quo.

But voter registration efforts in Mississippi and other parts of the black belt were met with such violence that the Kennedys' hope for a return to a more quiet time backfired. In 1963 we could see the beginnings of a strategy in the South for effective black electoral politics that would have a powerfully transforming effect on the society as a whole. Simultaneously, we observed that the civil rights movement was moving into Northern communities and, by so doing, demanding jobs and income as well as an end to segregation.

Rather than fight over the question of whether to have a new party or realign the Democratic Party, we said that the job of activists was to promote these local insurgencies and the initiatives sparked by the civil rights movement. And, the draft convention statement suggested that a heightened battle for jobs and freedom in the United States was the key to changing American policy in the world at large.

There was a particularly memorable moment for me and a lot of others at Pine Hill. That was a speech by Paul Potter. Paul was one of the founding circle of SDS, but he didn't make it to Port Huron because he had campaigned successfully to become an officer of the National Student Association, which was meeting simultaneously. Paul, in that role, had traveled with Tom Hayden to Mississippi and was beaten along with Tom by redneck goons some months before Port Huron. He was a remarkably gentle guy, one of the most beloved members of our crowd; he died very young, in the 1980s. Paul's talk at Pine Hill was an eloquently expressed vision of the university as a place where social movement and intellectual work might fuse—a place that could support and nurture those who wanted to move between research and action and fruitfully connect them. Paul had a knack for expressing social analysis in terms that reached to people's personal choices and dilemmas. The vision he was talking about connected with many of us in the room, who were facing big choices about how our lives ought to be directed. We could be in the university—but only if we consciously worked to make it a home for our political and moral values and goals. We could be activists—but we would be better as political actors the more we were intellectually engaged as well. For me personally, Paul was putting into words my own dilemmas, and from his words I was eventually able to define a life course.[1]


## A. J. MUSTE

DICK:

Tom and I and some others were invited to a meeting that took place at the Fellowship of Reconciliation (FOR) headquarters in Nyack, New

FIGURE 7.1. Dick speaking at the SDS Second National Conference, Pine Hill, New York, 1963

York, shortly after Pine Hill. We were to meet there with some of the leaders of the national peace organizations who wanted to get to know us
upstarts. These included A. J. Muste, who was a personal hero of mine.
The venerable Muste, who had started his political career in the World
War I era, who had been a Marxist labor organizer as well as a Christian
minister, who had adopted Gandhian nonviolence as a key element of
his perspective, was the director of FOR and had started other organizations like the Committee for Nonviolent Action, the Committee for
a Sane Nuclear Policy (SANE), and the Congress for Racial Equality
(CORE). Muste is one of the least well-known historically significant
figures in American history. He obviously had a talent for organizational
entrepreneurship—each of the groups he founded had a distinctive crucial role in the development of nonviolent peace and civil rights protest
and resistance. He drew around him a number of talented younger men
and women, who themselves became creative sparks for nonviolent resistance in the peace and civil rights movement. These included people like
Dave Dellinger, Bayard Rustin, David McReynolds, and many others. He
was the editor of *Liberation* magazine, which was an important resource
for our intellectual understanding. By the time of that Nyack meeting,
Muste had already indicated to us his interest and support for what we
were saying.

The peace leaders, or peace bureaucrats, as we sometimes called them,
who met with us included Homer Jack, who was the director of SANE (the
leading liberal anti–arms race organization), and others whom I cannot
recall. Some of these guys had a tendency to mistrust newly arrived activists
whom they had never heard of before. Some months before that meeting,
I remember having a conversation with a couple of peace leaders who said
they did not trust the Women Strike for Peace (WSP) group because they
didn't know who these people were. I understood the attitude, because in
intense political efforts trust is an important element in maintaining and
advancing one's work. The great journalist and one-time socialist youth
Murray Kempton once pointed out that it was possible to trust people on
the left with whom you had bitterly fought if you had a long relationship
with them, while deeply mistrusting those whom you didn't know even if
they seemed to be agreeing with you. One root of these attitudes had to do
with the deeply ingrained fear of communist infiltration; any upstart could
turn out to be a covert Stalinist.

All of that was both understandable and yet dismaying. After all, the best explanation for the appearance of "upstarts" was that the movement was growing! To have a movement that was simply made up of the same people always working together was obviously a dead end. Their distrust of upstarts was a sign that the older leadership in many left organizations had become totally habituated to being in charge of a holding company rather than a potentially dynamic center of activism.

Muste, who was at least a generation older than most others in the room at Nyack, had a very different outlook. Mickey and I first heard of him because of the Left forums he organized in New York after Khrushchev's speech—events whose purpose was to connect people even when there was sharp ideological difference or hatred, inviting Communist Party, Trotskyist, socialist, and pacifist leaders to share platforms. Despite all his frustrating decades in the swirling internecine warfare of American radicalism, he was still searching for ways to create a workable Left and to spark mass resistance.

At the Nyack gathering, Homer Jack and others in the orbit of SANE were understandably very excited by the prospect of a nuclear test ban treaty and Kennedy's receptivity to détente. Tom and I arrogantly laid out our view that the nuclear test ban treaty, which was then about to be signed, while a great achievement, was likely to increase the chances for war. This was a startling view, and Homer Jack, who had given his life to create this opportunity, turned red with anger. We explained that if the United States and the Soviet Union reached a détente, it made it more possible for the United States to intervene in local situations. I don't remember whether we mentioned Vietnam as one of those places, but maybe we did. Muste said: "Listen, Homer, to what they're saying—they have truth on their side!" Jack burst out in rage: "A.J.," he said, "you've been poisoning young minds for far too long!" Quite a moment in our own development as activists!

Bayard Rustin, who had come in late, took the floor, not to criticize us, but to emphasize "the need to build up mountains of discontent in the streets of American cities"—something he predicted was likely to happen in the coming months and years. So we saw Rustin at that point as allied to us in his emphasis on street action and civil disobedience as the main things to be doing at this point in time. I'm not sure if there was any result of that meeting except that we became, at that moment, part of the discourse

FIGURE 7.2. A. J. Muste, circa 1955

within the loose network of the Democratic Left and social movement leaders and thereby got the chance to presumptuously assert passionate challenges to the assumptions of our elders.

## FREEDOM IN THE SUMMER AIR

DICK:

In the summer of 1963, I wrote my dissertation. Mickey helped me a lot by buying (for $15) a used air conditioner, to cool the little room that I was working in that hot Ann Arbor summer. And she decided that, rather than hang around while I was holed up in that cave, she would go to the Atlanta SNCC office to help in the preparation for the great March on Washington, scheduled for August 28.

MICKEY:

In August 1963, Dick was busily finishing writing his dissertation. I had bought a room air conditioner (used and noisy) for our small spare bedroom, and Dick ensconced himself in there for the summer. I was mostly superfluous.

Tom and Casey had split up that summer, and Casey was living in Atlanta, working at the SNCC office. I was between jobs, so I decided to go visit Casey and help her in whatever way I could. I had never been south of Washington, D.C., and was filled with trepidation. When the Airporter bus deposited me at the terminal, right downtown, on Peachtree Avenue (no less), I was sure that each member of the crowd milling about me would recognize that I was (a) Jewish, (b) a lefty, and (c) going to the SNCC office—and promptly lynch me. Only Casey, who drove up shortly after I arrived, paid me any attention, and she took me to her apartment— safely in the black section of the segregated city. (In the days that followed, I always breathed a sigh of relief when we crossed whatever dividing line it was that indicated we were back, safe in the black neighborhood.)

Casey didn't really need my help, but I saw that the SNCC office could use some of my skills. Everyone was busily preparing for the March on Washington for Jobs and Justice, scheduled for August 28. Most SNCC folks thought that the march was a distraction from their critical work in Georgia, Alabama, and Mississippi, but participation was indeed mandatory. John Lewis (now the venerated U.S. congressman from Georgia) was then SNCC president and was scheduled to speak at the march. The office manager was looking for someone who could type up his speech, preferably on a mimeograph stencil so it could be duplicated. This was not such an easy feat in those days, and those in the office who were experienced with stencils were busy doing other important work. "I can do that," I piped up, having learned to cut mimeograph stencils when I was thirteen years old, at Camp Kinderland. They set me up at a ribbonless typewriter, and I went to work. When I had finished, the speech was mimeographed and copies were distributed to members of the march committee, including Bayard Rustin, Martin Luther King Jr., and Walter Reuther. I frankly don't remember what John had written that caused such consternation among the "adult" civil rights leaders (attacks on the Vietnam War, I think, and something about "blacks [not 'Negroes'] in the streets"). There ensued quite a to-do, exacerbating growing rifts between SNCC and the civil rights movement's older guard. John had to finally revise his speech, modifying what had caused the stir. Perhaps, if I had not been there, no mimeographed copies would have been made available, and John would have been able to say what he wanted to. Of such trivia is history made . . .

DICK:

I worked away on the dissertation, in splendid isolation, and had a draft completed by summer's end. That freed me to drive with others from Ann Arbor to Washington, D.C., in time for the big march. Mickey and I met up in the midst of the large, boisterous SNCC delegation, with whom she'd come up from Atlanta.

MICKEY:

Casey and I and three other SNCC workers drove up to Washington from Atlanta in an "integrated car"; that is, we were black and white folks. Through Georgia and the Carolinas, the black passenger lay on the floor of the car so that he would not be visible from the outside. It was my first experience with this region of America. On the other hand, through the car radio (in Virginia, I think) came the strains of Peter, Paul and Mary singing Bob Dylan's "Blowin' in the Wind." We were ecstatic. Something was indeed blowin' in the wind.

DICK:

The march was of course inspiring, in part because it was a huge mass of people, both black and white—the largest demonstration that any of us had ever experienced. SDS people felt part of it, because so many of our own members had been south and were accepted, at least to some extent, as compatriots and comrades by the SNCC people. Robb and Dorothy Burlage were living in Washington at that time, and so a lot of us piled into their apartment the night before the march sleeping twelve abreast across a bunch of pulled-together beds. It was one of the many moments in that time when we were deeply bonding with our brothers and sisters.

Right after the march some of these folks embarked on a cross-country drive to Bloomington, Indiana, for an SDS National Council meeting. Casey and Sharon Jeffrey were fellow passengers on that exuberant journey. As we drove through rural border country, Casey would shout out the window "Rise up!," while we sang all the freedom and labor songs in our repertoire. We were in a "freedom high" state of mind.

The most famous picture of SDS is often used as if it depicted the Port Huron founding, but it was actually taken at the Bloomington national council meeting. We didn't imagine that the photo would have any historical significance; it shows almost all of us with fists raised in a sardonic tribute to the Left heritage (but most raised their right arms, demonstrably ignorant of the correct left-fisted ritual display).

One memory from the summer of 1963 was that mainstream pop music began to reflect our own consciousness. The most popular song that summer was "Blowing in the Wind," Dylan's anthem, as performed by Peter, Paul and Mary. To us, its popularity was a significant harbinger. By the time Dylan's *Freewheelin'* album came out in May 1963, the SDS crowd heard him as our voice. We never expected that one of his politically oriented songs would become a big popular hit—let alone that he'd become the icon of the youth culture. In 1963 his songs, and occasional forays into scenes of protest including Mississippi and the Washington march, led us to see him as our own.

The Bloomington meeting was a scene of what we called "musical beds." Mickey and I, as the "mature" married couple, were not immediately privy to many of the romantic complexities that were developing in the SDS world, and we ourselves did not, of course, take part. We were astonished to learn, after the time there, the extent to which the manifold couplings in Bloomington resembled a French bedroom farce.

By 1963, in Ann Arbor, our apartment was something of a haven for the SDS crowd. We enjoyed watching TV drama shows, especially the few that actually were addressing social concerns. These included, most notably, *Naked City*, a pioneering police show based on an early 1950s film by Jules Dassin, who'd been blacklisted soon after, moving to Paris, where he (this Jewish guy from the Bronx, a Camp Kinderland alumnus) was transmogrified into a famous French movie director. *Naked City* on TV, like the movie on which it was based, was notable for its use of real street settings rather than sets, and it had a gritty, socially conscious feel to it. Even more politically adventurous was a short-lived program called *Eastside/Westside*, which starred George C. Scott as a social worker who, in the course of the series, becomes a political activist. His character's secretary was played by the great African American actress Cicely Tyson. *Eastside/Westside* each week featured a story that illuminated urban ills, with a surprising emphasis on questions of race and about protest. We persuaded our SDS friends that it might be fun to gather in our living room on the nights that these programs were on. We had a soft rug on the floor, and people could lounge about and watch TV programs and talk about them. Todd Gitlin had moved to Ann Arbor that summer, ostensibly to go to graduate school, but also to take up his role as SDS president. Todd was one of the regulars on our carpet, and we take some credit for his eventual emergence as a leading expert on popular culture and television, about which has written so widely and influentially.

At twenty-three and twenty-five, respectively, Mickey and I were surprised to be adopted as parental surrogates—but felt privileged to take this sort of role in the lives of these multi-talented, intriguing, and dynamic young people.

DICK:

I completed my dissertation in the fall of 1963, was awarded the PhD, and was ready to embark on an academic career. I didn't go into the job market immediately, since I finished the dissertation after the usual hiring season. Instead, I worked in 1963–64 as a research associate at the Center for Research on Conflict Resolution (where Mickey was "center secretary"). The center had been established a few years earlier by a rather distinguished group of social scientists, including Kenneth Boulding and my mentor, Daniel Katz. I was fortunate to be able to get a research fellowship to work closely with Katz and Herbert Kelman, another outstanding social psychologist, who had recently come to Michigan from Harvard. We worked together on a study of American perceptions of nationalism and the ways that nationalism did or did not play a part in people's identity. I launched a pretty decent survey, using a sample drawn in Ann Arbor, aimed at testing some ideas about these matters. It was work that I was excited by at the time, but it never got much notice, since I didn't devote myself systematically to writing it up (though there were a couple of articles we three co-authored).[2]

MICKEY:

In the fall of 1963, I decided to drive to New York to see my mother. Dick was teaching and couldn't go, but Todd Gitlin, SDS president at the time, wanted to go to the SDS office in New York and also visit his parents, so he and I made the ten-hour drive together. We arrived in the late afternoon and went down to the office, which was on Nineteenth Street, near Fifth Avenue. We found a parking spot on Fifth Avenue, in front of the building that housed the New York SNCC offices, and made our way to the SDS office. After a few hours, we returned to the car—to find the doors unlocked and our suitcases missing. "Oh well, the mean streets of New York," we thought, and Todd went to his parents' home and I went to my mother's, where I called the police to report the theft (for insurance purposes). A short while later, my mother's phone rang, and it was someone in the SDS office calling to tell us that the building janitor had found the suitcases on the back stairs and thought they belonged to SDS folks. (Why he thought that was never explained.) I picked up Todd at his parents' (like my mother, they lived in the Bronx), and we tore back downtown. The suitcases were indeed ours; mine had a funny lock, so that it couldn't be opened without first squeezing it shut, and when I opened it, it appeared untouched. Todd found nothing missing in his—except his address book! We were certain that FBI agents had recognized our car at the SNCC office, tailed us, stolen the luggage, taken what they were after—a list of SDS and other "subversives'" names—and, like good boys, had returned our goods. We could never prove that, but we could find no other explanation.

DICK:

The nationalism survey influenced my own political perspective. What I was hearing from our survey respondents reinforced my hunch that the emergent—and really dominant—consciousness in America was not based on patriotism as defined by the right-wing. Instead, Americans typically were most concerned about their lives, as embedded in family and work and community, and were not easily mobilized by nationalist symbols. Most of the time, I conjectured, the American majority responds to the threat of war as a threat to the fabric of daily life, rather than as time for nationalistic rallying. There was space, I felt, for the peace movement to frame opposition to war in ways that might reach into majority American consciousness. Moreover, I found that a substantial percentage of respondents to our community-based survey were people who had a cosmopolitan experience—travel and education were providing exposure to other cultures. Such exposure, my data showed, was associated with a disdain for narrowly based nationalism and support for internationalist policies. More than fifty years later, it seems even more the case that flag-waving patriotic and nationalist appeals, although they appeared effective in times of great threat, such as after 9/11, don't in the long run mobilize the energies and support of the American people for militaristic policy.

At the same time, I was of the view that the American Left should claim its legitimacy and frame its vision and strategy in terms that appreciated the national past. American leftists, especially those who have broken away from conservative traditions, are prone to thinking that America is best understood as an imperial power needing to be opposed, or that the truly valid ways of life can be found everywhere else but in the United States, or that American nationhood should be deconstructed. America as an empire, built on genocide of Native Americans and on mass enslavement of Africans, certainly inspires angry anti-Americanism, an anger reinforced by many versions of Americanism that blindly or willfully proclaim American superiority or "exceptionalism." My survey results in the early sixties suggested that the majority of Americans, however, aren't defined by or motivated by those sorts of "Americanisms." The Left that struggled to find itself in the 1930s as "twentieth-century Americanism"—the Left into which I was born—was onto something back then. The Popular Front of the 1930s (much derided in the New Left) provided clues to how a progressive patriotism might be part of the scaffolding for a majoritarian progressive coalition.

That work in Ann Arbor made me think I might have something to offer to the New Left—as a sociologist—as well as an activist.


## JFK MURDERED

DICK:

Everyone remembers 1963 as the year that John F. Kennedy was assassinated in Dallas. Even though we were, to say the least, ambivalent about Kennedy's policies vis-à-vis the Cold War and civil rights, we were, of course, fascinated with him. He had begun to change direction, we thought, in June of 1963, when he delivered a remarkable speech at American University in which he called for a new chapter in U.S.-Soviet relations, anticipating achievement of the nuclear test ban treaty and speaking much of the language of peace groups like SANE.

Although he and his administration were dismayed by the March on Washington and tried to prevent it from happening, they could not publicly disavow it. Responding to the pressure of dramatic confrontations in the South, the Justice Department began to lend support to Southern freedom fighters. Behind the scenes, and unknown to us at the time, the Kennedys had agreed with J. Edgar Hoover that Martin Luther King Jr. should be put under surveillance, and they bought into Hoover's claims that King was actually in thrall to the Communists. SDSers who were close to SNCC had enough firsthand experience to believe that the Kennedys were determined to control the civil rights movement rather than simply respond to its moral demands.

There were, accordingly, many reasons for our ambivalence with respect to the Kennedys, but nothing could be more shocking than to have JFK shot down in that motorcade on the streets of Dallas. It was quickly reported that groups of people in the South, including schoolchildren, applauded the news of Kennedy's assassination, and, like many, we saw this response as a logical culmination of right-wing hysteria that had been sweeping the South in general and Texas in particular. Tom Hayden came over to our place almost immediately, and we were glued to the television in the hours and days after the shooting. Tom was deeply affected by what was happening. He identified with the Kennedys deeply—with their Catholic roots and their capacity to affect history—even though he was highly mistrustful of their Machiavellian approach to social movements.

Figuring out the political, cultural, and social meaning of the assassination and the subsequent murder of Lee Harvey Oswald was our main preoccupation that weekend. We debated whether it was best to assume that some kind of conspiracy lay behind the assassination or whether Oswald could have been the lone assassin. My sociologist self invented, on the spot, a new social type that I called the "lurker." "Lurkers" are people like Oswald—very poorly integrated into normal society, their whole life story one of marginalization and alienation. Lurkers, I imagined, may be very tempted to do some kind of grandiose, highly visible public act in order to validate themselves. Later, as we learned about Oswald's personal history, his restless urge to stand out in history became even clearer. So it's always seemed to me quite plausible that Oswald did act alone, in the context of a climate in which hatred of Kennedy was widespread and profound and manufactured by right-wing operatives.

At the same time, the possibility of conspiracy seemed very real. For example, I remember distinctly hearing the surgeons on television reporting that the bullet hole in Kennedy's throat was an entry wound, which gave plausibility to the idea, which was soon voiced, that a second shooter was positioned on the grassy knoll facing Kennedy's approaching motorcade—since Oswald's shots had to come from above and behind. More blatant was the experience on Sunday morning of that weekend as we watched the telecast of Oswald being brought down to the basement of the jail for transport to the court. I said, jokingly, "He's going to be shot there," and, incredibly that's what happened. That one could imagine and then see Oswald being done away with reinforced the idea that something beyond a lurker acting alone was needed to understand this event. "Lurkers of the world unite!" I joked. Both Oswald and his killer, Jack Ruby, fit the social type I had been inventing.

For a while afterward, I was an avid reader of many of the books about the assassination. A leading questioner of the official story of the "lone assassin" was a good friend of SDS, former New York State Assembly member Mark Lane, who pioneered the notion that JFK was killed by an elite conspiracy. I've always been of two minds on the matter: while I think it's plausible that Oswald acted alone, I think there's very good reason to try to determine whether there was an assassination plot. Maybe the most plausible accounts are those in fiction. There is Richard Condon's great novel *Winter Kills*, and then there is Don DeLillo's rich novel about the assassination, *Libra*. Both compel belief that conspiracy in this instance can readily account for what we know as the "facts" better than the "lurker"/lone assassin story. But more importantly, DeLillo gives us a framework for understanding the assassination as a major episode in an ongoing cultural/ political war in the United States. It's a war that is being played out not just in political debate and mass mobilization but in the machinations of government intelligence organizations, which have both the power and the means to manipulate events, under cover. So whether or not there was a specific conspiracy in this case or in the later assassinations of King and Bobby Kennedy, the machinery for such operations exists in the national security apparatus. Such considerations became a necessary underlying theme in our political lives in the decades that followed.

In any case, the bright promise of that summer, for which "Blowin' in the Wind" was part of the soundtrack, had turned into a very cold November, in which death and violence were looming in ways we had not before been willing to face. That was the same month that America's puppet leader of South Vietnam was assassinated, just shortly before the killing of JFK. Vietnam was in our minds at that time, but only as one of a number of trouble spots, where, we thought, the threat of wider war might flare up. Kennedy's assassination, and the unresolved circumstances surrounding it, marked the end of our innocence. If once we had thought that reasoned debate and sincere, well-meaning protest could change the course of the government and the national elite, doubt about the sufficiency of decency and idealism now dominated our conversation.

At the same time, the pace and potentials of SDS were getting more promising every day. SDS had a close relationship with the UAW's national leadership, which, of course, was based in Detroit—a short drive from Ann Arbor. One of the founding leaders of SDS was Sharon Jeffrey, whose mother, Mildred (Millie) Jeffrey, was among UAW leader Walter Reuther's closest aides and confidants. Millie Jeffrey appreciated us greatly, and we were thrilled to get to know this exceptional figure in labor (and Michigan) history. She and other UAW staff were very helpful in getting support for SDS from the union.

After the summer of 1963, we succeeded in getting a grant from the UAW for what was called the Economic Research and Action Project (ERAP). The UAW thought that it was funding SDS so that we could advance a pro-union agenda on college campuses and an educational program in favor of full employment and other economic issues. But such an educational effort didn't match the yearning within SDS for direct action.

The nature of ERAP was to be debated at the next meeting of the SDS National Council, scheduled to be held New York during the Christmas break. It turned out to be another of those fateful occasions in the development of SDS and in our shared lives. Truly memorable was that certain persons of mythical proportions, who happened to be in the city, were invited to come by to greet the new SDS. One of our new and very active members, Jeremy Brecher, was a family friend of Alger Hiss. Hiss was, of course, one of the main targets of the postwar Red Scare, charged and ultimately convicted of perjury related to alleged espionage in the 1940s. It was his case that launched the career of Richard Nixon as a foe of the Red Menace and helped determine the Cold War discourse in postwar America.

Hiss, after three years in prison, had embarked on a private, under-the-radar, life, but Jeremy invited him to come by to greet the SDS National Council. I'm unsure whether many of those present really knew much about Hiss, but it was fascinating for us to have the chance to talk to him for a few minutes in a group situation. I can't recall the content of that interaction, but Hiss's appearance at the meeting was a symbolic flaunting of the LID code. We were welcoming in our midst someone who'd actually been convicted of aiding the Soviet cause.

When I was a kid, I had a deep and obsessive fascination in all of the happenings of the McCarthy years and had learned a great deal about the Hiss case. Hiss was of particular interest because he'd been a well-liked and prominent member of the foreign policy elite (and therefore his disgrace helped tarnish the entire New Deal legacy). He maintained, until his death, that he was innocent of the charges against him, and there was quite a literature debating the case. Indeed, I renewed my interest in Hiss some years later during the Watergate affair, when Nixon had been quoted as saying that his treatment of Daniel Ellsberg was based on his earlier targeting of Hiss.

It wasn't at all clear what Nixon might have meant when he said that. But Hiss had worked hard over the years to show that evidence used against him had been forged and planted—and it was clear that Nixon's crew of "plumbers" had tried to do just those things to Ellsberg after his leaking of the Pentagon Papers. The Hiss case involved all kinds of weird and fascinating details, including microfilms hidden in pumpkins in backyard gardens, but what intrigued me during the Watergate affair was the relevance of Hiss's claim that material allegedly typed on his typewriter and given to confessed Soviet spy Whittaker Chambers was in fact forged. Apparently, White House operatives had tried to forge materials to be used incriminate JFK in the murder of South Vietnam dictator Diem. To my knowledge, no one has tried to connect these various dots, and conventional wisdom now assumes that Hiss was indeed a Soviet agent of some sort. But even the phrase *Soviet agent* may be more ambiguous than it seems, given that at the time of Hiss's alleged "crimes" the USSR was not an enemy—and it's never been made clear what the content of the information Hiss allegedly gave to self-proclaimed Soviet spy Whittaker Chambers was about. I've always wished that a new generation of historians would look with fresh eyes on the whole matter of U.S. Communist Party involvement in Soviet espionage.

Anyway, we met Hiss for a brief moment in the SDS National Council meeting in 1963. A more significant encounter when Bob Dylan showed up for an hour or so. One of the people who'd been drawn to the SDS circle was Danny Kalb, an admired guitarist in the folk rock world, who was part of the New York SDS group. Kalb was a friend of Dylan's and thought that Dylan would be interested in what we were up to. So he told the council that, at a certain time, Dylan would be arriving at the meeting. We discussed how to greet him, deciding to be cool and take no notice of his arrival, even though we were in total awe of young Bobby.. We agreed that we would recess the meeting soon after his arrival, and then a small group of us were delegated to talk to Dylan in the hallway. I was one of those, for some reason, who was in that little "delegation."

We let Dylan know that we hoped to somehow involve him in our work. We thought, rather crassly, that he might do some fund-raising concerts for us, and someone gently tried to raise that with him when he said he was interested in helping us. He responded that what he really wanted to do was go out and organize with us. He said that he had been in Harlan County, Kentucky, where a miners' strike was famously happening, and he had been down to Mississippi for events there, and so he thought that he could play a role at least for a few minutes as one of the gang of organizers. But then, he said, "Please don't consider me a politically reliable person. I am not." "In fact," he said, "I've been seeing a shrink to figure out my emotional instabilities." To illustrate, he told the story, which has been published in several versions, of what had happened just a few days before his meeting with us. He'd been invited to get an award from a left-wing organization called the Emergency Civil Liberties Committee. He thought he had been invited to sing, not realizing that he was expected to say something rather than to sing. He came out from the wings to see a room full of "bald-headed overfed people" (as he put it) who were having a banquet, and he felt quite alienated from this crowd. That was just a week after the Kennedy assassination, and Dylan found himself saying to this assemblage that he understood Oswald's impulse to kill the president, or words to that effect, whereupon he was booed off stage. In telling this story to us, he was apologetic and upset with himself. Perhaps that event compelled Dylan to examine, more than he had previously, the implications of taking political stands and the dangers to art and psyche that might follow. Soon after meeting with us, he wrote a long poetic apology to the Emergency Civil Liberties Committee and another to *Broadside* magazine. In these, he was declaring in effect: "I am not the kind of person who can be seen as a committed engaged political activist, even though I've been singing as if I am."

Anyway, he did give us some contact information, but we were never able to make any further connection with him. I'm not sure how much people in the SDS leadership tried to continue that contact, but it never happened. There were some on the left who saw Dylan somehow as a renegade, who compromised politically once his commercial potential began to be realized. My five seconds with him led me to see him, instead, as an artist wanting to be understood through his songs and no other way.

The most memorable debate at the national council meeting was about what ERAP was to be. Al Haber, having solicited the grant from the UAW, urged that we fulfill its terms by setting up an educational program focused on economic and labor issues and aimed at college students. Tom Hayden took the view, which turned out to be quite prophetic, that it was very important for SDS to undertake an organizing program that would in some way parallel what SNCC was doing in the South. He argued that it was possible to recruit college students to go into urban slum neighborhoods in the North and concentrate on organizing poor whites, in the hope of building what he called "an interracial movement of the poor." It was quite a vigorous debate. Tom was proposing to take SDS in a very new direction—away from the campus and into the outer world—indeed into the most difficult neighborhoods of society.

The national council voted for Tom's version and that changed history as far as the New Left was concerned. The decision meant that we had to create an ambitious apparatus for recruiting and training groups of students, that we had to (carefully, if we could) select some urban neighborhoods for them to go into on a full-time basis, and that we then had to have several groupings of SDS-sponsored people operating in those neighborhoods over time. It was a remarkably ambitious program, especially when you realize (which we hardly acknowledged) that those who undertook it had little basis in experience or knowledge to do this work.

One of the people who took charge of it was Rennie Davis, a dynamic, charismatic guy, who was then at the University of Illinois, in Urbana, and who turned out to have remarkable skills as an organizer. Rennie moved to Ann Arbor and set up shop at the Center for Research on Conflict Resolution, which, rather boldly and most generously, provided us with space— and use of the center's mimeograph machine and other facilities in the evenings. The center at night soon became a bustling scene, staffed largely by several young women whom Rennie recruited, producing hundreds of mimeographed copies of a series of pamphlets that laid out a rationale for the organizing project. A training camp for student volunteers was scheduled for June 1964. By that summer, well over a hundred students had been trained and assigned to ten Northern cities, to set up communal apartments and figure out how to organize in some of the poorest urban neighborhoods in America.

# 8 ▸ OUR SIXTIES

## Making History Together

DICK:

One day in fall of 1964 I was hanging around the office of the social psychology program and Ted Newcomb came out of his chairman's office and asked whether I might be interested in a job opening up at the University of Chicago in the sociology department.

The Michigan social psychology program was unique in its fusion of sociological and psychological approaches to the field of social psychology. We were encouraged to believe that we were qualified for social psychology positions in either sociology or psychology departments. Although my own training was rooted in the psychological traditions of the field, I was instantly attracted to the Chicago opening because of my growing political engagement. If I wanted to contribute to social change, it was in sociology where I belonged. The University of Chicago had one of the premier sociology departments in the country; indeed, Chicago was the place where sociology was founded as an academic discipline, and the department there still retained an aura of distinction. Soon after that exchange with Newcomb,

I got an invitation to come visit the department at Chicago. I spent a whirl-wind day making the expected rounds of meeting and greeting various members of the department, and I gave a talk about my dissertation to the social psychology group. There was of course a lunch, with most of the members of the department in attendance, at the legendary Quadrangle Club—the University of Chicago faculty residential and dining institution in Hyde Park.

One of the people I met at that interview was Morris Janowitz, who a few years before had been in the sociology department at Michigan. I never knew him then, but he had a reputation as being abrasive and controlling. Janowitz was born and raised in the streets of New York in the 1920s and 1930s and prided himself on displaying an aggressive street style inside gen-teel academic halls.

In the lunch conversation, Janowitz, who was sitting next to me, insisted that the civil rights movement, just then reaching full-blown mobilization (it was 1964) was not providing the path to racial equality. He said that he was much impressed with new federal legislation supporting vocational training and wondered if SNCC's recruitment of bright Negro youth away from pursuing college opportunities might be tragic. As you might imagine, this conversation made me quite nervous about the climate in the depart-ment at Chicago. Nevertheless, my careerist self, of course, wanted their job offer. I had other feelers from major sociology departments or social psychology programs at that point in time, so I felt confident about my "marketability."

In those days, academic positions in major departments were allocated almost entirely by the old boy network. I imagine it worked in my case as follows: As far as I could tell, there was no open search with competitive applications for the position at Chicago. Instead, someone at Chicago had let Ted Newcomb know that there was a job in social psychology. Newcomb let me, as one of his prized students of the moment, know that this job existed and asked if I wanted it. Newcomb then relayed my interest back to his Chicago colleagues. It wasn't long before the job offer came to me. I don't think any other candidates were interviewed for this slot.

The idea of working in a movement rather than an academic context cer-tainly had been on my mind as I figured out my career trajectory. Some movement projects at that time were looking for academically trained researchers. For example, the effort to organize the mine workers of Harlan County, Kentucky, had let it be known that they were looking for someone with academic skills. The Institute for Policy Studies in Washington, D.C., was a recently founded think tank whose leaders I greatly admired. These included Arthur Waskow, Marcus Raskin, and Richard Barnett; they were deliberately creating an intellectual framework on the left outside of academia. The institute was an attractive place, and I wondered with Mickey whether that was where I should be applying. Her view—very strongly expressed—was that it was important for our lives to have a stable way of making a living. The last thing she was interested in was the kind of inherently insecure existence that a freelance activist intellectual was likely to have. The mood within SDS was that one should be devoting one's life to organizing and activism; careerism was anathema.

Mickey, with her strong working-class roots, felt that trying to have a decent job was an overriding consideration. She didn't feel guilt over her privilege—she didn't see herself as privileged. Indeed, some of our comrades who came from privileged backgrounds had no great need to worry about issues of livelihood at all, given the status and comfort of their families. Their relative freedom fused with middle-class guilt made the life of the freelance organizer powerfully compelling.

Mickey and I felt that our shared commitment to family and a stable personal life had a certain political validity. If you were going to try to work with and relate to the mainstream of American life and culture, it made sense to live a life that had some resemblance to mainstream norms. Indeed, our shared red diaper experience contributed to this perspective. Both sets of parents worked full-time and had stable family lives, and yet they had the commitment and sense of direction to be fully engaged in the political. We understood the value, and admired the courage, of the young, dedicated organizers whose political world we shared; it was clear that their single-minded commitment was necessary if there was to be a movement. At the same time, we thought the movement ought to be able to include and speak to those who shared the everyday lifeworlds of working- and middle-class Americans.

Mickey's perspective on my future was shared, ironically, by other comrades in the SDS world. More than one person, including, Tom Hayden, saw me as making my best contributions as a teacher and an academic, rather than as an organizer. I didn't know if that was a compliment to, or a critique of, my personality and style, but I was willing to accept these opinions as further validation of the academic rather than the organizer path. So I accepted the offer from Chicago, and we planned to move there during the summer of 1964.

MICKEY:

In 1963 Dick finished his PhD and began to think about a job. He was considering trying to connect with the Institute for Policy Studies in Washington, D.C., a left-wing think tank, run by Arthur Waskow and Marcus Raskin. It seemed a way for Dick to be working for the "movement" but also making use of his research skills and intellectual abilities. I did not want Dick to take that kind of job. Part of my upbringing had contrasted the life of those in the leadership of the International Workers Order (IWO) or the Communist Party with that of those in the rank and file. My parents were workers and made significantly less money and lived a more modest lifestyle than their leaders. They gave some of their meager earnings away to various institutions of the Left—which paid the leaders' salaries—and I always found that to be a bit jarring. I never wanted to be what we facetiously called "full-timers" (or the labor movement called "pie cards"), living off the movement. To me, movement work should be avocational, while one worked for "the man" to make a living. I knew that people working for SNCC in the South and SDS organizers were living on peanut butter—but I didn't feel that I could do that, either. I had grown up with too much of a working-class mentality, in near poverty, to ever be able to accept voluntary poverty. But the Institute for Policy Studies job paid a good salary—provided that foundation grants kept coming in and wealthy benefactors kept supporting it— the uncertainty of which disturbed me. I felt the need to work for a secure institution, with a decent salary, a pension plan, and some sense of permanence, not to have a job dependent on the political whims of the moment— or contributions of people like my parents.

Some years before, when Dick was applying for a fellowship, I had seen a questionnaire he had filled out that asked him to rank a number of factors in his professional life: teaching, research, family, institution, and so on. I remember being surprised and pleased when I saw that he had ranked family first. It seemed to me that one could not put family first and also work "full-time" for the movement; it required something equivalent to being in the military—willing to sacrifice oneself and all one had for the "mission" at hand. Although I understood that such sacrifices were necessary (someone had to do that work), that was not the life I wanted for us.

Equally important was my genuine belief that Dick had more to offer the movement (and the world) as a teacher, a mentor to generations of college students, who, at that time, seemed to be going about the business of changing the world. Whether they succeeded or not, I believe I was correct in my assessment of Dick's role, and our future was determined by our decision to seek a faculty position at a university.

In those days, the "old boy network" was in full force, and, on the recommendation of his adviser, Dick was simply offered a job in the sociology department of the University of Chicago. We had visited Chicago, driving from Ann Arbor, and were impressed with the "Second City," viewing it as truly comparable with New York (our standard for a city) and not a backwater like Philadelphia, Boston, or Detroit (the only other cities we had been to at the time). We were excited about the move—though very sad about leaving our good friends in Ann Arbor. I kept asking why Dick couldn't get a job at the University of Michigan, and he kept explaining that institutions didn't hire their own PhDs, for fear of a kind of ingrownness, a lack of diversity (in the old sense).

I went to Chicago in June of that year, to find an apartment. The only member of the department I knew at all (from American Sociological Association meetings) was a younger, rather staid, uptight assistant professor (who later became something of a hippie and moved to California; I always imagined him as a staid, uptight hippie—long hair and a button-down shirt and tie). He lived in a kind of gated apartment community, in a lush (in June) garden setting, but there wasn't anything available there. Finally, I contacted the University of Chicago housing office and found a large apartment in a university-owned building in the Woodlawn neighborhood, south of the Midway, across from the university and right behind its Center for Continuing Education. We had been planning to have a child once Dick was finished with school and had a job—after all, I was already twenty-four years old! (Those were different times. . . .) So we needed an apartment with a "baby's" room. Dick's desk could go in the "dining room"—a room neither of us had ever experienced before. I got the Housing Office to paint the apartment and refinish the wood floors—for a small increase in the rent (which brought it to $165 a month).

We moved our meager possessions from Ann Arbor (we had bought "light-weight" unfinished furniture in anticipation of moving it ourselves, but we finally used University of Chicago money to hire a mover), spent the summer again buying stuff to create a "grown-up" household, and then set off for a vacation trip to California! (My brother, Hershl, had been transferred there by Filon, the Standard Oil subsidiary, for which he served as a public relations guy, and we planned to stay with him and his family, in Los Angeles and then visit friends in the Bay Area.) We took the train from Chicago

to Los Angeles, in an effort to see something of the country—but we invariably traveled through the best places at night and didn't see as much as we
had hoped out the train windows.

California at that time was an idea, a concept, a way of life—more than
just a state. Everything seemed different—the light, the colors, the way people
lived, dressed, and ate—all was somehow magical, at least to transplanted
easterners. We spent some time with Hershl and May, my sister-in-law, and
their daughters, and, borrowing a car, we went to Disneyland (without the
kids) and also to Santa Barbara for a day. All we knew of Santa Barbara was
that it had received much publicity as the "home" of the John Birch Society.
(The local newspaper had indeed won a Pulitzer for its exposé of that nefari-
ous, extreme right-wing group, whose program labeled Eisenhower a Communist and called for the impeachment of Chief Justice Earl Warren.) As
we toured around its lovely homes and environs, Dick said, "No wonder the
Birch Society is big here—they have a lot to protect!" No way could we
have dreamed that we would one day make Santa Barbara our home!

Finally, we took the train up to Berkeley, where we stayed with Herb and
Becky Mills, early SDSers. Becky had been at Port Huron, as a student.
Herb had been one of the leaders of the Berkeley student movement in the
late 1950s and early 1960s and had met Tom Hoyden when he traveled to
California in the summer of 1960.

Herb went to work as a longshoreman (while he wrote his doctoral dissertation about the work on the docks), and he gave us an intensive tour of
Oakland and San Francisco. Wow! Here was indeed another city worth its
name. We took the cable car from its terminal at Market Street to Fisherman's Wharf and saw the hills, with their multicolored houses perched on
them, sparkling in the sunshine of a September day, with Coit Tower and
the bay glistening, too. I began to cry; somehow the sight of all that beauty, of
a different way people could live, moved me greatly. Herb's enthusiasm about
the work and the guys on the docks was also infectious—especially since we
were familiar with the long, left history of the International Longshore and
Warehouse Union (ILWU) and its attempts to democratize the workplace.
Here was an America that seemed to encompass the left tradition!

We arranged a meeting on the University of California, Berkeley, campus
with the leaders of the small SDS chapter there. We sat in a cafeteria overlooking Sproul Plaza, while those SDS guys complained: "Students here
are totally apathetic.... It's impossible to get them to do anything!"
That was, of course, about two weeks before actions were taken against

discriminatory car dealers near the campus and the subsequent emergence of the Free Speech Movement in December.

We returned to Chicago, where Dick began to be a professor, and I got a job at the La Rabida Institute of the University of Chicago, working on developing a vaccine against the streptococcus organism that causes rheumatic fever (which we never quite managed to achieve). I liked the work and the staff there. We worked in the basement (again!) of a hospital for rheumatic children and were quite dedicated to our quest. I was, in fact, pregnant when I started working there, but I didn't let on, because I was afraid I wouldn't be hired. (Pre–civil rights for pregnant women!) I wore a lab coat—yet in the sub-zero conditions of a Chicago winter, my boss told me that I could not wear trousers to work. "You can take them off when you get here. Bring a skirt." I was also afraid to mention that I was pregnant even when, after a few months of work, we all tested our vaccine on ourselves to see if it produced any untoward reaction!

Our baby was due in mid-July, but at eleven o'clock on the evening of June 2, my waters broke and off we went to Chicago Lying-In Hospital. I was not in labor, and we naively thought that since I was six weeks early, I would be permitted to leave the hospital the next day. Dick was told to go home and he'd be called when labor was underway. June 3, 1965, dawned with John Glenn suiting up for his orbit of the earth and me in active labor. Dick woke up, took his shower, ate breakfast, read the paper, and, when he finally called, was informed: "Your wife is in very active labor!" He made it to my room just before I was whisked away to the delivery room. (Fathers were not allowed in delivery rooms in those days.) At nine thirty that morning, our baby boy was born. The staff later told me that they were concerned since he was so early (and was facing the wrong way), and they had prepared an incubator. But they turned him around (leaving a black-and-blue forceps mark on his face, which soon healed), and he was a healthy five pounds, twelve ounces, so they just put him in a "warmer" bed. He had no eyebrows or eyelashes (they would soon grow in quite lushly, thank you), and a wonderful pediatric nurse had to coax him to develop his sucking reflex—but otherwise all was well, and we took him home after a few days. We named him for my father (Charles) and for a New Left hero—C. Wright Mills: C. Wright Flacks—called Chuck! (Years later I was at some sort of touchy-feely event and each member of the audience was asked to turn to a neighbor and tell of the most exciting thing that had ever happened to them. Unhesitatingly, I told about giving birth to Chuck.)

We are proud to announce the birth of

**CHARLES WRIGHT FLACKS**

who was born at 10:30 A.M. on June 3, 1965, and weighed 5 lbs. 11.5 oz.

He was given the name of his grandfather, the late **CHARLES HARTMAN**; and of the late **C. WRIGHT MILLS** — two rebels, two men worthy of emulation.

He eagerly kicked his way into the world six weeks before anyone expected him. Does the world deserve his eagerness? He needs a world of love and hope and freedom.

Will we ever deserve the eagerness of babies? Please, let us try.

His parents,

**RICHARD and MIRIAM FLACKS**

FIGURE 8.1. Chuck Flacks's birth announcement, June 3, 1965

FIGURE 8.2. Mildred and Sonia *kvelling* (swelling with pride) over their first grandson

I was now a young mother in a city where I didn't really have any friends (except for Bob and Marion Ross, former Michigan undergraduates, who had married and moved into the apartment above ours—they were now graduate students at the University of Chicago). For the first time in my life, I had no place to go in the morning: no school, no job (not wanting to face new motherhood with working full-time, I had quit my job when Chuck was born), and no role to play in any movement. I did establish a relationship with another faculty wife in the building, who had four kids under six years of age, each fifteen months older than the next—but she was pretty busy. . . . That I was out of my milieu was brought home to me one afternoon a few months later: I was sitting in my neighbor's apartment while Chuck was napping, when I saw through the window two men in suits and hats who were unmistakably FBI agents. "Uh-oh," I said. "Here comes the FBI." My neighbor looked at me as if I were insane. I left her apartment and greeted the men at the front door of the vestibule (they were indeed FBI).

"Can I help you?" I said, cordially.

"We're looking for Dick Flacks. Is he here?"

"No." I said.

"When will he be back? Can we reach him?"

"He's on the campus," I said. "I'm not sure where."

"Can we come up and use your phone?"

"There's a pay phone right at the corner."

"You don't understand," one of them said. "It isn't him we want to talk about."

"Do you think that makes it better?" I said, angrily. "I don't want to talk to you. Please leave."

And they did. My neighbor observed all this, openmouthed. I really don't know who she thought we were . . . nothing good, I'm sure. (The Feds were in fact checking out former SDS president Todd Gitlin, who had applied for conscientious objector status and had given Dick's name as a reference who could vouch for his sincerity. Dick had many conversations with agents, about many conscientious objector applicants. Rumor later on had it that one of the agents, who spent all his time on these C.O. interviews, eventually quit the FBI and became an anti-war activist!)

When Chuck was about a year old, I got a call from John Scott, director of research at the Survey Research Center at the University of Michigan Institute for Social Research, where I had worked briefly between biology jobs. They needed a Chicago area supervisor to oversee the collection of survey data in "Chicagoland." He remembered my qualifications as an "osmotic" sociologist and offered me the job. I realized that I could work from home in the afternoons (while I hired someone to look after Chuck) and that here was something to help me escape the "mommy role." By this time, the SDS office had moved to Chicago (mainly to get out of the left-wing hothouse of New York and become part of the heartland) and had an active project—the Economic Research and Action Project (ERAP)—an attempt to emulate SNCC with white workers in Northern cities like Chicago, Cleveland, and Newark—in the Uptown neighborhood of the city. The "revolution" seemed to be going on full force, while I was on the sidelines. Here was an opportunity to participate in the wider world, at least—and I also was able to hire a number of the ERAP SDSers as interviewers for the Michigan research institute. There were two research projects that I remember working on. One was under a contract with the UAW, which was considering an early retirement plan in an effort to open jobs to younger workers. The union wanted to better understand how its older workers viewed retirement and whether such a plan would find favor with them. I was very excited to have the opportunity to do some interviewing myself (in addition to training and supervising others) and visit the homes of UAW workers in the area. I was a part of the revolution! (sort of). Of course, I was shocked to learn that the UAW members had a very unrealistic view of what the reduced income of retirement would mean and had very vague ideas of what they would do every day after years on the factory floor. In the end, I don't think the union pursued its plans.

The other study was by a criminologist at the University of Michigan and involved interviewing randomly selected residents in the two areas of Chicago that had the highest crime rates: the white area of the Gold Coast, near Lake Michigan, and the black ghetto of the West Side. That proved to be a near impossible task—as a little prior reflection would have revealed. The Gold Coast was populated by elegant apartment buildings, with equally elegant (and tough) doormen. Our interviewers would appear and respond to the question "Who do you want to see?" with "Whoever lives in apartment 12C." The doormen were not impressed, and we had a very difficult time getting in at all. When we did, we would explain to the person who answered the door at 12C that we there doing a study of crime victims (or possible) victims in their neighborhood. Quite a few apartment doors were closed in our faces. On the West Side, we had only one or two (black) interviewers, one of whom turned out not to be bothering to do interviews, but answering the questionnaire himself! In those days, the response rate for the institute's surveys was over 90 percent; we managed about 78 percent—and the principal researcher was furious. (Today's response rates—on the telephone!—rarely exceed 50 percent and are often much lower.)

My neighbor (who had watched me deal with the FBI) was in a community theater group, the Music Theater of Hyde Park. She asked us to buy tickets to attend their performance of *Kiss Me, Kate*. We agreed to go—really, just to be neighborly—and didn't expect much. We were quite floored with the quality of the performance—and, since I missed the singing and performing of my early days (and since I still felt a bit out of the mainstream of life), I decided to join the group—especially given that their next show was to be *Fiorello!* Now I had rehearsals to go to, new people to see, and a role to play (literally!)—so that when the University of Chicago campus erupted in "revolution," I didn't feel quite so alienated and "out of it." I was in the chorus of the productions, never really a star. But I persuaded them to do *Finian's Rainbow* as their next production—during which I was pregnant, so I worked backstage, doing props and special effects (including the leprechaun's magic—great fun!). By the time of the next show (*Guys and Dolls*), I had a speaking part and was acting as producer! I believe that my activity with the Music Theater helped stave off postpartum psychosis and the idiocy of separated, non-communal motherhood. I also think that each of us has a need to express some sort of creativity, to explore some talent that lies within all of us, and we too often suppress it in the pursuit of "more important" things. My early experiences in camp and *shul* and the Jewish Young Folksingers encouraged that self-expression, and I was missing it in my young motherhood years.

## SDS: FROM CAMPUS TO STREETS

DICK:

One of SDS's interests, reflected both in the Port Huron statement and in our programmatic activities, was what we called "university reform." This phrase expressed the fact that on a number of campuses, including the University of Michigan, students were trying to overturn long-standing campus rules governing student life. At Michigan in the late 1950s, the dean of women, Deborah Bacon, had an undercover spy apparatus. She wanted to get reports about students who were engaged in interracial dating, as well as in other transgressions of strict rules aimed mostly at women students, and she would report back to the parents of those who transgressed. One of Tom Hayden's early campaigns when he worked on the *Michigan Daily* was to expose Dean Bacon's practices.

The absurdity of parental rules (members of the opposite sex allowed to visit in dormitory rooms with doors partially open and three feet on the floor, for example) and the idea that the university operated in loco parentis became large issues in the 1950s and early 1960s for students across the country. So one meaning of university reform was simply to enable students to be treated as adults. By that time, many students' parents were already treating them in ways that allowed for more autonomy and self-determination than the typical college rules were allowing. In any case, there was a climate rife with hypocrisy and deceit caused by such rules. Students had developed a long tradition of subterranean resistance to the parental regime.

Doing away with that regime was a piece of a broader vision of student empowerment that was both inspired by and implemented by participatory democracy. The Port Huron Statement eloquently talked about the ways that the university curriculum failed to address the big questions and the deep meanings that many students hoped to come to grips with in their classes. There was, in that period, a sizable academic literature criticizing higher education for its increasingly specialized and technocratic qualities and bemoaning the decline of liberal education as a central value, the massification of education, and corporate and military influence on research.

All of this discourse provided intellectual scaffolding to SDSers in shaping our university reform perspective. In early 1963, SDS convened a national conference on university reform at Brandeis University. I drove in our car with Tom Hayden and Bob Ross to Boston in a blizzard to get to the Brandeis event; having finally learned to drive just a few months earlier (the driving was itself a big deal for me).

Although largely unmentioned in SDS histories, it was a memorable weekend for those of us who were there. One highlight was a debate between Paul Goodman and I. Milton Sacks, then a dean at Brandeis. It was the only time I saw Goodman in person. Goodman's anarchist pacifist perspective, and his effort to live the life implied by his values, had become powerfully influential for folks like us. As so often in life, the hero in person loses something of his aura. Goodman onstage displayed an irascible heckling of the young for their ignorance of history, while offsetting his unpleasantness with his capacity for seeing the world in new ways. Although I saw him as personally difficult (maybe impossible), he remains to this day one of my intellectual heroes. His quest for practical utopian thinking, his concrete critique of centralization, and his visions of decentered society—all of these and more were ideas that I deeply internalized.

At Brandeis, we of course thought that Goodman wiped the floor with Sacks, an ex-Trotskyist neo-conservative whose work revolved around justifying U.S. policy in Vietnam. Sacks, I recall, simply provided conventional apologetics for the university as we knew it; Goodman was urging us to take control of our education and our lives, while doubting that students anymore even knew what an authentic education might consist of.

Also onstage at the Brandeis conference was a group called the Freedom Singers—four young black performers who were full-time SNCC organizers. They had banded together a few months earlier, with the encouragement of Pete and Toshi Seeger, to tour America, singing the freedom songs that were helping to fuel the Southern struggle. Their tour was a way of raising awareness of what that struggle was about and, not incidentally, was a tool for fund-raising and for recruiting sympathy and support. I think the Brandeis conference was something of a debut for them—and their performance had the intended effect of making strong emotional linkages between the Brandeis student crowd and the Southern movement. Bernice Reagon, the lead voice in the quartet, helped inspire and ultimately document the singing of the Southern movement—and went on to be one of the most creative figures in the making of music that serves social movements.

As the conference drew to a close, there was the spreading murmur among the conference attendees that philosopher Herbert Marcuse was about to make an appearance. At that time, I barely knew who Marcuse was, but I was amused and bemused by the hero worship that was evident as the Brandeis students literally sat at his feet, while he delivered an impromptu critique of the Cold War university in sonorous Germanic tones. I couldn't help feel that there was a striking contradiction between the students' disdain for authority and their idolization of Marcuse. Still, somehow his charisma and his staunch radicalism provided inspiration for anti-authoritarianism.

The Brandeis conference was not in itself a politically momentous occasion. It wasn't until the fall of 1964, at Berkeley, that the critique of the university being voiced at Brandeis turned into collective action on a significant scale.

But the weekend in Boston proved to be a time for making personal connections that had political consequences. At some point, the SDS crowd at the conference went over to Quincy House at Harvard, where we met Todd Gitlin and other Harvard student politicos in Todd's dorm rooms. I'd seen Todd and his friends in February 1962 at the Washington anti–arms race march, which they had helped initiate. I was somewhat in awe of their precocious command of arcane policy and also of their easy assumption that they had access to power. That weekend, we found out that SDS's broader and more penetrating vision and perspective were deeply attractive to Todd and his circle. But the Harvard students' self-assured elitism astonished me—we spent quite a bit of time as we lounged in the dorm talking about what "we" could do to replace Lyndon B. Johnson as the 1964 vice presidential candidate. Somehow it was felt in the room that we had a chance to get progressive Pennsylvania senator Joseph Clark on the ticket instead; I found it incredible that this group of twenty-year-old college kids believed that they had a chance to help make that happen.

Meanwhile, Tom's marriage to Casey was on the rocks. Mickey and I had gotten to know Tom and Casey quite well in the several months since they had moved to Arch Street in Ann Arbor. I'd begun to work with Tom on writing projects, including the follow-up to the Port Huron Statement, and in those months we spent many hours in intense conversations about the state of the world and the new organization. Tom's personal aloofness was famous in the SDS circle, but the disintegration of Tom and Casey's marriage was obviously emotionally devastating for him. So, during the long car trip from Ann Arbor to Boston, Tom opened up about his vulnerabilities and personal confusions. He and Casey had imagined an "open" marriage, but as soon as he began to practice that, he learned that it was a fantasy. Mickey and I represented, after four years of marriage, a haven of stability for Tom and other SDS comrades. But we never wanted to serve as role models for others. Anyway, in the car, Bob Ross and I offered Tom at least a moment where he could voice personal anguish and, by doing that, maybe gain some perspective. After a few tries at reconciliation, the couple decided to part.

SDS interest in university reform was soon overshadowed by the decision to recruit students to the ERAP projects. On the one hand, we were committed to trying to engage students in efforts to change their universities, while, on the other, we were mobilizing students to devote their energy to off-campus activism for social change. Although these two directions seem contradictory, to us they were intertwined. Both dimensions of student activism needed to be nurtured. We didn't in those early years have much expectation of a mass student movement, in any case; instead, we hoped to connect with and channel the energies of the small proportion of students in the country who were politically aware and socially conscious.

The ERAP leadership identified ten urban communities for possible organizing projects, to begin in the fall of 1964. Tom had decided that he was going to move to Newark to take the lead in a project there. Paul Potter and Sharon Jeffrey were committed to moving to Cleveland, where there was a prospect of working with welfare mothers. In Chicago, a young Michigan student named Joe Chabot had been spending some time scouting the possibility for a movement of the unemployed in Uptown, at that time a neighborhood destination for Appalachian white working-class immigration. Joe moved to Uptown after trying and failing to organize people at unemployment compensation centers. He quickly realized that people on those lines were looking for jobs and not very interested in identifying with the "unemployed."

By June 1964, ERAP had recruited something like one hundred students to work in the various cities, and most of these came to Pine Hill, New York, the location of the next SDS convention, to participate in several days of training. The passion of the students who arrived there to do that work was remarkable. The ERAP idea fit with a wider mood, which was quite pervasive among socially aware white students at elite colleges. The mood was fueled by considerable guilt over privilege, and it was focused, of course, by the civil rights movement. The Southern movement provided both moral challenge and opportunities for involvement for white upper-middle-class students. ERAP was started at the same time that SNCC had recruited hundreds of students to go to Mississippi for the summer, where they were to engage in intensive voter registration and educational efforts in the heart of the black belt. At the beginning of June, the news came that three of the Mississippi volunteers were missing (their bodies were found some weeks later). Meanwhile, the Kennedy administration had started the Peace Corps, which was attracting tens of thousands of volunteers to go all over the world for various kinds of service. And in the same period, several thousand college students were participating in the Northern Student Movement's intensive tutoring programs for urban ghetto children.

So the SDS initiative was part of a diverse effort by many college students to leave their comfort and their privileged sanctuaries and share the lives and circumstances of poor people in many different places. I remember walking with Tom around the ERAP training camp in Pine Hill in June 1964. Tom, who was himself passionately committed to attacking middle-class privilege in his own life and in the lives of others, remarked about a "fanaticism" that he experienced in the ERAP workshops. He told me about how a group had decided that they should live on the same food budget that welfare recipients of the community lived on, and he went on to remark that he wasn't sure he could keep to that kind of discipline.

Tom was excited by this passion but not sure what to make of it. One might assume that many of these young pioneers of community organization were naive, filled with idealistic illusion. One might reasonably question the motives of privileged youth making such forays into the slums. I think, however, that most of those who volunteered for SNCC's Mississippi Summer or Newark projects or the other ERAP initiatives had a fairly good sense of what they were getting into, even if they lacked clarity about what exactly their roles would entail. Most were quite aware that their motives very much included an urgent need to make their own lives "real" and knew that they had to be mindful of how their privilege would inevitably affect their capacity to be positive actors in the situations they were entering.

The ERAP concept (to enable students to become organizers in poor communities) borrowed a lot from SNCC, but the organizational goals that SNCC had in the South were certainly not the same as those required in Northern community organizing. Both efforts aimed at finding means to empower such communities. SNCC's strategy focused on the power of the ballot in black majority communities. ERAP envisioned the creation of community organizations that, in some respects, would be modeled after labor unions. The idea was to create an organization that could challenge and bargain with the welfare, housing, and school bureaucracies and other institutions that affected the daily lives of poor communities. Much of what we wanted to do resonated with the work of Saul Alinsky in the organizing efforts that he initiated, beginning in the 1930s in Chicago. But more than Alinsky, who typically focused on a particular community's interests and deliberately avoided embedding that community's concerns in any larger political agenda, we thought that these local ventures were to help develop an effort to create a new political coalition for change at the national level. We wanted to empower people in their communities. We also wanted to rewrite the social agenda of America.

My and Mickey's move to Chicago in the summer of 1964 was paralleled by the initiation of the Jobs or Income Now (JOIN) project in Uptown. A group of people, including several close friends of ours, moved to Chicago's North Side at the same time as we moved to Hyde Park/Woodlawn. Rich Rothstein, Rennie Davis, and, later, Todd Gitlin and his then partner Nanci Hollander and quite a few others showed up in the months that followed. Simultaneously, there was a decision to move the SDS office from New York to Chicago; the national SDS office was opened on Sixty-Third Street, just a few blocks from where we lived on Kimbark and Sixtieth. So our move to Chicago turned out to put us at the geographical center of an increasingly visible and rapidly growing SDS.

Still, pretty soon after getting to Chicago, I made the decision not to remain in the formal leadership of SDS. I didn't think a faculty member should be on the board of a student organization (in fact, I strongly advocated that the entire leadership of SDS needed to rotate and that the "old-timers" (now in their twenties) should help create an "adult" organization). However, I worked closely with the JOIN project, hoping to figure out how, as an academic at the university, I might be able to help.

To prepare our move, Mickey traveled to Chicago to look for an apartment and found one in university-owned housing on Sixtieth and Kimbark. It was across the Midway from the main campus of the university and on the border of the Woodlawn neighborhood. Because it was university-owned, the rent was exceptionally affordable (something like $160 a month). It was on the second floor of a courtyard building and, like many of the old Hyde Park apartments, was charming and even elegant, with lots of dark wood paneling and wood floors and interestingly shaped rooms. Gas lighting fixtures suggested that the apartment building dated from maybe the late nineteenth century.

In early summer of 1964, we met the moving van in Chicago, installed ourselves in our new apartment, and soon thereafter departed on our first cross-country trip. We were heading for California, where Mickey's brother, Hershl, and sister-in-law May and their two young girls had been living for a couple of years. We took the train across the country, which gave us a chance to see glimpses of the great West.

Hershl and May spent several days showing us around, as we drove from Hollywood to Mount Wilson. I marveled at sites that I had imagined and visualized in my childhood days of avid radio listening—Hollywood and Vine, the May Company, La Brea tar pits, and so on—places whose legends (purveyed on *The Jack Benny Show*) far outweighed their remarkable nondescriptness. More enticing, of course, were Malibu, Griffith Park, and Mulholland Drive. Southern California then was the land of popular dream, and Hershl and May's tour gave us a good chance to experience the strange mixture of smog and sun, of fantasy and fact. We never dreamed that we'd return to this place to actually live.

After a week or so, we took the train to the Bay Area. We had made some dates to see the small band of SDS members at Berkeley. In those days, a visitor from the movement in the East was not a common experience.

We arrived at Berkeley in early September and met our little group of SDS compatriots on the terrace of the student union overlooking Sproul Plaza. I had noticed, when we got to Berkeley, a news story about a pamphlet that had been distributed on campus a couple of days earlier by someone named Brad Cleaveland. This pamphlet was described as a ringing critique of the University of California administration's authoritarian rules and called for "open, fierce rebellion" and even civil disobedience to transform the university. Somebody in the group declared that, although there had been a good deal of activism in the spring about civil rights, it was not likely to resume. There seemed to be general agreement that the student movement might be played out here. I brought up the Cleaveland pamphlet, and all agreed that he was a sort of loner whose ideas were not likely to get much reception among Berkeley's students. We talked about the prospects for establishing an SDS chapter in Berkeley and the sorts of work it might try. I wrote some kind of report back to the SDS office about the situation in Berkeley that emphasized the belief by our members that not much was happening. That was exactly two weeks before the biggest student uprising in American history occurred, beginning about one hundred feet from where we had our lunch meeting.

I'm referring of course to the Free Speech Movement uprising in Berkeley that began when the university administration sought to stop students from recruiting on campus for civil rights campaigns in the Bay Area—campaigns that were irritating to the business employers being targeted. The University of California then had a rule that political advocacy was not permissible on the campus. A good example of the scope of that rule was an episode in 1956 when Adlai Stevenson, campaigning for president, was required to speak off-campus from a sound truck on Telegraph Avenue across the street from crowds assembled on the campus. Despite such absurdity, student activists at Berkeley had complied with those rules and thought that they were in compliance when they set up tables in support of various causes on the sidewalk on Bancroft Way in front of the campus entrance.

In 1963–64, the university administration received complaints from major corporate figures in the Bay Area that the campus was a staging ground for direct action campaigns aimed at employer discrimination. One of the key complainers was William Knowland, the publisher of the *Oakland Tribune* and a former U.S. senator from California.

The capacity of disadvantaged groups to gain power is often facilitated by the stupidity of those in authority. That generalization was often validated in the 1960s, and the events in Berkeley in 1964 provide a rich array of examples.

Before the fall semester in 1964, a student affairs administrator noticed that Bancroft Way, where student organizations traditionally tabled, was actually part of the campus and not public city property, as people had always assumed. And so an edict banning political movement solicitation from that area was issued just in time for the start of fall classes. All of the political groups, from right to left, that used that strip resisted, refusing to take down their tables. A police car was driven to the area to arrest one of the people who was resisting, and that car was suddenly surrounded by an ever-growing mass of students, who sat down around it, preventing it from moving for some fifteen hours. They used the roof of the police car as a platform for speaking. The hours of occupation and speaking created the social space for what became the Free Speech Movement. In that time and space, the grievances and demands of the movement were articulated, and hundreds who stayed the night became committed to them. The students demanded not only the right to have their tables but also an end to the restricted speech rules that were then operative and more or less taken for granted. In effect, they sought the same rights of free speech on campus that they had as citizens off the campus—and that included the right to advocate civil disobedience and to recruit for nonviolent direct action in behalf of just causes. This campaign was resisted by the University of California administration. As both Chancellor Edward Strong at Berkeley and Clark Kerr, president of the University of California system, opposed the student demands, and authorized punitive moves against protesters, student support for these demands grew powerfully. In December 1964, hundreds of students occupied the university administration building (Sproul Hall), and Governor Pat Brown ordered the police to arrest them, dragging them out of the building when they passively resisted. This scene ignited the campus and led to a general strike of students, which received worldwide publicity. One of the key leaders of the Free Speech Movement, Mario Savio, was dragged offstage at a large official gathering at Berkeley's Greek Theater as thousands in the amphitheater sat stunned. As the semester drew to a close, the faculty senate endorsed the movement's demands.

The protests at the Berkeley campus that fall and winter were not the first time, by any means, that American students had done direct action on their campuses. Indeed, even in the 1950s, there had been some instances of students occupying administration offices to protest racial policies. When Mickey and I were students in the fifties, there had been mass refusals by students to cooperate with civil defense drills that required people to take shelter in rehearsals for atomic bombing. But the Berkeley mass arrests and general strike were certainly the most massive and concerted action by a student body in American history. And the Free Speech Movement turned out to be but an episode in the development of a mass student movement over the rest of the decade.

We in SDS had not anticipated that the mass of students would respond to the politics that we were promulgating. In the early days of SDS, it was assumed that the majority of American students, who were from affluent backgrounds, would not support liberal causes. Indeed, surveys of political allegiance done in the fifties and up through the mid-sixties indicated that, on large campuses, including supposedly liberal ones like the University of Wisconsin, the majority of students said that they were Republicans.

My own research on student attitudes and attitude change was in line with other social science research that showed a tendency for students at elite colleges, on average, to become more liberal in certain respects in their years in college, but those kinds of changes were very varied and depended on the nature of the campus climate and were not necessarily universal even on a particular campus. For example, a study at Cornell University in the fifties showed that, although social science and humanities students tended to become more liberal, fraternity members and science majors tended to become more conservative, if they changed their political stance at all. So we in SDS never imagined that the white students of America, to any significant degree, would have any inclination to political protest. Our main hope was to be able to bring together that fraction of the student body that was politically interested and liberal, to support the agenda we had begun to formulate.

What happened in Berkeley in 1964 transformed our expectations about the student potential for agency. Indeed, much of the commentary on the Berkeley events (and there was a lot of commentary) began to suggest the possibility that "alienated students" might band together and become a force for change. Indeed, rather presciently, Clark Kerr in his classic book

*The Uses of the University*, written a few years before the Free Speech Movement, had anticipated the possibility that students in the "multiversity," as he called it, might rebel. It was Kerr who noted that undergraduates, by the nature of the multiversity, were herded into large classes and subjected to a mass education process that did not necessarily provide them with fulfillment. Mario Savio thought that Kerr was advocating a "knowledge factory." It is one of the fascinating aspects of the Berkeley story that Kerr was indeed an architect of the corporate transformation of academia even as he wondered about the social and human consequences of what he was bringing about.

A new staff member of SDS, Clark Kissinger, who had been a student at the University of Wisconsin in Madison and was now working in the New York office, had the fortunate insight that SDS, although not organizationally involved in the Berkeley protests, could provide a national platform for Berkeley activists to speak to students across the country. SDS, in the early months of 1965, sponsored such a speaking tour for a couple of the Berkeley Free Speech Movement leaders.

That summer of 1964 was of course an exciting time for the movement and for the political world in general. It was the summer of Mississippi, culminating at the Democratic convention in Atlantic City, New Jersey. Mickey and I were preoccupied with our move to Chicago after our cross-country trip, but we of course followed the summer's drama avidly.

Mississippi Summer was a project, sponsored by the major civil rights organizations, with SNCC field staff at the core, to recruit a thousand Northern white students to participate in efforts to organize voter registration and community education programs in Mississippi, the notorious bastion of white supremacy, enforced by police and vigilante terror—a state where virtually no members of the black majority could vote and where the vast majority of the black population lived meagerly as sharecroppers or in other marginal roles in impoverished rural towns.

It was probably the most ambitious and creative project for social change ever launched in the United States. I was gratified to be asked, in the spring, to interview Michigan applicants for the summer project—since the organizers wanted to be assured that those who were coming knew what they were taking on (the likelihood of miserable jail time and even death) and had the appearance of being able to cope with the multiple social and personal challenges they would face. For me, what was most striking about the interviews was that the kids stressed that they *had to go*—they all spoke about the moral imperative they felt to do their part in the Southern struggle.

It was one of many experiences I had in those years that made me want to try to figure out where this sort of passion, on the part of privileged, well-off youth, was coming from. It was the same sort of passion that drove participation in the Peace Corps and other efforts, by middle-class young people, to change their lives in hope of service to those in need.

In the end, some one thousand Northern volunteers went to Mississippi that June. As they were being trained, news came of the disappearance of Michael Schwerner and Andrew Goodman, two Northern volunteers who had joined the freedom movement some months earlier, along with James Cheney, an "indigenous" volunteer. Some weeks later, their bodies were found in the Mississippi River. The deaths of two white youth not only upped the ante for the project participants but helped achieve one of the project's political goals—to arouse the conscience of middle-class white America and help force federal intervention to overcome the long-ignored oppression and suppression of Southern blacks.

Mississippi Summer was a watershed moment for politically conscious young people like ourselves. The courage and commitment of our peers who went south was a spur to our own will to take risky and sacrificial action. Another inspiring feature of the project was the creation, throughout the state, of a network of "freedom schools" that made use of the skills and energy of the summer volunteers and brought a curriculum providing both skills and consciousness to black children there. The freedom school effort inspired many other alternative schooling and engaged teaching projects and helped many of us develop more concrete conceptions of how education—including higher education—might be transformed. One immediate reverberation of Mississippi Summer was the Free Speech Movement in Berkeley. Mario Savio and other members of the movement came to Berkeley right from the South, determined to continue the struggle.

There was a specific political goal in the Mississippi project—to replace the explicitly white supremacist Mississippi delegation at the Democratic National Convention in Atlantic City that August. An interracial delegation, elected in a self-organized primary campaign, came to Atlantic City, to testify about the brutal suppression of their voting rights and demanding that they be seated. In the end, their liberal and labor supporters in the party leadership gave in to Lyndon B. Johnson, and accepted a symbolic gesture that left the Freedom Democrats in the cold. That episode, I believed, was a crucial radicalizing experience for the new generation of activists. Our hopes for alliance with the established liberal-labor leadership were greatly weakened. A more militant, independent, and angry stance, already present in SNCC, was taking shape.

## ON TO CHICAGO

DICK:

Mickey and I returned from Berkeley by train to Chicago in September and prepared to start an entirely new chapter in our lives—me as I learned how to become a professor at one of the least politically hospitable elite academic institutions and Mickey as she found her footing as a researcher in an impersonal new urban world. For both of us, it meant beginning our first truly grown-up household.

The University of Chicago was well known for having a split character. The graduate departments of the university, including the sociology department, were primarily aimed at educating graduate students and advanced undergraduates in their disciplines. Under the leadership of the child prodigy president, Robert Hutchins, an undergraduate college had famously been established in the 1930s. Its aim was to provide a "general education" that was highly cross-disciplinary and based on the "great books" of Western civilization, using dialogical pedagogy.

In the late Hutchins era and especially after, there had been considerable warfare between the graduate faculty and the faculty in the college—a warfare that is significant for understanding the evolution of American higher education in general. By the time I arrived, the Hutchins practice of hiring faculty solely to teach at the college had largely disappeared. My own appointment originally was in the graduate sociology department, but one of my younger colleagues in sociology, Don Levine, urged me to consider teaching in the general education program as well. This suggestion appealed to me.

I joined the faculty group teaching Social Science II, excited by its reputation as a highly stimulating teaching and learning experience for faculty who were involved. Teaching social Science II involved working with a section of thirty students for the entire academic year. The faculty who were responsible for the sections planned intensively for each year's syllabus. The syllabus, in Hutchins style, was constituted largely of a set of readings based on the great books of sociology, anthropology, social psychology, and related fields. The course covered Sigmund Freud and Karl Marx, Bronislaw Malinowski and Max Weber, and a great deal else. The teaching staff for the course met each week for intensive discussion of the reading. That staff was predominantly young and drawn from the various disciplines. Teaching Social Science II added to my work load, which included a lecture course in social psychology and a graduate seminar, but it all appealed to me greatly.

My encounters with Morris Janowitz before being hired had made me aware of the likelihood that I was entering a conservative and academically traditional environment that would not necessarily be hospitable to my political interests, let alone the democratic academic style that I had experienced in the social psychology program at Michigan.

Before we moved to Chicago, in fact, I had a little encounter with Janowitz in Ann Arbor, where he was visiting briefly. He wanted to meet to welcome me to Chicago. He asked about my interests, and I told him that I was interested in the emerging left-wing intellectual life represented by developments such as the Institute for Policy Studies in Washington, D.C., and the Committee of Correspondence, a project of Harvard-based intellectuals whose various exchanges in the early sixties were influential for SDS. Janowitz expressed the view that people like Erich Fromm, David Riesman, and others whom I had named were "thugs," who were not going to be interested in sociology, in his opinion. He wanted me to know that, although he was an age peer of sociologists who as undergraduates at CCNY had been Socialists, he himself had never been one and was rather proud to say it. I couldn't help but feel at that moment that he was not only communicating about his own views but also laying down rules that he expected me to comply with. In a nutshell, he was saying, the sociology being done at Chicago was not to be oriented in a leftward direction.

Somehow I was not very intimidated by this discussion, nor was I, later, in my first conversation with Philip Hauser, then chair of the sociology department. While I was settling into the department, I took a drive with Hauser and mentioned to him that I was planning to teach in the college. "Well," he said, "that's probably a good thing. We've never had a sociologist in the college." This comment was startling, considering that some of the great figures in sociology, including C. Wright Mills, David Riesman, Everett Hughes, and quite a few others, had famously taught Social Science II in the 1950s. I, at the time of our first encounter, was stupidly ignorant of the fact that Hauser had previously been at war with the qualitative sociologists who had helped define what was called the Chicago school. Hauser, an esteemed demographer, was a major exponent of quantitative and "scientific" sociology and was eager to end the influence of the more humanistic, qualitative, and even literary approaches of the people whom he had defeated in the internecine warfare of the late 1950s and early 1960s. He wanted the very young and junior me to know that the department culture had drastically changed.

Before I had embarked to my job at Chicago, I had a conversation with one of my mentors, Daniel Katz, whom I admired both for his intellectual accomplishment as a shaper of social psychology and for his humane and democratic values. Katz warned me that the Chicago department was run by a group of men who had a "baronial" perspective and that it was important for me to avoid being subject to their control. "Think of yourself as already a full professor when you're there," he said. "I mean, don't follow any senior professor's agenda. Chart your own path." That was some of the best advice I ever got in my career; I quickly saw the relevance of it, given the kind of implied warnings that Janowitz and Hauser, the two most powerful figures in the Chicago department, had given to me, right at the start.

Meanwhile, SDS was moving to Chicago as well. One of the primary ERAP projects was under way, in Uptown—it began as an attempt to organize the unemployed as they lined up at unemployment centers but shifted quickly to an effort to work with Southern whites who had migrated to Uptown. The aim was to form a "community union" like the ones that were supposedly being developed in Newark and Cleveland. The "union" was to be called Jobs or Income Now, or JOIN, a reference to the idea of a guaranteed annual wage that was being discussed at the time. Lee Webb, who had been one of the leading staff people in SDS the previous year, moved to Chicago to take over the JOIN project. Soon other top leaders of the organization were in Chicago, including Rich Rothstein, Todd Gitlin (a former SDS president), Rennie Davis, and others. In my first months in Chicago, I spent time with the emerging project team. I can't recall being able to contribute very much, and what evolved was a sort of liaison role, helping to figure out ways to help link the project with existing liberal/labor networks in the city and how to bring about academic and middle-class awareness of the whole issue of unemployment and jobs and living conditions for poor whites.

The central ERAP idea of bringing college kids to live in a Chicago neighborhood, which was populated almost entirely by Appalachian and

Southern whites, and having these young people be able to reach out and mobilize the community was, in retrospect, clearly naive. I remember coming up to the JOIN apartment one hot summer day and noticing that quite a few of the summer volunteers were rather morosely lounging around, looking rather aimless. In the moment, I felt a wave of impatience and a bit of disdain for their seeming lack of engagement. Only later, it occurred to me that a lot of these kids were likely paralyzed by considerable fear about being out in those streets, trying to communicate with and organize among people with whom they had little common ground. But the culture of the collective made it impossible for those fears to be voiced—that culture demanded both commitment and self-assurance, which many volunteers could neither feel nor admit to lacking.

Still, some of those who stayed full-time had those qualities and found ways to connect with "indigenous" people and help some of the latter assume leadership. JOIN never became a community union in any real sense, but, over time, forms of protest and of developing social capital were happening. A lot of those early efforts are documented in a book that Todd Gitlin put together with Nanci Hollander, called *Uptown*.[1]

The JOIN project became part of a city network/coalition inspired by the war on poverty and by the civil rights movement's move to the North. The vision of a community union, acting in the urban neighborhood like a labor union, didn't get fulfilled. But JOIN was a facet of a fermenting political culture in Chicago, and many of the JOIN organizers went on to lifetime work carrying forward the logic of their early commitment.

Meanwhile, the national SDS office, led by Paul Booth and Clark Kissinger, had moved from New York to Chicago as well. So, even though I had stopped being a national leader of SDS, I was quite happy to have a lot of SDS comrades now in the same city, and I continued to be involved in some of the organization's national projects, even though I was no longer officially on the SDS National Council.

In fall 1964, Mickey found out that she was pregnant. It was not a surprise, since having a family was something that we had planned. Our new family priorities led me to decide not to go to the SDS National Council meeting that December (the first time I missed a major council meeting), which was held in Washington, D.C.

It turned out to be a fateful meeting. Just before it convened, SDS national leaders had heard from reliable sources that the Johnson administration was contemplating a major escalation of the Vietnam War. The war was going badly for Johnson, as he sent an increasing number of American troops to serve officially as "advisers" to the South Vietnamese regime, but more and more were being killed and wounded. That regime was extremely unstable and unpopular and the pressure was on either to terminate the involvement or to escalate it so that American power would take over the responsibility of fighting the war and winning it.

The national council debated what, if any, role SDS could play, if this escalation was indeed happening. A decision was made to mobilize a national demonstration in Washington to take place in April 1965. That was a big move for SDS, which up to that point had been almost entirely focusing energy on local organizing and domestic issues.

In its first couple of years, SDS's line, which I helped push, was that the best way to change American international priorities was to force the elites to focus on the internal, domestic crisis. That analysis was supported by events during the first months of the LBJ regime. Almost as soon as Johnson took office after Kennedy's assassination, he embarked on an economic program that included the so-called war on poverty, the passage of Medicare and major measures in education. Johnson quite brilliantly had used the national mood following the JFK assassination to move this very significant reform agenda, which would otherwise have been resisted. This effort on his part helped him politically to overcome his image as a conservative Southern politician.

SDS was quite engaged in the idea that, through the ERAP projects, we were in the front line of making the war on poverty a living reality that would actually help poor communities. Our organizing work was strongly influenced by a central argument that social scientists and social workers were making that emphasized strategies for empowering poor communities, so that the voiceless poor could find voice. Overcoming poverty required a redistribution of power and resources—and that could happen only if poor communities were organized. These ideas were inscribed in the official war on poverty legislation, which required "maximum feasible participation" of poor people in the implementation of programs at the community level. That legislation provided an opening for ERAP projects—to focus energy on demanding participatory democracy and organizing to make it happen.

This strategy was particularly effective in Newark, where Tom Hayden and others organized the Newark Community Union Project and challenged the old-line Newark political machine over control of federal poverty projects in that city. Similar sorts of organizing were happening in Cleveland, Boston, and Chicago in poor white communities.

So the idea that SDS should focus energy on the war in Vietnam was something quite unexpected in terms of the priorities that Tom and other ERAP staff were implementing.

But the rumors of escalation proved to be valid. Even though Johnsons had promised during the fall election that such escalation would not take place, thereby defining Barry Goldwater as a warmonger, it was clear, even before the election, that plans for escalation had been developed. In August 1964, claiming falsely that American ships had been attacked by North Vietnamese vessels in the Tonkin Gulf, Johnson had ordered retaliatory bombing of North Vietnam, but it was not yet declared to be a full-scale escalation. After LBJ's inauguration, systematic bombing of North Vietnam did begin in February 1965, just as we had feared a couple of months before. The decision to organize a national anti-war demonstration, made in December, took on a more desperate urgency.

The SDS march, planned for April, was preceded, however, by another, enormously creative, anti-war mobilization. That was the "teach-in" movement, which was initiated in Ann Arbor, SDS's hometown.

In response to the February escalation, a group of faculty, including those with whom we'd worked closely when we were in Ann Arbor, wanted to respond to the bombing of North Vietnam and the war policy. At first, they discussed the idea of a work stoppage. That, of course, would have been dramatic, but it would have perhaps caused a loss of jobs and otherwise threatened many of the younger faculty and staff. A compromise strategy was then decided on. The idea was to "teach in" rather than strike; beginning in late afternoon, a variety of workshops and lectures would be created to engage participants in learning about all aspects of the war situation, calling on the diverse expertise of campus scholars and teachers. The plan was to run these through the night. They had no idea at the outset what the turnout of students would be, but when the event actually occurred, masses of students did take part and large numbers of faculty as well.

This action in Ann Arbor quickly spread across the country. Remembering now how quickly teach-ins sprouted up on hundreds of campuses within days after the Ann Arbor event, I'm struck by the fact that this happened before the Internet and today's social media. It's certainly true that social media now enable the rapid development of mass action on a global scale, but it's useful to note that, fifty years ago, both the sit-ins in the early 1960s and the teach-in in 1965, were locally initiated protests that diffused rapidly, using more primitive technologies like the telephone and the U.S. Postal Service. In those days, many learned the power of informal social networks and came to see that such networks were absolutely crucial if social movements were to happen.

A few days after the Ann Arbor teach-in, I took the initiative in organizing a similar event at the University of Chicago. Some of the most distinguished faculty at Chicago who had expertise relating to the war agreed to participate. These included the great political scientist Hans Morgenthau, who had been famed as a conservative realist until that point in time. Morgenthau became a severe critic of Johnson's war policies (and his stance was undoubtedly a powerful influence on the intellectual world). Gilbert White, the well-known geographer, who had done quite a bit of work on the Mekong River delta, also participated, along with a number of other, younger faculty and graduate students. Hundreds of students stayed through the night in a variety of workshops and panel discussions. I was of course exhilarated by all this, feeling not only a sense of personal accomplishment but hope that an effective opposition to the war policy might become possible.

The teach-in was not just a breakthrough in opposing the war itself. It was a pedagogical breakthrough. There was a sense everyone shared, that this kind of relationship between students and faculty around a current crisis situation was an extraordinary learning experience for all concerned. The Port Huron vision of a college campus as a place of free discussion and deep education on the big issues of the day was realized in the teach-in moment. And in the process, the knowledge and the expertise of academic scholars were made directly relevant to democratic social action.

Moreover, the teach-ins were creating an alternative channel for getting information about the war to large numbers of people. There was no way you could get that information by relying on mainstream news at that point in time. There were a few journalistic outlets for anti-war analysis and depth reporting on the actual facts of the war—the *New Republic* was one such outlet, and *I. F. Stone's Weekly* was another. These were crucial resources, but were able to reach only a few thousand readers.

There were not many other places in the media where one could get a reliable understanding of what the war was about, and such information was needed if one was to formulate a position. You had to know about the history of Vietnam and its centuries of resistance to foreign invasion. You had to know, in particular, about the successful Vietnamese resistance to the French empire. You had to know the role of the United States in sabotaging the Geneva agreements that had ended the French war. You had to know about the nature of the communist regime in North Vietnam and the nature of the South Vietnamese government, about Laos and Cambodia, about the relationships and tensions between China and the Soviet Union, about the mineral resources in the region. All those matters were beginning to be explored in depth on American campuses during the teach-ins. That the anti-war movement started on the campuses had much to do with the fact that thousands of faculty and students came to see the war policy as fundamentally based on lies and therefore both morally and practically deeply wrong—perceptions rooted in knowledge that was simply unavailable to most Americans in the early Vietnam years.

The SDS March on Washington, on April 17, 1965, was the largest student mobilization in the United States since the 1930s. More than twenty-five thousand students came. That number is insignificant compared to the anti-war mobilizations in Washington of the late 1960s, which drew upward of half a million participants. But, at the time, it was seen as an unexpected and dramatic show of student force.

The march culminated at the Washington Monument, where there were speeches and performances that helped shape the emerging movement and helped define SDS politically. Phil Ochs, who by then had become the most political of the new troubadours, performed a song he had written, "Love Me, I'm a Liberal," which satirized the hypocrisy of mainstream liberals when confronted by more radical challenges. A key speaker at the rally was Senator Ernest Gruening, from Alaska, who was an eloquent critic of the war policy and was one of only two senators who had voted against the Tonkin Gulf resolution. Gruening spoke before the Ochs song, and I. F. Stone, the noted journalist and hero of SDS, came on right after Ochs's performance. Stone was enraged by the song and declared, "I am a liberal like Senator Gruening, and I will be around here a lot longer than some of the pseudo-Marxists who claim to be so pure will be." Ochs's song was decidedly on target, we thought, but Stone's embrace of the "liberal" label and his bitter observation about political integrity rang true then, at least for us, and even more in retrospect.

But the most important speech was made by SDS president Paul Potter. It became known as one of the classic speeches of the 1960s. In it, he famously asked questions about the nature of American society, as revealed by what we were doing in Vietnam: "What kind of a system is it that leads to the burning of children with napalm in Vietnam?" At the end of a litany of such frightening questions, he said: "We must name the system." That phrase—which declared our opposition to a "system," reflected and redefined SDS's political stance quite dramatically. Paul didn't, in fact, "name" the system. That ambiguity was characteristic of us early new leftists; we eschewed the vocabulary of Marxism and so did not declare our opposition to the classic names—"capitalism" or "imperialism." (Mickey, in a moment of cynicism, suggested "Irving" as a name for the "system.") Naming the system in Marxist terms would, we felt in our gut, pigeonhole us ideologically. And we sensed that those terms, which were rooted in class analysis, didn't capture the ways that the system was shaped by militarism and the national security apparatus and by racism. Nor did class analysis adequately define the cultural and psychological dimensions of the "system" we were committing ourselves to oppose. Paul's phrase brilliantly condensed both the radicalism and the tentativeness of the New Left's ideological quest.

In the three years after Port Huron, SDS had been functioning without any national media attention. The *Nation* magazine had run an important piece about SDS by reporter Jack Newfield, who was personally close to Tom Hayden and others in SDS, but the *New York Times* never mentioned the organization until February 1965, after the Newfield piece appeared. The respected civil rights reporter for the *New York Times*, Fred Powledge, came to Chicago to interview several of the SDS leaders and the *Times* ran a major front-page feature by Powledge about the New Left on March 15, 1965. ("The Student Left: Spurring Reform; New Activist Intelligentsia Is Rising on Campuses," read the headline.)

Up to that time, we had not counted on—or even thought much about—achieving visibility in mainstream media, but once we were on the front page of the *New York Times* our own self-understanding began to change.

The April 17, the March on Washington produced a level of publicity that we had not imagined. In those days, primary popular sources of media attention were the weekly pictorial magazines, *Life* and *Look*. Both featured big spreads with large photographic displays of the march and stories about SDS. Within days, similar coverage appeared in other national magazines. It wasn't long before the SDS office folks reported getting many requests for membership. It was the first time that people wanted to join SDS without having actually met anybody in SDS and, really, without actually having read the material that SDS itself put out. Suddenly, people were interested in the organization on the basis of how it was depicted in the national media. Those first depictions were favorable, but they were inevitably shaped in ways SDS itself did not control.

Of course, everyone was elated by the surge of interest—and hence impact—we were suddenly seeing. That initial euphoria prevented anyone from sensing dangers inherent in being in the media spotlight.

The April march against the war signaled the birth of a grassroots movement against the war. But the march also was a significant episode in the evolution of the American Left in general. The march had been opposed by some of the leading figures in the Democratic Left. It awakened some of the same deep tensions that the founding of SDS had caused three years earlier in the LID. Just before the march, a group of respected left-wing elders issued a statement attacking the terms of the march. What upset them in the first place was that SDS made no rules about who could or could not participate. So, for the first time since the 1930s, it was possible for actual Communists to march in the same parade and attend the same rally as all varieties of other left groups. That non-exclusionary policy violated the standing rules of the established socialist and pacifist organizations. (An exception was Women Strike for Peace [WSP], which was founded when the Cold War threatened the planet and which prided itself on its willingness to work with everyone, regardless of past or present political persuasion. This was the first in an ongoing solidarity between SDS and WSP—the two *anti-*anti-communist peace organizations—and resulted in cross-fertilization of ideas between them.)

Furthermore, the demands of the march focused on *ending* the U.S. military engagement in Vietnam, not on achieving a negotiated end to the war. The official liberal left position on the war was that there should be a negotiation between the United States and North Vietnam, and it was certainly averse to an outcome that would unify Vietnam under communist rule. But that outcome would surely be the result if the United States pulled out.

The SDS position, which eventually became the consensus stance of the anti-war movement, was that the United States should pull out. The Johnson administration, in fact, was putting forward that it were ready to negotiate. But the North Vietnamese and the National Liberation Front of

South Vietnam were not willing to negotiate until the United States made a plan to actually withdraw its military involvement. For us, and the campus-based anti-war movement as a whole, American involvement was inherently illegitimate, as was the South Vietnamese government that the United States had installed and was propping up. So the march was accused of being pro-communist, even by putative allies of SDS on the left. The *New York Post*, then under the editorship of the liberal James Wechsler, had a particularly nasty editorial attacking the march. Undoubtedly, that editorial helped inspire Phil Ochs to continue to sing his sardonic song satirizing liberals.

Nevertheless, we marched, and, despite these attacks, Senator Gruening did speak and the march drew an unprecedented number of students and others in protest of the war. In effect, SDS won the argument within the Left about how to build a coalition in the 1960s. A New Left politics had to get past Cold War liberalism and make it possible for all who agreed with a specific set of goals to participate in campaigns and mobilizations to achieve them. In later years, anti-war marching on Washington was taken over by leadership coalitions, which developed the boring and alienating practice of filling the platform with speakers representing every stripe and sect who were members of the coalition, presenting a litany of clichéd exhortation that you learned to pay little attention to. But that SDS April march on Washington was an experience in both its physical manifestation and the quality of the platform speaking, which itself was memorable and impactful.


## MAKING LIFE IN CHICAGO

DICK:

Our baby son, Chuck, was born on June 3, 1965. We named him Charles, after Mickey's father, who had died of a heart attack the day after she left her parental home for Ann Arbor in 1960. And it seemed fitting that his name be Charles Wright Flacks, to honor the legacy of C. Wright Mills, my intellectual hero (who had died just a few weeks before the Port Huron gathering in 1962). Chuck was born six weeks early (but he was big enough so that it was not a clinically premature birth). I'd postponed trying to put together the crib (my self-doubt in mechanical matters often paralyzed me in carrying out such tasks). But I was able, with a little struggle, to set it up all by myself—the sort of thing that helped me, as a new dad, feel part of the process and, incidentally, was gratifying because I was actually able to do it.

For me, a big personal surprise was how focused I wanted to be on the new baby. We both found ourselves wanting people to come and see and *kvell* ("derive joy," especially from children), but I recall wanting desperately for visitors to go already—their very physical presence seemed somehow contaminating. I had worried in advance about how our lives would change once the baby arrived—no more casual movie nights or long hours schmoozing with friends, no more freedom of being young in the city. The surprise was how I didn't care about all that once the baby was in our lives—how engrossing the newborn was.

I was beginning my second year as a professor that fall. Around that time, *Life* magazine had carried a story about the life of a first-year professor. The article was pretty accurate about how overwhelming it was—the many demands that are made on your time, without any clarity about how you're supposed to organize yourself or how to decide on priorities. At Chicago, for example, the practice among members of the department was to distribute to everybody else your latest writing. My desk soon was piled with stacks of paper, making for ever-greater anxiety about whether I was supposed to read all that stuff and be ready to converse with colleagues about it. Not to mention the intimidating output that at least some colleagues were displaying. In addition to teaching, faculty life involves a great many meetings, having to do with governance of the department, or the planning of curriculum.

The teaching load at Chicago, as befitting an elite private university, was somewhat less than one might find at a public university, but the new faculty member is faced with a much more demanding set of issues. For one thing, you're starting to teach, from scratch, courses that have large enrollments compared to those taught by more senior colleagues. Alongside that was the fact that a number of graduate students gravitated to me. It was gratifying as a very junior professor to be quickly attracting a following, but graduate student mentoring takes quite a bit of time and emotion, I was learning.

My involvement with the SDS founding cohort provided me with what I thought was an intriguing set of questions that whetted my curiosity as a social psychologist. I was struck, from the outset, by how many of our comrades came from very comfortable, and even elite, social backgrounds and attended the most elite colleges. What might explain their intense desire to merge their fate with that of the poor and the disenfranchised? Why commit oneself to organizing work in communities of disadvantage rather than pursue the opportunities for status and privilege that their backgrounds and their educational attainment made possible for them? Why be attracted to ideological perspectives aimed at discrediting and overthrowing those very structures of privilege that their own families and they themselves were beneficiaries of?

An easy possible answer was that these people were unable to compete in such arenas, and so they turned to rebellion. But the reverse seemed to be true. Port Huron was a gathering that included quite a few student body presidents and college editors from these elite schools. The Harvard peacenik crowd was a collection of quite successful students. Anyone who encountered early New Left and civil rights activists found them personally impressive, brilliant, articulate, and talented. They weren't losers, nor did they think of themselves that way.

A dramatic moment at the SDS convention in Pine Hill in 1964 had clinched for me the need to do some serious research: As the conference came to a close, Robb Burlage jumped on a chair and in his rich Southern drawl began to parody a Southern preacher. He called on those assembled to "repent their sins" by pledging money for SDS. Everyone gathered around and began to respond to his call. The sins they confessed were the occupations of their fathers. One was the son of a publisher of a major newspaper. One was the son of a dean of a law school; there were daughters and sons of prominent surgeons and psychiatrists and many lawyers.

Everyone was of course in blue jeans and raggedy clothes. They were winding up a gathering where most had committed themselves to spend their days working in poor communities. Why were these offspring of elite backgrounds making a strong commitment to social justice—and why would they welcome the chance to define their backgrounds as "sinful"?

The more I pondered these observations, the more I came to feel that studying these seeming puzzles about the personal origins of activist commitment might be significant, not only in telling the story of this activist generation but in shedding light on the social and psychic conditions that promoted political engagement in general.

## STUDYING THE LIBERATED GENERATION

DICK:

One of my most fruitful encounters at the University of Chicago was with a leading figure in the field of human development, Bernice Neugarten. Neugarten had heard about my interest in youth and politics. She was interested in generational relations within families, and she offered to sponsor a project that I would lead that would explore the relationships between young activists and their families. It was an extraordinary opportunity for me—her interests beautifully meshed with the questions I wanted to examine, and her concern with family relations was an excellent way to focus a research effort. We designed a study that involved identifying fifty young white people who were active in civil rights or anti-war organizations and activities. The plan was to identify such students, relying on various organizational membership lists, and contact them for face-to-face interviews and also contact each of their parents for similar interviews. For reasons of convenience and cost, those we interviewed had to be based in the Chicago area (although the students might be attending schools in other parts of the country). A crucial dimension of good research, of course, is to have control or comparison groups, and so we figured out ways to match each activist student with a counterpart college student (of the same gender) who was based in Chicago and whose family lived in the same neighborhood as the activist with whom he or she was paired. We ended up with fifty student activists and their parents and fifty other students (whose political engagement was unknown), selected from college rosters of roughly similar kinds of schools and their parents.

It was the first full-scale systematic study of student activism in the 1960s. The study was unusual in its design: most research on the childhood political development of adults relied on participants' reports about their parents' attitudes and practices. Neugarten's research funding enabled us to obtain firsthand accounts from the parents as well as from their sons and daughters. It was a design that produced a rich array of data. We explored at length attitudes on particular issues and also deeper matters of value and aspiration. The parent interviews focused not only on comparing students and parents' political views but also on trying to understand the values and expectations that the parents asserted to be central in raising their children.

The initial publication of that research appeared in an article in the *Journal of Social Issues*, titled "The Liberated Generation: An Exploration of the

Roots of Student Protest.[2]" It turned out to be the fourth most widely cited article published in sociology during the sixties. Because it was pioneering research, and because it dealt with a topic of major public interest, it set the stage for a great many other studies that replicated it and modified our initial findings. The finding that received the most attention was that student activists came overwhelmingly from liberal homes; the activists' parents told us that they were supportive of and encouraging of their children's interest in participating in social change, even if many were worried about risks and even if many of the students defined themselves as more "radical" than their parents.

Over time, I wrote a great deal about the meaning of these findings, and the story we told to give context to these findings contributed to the vast public discussion about the social and personal sources of student activism. Our research helped define a social and cultural division in the upper middle class. Traditional upper-middle-class families (typical of our control sample) were headed by relatively conservative fathers whose livelihood was likely to be in business, and the mothers tended to be domestically oriented. They were likely to tell us that they wanted and encouraged their children to be successful financially and occupationally, and they tended to uphold traditional family values. Activist parents were likely to be professional (and activists' mothers as well as fathers were professionally employed). The parents saw themselves as liberal politically and culturally. The values they espoused emphasized life goals for their children focused on promoting human welfare and on living lives of "meaning" and "fulfillment." Some of these parents told us that they had striven successfully in their careers and that they wanted their children to care more about making the world better and on living life fully rather than about material success and upward mobility. They also tended to emphasize their own tolerance for and even support of their children's desire to break with social convention rather than conform.

I concluded that the activists we interviewed, who were drawn from the first wave of student activists in the sixties, were likely to be carrying out, rather than breaking with, the values and expectations they learned from their parents. They were raised with strong pressure to make something of their lives—not in terms of fame and fortune but as creative intellectuals or artists or political actors. The civil rights movement, and the New Left that emerged from its inspiration, provided a home for such aspirations—a way of making a difference in the world, while helping resolve the guilt they were raised to have about their relative privilege. In a sense, the student/youth political and cultural movement was a product, and an evolutionary moment in the development, of what some were calling the "new class"—those whose capital was their advanced education and professional training. In the 1960s, it became intellectually fashionable to believe that the key agency of change in "post-industrial" society was going to be the new educated class, rather than Marx's proletariat. Our studies provided empirical support for this hypothesis.

My quest for psychologically oriented factors in the making of political commitment might seem surprising. You would think that, as an activist myself, I would be arguing that students were responding to the civil rights and the war issues—that the nature of these issues itself explained their protest. But a reading of history, and my own experience as an activist, inescapably suggested that movements are not simply the response of a group of people to a grievance or a particular condition. Movements typically begin when a few people step out of their ordinary routines and individual life concerns in order to find ways to take collective action challenging the status quo. Perhaps there were experiences rooted in personal development that could help explain the origins of such relatively uncommon energy and will.

Our research, soon buttressed by a lot of other studies, identified such a patterning in the life stories of white students who responded to the call of the civil rights movement, who helped found SDS, who started protesting the arms race. It was not what conventional wisdom might have expected—these were not losers or the "alienated." They were not rebelling against parental authority. For the most part, they were fulfilling values or traditions that their parents had inculcated or encouraged them to honor. As the movement grew toward the end of the 1960s, its ranks were filled by large numbers of students from more conventional and conservative backgrounds. It became a mass movement channeling a pervasive anger at authority in general, and racism and war in particular, that attracted the support and fervor of young people coming from many social places.

The sixties movement of white students began as an expression of a particular subculture of young people, many of whom shared a distinctive set of experiences in their families. These early activists helped create a framework of belief and action that increasingly attracted students and youth from across the spectrum of class and culture, because, as the decade went on, the social and political crisis confirmed the critiques and warranted the action that the early New Left helped promote.

## FEELING THE DRAFT

DICK:

In February 1966, General Lewis Hershey, the director of the Selective Service System, declared that henceforth student draft deferments would be based on students' academic performance rather than simply one's status as a student. My own experience, probably shared by lots of others, was that the student deferment essentially meant permanent exemption from military service. Undergraduate deferments would be followed by graduate and professional school deferments, and then marriage or various occupations would extend deferment until age twenty-six, the age limit for service.

Hershey indicated that there would be an exam given to all college students and that people below a certain threshold score on that exam would be subject to the draft. Moreover, he stated that universities would be required to send to the Selective Service System a ranking of their male students and that students whose class rank fell below a certain threshold might also be subject to the draft. That proposal was extremely threatening not only to students but to faculty as well. Suddenly the grades we were giving were not only going to be significant for students' professional career prospects, a fact that always has inherently distorted the educational value of grading. Now student grades were also going to become matters of life and death.

Almost immediately, some of us Social Science II faculty began to discuss how we were going to respond to this situation. I and some other colleagues decided to meet with University of Chicago president Edward Levi to ask that the university not cooperate with the Selective Service System. He agreed to meet with us but was incredulous that "faculty would be asking the university to commit civil disobedience." Moreover, he argued, such a move would mean that the university was taking sides in a policy debate. The university mission was to maintain its neutrality with respect to public policy issues, he strongly asserted. Some of us argued in response that, by cooperating with the draft system in the proposed fashion, he was hardly being neutral—university resources would be serving the classification needs of the military. My personal political view was that, if we could get universities to resist Hershey's plan, it would be a significant statement with respect to the legitimacy of the draft itself and the legitimacy of the war policy. Levi certainly saw that the university's taking such a stand would be quite fateful in a political sense; it would certainly have political consequences for the institution, if not for the war policy. Still, we felt that there were strong moral issues having to do with the abuse of the grading system that might lead the administration and faculty colleagues to consider that some sort of resistance to or questioning of the policy was in order.

Some of us on the faculty pledged that we would try to refuse to turn grades into the registrar—we would give students their grades directly, but we would not want to make them official if they were going to be used for the purposes of military classification. I accordingly didn't turn in my grade sheets at the end of the spring quarter—I did so, after my classes had voted in favor of my refusal (and I made it clear that any students who wanted their grades officially recorded would be able to have that done).

Students, of course, were threatened by the new policy. Hershey's announcement really mobilized the student body around the country. The general had made the most significant government action inspiring mass participation in anti-war protest until Nixon's invasion of Cambodia and the killings at Kent State five years later.

SDS declared quite quickly that it was going to organize around the Selective Service exam. SDS prepared a counter exam that, for those who looked at it, would help educate them about the war, and it was distributed in the form of leaflets as people went into the exam. But at the University of Chicago, the SDS chapter decided to call for an occupation of the administration building, demanding that the faculty proposal that the university refuse to turn grades into the Selective Service System be honored.

The 1966 student occupation of the University of Chicago administration building was one of the first such mass actions to occur nationally in the aftermath of the rebellion at Berkeley and one of the first mass demonstrations against the draft. Nearly one thousand students occupied the building for three days, in a remarkable pedagogical as well as political happening, not only for the students involved but for the campus as a whole. Faculty on several sides of the issue engaged in public debate and small group discussion inside the building. In a mass participatory democratic decision-making process, the body voted to vacate (while the administration had decided not to try to use force to remove the protesters). Eventually the

Faculty Senate voted to abolish class ranking of males. It was not a direct refusal to cooperate with Selective Service but that vote back handedly acknowledged the thrust of our protest.

The anti-ranking protest, while not able to compel the University of Chicago's resistance to participation in the processes of military classification, provided impetus to a rapidly developing draft resistance spreading on American campuses. A number of sit-ins like the one at Chicago were staged across the country. More significant was the emergence of a "Hell No, We Won't Go!" movement—in which thousands signed public pledges, often featured in college newspapers, not to serve if drafted.

As part of its response to the protests, the University of Chicago sponsored a national conference on the draft, attended by a number of luminaries, including Ted Kennedy, young congressman Donald Rumsfeld of Illinois, Margaret Mead, and several key Department of Defense officials. I was invited as a more or less token voice of the anti-draft resistance, along with our friend Paul Lauter, then a staff member of the American Friends Service Committee in Chicago. The invited participants were placed around a huge roundtable (eerily resembling the war-room setting of *Dr. Strangelove*), with an audience of spectators looking down on the panelists, who were arranged alphabetically. The seating arrangement meant that I was seated next to Milton Friedman, then a luminary of the Chicago economics department. Friedman was small, bald, avuncular, and affable. True to his libertarian faith, he argued early in the proceedings that the draft was a form of involuntary servitude—"selective slavery" I think he called it. Friedman, of course, was all for the maintenance of a massive defense establishment (which I learned in another public encounter with him was necessary for the destruction of communism, despite the ways its existence violated free market principles). He thought that you could recruit a volunteer army, adequate to the task, simply by making sure that you provided enough incentive for people to join. My own political view was that the draft made it too easy for the president to engage in and escalate a war—as was happening in Vietnam—and that having to employ a volunteer army would be a significant constraint on future presidents' readiness to commit to war. But Friedman and I agreed on the immorality of the draft and also in strongly opposing ideas for "national service" (a vision of a compulsory service requirement for all American youth that would include a variety of nonmilitary as well as military options). National service ideas were supported at the conference by Margaret Mead as well as Morris Janowitz. Mead was an entertaining presence—she carried a walking stick that was taller than she was (gleaned from one of her anthropological sojourns), and she publicly moaned at the conference about how, in her day, people were eager to pay taxes and serve the nation and now all that was lost. Janowitz, having submitted a lengthy proposal for national service, absented himself from any of the conference debate about the idea (such withdrawal from debate, I learned over the years, was his style). Donald Rumsfeld, I remember as a skeptic about the military budget and about the draft. He was part of a group of us who wrote a statement calling for a volunteer army to be included in the conference record.

I'm willing to believe that this conference provided some impetus to the eventual change in national policy having to do with selective service, but of course the real fuel for that was the growing draft resistance. By 1966, a number of young men, unable or unwilling to claim conscientious objector status, had heroically refused to be drafted and were serving time in prison. For me, their sacrificial stance was a strong spur to action. Even if one were unwilling to match their sacrifice (heavy prison terms), it created moral pressure to fulfill an obligation to resist the draft as well as the war.

Such resistance was of course a central historical focus of American pacifism. Some of the leading pacifists of the sixties, like Bayard Rustin and Dave Dellinger, had been incarcerated for conscientious objection during World War II. In the Vietnam era, Quakers and other religious pacifists launched draft counseling centers and distributed material enabling young men to learn about the possibilities for conscientious objection. Recognition of conscientious objection status was determined by local draft boards, and until the Vietnam era it was assumed that only those with demonstrable religious objection would be allowed to do alternative service. But many SDSers petitioned their draft boards with claims based on philosophical opposition to war, and some made their claims, based on opposition not to war in general but to the Vietnam War, because of its unjust character. As a professor, I was asked to write letters of support for individuals seeking conscientious objection status and even, on occasion, was visited by FBI agents, who were assigned the task of verifying such claims. As the years went on, increasing numbers of local boards granted the status on nonreligious grounds, maybe because it seemed prudent to keep youths with such dissenting attitudes out of the army.

More politically important was the growth of an increasingly determined mass draft resistance. It wasn't long before draft card burning became a mass action, featuring many collective card burning rituals. I think most of us came to feel that the draft cards in our pockets contaminated us physically and spiritually. Although past draft age by the mid-1960s, I publicly identified with the movement, speaking at "We Won't Go!" rallies and press conferences, expressing solidarity with draft resisters. I was frequently moved by the courage of young draft resisters, many of whom emerged from nowhere to express their defiance and participate in organizing against the war.

SDS tried initially to take the lead in the draft resistance effort. In the fall of 1965, internal documents discussing possible strategies for anti-draft activity were suddenly exposed in the national press. SDS was being accused of potential "treason" on the floor of the Senate and in huge headlines in newspapers like the *Chicago Sun-Times*. SDS membership ballooned on many campuses, fueled by the publicity. Paul Booth, as national secretary, called a press conference at the National Press Club in Washington and responded to the accusations, declaring that SDS wanted to see the government recruit people to "build rather than burn" (build America rather than burn people in other countries). That initiative by Paul (which I thought moving and politically brilliant), provoked considerable anger within the organization. He was attacked because he undertook his initiative without extensive consultation and democratic decision, and especially because the language of the statement he read seemed filled with liberal platitudes (rather than revolutionary rhetoric). This conflict meant that SDS lost its capacity as a national organization to take the lead in opposing the draft because our ability to speak on the issue became paralyzed by internal debate. As a result, an independent network of draft resisters grew up all across the country with a very strong local center in Chicago, and draft resistance became one of the important strategic levers in opposing the war.

There has grown something of a myth that attributes the movement against the war in Vietnam to the draft itself. People are even ready to argue nowadays that, if only we had a draft, there would have been more young people in the streets opposing the wars in Iraq and Afghanistan. There may be some truth in that, but I've always opposed that line of reasoning. For one thing, from a democratic point of view, the draft is, to me, clearly an abomination. The idea that the state can conscript young people's lives and force them to train to kill is deeply repugnant. Furthermore, the coercive effects of the draft extended beyond those actually drafted—the structure of deferments was designed to channel young men into socially desirable or governmentally preferred occupations. In the midst of the anti-draft fever, someone in SDS uncovered a document, circulated in the Selective Service System, titled "Channeling," which stated that the purpose of deferment was indeed to compel young men to choose occupations defined as desirable by the state, ones that they might not otherwise choose. Paul Lauter, Florence Howe, and I wrote an article for the *New York Review of Books*, in which we made this document publicly visible and discussed the draft and resistance to it.[3]

SDS had a very significant convention in June 1966 in Clear Lake, Iowa. We'd missed the previous year's gathering, timed for the arrival of our baby, but Mickey and I went to Clear Lake, participating in workshops and connecting with our crowd, while coming into contact with a new leadership group that was not connected interpersonally with the founding leadership. It was the first time, since Port Huron, that people not groomed or recruited by "founders" were seeking control. The new group came to be called Prairie Power, and its members had helped create SDS chapters in the Midwest and Texas. They included people such as Greg Calvert, Carl Davidson, and Jeff Shero, all of whom soon became SDS national leaders.

My own feeling was very strong that those who had led the organization at the beginning needed to allow for a new generation of leadership. I had quit the SDS National Council when I got to be a professor, because it seemed to me absurd for a professor to be in the leadership of a student organization (it smacked to me of the old Communist Labor Youth League [LYL], whose national leaders were, invariably, at least in their thirties). Our Port Huron compatriots all had moved well beyond undergraduate status by 1966. Most of the founding leadership generation was working in the various ERAP projects as organizers. I argued strongly the need to develop a new organization that would be what we shorthandedly called the "adult organization"—a more comprehensive New Left entity that anyone could join whether a student or not. Even before 1966, I participated in committees to explore that possibility—but little progress was made to figure out how to create a national organization.

At Clear Lake, some "old guard" leaders sought to retain their positions, but, rather than participate in the plenary floor fights, a bunch of us gathered in one of the bunks in camp for an evening of fun, beer, and storytelling, joking and reflecting that we were the first old guard in history to give up power without a fight.

That episode was really a symptom of the larger fact that SDS had grown enormously, not only in numbers but in its reach around America. There were dozens of chapters all across the country; people were joining and leading the organization at many levels. Many had not had even a personal acquaintance with most of the founding generation. It was a sign of the organization's vitality—a promise for its future—that highly articulate new people were eager to take over.

The prairie leaders, however, were not imbued with the New Left sensibility that the founding generation shared (whatever our differences). It wasn't too long after Clear Lake that Calvert and Davidson were expressing a more militant and, to my ears, doctrinaire leftism. One thing that we had tended to avoid was to identify ourselves with Third World revolutionary movements and the vocabulary of such movements and their supporters. Calvert and Davidson modeled their appearance on Che Guevara. They made a big point of explicitly renouncing Port Huron as "liberal," of wanting to build an SDS that might envision "revolution." Since I'd already decided to pursue political roles outside of SDS, I wasn't deeply distressed by the new generation, even if I was troubled by the eclipse, within SDS, of the New Left vision that I had helped shape and continued to work for.

## THE PERSONAL AND THE POLITICAL IN WARTIME CHICAGO

DICK:

I found much to do in Chicago from that point on. My primary interest was in becoming more fully engaged in city and neighborhood, rather than in national, political efforts. I had started a routine of speaking two or three nights a week in different parts of the city to various organizations, from the Kiwanis Club to Jewish temple groups. My talks were either about the war or about the student movement, making use of my own research. Mickey was at home with Chuck those evenings and was working part-time. She never seemed that irritated that I would be out speaking (not to mention the other nights when there were meetings to go to).

From the beginning of our marriage, we had decided together that although I was fully engaged in my academic career efforts, my time should be balanced between my work and politics, on the one hand, and personal connection with Mickey, on the other. In Ann Arbor, unlike a lot of my graduate student peers, I went home for dinner and stayed home in the evenings rather than go back to the office. Weekends were a chance to be together for relaxation and social activity rather than a time to work.

I was privately critical of other graduate students and faculty, for whom working overtime seemed to take priority over family time (as well as political engagement). I vowed from the beginning that that wasn't who I was going to be. That vow expressed our shared decision. It was obvious that Mickey was not about to be a quiet supportive spouse, helping me do my career, while she suffered the boredom and burden of domesticity. Yet when the baby was born, she was not averse to being home for that first year. She got work grading exams for a correspondence college program—work she could do at home when she had time. That changed after about a year, when she got a good job doing social research in Chicago, and we hired a nanny to come look after the baby in the afternoons, when Mickey was working.

Our apartment was in a three-story building with three wings surrounding a little courtyard. Our downstairs neighbors, Carol and Ross Lathrop, had four daughters, and we began an arrangement with them, which soon became part of the 6029 Kimbark Avenue practice: we set up an intercom system so that the Lathrops could look after Chuck on evenings we both wanted to go out. The intercom allowed them to hear any baby cries, and of course one of the Lathrops would check on him periodically during the evening. I don't think we did this too often at first, but it became a routine in the building as other couples with young children joined in this little network. We would reciprocate with the other families in this kind of remote-control babysitting arrangement.

During the five years we lived there, we created a pretty good neighborly network, and several close friends also got apartments in the building. Bob and Marion Ross moved in upstairs. Bob had been an undergraduate at Michigan when I was a graduate student, and he was one of the pioneer founders of SDS. He was a campus leader in student government and helped start the SDS chapter in Ann Arbor, and he was vice president of SDS in the year before Port Huron. Bob and Marion married when they both came to Chicago for graduate school (one of the first SDS leader marriages at the time), and he entered graduate school in sociology at Chicago. The Rosses are among our oldest friends, having shared both political and personal life in those days, and of course we are still in good touch a half century after and three thousand miles apart.

The Lathrops moved out at some point, obviously needing a house big enough to accommodate their four kids. Their apartment was rented by Joan Wallach Scott and Don Scott. Joan, who subsequently became one of the leading feminist scholars in America, had been a childhood friend of mine. Joan's parents, Sam and Lottie Wallach, were good friends of my parents, Dave and Mildred. Sam was one of the top leaders in the Teachers Union and in one of the first groups purged in the early 1950s Red Scare. They shared an avid tennis interest with Dave and Mildred, and so the two families often spent Sunday afternoons in the fall going to various Long Island parks where there were public tennis courts. On those September afternoons, we children were left to fend for ourselves, while our parents played doubles. Joan and I crossed paths through much of childhood—at summer camps and family visits and in the swirl of the movement.

Joan and Don had been history graduate students at the University of Wisconsin, and both had gotten their PhDs there before they moved to Chicago, where Don was hired by the Chicago history department. Joan was raising a young son, Tony, of about Chuck's age. Tony and Chuck became friends of course and had a good deal of playtime together in that year or so when we were neighbors on Kimbark Street. Tony Scott, incidentally, grew up to be A. O. Scott, the highly respected film critic for the *New York Times*. Perhaps his future was foreshadowed when he led Chuck in playing various pretend superhero games, trailing old pillowcases behind them, as capes, and jumping off the back of a couch, yelling "The dymanic [*sic*] duo!"

From the outset, Mickey and I have been bound together by shared tastes in culture. From the start of our being together, we've always set aside at least one night a week to go out to the movies. Living in Chicago, we found, made this routine not so easy. Apart from the babysitting problems was the fact that, surprisingly, Hyde Park at that time had exactly one movie theater, with a not-always-exciting bill of fare. Of course, the university film society helped, and there were occasional special outings downtown for shows and films and a dinner out.

We also shared an intense love of music—especially "our" music—the music of the folk revival, promoted by Pete Seeger and the left-wing People's Songs crowd. Before we met, we each as teenagers went separately to Weavers concerts and to hootenannies in the city, and our camp life was richly infused with folk music and the politicized contemporary songs derived from the social movements of past and present and preserved in red diaper babies' cultural lives. Mickey liked doo-wop more than I did; I liked jazz, and she didn't—but these taste differences were set aside in the explosion of new songwriting and folksinging. College campuses were primary venues for the performances of people like Phil Ochs, Judy Collins, Joan Baez, and many others. The University of Chicago had a very active, long-standing, folk music society that put on a number of events each year. Bob Dylan, by the mid-sixties, was becoming a superstar, and we went downtown to a memorable concert at Orchestra Hall in 1965. It was one of our peak musical experiences—Dylan performed, one after another, some of the greatest songs ever written—songs that, at that time, we had not heard before: "Mr. Tambourine Man," "Gates of Eden," "Chimes of Freedom." You couldn't help being in awe at the songs, the poetry, the intimations of genius.

But our most typical Saturday night pleasure was hanging out in our apartment with close friends. SDS comrades, especially Rich and Vivian Rothstein, were regulars. Rich and Bob Ross had gone to the London School of Economics for a year after Port Huron, and Rich, who'd graduated from Harvard, came back highly committed to full-time work in the movement. He had taken over leadership of the JOIN project in Chicago's Uptown neighborhood and had established very extensive networks within the labor leadership in the city as well as in the community. Vivian worked on the JOIN project for a while and then got other organizing work in a white working-class community in the Chicago area. We started a ritual on Saturday night of tuning in to the wonderful three-hour radio show on the main FM station—WFMT—called *The Midnight Special*, which coupled the kinds of music we loved with a rich array of satirical comedy. Recordings of Joan Baez alternated with sketches by the comedy duo of Mike Nichols and Elaine May. It was a pure delight to share this with close friends, and Rich and Vivian often came down from the North Side to join us. We'd order in pizza, of course, and have some wine. And it was a big surprise when, one evening late in our Chicago lives, Rich brought a baggie and induced us to try some grass. The surprise came because, in general, Rich was one of the straightest members of our crowd.

Something that was not on our social calendar very much was social events with members of the sociology department. I'm not sure whether we were personally simply not being invited or, more likely, the department itself was not very convivial. I was sure that most members of the senior faculty hated one another—it wasn't the usual intradepartmental factional warfare, but something closer to a low-intensity war of all against all. The likelihood of warm social evenings was very, very slim in that crowd, and there were hardly any young faculty in the department who were coupled and likely to entertain.

I never minded that our social life was not oriented toward the campus in those years. The prospect of spending an evening with academic colleagues was always a source of tension, because no one knew exactly, at that point in history, what the decorum was. Traditions of academic stuffiness and formality persisted, but this was the sixties and much of that tradition was breaking down. But there were a few memorable dinner parties, which we'll describe farther along in the University of Chicago story,

We gradually got involved in the politics of the neighborhood. Hyde Park was famously a community with intense political involvement. We joined the Hyde Park Co-op. The Co-op was a legendary supermarket, and the Co-op board ran not only a very large supermarket but a credit union as well. For some reason, Mickey decided to run and was elected to the credit union board, and so that became one of her activities. As is often true about such enterprises, the credit union struggled with a lot of contentious issues, so it turned out to be more emotionally fraught than she had bargained for.

Meanwhile, I got involved with other organizations in the city. I was appointed to the board of the American Civil Liberties Union (ACLU) of Illinois and to the Chicago SANE board. The ACLU in Illinois was a particularly creative organization at that moment. Its staff director, Jay Miller, was eager to have the ACLU engaged with issues of poverty and the rights of the poor, along with more conventional civil rights and civil liberties matters. I think he wanted someone like me to be on that board in order to bring a fresh, New Left/ERAP perspective.

Because of my connection to ERAP, and my identity as a sociologist, I became very interested in the intensifying policy debates relating to poverty. I taught a course in the University Extension Division (in a downtown evening program) on the war on poverty and was able to add such issues to my repertoire of topics for community-oriented speaking around town. ERAP was an experiment in the forefront of that debate; it was consciously implementing the argument that poverty was rooted in political powerlessness. The federal war on poverty, with its official embrace of maximizing participation by poor communities, was both a stimulus and target for grassroots organizing, and ERAP projects were trying to make use of the opportunity. In Newark, the Newark Community Union Project dominated the local poverty board; in Cleveland, the ERAP project was organizing welfare mothers to demand their rights vis-à-vis the welfare bureaucracy, and the JOIN project in Chicago was making similar moves.

The SANE board included a number of longtime left activists in Chicago. Notable presences were Sidney and Shirley Lens. The Lenses had been active Trotskyists and labor activists since the 1930s. They were prime movers in the Chicago Left, respected for their wisdom and experience, despite their sometimes irritating interpersonal styles. Sid was very interested in cultivating relationships with the SDS circle, and these were helpful in enabling us to connect with the Old Left veterans of the city. Some of those were people who remained active in the labor movement, and some were venerable Hyde Park activists who had been in one or another socialist, pacifist, or Communist Party organizational context prior to the sixties. I was pleasantly surprised to see that, by the mid-1960s, the generations and the factions of the Left in Chicago were able to come together to a considerable degree, even with the old wounds and bitter differences in their memories.

## CHICAGO'S SIXTIES MOVEMENT

DICK:

Chicago progressive politics through the 1960s was a kaleidoscope of experiment and struggle. The city was ruled by the machine as a one-party dictatorship—we liked to say that there was not much difference in the way that Chicago and Moscow were governed. The machine was determined to manage and control all the politics of the city, not simply to guarantee its one-party electoral rule but to co-opt or suppress potentials for dissent. The rising civil rights movement could not be so contained (especially since the minority population of the city was also growing). This was a time when Martin Luther King Jr. and other Southern activists began to look north and to economic justice as well as racial justice as the framework for organizing African Americans. The huge black communities on the South Side and the West Side were increasingly restive with the old-line Democratic Party political rule. Young independent political leaders were emerging and trying to ally with white progressives and labor people in search of a coalition that might begin to challenge the power of the machine.

These efforts focused a lot on the Chicago public schools, a highly segregated system, with deep inequities in the treatment and support of black and white neighborhoods. We had little personal involvement in the school struggles, but we tried to do our part in supporting organization in the Hyde Park neighborhood that could help a citywide political reform.

In our years in Chicago, the reform movement was largely frustrated. Still, that time was the seedbed for much of the transformational politics that did happen in that city in the decades following the 1960s. That post-sixties ferment was greatly aided by many veterans of SDS, who became significant organizers in the political and educational reform movements that help define Chicago to this day.

As time and struggle went on, we participated in widening circles of progressive activists across the Chicago region. For example, I got to know a number of priests and ministers taking initiative for progressive change. The promise of the religious community upsurge was brought home to me one day when I was asked to speak at St. Mary's of the Lake Seminary, located forty or fifty miles from Chicago. My talk keynoted some kind of all-day event. I was accompanied on the drive out there by Nick von Hoffman, the acerbic columnist for the *Chicago Daily News*, who covered the civil rights and other movements with vivid flair. We arrived to have lunch with several hundred frocked seminarians. Our lunch table companions let us know that they were forbidden to listen to the news on the radio or read newspapers. They lived in a strikingly insulated world. Still, this daylong retreat was happening, and Nick and I somehow had been invited.

When I got up and started to talk about participatory democracy as a vision of people in institutions being able to have a voice in the decisions that affect them, the seminarians, all in their black robes, leaped to their feet, applauding wildly. I was seeing with my own eyes the ferment that was happening within the Catholic Church globally as well as in the city of Chicago.

We got to know a number of people who were veterans of the labor wars in Chicago. Most impressive was Jesse Prosten. Jesse and his wife, Anne, were longtime figures of the Left in the city. Jesse was the chief organizer of the United Packinghouse Workers of America (UPWA), a union with a notable progressive tradition that, in the thirties, organized the meatpacking houses. The meatpacking industry of course had been at the heart of Chicago's economy for decades, but it was in serious decline by the time we came. The UPWA was one of the Left-led unions that had survived the Red

Scare, and Jesse, despite his Communist Party ties, had maintained his leadership role in the union through the McCarthy era.

Jesse was one of the wisest human beings I've ever met. His sagest observations had to do with how someone who was politically vulnerable in an institutional setting can maintain his or her institutional position while acting with integrity and principle. He once told me that it was very important to be above reproach: "Don't even take a box of paper clips out of the office, because anything you do that violates the rules can be used against you" by those who are unhappy with your presence in the institution. As a radical within the University of Chicago, I resonated with his admonitions. Jesse, redheaded, earthy, and tough, was the epitome of the organizer, fusing macho swagger with a deeply caring and moral being. He was beloved by all of us in the SDS crowd who got to know him in that period—a human bridge to the Left past and to the grassroots leadership in the city during our time there.

The head of the UPWA was Ralph Helstein, who had come to the packinghouse presidency from his position as general counsel of the union—rather than rising from the factory floor. Helstein was one of the most progressive union presidents in the AFL-CIO at the time, and was a strong backer of Martin Luther King Jr. For some reason, in the spring of 1964, Todd Gitlin and I were delegated to go visit Helstein as part of an effort to get the union to increase its financial support of SNCC in Mississippi. Maybe one reason we were asked to do so was our friendship with Nina Helstein, Ralph's daughter, a University of Chicago student, who traveled in SDS circles.

Helstein's response to our appeal was to opine that what SNCC leader Bob Moses was trying to do in Mississippi was not possible. Helstein declared that, from the 1930s on, the union movement had learned that you cannot really organize agricultural workers, and he expressed doubt that farm worker leader Cesar Chavez could be successful in California, let alone Moses in Mississippi. We were annoyed, to say the least, with Helstein's attitude. He lived in a custom-built, architecturally designed house in the heart of Hyde Park that seemed incongruously lavish for a labor leader. Helstein did not make a good impression on us, lounging in material comfort and deciding who could and couldn't be organized. I've never been sure whether he did get money flowing to Mississippi. Probably he did, but the conversation was one of many that we in the SDS had with old-timers who seemed complacent or condescending in the face of our sense of urgency and new possibilities.

Helstein's observations about the difficulty of creating viable organ-izations of farmworkers were actually well taken—later developments in both Mississippi and California pointed up some of the problems he had talked about. Fortunately for history, however, Bob Moses and his fellow organizers persisted despite the pessimism of some elders. Moses's dream in Mississippi was to build a grassroots force, not only in the cities but also in the rural areas, which could enable the black majority of the state to gain political power as well as to build institutions of self-determination and eco-nomic sustainability.

Moses paid visits to Chicago during that period. At some point, we hosted a small gathering with him. He was one of the most impressive human beings I've ever encountered. His charisma came from his very quiet, mod-est way of speaking, conveying a degree of thoughtfulness that was over-whelmingly persuasive and affecting. He said, on that afternoon in 1965, that the grassroots organizing effort in Mississippi was in a race with the migra-tion of Mississippi blacks going north. So the vision of black power in Mis-sissippi was up against the rational desire of many blacks to leave the state altogether. "Could a black majority be sustained in the face of that strong trend?" was the question that he was wrestling with. Black electoral power did come to pass in Mississippi, which now has one of the largest propor-tions of black elected officials in the country—even if the utopian vision of agriculturally based communal control didn't come to pass.

Another person we were privileged to get to know in Chicago was Studs Terkel. In those years, Studs was well known in the city for his daily inter-view program on WFMT. Because tuning in was a regular habit of many people in the city, Studs was long established as a beloved figure. He became supremely famous about the time we got to know him, after he published books based on the interviews that he'd been doing on the radio, starting with *Division Street, America*.

Studs's radio show had been running for fifteen years by the time we got to Chicago. My early impression of Studs on the radio puzzled me. He always was asking what I deemed "stupid" questions; for example, "How does it feel to be who you are?" he might ask an opera star. After a while, I understood that his questions were designed to elicit as much from the people he was interviewing as possible. He was able, using a naive pose, to break through the packaged responses they were likely to have and to get them to speak spontaneously. These interviews turned out to be a national treasure, stored in his many books and in an archive of his forty-five years of radio programs.

Studs, like Jesse Prosten, embodied the possibilities for a humane and democratic Chicago. A veteran of the thirties, he deeply appreciated the young generation of black and white activists and came at everything with an effervescent enthusiasm that infected those who heard him on the air or in person. Studs's books, and his radio work, directly descended from the best of the popular cultural front of the thirties—an era that, throughout the fifties and much of the sixties was regarded with disdain by cultural arbiters including many left intellectuals. The disdain was based on the perception that the Popular Front expressed a naive or disingenuous populism, and a shallow politics, that covered up the dark sides of human nature and of democracy and was blind to the crimes of Stalinism.

Studs was a child of that era, and he helped rescue its core cultural project. His books created a mosaic of American voices, describing the conditions and responding to the major events and crises of life and history. His artful structuring of these materials helped to make us see that an appreciation of the people in the fullest range of their expression need not be simply sentimental but, in fact, provided some deep insights into how personal life is embedded in history.

People like Jesse Prosten and Studs Terkel showed me, and I think others in the New Left generation, how much we actually could learn from grizzled veterans of the Old Left. And, indeed, how much the visions and hopes we had for a New Left had deep connection with political and cultural experiments that came before us. These were people who had struggled through the many disillusionments and betrayals of their political lives and had learned how to learn and to teach.

At the time, Jesse and Studs and some other old leftists we worked with in Chicago seemed to me quite different from my parents, who I tended to perceive as locked into and blocked by their party identities. A decade later, when my parents came to live close to us in California, I came to see them— and many of their friends—as members of a political generation that weathered betrayal and failure and rather than being bound by their pasts had continued to develop into their old age. Studs and Jesse were exemplary— but, we came to see, were hardly isolated members of that generation.

In those years in Chicago, I was able to encounter many of the more venturesome people who worked in the media. These included Nick von

FIGURE 8.3. A "stroller brigade" leading the Chicago Peace March, 1968; Flacks family at left end

Hoffman, who had helped, in the pages of the *Chicago Daily News*, to highlight the various social movements in the city. Nick wrote some fairly cynical pieces about the SDS crowd, rooted perhaps in his experience as a community organizer—he had started as a key staffer for Saul Alinsky.

More personally relevant were friendships with a group of journalists who worked for the major dailies, but who became a collective of media critics and eventually published a magazine called the *Chicago Journalism Review*. These were working reporters who identified with the movement and whose radicalization was spurred by their experience with the political machine of Richard J. Daley, culminating in the police riot at the Democratic convention in 1968, where press badges were invitations for assault by cops.

Chicago, in those years, had four dailies. These included the *Chicago Tribune*, then the embodiment of quasi-fascism; the *American*, descended from William Randolph Hearst's gutter journalism; and the *Sun-Times* and the *Daily News*—morning and evening papers founded by Marshall Field. These last two were the newspapers that featured work by more critical reporters, epitomized by the fearless Mike Royko. The dailies, along with some weekly neighborhood and alternative newspapers, were joined by a number of talk radio and TV programs. I look back at Chicago in those years as having a considerable public space, despite the monolithic political dictatorship of the Daley machine.

As I expanded my social network and became a visible public voice of protest and dissent, I came to be a fairly regular guest on local radio and TV talk shows then very popular in the city. Irv Kupcinet, veteran columnist at the *Sun-Times*, had a program called *Kup's Show* that went on for hours on late Sunday night TV. People of many different stripes with many different axes to grind were invited to sit around a coffee table and talk to each other on the air. One time I shared the table with a starlet or two and the Reverend Jesse Jackson.

One memorable appearance: I was a guest on a radio talk show with Milton Friedman, with Vietnam as a central topic. I challenged him for never questioning the size of the military budget, even as he demanded limited state activity in every other sphere. Friedman stated that it was important to defeat communism before you could whittle away at the size of the Pentagon. A couple of years later, when he became a strong critic of the military draft, he adopted a stance more consistent with his libertarian free-market perspective.

Most memorable was an occasion when I was paired on a radio talk show with General Jimmy Doolittle. I was there as a critic of the Vietnam War. Doolittle probably was there to promote his memoirs, but he felt it incumbent on himself to declare that the answer in Vietnam was to bomb North Vietnam in order to destroy the food supply of the population. I said, "So are you really willing to cause starvation for millions of people in North Vietnam?" He responded, "Well, they are two legged animals." I replied (and I'm pretty proud in retrospect to have been able to do so) that I was very glad that most Americans did not share that kind of racism and that I doubted very much that the United States would pursue the strategy that he was proposing.

Like many of my SDS comrades who were also getting some media spotlight in those years, I certainly enjoyed the opportunity. Naturally, I thought that I might be making some difference in affecting the public discourse when I had these chances to speak. I felt this despite some hate calls and mail as a result of some of these appearances (that encounter with Doolittle was particularly productive of such vituperation). In the early days after Port Huron we expected little mainstream media attention—and accordingly didn't try to get publicity. By the mid-sixties, we were getting it—and eager for more.

It took a while for us to learn how the media spotlight created profound contradictions for the movement. Publicity helped build our ranks—but defining our purposes and impact in terms of that spotlight had distorting effects on the ways the movement operated, the tactics used, and the strategies envisioned. Gaining the media spotlight became a focal point of action—with far too little effort devoted to figuring out how to control how we appeared in its glare.

# 9 ▶ OUR SIXTIES

## Some Scenes from the Theater of "Revolution"

## MEETING THE ENEMY

DICK:

In the summer of 1967, Mickey and I decided to take our two-year-old, Chuck, on a jaunt to California to visit Mickey's brother, Hershl, and his family in Los Angeles.

While we were there, I received a message from Tom Hayden. He was convening a group of movement activists to travel to Czechoslovakia to meet with representatives of the Vietcong and North Vietnam, and he wanted me to participate. It was a startling call, not least because making the decision to go, and raising money for such a trip, had to happen very quickly. I ended up leaving Mickey and Chuck with Hershl and May, while I boarded a plane for New York to meet up with the rest of the people on the delegation.

It was an interesting and diverse group that was going to Czechoslovakia. There were several people who'd been active in SNCC and related civil rights activity. There were some of the old SDS crowd, including Tom, Rennie Davis, Vivian Rothstein, and Carol McEldowney. Some of the delegation represented pacifist organizations. There were quite a few journalists, including Andy Kopkind, whose work I truly loved. He was then a writer at the *New Republic*, and more than most professional journalists, he deeply appreciated the New Left and wrote eloquently about it. Christopher Jencks was there, who had already begun to establish himself as a journalist, as well as a leading sociologist of higher education. Others included Sol Stern, then at *Ramparts*; Carol Brightman, who ran a very influential little magazine called *Viet Report*; and Ray Mungo, one of the leading underground newspaper entrepreneurs. Reverend Malcolm Boyd, famous as a dynamic radical priest, also was in the group. Dave Dellinger, one of the guiding figures of the anti-war movement, was co-leader of the delegation along with Tom. We were going, we learned in New York, to Bratislava, Czechoslovakia, where we were to be met by Madame Nguyen Thi Binh, one of the top officials of the National Liberation Front, and a group of North Vietnamese government officials and leaders of various organizations in the north. Presumably, the Vietnamese would have some message addressed to the anti-war movement about how the war was unfolding from their perspective. In any case, just having a meeting between Americans and the Vietnamese enemy would be symbolically like making a separate peace, in the face of our government's war policy.

When we arrived in Bratislava we found ourselves in a modernistic labor conference center overlooking the Danube. The town, now the capital of Slovakia, had been badly damaged by bombing and other effects of war during World War II, effects still very obvious in 1967.

Meeting with the Vietnamese, of course, had a considerable impact on all of us. It became clear that the message they wanted to convey to the American peace movement was that our emphasis on the Vietnamese people as victims of the war starkly contrasted with their own view, which was that they were effectively resisting the military onslaught of the United States. They had defeated the French in 1954 and they were going to defeat the United States.

That was the message. We found it hard to accept, since the United States was the world's supreme military power and had atomic weapons, if necessary, as a resort. In an intense face-to-face small group session, a North Vietnamese military guy insisted to us that the United States wouldn't use its nuclear weapons. For one thing, he said, the Russians have the bomb and that will deter the United States. And for another thing, he asserted, "The American people would not stand for it." It was a remarkably positive view of the American people—more positive than we ourselves believed.

Their claim that they were going to defeat the United States was not, I felt, simply romantic bravado. They argued that they were able to defeat the American military because they were engaged in guerrilla warfare, which the Americans could not suppress. The more that the United States introduced troops and escalated the size of its presence, the more the Vietnamese people would unite against us. They described particular tactics that would be effective in hamstringing the American effort—tactics that relied on the cooperation of the peasant people who were the base of Vietnamese society.

They did not, of course, minimize the effects of the bombing on the people. One of the members of the delegation was a young woman who had been wounded by a cluster bomb, and they wanted us to know about this weapon. It was a particular type of bomb that did not explode but spewed sharp metal objects, whose only purpose was to penetrate human flesh. This girl showed us the multiple scars on her body. They had some medical means that they claimed could help people who were wounded in this way, but they wanted us to know the human costs of the American bombing strategy.

We didn't realize then that the import of this meeting, in part, was to prepare us for the Tet Offensive, which was to occur six months later. Tet demonstrated some of the truth that the Vietnamese were declaring—namely, that they could launch a military action that would seriously damage the United States' ability to wage the war militarily. The ultimate defeat, they predicted, would come because the American public would see that victory was not possible—just as the French people had decided in 1954. That prediction turned out to be valid.

For several of us, it was the first time we'd ever been in a foreign country. So an important dimension of the experience in Bratislava was the opportunity to encounter Czechoslovakia. Our Czech communist hosts had arranged a variety of official events that were insufferably uninteresting. One evening we were taken to the Opera House (a notable institution in Bratislava) for a performance of *La Traviata*, sung in Czech. During the first intermission, a couple of us went outside for some air. There in the Opera Square was a huge throng of young people. It turned out that the square was a gathering place for the many students of Bratislava (which was a locale for several colleges). I said rather loudly how great it would be if someone here spoke English. That attracted the attention of a young man, Tomas, who spun around and greeted us warmly in English. He quickly established that he was a very cosmopolitan guy who had traveled to other countries and knew something about the world. He offered to show us around town a bit, which we, of course, were eager to do. We went on a walk and passed the Culture Palace, a refurbished old building on the riverbank, where we heard the sounds of a rock band. Tomas took us inside to what turned out to be a rehearsal space for one of many rock bands in the cultural underground of Bratislava. They were singing in English, although they didn't know the language. So we learned that, in this highly controlled society, a youth culture with strong interests in what was happening in the West, was flourishing. The musicians invited us to their "cave" and so, fascinated and mystified, we followed them. It turned out that they had a kind of clubhouse in the cellar of a bombed-out building. We had to crawl through a tunnel to get to this room. The cave was illuminated by a green light bulb, and the place was plastered with Beatles posters. Their interest in the Beatles—and all things Western— was poignantly coupled with a gesture of welcome. They immediately passed around bread and salt, a traditional way to welcome guests. They had a tape recording that they wanted us to hear. It was a tape of the Beatles' new album—which we had not yet heard. They had just recorded it off Radio Luxembourg, which at that time was broadcasting into Eastern Europe music that was otherwise unavailable there. That's how I first heard *Sergeant Pepper*.

We talked about our opposition to the draft and the war in Vietnam, and they shared that opposition, because the war, they thought, was diverting resources from the needs of the Czech people. They wanted it to be over, as much as we did, but for somewhat different reasons. I was also struck by the admission that they were not particularly eager to come to the United States. They seemed more enthusiastic about Scandinavia as a place that represented an alternative to them. Another surprising political theme was their strong belief that the world had gone downhill since Khrushchev and Kennedy were gone. They wanted to know who we thought had killed Kennedy, and they somehow coupled that assassination with the death of the Beatles' manager Brian Epstein. Through the fog of controlled media, these kids were forging a countercultural sensibility, literally underground.

Several months later, Czechoslovakia exploded in rebellion. Our encounter with Tomas and the rock band allowed us an advance glimpse of the

Prague Spring. My immediate sense, from the conversation in the "cave," was that the apparent solidity of a severely authoritarian regime was an illusion. And it didn't surprise me, twenty years later, when Slovakia split from Czechoslovakia and declared its independence. One of the main threads of our cellar conversation had to do with a discontent rooted in nationalism. "Freedom" meant freedom of expression and personal opportunity, but it also seemed in 1967 to mean something about national autonomy.

As our guide that evening, Tomas provided his own intriguing insights into youth consciousness. He had been able to travel (more than I had believed possible), but he was pretty provincial as well. Early in the evening, he wanted to assure us that he understood that the "Negro problem" in America was trumped up by Communist Party propaganda and that, anyway, Czechs could understand it because, he said, "We have to deal with the gypsies." We, of course, sat him down and lectured him about racism in the United States and what we were about politically. I stayed in contact with Tomas for a few months after that, but we lost touch after the abortive spring rebellion.

Our meeting with the National Liberation Front in Bratislava has received little attention in histories of the anti-war movement, and perhaps the meeting itself had not much significance in terms of any immediate outcomes. Some members of our group were invited to travel to North Vietnam—and some of them, as a result, became even more actively committed to anti-war organizing on their return. Despite the presence of the journalists, little was written about what had transpired at the meeting.

One by-product of my experience in Bratislava was to gain an increased contempt for the communist bureaucracy in Eastern Europe. We were hosted by the official Czech-American peace organization, and its representatives were the ones who arranged several absurdly irrelevant events for us to attend. Early in the week, we were taken to Bratislava's old town hall, where various city officials delivered lengthy and empty speeches to us. Since that was the first morning I had ever been in a European city, I was restless, and so I decided to take a stroll. Leaving the official gathering was not, apparently, acceptable behavior. After walking a block or so, I felt a hand taking my arm, and it was a short Vietnamese guy, who I was to get to know well. He was Do Oanh Xuan, one of the key interpreters for the Vietnamese delegation. I later learned that virtually every American who went to North Vietnam had close encounters with him. He turned out to be a very sharp, sophisticated guy whose role was much more significant than that of a simple interpreter. He was in fact in charge of the North Vietnam Peace Committee. As we strolled, Oanh asked me why I thought we were taken to the old town hall, and I said I had no idea. He explained: "Well, that is the place where Napoleon signed a peace treaty back in the early nineteenth century, so it has symbolic relevance for the Czech government and party. They really want us to sign a peace treaty with the Americans, regardless of the cost to us." I was rather stunned by how casually Oanh opened up a gap between the Vietnamese's own view of the war and the official Communist Party line in Europe.

I had a number of other surprising conversations with Oanh as the conference days went on. At one point, he asked me if I had read Mary McCarthy's article on Vietnam in the *New York Review of Books*. It was of course a startling question. It hadn't occurred to me that the *New York Review of Books* was being followed by the North Vietnamese (though later I realized that if Oanh was a key official in maintaining liaison with the U.S. anti-war movement, he would have to be immersed in the American intellectual scene). He asked my opinion about various rather obscure factions in the anti-war movement. He declared that, although he was a Communist, he was first of all a Nationalist. He told me that he grew up near Halong Bay and that it was the beauty of that place that defined his resistance to the American and other imperial attacks.

More than forty years later, Mickey and I traveled to Vietnam and, of course, to Halong Bay. Actually seeing it helped me make sense of Oanh's declarations. And it was striking that our guide on that later trip made a big point of saying that Ho Chi Minh was more a Nationalist than a Communist. (Our guide told us a joke: Stalin invited Ho Chi Minh to the Kremlin. When Ho entered Stalin's office, he found two chairs. Stalin gestured that this one was for a Nationalist and that one was for a Communist and waited to see where Ho would sit. "I think I'll stand," said Ho.) Hearing that echo of Oanh's declaration made me wonder whether he, in Bratislava, was less unconventional politically than I had thought at the time.

We learned that week more than we had known about the way that the Vietnamese understood themselves. Their national identity is rooted in centuries of resistance to foreign invaders—not just the Americans or the French, but the Chinese. They made it clear that they would not subject themselves to any larger power. And that resistance to domination was the heart of their nationalist spirit as far as they were concerned.

We in the SDS were criticized for being pro–North Vietnamese and emotionally committed to a communist victory in the war. Tom Hayden, in a final speech at the conference, declared, as the followers of Spartacus had in the film, "We are all Spartacus"; we, anti-war activists, are all Vietcong. No doubt, we romanticized the Vietcong. Their lives were profoundly harder and their sacrifices greater than any of us could conceive; indeed, some of their delegation claimed to have come to Bratislava across very difficult and dangerous paths. Our emotional affinity had to do less with their ideology than with a belief, not simply romantic, that they were people who had risked themselves extraordinarily for freedom. I was personally touched, for example, by hearing that even members of the North Vietnamese elite were subject to intense bombing. A leading member of the North Vietnamese cabinet told me how, when bombing alerts happened, their families were deliberately scattered—children of one family exchanging with another—so that families would have less chance of being totally wiped out in an attack. Each of these attacks, of course, was ordered by members of the U.S. government, who had no fear of any personal discomfort as a consequence of the war they were conducting.

It was a war that cost two million Vietnamese lives, and those lives were lost not only to conventional bombs but to napalm and other chemical weapons—weapons that led to disfigurement and other major aftereffects, including large-scale environmental devastation. Despite all of that, our Vietnamese counterparts insisted, quite presciently, that they would, in the end, prevail. And part of their apparent faith in that outcome was their belief that the American people would not persist in a war waged in these ways for unworthy purposes. Indeed, they called us "sons and daughters of Lincoln and Jefferson"—an appreciation of American heritage that struck a chord with me, but was met with audible groans from some of our delegation.

After the conference, we traveled to Prague for a couple of days. It was, mostly, a sightseeing opportunity (which, given Prague's beauty, was well worth it, to say the least). I visited the old Jewish quarter, where four synagogues (some dating back one thousand years) and a cemetery are the remnants of a depopulated ghetto neighborhood. The walls of the Pinchas synagogue are covered with the names of Czech Jews killed in the Holocaust. Despite my very limited Yiddish, I was able to exchange a few words with one of the docents and had the realization that Yiddish, although seemingly the provincial and obsolete language of a particular Jewish time and place, helps sustain the global reach of Jewish identity. I wished that Mickey were with me—her knowledge of the language would have greatly enhanced that experience.

MICKEY:

I was left behind with two-year old Chuck in Los Angeles, where we had been visiting my brother. I had to take Chuck home alone on the plane. I was not happy about all that—but Dick and I had an informal sort of reckoning system, with arbitrary "points" awarded to the partner who made a sacrifice for the other. We agreed that this trip won me many, many "points"— though we never decided exactly how many, nor were they ever exactly reciprocated. We seemed to lose count of it all, but still refer to any sacrifice as earning "lots of points."

DICK:

One notable fact about the Jewish quarter is that Franz Kafka's house is marked with a plaque. Coming across this landmark helped explain the strange conversation I had with one of our Czech minders in Bratislava— when we asked what he thought about Kafka, his only comment was that he was the well-known Jewish writer. At the time, we marveled at how thorough the cultural controls were in a communist dictatorship—to see Kafka in that limited way! In Prague, we learned that his reputation, such as it was, had to do with the landmark made of his house in the Jewish quarter.

From Prague, we traveled to Paris, where we were hosted at a dinner by the North Vietnamese embassy, and we engaged in some further conversation with them, over a repast that I have always remembered as one of the two or three best meals I've ever eaten. We learned that the Vietnamese had fused the two great national cuisines of the world: Chinese and French. I wasn't clear what restaurant we had been taken to, although I believe it was Le Foyer Vietnam, which reputedly was owned by the North Vietnamese embassy. Years later, on a short jaunt to Paris, I tried to take Mickey to the same place but couldn't find it. I thought naively that it shouldn't be hard to find a Vietnamese restaurant in Paris—not realizing that, by then, every block on the Left Bank had one.

I roomed overnight in Paris with Dennis Sweeney, who was somewhat legendaryhone of the young white Northerners who had gone to Mississippi in 1964 and stayed there, not just for the summer but for a prolonged time. After Mississippi, Dennis returned to Stanford University, where he was a leader of draft resistance. He was a buddy of David Harris (who was well known as a draft resister and was Joan Baez's husband). Dennis confirmed a story I'd already heard—that in Mississippi, in the long days and nights of that struggle, and then in Palo Alto especially, he and his comrades dropped acid on almost a daily basis. Dennis shared this with me because I had noticed something about his behavior in social situations. He would withdraw into himself in a way that was hard to describe but very noticeable. It wasn't just that he was quiet. He seemed to be inside himself, virtually disappearing. I finally asked him about it. He said, "Well, I'm seeing movies in my mind . . . and I'm sure it's a result of dropping all that acid."

Dennis was one of those figures in the sixties who had a saintly quality. He had a sort of angelic aura, if a bit gaunt. Known for his heroic dedication in the Southern struggle, he was exceptionally gentle, soft-spoken, self-sacrificing—and very hard to penetrate. Years later, Dennis showed up in the office of Congressman Allard Lowenstein and killed him. Dennis was then hospitalized for many years because of his schizophrenia.

Lowenstein had been deeply involved with the Mississippi project. In fact, he was one of the originators of the idea of recruiting Northern students to go en masse to Mississippi to aid in voter registration and, by so doing, drew the national spotlight to the police state conditions there. Al worked hard, traveling to the major campuses, to recruit kids to sign up.

After Lowenstein was murdered, it became public knowledge that he had a practice of inviting young men—Dennis among them—to sleep with him. Clearly, his relationship with Dennis was fraught with emotional complexity. Dennis explained after he killed Lowenstein that he had voices in his head, that he had pulled his teeth out because he thought they were serving as radio transmitters, that the voice he was hearing was Lowenstein's. It had been rumored for a long time that Lowenstein, an early leader of the National Student Association, had connections to the CIA. Dennis's dementia led to an obsession: that the only way to get rid of that voice in his head was to kill Lowenstein.

One might take the whole Dennis Sweeney tragedy as emblematic of the sixties. There was the brave and self-sacrificing activism, there was the psychedelic abuse, and there was the descent into madness and violence. This plotline doesn't at all define our own personal sixties experience, but certainly Dennis's story ought to raise questions about the potential cost of seeking the totalistic self-transformation that was a central value of the movement and the counterculture.

## ESCALATING PROTEST

DICK:

I got back to Chicago after that fateful and fascinating trip more determined to devote energy to stopping the war. The most dramatic mobilization against the war began to gather almost immediately after my return from Paris—the great Pentagon march, in late October 1967.

We left Chuck with my parents in Brooklyn and went on to Washington, D.C., to participate in the national March on the Pentagon. The march was a dramatic moment, displaying the increased militancy of the anti-war movement, aiming to invade the grounds of the Pentagon. It fused the theater of the counterculture with the emerging revolutionism typified by the SDS style of political expression. The new leadership of SDS wanted to be particularly militant in these demonstrations, and so controversy and conflict swirled around the appropriate way to frame the march. The debates were swamped by the drama of what happened in the end. It was an iconic moment when thousands upon thousands of young nonviolent protesters circled the Pentagon, while armed and bayonet-wielding troops, including roof-top snipers, protected the building. The photos of young hippie women putting flowers into the barrels of the guns went around the world and served to define the situation in the United States—flower power versus bayonets. Norman Mailer's *Armies of the Night* offers a magnificent literary depiction of the Pentagon drama. One of the great books of that time, it depicts what it felt like, moment by moment, to be engaged in that dramatic protest, and intermixed with this narrative is a Maileresque exploration of the cultural meanings involved. Indeed, it's hard to separate his descriptions from what we actually experienced.

As we drove down to Washington, Mickey and I made it clear to each other that, because we had a baby at home with my parents, we were not to get into trouble. Imagine my surprise when she joined the throng that was charging beyond the military barricade to try to get closer to the steps of the Pentagon. Of course, she was hardly alone, but I really felt panicky that she might end up in jail. I remonstrated with her and we pulled back a bit, just before troops started to beat the young people occupying the Pentagon steps.

Soon after, we were walking arm in arm in the dark and a uniformed National Guard kid with his bayoneted gun accosted us, whereupon another young protester yelled to him: "Hey, leave those people alone. They're your parents!" I was twenty-nine, Mickey twenty-seven, and we thought of ourselves as young, but at that moment we began to realize that we were on the far edge of the age cohort then leading the movement.

That night, we met up with Paul Lauter and Florence Howe, our close friends and comrades in arms. Paul and Florence had been in Chicago during our time there. Both were academics, who had left teaching to work on the staff of the American Friends Service Committee in Chicago. They were cohabiting, and it's startling to recollect that they lost their positions with the Quaker organization because of this "illicit" relationship. Shortly before the Pentagon march, they had moved to Baltimore, where Paul had a job at the University of Maryland and Florence began her very visible career as a pioneering feminist scholar, at Goucher College, in the development of women's studies.

They were friends with the poet Denise Levertov and her partner, Mitchell Goodman. Denise and Mitchell offered their Washington apartment for people to crash after the events at the Pentagon, so that's where we ended up. The motley crashers included some of the most active young draft resisters. So we had a chance to personally connect with a group of guys who had seemingly come from nowhere to take brave action as draft refusers, combining that with dedicated organizing. These kids had not been "political"; they were coming from religious and military backgrounds, and their objections were genuinely conscientious in a deep sense. Adrenaline ran high that day and night; I'm pretty sure we barely got any sleep.

Looking back at those few weeks in the summer and fall of 1967, I'm astounded by the tempo and pace of our lives then. For me, it was a summer of a certain exaltation, having had the opportunity to be inside history, to be connected to people whose talent and capacity for risk was literally moving the world. In just a few weeks, I'd met with key people in the Vietnamese struggle, traveled with and formed bonds with a diverse crew of leading anti-war activists, and confronted cops at the Pentagon, swept up in the rising tide of resistance to the war. The excitement—both the danger and the exhilaration—was life-changing, and yet it was only the beginning of what increasingly appeared to be a revolutionary time.

MICKEY:

I was pregnant as 1968 began—something we had somehow planned despite the swirl of world events. I was now working at the University of Chicago's Industrial Relations Center. I was doing data analysis of questionnaires that had been given to staff and patients of various hospitals. It became apparent that the hospitals receiving the highest ratings from both staff and patients were the Catholic hospitals in the survey. It was clear that medicine as a calling proved of greater value than simply a rewarding career.

In June, I went to a conference in Pittsburgh on data banking. Most of the sessions were more technical than I had bargained for (or wanted), but there was one that particularly interested me. It was to be held at 3:00 P.M., so, after lunch, I lay down for a little nap. Of course, I slept through the whole afternoon, waking in time for dinner! That led me to believe that maybe it was time for this pregnant lady to quit work—which I did as soon as I returned home. Less than a month later, Marc Ajay Flacks was born, about three to four weeks early!

DICK:

In February 1968, the North Vietnamese launched the Tet Offensive. It wasn't hard to see that their sudden strikes at key sites, including the U.S. embassy in Saigon confirmed what they had been telling us in Bratislava about their potential to take military initiative that would demonstrate to the American people that the war was untenable. That was a moment when major media began to turn against the war policy. Walter Cronkite, the most credible mainstream news source in the country, took the unusual step of taking a strong public position on his network news program, declaring that the war was unwinnable.

The anti-war movement pace was increasing in many different ways. Large-scale mass mobilizations in Washington, D.C., and other cities were organized. At the same time, SDS was initiating campus confrontations focusing on the links between universities and the war effort. The numbers and the visibility of draft resisters were growing, and the overall militancy of the movement was becoming more and more explicit.

There was no doubt that such militancy was an inevitable product of the continuing escalation of the war, making ever more evident, to more and more of the young, its glaring immorality and futility, Moreover, confrontation and disruption were necessary strategically as well as emotionally. SDS leaders declared that the war had to be "brought home." Americans shouldn't be allowed to passively accept a war in their name, the cost of the policy needed to be made plain, and so resistance that disrupted the fabric of ordinary life was necessary.

I agreed with that perspective, but I was disturbed by the way radical resistance was being framed in movement rhetoric. It was being defined as a recipe for "Revolution," rather than as a crucial element in a struggle to end the war. An early example occurred at the time of the Pentagon demonstrations in October 1967. Mass uprising in Oakland, California, directed at blocking the Oakland Induction Center as young recruits were bused to its doors, turned into considerable street violence. People ran into the streets and threw stones and tear gas canisters at the advancing lines of police, deliberately refusing to use the forms of nonviolent resistance derived from the civil rights movement. Movement publications trumpeted the Oakland street action as a new level of resistance, as a kind of rehearsal for revolution. To me, such revolutionary rhetoric seemed a trap, providing justification for police state repression, while suggesting to the media audience that the movement was interested more in fantasy than in ending the war. Ghetto rebellion and campus confrontations were profound expressions of *resistance*—but, if it was "revolution," then it would have to be waged against the majority of the population.

## BACK TO THE DRAWING BOARD?

DICK:

In 1967 some of us old guard SDS types had decided to try an initiative to create a new formation that would sustain the New Left project and provide a political home for those of us who had moved in life beyond studenthood. And when we first started to talk, there was some hope that we could help create a new organization.

In any event, our group in Chicago took the initiative to call for a conference to take place in the venerable Circle Pines Co-op Camp in Michigan in June 1967. The conference was called "Back to the Drawing Board." We reached out to as many people as we could identify across the country who were our age and older to come talk about organization and potentials for the Left. Our intent was not to compete with SDS on its own ground, but to create a home for people who could not find it in SDS because of their age and station. We certainly felt, however, that the SDS leadership—Greg Calvert, Carl Davidson, and others who were setting the SDS direction—needed to support or at least accept what we were doing if it was to be legitimate. Their view, expressed forcefully, was that they would not support an event that would be laying the groundwork for a new organization. They seemed to accept the idea that people like us needed to sort out our political direction and perhaps initiate new projects, but they ruled out anything that would be designed to create a new organization. Their argument, which was compelling, was that if a full-fledged New Left national organization were initiated, its leadership should be with black and working-class activists, not with white middle-class, primarily academic, folks.

Accepting that argument, we went ahead with the conference with a more modest sense of what it might accomplish. Somehow Mickey and I were given responsibility for the logistical details of the event. Several hundred people indicated their interest in coming (outstripping initial expectations), and it was a remarkably diverse group of folks in their twenties, thirties, and beyond who finally gathered. The conference opened on a Friday night in a pouring rain with a keynote speech by Tom Hayden. In the middle of his speech, the doors burst open and in marched a strange, colorful group of men who called themselves "the Diggers from San Francisco." One of them declared himself to be Emmett Grogan, who had become a legendary figure in the Haight-Ashbury scene. They demanded, first of all, that if anyone in the room was a lawyer, he or she should go with them, because they had been stopped by the police and some of their members were being held. Somebody volunteered to go with Grogan, leaving behind Peter Berg, another well-known Digger figure and one or two others. They then proceeded to disrupt the planned agenda by staging a kind of guerrilla theater confrontation. Berg denounced SDS as a middle-class white organization with no potential for real effect on history. We needed to know that in San Francisco they had begun to create a free society and a free economy. They declaimed a mélange of anarchist revolutionary imagery and rhetoric, insisting that the future lay with them. Some of our folks tried to challenge their disruption of our event. Bob Ross asserted that, had the CIA wanted to disrupt us, this is what they would do. Bob was ridiculed quite mercilessly by Grogan (who had by then come back). Berg read a long poem written on brown wrapping paper that he had scrolled. The poem was replete with F-bomb expletives.

Mickey was in charge of registration, and as the evening went on it was clear that people were arriving and not signing in, but were speechifying about "fucking this and fucking that." She burst in on the proceedings in her most assertive style, interrupting the reading of the poem. Mickey blurted out, "There'll be no fucking at all unless people register!" It was a wonderful intervention that broke the high tension of the moment. The evening soon ended with the Diggers declaring that they had a car full of guns and bows and arrows and that in the morning they would be training us for armed struggle. That night I lay in bed, listening to the heavy rain, unable to sleep. I couldn't figure out what we would do the next day, given what had transpired and what the Diggers had proposed to do. But in the morning the sun came out, and most of the Diggers had gone on their way.

We realized that we had been subjected to a challenging piece of theater. Many at the conference were thankful for it because the confrontation certainly provided us with a firsthand experience of the newly emerging counterculture of the Haight as presented by its most political and creative organizers. That was a couple of weeks before the so-called summer of love was declared—we were in a sense privileged to have direct contact with the Diggers. Emmett Grogan in particular was already a legend. Two others at the conference, also to become legendary countercultural figures, stepped up there to embrace the Diggers. Abbie Hoffman was one; he'd come to Circle Pines from New York and had been active in the Mississippi movement and in Boston. It may well be that the most important historical outcome of the Circle Pines conference was that the moment of the Diggers' confrontation with SDS had inspired an epiphany for Abbie that eventually was fulfilled in the creation of the Youth International Party (Yippies). Abbie wrote later that the Diggers made him see how political theater might have real impact. And it inspired him to want to mobilize politically the rising countercultural mood among America's youth. Abbie and the Diggers saw that task as far more relevant than SDS's more strictly political and rational mode of operation.

Another person in the room who identified with the Diggers was Jim Fouratt, blonde, angelic, and waiflike. Like Abbie, Jim stayed at the conference after the Diggers had gone, and he soon made it clear that he was gay and began to talk at the conference in terms that anticipated the gay liberation movement. Like Abbie, his experience at that conference with the Diggers propelled him toward leadership of a political homosexual project. Within a few weeks he became such a leader, present at Stonewall and a founder of the Gay Liberation Front. He's spent all his life since in both the politics and the cultural life of Greenwich Village.

At the time, those of us who had organized "Back to the Drawing Board" considered it a failure.

MICKEY:

A high point for us, however, was the sight of two-and-a-half-year-old Chuck watching his father make various logistical announcements at lunch, standing on a chair. Chuck promptly mounted his booster seat and began waving his arms around.

DICK:

The conference certainly failed, if measured in terms of our initial goal. Indeed, I think we ended the conference feeling more confused and uncertain about what was to be done than we did going in. The revolutionary mood in SDS and in the black movement, the rise of the Black Panthers, the growing militancy in many parts of the society, the growing tempo of the war, the ghetto riots that had been particularly dramatic in Newark, where Tom Hayden had spent the previous several years—all of these and much more were challenging our suppositions about what kinds of politics and political action might be leading-edge.

Indeed, all ideas from the early sixties about a liberal-labor coalition and a new politics of domestic economic reform—all of that seemed to have been obliterated by the war, which was draining away the potential for domestic reform and public investment. The war deeply split the forces that would have made up a progressive coalition. On the one hand, the national labor movement leadership fully backed the war effort and therefore was totally estranged from the anti-war movement and the young. On the other hand, Martin Luther King had taken a big and controversial step by forcefully opposing the war just a few weeks before the meeting in Michigan. He did that despite urging from the more established civil rights leadership to avoid Vietnam.

The Circle Pines conference was bound to be inconclusive in terms of any effort to think about a long-term project of national left-wing organization. Thinking back all these years later, I realize that the historical meaning of that conference can be found in the invasion of the Diggers, and particularly of the coming-out of Abbie Hoffman and Jim Fouratt, who found inspiration for the political/cultural fusion that they so creatively pioneered in the months and years after. It was not that they were entirely right about how the Left should be constituted, but they each helped us see, in Circle Pines and long after, how limited the New Left of the early sixties had been in helping re-create and redefine American radicalism. They were harbingers of transformations in culture and identity that most of us had not begun to envision.

# 10 ▸ OUR SIXTIES

## 1968 and Beyond

## NEW UNIVERSITY CONFERENCE

DICK:

I began, in early 1968, to work with some other academically based radicals on the idea of creating a Left organization for those working in academia. The idea, which came to be called the New University Conference (NUC), was to bring together a network of radicals working in the university—particularly faculty and graduate students—who would try over time to formulate strategies, on the one hand, to relate to our work in higher education and, on the other hand, to help to link faculty with the student movement.

The founding conference of NUC was at the University of Chicago in March 1968. The conference attracted a good deal of participation from across the country, suggesting that our initiative made sense to a lot of people. The event itself seemed fruitful. I was one of the keynote speakers, along with Staughton Lynd. Staughton was one of the leading older figures in the anti-war New Left. He was the son of Helen and Robert Lynd, famous sociologists of the 1930s, and he had made a mark as an American historian focusing on bottom-up movement in the American Revolution. He was a long-standing pacifist, who wrote widely and eloquently in the vein of nonviolent revolution. In academia, while teaching at Yale University, he had begun to emphasize the idea that left academics should not follow the conventional demands of academic roles but should behave in a revolutionary fashion. He had given up his post at Yale, saying that he no longer wanted to be a teacher for the national elite, and moved to the more working-class-oriented Roosevelt University in Chicago.

In his talk to the NUC founding conference, Staughton advocated that we not try to work within the university as a terrain of action, but move outward into the larger world of movement protest. I gave a talk in which I stressed another potential path, which was to see the university as our workplace and to stress that we had a social change function as teachers and researchers and as workers within colleges and universities. I wasn't averse, of course, to the "outside" perspective; we ourselves were participating actively in wider movements. But I thought at the time—and still think—that the Port Huron vision of the university as a resource and a base for democratic social change ought to be a guiding framework for academics working in higher education.

Under the slogan "A national organization of radicals who work in, around, and in spite of institutions of higher education," NUC was founded. Sufficient resources were gathered to set up a full-time office in Chicago. Our good friend Rich Rothstein, who had been active in the JOIN project and doing some teaching at a community college in the Chicago area, agreed to become the full-time director of NUC. Its founding coincided with the greatest turmoil in the society and in the universities—a situation that eventually strained its organizational and political capacities to the breaking point, so that by 1972 NUC had disbanded. But in the interim, it did provide a home and a network for faculty and graduate students who were committed to support for the student movements then exploding around issues of race. NUC members were active in supporting the creation of black studies and other ethnic studies programs and in battling locally on issues of access and inclusion. NUCers pioneered transformational efforts in academe with respect to women's liberation. NUC founders went on to create academic feminism—women's studies programs, feminist theory, child care centers, policies on sexual harassment and affirmative action.

And NUC members began, in the late sixties to create "radical caucuses" in many academic disciplines—reshaping the leadership of professional organizations and deeply affecting those organizations' practices while, at the same time, doing the "New Left" intellectual work that changed the theoretical paradigms in a number of fields. NUC as an organization was often torn and paralyzed by internal debate—but we helped, I think, to nurture and inspire the ferment that marked academia in the years to come. I took part in much of that ferment—but, it turned out, not much in national NUC affairs, for reasons that will become evident as our story unfolds.

Just the same weekend we were meeting at the University of Chicago, another group was meeting in the Chicago area. They were New Left activists, led by, among others, Tom Hayden, Rennie Davis, and Dave Dellinger. The group was discussing actions to be taken that summer at the Democratic Party convention, to be held in Chicago in August. Tom, Rennie, and Dave had come to the conclusion that targeting the Democratic convention for anti-war protest was both necessary and desirable. The electoral campaign to oppose Lyndon B. Johnson was under way that spring, and, on March 16, Eugene McCarthy had won a surprisingly large vote in New Hampshire. Bobby Kennedy soon decided to run, and two weeks later Johnson announced that he was not going to run for re-election for president.

Johnson, at that time, could not go out into the country without mass demonstrations disrupting his capacity to speak. His only possible public appearances were at military bases. His unpopularity and the unpopularity of the war literally drove him from office. Watching him on TV on March 31 as he abdicated was a moment of rather exalted victory. LBJ coupled the abdication with a new offer for negotiation with the Vietnamese, and that coupling led them to take that offer seriously.

The Democratic convention was inevitably going to be a target for anti-war protest. Johnson's decision opened up the possibility that an anti-war candidate might be nominated, but LBJ's designated successor was Vice President Hubert Humphrey, who defined himself as a supporter of the war policy. No one believed that McCarthy could remain as a serious contender for the nomination, but of course Kennedy was a quite different prospect. His candidacy, though dismaying to those who had worked passionately for McCarthy, nevertheless came to be seen by many liberals and progressives as a vehicle for rescuing the country as turmoil and bloodshed grew.

New Left activists were divided on many matters of tactics and strategy, but they generally agreed that the war policy would be decided in the streets rather than at the ballot box. Whatever the potentials of that happening, the direct action protests had to continue, and the Chicago convention was inescapably a space and a moment for the next big wave. Somehow, I managed to stop by the preparatory meeting that weekend—I think for just a brief moment—but I had no intention of putting my time and energy into that effort.

After that meeting, Tom and Rennie decided to move to Chicago and set up residence to work on the summer demonstrations. It turned out that an apartment next to ours on Kimbark was going to be vacant because its renters were spending some time away from the city. So we got that apartment as a sublease for Tom and Rennie. We had a three-year-old and a new baby on the way. So we made it clear to them that we were not going to be swept up in their plans and activities, and, indeed, despite our proximity to the leaders, we were remarkably uninvolved in the buildup to the August events.

That Mickey and I were insulated from full engagement in the swirl and heat of what Tom and Rennie were trying to bring off indicates that we managed to preserve a certain island of domestic stability. It helped that Tom, who normally was determined to sweep everybody around him into his plans, respected our boundaries. Somehow our family was to be an exception from the rule that everyone had a moral obligation to become totally revolutionary, which tended at the time to be his line of argument.

MICKEY:

Somehow, we maintained that exemption throughout all our years with Tom. Maybe it was because of our early "adulthood"—a real home, with a carpet and a TV set—early in our friendship. . . .

DICK:

In fact, from our relationship with Tom Hayden we learned a lot about what we did NOT want to do politically. It wasn't that we disagreed for the most part with the moves he was making (at least as we interpreted them); it was that he was then making life choices that we quite deliberately did not want to make ourselves. Our desire was to have a personal life that was stable and that made sense for the sake of our kids and our own well-being; but as well, we deeply questioned a politics that depended on a movement that was rootless and did not connect to the everyday realities that most people in society lived. At the same time, the urgent need for resistance demanded an activism of the kind Tom was then living—full-time and ready to face danger and to take high risks. There were tens of thousands of young people at that moment who felt compelled to such activism and who indeed were coming to believe that the escalating crisis would leave little opportunity for private peace.

And despite protecting our space for normal life, we were inescapably involved.

In March 1968, right after LBJ's historic speech, I was on my way to Princeton University to take a part in a conference sponsored by the Woodrow Wilson School and the American Friends Service Committee on the war. It was a rare occasion because movement activists like Tom Hayden, David Dellinger, and others in the anti-war leadership were given a prestigious academic platform with mainstream scholars concerned about war/peace issues and Third World revolution. At that conference, I had the chance to encounter some leading characters in the growing intellectual opposition to the war. Susan Sontag, who by then had become a very eloquent critic of the war, as well as one of the most influential interpreters of the cultural turn in America, was there. One memorable evening, she ended up holding court in her hotel room. Sontag was a striking presence, and being able to schmooze with her and other notables felt, of course, like a privilege. Among those in the room was Eqbal Ahmad, the brilliant Pakistani radical, who was a fierce critic of American empire (and whom I knew a bit because he married the daughter of close Teachers Union comrades of my parents). I can't remember much that was discussed during the conference, but the event was an important confirmation of the growing rift between the academic and governmental establishment on war matters.

## MICKEY:

As Dick went off to Princeton for a conference on the Vietnam War, I felt the marginalization that is not uncommon to pregnant women (I was quite pregnant with Marc at the time)—seemingly separated from her own body, as well as from the slim people functioning around her, and yet concerned much more about what was happening inside her than about anything else. After a few days, he came back, raving about the conference and especially about Susan Sontag. For the first time in our lives, Dick was raving about "another woman," even commenting on how beautiful she was, describing her hair and blazing, dark eyes. I was, of course, not pleased and took an immediate dislike to Sontag—even though I knew nothing else about her. . . . For years, as she grew in prominence, we would jokingly refer to Sontag as "Dick's girlfriend."

Once, years later, we were going through my old CCNY yearbook, which included photos of the faculty in various departments. I had taken an elective course in esthetics (as a respite from the rigors of biology and chemistry) taught in the philosophy department, by a young woman who seemed barely older than we were and around whom various rumors swirled. I had at that time been reading works by a British Marxist philosopher (who was killed fighting for the Loyalists in the Spanish Civil War), Christopher Caudwell. For the term paper in the esthetics course, I wrote about his two books *Studies in a Dying Culture* and *Further Studies in a Dying Culture*. As he had, I used an avowedly Marxist analysis and handed in the paper with some trepidation (this was in 1959). The instructor gave me an A-plus and, much to my amazement, commented, "Have you read Lukács?" (I did know the name of this prominent Hungarian Marxist philosopher, György Lukács.) I had told Dick about this course and teacher (who was, it was rumored, a Sarah Lawrence graduate student and had had a child fathered by famed literary critic Philip Rieff). As we looked at the photos, Dick pointed to a young woman in the philosophy department photo and asked: "Is that your esthetics teacher? What was her name?" I replied, "Yes, but I don't remember her name." He exclaimed triumphantly, "That's Susan Sontag!"

Years later, this time at the University of California, Santa Barbara (UCSB), the Arts and Lectures program was hosting Sontag (by now a celebrated writer and critic) for a public speech. I knew that the program often relied on volunteers from the community to chauffeur guests around, and I called them to explain that Sontag had been my teacher and to offer my services. I picked her up at her downtown hotel one morning and drove her to the airport, where she was departing Santa Barbara. We were early, and so we had some coffee at the charming restaurant overlooking the runway. I told her the whole story, whereupon she exclaimed: "You're the one!! I've been dining out on the story of my student who wrote on Christopher Caudwell ever since!" A high point of my life!

DICK:

During one session at Princeton, where Tom Hayden was on the speaker's panel, I happened to be sitting next to a slender man, somewhat older than myself, who was rather frantically scribbling a lot of notes and mumbling to himself. I noticed that his badge identified him with the Rand Corporation, so his behavior was both weird and suspect. It wasn't until years later that

I realized that I had been sitting next to Daniel Ellsberg, just at the point in his life when he was beginning to rethink who he was. His frantic scribbling and mumbling was about things that people were saying that, he later recalled, hit home emotionally. Reading Ellsberg biographies in recent years let me know that, indeed, that Princeton conference was a key moment in his political evolution. Ellsberg's tortured self-transformation was, I think, emblematic of a process that a significant number of people of his age and station were going through in those days. There were, right then, quite a few collisions between history and individual life courses that led to sharp left turns.

Events in the larger society were everyday reinforcing such desperate feelings. Just four days after Johnson announced his abdication, Martin Luther King Jr. was assassinated in Memphis. In the immediate aftermath of that, rioting broke out in America's cities, most particularly in Chicago, where Mayor Richard J. Daley declared that police should "shoot to kill" those bent on arson and looting. All of us at Sixtieth and Kimbark were of course nervous, since we were embedded in the ghetto neighborhood of Woodlawn. Some of our neighbors packed cars and took off for what they thought were safe havens. Most of the uprising in Chicago in the days after King's assassination, however, took place on the West Side rather than the South Side. Our failure to panic turned out to have been wise rather than foolish.

A few weeks later, on April 23, there came news of a Columbia University student revolt led by SDS. SDS had exposed secret links between Columbia and the Institute for Defense Analyses, on research that furthered the Vietnam War effort. Simultaneously, black students were mobilizing against Columbia's deliberate effort to exploit and wall itself off from the Harlem ghetto in which it was embedded. Although the Columbia uprising appeared at first to be another episode in the many, many scenes on many, many campuses of student occupation of administration buildings and other campus sites, it quickly exploded beyond even that new normal. New York police were ordered onto campus and brutally dragged students out of buildings, causing many bloody injuries. All of this was featured on the front page of the *New York Times*, whose ties to Columbia contributed to the massive coverage the newspaper gave to these events. The strike at Columbia paralyzed the university and captured global attention. That attention was fused with the student uprisings in Paris, which began just a few days after Columbia. Ghetto rebellions, campus revolts, revolution in the Paris streets—not

to mention the continuing turmoil of the Cultural Revolution in China—
each of these separately was a dramatic rip in the social fabric, evoking
deep emotion and indelible memory. Taken together—they were making
1968 one of those great historic watershed years like 1848 or 1917. Despite
my skeptical attitudes toward the revolutionary rhetoric we were hearing
from our political comrades, it was hard not to ponder the possibility
that we were in the midst of earthshaking, and maybe even revolutionary,
change.

MICKEY:

When Chuck was approaching nursery school age, we decided to have
another child. Again, I began a new job just before I got pregnant—but
now, I didn't have to hide it. I was working as a research assistant at the University of Chicago's Industrial Relations Center, located just down the block
from where we lived. They allowed me to work half-time (which no science
lab would do) on a project investigating how patients and staff related to
various hospitals around the area. I was busily engaged in trying to create a
database of various factors—we had learned that staff attitudes were best in
the hospitals that patients also considered the best and that middle-
management styles were the most significant factors.

A month before I was due to give birth (my mother had just come to stay
with us until the birth)—it happened again: early labor! This time my
waters broke as we were all eating dinner, and we rushed off to the hospital.
I sent Dick back home to finish dinner and to put three-year-old Chuck to
bed. A few minutes after he returned to the hospital, our baby was born! (I
used to joke that I had perfected shorter pregnancies—our second son was
four weeks early and weighed nearly seven pounds—and lightning fast
deliveries. . . . I was probably created to have a dozen children!)

We named him Marc Ajay Flacks. The Marc was for Dick's grandmother,
Mary (again, courtesy of immigration officials who couldn't deal with the
"Merriam" version of Miriam), vaguely for Marc Chagall (hence the spell-
ing), and also for Vito Marcantonio (usually called "Marc"), the New York
congressman (protégé of Mayor Fiorello La Guardia), whose vote was one
of only two against the Korean War and who was an early hero of mine. On
June 27, 1950, Marcantonio, the only congressional voice opposed to U.S.
intervention in the Korean War, stated in Congress: "You only live once and
it is best to live one's life with one's conscience rather than to temporize or
accept with silence those things one believes to be against the interests of

one's people and one's nation." The "Ajay" was for A. J. Muste, a socialist/pacifist leader, who was another one of our heroes from the fifties.

DICK:

By the time of the California primary, we and others in our crowd had come to think that there was a possibility that Bobby Kennedy's electoral advances in the primaries would propel him to the nomination. It was not just his opposition to the war but also his overall social perspective that was beginning to excite us. He was sounding far more progressive than any previous candidate of a major party, and he was striking fire, among black as well as white voters. Working-class voters who had been otherwise departing from the Democrats and voting for George Wallace were supporting him in these primaries. Kennedy seemed at that moment to be the one figure in American politics with a chance of gaining power, who was able to appeal across boundaries of race to unify working people. He had begun his presidential campaign by consulting with Cesar Chavez and lending support to the farmworkers' struggle in California. He identified strongly with the plight of poor people, and his whole demeanor in the campaign was one of humility and caring. It wasn't the Bobby Kennedy that we had seen earlier in the decade, who had often been ruthless in his efforts to bring black leaders back into line (and who, it later was revealed, had authorized FBI surveillance of King). Ever since the Cuban missile crisis and the assassination of JFK, it was being said that Bobby Kennedy was undergoing some kind of transformation, and his campaign for the presidency reinforced that view.

Early in the morning on June 6, Mickey and I were awakened by Chuck, who had turned three a few days before: "Mommy, Daddy, they shot Bobby Kennity [sic]." By that time in his life, Chuck was able to get up in the early morning and turn on the TV cartoon shows by himself. That morning, the kids programs were interrupted by this news. We rushed to the TV ourselves to see the turmoil replayed on television. Another sudden overturning of the world was shattering our little household.

Tom Hayden was deeply affected by the Bobby Kennedy killing. Jack Newfield, the crusading New York journalist, who was a good friend of Tom and other SDSers, was working in the Kennedy campaign and had introduced Tom to Kennedy in a private meeting. Tom was invited to join the funeral party and appeared at the side of Kennedy's casket in St. Patrick's Cathedral, in New York City; he was onboard the funeral train that carried the casket to Washington, D.C. Tom's appearance there got a good deal of nasty comment from some "revolutionary" lefties, but Tom was able to respond to that criticism by saying that anyone who did not have a deep emotional response to this situation didn't have a heart—and maybe even said that he didn't want to be part of a revolutionary movement that lacked such heart.

Tom's mother called us while Tom was involved in these events, wanting to know where he was, knowing that he would be upset. She was worried that Tom was getting into trouble because of his political activity. We were able to reassure her—suggesting that if that were the case, he would not have been invited to the funeral party of Bobby Kennedy. She surely took some pride and comfort from that news.

## STRUGGLING IN THE STREETS AND SUITES

MICKEY:

The "police riot" at the 1968 Democratic convention was just a part of a years-long pattern of repression exercised against the Left in Chicago. In the spring of 1968—months before the August convention, we took pregnant me and two-and-a-half-year-old Chuck in a stroller to participate in the peace movement's annual Easter March—which had been started by peace-niks in the religious community as an annual Easter time anti-nuclear weapons march in the fifties, and now was focused on Vietnam as well. About halfway through the march, a wheel fell off the stroller, so we were forced to leave the march route and make our way back to our parked car. Only later did we learn that, a little past where we had left the route, a phalanx of police had intercepted the march and ordered everyone to disperse—an order they quickly enforced with batons against the mostly middle-aged, thoroughly nonviolent marchers. Truly a harbinger of things to come. . . .

DICK:

By early July, Mickey was in her eighth month of pregnancy, and despite the Chicago heat we were at home that summer trying to get some relief by occasional trips out to Promontory Point (known as "the Point"), overlooking Lake Michigan, where you could feel the breezes off the lake. Marc Ajay Flacks was born on July 10. He was, like Chuck, several weeks early. Mickey was remarkable in the ease of her deliveries—her water had broken the night before Marc's birth. I took her to the hospital and then went back home, where Mickey's mother was staying with Chuck. She needed some help to get Chuck to bed, and I thought there would be time for me to do that and get back to the hospital before the baby was delivered. But true to form, Mickey delivered before I could get back, so I never got to actually be part of the birthing of either of our sons.

While our family was immersed in a major moment of domesticity (including moving across the courtyard to a larger apartment with a bedroom for each kid) the city was experiencing a major moment in history. The Democratic convention seemed increasingly likely to be a scene of confrontation and turmoil.

Tom and Rennie were expecting and planning big drama. They and other organizers earlier tried to negotiate agreements with Mayor Daley and his minions to get some permits for spaces where demonstrations could occur. They managed to secure one permitted gathering—a rally in Grant Park in downtown Chicago. The Yippies (led by Abbie Hoffman and Jerry Rubin) had envisioned a big festival and campout in Lincoln Park where they hoped to nominate a pig for president, while hinting that they intended to spike the city's water supply with LSD. Daley and company were intransigently opposed to permitting such an event—let alone allow announced marches to the convention site (some miles away from downtown). In the buildup to the convention, it was decidedly unclear how many demonstrators would materialize—and the threatening posture of the mayor, manifested by the roughing up of hippies and reporters in Lincoln Park early in the week before the convention, may have deterred numbers from showing up.

The "police riot" that was the culmination of the convention week in Chicago—a display of seemingly out-of-control ferocity that the whole world watched on TV—was puzzling. Had demonstrations and hippie festivals been permitted, it seemed, after the fact, the world may have seen a rather sparse numerical turnout nicely managed by a tolerant mayor and party. But Daley seemed determined to carry out a crude enforcement of law and order. Most people explained Daley's brutality by focusing on his blunt authoritarian character, his obtuse irrationality.

Maybe that was it, but perhaps the mayor and his elite backers believed that they had reason for great fear. Earlier that spring, Morris Janowitz, chair of the University of Chicago sociology department, made himself available for a discussion of his recently released pamphlet titled *Social Control of Escalated Riots*. He told members of the sociology department that he had advised Mayor Daley that police violence against demonstrations would not be the best tactic for managing them. Janowitz advocated massive arrests rather than beatings as a form of social control in the event of riot. This sociological wisdom was accompanied by his expressed worry that the greatest danger would be a joint uprising by black and white youth. He thought that the convention marches and protests could ignite the ghettos of Chicago. This nightmare scenario may well have been what Daley and his minions were trying to avert by displays of toughness. It was Daley who, when rioting erupted in April after the killing of King, authorized police to "shoot to kill" those suspected of attempting arson or looting. And there were other early indications that police violence was likely at the convention. That spring, a peaceful anti-war demonstration downtown was met with remarkable force by the police. Mickey and I and Chuck were at that march but, fortunately for our safety, had left before the blowup. Many who witnessed the unprovoked police attack on that earlier march understood Daley to be sending a warning to our side: If you come to the Chicago streets, no matter how peacefully, you will get banged.

MICKEY:

The Democratic presidential primary campaign was in full swing, along with the anti-war movement. We had moved to a larger apartment in the same building in anticipation of Marc's birth, and the graduate students in the apartment next door had gone away for the summer and sublet the apartment to organizers of the Democratic convention protests, Tom Hayden and Rennie Davis. We were too busy with late pregnancy, birth, and a new baby to pay too much attention to what may have been happening next door, but we knew that thousands of young people would be coming to Chicago in August. Dick was planning to go to sociology meetings in Boston and then to an American Psychological Association (APA) meeting in San Francisco, dropping off Chuck beforehand at his parents in New York so that I wouldn't be alone with a newborn plus a three-year-old. (My brother, Hershl, who used to go to New York every Labor Day for some business meeting, would return to Los Angeles via a flight that stopped in Chicago and would bring Chuck back.) So I was alone with infant Marc in Chicago during the Democratic convention of 1968.

The first few days of the convention police assault centered on the hundreds camped out at Lincoln Park, far from the South Side neighborhood where I was nursing six-week-old Marc. On Wednesday, however, the

Chicago chapter of Women Strike for Peace had obtained a permit for a rally at Grant Park, opposite the Hilton Hotel, where many delegates were camped. I figured that this rally was going to be legit, so I bundled Marc into his carriage and made my way to Grant Park—early, so I could nurse him as I sat on the platform while sound checks were conducted. Then we joined the growing crowd on the grass.

Everyone now knows about the person who climbed the flagpole and lowered the American flag—he was actually a plainclothes cop who was giving the signal to the hundreds of riot police lined up at one corner of the park. As they began to charge, I began to move to, what I hoped, was safety. My first thought was the big ABC-TV truck parked in the center of the rally. Surely, I figured, cops would not want to be seen on national television striking a six-week-old and his mother. I suddenly remembered, however, that the media were prime targets of the Chicago cops. Also, tear gas had been fired at the crowd, and I had no idea how baby Marc would react to that (he was sleeping in the carriage). So I changed course and headed for the Lake Michigan waterfront, knowing that the wind would blow the tear gas toward the Hilton.

On a side road running along the park from the lake to Michigan Avenue, I found a squadron of National Guardsmen engaged in affixing bayonets to their rifles (which were apparently unloaded, we learned later). Somehow the image of Nazi Stormtroopers bayoneting babies flashed in my mind, and I screamed at the guardsmen: "Here, d'you want my baby for your bayonets? For shame!" They must have thought I was clinically insane.

As I made my way to my parked car (a little red Datsun station wagon), some guys with Red Cross armbands asked if I could take some people with bloodied heads to the hospital. (Nothing bleeds like even a superficial scalp wound.) "Sure," I said, loading Marc's carriage (which became a car bed—no child safety seats back then) into the cargo area, stuffed three or four bloodied youths into the car, and took off for the University of Chicago's Billings Hospital, located near our house (and where both our kids had been born). When we got there, I explained where we were coming from, and I asked them to treat the police victims and to send me the bill. (I never got one.) I then returned to the park to pick up some more victims. Marc, of course, slept blissfully through it all.

Arriving at home, I nursed Marc again and put him to sleep in his crib. The phone rang; it was Casey Hayden, saying: "Go to a pay phone and call this number, NOW! Tell nobody!"

266 MAKING HISTORY/MAKING BLINTZES

I called Marion Ross and asked if she could babysit for Marc while I "ran an errand." She came down from her neighboring apartment, and I ran out to the nearest pay phone. I called the number Casey had given me, and she answered. "Rennie [Davis] got his head bashed, and the cops said if they saw him on the streets, they would kill him. Can you come pick him up [on some corner in Uptown] and take him to your house—without being followed?"

I called Marion and told her that I'd be back in an hour or so. "Where are you going?" she asked. "I can't tell you," I replied. "Sure," she said.

I followed Casey's instructions and brought a bandaged Rennie home, opened the living room sofa bed for him, and he, Marion, and I watched the police riot unfold and the confrontation with the National Guard on Michigan Avenue. Rennie was weeping—at the ignominy of watching it all from our sofa bed instead of being in its midst. Marc continued to sleep.

While I was out playing cops and robbers, Dick called from Boston. When Marion answered, he asked where I was. "I don't know," said dutiful Marion and nothing further. Dick was not reassured, but he called again later and was relieved that Marc and I were all right.

DICK:

The American Sociological Association (ASA) convention was scheduled for Boston at the same time as the Chicago Democratic convention. As a result of the March NUC conference, I'd been working with some graduate students who had been part of the Columbia uprising that spring to create a framework of dissent at the ASA convention in Boston. I decided that I had to go to Boston since I was one of the initiators of what we called the Sociology Liberation Movement. For the convention, we had asked the ASA leadership to let us set up a table to distribute literature and to have a meeting room where we could gather people for discussion. We learned that ASA president Philip Hauser had invited Wilbur Cohen to serve as the keynote speaker at the convention. Cohen was a legendary liberal, often regarded as the father of the Social Security Act in the New Deal years; but at the time of the ASA meeting he had recently become secretary of the Department of Health, Education, and Welfare in the Johnson cabinet. We regarded his appearance there as an implied endorsement of the LBJ war policy, and so we decided to request that a spokesperson for the Sociology Liberation Movement be part of the panel Hauser was setting up and be given the opportunity to comment on Cohen's address.

Mickey stayed in Chicago with six-week-old Marc. En route to Boston, I had taken Chuck to New York, where my parents were happy to have him visit them in Brooklyn.

Louis Kampf, NUC comrade and a literature professor at the Massachusetts Institute of Technology, was a member of the Harvard Society of Fellows. He offered me the chance to stay at the society's house in Cambridge during my time in Boston (such invitations being a perk of being a member). On my arrival there, I was rather shocked to find a telegram from Hauser (to this day I have no definite idea how my whereabouts were known to him), asking me to show up at nine o'clock the next morning at the ASA suite in the Boston Sheraton. Hauser was chairman of the sociology department at Chicago when I was hired and one of its most powerful senior figures. He had done extensive public service in his past, heading the U.S. Census Bureau, pioneering research and training in demography, and heading a commission on segregation in Chicago's schools. He certainly did not like the idea that we were planning protests at his convention and particularly targeting his friend, Wilbur Cohen. (Cohen's son, Chris, was part of the early SDS crowd in Ann Arbor; those of us in that crowd always had great respect for Wilbur Cohen's pioneering role in helping construct the welfare state; the ASA protest was not about him as a human being but about the relationship of sociology to the warfare/welfare state.)

When I arrived at the penthouse the next morning, Hauser greeted me with this statement: "Let us make something clear—if there is any disturbance at this convention, the police will be called." I was quite shocked at this blunt threat, particularly since we had planned no disruption of anything at the convention, as I quickly pointed out. Others in the room, including Peter Rossi, who was also a prominent member of the Chicago sociology department and was secretary of the ASA at that time, calmed Hauser down, saying, "Phil, don't make threats." Hauser responded with something like, "I'm not threatening. I'm just giving the facts." In any event, I proposed to those assembled, who were the executive team of the ASA, the various "demands" that the Sociology Liberation Movement had decided to make: that we be given opportunity to distribute materials and schedule meetings of our caucus and to have a voice on the panel that was to respond to Wilbur Cohen. Much to my surprise, our last demand was agreed to, as were our requests for a table and a meeting room.

Our caucus convened soon after the convention began, and the turnout was good, with quite a number of graduate students and young faculty attending. An early agenda item was to figure out who was going to be the Sociology Liberation Movement respondent to Cohen. I think I was the one who proposed Martin Nicolaus, a young Marxist scholar working in Canada, who was exceptionally brilliant and eloquent. Nicolaus was noted for his bold and articulate style, and I argued that he was likely to rise to the occasion in terms of being able to state a sharp position and do so with conviction. Although he had little time to prepare anything in writing, his remarks were taped and later transcribed—and were widely circulated as a kind of manifesto for radical sociology, titled "Fat-Cat Sociology." Nicolaus declared, "The eyes of sociologists, with few but honorable (or honorable but few) exceptions, have been turned downward, and their palms upward." Instead, he imagined: "What if that machinery were reversed? What if the habits, problems, secrets, and unconscious motivations of the wealthy and powerful were daily scrutinized by a thousand systematic researchers, were hourly pried into, analyzed and cross-referenced; were tabulated and published in a hundred inexpensive mass-circulation journals and written so that even the fifteen-year-old high-school drop-out could understand them and predict the actions of his landlord to manipulate and control him?" It was an outrageous and crude impromptu speech, but its caricature of sociology's relation to power echoed a long tradition of similar critique. Robert Lynd, in the thirties, wrote a book about conventional sociology called *Knowledge for What?* And a decade before the ASA meeting in Boston, C. Wright Mills had called for a discipline that would nourish the "sociological imagination" as a resource for ordinary people.[1]

While Cohen spoke, members of the Sociology Liberation Movement stood with black armbands, wearing buttons that read "Knowledge for whom?," and faced the rear of the auditorium. That completely silent witness was the only visible protest we undertook, but I am certain that Hauser was in a rage.

Nicolaus's speech alluded to events unfolding in the streets of Chicago. That night we assembled in somebody's hotel room to watch what was happening in those streets, and we saw scenes of mass carnage that followed after a rally in Grant Park. I called home and my anxiety was greatly increased when Marion Ross answered the phone to tell me that Mickey was out, whereabouts unknown. Fortunately, I learned she was home safe soon after that call.

Those of us in the Boston hotel room, especially me, felt powerless and frustrated, but we figured out a way to respond to the events in Chicago.

Some of us decided to introduce a resolution at the ASA business meeting the next morning, to demand that any future conventions of the ASA scheduled for Chicago be moved to another location. It turned out there were already three planned meetings in Chicago for the next decade so our proposal had more than just symbolic meaning. Later that week, the business meeting of the ASA voted overwhelmingly to withdraw its convention from Chicago for the next decade.

Years later, in the mid-seventies, grand jury investigations and lawsuits managed to turn up large batches of information pertaining to the Chicago police force's relationships to political dissent and protest. Many of us who had been targets of the "Red Squad" got the opportunity to get our files, and I learned that, prior to the Boston meeting, Hauser had notified the Boston police that I was coming to the convention with the possible intent of disrupting it—which led the Boston police to ask the Chicago police for information about me. Hauser's threat of police action made in the penthouse of the Sheraton turned out to have been far from idle.

Nicolaus, whose remarks at the convention included an observation to the effect that we in the Sheraton were lucky not to be facing the barbed wire and billy clubs that demonstrators in Chicago were experiencing, had not been aware, of course, that the ASA president had asked the cops to put me (and perhaps others) under surveillance. Nor, perhaps, did most of the other leaders of ASA. In the months that followed, Hauser's hysteria about academic protesters in general and me in particular intensified.

Nicolaus, by the way, followed some unexpected paths. A few years after the ASA events, he became quite celebrated in Marxian circles as the translator of the previously obscure *Grundrisse*, in which Marx's mature philosophical perspectives can be found. At the time, one would have expected Nicolaus to be a leader in the neo-Marxian revival in American and European intellectual worlds. But Nicolaus, who never completed a PhD, may well have had career problems in academia. He ended up as a lawyer and has written quite a lot on issues of addiction and self-help, including *Empowering Your Sober Self*. His website suggests a person of unusually wide interests and talents (see http://nicolaus.com/mn/).

The Boston convention of ASA validated the strategy we had begun to formulate in NUC. It established the presence, within the discipline, of a challenging perspective that was organized, at least to some extent. We created a network of people who would continue the work of fostering a critical sociology. A journal was established, called the *Insurgent Sociologist* (now

*Critical Sociology*), and was based at the University of Oregon, where one of the Columbia radical graduate students, Al Szymanski, had just been appointed an assistant professor. A significant cluster of people vowed to continue organizing at ASA conventions and contemplating other activity promoting a radical sociology. The loosely organized radical sociology caucus was the first of many parallel formations that started up in the following months across the academic disciplines—formations that eventually helped reshape the content and practice of the academy.[2]

For some reason, I'd agreed to deliver a paper at the convention of the American Psychological Association (APA), convening in San Francisco the day after the Boston ASA meetings ended, so I quickly boarded a plane for California, while the turmoil continued in Chicago. My paper was scheduled on the opening morning of the APA meeting and had to do with student activism. I arrived in San Francisco on one of the hottest days in the city's history (97 degrees) and found that the dumpy (cheap) hotel where I was staying had no air conditioning. Still, I managed to get to my morning panel and was the leadoff speaker.

I told those assembled that I'd just come from the ASA meetings, which had voted to boycott Chicago because of the behavior of the police and Mayor Daley. As soon as we finished our paper presentations, someone in the audience stood up and said, "Rather than have a discussion of these papers, why don't we discuss how to organize APA to boycott Chicago!" Immediately, a statement to that effect was circulated to the sizable crowd gathered in that room. A committee was organized and, without lifting another finger, I had succeeded in initiating the process whereby the APA later that week engaged in a Chicago boycott. It was not a small matter, since, at that time, the annual APA convention was the fourth largest of any in the country. Its conventions sprawled across four or five hotels, with some ten thousand to fifteen thousand in attendance. So for the APA to boycott Chicago was actually a materially significant fact, one that got a good deal of press attention nationally as well as in Chicago. It was the easiest effective political action that I have ever attempted.

The night after my APA presentation, I flew back to Chicago. Mickey's brother, Hershl, had been in New York for several days and was able to pick Chuck up and bring him back to Chicago, and so we reunited after all these happenings, eager to occupy ourselves with our kids after the eventful and tumultuous previous twelve months. But the chance for a peaceful private time quickly vanished.

The fall presidential election was a dismal anticlimax. Despite universal left-wing loathing of Richard Nixon, few of us considered voting for Hubert Humphrey, given his unflagging public support of the war policy and his silence in the face of the police riot in Chicago. I wrote in the great come-dian and activist Dick Gregory; Mickey claimed to have written in my name. Nixon was of course elected, but to this day I can't feel regret about our failure to support Humphrey.

Some of our comrades of those years do feel such regret, but I haven't found a persuasive case that Humphrey's election would have moved the country in a positive direction. Indeed, it is not well remembered that the Nixon years witnessed some of the most progressive legislation of our time (including major environmental protection laws and the Freedom of Information Act) and the establishment of relations with Red China. So, even though I'm very much a critic of left-wing third-party-ism in national politics, punishment of the Democratic war party at the polls still seems like the right thing to have done—though I'll grant that further debate on this issue might be worthwhile given the perennial perplexities that electoral strategies create for progressive activists.

## THE UNIVERSITY AS A BATTLEGROUND

DICK:

That fall, a group of us on the University of Chicago faculty formed a chap-ter of NUC. We were just a small band, and much of our shared interest was in supporting the student movement, but we did begin talking about the university and its social role.

The sociology department at Chicago was remarkably conservative— even though it had been the pioneer department in constructing sociology as a discipline. The department, historically, had strong connections to the life of the city and to the poor communities of Chicago through the research and the political activity of many of its faculty. George Herbert Mead, one of the founding figures of American sociology, along with John Dewey and some others at the University of Chicago, was an active supporter of the labor movement in the early twentieth century and of the social work experiments of Jane Addams at Hull House. In the Robert Hutchins era, the university was seen as a center of resistance to attacks on academic freedom.

By the time I got there, however, the "Chicago school" of urban ethnography that had defined the department had been almost entirely erased as the result of internecine battling earlier in the sixties.

It wasn't entirely erased, however. Morris Janowitz continued to do a version of that work, but his efforts were shaped by his strong belief that sociologists needed to be intellectual allies of the powers that be. Janowitz did sponsor ethnographic research by graduate students—people like my close friend Harvey Molotch—which made significant contributions to the understanding of the then current race and class conflicts in the city. But whole areas of study that had been central to sociology, and especially to the classic Chicago school, were no longer taught.

One neglected matter, I felt, was the study of Karl Marx. We had some Marx readings in our Social Science II undergraduate syllabus, but there was no graduate course on Marxism in the university. I couldn't claim scholarly authority with respect to Marxism but, nevertheless, organized a graduate seminar that attracted students from a number of departments. It was not a bold step on my part—at Chicago you could teach whatever you wanted without questions from colleagues (or at least so it seemed to me). But I thought that it was an intellectual breakthrough for me: I was a social psychologist, not a macro-sociologist. To lead the seminar, I had to immerse myself not only in the Marxian texts but also in the newly burgeoning "neo-Marxian" literature. Marx was being revived in the sixties, and the European neo-Marxists were seeing him in new ways.

The participants in the seminar included some who were already more schooled in European critical theory than I. One member was Andrew Arato, then a political science graduate student at Chicago, who was soon to become an important theorist in this vein. For me, it was decidedly an instance when teaching was a way of learning and a path to intellectual transformation.

A recent hire in the sociology department was Marlene Dixon who had just gotten her PhD at the University of California, Los Angeles (UCLA). She joined the department in 1966, and she was part of our NUC group. Marlene, I think encouraged by my example, began to consciously inject into her undergraduate teaching in sociology perspectives that were at odds with the intellectual climate of the department. She had been trained in "symbolic interactionism" at UCLA. This theoretical tradition, which had its origins at Chicago in the early years, had been obliterated under the leadership of Philip Hauser in the departmental wars of the early sixties. There was nothing particularly radical about symbolic interactionism, but it did offer a coherent paradigmatic alternative to what was then dominant in the department and the discipline as a whole. It was a perspective that fostered qualitative, "humanistic," and philosophically grounded work, rather than the quantitative empiricism then predominant.

Marlene had a joint appointment in the Department of Human Development, a doctoral program headed by my colleague Bernice Neugarten. Marlene was coming up for a contract renewal in both departments, and the decision about that was being deliberated in the fall of 1968. Marlene was one of only a handful of women on the entire faculty, and most of these were in more or less feminized disciplines like human development, education, and social work. There were a few very senior tenured women sprinkled around the campus.

There were also a few senior women who were wives of senior male faculty, including sociologists Alice Rossi, Zena Blau, and Evelyn Kitagawa. These women were well published in the discipline, but they had no regular faculty appointment because of the prevalent notion that spouses could not serve in the same department without risking nepotism. I don't think there was any legal or formal barrier to such appointments (and indeed there were a few married couples with appointments on campus), but it was the prevailing rule. These three women in sociology were marginalized in career terms even though they were widely known as significant scholars. Such arrangements were taken for granted (including by some of the women affected).

In February 1969, it was announced that Marlene was not going to have her contract renewed. This decision was surprising; the renewal of a three-year contract was more or less routine, since normally in academia one was given six years before a tenure decision had to be made. Her termination was, accordingly, abrupt and early—and it was done despite the fact that her colleagues in the human development department, where her work was primarily centered, had recommended her renewal. The negative evaluation provided by the sociology department was determinative. Since she was a sociologist, the custom at Chicago was for the anchor discipline's decision to rule when there was this kind of joint appointment.

There was an immediate student reaction to this news. Marlene was a popular teacher, and her students, including SDS members particularly, quickly rallied for her and demanded an explanation for the decision. I was a junior (untenured) member of the sociology department, so I had no part in the department's decision, but I vocally supported the student challenge to her termination, since I knew that she was an effective teacher, that termination after three years was not necessary from a procedural point of view, and that she could easily be given further chance to prove herself.

Janowitz, then in his first year as chair of the department, convened a meeting of the entire faculty of sociology, including me. He wanted to issue a statement to be signed by the entire department, defending the decision to terminate her. The statement draft that he presented at the meeting argued, among other things, that her teaching in undergraduate courses had been carefully reviewed and found wanting. I asked Janowitz (in a tone of "naive" innocence) whether he had consulted with the chair of the under-graduate sociology program, and he said, of course, and I said that I found that information strange since, in fact, I was the chair of that program and had never been consulted about her performance. Whereupon a colleague piped up: "Get rid of that passage, Morris. You know we never talked about her teaching."

This exchange was the first of many revealing and enlightening episodes in the Marlene Dixon saga that then ensued. That meeting was the first time I'd been witness to a tenured faculty personnel discussion. The news that they had not discussed her teaching in evaluating her work was a startling confirmation of the widespread suspicion that teaching was not a criterion for advancement in a research university—even as official pronouncements claimed the opposite. It was also enlightening to observe Janowitz's capac-ity for fabrication on the spot—something he continued to display in the days to come. I also discovered, to my surprise, that I could stand up to his bullying style without flinching. That was a refreshing thing to learn about myself since, up to that time in the Chicago department, I had been largely silent in department meetings. My silence ended with that exchange.

When the meeting ended, we were asked to come back to the depart-ment office later in the day to sign the redrafted statement. I went home without reading or signing it. Later in the evening, Janowitz called to ask why I'd neglected to sign. iI told him that I hadn't read the final version He suggested that we meet in the lobby of a university building near my apartment so I could see the statement. We met, I read it, and I said that I couldn't sign it since I disagreed with the department decision in her case. "Aren't you a member of the department?" he asked. "Is signing this a membership requirement?" I replied. He hurried to assure me otherwise.

The student protest leaders decided that they were going to occupy the administration building, and 450 students poured into that building on January 30 (after 1,000 students had met and debated a strategy the night before), to demand student participation in university governance including faculty personnel decisions. Many of the graduate students in the sociology department took part in the occupation. The protesters planned to stay indefinitely.

The demand for student voice resonated with many University of Chicago students. For graduate students in a number of disciplines, the demand expressed their restlessness with the intellectual climate in their departments—a climate that often fused authoritarian style with a variety of elitisms—much out of tune with the swirling political dissidence and countercultural experiment of the period. The graduate students, and not a few Chicago undergraduates, wanted academic careers, but they were strongly alienated from the actually existing university. At the same time, the Dixon case revealed the patriarchal character of the university, anger at which was not assuaged when the administration set up a committee of women faculty to examine the Dixon matter. That committee was chaired by Hanna Gray, a historian (who, a decade later, became the first woman president at Chicago and the first woman to head a major university).

University of Chicago president Edward Levi had made a decision right at the start of the protest that the police would not be called to eject the students. He had observed far too often the consequence of police attacks on student sit-ins—most recently at Columbia, where the police brutality against students occupying campus buildings had provoked a huge strike. Indeed, one could speak by that time of a "Berkeley scenario"—students sit in en masse, police eject them with force, mass student strike follows, college president is fired. Levi quite consciously wanted to avoid that scenario. Instead, Levi managed to move the administration's key functions elsewhere on campus and left the building to the student occupiers.

It was the second time that Levi had to manage an administration building sit-in. The first had occurred when the Students against the Rank group had occupied the building for a few days to protest university cooperation with the Selective Service System. While that event was going on in 1966, I had received a call from Levi in my office. He loudly and angrily said to me on the phone: "Why do the students lie? You talk to them, so tell me why they lie!" I was a bit shocked at this outburst and didn't have much of an answer (I wasn't at all sure what "lies" he might have been reacting to). A couple of weeks after the "rank" protest, on the Memorial Day holiday, I was at home with Mickey, when the phone rang. It was Provost Levi asking me to come to his house for a conversation. Rather than immediately rush over, I decided to wait a decent interval, so I told him that I'd be there in an hour (even though I needed only ten minutes to get to his house). Mickey was immediately anxious, fearing that I was about to face discipline, but I doubted it, perhaps naively.

In any event, I went to Levi's house, finding him in a distressed mood. He made the following speech to me: "I want to talk to you because you talk to the students" (suggesting, peculiarly, that this was unusual behavior for a member of the faculty—but more likely meaning that I was conspiring with them). "I want you and others to realize that this university is vulnerable. It's a private university. We depend a lot on donations—large grants and dona- tions. If we become a target of these protests, we could begin to be hurt financially." He said:

> Furthermore, I myself feel worried about and vulnerable about my role in all this. I don't have to be president of the university—I could go back to my office in the law school. I don't need all this aggravation! I thought we had relations between the administration and students that would prevent another Berkeley here. In fact, Hannah Arendt herself had assured me that "there would never be a Berkeley at Chicago because you, Ed Levi, talk to the students." I decided this protest occurred because I had left too much responsibility for the deans, and they did not do a good job working with the students. But I've looked into the matter, and I now realize why students pro- tested. We don't pay enough attention to the undergraduates in terms of ame- nities! Do you know that many of the students don't have their own phones in their dorm rooms and have to go out in the hall to call home? That has to be remedied!

I said: "Well, I think that would be fine, but of course they were protest- ing the war and the draft and the university's complicity with that." He was exceptionally dismissive of that. He said that there was no rationality in thinking that the university was complicit (even though he had refused to consider ways to avoid sending student grades to the Selective Service Sys- tem). He said, "I don't think they would really expect us to do civil disobedi- ence as an institution, so it must be more mundane problems that they really are bothered by." It was a deeply instructive encounter for a twenty-eight-year-old junior professor, one in which I experienced the considerable moral blindness and somewhat deranged anxiety on the part of a person widely respected for his cool rationality.

In 1969, when the students occupied the administration building in the Dixon affair, Levi had his act together. He was determined to lead from behind, encouraging the senior faculty to appear to be the key defenders of the university. That wasn't hard to do since the student protest was directed at gaining a voice in faculty decision making—a demand that seemed to strike at the very heart of their professional privilege.

So the main statements defending and advancing the university's official position during this sit-in came from the Academic Senate leadership rather than from the office of the president. Day after day, as the sit-in went on, faculty leaders would call press conferences, where distinguished professors would spell out their anger at the protesting students. Several of these were émigré scholars from Nazi-occupied Europe, who repeatedly compared the protesting students in Chicago and the Nazi youth they had had to flee. One well-known scientist opined that there was a global conspiracy from Peking to Berkeley that the sit-in was a part of. The eminent psychiatrist Bruno Bettelheim made known his insights about the pathological character of the typical student activist.

The Academic Senate declared that students who were sitting in were in violation of university rules because they were "disrupting the mission of the university," and so there was established a faculty tribunal to mete out discipline for those who were violating the rules.

Since the offending students weren't to be arrested, the problem of how to identify the offenders had to be faced. Photographers were sent into the building to photograph protesters, and then senior faculty convened to look at the pictures and see whom they could identify. One of the very senior members of my department, early in the sit-in, saw me standing in the administration building lobby. He approached me and asked if I would help him identify the sociology graduate students who were participating, saying that he knew them by sight but not all their names. I said, "Are you actually expecting that I would cooperate with you in identifying students so that they could be disciplined?" His reply: "I want to see if you will." "Of course, I won't," I said. He said, "That's what I wanted to find out!" Several decades later, I had the chance to talk with this former colleague about the Dixon affair. His memory was that he was one of those in the department who opposed the authoritarian Janowitz and Hauser. I didn't discourteously remind him of the test he tried to impose on me.

As the sit-inners gathered, Janowitz, at a department emergency meeting, went on about how potentially violent these people were—how, in fact, having seen their anger, he feared that he would have his head broken by one of them. A few days later, Hauser declared that he couldn't get near the administration building, because of the odor that was emanating from there. I was surprised at the brutal stereotyping indulged in by some of the faculty. As in all highly polarized conflict, such stereotyping functioned to justify demands for repression that these guys, all liberals, would be unlikely to support when not so threatened. Still, their reiterated claims that values of civility were under attack by the students seemed to me remarkably hollow given their readiness to punish and their profound deafness to the student voices.

At some point that spring, I was invited to give a talk at Wesleyan University, then still an all-male college. There had been, a few weeks before, a student sit-in there, and one of its leaders, who hosted my visit, turned out to be the son of an official of the University of Chicago faculty senate—one of those most assertive in endorsing repressive punishment at Chicago. I couldn't help but add Oedipal rage (along with threatened privilege) to my inventory of Chicago professors' reasons for their ready resort to repression.

Quite regularly, I'd get notes from faculty colleagues across the campus. Their content was typically something like this: "Dear Professor Flacks, I have supported your dissents from the war policies and your defense of the student movement—until now. This University is the bastion of liberal values—a haven during the McCarthy years. I can't understand why you want to destroy it."

This sort of sentiment indicates that the privilege that so united and mobilized the faculty wasn't crass and narrow. Many of these felt in their bones that (a) intellectual life was the most important human activity and (b) it rested on very fragile and always threatened foundations. To defend those foundations, I thought that they ought to listen closely to the students' voices and even welcome their clamoring demands for dialogue and participation. Levi brilliantly had encouraged the faculty to be the cops, and so, despite their stated commitment to the ideal academic community, they became willing to identify for discipline those whom they had mentored (this in a university whose very raison d'être was based on mentorship).

Meanwhile, within the sit-in there was a considerable amount of fierce debate about its nature. The sit-in began with the demand that students have a voice in the governance of the university (and that Marlene Dixon be rehired). There were other demands having to do with the University of Chicago's relationship to the ghetto communities that surrounded the campus—a relationship based on a kind of semi-enlightened colonialism. But the prime motive for the sit-in had to do with the Dixon case. As the protest built, its feminist dimension came to the fore. On at least one occasion, the women activist students arranged a press conference that would involve only women reporters. Indeed, the Dixon affair deserves to be remembered at least because it was the first mass expression of women's liberation in the academic world.

As the days wore on, fierce debate among the students in the building came to revolve around the issue of student privilege. Within the national SDS, the influx of the Maoist Progressive Labor Party (PL), espousing a simplistic class analysis, threatened the SDS leadership. The response of that leadership to the PL challenge was to try to outflank the Maoists from the left. Who could prove themselves most revolutionary (and most vulgarly Marxist) became the heart of the contest.

In that context, there was a rising view within SDS inner circles that the student body of America was "petty bourgeois" and therefore privileged—and that a self-respecting revolutionary organization should not be one that was emphasizing student power (an emphasis that until then had helped SDS become the spearhead of the national student movement). Elite college students should not lead the movement. For the PL, elite students should subordinate themselves to working-class interests and culture (abandoning bohemian counterculture and supporting day-to-day-labor struggles). SDS leadership countered the PL line by defining the "vanguard" in terms of "revolutionary youth"—but it was youth of color and working-class youth whose leadership and interests needed to come to the fore.

So, at Chicago, the very demand of the sit-in, which had mobilized and electrified the student body as a whole, was one that was now questioned inside the occupation. SDS, which had been the leading edge of radicalizing and organizing the white students of America, was beginning to deny the political and moral validity of these very students. This seemed to me a remarkably bad turn of events, not only for the future of the organization but for the fate of the New Left project itself. Since I was spending my time on the wider campus, rather than twenty-four hours a day inside the

Administration building, I was seeing a rising tide of rebellion throughout the University of Chicago campus among students who were not directly part of the demonstration. Even members of the business school were picketing, and many other departments had intense meetings. Many students were participating in a far-reaching questioning of the nature of the academic profession and the university's societal role

That was particularly true for the sociology graduate students. This was the department that was the epicenter of the Dixon case, and many graduate students were active in the sit-in. The ferment in the department halls was palpable—marathon meetings, passionate manifestos, and elaborately worked-out proposals for department reform were the order of the day. It turned out to be a seminal moment in the evolution of the field of sociology, I have come to believe, because so many people with bright prospects in the field were engaged in this kind of critical examination of their role, questioning the theoretical and ideological frameworks that governed their work. These Chicago events were both symptoms of and inspiration for radical turns throughout academia—the very process that those of us who started the NUC had hoped might gather force. Many of the students in sociology who had been involved either in the sit-in itself or in the department discussions went on to reshape their own intellectual careers in light of these debates and experiences.

The sit-in ended after sixteen days, and it ended not with a bang but with a sort of whimper. The leaders emerged from the building, and at a big press conference they announced that they had been defeated, and renouncing the very student movement that SDS had helped create.

I thought that was a bizarre turn of spirit and rationality. I could not share the conviction of these younger folk that the times required them to get ready for revolutionary armed struggle. Their defeatism was rooted in their view that reformist social movements were futile—and that student protest was, in a sense, a way to reproduce rather than challenge social inequality. Their conclusions, I felt, were colored by considerable guilt over their own felt privilege—and fed by the rather insular social space they were inhabiting—not only inside the occupied building but in the cell-like social organization that was emerging in their ranks.

I did not think that their interpretation of events needed to be taken as the final word. To me, it was more important to witness what might be called the *conscientization* of many students—a growing mood not only of alienation from established authority and institutions but, equally, a determination by many to seek morally grounded and politically engaged life courses. An intriguing irony of the late sixties was that a far-reaching student movement was sweeping the country at just the time when its leading organization was disintegrating.

When the sit-in ended, the University of Chicago machinery for punishing the student participants went into full swing. Students who had been identified as part of the sit-in were systematically called before a faculty tribunal. They were presented with a choice: either to confess that they, in fact, had violated the university's mission and were now sorry to have done so or to insist on defending what they had done. If they defended their participation, they would be suspended or expelled; contrition would lead to absolution. In the end, some 140 students were expelled or suspended—the largest purge of student protesters in the sixties.

It's important to realize that this was a university that historically prized the mentorship relationship that students, including undergraduates, could establish with faculty members, and it was that mentorship relationship that was exploded in this proceeding. The students who were identified were those who had close enough relations with faculty that they could be named by faculty who viewed their pictures. It seemed to me a remarkable betrayal of the mission of the university—far more serious a betrayal, I felt, than the nonviolent occupation that the students had engaged in. Indeed, I took the position, rarely understood or endorsed by faculty colleagues, that the sit-in was an expression by many of the students who were most committed to the ideals of the university—it was a cry of the disillusioned—and a prod to the faculty to re-examine their practices in the name of those ideals. I thought that those of us who sided with the students were in fact something like worker priests in the Catholic Church—whose presence in the struggle embodied the message that the university was not completely lost.

My self-righteousness had been fed by numerous instances of what I saw as the rank hypocrisy of some leading faculty. One source of hypocrisy was the frequent invocation of the notion that university decisions were to be free of political bias—invocations that were uttered precisely when political bias was being practiced. So, in the faculty debate in 1966 over whether student grades should be made available to the Selective Service System, I was struck by the tortured reasoning of a very well-respected political scientist, explaining why the radical historian Staughton Lynd could be excluded from consideration for a faculty position. Lynd's politics disqualified him, he said. Lynd allegedly poisoned students' minds by questioning the value of conventional scholarly research. I sat there wondering how, if the gentle-man were serious, he could be so blind to the logic of his argument.

Morris Janowitz, by contrast, seemed to me best understood not as a hypocrite but, instead, as one who tended to view the academy as a field of combat. Morris had grown up in the streets of the Bronx, and I think he saw street fighting as a normal framework for human relations. He'd served in World War II as a military researcher and liked to remind listeners that he'd had shrapnel in his left calf (often pulling up his pants leg to show the scar). He was proud to continue to serve the military (and the police) as a sociolo-gist, presumably hoping that in that role he could enhance its institutional rationality. There's nothing particularly discrediting about that aspiration, except that he was always guided by strategic, rather than moral, perspec-tives in determining his actions.

During the Dixon events, Janowitz made a lunch date with me at the fac-ulty club. He asked me, in his blunt fashion, why I needed to stay in the university and suggested that if I were to choose to leave the university, he would help get me a research center in, say, Florida. I was amused by this, of course. He was making me an offer I couldn't refuse, perhaps modeling his leadership style after a stereotypical ward heeler in the Chicago machine. I responded that I had as much right to be in the academy as he did. I don't remember how the lunch ended, but I found in all my interactions with Janowitz that his bullying could be readily checked by an assertive response. I was really glad to learn that I had that kind of assertiveness in me.

There was a particular public occasion that fully dramatized the discon-nect between the university's claims and its practices. In the fall of 1968, the university staged a large public banquet in downtown Chicago to commem-orate Edward Levi's inauguration as president. It took place only a couple of months after the police riot created by Mayor Daley had convulsed the city. The guest list included many of the architects of the war in Vietnam, includ-ing Secretary of Defense Robert McNamara and National Security Adviser McGeorge Bundy, as well as the mayor of the city of Chicago just after he had presided over globally broadcast police brutality. SDS decided to stage a protest at that banquet, and I shared the students' anger about the com-memoration. I wrote a letter to the *Chicago Maroon* (the student newspa-per) in which I stated that I thought the banquet had been arranged by a master of guerrilla theater, wanting to demonstrate to the world how the university was tied up with war criminals and with the Chicago machine. Somehow some students managed to get admitted to the banquet, and they spoke out disruptively with some transgressive glee, before being escorted out. These students were spat upon and roughed up by some of the regents and faculty present at that event.

The national drumbeat of declarations about how destructive the student movement was to norms of civility needed to be balanced, I thought, by the fact that, when pressed, faculty and trustees of this very distinguished university had lost their capacity for civility and for rational discourse, even as they patted themselves on the back every day because of their claimed commitment to rational discourse and the disinterested search for truth.

I saw the students in those weeks as more exemplary of civility and rational discourse than the university leaders. A remarkable set of mass meetings preceded the occupation. On two or three evenings, at least one thousand people packed Mandel Hall for hours of debate. Our close friend and SDS comrade Bob Ross, who'd come to Chicago as a sociology graduate student, masterfully presided over one of those meetings. He summoned his years of experience in SDS and student politics to invent procedures that allowed for debate and decision making in this large and contentious crowd. Bob was one of those students suspended after the sit-in, but he eventually got his PhD and went on to be a leading intellectual figure in the global anti-sweatshop campaign, a close adviser to a state legislator, and a leader of the faculty at Clark University.

Another meeting was chaired by Jackie Goldberg, who had come from Berkeley—where she was active in the Free Speech Movement—to enter the graduate school of education. Years later, after working as a teacher in Los Angeles ghetto schools, Jackie was elected to the Los Angeles Board of Education, served as its president, and began a remarkable political career, serving on the city council and eventually as an representative in the California State Assembly, where she helped found the progressive and the lesbian, gay, bisexual, and transgender (LGBT) caucuses. Bob and Jackie are living demonstrations of the educational value of student activism, having developed singular fusions of passionate social engagement and remarkable political skill because of their schooling in the student movement.

The "civility" of the assembled students was evidenced by the openness of the discussions that happened in Mandel Hall. For example, my colleague and faculty friend Don Levine spoke at some length, passionately trying to persuade the students not to pursue their protest. For Don, the University of Chicago was sacred ground, a place that had liberated him, first as a student and then as a professor from small town provincialism, and provided him the space to develop as a deeply serious scholar. He expressed his fear that the university could be irrevocably damaged, describing a scenario where it would be moved out of the city and turned into a research institute, no longer troubled by unruly students and threatening urban neighborhoods. It was not a scenario he wanted to see—but one he thought plausible. Don was heard by the assembly, but his arguments turned out to be unpersuasive. Don's passionate speech was but one example of the numerous face-to-face dialogues that students undertook with faculty during those days, and the openness of the Mandel Hall meetings was typical of the dozens of intense meetings across the campus. As I say, I was repeatedly struck by the contrast between the student deliberations and the more emotionally overwrought behavior of many on the faculty.

In addition to lurid images of the students, a number of professors and administrators harbored fears about the neighborhood in which the university was embedded. The story of the University of Chicago and its relations with Hyde Park and the surrounding South Side black ghetto has been extensively told and retold. It's a story filled with all the contradictions that can be observed in many colonial relationships. In the days of the Dixon affair there was a genuine fear that the large, well-organized Blackstone Rangers gang or other groups might attack the university or somehow ally with the student protest. SDSers from the university met with black activists from the community to try to find common ground, on the theory that the sit-in might provide leverage for advancing community interests. To my knowledge, the fear on the administration's part that the wall it had worked hard to build between campus and neighborhood would be breached proved to be unfounded. In the years that followed, the university managed to acquire and clear large blocks bordering the campus and the Woodlawn ghetto, and today the population of Woodlawn is less than half of what it was in the 1960s. Indeed, a literal, not figurative, wall has indeed been built along Sixty-Second Street.

The events on campus were widely covered in the Chicago press—front-page news day after day. Prominent coverage of daily professorial press conferences was coupled with some serious attention to the voices of the sit-in. Many reporters in Chicago had been radicalized by the Democratic convention police assault on those wearing press badges, so quite a few of those covering the protests were eager to interview its spokespeople. One memorable moment for me was my appearance on the popular *Kup's Show* along with political scientist Hans Morgenthau and civil rights activist Jesse

Jackson and one or two Hollywood starlets. Another notable media experience for me was to be asked to write a piece for the *Sun-Times* Sunday magazine, counterposed with one by Bruno Bettelheim, on student activism. I thought making these mainstream media appearances was a contribution to offsetting the growing public anger at the student movement, . . . and I couldn't resist the opportunity to be in the spotlight—an impulse that was soon to cost me dearly.

The Dixon protests were widely reported in Chicago. Nationally, they were but one episode in the daily stream of stories about rebellious students. I think the main point about the Chicago protests that reached the national radar was that, uniquely, the police were not used to quell the protests and that they ended without "violence" and with the student leaders declaring themselves defeated.

Edward Levi's management of the protests enhanced his reputation as a "great" university president and certainly helped his subsequent selection as attorney general by Gerald Ford in the aftermath of Watergate and the Nixon impeachment. Of course, he was a very distinguished lawyer and former law school dean, and as attorney general he crafted a regulatory framework that claimed to rein in the FBI and government surveillance.

As far as I was concerned, the management of the University of Chicago protests was cynical and disastrous. Police violence was avoided, and one could certainly feel particularly relieved that the notorious Chicago police force was not deployed in this case. But I was deeply disturbed by the disciplinary process established when the sit-in ended. That the students' only effective defense against being suspended or expelled was to denounce their own participation was an invitation to lie—an invitation made doubly egregious by the fact that the students were called to account because their own mentors had in many cases fingered them. I was shocked at how a process that seriously compromised the integrity of the institution was supported by many colleagues.

At the same time, there were those who opposed or had reservations about the authoritarian institutional responses to the crisis. As the weeks went by, some colleagues made some public gestures of resistance. One amusing episode: I attended a department meeting in the Quadrangle Club (the faculty residential and dining club). When the meeting ended I encountered a group of students who were occupying an area of the ground floor, staging a hunger strike in protest of the disciplinary process, Of course, I knew many of those camped out there, and I approached them to wish them well and to see if there were things they needed that I might help with, whereupon I felt a firm hand on my back, pushing me toward the exit. It was the secretary of the club, telling me that, since I wasn't a member, I was being asked to leave.

I thought that was amusing since I was there in an official capacity as an invited participant in a meeting of the sociology department. I immediately went back to the department and sought out one of my colleagues who lived permanently at the club. I said to him, "I've just been thrown out of your club," and explained the situation. He, who had never shown the slightest sign of political interest, rose to this occasion, immediately circulated a statement to all our departmental colleagues protesting that their colleague, Professor Richard Flacks, had been ejected from the Quadrangle Club. I appreciated this gesture, especially since it was one of the few times that a senior member of my department had shown any sympathy for me during those particular months. I think many of the other department members signed this statement, and I eventually got some sort of apology from the club.

On May 5, 1969, several of us faculty concerned about the disciplinary proceedings staged a vigil outside of the Quadrangle Club. It was one of a series of efforts to mobilize concerned faculty—efforts that suggested a considerable number of younger faculty and a few senior members were indeed worried about the disciplinary process. In the end, however, more than 140 students, both graduate and undergraduate, were suspended for one or more quarters or expelled.

After the vigil was over, I went back to my office, where I had made an appointment by phone with someone stating that he was a reporter for the "*St. Louis Globe*." He had called my home on the weekend and offered to come right over. I put him off until Monday and said I'd meet him at my office. What happened when I got back to my office was quite fateful. A gentleman arrived with a tape recorder and placed it on my desk. It was not unusual for me to have an interview of this sort, and so I thought nothing untoward about it, except when he asked me what seemed to be a ridiculous question: "So what do you think of all this protest?" Suddenly the phone rang, and it was someone I needed to talk to. I turned away from my interlocutor. When I hung up the phone, I recall, the tape recorder fell to the ground, and I of course leaned over to pick it up. That's the last memory I have of this episode, since he struck me perhaps with an ax or hatchet, causing severe damage to my skull and cutting my right wrist, leaving me bleeding on my desk. Fortunately, a student arrived within a few minutes

FIGURE 10.1. Dick's office after the attack, May 5, 1969 (photo by Bob Richards)

after the attack and quickly got me emergency treatment. I was taken to the hospital in a semiconscious state, and Mickey was, of course, soon notified.

Although I had moments of some consciousness during the following week, I had lost a lot of blood and suffered some brain damage. In fact, at first the doctors at Billings Hospital had to say to Mickey that they were not sure I would walk again (one doctor scared her by saying that it was possible I would be in a vegetative state), but I regained full consciousness after a blood transfusion about a week after the incident.

Mickey suffered much more than I—having to deal with the frightening fact of the attack itself, with the uncertainty about recovery, and with the care of two little kids in the midst of all this. All of our parents, of course, came to help out with the kids, and soon Mickey was getting a lot of support from our neighbors and friends. Several senior faculty and their wives, including anthropologist David Schneider and Hans Morgenthau, offered help and support. It is worth noting that *no* sociology faculty members offered any help.

MICKEY:

On Sunday, May 4, 1969, Dick got a phone call from a man saying that he was a reporter for the "*St. Louis Globe*" and would like to interview him for a story on the student movement. The caller suggested coming over to our house, but Dick suggested that he meet with him at his office on the campus in the afternoon of the following day. That afternoon, I went to work at my new part-time job, preparing to train residents of Chicago's public housing "projects" to work as interviewers for a research project of the University of Illinois Chicago Circle campus. I was working on my training materials when I got a phone call. The young man said he was calling from the University of Chicago Hospital, and there had been an "accident," and Dick was in the hospital. He was very calm, and I was not unduly alarmed as I drove down Lake Shore Drive to Hyde Park. In fact, I imagined a whole scenario: a week or two before, University of Chicago students had occupied the university's faculty club, where the sociology department had some of its meetings. Dick had stopped to chat with the students on his way out of the club, whereupon another faculty member came over, took Dick's elbow, and asked if he were a member of the club. Upon hearing Dick say that he wasn't, but that he had been at a department meeting, the professor announced that he was the sergeant at arms of the club, and he firmly escorted Dick out of the building. As I was driving, I imagined that, on this day, the police had been called to the club, where I knew that a faculty vigil was happening, and that Dick had been involved in some sort of melee with the police. From my Chicago convention experience, I knew that the application of a police baton to the human skull often resulted in a particularly bloody wound. That was what I imagined had happened to Dick and was why he was in the hospital.

When I finally got to Hyde Park and pulled up at the emergency room entrance of the University of Chicago Hospital, I was greeted by Bob Ross. He looked ashen, and he told me that Dick had been attacked by an unknown person and had suffered injuries to his head and wrist. I hurried in and found Dick lying on a gurney waiting to be X-rayed, with his head and wrist heavily bandaged. He was conscious and spoke to me as if he knew who I was. He did seem confused, and I tried to reassure him that he was in good hands in the hospital and that I would see him after his X-ray. I found the fact that he was conscious reassuring—he was not lying in a coma. The doctors told me that after the x-ray he would be undergoing surgery and they would know better after that what the story was. . . . It would be at least a few hours, they said.

I had two little boys at home, being looked after by a young woman, a University of Chicago undergraduate who had been working for us for about two weeks. When I got home, I found that she was nearly hysterical (the university and the police had called the house and she had had to speak with them). She announced that she couldn't handle the situation and was quitting immediately!

Fortunately, she had been able to keep all of this from almost four-year-old Chuck, and he was simply happy that I was home early. I fed both kids supper and got them to bed. I then asked Bob's wife, Marion, to babysit, while I went back to wait for Dick to emerge from a six- or eight-hour surgery, accompanied in the waiting room by Bob and one or two other anti-war activist professors (no sociologists, of course). While we waited, the chair of his department was announcing to the press and the campus community that Dick had attempted suicide and that it "was a cry for help," and he was pleased that "we would now be able to help him. . . ." This chair, Morris Janowitz, seemed to me to represent the dominant sensibilities and political outlook of the vast majority of University of Chicago faculty: that they considered the students—especially undergraduates—"dirty and smelly" and an undue burden on the faculty (who had much more important research work to do and for whom undergraduates in the college were simply a way to help pay their salaries) and that the "mission of the university," the "life of the mind," was much more important than the anti-war activities of the students, who were endangering the university's very existence. Some of these distinguished faculty members were refugees from Nazi Germany and would compare the students to the Nazi Brownshirts who destroyed Germany's universities.

When the president of the university called me the next day to ask if there was anything he could do, Bob Ross suggested that I tell him to make a public statement contradicting Janowitz's lie—which he did.

As we waited, I learned the truth as it had been pieced together: Dick had been attacked by the so-called reporter, who had bashed in his head and tried to sever his wrist—probably both injuries caused by a hatchet. An undergraduate had arrived at Dick's office, apparently minutes after the attack, and called for a university security guard, who called for an ambulance, placed a tourniquet on Dick's right arm, and probably saved his life.

Later, when a committee of the ASA, meeting in Chicago, passed a resolution of "condolence" to Dick and his family, one committee member, Philip Hauser, a colleague in Dick's department, voted against doing so. That was the atmosphere at the famed university in Hyde Park—and I couldn't stand it!

Actually, I hated everything about Chicago in those days. One December, when Chuck was a year and a half, I came home with a carload of groceries. I couldn't carry both him and the groceries up to our second-floor apartment, so I left the car at our back stairs, took Chuck up and put him in his high chair with his favorite finger foods, and went back for the groceries. I found that a small gang of neighborhood boys—eight- or ten-year-old African American children—had grabbed my groceries and were running away with them. I gave chase, and they dropped most of the bags. I was angry, of course, but I realized that our building was a white interloper in the African American neighborhood of Woodlawn—separated from Hyde Park and the University of Chicago campus by the Midway, a grass and tree-lined boulevard. (Today, an actual ten-foot-high chain-link fence separates that university-owned building we lived in from the rest of Woodlawn.) We, the University of Chicago community, were the intruders in the neighborhood—and taking advantage of us seemed natural to me. Within the following weeks, we were the victims of a pocket picking—my wallet was taken while I was in line at a drugstore (and then returned minus its cash, but with all else intact—for which I was grateful) and a "home invasion"—a young man armed with a "zip gun" forced his way into our apartment and made off with my wallet (after socking me in the jaw when I tried to stop him). The second time, my credit and department store cards were used to buy obvious Christmas presents for the robber's friends and family—toys, a cheap watch, cosmetics, and so on. I understood what was going on, but I did not feel that I deserved to be the victim of the inequities in our society. I was also very worried about raising children in this milieu—not so much fearing for their safety, but not understanding how to avoid developing racism in them. How, if they grew up here, would they ever feel (as I had in Atlanta) that their safety and security lay in the black neighborhood?

In general, the state of "race relations" in Chicago at this time (1964–69) was, to me, akin to that in Mississippi. The city was totally segregated, with invisible walls seemingly between neighborhoods. Ironically, only Hyde Park had something of an integrated population—black and white united against the poor, it used to be called—which soon came up against the "wall" of Woodlawn. As New Yorkers, we were used to at least riding the subway with people of all races and nationalities and having a sense that we all lived in the same community; even if our neighborhoods were all one color, we met other folks at school and in the course of our daily lives. And my neighborhood, built around the old Communist Party "Coops," had many people of color; I went to college at CCNY in Harlem. African Americans were in my world—but in Chicago, they seemed to exist only as "the other."

When Martin Luther King Jr. decided that Chicago's time to change had come, in 1965, he began a series of marches through the city's streets. In June 1965, we took newborn Chuck in his baby carriage to march in downtown Chicago—with mostly black folks. A year or so later, King organized a march through Chicago's Southwest Side, a community of ethnic whites—working-class Poles and Slavs. I decided to go to this march as a "spy"—that is, I "hid" in my white skin, put on a skirt (instead of my usual jeans), and hesitated about wearing my sandals (though I finally did). I dressed one-year-old Chuck (in a sailor suit, I think), plopped him in his stroller, and went to stand on the sidewalks of southwestern Chicago (only a mile or so from Hyde Park/Woodlawn). What I observed will stay with me forever. Young matrons like me were standing on the sidewalk waiting for the marchers to arrive. They had paper shopping bags with them, filled with empty bottles of all sorts. The atmosphere was tense and ugly: at one point, a car came by, driven by an African American man. He had to stop for a red light, and the car was soon surrounded by a crowd of screaming women; they began rocking the car, meaning to overturn it. Fortunately, the light changed, and the car drove off—in a hail of thrown bottles.

When the marchers finally appeared, the crowd hooted and jeered. Their greatest wrath, however, was reserved for a group of nuns among the marchers. The young women on the sidewalk threw their bottles at them in a furious frenzy—maybe remembering the discipline exacted on them by nuns back in Catholic school. One woman exhausted all the bottles in her shopping bag, and as she began to throw her baby's bottle at the nuns, she was restrained by her friend. . . . I had never experienced such raw hatred—and I quickly retreated to my Hyde Park/Woodlawn "haven of civility," where the racist hatred was usually much more hidden. Needless to say, I did not feel at home in Chicago.

Part of our life in Chicago was the SDS JOIN project, a program to "organize the unemployed" of the Uptown neighborhood on the North Side.[3] Post-graduate SDS members were now engaged in a number of such projects in cities, including Cleveland and Newark, as well as Chicago; the goal was organizing "an interracial movement of the poor." They lived communally in an apartment in Uptown and were paid (as I remember) $10 a week; they ate mostly peanut butter and spent their time trying to organize the mostly Appalachian immigrants into such a movement. As before, it was difficult for me to relate to this project, even though some of my best SDS comrades were involved.

I was still skeptical of working for the "movement" instead of having a job with "the man," and I didn't see how middle-class "kids" would be able to effectively communicate with working- and lower-class "red necks." Although some bridges were built—actually more in cities where the projects were in black communities—the enterprise was generally less than successful. (Recently, I learned that some of the original JOIN staff had remained in Chicago and formed the backbone of the Harold Washington mayoral campaign. They are still important activists on the Chicago scene.) I hired some of those JOIN SDSers to interview for the University of Michigan Survey Research Center, but I generally kept my distance from the project.

Dick was more involved—but I think everything soon gave over to the exigencies of the anti-war in Vietnam movement. SDS organized the first national demonstration against the war in April 1965. For students, it was spring break—but I was working at the La Rabida Institute and was six months pregnant. I decided to go anyway and heaved myself up onto the chartered bus for Washington, D.C. (I called my boss from a turnpike rest stop, pretending to be at home with a sore throat.) I'm very glad that I went, because we were "in at the beginning" of the massive anti–Vietnam War movement: we had expected maybe five thousand people, and about seventeen thousand showed up! SDS resident Paul Potter gave a truly brilliant speech, at which he said that we would never eliminate the wars like Vietnam unless we learned to recognize the "system" that produced them, and he urged us to "name the system!" (I suggested "Irving"; I was my usual somewhat cynical self.)

As a result of that march, SDS became the de facto leader of the anti-war movement, and Dick became a major lecturer on the Chicago circuit, going to one event after another, one meeting after another—mostly while I was home with baby Chuck. We were also short on cash (the University of Chicago, being so prominent, paid its faculty peanuts, and it kept all salaries secret), so I became one of many, many junior faculty or graduate student wives working from home, grading papers for a correspondence high school GED (general equivalency diploma) program. My biology degree, again, got me a (very small) salary to help put food on the table. I don't remember feeling particularly resentful about being left out of so much that was happening around me because, as I've noted, I wasn't terribly enamored of most of it. I also felt that I had no "credential" in a student movement, being neither student nor teacher. I did accept a fairly typical female supportive role: I kept the home fires burning while Dick went off to war (against war). I also remember welcoming the SNCC and JOIN refugees living on peanut butter to our home for a good dinner, although some of them got a little sick from eating the unaccustomed food!

This was also the time when the women's movement was born—second-wave feminism. I had read Betty Friedan, of course (Dick's response had been: "What makes her think men have it so good?"), but I came from a different tradition. My parents had both worked (until my mother became legally blind) and had used day care for my brother back in 1933. But it was more than work—it was the notion that I came to understand: a certain amount of shit exists in life—whether it be literally in a baby's diaper or the drudgery of cleaning, cooking, and making a home life. Those tasks, that shit, ought to be (and was, in my experience) shared by both husband and wife. My mother used to tell of showing up unannounced at the apartment my father shared with his sister (before my parents lived together) and finding "Hartman" (as he was known to my mother) in an apron with a dust rag in his hand; she told this story quite proudly. . . . The Communist Party Left proclaimed, at least, a basic equality between the sexes, and our heroes included the storied women tractor drivers of the USSR. In addition, I was a tomboy as a kid, and I always felt inferior to no man—in any sense. Whatever had to be done, in any setting, he could do or I could do—no difference. And work, to us, was what put food on the table and wasn't thought of as a "career." Being a college graduate simply made possible having an easier job than sewing machine operator. I carried this working-class sensibility with me always (still do, I think) and felt it differentiated me from most of the SDSers and folks in the New Left movement(s).

I also perceived the early young feminists in Chicago as looking down on marriage and family, seeing it as a betrayal of feminist consciousness. Merna Villarejo, a young science graduate student at the University of Chicago (now a renowned biochemist and professor—and mother—and was herself a red diaper baby and was also married to one), and I even wrote a "defense of motherhood" article for some feminist newsletter—which achieved some level of fame (or infamy!). While I understood that "sisterhood is powerful," I certainly did not feel at ease with or close to my sisters in the Chicago feminist scene. In fact, their strident militancy (as I perceived it) was one more strike against the city of Chicago.

DICK:

The story of the attack on me was big front-page news in Chicago newspapers and made national news as well: Founder of SDS brutally attacked, professor brutally attacked, and so forth. In a cliché of the city's yellow journalism, Hearst's Chicago newspaper, *American,* tried to sneak photographers posing as doctors into my room in the intensive care unit. But the hospital and university had wisely arranged twenty-four-hour security protection.

When I awakened, a week after the attack, I somehow had the sense that it had been a political incident, even if its origination was at that time opaque. The fact that the attacker had been posing as a newspaperman and asked me a question about the protests was evidence of something political. I wasn't sure what might have motivated the attack but conjectured that the considerable notoriety in the local media as a defender of protesters made me a visible target. It was several years later that a plausible scenario to explain the attack was pieced together.

I spent a month at Billings Hospital recovering from my injuries. The recovery involved not only surgery on my skull but also blood transfusions and a good deal of physical therapy to get me walking again. I left the hospital with a brace on my leg and a catheter for my bladder, so I was hardly fully recovered, but I was happy to get out of there. One thing that kept me going during that month was the fact that we received literally hundreds of letters, cards, and telegrams from people all over the country who were expressing their support, their sympathy, their solidarity. These messages quite tangibly helped me set aside the pain and discomfort.

I was released shortly before graduation day at the University of Chicago. Activist students had organized a counter-commencement and I was very gratified to be asked to speak (along with Benjamin Spock). I wasn't in any condition to physically go to the ceremony (held in Rockefeller Chapel), but I made a brief recording, which was played there. Before the event, Spock showed up for a visit to our apartment. We'd met him briefly at an earlier occasion, when we were visiting Ann Arbor with baby Chuck and were able to get the personal, hands-on blessing of our baby from the world's most famous baby doctor. Now, baby Marc got it too! All this attention certainly helped my recovery!

There wasn't unanimous solidarity from my colleagues, however. Immediately in the aftermath of the attack on me, Janowitz declared, to various people, that I had attempted suicide—and that maybe now I could get help for my emotional distress. That was a shocking thing for him to have made up. It's possible that he sincerely believed that account, yet it's hard to imagine how he could have, since the evidence of an attack was straightforward. The day after I was hospitalized, the department voted a message of sympathy, with the abstention of Philip Hauser, who stated something to the effect that this was chickens coming home to roost. I found it hard to believe this story, until not long after, I was told by more than one participant, that Hauser had said similar things at a national council meeting of the ASA when members discussed a motion of solidarity with me. Hauser's hatred of me probably dated from the time he believed that I wanted to disrupt his convening of the ASA. A few days before the attack on me, I encountered him on the street; he spit at my feet, muttering about me and my little Maoists, before crossing to get away. It's emblematic of one facet of the sixties generational upheaval that someone of great professional stature, and with a history of active support for social justice, could become a sort of raving fascist when his authority was called into question.

I have to say that I certainly provided some discomfort for my colleagues. My vocal and active opposition in the Dixon matter was exacerbated by the fact that earlier in the year I had received an offer of tenure from the sociology department at UCSB. I told Janowitz of this offer and asked if the department could review me for tenure and match the California offer. This meant that, beginning in March, the department (and the undergraduate college independently) was in the process of evaluating my case, with a decision target date that turned out to coincide with my hospitalization. It was certainly not an easy matter for them to decide—I had a very short list of publications, and now I had become a martyred victim, in the wake of great turmoil resulting from the earlier Dixon decision. I wanted them, however, to do this review—as a test of whether their claims of objectivity in assessing the quality of intellectual work might hold up. Although I'd published little, I did have a co-authored book (based on the Bennington College work I'd done with Ted Newcomb) and a couple of very widely cited articles based on my research on the social psychology of student activism. The research project we had launched was decidedly pathbreaking, and I knew that the project's design, its findings, and the interpretive framework I had developed for it certainly made a case for tenure—as indeed the department at UCSB had recognized. I was, objectively, a rising star—and had been told as much a few months earlier by a couple of younger tenured colleagues.

The outcome of the vote, which, as I recall, was conducted while I was nearing the end of my hospital stay, was interesting and peculiar. I was awarded tenure as a professor in the college but promoted to "associate professor without tenure" in the sociology department, a position that I believe was unique in the university at that time. So, technically, this offer did not match UCSB's; I could stay at Chicago if I so chose, but I had grounds for leaving based on my public assertions about "matching" being required.

Actually, even before that vote, Mickey and I had decided we were going to go to California. We had strong family reasons for the move: her brother, Hershl, and his family lived in Los Angeles, and her mother was alone, living in the Bronx. It made sense to move to Santa Barbara so that her mother could come out to join her children and grandchildren in Southern California. Also, after the fact that I was almost killed in Chicago, it seemed extremely logical that we would go to a more restful and seemingly more insulated environment like one that Santa Barbara could provide. And the UCSB department was making a name for itself in its fostering of critical and innovative perspectives on the discipline and on society. Intellectually, it promised me a home that I never could have in the Chicago sociology department.

A lot of the graduate students, however, were extremely upset by the department's decision not to offer me tenure, and their effort to find out why resulted in still another example of Janowitz's great capacity for fabrication. They confronted him, asking to know why I had not gotten tenure in the department, and he said that my letters from outside evaluators were deficient. For example, he said, Barrington Moore (a noted social theorist) had written a letter evaluating my work, which did not endorse me for tenure. But Moore had sent me a copy of his letter, which spoke enthusiastically about my work, though lacking a direct statement for or against tenure. Perhaps, on the one hand, this assessment could be read as Janowitz claimed; on the other hand, it most certainly could have been used to make the case for tenure as well! More problematic was Janowitz's claim that Kenneth Keniston had failed to write a letter for me. A letter from Keniston was particularly important, because at the time Keniston, at Yale University, was the leading figure in research on understanding the social psychology of student activism, and therefore his evaluation was the single most important one needed for my case. I called Keniston when I heard what Janowitz had claimed and asked him whether he had been asked to write a letter for my tenure review. He told me that he had not been asked for an evaluation by the sociology department; he had been asked only by the college—and had written an enthusiastic letter. Janowitz, responding to graduate student protest, simply fabricated the basis for the department's failure to award tenure.

A few days after getting out of the hospital (and just after having my catheter and urine bag finally removed) and just after having told the department (and the press, which had asked) that I was leaving, I got a call from Janowitz asking me to come see him in his office. It was one of the strangest conversations of my life. First he wanted to tell me that I would have gotten tenure a year from now in the department. He stated that only one member of the department had made a point of voting against me for political reasons, and he named Hauser as that person (thereby violating one of the cardinal rules of academia protecting the confidentiality of professorial reviews). I remarked that he had not told me that I could've gotten tenure a year from now until after I resigned. I have no way of knowing whether his "prediction" would have turned out, but I couldn't help being privately glad to believe that I in fact qualified for tenure in this most elite of sociology departments.

He went on to urge that he and I remain colleagues; he was worried about the future of the discipline because so many in the New Left were sociology majors who might disrupt the collegiality necessary for the preservation of the field. He remarked that Barrington Moore, despite his Marxism, remained a good friend and colleague, and he hoped that he and I would continue to have that kind of relationship. I didn't say what flashed through my mind—"If that's what you actually want, you'll need to stop lying and bullying." He went on to say that he understood why I needed to leave Chicago and thought it was similar to the situation that led him to leave the University of Michigan sociology department and move to Chicago. He told me that he needed to leave Michigan because of his relationship with a senior professor, Albert Reiss, which he described as Oedipal; it was understandable to him that I needed to establish my autonomy just as he had needed to. There was one difference, he said, between his departure from Michigan and my departure. In his case, he said, he did not call a press conference to announce his decision. I told him that I did not call a press conference either, but that the press was naturally interested in my decision given what transpired here. To this day, I haven't fully decoded the message he might have been trying to send.

Janowitz was hardly typical of academia. As I said earlier, I think he was proud of the fact that he knew how to operate as a kind of street mobster rather than behave as a genteel scholar. He made no effort to conceal his intention to control students and the department terrain; indeed, his election to chair of the sociology department had been delayed because of the mistrust and possibly hatred some senior members felt toward him. His modes of control included a bullying style (which shriveled when he was challenged, as is often the case with bullies) but also a kind of benevolent paternalism directed at graduate students. One of the sweet ironies of those years for me was that many of Janowitz's students were radicalized during that period, in part because of the wider events and movements of the time, but also in reaction to him. Within two or three years after we left Chicago, some of the most respected senior figures in the department departed as well, including Peter Blau, Peter and Alice Rossi, Bill Hodge, and Nathan Keyfitz. Perhaps they also had Oedipal problems with Janowitz.

There's a final chapter to the story of my relationship with Janowitz that occurred twenty years after I left Chicago. I had the chance to return to Hyde Park for the first time since leaving. My book *Making History* had recently come out, and, much to my pleasure, former SDS leader and Weatherperson Bernadine Dohrn, by then well established as a force in Chicago, offered to help me get the book promoted in Chicago. She arranged a book signing in the 57th Street Seminary Co-op Bookstore. It was a very pleasurable afternoon. Many people whom I knew back in the day came by to give greetings, the turnout was good and nostalgia filled the room. Just at the end of our allotted time, a youngish woman came in, trembling with, it turned out, anger. "How dare you come back to this community you had tried to destroy," she blurted out. "Let alone to this bookstore!" I was taken aback, to say the least, and asked her who she was. She told me that she was Morris Janowitz's daughter and that my appearance in the bookstore was particularly inappropriate, since her father had helped found the store in the 1950s. She said that when she was a teenager back in 1969, she shared the movement's evaluation of her parents. She thought they were war criminals then, but over time she learned that they were the true heroes. "You, I realized were the villains!" she said. She reported to me that her parents received threats in the mail and on the phone. When I denied knowing about that, she said, "You're the one who stimulated and inspired the threats!" I thought that was ironic, to say the least. I was the one who'd been assaulted. He was the one who tried to depict the assault as attempted suicide, I tried to tell her.

Bernadine Dohrn was seated at the table next to me while this exchange was happening. Hearing this verbal attack, she burst out: "Here, I, Bernadine

Dohrn, queen of violence, have never been attacked in person like you, mild mannered professor, just were!"

When I got home a few days later, I learned from a *New York Times* obituary, that Morris Janowitz died the day after my encounter. Rebecca Janowitz, out of loyalty and stress, found a way to deal with her grief and to speak for him at that moment.


## WHO ATTACKED ME AND WHY?

DICK:

In the 1970s, largely in the aftermath of the Watergate scandals, there was a burst of legal action and investigative reporting aimed at unearthing illegal or questionable government surveillance and undercover practices in the 1960s. A particularly ambitious project was based in Chicago, and a few years after leaving the city, I received a batch of material from this committee—copies of leaflets, news clippings, and photos concerning a group called the Legion of Justice. The material provided circumstantial evidence suggesting that the legion may have been behind the attack on me.

The most striking evidence was a copy of a mimeographed flyer announcing a Legion of Justice rally to be held at the *exact time that my assailant came to my office.* The rally was held at the University of Illinois Chicago Circle campus, and it was billed as a protest against communist-sympathizing professors. There was mention of people who wore Vietcong rings. That was an interesting tidbit—the slashing of my right wrist perhaps was motivated by the fact that I indeed was wearing the ring I'd received from the Vietnamese in Bratislava—a ring made from metal supposedly crafted from a downed U.S. bomber. The materials indicated that all the known Legion of Justice activists were visibly present at that rally. It has seemed quite plausible to me that the rally was staged to provide these activists with alibis concerning the assault on me. That the legion was connected to the national vigilante network called the Minutemen made it possible for them to import a hit man from elsewhere to do the deed and make a quick getaway.

The Legion of Justice seems to have started in 1969 at about the time the sit-in at the University of Chicago began. One day the administration building was invaded by club-wielding men who proceeded to beat up some of the students inside. They identified themselves as the Legion of Justice. A right-wing political figure, Thomas Sutton, claimed to be the group's founder and leader. Over the next couple of years, the legion claimed credit for various acts of vandalism and disruption directed against left-wing and anti-war groups, They never claimed connection with the attack on me (possibly since the attacker would have been guilty of attempted murder), but I've come to assume that they were involved. By the mid-1970s, connections between the Legion of Justice and the Chicago police "Red Squad" were well documented. That connection echoed similar linkages between police and private vigilante and death squads in many parts of the world— with police suggesting a target for criminal attack and the private groups administering "justice" and also doing undercover spying that the police agencies were not authorized to do.

In 1975 Congress established a committee chaired by Idaho senator Frank Church to investigate illegal activities of government intelligence agencies. I was contacted by committee staff who told me that I had been one of several dozen SDS leaders targeted by the FBI under its secret Counterintelligence Program (COINTELPRO). The program, aimed at disrupting organizations the FBI deemed subversive, used various undercover and deceptive tactics— break-ins, threatening anonymous communications typically designed to foment mutual distrust among organizational leaders, and efforts to cause trouble for individual activists. Committee staff members visited me in Santa Barbara and showed me copies of memorandums signed by J. Edgar Hoover authorizing the sending of letters to the University of Chicago Board of Trustees and signed "concerned alumus [sic]." The letters included a detailed listing of alleged subversive activity on my part and urged that they consider whether I belonged on the faculty. Hoover's memo suggested that having me fired was a goal of this effort. I found the letters amusing, especially since the word *alumnus* was spelled *alumus*; I doubted that University of Chicago officials would pay much heed to an anonymous correspondent who couldn't spell.

Shortly after getting this stuff, I was called by a *New York Times* reporter, asking if I was the same Richard Flacks who had been a professor in 1969 at the University of Chicago. The "concerned alumus" letter had become public. Edward Levi's appointment as attorney general was being considered by the Senate Judiciary Committee, and he revealed that he'd been the target of COINTELPRO activity, explaining that he had received this letter about me. The *Times* reporter was interested in something more—the fact that the COINTELPRO action against me was dated just a few days before I was physically attacked. He wanted to know if there might be a connection. I said I had no idea, but he wrote the story so that a connection between my targeting by the FBI and the attack could be inferred.

Since I was in fact a target of FBI surveillance at the time, what did the FBI know about the assault? And once it happened, how did they react? It was possible, under the recently adopted Freedom of Information Act (FOIA), to get copies of one's FBI files. And, out of the blue, I was contacted by Maryann Mott, General Motors heiress, who was becoming known as a very generous philanthropic supporter of progressive causes. Maryann had been talking with mutual friends and wanted to offer funding for me to hire a lawyer who would launch an effort to get my FBI materials.

We undertook that effort. After some months, we received copies of the file from the FBI's national headquarters. These were rather heavily redacted—the FOIA allowed the FBI to withhold information that might compromise their methods or name their undercover sources. But more obvious than the redactions was the fact that the files were incomplete—they were by and large summaries of information evidently detailed elsewhere but not provided. So we made a broader and more penetrating series of FOIA requests, directed at each of the local FBI offices in places I'd lived, asking for all files about me in each locale. After many more months, I received a large carton, which was maybe three feet high, filled with documents and, most usefully, containing an index of every document in my files, including those that had been withheld.

I learned that the FBI opened a file on me when I was ten years old—I was after all a camper at Wo-Chi-Ca, an undoubted communist front. I was from then on a subject; when I went to Ann Arbor for graduate school, for instance, the FBI inquired after me with my landlord and with school authorities. Apparently, they opened a different file when SDS became a target, and it took them some time to merge my two dangerous identities. From the early sixties on, there were many inquiries about me personally or, at least, as part of more extensive investigations of things I was involved in. My file became a fairly good repository of news stories about me, interspersed with transcripts of phone conversations (labeled as reports by unnamed informants). My only potentially unlawful activity that was noticed was my public advocacy of draft resistance (a crime for which, in fact, Benjamin Spock and others did face trial).

But what didn't appear in the hundreds of documents was any FBI report relating to the assault (though a few news clippings about it did show up).

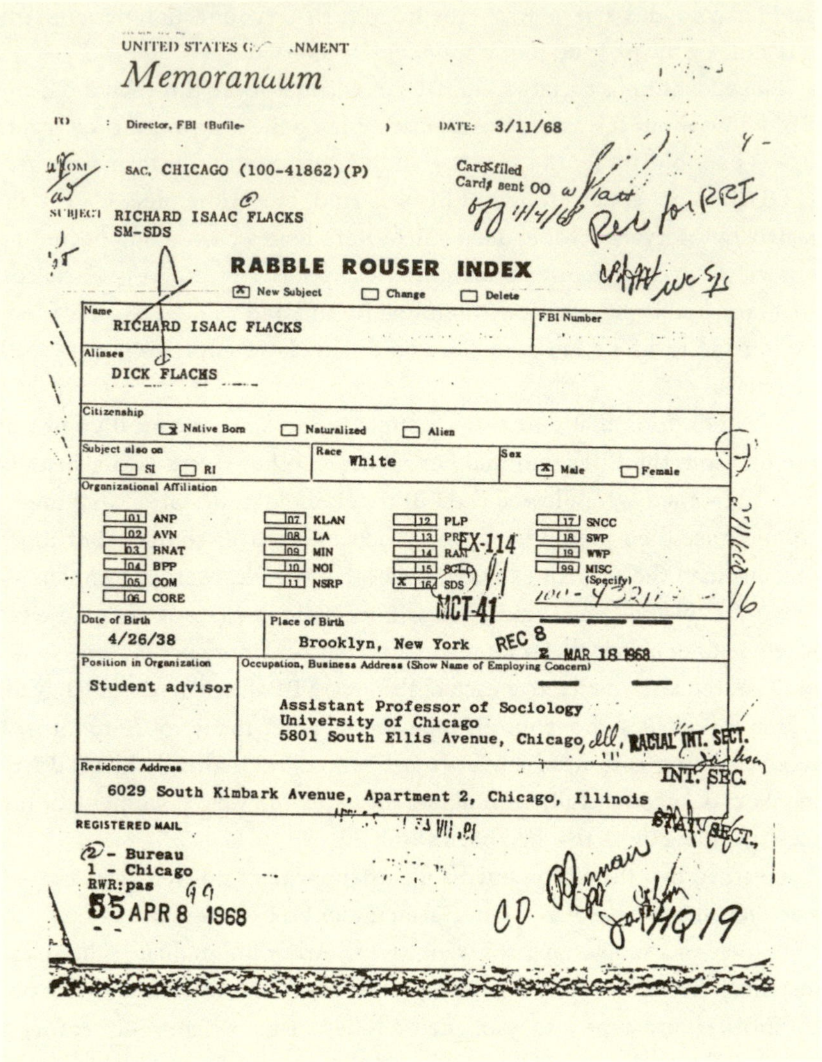

UNITED STATES GOVERNMENT

*Memorandum*

TO : Director, FBI (Bufile- )

DATE: 3/11/68

FROM : SAC, CHICAGO (100-41862)(P)

Cards filed
Cards sent

SUBJECT: RICHARD ISAAC FLACKS
SM-SDS

**RABBLE ROUSER INDEX**

☒ New Subject ☐ Change ☐ Delete

| | |
|---|---|
| Name: RICHARD ISAAC FLACKS | FBI Number: |
| Aliases: DICK FLACKS | |
| Citizenship: ☒ Native Born ☐ Naturalized ☐ Alien | |
| Subject also on: ☐ SI ☐ RI | Race: White |
| Sex: ☒ Male ☐ Female | |
| Date of Birth: 4/26/38 | Place of Birth: Brooklyn, New York |
| Position in Organization: Student advisor | Occupation, Business Address (Show Name of Employing Concern): Assistant Professor of Sociology, University of Chicago, 5801 South Ellis Avenue, Chicago, Ill. |
| Residence Address: 6029 South Kimbark Avenue, Apartment 2, Chicago, Illinois | |

Organizational Affiliation: 01 ANP; 02 AVN; 03 RNAT; 04 BPP; 05 COM; 06 CORE; 07 KLAN; 08 LA; 09 MIN; 10 NOI; 11 NSRP; 12 PLP; 13 PR; 14 RAM; 15 SCLC; ☒ 16 SDS; 17 SNCC; 18 SWP; 19 WWP; 99 MISC (Specify)

EX-114

REC 8

MAR 18 1968

RACIAL INT. SECT.

INT. SEC.

REGISTERED MAIL

2 - Bureau
1 - Chicago
RWR:pas

55 APR 8 1968

FIGURE 10.2. Sample page from Dick's FBI file. In addition to being listed in the Rabble Rouser Index, he was on the Agitator and Security Indexes.

That prompted us to sue—because the document index we received indicated that there were in fact materials filed at the time of the attack that were not provided to us initially. We instituted a suit to get documents relevant to that assault and asked that my lawyer be able to interrogate the Chicago agent in charge at that time. Judge John Sirica granted the latter request (somewhat

# Chicago Tribune

## THE WORLD'S GREATEST NEWSPAPER

### Saturday, December 20, 1975

# Ex-U. of C. prof may sue FBI for conspiracy

By Peter Reich

A FORMER University of Chicago professor who was the target of an FBI smear attempt seven years ago, says he may sue the FBI for conspiring to deprive him of his livelihood.

The professor, Dr. Richard I. Flacks, now is chairman of the sociology department of the University of California at Santa Barbara.

He told The Tribune in a telephone interview that he is also thinking of filing suit to find out "if there were any other FBI actions against me."

IT WAS DISCLOSED in Washington Thursday that FBI counterintelligence agents in 1968 wrote an anonymous letter to University of Chicago officials accusing Flacks of "working for a group that will support and provide leadership for student rebellions."

The letter—signed "Concerned Alumus" [sic]—asserted that "it is difficult to understand why the University . . . would want to continue to employ an individual who is working for student rebellions."

Flacks had been an official of the radical Students for a Democratic Society, was a participant in scores of campus and Anti-Viet Nam War demonstrations, and had publicly urged students to resist the draft.

ON MAY 5, 1969, FLACKS was severely beaten by an assailant who entered his office in the Harper Library, 1126 E. 59th St., under guise of seeking an interview. Flacks suffered a fractured skull and a severely cut wrist.

The attacker was never apprehended.

Flacks said he has always believed his assailant "was a member of a vigilante group," and added, "I prefer to believe he had no connection with the FBI." The FBI's mailing of the anti-Flacks letter was made public last Thursday by Atty. Gen. Edward Levi in testimony before the Senate Select Committee on Intelligence.

Records show that on July 26, 1968, the special agent in charge of the FBI field office in Chicago had requested permission of his superiors to send an anonymous letter discrediting Flacks to the University of Chicago board of trustees, and to The Tribune. Permission was granted.

HOWEVER, NO ONE at The Tribune can recall receiving such a letter.

Flacks said he was unaware of the letter until recently, and that, apparently, the letter resulted in no action by university officials.

He said he left the University of Chicago of his own volition, in the fall of 1969.

Flacks, 37, is married and the father of two children. He says he is still active in politics, currently serving as chairman of a Santa Barbara County committee to elect Tom Hayden, former student radical leader and husband of movie star Jane Fonda, to the U.S. Senate.

Richard Flacks

x-fac

FIGURE 10.3. *Chicago Tribune* report of Dick's action against the FBI

surprisingly, since the FBI assiduously tries to protect its agents, especially retired ones, from this sort of thing). And the judge declared that he would review each of the withheld documents that we suspected might be relevant, to see if in fact they were.

Judge Sirica declared that some of the documents shouldn't be turned over to us since they would unnecessarily jeopardize FBI procedures and informants and weren't relevant to the suit. He either inadvertently or slyly gave as an example a document indicating that the person who chauffeured Spock on the day he visited us was an undercover FBI informant—and, the judge said, we did not need to have that document. Of course, by saying that, the judge, in fact, blew the cover of the informant in question, who turned out to be an undergraduate who had sought opportunities to take independent study courses with me. He soon surfaced as an involuntary witness in some proceeding; he had infiltrated both SDS and the communist youth group, the DuBois Clubs, and in that undercover role had been one of the rare African American members of these Chicago chapters.

There was one document the judge turned over. It revealed that a "previously reliable informant" had declared that members of the Chicago police were involved in the assault on me. The document concluded that the informant could no longer be regarded as reliable. This was the closest thing to a "smoking gun" that our foray into the files turned up. I wondered whether we had grounds to pursue a legal action against the FBI. Hadn't they withheld evidence of a crime? Hadn't I been subjected, from childhood, to surveillance that violated my rights? My lawyers thought that such a suit would be very costly and probably fruitless.

By 1976, we were not eager, in any case, to get further immersed in the matter. We considered for a while whether it might be a good idea to hire a private investigator, who could penetrate the right-wing world in Chicago to see what else might be learned about the story. But I felt strongly that I wanted to live life fully and forwardly and not get obsessed with uncovering the assailant's identity and the precise provenance of his actions. The lawyers may well be correct—we would find such an exploration both frightening and futile. And, at the time, there were a number of systematic investigations and legal actions that were fruitfully exposing—and generating useful regulation of—the misdeeds of government police agencies.

I'm writing this account almost forty-eight years after the attack. I still bear its scars: an indented skull, an inability to hop on my left leg, and a right hand that's only partially functional. But apart from limiting my ability to (badly) play tennis, piano, and guitar, I've not felt handicapped or significantly damaged.

I learned some lessons from the experience about the relationship between movements and media spotlights. It was, after all, odd that the attack was aimed at me, the mild-mannered professor, and not the self-proclaimed white revolutionary leaders who were in Chicago at that time. I think I was a target of choice for two reasons: one, there may have been a perception that professors were sort of puppet masters of student protest, and, two, I had not been avoiding opportunities to be quoted in justification and support for what the students were up to. I didn't realize at the time that all of the "excesses" and outrages done in the name of the movement—including the things that were done in its name that I opposed—would nevertheless be heaped on the head of someone like me. I was in the spotlight as a defender of the movement, but had in reality no voice in determining the direction or behavior of its participants. Maybe, I began to think, this wasn't a tenable position to be in! I came to realize that the media spotlight provided not only a chance to speak for the movement but a far too tempting seduction that might turn out to be a trap. One's health—both political and personal—might well depend on resisting that seduction.

## A WORD ABOUT MARLENE DIXON

DICK:

Fifty years ago, in the midst of all the tumult, I entertained the thought that the sit-in and all its reverberations could best be depicted as an epic novel. I never tried to produce such a work, but if I had, I think its core would be defined by two strange characters: one was Morris Janowitz, whom we've already met. The other was Marlene Dixon.

I met her first when she arrived at the University of Chicago in 1966. She was a big-boned and chubby woman, with oversized glasses, who wore, as I recall, tailored suits (which were not flattering to her figure), presumably to suggest a rigorous professionalism. In other words, she was pretty uptight and pretty anxious. And no wonder—not only was she the relatively rare woman, needing to impress a coldly indifferent, if not disdainful, male hierarchy, but her working-class background surely added to her insecurity. Moreover, she confessed, she'd done a dissertation on a dry, easily forgettable subject because her mentors thought it was the quickest way to get done and out into the job market. But that sort of advice is shortsighted—how might she find the inspiration she'd need to turn out publishable work based on a dissertation she pretty well despised?

Marlene had one seemingly good professional benefit at Chicago: she was a member of the interdisciplinary Department of Human Development, which had senior women on the faculty, a generally liberal and nurturing set of colleagues, and a number of mature women graduate students. So she spent her time there; in fact, I think her salary was budgeted to that department. Her undergraduate teaching, however, was done in sociology, largely out of the sight and awareness of the senior sociology faculty.

I'm sure I encouraged Marlene to find ways to be inspired in her teaching and not think that adherence to a conventional curriculum was a good strategy for success, let alone fulfillment. And soon she was letting her socially critical side find expression in her classes and in her intellectual projects. She did at least one act of public defiance. According to the *Chicago Maroon*, writing about it forty years later: "During a faculty procession at the inauguration of Edward Levi, the University's eighth president, the openly Marxist and feminist Dixon opted to stand alongside the 100 students chanting 'Work, study, get ahead, kill!' outside the main entrance of Chicago's Conrad Hilton instead of entering the hotel with her colleagues."

I'm not sure whether her act of solidarity with the students actually occurred at the Hilton or, more likely, at an on-campus ceremonial procession, but when her contract was terminated, this act was taken to be a reason. In any event, she became a cause célébre, and I was her chief adviser. I urged that she not get out in front of the student protest if she wanted to have an academic future. The protest had to be the work of the students, and in truth it was. There was no way politically or personally that she would gain by being seen as its leader. Still, she was the recipient of a good many threats, and, as it usually did when targeting persons it disliked, the *Chicago Tribune* published her address. I suggested that she move out of her apartment and asked our close friend and neighbor Joan Wallach Scott if she could stay with her and family for a while. The Scotts were willing to have her stay there, and Marlene arrived at their apartment, plopped down on the living room couch, declared that she would "require" a case of beer, and requested Joan's company to help her find an appropriate outfit for a press conference. I suddenly realized that I might be a Dr. Frankenstein: this was a new Marlene, assertive, self-important, dominating—and needing a good supply of alcohol. I hadn't really seen this Marlene before.

In general, however, Marlene followed my advice and stayed out of the limelight. When Hanna Gray's committee supported her termination, they had recommended that she be given an additional year's appointment—an offer Marlene promptly rejected. At some point, Marlene took off for a West Coast vacation trip (maybe she had gotten a leave from the university), returning to visit me in the hospital. By then she was even more bubbly and assertive. And I think by then she'd decided on a new, historical role for herself: she was going to be the first female Lenin—the Lenin of feminism.

She got an appointment at McGill University in Montreal for a while, but she decided in 1974 to move to San Francisco. There she established her own party—Democratic Workers Party—which she led in the classic Leninist style. It was one of a number of such new Communist parties in that period, but was distinctive in that it emphasized critiquing feminism from a class point of view, as well as her ability to recruit and dominate a considerable number of PhDs and MDs. Despite its proletarian name, her organization, which went through several permutations, was largely populated by professionals, maybe because of Marlene's way of evoking guilt in privileged folk. DWP and its successors had some success organizing and institution building, but its cultish quality was its undoing, since Marlene often markedly shifted her line and required her followers to faithfully take every turn. Eventually, while she was traveling abroad, there was a rebellion; Marlene was expelled and the party dissolved. Marlene was brilliant, but unstable, to say the least. The rebellion was fueled by her alcoholism, and her story ended up as a sort of caricature of left-wing sectarianism. A good study of it can be found in a book by Janja Lalich, *Bounded Choice: True Believers and Charismatic Cults.*[4] Marlene died in obscurity in 2008.

The sixties ended, conveniently enough, by the summer of 1969. I was, fortunately, in no shape to personally witness certain other Chicago happenings that symbolized that ending—particularly a crazed SDS convention that signified the organization's collapse into warring sectarian factions and presaged the formation of the Weatherman—that faction of SDS leaders who decided, out of guilt over their own privilege, to set up a revolutionary underground. I was struck, when this was happening, at how many of the Weathermen were the sons and daughters of elite parents or the beneficiaries of elite education. Many of them were deeply affected by witnessing firsthand poverty and oppression in the American South, in Northern ghettos, or in Latin America—and they were deeply affected by the black revolutionary challenge that was rising in those years, which led them to want to short-circuit the social change strategies that were based on mass mobilization and community action and characteristic of the movement until then. Organizing was too slow and, strategy itself was a distraction from a determination to suicidally make oneself into a brick to be hurled at the imperial facade.

That way of thinking, I believe, was rooted not only in guilt (assuaged by a readiness for suicide) but also, ironically, in their privilege—it was natural for some of these folks, born into high status, to believe they had the right to take history into their own hands, rather than work within a democratic framework.

In that, they reminded me of similar patterns by children of privilege in many other pre-revolutionary situations—like the nineteenth-century Russian students who were eager to assassinate members of their parents' aristocracy.

I offer one anecdote to show how the nascent Weather-attitude manifested itself to me: In the spring of 1969, after the sit-in, I was interacting with my fairly large undergraduate class about the events and gave them my perspective. My graduate teaching assistant leaped up, interrupting me to say that I should stop feeding them my line—he had a different perspective (and I don't remember what the substantive issues might have been that divided us). This was a guy who was notable for his intellectual demeanor; I couldn't help but think that in an earlier time he'd have been the perfect *yeshive bocher* (Jewish religious school youth). When the class ended, I asked him what he was up to. He said, "I have to turn myself into a thug!" He was identifying with the Weathermen and had become convinced that armed struggle was necessary and inevitable. So he said he had to transform himself. His bold intervention in class was a way of practicing for that, and he proudly told me that he and a couple of others had pushed a leading conservative faculty member around the day before—all part of the thug-making self-transformation. He later in life regretted his Weather moment—but the emotions he expressed at the time were not untypical at Chicago, Columbia, and other campuses by 1969.

## STICKING WITH IT

DICK:

Somehow, the onrush of very disturbing, grotesque, and scary experiences of that time didn't leave Mickey and me with any desire to opt out of the political—or the academic—world. But we knew we were very lucky to be able to move to the beckoning paradise of Santa Barbara, California. A few days after Neil Armstrong walked on the moon in July 1969, we boarded the plane for Los Angeles.

# 11 ▸ MOVING TO CALIFORNIA

DICK:

My parents flew with us to California, while our belongings traveled by moving van. We were renting the house of our new colleague, Bill Chambliss, who was on sabbatical in Africa. My parents decided to camp out in the Santa Barbara house; meanwhile, before the moving van arrived, we spent a week with our Chicago friends Don and Merna Villarejo, who had moved to Los Angeles the previous year.

That week in Los Angeles was a sweet entry into life in Southern California. UCLA had a sort of country club setup for faculty and staff families, so much of our time was spent by its huge pool. It was a time when California was a mecca, embodying possible futures for the rest of America. Its attractions were immediately evident, so we were gently eased out of the madness of our Chicago days.

The Chambliss house was the first house that either Mickey or I had ever managed. Both of us had grown up and lived, until then, in rented apartments and, until coming to California, hadn't even imagined that we'd be homeowners. We had to take instant charge of the Chambliss house and its acre-size backyard, with a number of orange, lemon, and other fruit trees and a lawn that had to be mowed. We had to learn to operate a sump pump when it rained, since the little basement inevitably flooded. We had to learn how to cope with a leaky roof and walls. (There was a lot of rain that winter as it happened.) And we had to take care of a large black Labrador retriever, who aggressively barked at children and disabled folks and other helpless beings who dared to pass the house on the road.

Much of the burden of all this caretaking was on Mickey. Even though the brace was off my leg and my bladder was functioning normally, I still was pretty shaky. I'm still, decades later, in awe of her patience at the time, even though her highly urbanized, working-class self was hardly sure she could handle the house along with me and the children (ages four and one). To paraphrase the old soap opera tagline, Could a young girl from the Bronx find happiness in a Santa Barbara paradise?

Still, there's nothing quite so enticing as that first immersion in Southern California climate and the physical beauty of Santa Barbara. There was something idyllic about the scene: the house, surrounded by fruit trees and its large yard, fronting on a more or less country road without side-walks, the fragrances and the bird sounds in the air. And there were the enticements of the beach and ubiquitous swimming pools we found at the homes of new friends. So in the first few weeks of our arrival, we reveled in this new world.

On the day we arrived, we were greeted by Harvey and Linda Molotch at their beautiful little house in Montecito. Mickey will tell about how intimi-dating it was to see their place in the midst of the mess that she felt we were in. Harvey had been a student of mine at the University of Chicago and we had known him previously in Ann Arbor because, as an undergraduate, he worked on the *Michigan Daily* when Tom Hayden was its editor. Harvey had come to Santa Barbara, hired by the sociology department, a year before we arrived. It was he, more than anyone, who was responsible for our decision to move; he stressed, in several letters, both the beauty of the community and the attractiveness of the department itself.

Before we departed Chicago, Harvey sent us information indicating that my appointment at UCSB was quite controversial in the community. The local daily, the *Santa Barbara News-Press*, was filled with letters denouncing my hiring. After all, by 1969, SDS was universally defined as an organization that promoted revolution and violence—and I was said to be one of its founders.

FIGURE 11.1. Mildred and Dave Flacks on their neighborhood tennis court in Goleta, California, 1980s

Santa Barbara's Republican representatives in the state legislature undertook to make an issue of my appointment and their campaign helped stir up quite vocal opposition. There were ads taken out denouncing me in the newspaper and six weeks of continuous attack in the letters column. While I was still in Chicago, a Los Angeles TV news program sent a reporter to interview me on camera, and several of the leading newspapers in the state did phone interviews with me.

Finally, after six weeks of featuring the public outcry, the *News-Press* decided to end its campaign by having a reporter call me for an interview. He asked whether in fact I was an advocate of violence and revolution. I told him that I had never advocated violence, that I was a believer in nonviolent action, and I noted that I had left SDS some years earlier.

The reporter indicated that the *News-Press* had been approached by university officials, who felt that the anti-Flacks campaign was hurting their financial contributions and their standing in the community and pleaded for the campaign to stop. The interview was designed to end the controversy and the newspaper published an editorial, along with the story about the interview, declaring that it was time to wait and see whether the professor really does believe in nonviolence. No further letters were published.

MICKEY:

I was struck by the civility and "niceness" of the Santa Barbarians. As is usual when one moves to a new town, there are many occasions when you are asked to give your name and address—utility connections, new store charge accounts, and so forth. I had some trepidation because of all the publicity about Dick, "the radical professor," and I steeled myself for unpleasantness. On the contrary, a frequent response after I gave my name was "Welcome to Santa Barbara, Mrs. Flacks!"

One exception was at the Department of Motor Vehicles (DMV). . . . I went to take my driver's test in order to get a California license. The instructor told me that I had failed the driving test. I (whose driving was a source of great pride) sputtered: "This is the fourth state in which I've applied for a license, and I've NEVER failed!" "Well why don't you go back where you came from, Mrs. Flacks?"

When I got home (having driven with my Illinois license), I called the DMV and asked to speak to a supervisor. "I think I've been discriminated against on my driving test," I complained. By his concerned response, I realized that he assumed I was African American. "Oh, please come in

tomorrow at 11:00 a.m., and I'll give you the test myself," he said, solici-
tously. I did, he gave me the test, I passed, and he apologized for any problem. The first DMV guy was obviously an anomaly.


## SOCIOLOGY UCSB STYLE

DICK:

The UCSB sociology department had been established as a graduate program in the mid-1960s when UCSB became a full-fledged campus of the
University of California. The first social science dean at UCSB was noted
sociologist Don Cressey, who was imported from UCLA, where he had
chaired the department in the sixties. He and David Gold were pioneering
figures in the UCSB sociology department. Their aim was to build a doctoral program in sociology (the school until the early sixties had been an
undergraduate college). Both Don and Dave had received their education
and started their practice of sociology in the 1950s, and so their own personal perspective on the field tended to be very mainstream. But Dave, serving as chair, despite his very conventional take on the discipline, realized
from the start that to build a distinctive department the best strategy would
be to recruit people who were unconventional in many ways. There was no
point, he thought, in constructing a department that looked like a standard
issue mainstream program. Instead, he sought out people who were, in one
way or another, at the cutting edges of the discipline. For example, Aaron
Cicourel, who had made a name for himself as a critic of conventional
empirical methodology, was an advocate of an emerging perspective in the
field that called itself "ethnomethodology." Dave hired several students of
the leading figure in ethnomethodology, Harold Garfinkel at UCLA,
including in particular Don Zimmerman, who was a pioneer in conversation analysis. Dave recruited others who were doing research on issues and
topics that were excitingly not conventional. Tom Scheff arrived, already
established as a leader in the critical study of what then was called deviant
behavior. Bill Chambliss was becoming well known as an exponent of critical criminology. John Baldwin, a young researcher on animal behavior, had
just completed fieldwork in a Latin American jungle studying monkey colo-
nies. Dave found me appealing as a young radical sociologist, who had done
empirical research of significance and who was clearly someone trying to
stake out new directions for the discipline.

From that depiction, one might be able to tell that the sociology department at Santa Barbara was almost the polar opposite, in terms of its internal dynamic and perspective, of what I had experienced at the University of Chicago. It was a department that was branding itself as critical—of the discipline, of conventional modes of academic operation, and of the society at large. It's important to stress, and I will say more about this subject later, this was not a "radical" department in a political sense; it was, rather, an intellectually very diverse department in terms of the interests and outlooks of its members, but all of them shared a restlessness with the discipline as it was then constituted. There were maybe four or five other departments of sociology in the United States that had a somewhat maverick climate, but I daresay that none of them was as intellectually diverse, and none tried to fuse critical perspectives with a commitment to scholarly rigor.

Tom Scheff was chair of the department when I arrived. He insisted, given my physical condition and all that I had been through, that the first quarter of teaching would be a very light one—"Just have a little graduate workshop of some sort. Don't worry about preparing a class." That was something of a relief—we really did need some time to settle in and to regain some physical stamina.

## A SPIRIT OF REBELLION

Soon after the quarter started in the fall, I began to make connection with student activists at Santa Barbara. The previous year had been one of considerable turmoil on the campus. Before 1968, UCSB was known as a party cum surfer college and politically lagged well behind the more activist University of California campuses. In 1968 the small contingent of students of color on the campus began to organize, demanding recognition and voice—no doubt inspired by black and Chicano student protests around the country. Black Student Union members seized the campus computing center demanding a black studies program, the hiring of faculty of color, and more attention to campus access for minority students. This action turned out to be largely victorious; the campus administration and faculty leadership negotiated with the students, with agreements that did eventuate in the formation of a black studies program and a Center for Black Studies Research. Then, in April 1969, an intercollegiate conference of Chicano student activists met at UCSB and adopted the "Plan de Santa

Barbara," which served as a manifesto for Chicano studies at UCSB and across the country.

Soon after that, campus radicals, led by the SDS-affiliated group on campus, took over the University Center—the student union—and proclaimed a "free university," within which they set up all kinds of classes and workshops, occupying the building for several days. Late that academic year, in the midst of this newly activated environment, my appointment was announced.

In 1969–70, the campus newspaper, *El Gaucho*, was edited by Becca Wilson, one of the leading figures in the campus Left; at the same time, some of the officers of the student government were actively engaged with the Radical Union (as the SDS chapter was called). The character and tone of student life at UCSB was certainly shifting.

At the start of the fall quarter of 1969, it was announced that a young anthropology professor at UCSB, Bill Allen, was not going to have his contract renewed. Bill was a very popular teacher, who taught a lecture class populated by hundreds of students. Bill attired himself in a countercultural fashion with a bushy red beard and tie-dye. He was an ex-Marine who had been a UCSB undergraduate; he came back from the service and did his graduate work in the anthropology department. As he became increasingly "countercultural," he undoubtedly alienated some senior members of that department—while attracting a growing student following.

The decision not to rehire him, which, like the Marlene Dixon case, normally would have been a more or less routine thing to do, was the spark that ignited a campus-wide movement, whose demand was quite modest—that there be a public hearing, so that Allen and the students could know the reasons for his dismissal. It was widely suspected that it was politics more than his own accomplishments (or purported lack thereof) that was the decisive factor.

By the end of the fall quarter, the Radical Union had collected what they claimed were 7,776 signatures on a petition for an "open hearing" for Bill. The administration paid little heed to this demand, and so, in January 1970, students began to physically protest Bill's case. A call for students to surround the entrance to the administration building, which was on central plaza of the campus, resulted in a crowd of thousands of students who occupied the space for a couple of days. Campus police were called to clear the plaza, and they did so with some roughness. It was the first police-student confrontation at the historically placid campus. As a result of that police invasion, radical leaders called for a campus strike, which pretty well paralyzed the campus for several days.

The majority of undergraduates at UCSB lived in the (adjoining) community called Isla Vista. When the Santa Barbara campus was established as a branch of the University of California system, it was situated on a former Marine base adjacent to a sparsely populated piece of land that overlooked undeveloped and pristine beaches. Local developers saw the opportunity to capitalize on the need for housing for a rapidly growing student population, and so almost overnight a village to house thousands of young people was constructed; the county board of supervisors, guided by developer interests, adopted zoning rules that relaxed standard density requirements, so that a very compact, dense, student residential world was instantly created. Land values skyrocketed from $2,000 to $100,000 per acre, and dense building was allowed on the bluff overlooking the Pacific Ocean—a bluff that was notoriously unstable. All this feverish development was a marked contrast to the long history of local effort to protect the fabled beaches and idyllic way of life from destructive overdevelopment.

When the campus was initially planned, university administrators were advised by a well-known planning firm to ensure that the student residential community at UCSB be operated under university control; other University of California campuses developed in the sixties, especially at Santa Cruz and San Diego, were successfully planned in that fashion. But local developer interests insisted that student housing be turned over to the private market, and they prevailed. Indeed, campus administrators helped set up a special local bank to serve as the financial center of this development, and the administration acquiesced to the high-density zoning that the developer interests promulgated. The result, by the late sixties, was an obviously jerry-built Isla Vista, inhabited by fifteen thousand people under age twenty-five and hardly anyone older. The university largely adopted a hands-off attitude toward the community and, accordingly, there were very few amenities and services.

Isla Vista, by the time we arrived, was a world largely created by the students themselves. Given the rising cultural tides of the 1960s, it became a haven for the drug culture and a heaven for hippies. Inevitably, the unauthorized practices of the members of the Isla Vista scene inflamed a police force whose members had little inclination or training to understand any of it. It was in this social environment that the spark of Bill's dismissal was ignited.

There had already been troubles with the police. Just a couple of months earlier, Black Student Union leaders who had been involved in the campus uprising in the previous year were arrested on widely disbelieved charges (such as nonpayment of rent). Meanwhile, student run-ins with the police relating to drug or traffic offenses were routine.

The Bill Allen demonstrations were taking place as the trial of the so-called Chicago Conspiracy 8 was reaching its conclusion. The "conspiracy" trial, of the organizers of the protests at the 1968 Democratic convention, was a dramatic one for many young people in America, since several countercultural heroes had appeared on the stand, and the defendants themselves, especially Abbie Hoffman and Jerry Rubin, were achieving iconic status in the youth culture. I first saw evidence of that when Tom Hayden (who was one of the Chicago 8) spoke at UCSB in January 1970. Organizers of his talk expected a couple of hundred to turn out, but the auditorium of one thousand was packed and crowds overflowed into the plaza in front of the building. Something was happening in the wider student body that caught the political activists by surprise.

Soon after, student leaders at UCSB invited Bill Kunstler, the lead attorney for the Chicago 8, to come speak on campus. I was surprised to learn that he had accepted, given his preoccupation with the trial, but nevertheless Kunstler showed up on February 24 and spoke to the largest political gathering in the history of Santa Barbara, at the campus football stadium. Kunstler gave a rousing speech in which he urged mass protest against the war and a defense of free expression but made a point of opposing "picayune violence." He held up a copy of that morning's *Chicago Today*, which bore the headline "Kunstler Speech Sparks a Riot"—rather astonishing since it appeared before he had actually spoken.

It was already a volatile situation—the day before, some students had been arrested in the streets of Isla Vista as part of a police crackdown on troublemakers, including a well-known black activist named Lefty Bryant. As the students streamed out of the stadium, a young man, shirtless, swinging a wine bottle, was suddenly attacked by a group of police, who presumed that what he was carrying was a Molotov cocktail. This attack occurred in the plain view of thousands—who immediately responded by counterattacking the police.

The student-police conflict after the Kunstler speech escalated over several hours, and it was in the chaos of that escalation that a group pushed a burning trash dumpster into the Isla Vista branch of the Bank of America, setting the building ablaze. By that time, police had withdrawn from the area under a hail of rocks and burning bottles, and the fire department apparently did not want to enter that scene.

By the next morning, the obscure community of Isla Vista was the subject of a worldwide news story—it was the place where the Bank of America building had burned. There followed several further days of rioting. The arrival of the National Guard, along with a drenching rainstorm, quelled the uprising. By then, the community was under martial law, ordered by Governor Ronald Reagan.

I wasn't an eyewitness to most of what transpired in the Isla Vista streets in those days. But I did have a fortuitous chance to get some insight into students' political emotions in the hours between the Kunstler speech and the burning of the bank. In the fall, the sociology department had offered a large course on the nature of the university. The fall course was centered on weekly talks by faculty members, and each of us led a discussion section as well. Students in my section wanted to continue the conversation, and so I sponsored a freewheeling discussion class in winter quarter. For various good pedagogical reasons, we decided to convene the class in student apartments, and by coincidence, the first of these was scheduled to meet in the late afternoon in Isla Vista, after the Kunstler event. As I made my way to the oceanfront apartment building, one could see the hubbub in the streets in the center of town—some stone throwing at cop cars and lots of excited milling. Members of the class filled the apartment living room—and, of course, all we could talk about was what was happening in the streets. Class members were restlessly coming and going, so we were getting a stream of reports about the feverish escalation of activity. A discussion began about the politics of it all. More experienced activists argued that rioting and attacks on buildings, including the bank, were bound to be politically damaging: Weren't they mindless? Wouldn't they just give the "pigs" reasons to attack us? It was intriguing, at the same time, to hear what a number of relatively apolitical kids were saying—"This is a way we can be taken seriously! This will force them to pay attention to what young people want!"

I was struck by the realization that the spirit of rebellion was exciting kids who had grown up in the very heartland of comfort and the mainstream of the culture. The Isla Vista uprising, I came to believe, was much more the doing of the "golden sons and daughters" of California than of left-wing "agitators" and "revolutionaries" (as the media and the authorities were claiming).

Everyone on the scene that night made a big point of telling me to get out of Isla Vista before it was too late. They were sure that the police viewed me as notorious and would love to get their hands on me in these circumstances.

I was, for some reason, less worried about that than they were—and I was probably wrong to be blasé. After all, when Tom Hayden had come to town a few weeks earlier and stayed at our house, we were followed by several police cars everywhere we drove. Indeed, some years later, I learned that one of our neighbors had taken it on herself to file weekly reports on our doings to the police. Most disturbing was to find out that one of the graduate students in sociology was a sworn member of the sheriff's department and, the student told me, had regularly reported on me ("But I always made it clear that you weren't a danger," he shared). And it eventually came out that the intelligence unit of the sheriff's department had actually predicted that my coming to UCSB would foment civil unrest (that report also claimed that there were several dozen Marxist professors at UCSB). So I guess I was fortunate, after all, to have taken the students' advice to get out of Isla Vista that night!

The events of February were the beginning of months of turmoil at the UCSB campus and in Isla Vista itself. The once seemingly sleepy party school was transformed, in terms of both its national image and the emotional climate of the place, into a center of revolutionary upheaval. This climate led to further publicity about my presence on the campus. The *Santa Barbara News-Press* resumed its anti-Flacks crusade by alleging without any evidence that I had something to do with the invitation to Kunstler to come to campus and therefore bore responsibility for the riot. I was upset and angry at this editorial since, ironically, I had had nothing to do with the invitation to Kunstler, let alone any of the organizing that had been taking place. My physical condition, if nothing else, prevented me from being actively engaged in such activity. The *News-Press* effort to connect me with the riot appeared in stories about Isla Vista across the country.

Accompanied by Harvey Molotch, I went down to talk to the editor, sternly declaring that they needed to retract this editorial because it was extremely threatening to me and my family to have these allegations published. I said that I'd have to find "other means" to counter what they had written—meaning that I might have to sue, but he possibly (or probably) thought I'd be able to order my minions to burn the newspaper's offices down!

The result of that encounter was that I was given the chance finally to speak for myself in the pages of the *Santa Barbara News-Press*. Some days later it published an op-ed article I'd written giving "my side."

Nixon's invasion of Cambodia in the first days of May prompted nation-wide campus demonstrations. Students were mobilizing even on campuses that had seen relatively little protest. One of these was Kent State University in Ohio. There, Governor James Rhodes called out the Ohio National Guard to quell protests; on May 4 guardsmen fired dozens of rounds at an unarmed mass of students, killing four and wounding a number of others. These events were soon followed by a National Guard assault on dormi-tories at Jackson State, a black college in Mississippi, during which two stu-dents died and others were wounded. Millions of students and faculty went on strike during this period, in what was the largest mass protest in U.S. history.

These events—the killings and the massive confrontations—turned the tide of popular feeling about the generational revolt and the student move-ment. Blame for these events began to focus on the inflammatory words of Nixon and Spiro Agnew, his vice president, and Ronald Reagan. Reagan was quoted as saying: "If it takes a bloodbath, let's get it over with. No more appeasement."[1] Nixon talked about the protesters as "bums" just before the Kent State massacre. Agnew had been bloviating for months about the "criminal Left" and the need to separate and discard the protesters from society.

The growing backlash against such sentiments was largely among those whose age and class made them likely to be relatives and acquaintances of college students. My reading of the century-long history of student move-ments around the world made me aware that severe repression of students often led to public soul-searching and to an erosion of the legitimacy of regimes that had repressed them. After all, those being beaten and jailed included offspring of elite or relatively advantaged families, likely to be furi-ous that their kids were being attacked—and at the same time having politi-cal clout to make their anger consequential for those in authority.

This process was very evident in June 1970 when the third "Isla Vista rebellion" was quelled by a massive police occupation of the community, coupled with a very harshly enforced curfew. In response to the police onslaught, a group of faculty, clergy, and other adults joined with students to violate the curfew with a nonviolent occupation of a park in Isla Vista.

Police broke up that protest by arresting hundreds and pepper-spraying many others. A large number of students were incarcerated in a newly opened county prison, not fully equipped to handle their influx. Suddenly, hundreds of their parents descended on the community in outrage at the treatment of their offspring.

The police behavior was publicly criticized by conservative local media commentators, who, until then, had been enthusiastically demanding stern discipline. Soon a so-called blue-ribbon committee of Santa Barbara citizens was formed to investigate what happened in Isla Vista; the Board of Regents of the University of California established its own commission to investigate the uprising and the way the university had responded to it; and the president of the Bank of America, Louis Lundborg, came to Isla Vista to listen and learn. Lundborg eventually wrote a book called *Future without Shock* in which he declared that he had discovered that the students had a real point about the war and many of their other criticisms of authority in society were, he had come to believe, valid.[2]

This Lundborg book was a small example of a wider process in the country—very popular media efforts to "understand" the young and to acknowledge the validity of countercultural criticism of the state of things. Best sellers like Charles Reich's *The Greening of America* defined the youth revolt as the wave of the future, while Margaret Mead declared that we had entered a new era in which the young would be teaching the old about how to live.[3]

I was intrigued when, in the 1970 congressional elections, there was a surprising turn away from the Republican Party, despite Nixon's and Agnew's fevered exhortations about the barbarian hordes. I felt at the time that the electoral shift had a lot to do with a middle-class backlash against the generational polarization of society. As more and more people began to experience, in their own families, the impact of the anti-war protests and countercultural experiment, the GOP strategy of polarizing against the young was backfiring.[4]

## A SPIRIT OF REBELLION—BEYOND THE CAMPUS

DICK:

Those first years of the seventies, then, were a contradictory time politically. On the one hand, efforts to repress the sixties movements and to stir up

FIGURE 11.2. Dick, with Marc on his shoulders, and other UCSB professors at an anti-war march on State Street in Santa Barbara, 1970

backlash against them were quite intense, as grand juries were convened, aimed at prosecuting leaders and sympathizers of the "revolutionary Left." On the other hand, both locally in the Santa Barbara community and nationally, political ferment and cultural experiment accelerated.

Santa Barbara was emerging as a center of environmental consciousness in the aftermath of the great oil spill of January 1969—a catastrophe that soaked the beaches of this beautiful resort community with oil leaking from a major well blowup. Images of oil-drenched birds circled the planet. A grassroots campaign led by an organization called Get Oil Out (GOO) sparked a far-reaching community mobilization to try to stop further oil development in the Santa Barbara Channel. That campaign began a widening effort in the Santa Barbara area to construct a politics based on environmental values and to create an institutional framework that would support those values. The Santa Barbara oil spill is often credited as the beginning point for Earth Day: Senator Gaylord Nelson, the initiator of Earth Day, claimed that the oil spill inspired him to propose a national mobilization, modeled after anti-war mobilizations.

We were struck with how environmentalism opened possibilities for political innovation on a local level that had a great deal of promise in creating vision for new paths for social change. Santa Barbara had been governed for decades by Republicans, who dominated every level of representation (Congress, the state legislature, the county board, and the city council), favoring pro-developer, pro-business, pro-growth policies.

By the late sixties, a new politics was emerging. It was partly made possible by demographic change. The university's growth brought more liberal voters and political activists to the area. The university's presence enabled engineering firms (fueled by the defense budget) to set up shop in the rapidly growing suburb called Goleta, in which UCSB was embedded. The influx of academic and scientific staff created a rapidly growing constituency favoring environmental perspectives and resistant to suburban sprawl. And by the early seventies, there were a considerable number of UCSB graduates who decided to stay around, attracted to the region as a place to settle. Among its attractions were its emerging political and cultural possibilities.

Goleta, in the late sixties, became the second-fastest growing urban area in America. By the early seventies, many in the region had come to see continuing growth as unsustainable given the limited availability of water in semi-arid Southern California, as well as the threatening smog, the congested traffic, and the ballooning public costs that were outrunning the financial benefits of growth. If oil development continued (which itself would grow the population), Santa Barbara would inevitably end its attractiveness as a tourist destination and as a haven for the knowledge industry. Indeed, the community shared a deeply held conviction that this coast ought to be protected, that its industrialization would be a world-scale tragedy.

So, threat, demography, and vision converged to provide energy for grassroots activism and receptivity for a new politics.

Meanwhile, on campus, a similar visionary perspective was taking hold. Many radical student activists were saying something like the following: "The riots resulted from the fact that we had no voice in the political arena; we are subject to the draft and other kinds of constraints without having the right to vote and without having power locally in the setting of rules and the making of policy. What we learned in this year of turmoil was that confrontation and destruction may get attention, but something more stable is needed to really carry forward our perspectives and interests."

Even before the passage of the franchise for eighteen-year-olds, Isla Vista developed a shadow government based on the youth of the community, constituting a community council for which all residents aged sixteen years and over could vote. The council, in its early days, was at least symbolically representative—and university authorities decided to provide some financial support so it could be staffed. Under its aegis, other community institutions were formed in the years after the bank burning: a planning commission was created to monitor development within the Isla Vista community; a credit union was established as an alternative to the hated Bank of America; a food co-op was started, along with Isla Vista's first medical clinic, a child care center, and a youth recreational project. Intriguing, if ephemeral, grassroots structures came into being—block organizations, skills exchanges, community gardens, a monthly newspaper.

Meanwhile, the university hastily reversed its long-standing attitude of neglect of Isla Vista by providing some significant funding to house and staff the student-led ventures in community development and to reform policing—enabling creation of a foot patrol (ending patrolling by police cars) and a coordination of campus and county sheriff police forces.

The passion for collective experiment and community voice in Isla Vista paralleled developments across the country. In many college towns and youth-based neighborhoods, similar kinds of institution building were going on. Free schools were sprouting up everywhere, based on experimental education models like Summerhill[5]; free clinics, based on the idea of providing medical care for all and on alternative as well as conventional medical practices; free legal collectives where lawyers and law students and interns could provide legal help needed for those up against difficulties with respect to protest, drugs, landlords, employers, and so forth.

At the same time, the women's liberation wave was gathering force in Santa Barbara (and all across the country, of course). Under the radar, consciousness-raising groups were forming that brought together women of varied ages to talk in deep ways about their lives, their relationships, and their potentials.

If Mickey and I had thought we were going into retreat by moving to Santa Barbara, we were instead swept up in the activist surge. Veteran activists of the 1960s, like ourselves, were now of an age and inclination to figure out how to settle in for a long haul and were everywhere moving into local communities with the idea of organizing a new politics and implementing New Left values in practical ways.

Mickey and I were so inclined before most of our peers. In the late sixties years of revolutionary rhetoric and apocalyptic imaginings, our stability as spouses and parents often made us feel uncomfortably bourgeois and out of phase. But after the apocalyptic moment that marked our arrival here, we served as kind of semi-parental figures for a growing number of younger people who were deciding to stay in Santa Barbara after they left UCSB, eager to see what was possible, politically and culturally, in this once conservative town. Our living room became a meeting place for regular gatherings of what we came to call the Thursday Club.


## THE THURSDAY CLUB

DICK:

These meetings at first were brainstorming sessions about what could be done in a place like Santa Barbara to create new politics and new social possibilities, now that we all agreed that the Revolution was not, in fact, at hand.

At some point it was suggested that participants start to define specific projects that, given our skills and interests, might be of value or interest to the wider community population. Soon small subgroups formed around each of these project ideas, tasked with developing concrete proposals and plans.

An early proposal was that the community needed a weekly publication that would serve as an alternative to the mainstream daily newspaper and a voice for the new generation, while providing content that could be of interest or use to anyone, regardless of age or ideology. The newspaper collective included several people who had been leaders in the Isla Vista/UCSB scene; they had created an occasional newspaper of revolutionary tenor in Isla Vista. They called it the *Strategic Hamlet*—a very clever name for the publication, referring ironically to the concentration camps that American occupiers had set up in Vietnam but conveying the idea that Isla Vista might be a strategic center for revolutionary ferment. The *Strategic Hamlet* folks (many of them also members of SDS in the late sixties) came to see that the "revolutionary" rag that they were putting out was not going to be sustainable, nor would it stay relevant, as the fervor of revolution began to wane. So they decided to start a weekly that would be addressed to the wider public and that would meld investigative reporting and cultural coverage. It would include a calendar of events that would be useful for anybody (and meet a need poorly addressed by the *Santa Barbara News-Press*) and features like a countercultural horoscope, hippieish comic strips, and graphics—as well as commentary, exposé, and reportage. The plan was to attract advertising and become sustainable financially.

The result was the *Santa Barbara News and Review*—one of the pioneer ventures in what nationally became the underground (or alternative) press. The *News and Review*'s content paralleled that of the many other similar weeklies that sprouted in the mid-1970s around the country. It was relatively unique, however, in its internal structure, since it was organized as a worker-owned collective. Everyone who was on the staff had a voice in the operation and ownership of the newspaper, an arrangement eventually formalized by a corporate charter that legally inscribed the worker ownership model. Essentially, everyone who worked on the newspaper got a voting share for each six months of employment. Voting rights were retained by all who had worked there for at least six months, even after they moved on.

I was honored to be appointed as the trustee of the *Santa Barbara News and Review*; my role was to ensure that the worker ownership model was adhered to and effectively operating.

Financially, it took some years for the newspaper's business model to become at all sustainable. Most of the full-time reporters had to take other jobs in the early years. But the bet that the weekly would be able to survive based on advertising revenue did pay off; eventually, the newspaper was able to support a full-time staff of reporters and production people. And it served as the information hub for the intensifying countercultural swirl of enterprises, services, and cultural activities that characterized the daily life of Santa Barbara, while helping the emerging political left wing of local politics find out about itself and define its issues.

The newspaper project was only one of a number that were developed at meetings of the Thursday Club. One idea that was floated was to create a community environmental structure that would promote environmental practices—recycling, community gardens, green building, and the like— and articulate an embracing vision for a sustainable region. This idea became the Community Environmental Council. Now recognized globally as a model for community transformation, the council continues to be the leading force for sustainable policy and practice in this region.

A law collective was formed by a group of young progressive lawyers, together with several activists who were interested in being paralegal interns, to serve political and other needs of young people in the community primarily, but also to provide legal services for the poor. A free school was created, whose intention was to provide alternative education on a full-time basis—UCSB students were recruited as teachers, who would get course credit for working at the free school.

I was inspired by all this to develop academic content and credit for work in alternative institutions. So, in addition to the brainstorming in our living room, I had the chance to work with a wide number of the young activists who were creating institutional experiments. My role, often, was to ask the practical questions that youthful romantics might prefer to ignore. But that romanticism was necessary if there was to be energy for achieving the improbable. And there was real achievement in the fostering of institutional change and in enabling many of the participants to develop their capacities, skills, and identities for long-term participation in social change.

## NEW COMMUNITY POLITICS?

DICK:

Alongside alternative institution building, we were caught up in working for a new community politics. The George McGovern for President campaign in 1972 was an important harbinger and seedbed of political change in the Santa Barbara region. The McGovern effort had a strong following in Santa Barbara, especially on campus. Despite its disastrous national outcome, the effort to promote that campaign locally was an important spur in Santa Barbara for new electoral initiative. One example was the decision by a young schoolteacher named Gary K. Hart (not the Hart of Colorado who was a famous McGovernite). Our Hart decided in his twenties to run for state assembly in a historically Republican district. He had been a supporter of draft resistance and participated in the student movement in the 1960s at Stanford, and he came back to Santa Barbara, where he had grown up, to teach school. Although his first political ventures were not successful, they helped him establish a base, leading eventually to long and celebrated service in the state legislature and as secretary of education in California.

Hart's campaigns marked the beginning of a major electoral shift toward the Democratic Party in a region that had long been safe GOP territory. Liberal Democrats have controlled the legislative seats that represent the coastal region centered on Santa Barbara ever since. Sometimes, over the years, those elected have been heard to call Mickey and me their "conscience"—usually meaning that we've been able to remind them of their duty to heed the voices of grassroots progressive movements rather than dance to the relentless drumbeat of business donors and lobbyists.

Simultaneously, environmentally conscious, anti-growth activism took control of various nonpartisan governmental bodies. One of the first successes of this new coalition was to elect its candidates to the Goleta Water Board, when some bright people in Goleta discovered that the water board—hitherto a very obscure entity—could be a fulcrum for slow growth policy. They effectively stopped housing development in Goleta by declaring a moratorium on new water hookups on the grounds that the pace of development was threatening the future water supply of the whole region. Soon after, the Citizens Coalition was formed in the city of Santa Barbara, and it challenged and overcame the prevailing Republican control of the city council. Mickey got involved in the Citizens Coalition, much enjoying the diversity of the folks she got to know there. Coalition leaders and candidates were not necessarily liberals in the usual sense, but they all shared a slow growth and environmentalist perspective. One of the four Citizen Coalition candidates was Leo Martinez, the first Latino to be elected to the Santa Barbara City Council.

The Citizens Coalition validated our decision to focus our political energy on building and organizing on a local level. That "local" perspective seemed to us a way to enable progressives to reach out beyond the narrow boundaries that defined the movement of the sixties. We found that people, regardless of their ideological labels, were willing to join together around issues of common concern that affected the community's welfare. Resistance to growth was one important focus for such coalition building. The oil spill, which had so threatened the very existence of the community, certainly spurred such coming together. People who professed to be ideologically free-marketers were quite willing to see property rights regulated and controlled in the interest of preserving Santa Barbara.

In the seventies, conversation about democratic regulation of economic activity was welcomed by people across the ideological spectrum. A strong majority of people in the community were quite ready to vote for restrictions on the oil industry and to vote for politicians who would enforce such restriction. They were quite ready to vote for land use regulation to constrain development that fostered population growth or that would infringe on the quality of life of the community. Many large-scale developments in this highly desirable region—hotels, corporate headquarters, upscale housing projects, and so forth—were vetoed by popular vote and by political leaders who were willing to do that vetoing, knowing that they had majority support.

In the seventies, we began to imagine that many communities in the United States would look for versions of what we were calling "economic democracy"—a governmental model based on a direct voice for the community in the economic decisions that affect its future. We came to believe that progressive activists could work at the community level for democratic process and community control regardless of the state of national policy. Struggles for economic and social democracy locally situated could be transformative for the society as a whole. So even though the Republicans swept the elections of 1972, leading many to assume that the country was shifting to the right, Santa Barbara was moving in quite the opposite direction. Here, liberal political candidates were winning office, environmentalists were dominating the discourse. A region once seen as a right-wing bastion was now being led by environmentalists, feminists, and former antiwar activists. In my always romantic view, we could be, in our community, acting out the beginnings of an alternative future.

## LEARNING TO LOVE CALIFORNIA

MICKEY:

The Santa Barbara campus of the University of California (UCSB) had been courting Dick for a number of years. He didn't pay much heed to the courtship because he was an assistant professor in one of the world's leading sociology departments, and UCSB seemed to be something of a backwater. . . . Besides, wouldn't it be a cop-out for a sociologist/radical to leave a dynamic urban area for a beautiful resort town in Southern California? In 1968, though, a newly minted PhD from the University of Chicago took a job at UCSB and reported that it really was a wonderful department, full of quirky, non-doctrinaire, "new style" sociologists, and that it was really OK living there—Los Angeles was only ninety miles away! In early 1969, UCSB again courted Dick, this time offering him a tenured position. He would be up for tenure at the University of Chicago the following year, and being able to present an offer of tenure from another university was a nice card to play. He was far from sanguine about getting tenure in the department that was so hostile to much that he believed in and was working for.

The sociology department's tenure decision was being made while Dick spent a month in the hospital following the attack. Meanwhile, the University of Chicago's anthropology department, whose leading professors had been about the only faculty members who were warm and friendly to us, offered Dick a tenured position—for which he was very grateful, but felt totally unqualified. We were still waiting for the sociology department. By this time, we were quite ready to leave Chicago. Harvey Molotch, the new PhD who was at UCSB, was really urging us to come; my mother, who was alone in New York (my brother and his family having moved to Los Angeles), would likely move to California if we did; even Dick had had enough of the Windy City and its university, with its faculty that, I felt, consisted primarily of right-wing snobs. (I used to observe that Hyde Park had only one movie theater and that a typical faculty Saturday night consisted of a string quartet concert in someone's home, followed by dinner served by hired African American staff at about 10:00 P.M.—not really our style!) The department finally announced its decision just before the deadline that UCSB had given us: Dick was given tenure in the college (the smaller, undergraduate part of the University of Chicago), and the tenure decision for the department would be delayed one year. This meant that he could stay if he wanted to—even forever if he wished, but it was hardly a ringing affirmation by the department. We soon let UCSB know that we were coming! I was overjoyed!

Dick was, at this point, a semi-invalid, with a brace on his leg and a hole in his head. His parents had come to be with us in Chicago as soon as their school year in New York ended. They helped us pack, took care of the kids while I dealt with the myriad details that had to be attended to. (One was the thirty-plus parking tickets I had accumulated on my visits to see Dick in the hospital. I had figured that Dick's being there was, somehow, the University of Chicago's fault, and the university virtually owned the Hyde Park streets around the hospital, so I had the right to park there. A lawyer suggested that since I was leaving town, I was probably right!) We arranged for a moving van (which UCSB was paying for) to take our belongings, books, and furniture, and the six Flackses flew off to the West.

It would be a week before the moving van would arrive at our rented house in Santa Barbara (owned by a new colleague of Dick's, who was off to Africa for a year), so we would be staying with the Villarejo family, since Don Villarejo, with his newly minted PhD in physics, had taken his first job at UCLA. The senior Flackses (Dave and Mildred) went up to Santa

Barbara to camp out at the house and wait for the movers. When the moving company called, my brother drove us and the kids (a graduate student was driving our little Datsun station wagon across country for us) to our new home. When we got there, to the first non-apartment I had ever lived in, we found a three-bedroom home with a large black dog (part of the deal) complete with a yard and a horse corral. The "landlord" was six thousand miles away, and we knew nothing of heating systems or plumbing or grass cutting. My father-in-law had thoughtfully compiled a three-page list of the things that I would immediately have to take care of. . . . The weight of everything that had happened and was about to happen was seemingly on my shoulders, and mine alone: Chuck was four, Marc was one, the street where the house was situated seemed to be in the country—with no sidewalks—and I was in a place where I knew almost nobody and had a semi-invalid, infamous husband living in the home of the John Birch Society! Before my brother left to go back to Los Angeles, Harvey Molotch came over and invited us all over to his house in Montecito—the tony suburb to the south. He took us there via the "scenic route," a curvy, winding road across a ridge, which is sometimes referred to as "the Riviera"; Marc, who was sitting on my lap (years before mandatory car seats), promptly threw up. While I remained in the car, my brother went in to fetch towels for cleaning Marc and me. He came out of the house, a former carriage house that Harvey and his wife, Linda, had remodeled, and gushed, "It's like something out of *House and Garden* in there!" At that, for the first (and only) time since Dick was injured, I lost it—I broke into uncontrollable sobs. . . . How could I possibly manage all this and thrive in this totally unfamiliar atmosphere?!!

In addition, Harvey had thoughtfully sent to us in Chicago the editorials and letters to the editor in the pages of the *Santa Barbara News-Press*, the local daily. The attack on Dick had been national news, and in California the story was that this radical, troublemaking professor had been given "lifetime tenure" at UCSB—without the approval of the regents, among whom was the governor, one Ronald Reagan. (For a few months, the Regents of the University of California had given up their authority to approve/disapprove tenure and other faculty decisions. It was during this time that Dick was hired.) Another regent, Mrs. William Randolph Hearst (Patty Hearst's mom), suggested that Dick should be fired, if not for his politics, then for "being a person of low moral character." Reagan, when asked to comment on the Flacks appointment, made one of his better quips: "They tell me he

[Flacks] is a competent sociologist," he said. "But this hire is like hiring a pyromaniac to work in a fireworks factory because he's a competent fuse maker."[6] The editorial pages of the local newspaper were filled with varying attacks on Dick or criticism of the university. On July 4, shortly before we arrived, a local nursery owner placed a display ad asking: "Are you a REAL American? Or, like Prof. Flacks, a 'watermelon' American (green on the outside, red on the inside)?" Every day, a new letter or editorial appeared—and Harvey had sent them all.

So it was with a good deal of trepidation that we moved into our new home. The first days in a new town require one to give one's name many, many times over—to the power companies, the water provider, the elections registrar, and so forth. I did so with some hesitancy, expecting some reaction—positive or negative. I had no hostile reactions those first days, no reactions of any kind; most people, I thought, don't read the newspaper or remember or care. One young man, a shoe salesman, I think, smiled when I gave him a check and said, warmly, "Welcome to Santa Barbara, Mrs. Flacks!" A few months later, however, we returned home one day to find a note, barely legible or comprehensible, saying something like: "Your yard is as messy as your brain; someone ought to clean both of them up!"

We did get a phone call from a woman who ran the local parent-child workshop (a program of the local community college), in which parents of preschoolers along with the community college's students worked as teachers in a nursery school. She obviously knew exactly who we were and was calling to invite us to send Chuck to the school. I was very touched, but I explained that I was hoping to find work and would not be able to participate as a parent/teacher.

We were also warmly welcomed by the members of the sociology department—unlike at the University of Chicago. We immediately had a dinner invitation from the chair, and various faculty members called or dropped by during those first few weeks. Harvey was especially helpful, as were many other sociologists. Dick could not drive (because of his semi-paralyzed leg and severely disabled right hand), but many colleagues would come by and pick him up and bring him back. What a difference from Chicago!

I looked for part-time work and applied at UCSB for a job in a research lab but was told that everyone wanted a full-time staff research associate. I knew that, for my own sanity (as well as the added income), I had to find some sort of work. The wife of a sociology colleague worked part-time as a clinical technician in the laboratory of the local county hospital. The pathologist who headed the lab agreed to allow me to train as a clinical technician on a part-time basis (which was, in fact, strictly against state policy). I was to work every afternoon. I was able to find a woman on our block who took in babies and toddlers to care for, and she took Marc for each afternoon. These were the days of alternative schools, and the local Community School, established at an activist's home, was open to four-year olds. Chuck began to attend all day—and he loved it! There was a young man teaching who was a musician (as well as the math teacher). Chuck fell in love with him and was delighted to spend weekdays at the Community School.

I was liberated from my semi-rural isolation! I believe that it is this isolation that is the worst part of stay-at-home moms' (or dads') burden. In a different century—and even in my own childhood, "villages" did raise children. Women spent many hours each day in the company of other women like themselves, both working together and socializing—just as their husbands did at their workplaces. Also, I was happy to be back in a scientific setting, where there was one true answer and my job was to find it. How different that was from the turmoil around us brewing in the student community!

Even the non-student community was beginning to become involved in the anti-war movement. A group of women, mostly faculty wives, poured blood on the files of the local draft board. They were arrested, and they refused bail for a few days, remaining in jail as a further protest. A meeting was called at the home of one of them, who was a sociologist's wife. I attended and, speaking from my long political experience, laid out a possible plan of action we should take. I no longer remember, in fact, what I was advocating, but it prompted sociologist friend Harvey Molotch to exclaim: "The *News-Press* was right!" (I felt complimented and empowered—a nice feeling.)

Some faculty and graduate student wives also started a consciousness-raising group at around this time. We called ourselves "Jewish radical feminists," though we weren't all Jewish, some were not radical, and most were not feminist. Dick facetiously dubbed us "the Pink Ladies." He was also asked to write an article (about the student movement) for *Playboy* magazine. He started to refuse in outrage, until they said: "You haven't heard what we pay." Upon being told that he would receive $3,000, more than $1.00 per word, he replied that he'd have to consult his wife's consciousness-raising group. When the women of the group heard about the $3,000, they agreed—if he would contribute half to the women's movement—which we were happy to do.

The riots in Isla Vista—both police and student—went on without my participation. My only "action" was to force my way through a police line surrounding the administration building because it was payday, and I wanted to go to the accounting office to make sure we would be paid; if not, THEN I would riot! I felt a bit alienated from the whole thing—again, because I was neither a student nor a faculty member nor an Isla Vista resident. We left our rented "house in the country" and moved to a suburban tract four-bedroom plus "family room" home (though located within the city of Santa Barbara). I had searched for a house that was in what I was told the best school district in town, that had a real sidewalk in front of it (so our kids could learn to skate and ride a bike), and that had either a pool or a pool-size backyard. This last requirement was because Dick was still wearing a brace on his partially paralyzed leg, and I thought swimming might be the only exercise he could manage. Our realtor was a local progressive who was worried that, given all the hullabaloo about Dick's appointment, we might not find a local bank that would give us a mortgage. Actually, we had no problem and financed a house (with a down payment from Dick's workers' compensation settlement from the University of Chicago—he was, after all, attacked in his campus office). The bank was happy to lend us the money; the house cost $39,000, or three times his annual salary in 1969, which was $13,000!

Soon after we moved in, I told Dick that I couldn't tolerate the "avocado green hi-lo" carpet that was in almost every room. I wanted to spend what, for us, was a significant sum of money to buy new carpeting. He was very dubious: "What if the university shuts down or I lose my job?" I told him that, in that case, new carpeting would make the house easier to sell. "What?" he exploded. "Nobody is ever going to want to buy a suburban tract house like this anymore! People will want to live communally!" (Thus spake the sociologist.) We bought strawberry red carpeting, and a young woman in my consciousness-raising group was relieved because at least the "bourgeois" wall-to-wall carpeting was red!

The school district was considered the best, although it had the same demographic of students as most other schools in the area. It had been recently developed and consisted of only three elementary schools, one of which was located two blocks from our house; just about all the kids walked to the school (ah, the good old days . . . ). The district school board was made up of five parents, elected by the residents of the district. The principal of our school, John Ehrenborg, had been hired before the school was even built, had supervised its construction, and had hired all its teachers and staff. (This area was, at that time, one of the fastest growing in the country—principally because of the growth of the university and the defense think tanks and contractors that surrounded it.) The school's teachers were a bit concerned when we registered Chuck for kindergarten. (He already had a "curriculum vitae" that included the University of Chicago Laboratory Nursery School and Santa Barbara's "free" Community School, as well as being the son of the infamous "Prof. Richard Flacks, 31, with lifetime tenure," as the *News-Press* put it for about two years—long after the professor was thirty-one.) They had a meeting to discuss what Chuck might be like! Instead of the wild, long-haired, unruly kid they expected, they got Mr. Responsible, almost Goody Two-Shoes. When Chuck had been in Chicago's Laboratory Nursery School at age three, his teacher told me that she never had to worry that she might overlook some kid who was in distress—hurt, crying or otherwise unhappy—because Chuck would always come and tell her. I had swelled with pride at this news and felt that the essential part of our parenting was already successful. . . . Concern and a sense of responsibility for others was part of his character. I told his kindergarten teacher and the principal: "I'm sending you a kid who loves learning, who is turned on by it. All I ask is that you not turn him off." And they didn't.

One day, when Chuck was in third grade, Sharon Jeffrey, a fellow SDS founder, was visiting, getting a little rest and relaxation from her work in Cleveland's ghetto. We were going over to Chuck's school to pick him up for an outing. We got there a bit early and heard, drifting out of the classroom, the sounds of childish voices singing "Blowin' in the Wind." Inside the classroom the walls were festooned with borrowed prints of Van Gogh paintings, including *Starry Night*. After the Dylan song, the teacher played Don McLean's recording of "Starry, Starry Night" and wrote the words on the white board. She used this as a lesson on poetry, leading a discussion about both Van Gogh's life and death and how the song expressed the singer-songwriter's feelings about him. She put Van Gogh's birth and death dates on the board and built a math lesson around figuring out how old he was when he died. Needless to say, both Sharon and I were absolutely blown away. This teacher, Judith Sims, was the best teacher I ever saw. She later organized parents in a downtown neighborhood to get a magnificent new playground built to replace old, unsafe equipment that the city had simply removed. She also later developed a garden-based curriculum on environmentalism and sustainability that has been emulated all over the country. This was a public school, with kids from both middle- and working-class families (99 percent white, of course—but the district later reached out to encourage transfers by minority group children—and it now is somewhat integrated).

Dick and I learned from this experience that "smaller is better" (often). The three-school district, the power of an individual principal with a truly progressive vision of education, the small classes possible in those days, the participation of parents in the classroom and in the district policies—all taught us what society based on "participatory democracy" might look like. We also learned that our world, at least, this little community in Southern California, a climate and cultural paradise, was truly changing. The 1960s flowed into the 1970s with an explosion of new forms of living, of what popular culture was and could be, of how the sixties activists would further transform themselves and (at least, parts of) society.

In September 1970, as the "revolution" was raging around me, I finally got a full-time job as a staff research associate in the genetics and molecular biology section of the biology department at UCSB. I was working for a professor/researcher who was using a single-celled microorganism, *Tetrahymena thermophila*, a cousin of a *Paramecium*, to do experimental genetics. It had been five years since I'd worked in a research lab (the clinical lab work at the county hospital was quite different), and, though I felt a little rusty, I again enjoyed the precision of doing science. When the student world seemed to be exploding around me, I could escape the chaos of those days by staring into my microscope—and feeling that our basic research might not only advance scientific knowledge but be useful someday in helping humanity. We still continue to learn new functions of and for microorganisms—from ulcer causing to oil spill devouring. (So far, *Tetrahymena* have not been notable for anything—but who knows?)

One contribution I made was, in fact, a function of my being a wife and mother; it would not have happened if I were not always worrying about being home for the kids. *Tetrahymena* mate by forming pairs and swimming as an attached pair for up to twelve hours. During this time they exchange genetic material, thereby giving rise to "offspring" that are genetically different from either parent. (They can also divide by themselves, creating "daughter cells" that are genetically alike—but that's another story.) The

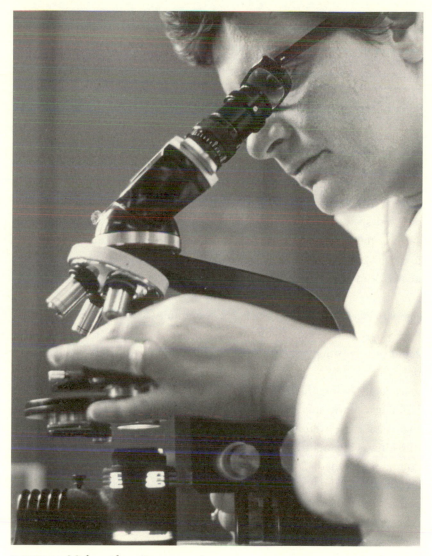

FIGURE 11.3. Mickey at her microscope, circa 1975

mating and genetic exchange take place in a "starvation medium," containing various salts, but devoid of nutrition. The literature always recommended isolating the mating pair (into its own drop of nutrient material) at six to eight hours after the beginning of mating, assuring that the genetic exchange would be complete and providing the opportunity for a new clone to grow. As I watched the mating pairs, I saw that nearly 100 percent of the mating took place after four or five hours. Not wanting to begin the laborious process of isolating the pairs late in the afternoon (or after coming in at dawn), I began to isolate the pairs after about four or five hours. Upon testing to determine the genetic makeup of the subsequent clones, we found some screwy results. Investigating further, we discovered that "feeding" the mating pairs at precisely four hours and fifteen minutes yielded a genetic reorganization in each "offspring" that wasn't previously known and accounted for our results. This was a new useful technique in *Tetrahymena* genetics that was found only because I couldn't stay late or come in too early—I had a family to see to!

A few months before our arrival in Santa Barbara, in January 1969, the nation's first major oil spill blackened the pristine beaches of the community and spawned the environmental movement. Along with the growing anti-war movement, it contributed to a new sensibility in the community, a more progressive outlook. What had been a city of the "newly wed and nearly dead" for a generation was now becoming home to many graduates of the sixties movements, and a new generation of UCSB faculty and staff was increasing its presence in the community, as well. Despite the staid, conservative, lily-white neighborhood we lived in, I began to feel that there could be interesting political developments among the adult population of the area.

Actually, before the oil spill, in 1968, a Los Angeles developer proposed building a condo apartment building on a bluff overlooking the ocean. (At that time, there were no regulations governing oceanside development.) The lot was apparently zoned for such residential development. A citizens committee formed, Committee for Shoreline Preservation, and circulated an initiative, rezoning the property for a park. Thousands of signatures were gathered, and a major battle ensued. Many people who signed the initiative had failed to write their zip codes on the petition. Two elderly ladies from the committee, Selma Rubin and Anna Laura Meyers, painstakingly added the appropriate zip code wherever it was missing. When the petitions were filed, the county's district attorney, part of the old boy power structure of realtors and businessmen, promptly arrested them, charging forgery (or petition falsification, or some such thing). They were promptly bailed out, but the charges were pursued to a trial, where they were found not guilty. The district attorney appealed the decision—all the way to the state supreme court in his pursuit of these two "criminals"! (He was subsequently defeated by a new breed, a Democratic district attorney, and moved to rural Northern California.)

Another oceanfront property, the site of an abandoned nursery and the largest piece of privately owned undeveloped oceanside property in the state, was ripe for development. Many developers had tried to obtain and build on it, only to be thwarted by the owners' price and some city regulations. After more than twenty years, in the 1990s, another committee (Preserve the Wilcox Property, as it was known) was formed, and it initiated, first, negotiations with the owners to offer the land at a reduced price and, second, a community-wide campaign to raise funds to buy it and turn it over to the city for a park. Their efforts were successful; over $2 million were raised—topped off by a generous donation from the Kirk and Michael Douglas families (Michael Douglas lived in the area). The Trust for Public Land purchased the property—and the Douglas Family Preserve now will remain as a public park.

This tradition of generous wealthy benefactors dates back to the 1920s, when Santa Barbara, which had been a watering-hole spa for the world's wealthy, became home to, typically, second sons of eastern industrialists. The first sons took over the family business, and the younger sons—often of an artistic or even bohemian bent (and possibly gay)—came to Santa Barbara, where they took civic pride in contributing to the community. Long stretches of oceanfront were bought and donated to the city for parks; museums were created, and, after a devastating earthquake in 1926 laid waste to the downtown, it was rebuilt in a uniform Spanish colonial style, with buildings of great beauty and architectural distinction. This tradition was seized on by the newcomers of the 1960s and 1970s to help preserve Santa Barbara as an "oasis of refinement" midst the ticky-tacky of growing Southern California.

In 1972 the seven-member city council was populated primarily by real-estate professionals and downtown businessmen, elected at large. With the growing university, there was an increasing demand for housing—both in the city and in the nearby unincorporated Goleta Valley. Any and all proposals that developers brought forward seemed to be approved by the city council—often on appeal from a planning commission denial. People began to feel that the community was being given away to overdevelopment. An ad appeared in the *News-Press*, inviting all interested residents to a meeting at the local Red Cross facility to discuss an upcoming city election and the issues it raised. I spoke at that community meeting (about the need for a racially integrated community, as I remember) and found myself on the elected steering committee of what would become the Citizens Coalition. I helped write the platform and bylaws, and became vice chair of the organization.

## CITIZENS COALITION DECLARATION OF PRINCIPLES

MICKEY:

The following is an abridged version of the coalition's declaration, which was published as a mock newspaper, and sent as an election mailer to every registered voter in the city. In the original, each heading below contains a paragraph detailing its meaning.

> The City election this spring will mark a crossroad for Santa Barbara. The directions in which the new City Council moves will have profound and lasting effects on the life of our city. The Citizens Coalition was created to seek out, select and support those candidates who seem most likely to serve the citizens of Santa Barbara as members of a competent, effective and forward-looking City Council.
>
> To promote and ensure a city of beauty and harmony, prosperity and justice, we the Citizens Coalition and, indeed, the people of Santa Barbara seek and require:
>
> A City Council That Is Responsible and Responsive to the Needs and Wishes of All Constituents
> A City Council That Plans for the Future
> A City Council That Understands the Meaning and Value of Culture and Recreation
> A City Council That Understands That Community Programs Are Vital to the People
> A City Council That Inspires an Attitude of Respect
> A City Council That Will Encourage Responsible Business Activity
> A City Council That Conserves the People's Money
> A City Council That Supports the Public's Right to Know

By a fluke, four of the seven seats were up for election at one time, and the coalition ran a vigorous campaign that elected all four of our endorsed candidates. Boy, this was easy! A lot better than Democratic Party politics in Chicago or even Ann Arbor! (California local elections for councils and boards of supervisors are nonpartisan.) This was hardly a left-wing coup; Dick accurately described our four new councilmembers as a defense engineer, the wife of a retired U.S. Army colonel, a realtor, and one ringer—the first Latino (Chicano, we said then) councilmember, a union plasterer, who later left the area for New Mexico, where he ran for office as a Republican. One of the first acts of the council was to commission a study on the impacts of growth, conducted by Harvey Molotch and Rich Appelbaum (another sociology colleague), with the assistance of (mostly unpaid) community members. This study, done before the era of desktop computers, was also assisted by a sympathetic executive at the local office of a major defense contractor, on a room-size IBM computer, and written on electric typewriters. It was, in essence, an environmental impact analysis, done long before anyone had heard the term. It analyzed the impacts that various population levels might have on the city—culturally, environmentally, economically, and socially. It found that the most minimal impacts would occur if the zoning were configured to allow building to accommodate a population of eighty-five thousand—an increase of about six thousand from the existing population. The study was groundbreaking—in its methodology, assumptions, and conclusions. It was titled "The Impacts of Growth," and every planner educated since 1975 has heard of it.

The city, in an update of its general plan, enacted the zoning that was designed to limit the population to eighty-five thousand, and "no growth" became the mantra of the local environmental movement. The oil spill had taught the community that corporate interests were often antithetical to residents' "quality of life" and could be (more or less) successfully fought; now, we could fight developers, as well.

Politics had changed in Santa Barbara. In relatively short order we elected an environmental majority to the board of supervisors (the county's governing body) and a progressive Democrat to the state assembly and, later, the state senate. The new growth in the area has resulted in a majority of 58 percent registered Democrats in the city, and the area has lost its reputation as a conservative backwater. We believe that we played some part in making that happen. We found that speaking at local governmental meetings had some impact. It was reported in the newspaper and was often paid attention to by elected and appointed officials. I was asked by a progressive personnel director to help draft the city's affirmative action plan and later served as chair of the Santa Barbara County Affirmative Action Commission. We began to joke about "socialism in one small city. . . ."

The redevelopment of Stearns Wharf after a destructive fire provides an example of our brand of "socialism": under much debate at a series of city council meetings (with much public participation) was what kinds of businesses—stores and/or restaurants—would be permitted on the city-owned wharf. Of great concern was the notion that there be businesses that would attract all classes of people: a touristic T-shirt shop as well as a fine arts store, a longtime tenant coffee shop as well as a gourmet ice cream store, a fine dining restaurant as well as a locally owned hamburger joint. . . . Such decisions are not often made in such a participatory manner, and we (once again) felt proud to live in the community. As the years have marched on, we've come to expect such democratic participation in planning decisions—and we've, by and large, not been disappointed.

My affirmative action work led to a fun time for me and Dick. The American Psychological Association (APA) was to hold its annual meeting in Honolulu, Hawaii, in 1971. Dick was a board member of the Society for the Psychological Study of Social Issues (SPSSI) and was invited to attend the meeting, with all costs covered. There was some protest that holding the meeting in Hawaii made attending it difficult or impossible for graduate students and others whose expenses were not paid by some institution. Dick, therefore, was not planning to go. We got a call from Rebecca Mills, a fellow SDS founder, who worked in Berkeley as an affirmative action consultant. She was scheduled to speak at the APA meeting, to the occupational psychology section. She couldn't go and wondered if I would like to speak in her stead. No expenses were to be paid, but I wouldn't simply read her paper, but would make my own remarks. Now we saw the whole thing as a boondoggling lark and decided to go. I spoke informally, without actually writing a paper, and speculated on what could happen in the workplace if the goals of affirmative action were achieved and offices were "overrun" with women. I imagined on-site child care provided by employers, nursing stations throughout the offices and factory floors, and a warmer, friendlier atmosphere in the nation's corridors of business power. Mostly, the industrial psychologists blanched at all these thoughts, and I have since been warmed by seeing some of them come to pass—though not, unfortunately, the last dream. . . . We loved Hawaii, and we've since returned many times, with the kids, and by ourselves. We chose to celebrate our fiftieth wedding anniversary on Maui. (People say, "But you live in Santa Barbara! Why do you need Hawaii?" To which I reply, "The beach in Hawaii:Santa Barbara = Santa Barbara beach:Coney Island!")

## RAISING PROGRESSIVE, JEWISH KIDS
## IN SANTA BARBARA

MICKEY:

The one thing we really missed as we settled into Santa Barbara life was a significant secular Jewish community, like the one in which we had grown up. Especially as our children began to "come of age," we wondered if and how we could be successful in transmitting the knowledge and values that were so important to our politics and our lives. We did send our kids back East to Camp Kinderland (which was and is still going strong), but with limited success: they, as Californians among kids from New York or Boston who saw and knew each other all year, were too much the "outsiders" to really absorb all that Kinderland had to offer.

I knew a few other families with some of the same background and quandaries and decided to get them together to start a secular Jewish "Monday school." Some of the young women among the "Pink Ladies" agreed to be teachers, and we got after-school space on Monday afternoons at our local elementary school (after we assured the school that the program was not religious but cultural and was open to all) and a curriculum from my brother, Hershl, who was director of a large such school in Los Angeles (the Sholem School). The parents agreed to pay the fees needed to pay the teachers, but didn't really step up to participate in helping create and run an institution, no matter how small.

I eventually tired of doing most of the work, and the "school" fell apart. I did continue teaching a small group of twelve-year-olds, a sort of pre–bar/bat mitzvah class. I taught about twentieth-century Jewish American history and, for a "term paper," asked them to interview their grandparents (or other older relatives) to trace their own history. For my own kids (who were in that class), I asked each in turn what aspect of Jewish history or culture interested them most and helped them prepare to deliver a *droshe* (exegesis or speech) for their bar mitzvah in our large backyard, sans rabbi or prayers or blessings. Their friends, of course, were having more traditional bar mitzvahs at this time, and we would often go to the service in the local Reform temple, seeking something in the traditional service that resonated with our values. I found that the grandfather's (usually) handing the Torah to the bar/bat mitzvah as a symbol of the passing on of lore "from generation to generation" (as the Passover Haggadah states each year) met that criterion. At our kids' bar mitzvahs, instead of the five books of Moses (the

Pentateuch, or Torah), five different members of the family presented the bar mitzvah with a "book" or other symbol of his history and tradition. For instance, my mother, Sonia, gave Chuck my father's tailor's shears, which my brother had mounted on a plaque, in "memory of Charles (Yekhiel) Hartman, who was proud of his craft and of his class." Sonia presented it sort of in the name of the international working class, which would one day triumph! There wasn't a dry eye in the house as Sonia reminded Chuck to be a "credit to his family, to his people, and to humanity." I felt that we had passed it on. At the end, Chuck recited Hershl's "Credo for a Secular Bar/ Bas Mitzvah":

**I am I**

**I am a human being**
Nothing that touches other human beings is strange or foreign to me.
All women and men are my sisters and brothers.

**I am an American**
The dreams of the millions who came here, who sweated, struggled and died for their dreams . . . all this is my heritage. The dreams are not yet fulfilled. There-fore, my heritage is my responsibility: to carry on the struggle for the dream.

**I am a Jew**
My roots are deep in the millennia that formed my people's culture. My people is not chosen: it is unique, as every people is unique.

The freedom dream of Moses is my heritage, and the picket lines of the sweatshops. I am a descendant of the Prophets, and the uprisings in Europe's ghettos and death camps. My inheritance is in the songs of Solomon and Hirsh Glick, in the wisdom of Maimonides, Sholem Aleichem and I. L. Peretz, in the heroism of Masada and Hannah Senesh. The beauty of my people's dreams finds voice in Yiddish, in Hebrew, in Ladino and in all the languages of the world.

**I am a Jew**
Every person must have roots and these are mine.

**I am I**
My eyes and hopes are on the future. My identity and my strength come from the past and from the present. From the heritage of all our yesterdays I will help build a humane tomorrow for humanity.

Text by Hershl Hartman
For the Jewish Secular Conference

When Marc's turn came, three years later, our program introduction read as follows:

> Welcome to the 2nd (and last) triennial Bar Mitzva at the Flacks'. Again, we want to share with our community of friends and family elements of the tradition of our parents, in which we were raised, and in which we have tried to raise our children. The occasion of Marc's 13th birthday provides an opportunity to celebrate this tradition.
>
> Our tradition is a secular, Jewish one: it includes elements of our ancestral past (i.e. the ritual marking of passage from childhood to adulthood), the Prophetic tradition of Elijah and Isaiah is part of it, the Yiddish language and the verbal and musical literature created by people whose mother tongue was Yiddish plays an important role in it. The prophets of recent centuries are also a vital part of our tradition: the legacies of Jefferson, Marx, Eugene V. Debs, Emma Goldman, ML King and C. Wright Mills have become entwined with our own roots in the ghettos of Eastern Europe and New York, to produce the flower of progressive, Jewish secularism, which we are trying to transplant into the warm, but not always hospitable, soil of Santa Barbara.
>
> Marc Ajay Flacks was named for his great-grandmother, Mary Flacks, for the artist Marc Chagall, for Congressman Vito Marcantonio, and for pacifist-socialist A. J. Muste. The values embodied and expressed by all those people are part of the tradition we share with you today—as well as the joy of 13-year-old Marc!

Marc decided to recite a new translation (by his mother) of the piece by Sholem Aleichem on which "If I Were a Rich Man" (from *Fiddler on the Roof*) is based, and the house was again brought down by my singing—with my mother!—a charming Yiddish lullaby about a baby who very much reminded me of Marc. It ended with the (translated) words: "'Twill take much work and mother's tears, / Until a *mentsh* emerges from you!"

While we were proudly asserting our Jewish and left-wing identities, we very much wanted to make sure that our kids would not feel too much like strangers in a strange land. We felt that maintaining that identity in the face of forces for assimilation would make them stronger, but we wanted them to feel that they "belonged" as well. Chuck joined a community swim team and a wrestling team and played flag football with his buddies. Later he was a star in the junior high and high school musical theater scene—and was the toast of his junior high when Jane Fonda (who was married to Tom Hayden; they'd bought a ranch in Santa Barbara that served as a children's camp and progressive conference center) came to see him in *You're a Good Man, Charlie Brown* and came backstage!

In elementary school, he was one of about three Jewish kids in the entire school. When he came home singing all the usual Christmas carols, I protested to Principal Ehrenborg that he should "put the Christ back in Christmas, the 'Kh' back in Hanukkah, and get them both out of the public school." Thereafter, the school celebrated "winter holidays around the world," and the school secretary, whenever she saw me, would say "Here comes the Grinch!" (I think she said it in admiration. . . .) I must admit that, first, I accepted an invitation to come to Chuck's class and talk about Khanuka; it was 1973, and I told the story of the Maccabees as if they were the Vietcong, fighting imperialism, and made sure to draw the parallels. The kids seemed impressed! Chuck did not seem at all embarrassed by his mother and went on to be a political science major at the University of California, Santa Cruz, and a master's in public policy from Harvard's Kennedy School. He currently is coordinator of Santa Barbara County's programs for the homeless.

Marc went whole hog with this "belonging" stuff: first, he beat up a kid in fifth grade who had called him, derisively, "You Jew!" (His teacher couldn't understand why he was so angry; she said that she wouldn't mind if someone said to her "You Christian!"—an atypically dense teacher at that school, who couldn't understand Marc at all.) At Santa Barbara High School, which was the most integrated school in the area—about 60 percent Latino, plus kids from the wealthy Montecito suburb, along with us middle-class Anglos—Marc became a star defensive end on the football team, as well as "spirit leader," a school-wide elected position, and was also a member of the elite choral group. He was known, seemingly, by the whole school, and for years couldn't walk down State Street without being hailed by Santa Barbara High School alumni. All of this helped him get into Wesleyan University, from which he graduated in 1990. He is now a PhD sociologist (the family business?), teaching at a community college in Northern California.

We also did not—contrary to the fashion then current—try to shield our kids from popular culture. We ourselves had grown up with the Lone Ranger and the Green Hornet on the radio, Superman and Batman in the comic books (though we weren't allowed to buy them—we had to make do with leftovers from other kids), along with Howard Fast and Paul Robeson and Yiddish literature, and we felt that being an integrated part of the surrounding community required a common vocabulary with its members. Much of this vocabulary stems from the popular culture. The only thing we wouldn't let the kids watch was the TV news during the Vietnam war … too scary. We also provided the 1970s–80s versions of Fast and Robeson, as our family listened to recordings of and sang the songs of Pete Seeger and Woody and Arlo Guthrie and (early) Bob Dylan and the Freedom Singers and all of it! I would often return hoarse from a long car trip of singing with the kids. (Their Camp Kinderland experience helped with this, also.)

Also contrary to the fashion then current, we believed that our kids would benefit from being looked after—at least some of the time—by persons other than their parents. We were fortunate that Dick's parents, Dave and Mildred, retired in 1972 and moved to Goleta (actually, to Isla Vista!). Both were schoolteachers as well as grandparents and genuinely enjoyed caring for the kids. In September 1973, we even went off for more than three weeks to an American Sociological Association meeting in New York and then to the USSR and Warsaw and Paris and London, while Dave and Mildred stayed in our house with the kids. But we also hired various babysitters, and Marc, from the age of two, went to the UCSB Childcare Center that we helped to establish, until he started kindergarten. We jokingly said our kids were being subjected to "benign neglect," and we felt they benefited from it. I hope so!

Many of the hip, progressive parents of that era believed in in-home schooling, or parent participation nursery and elementary schools. I, however, ever the "working-class contrarian," wrote an article for the alternative schools newsletter on "why we send our kids to public school," outlining our position and suggesting that alternative schooling was simply elitist unless it was part of public schooling. Even as that has become more and more the case, especially with some charter schools, I still believe that kids from "alternative" families should be in the public schools—both for their own and for the school's benefit. This is not to say that parents should make their kids fight the battles that the elders should be fighting or that kids should be subjected to abuse in a racially divided school. But part of the decision about where to live, I believe, should consider what the neighborhood public school is like and can our kids thrive there. (Kids from progressive families can probably thrive anywhere.) Similarly, if neighborhood schools are to improve, they need the help of progressive parents who are adept at questioning authority and willing to play a role in their child's public school. Segregating ourselves is not the answer.

# 12 ▸ A LONG MARCH?

DICK:

The community-based politics that we were undertaking in the 1970s in Santa Barbara would have seemed surprising and strange to people in the movement in the late 1960s. In those years, the dominant voice within the movement was speaking a rhetoric of "revolution," as in the following kind of talk (with my own paraphrasing) that was prevalent: "America as we know it is intransigent. The war escalates in the face of the huge mass mobilizations, in the face of draft resistance, in the face of articulate public opinion. At the same time, the apparatus of repression is evidently strengthening. The war drains away the potential for progressive domestic policy and the leaders of progressive reform (King, JFK, RFK) are being eradicated. Isn't the United States of America a giant imperial octopus that is exploiting the world while reinforcing class and racial oppression? Conventional politics won't change this, and Malcolm X and the Black Panthers are right—neither will nonviolent direct action. The armed struggle of the National Liberation Front in Vietnam, however, is defeating the American empire."

The revolutionary mood and mode was very hard to question within the movement: any sign of such questioning was taken as a sign of weakness, revealing a lack of commitment, an expression of privilege, a betrayal. But, of course, there was a big problem: besides the ways that this line of talk alienated most Americans from the movement, and besides the fact that it provided a justification for police crackdown on the movement, the problem was that it was proposing a transformation of society *against the majority*.

The Weatherman faction of SDS fantasized a kind of solution to that conundrum. They seemed to believe for a time that black America was ready to rise up, that there were in addition a significant number of youth (both of color and white) ready to tear down authority, and that the revolutionary upsurge of these sectors could be sparked by bold (and possibly suicidal) direct action. Such an upsurge would surely win the support of the majority of the world's people, they asserted, even if the American majority opposed it. In short, the revolutionary perspective, when thought of in any strategic terms, meant abandoning hope of getting the majority of white people to support progressive change and, it seemed to me, was envisioning a kind of self-sacrificing revolutionary suicide for white activists. Weather members enacted this scenario, going underground and plotting terrorist moves that were ultimately self-defeating and self-destructive.

I thought (and wrote a little in this vein): this was a politics rooted in guilt. It was honorable for these folks, many born into very wealthy, or at least very comfortable, circumstances to feel guilty about their privilege and to search for ways to explode it. But such guilt—which earlier in the sixties had led many of them into deep engagement in civil rights and anti-poverty struggles—rather than being a resource for long-term struggle was turning into a politics of destruction. And, ironically, the underground terroristic course they took, it seemed to me, was an acting out of the elitism they thought they were overcoming. They would make history no matter what the interests and feeling of ordinary people.

In the late 1960s and early 1970s, after we'd settled in Santa Barbara, the revolutionary mood was widespread, but it was being expressed in more cultural and anarchist terms. The burning of the Isla Vista Bank of America was an act of spontaneous rebellion. After the fact, it got defined by ideologically oriented movement activists as an exemplary action in a revolutionary trajectory. When that definition was proclaimed by visiting revolutionary personages, it wasn't well received. Radicalized students wanted to know about action alternatives that didn't have to result in their own self-destruction.

In those years, I was constantly struck by just how much students were ready to imagine impending apocalypse. In my classes, I developed an exercise asking students to imagine where the world would be in ten years. The typical responses emphasized the likelihood of nuclear war or of an environmental catastrophe of such proportions that it would deeply threaten the capacity to live in normal ways. More politically minded students assumed that a civil war or fascistic police state lay ahead.

I was troubled by the thought that, however horrific, these scenarios had a certain appeal. For young people at that moment, imagining the apocalypse enabled them to avoid the need to figure out their own personal choices. History would decide their fate. The counterculture, the youth revolt, challenged those affected to determine how their lives in the long term might be lived, but neither the movement nor the society at large offered coherent paths. For a lot of youth at that moment, apocalypse offered the promise of living in history—and maybe never having to grow old.

I couldn't absolutely deny that the chaos of that period wouldn't further intensify or claim that social breakdown or upheaval was impossible. But as a teacher—and as someone committed to social change—I worried that the apocalyptic mood was not functional for people who would, after all, probably live for a few more decades. I wanted to encourage them to think that their energy and creativity could make a newer world possible. In the climate at the start of the seventies, it was difficult to engage students in serious conversation about the longer run.

MICKEY:

I felt the same way about the women's movement. Did these young women really believe that they would all be lesbians, spending their lives separate from men, not marrying or raising children? Did they all believe they would have fabulous careers (à la Gloria Steinem or Germaine Greer or Jane Fonda?) and never need to worry about simply making a living? It seemed to me that many of the women in, say, the Chicago women's lib movement, did think this way, and I did not really want to engage them in argument, but felt quite alienated from them. In California, Berkeley "women's libbers" seemed also to be of that ilk. They organized a California conference, held in Santa Barbara, where they came and berated all women in relationships with men as being "male identified"; I certainly was proudly such!

DICK:

In the last chapter we talked a bit about how conversation about the longer run eventually came to typify those who had been radicalized in Isla Vista in the late 1960s. But there were tragic outcomes as well. There were some who gave themselves to acts of violence in which they died or ended up going to jail for long, long sentences (and some of latter are still in prison). Some young people of promise were wrecked psychologically—wreckage that some were able to climb out of and others not.

Another waste to me was the fact that some onetime New Left activists were drawn to the old and, I think, discredited the idea that revolution demanded and could be led by a "vanguard party." So several "new Communist parties" were formed in the late 1960s and early 1970s based on variants of Maoism, presumably because it appeared that Mao Tse-tung, in fact, had found the true path to revolution. These revolutionary sects, like the original Communist Party, attracted and helped shape some very talented organizers. However out of touch they were with reality, these parties encouraged members to go into factory work and strive to exercise leadership on the shop floor. As the Chinese communist leadership jettisoned Maoism (and socialism), the new Communist parties disintegrated—but some of their former members continued their dedicated engagement with the labor movement. Indeed, some of the most respected figures in the contemporary labor movement today had such beginnings (including some who had been my students at the University of Chicago and at UCSB).

The Thursday Club at UCSB created the space within which "revolutionary" student activists could figure out projects and paths for the long-term struggle. It's one local example of what turned out to be a national trend in the early 1970s—the coming together of sixties radicals to figure out how their personal life courses could be entwined with social transformation.

Some people have written about the New Left as a tragic story, in which the bright promise of the early 1960s was degraded and destroyed by the end of the decade. Our experience was quite different. Despite the collapse of SDS and SNCC, and the turn toward madness evinced by the Weatherman and Maoist sects, I'd argue that the spirit of the New Left was carried forward in projects, counter-institutions, and local organizations in dozens of communities (many, like Santa Barbara, once conservative bastions) and in the form of new social movements—feminism, environmentalism, gay liberation, and related developments. The vision of grassroots democracy that had been expressed by SDS and SNCC was, in the 1970s, being put into practice in the wider world.

## TOM HAYDEN RUNS FOR SENATE

DICK:

An important moment in the New Left's turn toward long-term political engagement was the decision by our SDS comrade, Tom Hayden, to run for the U.S. Senate in the California Democratic primary in 1975.

After the Chicago conspiracy trial, Tom had gone to Berkeley, where he became identified with the revolutionary ferment of the late 1960s there, sharing both the fantasies and frustrations of the Red Family and the countercultural whirl in which that collective was embedded.

Eventually, however, Tom partnered politically with Jane Fonda and others in an effort to stop the war in Vietnam. They embarked on a strategic effort to focus on Congress and see if a congressional majority could be built to stop appropriating money for the war. Jane had led a project aimed at mobilizing anti-war sentiment among GIs; she had done a very successful set of tours with other show business people, a kind of counter USO (United Service Organizations) effort called Fuck the Army (it could also mean Free the Army), or FTA. It was surprising, given her national celebrity and notoriety, when she became romantically involved with Tom—not the image of a movie star's romantic partner, of course. We were excited by making a connection with her; for one thing, Mickey had always been a big fan of Henry Fonda, particularly his role as Tom Joad in the *Grapes of Wrath*. It was a peak experience for Mickey to be able to tell Jane Fonda how much she loved Henry's performance. At Tom and Jane's wedding, Jane took Mickey by the hand and led her to Henry: "Tell him," she said, "about how you feel about his Tom Joad!" When Henry died some years later, Mickey sent Jane a condolence card quoting Tom Joad's final speech to Ma Joad: "I'll be there, Ma. . . ." Jane put it on her "official" announcement of Henry's death.

One day, early in 1975, we visited Tom. Jane was on location, and he was babysitting their two-year-old son, Troy. Tom seemed, on the one hand, sort of feckless, not wanting to be consigned to a house-husbanding role and, on the other hand, intrigued by the possibility that the sixties generation might become a potent electoral force. He declared to us his interest in possibly running against John Tunney, the incumbent California Democratic senator in the June 1976 primary.

Even though George McGovern's presidential campaign in 1972 had a disastrous outcome, the aftermath turned out to be rather hopeful. The monumental unravelling of the Nixon administration created unexpected space for the Democrats nationally; meanwhile, Tom could imagine an accelerating development of a progressive force within the Democratic Party in California. His candidacy could help crystallize such a force; given his recognition as both an anti-war leader and Jane's husband, he assumed that he had a potential base—and Jane would be a formidable fund-raiser.

Mickey and I certainly wanted to support this effort; by fall of 1975, we were working hard to organize the Hayden enterprise in the Santa Barbara region. We were proud that Tom carried Santa Barbara County in the June primary as the result of a local campaign that had a good grassroots volunteer army and that could capitalize on the burgeoning youth voting bloc in the region. Statewide, Tom got more than a million votes, which was generally seen as a surprising achievement for a notorious radical activist. The Hayden vote seemed to suggest that there was a sizable progressive political base, undoubtedly concentrated in the under-thirty generation, but destined to grow. Of course, it helped that Tom's campaign had the backing of Jane Fonda, who was able to raise a lot of money—and it was a particular benefit to have Henry Fonda make television commercials supporting Tom.

An important aspect of the campaign was the development of an ambitious program. Derek Shearer, who had coined the phrase *economic democracy*, and done much writing to help define it in policy terms, led a team that included our friend Bill Domhoff, the leading sociological researcher of the "power elite." In the late 1960s Bill had argued, without much immediate effect, that the Left ought to base its electoral strategy, not on futile efforts to start third parties, but on running strongly articulated campaigns in Democratic primaries. Bill had come to the Left in the 1960s out of a career as a psychologist studying dreams. He was much the all-American boy, having served as a batboy for the Cleveland Indians in his youth; stocky and muscular, he reminded one of Mr. Clean. He and his family spent a year in Santa Barbara in 1970–71 when he was a visiting professor; we'd become good friends. The Domhoffs had four kids—and their two boys were the same ages as ours. Family trips to Santa Cruz (where Bill was a faculty leader) helped sustain our friendship.

Bill's fusing of vision and hardheadedness—and his lack of leftish ideological baggage—turned out to be a real asset to writing a new Hayden campaign manifesto. We called the pamphlet *Make the Future Ours*.

Tom's campaign wasn't the only significant electoral effort deriving from the anti-war movement and the New Left. In college towns, new coalitions led by New Left veterans were winning control. Most dramatically, this was happening in Madison, Wisconsin, where former student leader Paul Soglin (whose mother lived in Santa Barbara and was part of our secular Jewish group) was elected mayor, reflecting and propelling the radicalization of the state capital. You could see similar things happening in Ann Arbor, Berkeley, and Santa Cruz.

Less expected was the rise of a powerful left force in Santa Monica, where Derek Shearer's wife, Ruth Yannatta Goldway, was elected mayor, and Santa Monica's rent control movement took over the city government. Derek, a young journalist, but too young to have been active in the sixties, had gone to Yale, where in the late 1960s he befriended and got to know Bill and Hillary Clinton (Derek's sister was dating, and eventually married, Bill Clinton's roommate, Strobe Talbott). Derek's father, Lloyd Shearer, was the founder and editor of *Parade Magazine*, the Sunday supplement to most of America's newspapers. Derek was at ease with people of every station; he combined an easy familiarity with the ways of the powerful with a kind of rational populism. Ruth, daughter of the well-known Marxist intellectual David Goldway, had helped spark a grassroots consumer movement in Santa Monica. Once they married, Derek helped make her the mayor as the Santa Monica electoral machine was gathering force.

When we first laid eyes on Ruth (before that we thought that, given the name Yannatta, she was maybe Japanese) at a Santa Barbara conference about new economic ideas, we realized that she was Ruthie Goldway, whom we both knew from camps Wyandot and Kinderland. It was a pleasure to see her in this leadership role and to become close friends with Derek and Ruth. They loved giving book parties and other entertainments, and their Santa Monica house became a salon for progressive activists and intellectuals.

Derek's use of the phrase *economic democracy* helped crystallize the Hayden campaign's purposes. It built on the Port Huron concept of participatory democracy, arguing for a politics that went beyond the welfare state, beyond the provision of a social welfare for workers and the poor, toward a politics that aimed at curbing corporate power, creating mechanisms of regulation and planning at the local and national level, and building up alternatives to private banks to create enterprises and promote economic development under public control. Similar ways of thinking were emerging in Europe under labels such as "Euro socialism" and "Euro communism"; elements of the European Left were trying to reach beyond the established framework of welfare state politics (a politics already beginning to falter because of budget crises, among other factors). It seemed as if the Western Left was coming to a shared new perspective: the welfare state had saved capitalism after the Depression and World War II, but it was not adequate for dealing with environmental destruction and for sustaining social justice. And revolutionary socialism had proven to be an ideological and political dead end. But something new might be in the offing: an agenda of structural reform aimed at democratic control of the economy might be the basis of a rising electoral Left.

The Hayden campaign was an opportunity to begin to express and test these ideas. More importantly, it laid some groundwork for development of networks of activists and academics that advanced economic democracy in policy and in politics.

When Jimmy Carter was elected president, one of the innovations in his administration was the establishment of a national co-op bank—a federally funded center for providing financial and technical support to consumer cooperatives. Derek Shearer was appointed to its founding board. Other Hayden campaigners got posts in other Carter programs. The VISTA (Volunteers in Service to America) program, for example, provided a federal government framework for funding community-based organizer training that could enhance citizen action. It was initially headed by Marge Tabankin (who has said that she joined the New Left upon hearing a speech as a teenager by Tom Hayden); in California, it was headed by Hayden campaign activist Loni Hancock, who later became mayor of Berkeley and then a California state senator.

In California, after Tom's defeat, he and others who had worked on his campaign founded a new political organization, as planned. It was called the Campaign for Economic Democracy (CED). Mickey and I helped organize a founding CED conference in Santa Barbara that drew hundreds of community activists, progressive elected and appointed officials, and policy-oriented academics. CED's aim was ambitious—to create a policy agenda for California, a network of community-based organizations, and a strategy for electing progressives at every government level.

FIGURE 12.1. Tom Hayden (1939–2016)

These CED plans were not a strategy unique to California. A loose national network had formed even before 1975—awkwardly called the National Conference on Alternative State and Local Public Policy (we called it ASLAP). It was based at the Institute for Policy Studies in Washington, D.C., and staffed by some SDS veterans. Mickey and I attended annual ASLAP conferences and encountered some people who later became national political figures, including Barney Frank, Bryan Dorgan, Miles Rapaport, and many local activists who had led successful campaigns that were establishing progressive city councils, not only in the small university towns where such campaigns had started, but in larger cities like Austin, Texas, and New Haven, Connecticut, as well. Ideas that were generated by the conferences and in ASLAP publications became resources for local action. Mickey and I took the lead in California in organizing a couple of statewide ASLAP conferences, and these helped foster a number of networks with respect to housing, health care, and environmental policy. The Santa Barbara conference that launched CED was at first envisioned as an ASLAP event—but we were willing to merge with the CED plan.

For us, that founding conference was memorable:

MICKEY:

The founding conference was held on a weekend in Santa Barbara, at the beautiful Santa Barbara City College campus, overlooking the downtown beaches. Friday night was to be devoted to a cultural event starring Henry and Jane Fonda, George Takei, and others of note, doing various readings. When I came home from work that Friday afternoon, I found James Garner (one of my favorites, who had chauffeured Henry up from Los Angeles) sitting in my living room, playing with our kids. At Dick's desk in his study sat Henry, studying his script for the evening's reading. At the dining room table, Sam Brown (later to be elected state treasurer of Colorado) sat scribbling some notes for a speech he was to make that evening. Henry emerged from the study and saw Sam's scribbles; we saw them, too, and reminded Sam that he had only ten minutes to speak and already had two or three pages of notes. "You're going to speak for ten minutes from THAT?" Henry exclaimed incredulously. . . .

DICK:

We began to see in the mid-1970s that our efforts at local political organization and activism were part of a national movement. It was a decentered

FIGURE 12.2. Mickey, serving as MC, welcoming Berkeley congressman Ron Dellums to keynote the founding conference of the Campaign for Economic Democracy in Santa Barbara (photo by Anne Marie Staas, c. 1975)

movement, very loose and not coordinated, but nevertheless offering a bottom-up process that might lead toward new directions for the society as a whole.

CED took shape, however, as a quite structured operation, with a central staff and a statewide policy direction. Local chapters were required to follow the statewide agenda and support its structure. This setup turned out to be difficult for us to commit to. Before CED established itself, we'd been leaders of a diverse group of Santa Barbara activists who had set up a new local organization, Network, a successor to the Citizens Coalition. The coalition had been an ad hoc group that served at election time to sponsor candidate slates supporting anti-growth, environmentalist positions. We saw the need for a continuing organizational structure, with a membership base that could support a staff that could advocate and lobby in local government. Local development interests were stepping up their own political efforts, in alliance with the oil industry and others that hoped to defeat or dilute the environmental majority in the region. One of their talking points was that growth and environmental regulation hurt poor and working people—costing jobs and raising housing prices.

Network forged another view: that environmental protection was crucial for everyone and that democratic planning could foster a local economy from which all could benefit. Our immediate aim was to persuade environmentalists to adopt such a perspective. We wanted to overcome what was getting to be called Nimbyism ("Not in my backyard")—an attitude easily able to lurk inside the anti-growth politics that we were then speaking for. If, for example, you want to restrict population, we argued in contrast to Nimbyism, it was imperative to promote publicly subsidized housing for low- and middle-income folks—while blocking expansion of luxury and higher-end development.

## THE LONG MARCH STRATEGY

DICK:

The German New Left leader Rudi Dutschke had enunciated the strategy of the New Left as embarking on a "long march through the institutions of society." This was a play on the "long march" of Mao's Chinese People's Army; to us, it neatly stated what we were about—to make democratic transformation step by step, focusing on the communities and institutions in which we were embedded. It was a different kind of work than the "revolutionary apocalypse" so intensely imagined by young radicals a few years earlier.

It's important to see that a fundamental premise of the long march strategy was that the national welfare state that arose out of the New Deal would be preserved. For example, if there was to be housing for low- and moderate-income people, there had to be governmental subsidy for it; there was no way that the private market by itself could create affordable family housing even for middle-income people. Free marketeers claimed that expanding the housing supply would keep prices affordable. This claim, we knew, was not going to affect housing prices, especially in places like Santa Barbara; we could see that growth-oriented coastal communities were experiencing the same price inflation in housing as our growth-controlled region. There had to be significant public housing investment, nationally and locally, if average, let alone poor, families were to be able to rent or buy the housing they needed in the communities where they worked. The private market couldn't adequately supply the housing needs of working- and middle-class families.

Economic democracy as vision and program requires the maintenance of a vibrant public sector, in which the social safety net is in good shape and public investment in public goods is taken for granted for a healthy economy. Having come of age in postwar, post–New Deal America, we took these assumptions for granted. Our aim was to build on them, so that communities would have resources to control and plan their futures rather than be at the mercy of corporate and national government bureaucracies. We took for granted that there would be no political possibility to diminish or undermine the legacy of the New Deal. But the welfare state reinforced a top-down, bureaucratically organized society. Welfare benefits could weaken working-class solidarity and collective action. A powerful state, politically buttressed by government benefits, we believed, was allying with corporate elites to control the futures of ordinary people from above.

In the 1970s, therefore, it seemed that the political battles of the future would have to do with the degree to which corporate control over life and society could be offset by other institutional centers of initiative.

It was obvious, when it came to environmental issues that the future had to be one in which corporate power was controlled and regulated in ways that would enhance and protect the environment in all of its many ramifications. Well before global warming came to be the central focus of environmental concern, in Santa Barbara many were learning to talk about a "soft energy path"—replacing fossil fuels with a solar-powered economy that would be good for the planet and also for livelihood. The Santa Barbara oil spill compelled many in our region to become aware of such new thinking, finding the language to oppose further oil development, imagining Santa Barbara as a global leader on the soft path.

At some point, someone coined the phrase "Think globally, act locally." Like the "long march," it perfectly expressed and validated the politics we were doing. Indeed, strategies aimed at somehow fighting for national power seemed fruitless and pointless. Tom Hayden had the opportunity to visit Jimmy Carter in the White House, and he asked Carter whether it might be true, as Tom believed, that corporate power and the power of Wall Street was greater than the power of the presidency. Carter said, in effect, "That's what I've learned in my years in office so far."

It was a striking confirmation of what was in our bones: that progress in this country toward democracy might be more possible on a local level. Our localism contradicted liberal shibboleths about the inevitable backwardness of local politics and the necessity for federal power to institute change.

The battle for civil rights in the 1960s was necessarily about forcing federal power to overcome state-based white supremacy; the need to restore the economy in the Depression and to provide protections for working people from the crushing devastation of the marketplace demanded federal power and programs.

The question of oil development off the coast of Santa Barbara featured something different: federal power typically sided with the oil industry against local desire to control it. In the years after the 1969 oil spill, somehow our county government, allied with strong grassroots citizen mobilization, achieved agreements with the oil companies that regulated them far more effectively than federal government oversight had done. The same story could be told with respect to nuclear energy and with urban development.

By the early 1970s, in California, environmental legislation and citizen initiatives were providing new rules requiring environmental impact review of development, forcing developers into direct negotiations with environmentalists and resulting in the vetoing or significant modification of potentially destructive projects relating to land use and energy development. The struggle over these things never ends, but the balance of power has shifted a bit toward democracy with respect to such decisions—at least in our coastal California world.

An aside to you, the reader: Can you forgive these paragraphs of rather abstract analysis? I'm hoping that they'll help explain why the impulse to focus political action in our community seemed so persuasive, so right in those years.

## COUNTERCULTURAL CONTRADICTIONS

DICK:

Many members of the Thursday Club had been active in Isla Vista in the period after the year of bank burning and rebellion. In the first years of the 1970s, an exhilarating spirit of experimentation and social entrepreneurship was in the air in that unusual town. Given the countercultural climate of the youth ghetto, all kinds of social ventures seemed possible. The big idea was to make Isla Vista a fully legal city. If that had happened, a number of promising ideas about policing, justice, tenant rights, environmental planning, and social enterprise might have borne fruit—given the political and economic power that a city provides. Isla Vista cityhood was opposed by the powers that be, including the university, apartment owners, and county government. Apart from this powerful opposition, the life-cycle needs of most people living there made for a serious contradiction. It wasn't just that the student population turned over constantly and inevitably. It was also that even committed Isla Vista activists were only rarely able to settle down to live in this densely populated town of rather ticky-tacky apartments—where almost everybody was between seventeen and twenty-five years of age. After a while, most found it too constraining—a life with limited privacy and diversity and, ironically, where social permissiveness made a lot of demands on people to prove how free their spirits were.

The Thursday Club allowed some of these Isla Vista expatriates to further develop their social creativity even though they'd moved out of the Isla Vista scene. Seeds planted on a Thursday evening sprouted into a legal collective to represent youth, tenants, and political dissenters; the *Santa Barbara News and Review*; and the Community Environmental Council, aimed at both policy and instituting environmental practices like community recycling and urban agriculture. Many such projects were short-lived, given the lack of reliable financial support and given, again, the life cycle pressures (toward settling down and family), while other projects have grown into major permanent institutions. As these projects emerged and their participants became immersed in them, their time and the need for the Thursday Club ran out.

In the years since, the Santa Barbara region has been the site of literally dozens of projects, enterprises, and organizations that were created by activists and artists influenced by countercultural values. The history of the past fifty years in our town has been fundamentally shaped by the rise of these. A random list of important ones includes an alternative newspaper, community environmental development, a nonprofit environmental law firm, a farmers market, an international film festival, a Chicano community center, a multimillion-dollar progressive alternative to the United Way, the Women's Political Committee (whose endorsement of candidates for office is practically a requirement for election), a Pride foundation, student housing co-ops, a campus radio station, community access television, and much else.

Thinking back over these decades, I'm a little surprised how much my life has been shaped by the time that I've spent helping facilitate this local social entrepreneurship. In the early years, I enabled quite a few students to get academic credit for "interning" (as it is now called) in the development and staffing of some of these projects. I've served on a number of boards of these groups, helping them get the resources and support needed to sustain themselves. And Mickey and I were in on the ground floor of several of these.

These roles were greatly enabled by the fact that I was a professor of sociology. We professors, first of all, have a good deal of control over our daily time—and that makes it possible to go to meetings and otherwise devote energy to such projects. Because I teach sociology, it seemed to me that such activity was not only possible but necessary if I was to make a claim to understand the social world I was in. Moreover, I could claim some expertise in social organization that might be a resource for those I was working with.

In the end, I may have gotten more out of this activity than I gave. That's one of the joyful sides of civic engagement—it's a way to claim that your life has value. Building social institutions, like any construction work, enables you to point to something in the world and say, I helped put that there.

# 13 ▸ SOCIALISM IN ONE CITY

DICK:

In the 1970s, when economic democracy as a set of ideas, a program, and a vision and as an organizational framework was at its peak, we used to joke (but not only jokingly) that our goal was to make "socialism in one city." That is, of course, a play on words used in the aftermath of the Bolshevik revolution, when many Bolsheviks declared that it was possible to make socialism in one country rather than wait, as Leon Trotsky thought, until the workers of the world had in fact united and made revolution globally. Stalin made sure he won that argument—though in retrospect Trotsky sure had a point.

Santa Monica, where Tom Hayden lived and Ruth Yannatta Goldway was mayor, had come to be called the People's Republic of Santa Monica, largely because of its strong rent control policies. Whole books were being written about the left-wing reform movements aiming to take over American cities. Berkeley, the town at the heart of the sixties student rebellion, was probably the first to elect self-proclaimed radical majorities to its city council. One of my intellectual heroes, Ed Kirshner, was a Berkeley-based city planner who tried to spell out for the city's development a program that he based on a vision of public enterprises that might help support themselves and support a wider public sector. If one could municipalize electricity, gas, cable TV, and other utilities and invest public funds in consumer co-ops and the like, one could begin to transform, on the community level, the way the economy actually works. One could create jobs without the need for corporate dependency and empower community members to make key economic and planning decisions with resources to implement them. Ed even imagined the benefits of community ownership of land, in which developers would have to lease land from the community and therefore be subject to its control.

Ed had a rare capacity to be both visionary and hardheaded planner. I'm not sure what elements of his vision actually became policy in Berkeley, but in his time he became a wonderful consultant to communities seeking ways to develop affordable housing despite the lack of adequate public subsidy. In later years, Ed gave all that up to become an artist. But no one contributed more to making a plausible case for what the old-time Socialists called "municipal socialism"—a case for this as a strategy for societal as well as local change.

I'm still guided by this perspective, and it's worth mentioning right here that its essence has been taken up and organized for by another intellectual hero and friend, Gar Alperovitz. Gar started out as a legislative aide in Washington, D.C., in the sixties and, along with his colleague Arthur Waskow, was a strong and useful friend to the early SDS. He was active in ASLAP, as was Ed Kirshner, and, in that context, formulated a policy framework that he's been working on to the present day. Gar has exhaustively documented the many ways in American history that localities have gone beyond conventional market and capitalist rules to solve community problems. As I write this, Gar has launched a new political initiative called the Next System, aimed at demonstrating and fostering such community projects. Gar calls his vision the "pluralist commonwealth." This term encapsulates the same kind of vision as "participatory democracy"—and both terms seem too opaque and academic to be taken up by a popular uprising. But it's rooted in an appreciation of the valid mistrust that Americans have of the power of the state as well as of the megacorporation. It is an effort to continue what we at Port Huron were trying to do—to reimagine "socialism" as a decentralized framework that would encourage and be grounded in local initiative.[1]

In the 1960s New Left, we were sure that "socialism" had to be jettisoned as a label for our dreams. For most Americans, socialism meant an authoritarian system, an importation of unfreedom from foreign and even enemy places. A virtue of "participatory democracy" as a label for our vision is that it sheds the baggage that the word *socialism* inevitably seems to carry. I like to say that I'm a Socialist on Tuesdays and Thursdays and a participatory Democrat on Monday, Wednesday, and Friday. On the weekend, I might be an anarchist or a Jeffersonian Socialist. Underlying all these labels is a shared vision of social control of the economy that supersedes private power—but if it is to be democratic, that control has to be local and accessible to community will. That Bernie Sanders could win a vast popular following while calling himself and his program "socialist" really challenges the way SDSers thought about the matter. It seems that the newest Left is emerging with a clearly stated aim of going beyond capitalism—and that "socialism" provides a label for that. Ironically, what Sanders called a socialist program was a collation of social democratic goals already implemented in European countries that are not socialist. He avoided discussion of alternatives to private ownership, community control, and workplace democracy which are central to the "next system" way of thinking Still Bernie is showing that advocating vision and program beyond politically possible reforms and normalizing socialistic ideas can, for the first time in our lifetime, be the basis for popular politics. And his campaign has stimulated many to think about the long run visionary—after a couple of decades in which such thinking seemed to have vanished.

In the day-to-day of local political activism, one doesn't think in such visionary ways. In fact, that day-to-day is often frustrating—there's an enormous amount of petty detail about procedure and policy that one has to know about, and unexpected blockages and sidetracks are almost always going to happen. In the midst of such frustration, I not infrequently wonder whether we're spinning our wheels while the world spins out of control. Writing this, though, gives some opportunity for a bit of the long view, and thinking back over more than fifty years in the local scene, we can both see definite change in hoped-for ways and learn something of the limits of the "think globally, act locally" long march.

So here's a bit of an inventory of the changes attempted and some outcomes during our time in Santa Barbara. This isn't about taking personal credit for any of that, but to let this writing help record some of the history we've lived through and shared in our place and time.

## OIL

DICK:

The most important struggle in these years has had to do with energy development. We arrived in Santa Barbara just a few months after the great oil spill of January 1969. It was evident as soon as we got there that the oil spill had affected the community deeply. New organizations to promote environmental values had suddenly emerged, and there was an evident mobilization of people politically to protest oil development in particular and promote alternative energy—and this was happening in an area long thought of as a wealthy bastion of conservatism. The founding organization of all of this was Get Oil Out (GOO). Oil has never been "gotten out" of the Santa Barbara Channel—there are still oil rigs out there, and drilling is going on. But the anti-oil movement in Santa Barbara, which now encompasses the entire coast of California, has succeeded in preventing new development of oil lands off the coast in both federal and state waters.

This stoppage is not permanently guaranteed. It's not nailed down or carved in stone, and there are circumstances, no doubt, in which drilling could once again escalate, but it's a political achievement to have been able to stop the oil industry's development.

In the coastal region of Santa Barbara County the great majority of people will support politicians only if they are anti-oil. The county as a whole presents a bizarre political mix. The much more conservative North County area, which controls two of the five seats on the county board of supervisors, is politically dominated by those who are willing or eager to see further oil development, and so there has been a continuing battle for control of the board majority—and for the fate of the oil industry in the region.

Oil threatens the South Coast economically as well as environmentally. The economy of the South Coast is highly dependent on it being maintained as an attractive place. There's a vast tourist industry that depends on this, but so do the university and the technology companies (Santa Barbara is known as "Silicon Beach") that make their home there.

Here's a story I witnessed firsthand. In the 1980s, the Atlantic Richfield Company (ARCO) announced plans to develop an oil lease it controlled that was five miles off the beachfront of UCSB. Chancellor Robert Huttenback undoubtedly thought that the university could benefit from some of the money that the oil company would dole out in compensation for the noise, the air pollution, and the threat of oil spill that its industrialization of the coastal waters would produce. As the ARCO plan became known, many people in the community and on campus—students, faculty, and some in the administration—thought that Huttenback was trying to make a fool's bargain.

Fortuitously, Huttenback was forced to resign in the midst of this (for a description of his demise, see chapter 14). And in the year between his departure and the appointment of a new chancellor, retired University of California, Irvine, chancellor Robert Aldrich was put in charge. I was then a leader in the academic senate, and so I participated in meetings among faculty and administrators that threshed out a campus position on the ARCO project. Aldrich heard the voices of the community and the campus and agreed to reverse the path toward oil development. Of course, the power to do so lay in state agencies quite distant from the campus chancellor. A complicated political dance ensued, which resulted, finally, in a vetoing of the oil drilling proposal by the California State Lands Commission.

I was struck by this particular episode, given the power of the oil corporations and their assumed power over political bodies like the lands commission. My instincts as a political sociologist made me privately expect that big oil would win—even as we worked hard to stop the project. (Mickey believes that this is an existential hallmark of our lives: "they" will probably win, but we keep fighting anyway.) Somehow the politics of resistance to oil had gained sufficient weight that the voice of the community, along with the voice of the university administration and faculty, partnering with some key Democratic figures in the state government was sufficient to stop this particular oil proposal. And the economic value of the university (clearly jeopardized by the intrusion of oil drilling) certainly was a key factor in the final decision.

A few years later, a similar incident concerning the university and oil occurred, when new chancellor Henry Yang came onboard. Mobil Oil Company had a plan to drill on land near the campus, and to do this it required campus approval. Of course, this proposal was seen as outrageous by many faculty members and in the surrounding community. Yet Yang was being pressured by members of the legislature and the university's regents to go along with Mobil Oil. At first, Yang handled the matter by appointing a faculty committee to advise him on what policy he should take, but in the midst of these deliberations he decided to veto the proposal altogether. It was a bold move to challenge the pro-oil pressure, and Yang, to this day, speaks with pride about having made it.

Aldrich and Yang realized that the threat of oil industrialization near UCSB would be destructive to the university. Its capacity to continue to grow as a globally significant research center and to attract faculty and researchers and graduate students depended on its ability to maintain the quality and beauty of the environment surrounding it. That rather direct interest merged with the strong environmental consciousness present in the student body and in the community and the faculty as well.

Somehow, the Santa Barbara coastal population has developed considerable power to veto the stated aims of the oil industry, although not yet to stop all oil production in the region. In May 2015, a corroded oil pipeline spilled one hundred thousand gallons across beaches on the coast—an event that got worldwide press even though the size of the spill was smaller than historic disasters of this kind. This disaster reinforced the conviction, shared by almost everyone living in the area, that oil companies can never be trusted to provide even the protections they are required by law to deliver. The 2015 spill ignited new protests in the streets and courts; one recent result was a decision by a major oil driller, Venoco, to end its offshore operations and dismantle its long-operating drilling platform.

The experience of the decades since the 1969 oil spill tells us that there is more political power in a locality like Santa Barbara than one might think. Where that leverage comes from isn't altogether clear, and for communities that are situated atop valuable resources the capacities to offset their exploitation ought to be systematically analyzed. All over the planet, communities of many kinds are engaged in resistance to corporate exploitation and often with success. Santa Barbara's history might provide some clues about how that success can be achieved and sustained. It's a special and distinctive place for sure—but its story does have relevance for the world resistance to corporate globalization in our region[2]

These cases illustrate the continuing battles with oil companies that help define Santa Barbara's history. And oil isn't the only energy resource around which such battles have raged.

In the seventies, Governor Jerry Brown supported the installation of a huge and potentially explosive liquefied natural gas storage facility up the coast. Grassroots protest and legal action (including challenges by Chumash Indians claiming the site as a sacred place) defeated what was seen as a dangerous installation. Less successful was the mass uprising against the Diablo Canyon nuclear power plant in San Luis Obispo County—which mobilized mass occupations and intense activism. The Diablo Canyon power plant got built—but its opening turned out to be the end rather than the beginning of further nuclear plant development. It is now slated for dismantling.

Had there been no resistance, the entire central coast of California would by now have become an industrial belt—resembling New Jersey, perhaps. From that perspective, the environmental movement that was ignited by the 1969 oil spill changed the future.

In the same years, the region has had some success in promoting alternative energy policy and practice. There has been a good deal of development of solar power in the area. It is helpful that there's at least some sunshine almost every day; with federal and state tax benefits for solar installations and the formation of various kinds of private and semi-private solar companies (some with the active sponsorship of the Community Environmental Council and other groups), Santa Barbara is among the top ten solarized towns and cities in the state.

A few years ago, our friend Walter Kohn (the late Nobel Prize–winning physicist at UCSB) decided (at age eighty-five) to devote his time to promoting rooftop solar electricity installation. His example inspired us to follow suit. The installation was costly on paper, but we learned that a lot of those costs are offset by tax benefits and by the fact that home solar electric installation can pay for itself over time—not only reducing electric bills, but actually allowing the homeowner to sell back to the electric company surplus electricity. Despite the utility corporations' efforts to resist solar conversion, these public subsidies have continued. Currently, we're working to establish Community Choice Energy—a publicly owned company to acquire renewable energy sources that the utility will be required to buy. The environmental leadership in our region wants to make Santa Barbara a forerunner in electric car use, and needed charging stations and other facilities are springing up to make this feasible.

## LAND

DICK:

Alongside oil and other energy development, our community-based networks and movements have focused on land use and on housing planning and policy. Mickey and I—and especially Mickey—cut our political teeth in Santa Barbara as a leading member of the anti-growth Citizens Coalition. That was part of a regional movement soured by the very rapid population growth of the sixties, especially in the suburban sprawl of Goleta, where the opening up of the university campus and the emergence of defense research firms brought a big influx.

MICKEY:

As a summary of our community work beginning in the 1970s, I offer my "political resume," which I have updated pretty much to the present day:

### MIRIAM (MICKEY) FLACKS

Current occupation: Retired

Previously: Editor, *Environmental Periodicals Bibliography*, published by the International Academy at Santa Barbara, 1988–92

> UCSB, Staff Research Associate in Molecular Biology, 1970–87
>
> University of Chicago, La Rabida Institute, Research Assistant
>
> University of Michigan, Survey Research Center, Chicago Area Supervisor
>
> University of Michigan, Mental Health Research Institute, Research Assistant

Education: Bronx High School of Science, Bronx, New York;

> City College of New York, New York, Bachelor of Science degree

Personal: Married to Richard Flacks since 1959 (and counting); Mother of two, Grandmother of six

COMMUNITY SERVICE (VOLUNTEER ORGANIZATIONS)

1962–69:

Ann Arbor, Michigan, Active in anti–Vietnam War movement and New Left (SDS)

Chicago, Illinois, Hyde Park Co-op Credit Union, Board of Directors

1970s:

UCSB University-Community Child Care Center; Founding Board Member

Citizens Coalition (environmental electoral organization), Vice President

Santa Barbara Jewish Secular School, Teacher

Santa Barbara City Affirmative Action Committee

1970s–80s:

UCSB: Ombudsman's Advisory Committee

Biology Department Biohazard Committee

Bus Transportation Committee

American Federation of State, County and Municipal Employees
(AFSCME) Local, Executive Board, Member

Hillel Foundation, Community Advisory Board President

1980s–90s:

Santa Barbara Jewish Federation, Board of Directors, Newsletter editor,
Executive Vice President

American Civil Liberties Union, Board Member and President, Santa
Barbara Chapter

Jewish Secular Humanist Society, Chair

Network (Citizens' Lobby), Executive Committee

*Santa Barbara Independent* "Local Hero" (with Dick)

Santa Barbara Women's Political Committee, Board of Directors,
Newsletter Editor

Santa Barbara County Affirmative Action Commission, Co-chair

Environmental Defense Center, Board of Directors

Citizens Planning Association, Board of Directors, Vice President

Community Housing Action Group (CHAG), Co-convener, American
Planning Association Award

Santa Barbara County Action Network (SB*CAN*), Founding Member and
Board Member

2000s:

Economic Community Project, Board of Directors

Santa Barbara County Housing Authority, Board of Commissioners

City/County Affordable Housing Taskforce, Member

Election Campaigns, Database Coordinator

SB*CAN*, Housing, Open space, Transportation Committee (HOT Hero,
2008)

Santa Barbara for All (SB4ALL), Co-chair

Rental Housing Roundtable, Member

2010–present:

Coastal Housing Coalition, Conference Planning Committee

County Housing Authority, Board of Commissioners, Chair

Santa Barbara Tenants Union, Organizing Committee

SB*CAN*, HOT Committee

Santa Barbara County Democratic Central Committee

SB4All (Housing Advocacy)

---

DICK:

By the mid-seventies, as anti-growth forces took over Santa Barbara's city council, we were among those arguing for the need for a solid and persuasive foundation to arguments against growth. The city council commissioned Harvey Molotch and Rich Appelbaum, our close friends and sociology department colleagues, to undertake what became an ambitious and nationally well-known study of the "impacts of growth"—a study that examined everything from traffic to water quality to determine optimal population targets for the city. The city, as a result, was radically downzoned—beginning an ongoing process of shaping zoning and planning in the city in tune with community needs and resources rather than the traditional imperatives of what Harvey famously called the urban "growth machine."[3]

Such policies and politics have dominated the entire South Coast's history over the past forty years. In Santa Barbara, every commercial and housing development is scrutinized by citizen activists in terms of impact on traffic, air and water quality, public services, and the like. Growth has continued in these years; some questionable developments get approved but, as with energy development, the community consciousness redefined the future in ways contrary to the developers' goals. Indeed, some major developers have either left the business or learned to adapt their plans rather than fight the community's will. As with energy, that will has to some degree trumped the logic of private profit and a free market.

These are examples of "socialism in one city" politics. There has been at least one major negative to this politics—it can't really control private investment that creates new jobs, especially "clean" service jobs. The zoning policies restrict the size of the population living in the region—but both low- and high-paying jobs continue to be created by the expanding technology, hospitality, and health care industries and the university. At the same time, people working in existing jobs retire but continue living in the area. A restricted housing supply (the vacancy rate is close to zero) and a growing economy have meant that tens of thousands of people are commuting to their jobs—many driving more than fifty miles each way. Meanwhile, to make matters worse, wealthy types are in the market for investment or second homes, Airbnb-type short-term rentals are common (even though illegal), increasing numbers of students flock to the area to attend Santa Barbara City College (a local community college with an international reputation), and language schools attract the offspring of rich overseas families who want to practice their English in the Santa Barbara playground—all of this using up the limited availability of rental apartments and making for wildly inflated housing prices. The community college has recently initiated a program whereby students who graduated from a local high school and live at their old address (typically, at home with their parents) receive a full scholarship for two years (tuition and books) provided that they attend full-time and carry a full load. This program may encourage local students to attend the community college and discourage "out-of-towners."

Our society lacks a legal foundation for community planning that includes capacity to regulate the local economy so that investment can mesh with community-defined need. And, unlike major European countries, the United States has no fully developed housing policy that would regulate the cost of housing to meet the needs of working families. A sustainable future depends on people getting out of gas-driven cars, living close to where they work, and walking and biking—rather than commuting. The struggle to make that future possible is now the central theme of local politics in Santa Barbara—but it runs up against the "jobs/housing imbalance" I've described.

## THE NEW URBANISM

MICKEY:

As time has passed, things in Santa Barbara have changed—and we with them. The new image of Santa Barbara—as a vibrant, exciting place to live—along with the growth of the university and a "Silicon Beach" information technology (IT) industry has created many jobs and filled them with people brought from elsewhere, or recent UCSB graduates, or children of the 1960s "settlers." Unfortunately, as elsewhere in coastal California where residents organized to stop growth, there is insufficient housing affordable to these folks. "The Impacts of Growth" study found that, by and large, it is not simply the attractiveness of a place that brings new people, or the availability or price of housing, but that they come for jobs. That has indeed happened—the older residents, many of whom have retired from jobs at UCSB or the ancillary industries, have remained in their homes or, at least, in the area. The zoning put in place in the 1970s has not stimulated new residential building, despite the boom in the housing market. (On average, one hundred units per year have been built—mostly high-end condos.) Also, the city of Santa Barbara is pretty well built out—there simply aren't large swaths of land on which to build new tracts of single-family homes. The result has been thirty thousand car trips a day into the area from adjoining communities like Ventura and Oxnard to the south and the Santa Ynez Valley, Lompoc, and Santa Maria to the north. Studies are still incomplete, but estimates indicate that as much as one-third of the workforce of the South Coast (Santa Barbara, Goleta, and Carpinteria) lives elsewhere. This situation is unhealthy for the community, in that these commuters are not really a part of the community: they don't hang out after work, or send their children to local schools, or coach Little League, or stick around to go to concerts and shows. Santa Barbara is not Manhattan, where commuters also descend and leave each day, because those folks go to communities that are an integral part of their lives. Folks are living in Ventura only because they can't afford to live in Santa Barbara—and there are no options like Brooklyn, Queens, the Bronx, or Staten Island. (Actually, Goleta is a little like an outer borough—but Santa Maria and Ventura, each about forty-five miles away, are not.)

Here is my favorite concrete example (from our own lives): when Dick first started working at UCSB, he earned $13,000 a year. We bought the house with four bedrooms plus a family room in a suburban tract on the edge of the city for $39,000. The bank was only too happy to give us a mortgage, because they believed that a house should cost about three times one's annual income. Today, with Dick retired, his job at UCSB does not retire with him; someone must be hired to replace him if students are to be taught. That person today would earn about $85,000 per year; our old house would sell for about $1 million. There is no way that the new professor could afford that (or practically any) house in Santa Barbara.

So with no possibility for growth in population, Santa Barbara exports the housing needs of its community to neighboring cities. This was, in fact, predicted by "The Impacts of Growth" study, and it doesn't seem fair to us or to our neighbors.

I have become something of a housing maven since I was asked by my county supervisor to serve on the Housing Authority Board of Santa Barbara County. The Housing Authority is a federal/state agency, charged with providing "safe, sanitary housing" (from the 1937 Housing Act) affordable to those in Santa Barbara County with an income of less than 80 percent of the area median income. We have built or acquired more than one thousand units of such housing in the county—known elsewhere as "the projects"— though ours bear no similarity to that image, since they are usually the nicest, most attractive units on the block. (The city of Santa Barbara has its own Housing Authority, headed by a UCSB sociology student of the early 1970s, with units numbering about 14 percent of the total housing units in the city.) This tenure has provided me with much information and insight into how federal, state, and local laws affect the housing situation and an understanding that there are no subsidies for housing for folks making more than 80 percent of area median income—which in Santa Barbara County is about $60,000. Standard assumptions are that the private market will provide housing affordable (i.e., monthly cost being no more than 30 percent of monthly income) to the "middle class." The housing "bubble" (which has never really burst in our area) plus the large number of retirees and second homes for wealthy Angelenos has assured that the middle class is effectively priced out of the market—hence the commuting and also a fair amount of doubling up (more than one household sharing a home). The zoning laws and the reluctance of capital to invest in housing have made "the market" a totally inadequate solution.

The anti-growth sensibility has erroneously focused on housing, rather than jobs, as a control. This sensibility is deeply ingrained in the many veterans of the 1970s anti-development wars, and, I must say, it meshes nicely with a natural tendency of older, relatively well-heeled and settled folks to resist any change and to worry about "those people" moving into their neighborhood or city. A recent struggle to incorporate the principles of "smart growth" (compact, dense development in walkable urban areas, well served by public transportation) and "sustainability" (reducing commuting and local auto use, as well as enacting policies that reduce energy use) into a general plan update was met with staunch opposition from some of the no-growthers with whom we had once allied. The sands had shifted, and strong environmentalists and progressives now supported zoning that would help provide the housing that met the goals of sustainability, while folks who had identified their no-growth perspective as environmentalist now opposed housing the firefighters, police officers, nurses, teachers, and plumbers who can't afford housing in the community. In addition, developers are aware of the worldwide trend of people coming back to cities, seeking "community," and reversing the post–World War II trend of a suburban house with yard and picket fence—an idealized view of onetime rural habitation. Article after article in the press documents the trend toward smaller units in urban neighborhoods, mixing commercial, residential, institutional, and even industrial uses in a single neighborhood or building—and architects and developers are only too happy to design and build them.

In Santa Barbara, we are fortunate to have a few developers who are willing to forgo maximizing their profits in order to build this type of housing. The city has also enacted "inclusionary zoning" policies that require at least 15 percent of all new construction to be restricted (in perpetuity) for those with incomes up to 120 percent of area median income (and even up to 200 percent!). All of this is, of course, anathema to local conservatives, whose ranks have been swelled by former anti-oil, no-growthers. Of late, a city with a nearly 60 percent Democratic registration has barely managed to eke out a 4–3 majority on the city council. My hope is that we will be able to persuade a strong majority of the electorate to support this "new environmentalism."

We have "walked the walk." After the kids had graduated from college, Chuck was married and working in Sacramento, and Marc was in graduate school at the University of California, Santa Cruz, we decided to realize our longtime dream to leave our suburban tract home on the edge of the city and move downtown into a smaller house in a more urban neighborhood. Dick was a bit skeptical that we would find a place we could afford, but he looked forward to weekend activities of house hunting. On our first such weekend, we passed a two-story house, right across the street from a series of public parks; our realtor (who was a University of Michigan graduate and a liberal) said that it was a duplex, with both units rented as apartments, and that he would have to arrange an appointment for us to see it. We agreed, and the following Tuesday we met him at the house. The downstairs apartment smelled bad, the walls were covered in wallpaper that would have hastened Oscar Wilde's death ("Either that wallpaper goes or I do," he is reported to have said on his deathbed), the carpet was an ugly green, and some very strange, cult-like people were living there. Upstairs, a young postdoctoral couple was living in a two-bedroom, two-bath apartment that was divided by the entry hall, with a giant bedroom and attached bath essentially separated from the rest of the apartment. Dick saw his office in this giant bedroom, but wondered what we needed an extra upstairs kitchen for? Mort, the realtor, and I pointed out that we could rent out the remainder of the apartment as a one-bedroom, one-bath unit.

Despite the ugly appearance of the units, Dick and I, independently, fell in love with the house in a way we had never felt about our suburban home.

That was in 1992, a period that had seen a recession in the housing market, so the house was available for what we could afford—especially since

Dick's parents, Mildred and Dave, had recently died, and we sold their Goleta house very quickly, splitting the proceeds with Dick's sister, Nancy. A state policy that the county had adopted in an effort to get seniors to move out of their longtime, large houses allowed people over fifty-five years old to keep the property taxes on their old homes (kept artificially low for twenty years through Proposition 13, the beginning of the "tax revolt") and meant that, although the new house cost more than what we sold the old house for, only the part we didn't actually live in would be considered for property taxes at the new rate. It was our first indication of the advantages of rental property ownership. We decided then and there that we would rent the upstairs apartment to the "deserving poor"—either graduate students or people who worked as community organizers—at substantially below-market rates (about 50 percent below). We like to say that we did this to forestall the earthquakes that would result from our communist parents rolling over in their graves at our being landlords. . . . In fact, the tax advantages of rental property are quite substantial—and we, only somewhat reluctantly, joined the rentier class.

We have loved living there.

We see a lively street, we live among people of color, most of our neighbors are renters, we hear the sounds of traffic (a lullaby for New Yorkers), we are across the street from a beautiful urban park and, most of all, we walk almost everywhere. The downtown, with all it has to offer—meetings at city hall or the county building, museums and galleries, restaurants and movies, the library and stores, and a real sense of place—is within a twenty-minute walk. We use only one car, and that mostly for trips to Los Angeles and Goleta (or our old neighborhood!), putting no more than eight thousand miles a year on our old 2000 Maxima (finally replaced two years ago). Our dream now is to have more friends join us downtown so that we can share a driving-free community as we age. Living where we do also helps us to understand the advantages of the "new urbanism."


## COMMUNITY EMPOWERMENT

DICK:

One thing our decades of local activism has made clear is that community movement is most likely to make sense when there are laws—set at the state and national levels—that can be used to enforce community needs and demands. The California Coastal Act (passed by popular vote in 1971) has been a powerful tool, allowing the environmental movement to have a voice and even to win agreements on local developments in the coastal zone. State laws requiring environmental impact studies as part of the project approval process have been a crucial factor in empowering community and environmental activists to veto or reshape many otherwise threatening developments. In our region, the passage of these laws led a group of activists and lawyers to create the Environmental Defense Center—a nonprofit law firm whose practice has resulted in innumerable gains in the interpretation and implementation of law in ways that serve community interests and needs. The center works intimately with activists and community groups to foster rather than replace grassroots activism.

Somehow, in the 1970s, I became interested in cable TV as a political issue. Because of its physical location, Santa Barbara never was able to get most broadcast television, and so the community from the fifties on was almost totally dependent on cable for its television reception. The local cable system was begun by local entrepreneurs, but the system was purchased by Cox Cable of Atlanta, Georgia, late in the seventies. In those years, the local cable operations were regulated by city and county government, which licensed the cable company, had approval power of its rates, and tried to ensure that cable service would be universally available. Federal Communications Commission (FCC) rules, moreover, which were written in the seventies, required cable operators to provide channels for local government, schools, and "public access" (meaning a facility where any member of the public could be trained and could produce programming free of editorial control).

The city appointed an ad hoc committee to advise on cable TV policy, and somehow I found myself a member of that body. In that role, I learned that the local system was a cash cow for Cox Cable—a monopoly with relatively low overhead and a captive audience of something like 90 percent of the city's households. I worked with some other media activists to create a citizen watchdog group. We challenged Cox's demands for higher rates (saving Santa Barbarans hundreds of thousands of dollars) and worked to compel the cable company to create the federally mandated public channels—and studio facilities to enable citizens and schools to program. We were able to outsmart the Cox folks—especially because they had to get city and county renewals of their license—so that the channels and facilities we wanted came into being.

When the National Co-op Bank was established during the Carter years, we saw a new opportunity—maybe we could get some public financing from the bank to create a consumer-owned cable company. When our proposal was given prominent publicity in the local press, cable co-op meetings were packed. And in spite of the "socialistic" nature of the proposal, those thronging the meetings included a good many retired military, ex-bankers, and other conservatives. The people who turned out loved the idea of a cable company that was locally controlled, whose revenues would stay local, and where they could have a voice. The sentiment at those meetings excellently exemplified Gar Alperovitz's contention that all through history Americans have valued community and democracy ahead of ideology about corporate property rights when these conflicted with community interest.

Our proposal wasn't funded by the National Co-op Bank (which did support a cable co-op in Davis, California). The cost of acquiring the Santa Barbara system made our plan unfeasible. Then, in the Clinton years, all of the laws that had empowered communities to regulate cable TV were replaced as a mania for "deregulation" dominated public discourse—and the capacity for local citizens to effectively regulate its cable system went away.

As community TV cable visionaries, we had at least one final project. Cox had established a public access facility, but the new federal rules made the company less willing to continue to operate it. With the help of city and county staff, we designed a nonprofit public access company to take over the operation, with an agreement by Cox to help sustain it financially for several decades.

That story, like virtually all of the episodes in our local activist history, is filled with complexity and ambiguity. Something like twenty-five years of effort had a reasonably progressive result—but yet the more far-reaching and visionary possibilities we worked for depended on rules and resources that higher public authority could provide. But such positive supports for community empowerment were only sometimes available—and increasingly, local anti-corporate plans have been frustrated by the ability of powerful corporate interests to rewrite government policy on the national level.

One of the biggest engines of development in the region is not a private corporation. It's UCSB. (The university is now the largest employer on the South Coast.) Like most up-and-coming universities, it has many reasons to grow both its student population and its overall research enterprise. Population growth statewide is of course a pressure on the university to expand the undergraduate enrollment; The University of California system is the elite public university in the world, and it offers real opportunity to first-generation kids for a life of wider horizon than their parents had—and a real bargain financially to the more privileged families whose offspring can get a good education and a reasonably prestigious credential at a price that is still a bargain for the wealthy. But UCSB is pushed toward growth for other reasons—like expanding its graduate training and the rising curve of the research dollars its faculty has been achieving.

More students mean more faculty and staff—and most of these have families. More students, faculty, and staff mean a bigger market—and so university growth has a multiplier effect on the local economy and its workers. And, historically, the University of California as a state institution has been largely free of local control, so most of the University of California campuses have been able to grow without a lot of effective resistance in their localities.

UCSB development is regulated by the Coastal Act. And that act creates a political framework that does give citizens groups and local governments leverage for challenging UCSB growth plans. In the late 1980s, community voices forced the campus to agree to an enrollment cap of twenty thousand. Once again, community action reshaped the goals of a powerful institution, after a considerable amount of protest and litigation. In the past few years, I've been a leader in a new community effort to help shape UCSB growth—a story I'll save for a later chapter.


## THE BALLOT BOX

DICK:

Sometimes, progressive activists have been frustrated not only in confronting powerful institutions, but also because we've failed to persuade electoral majorities (whose perception of some issues has been colored by big campaign money). In the 1980s, for example, several efforts to get citizens in the city of Santa Barbara to vote for rent control were defeated at the ballot box—even though the majority of the city's population lives as renters. Landlord interests spent a lot to discredit rent control—and some of their arguments resonated with the feelings of some renters who imagined themselves as future property owners—as well as some who believed that rent control might lead landlords to allow housing quality to deteriorate. Rent control was successful in that period in several other California cities—leading the landlord lobby to push through state legislation that has crippled the ability to effectively control rents. My sociology colleague Rich Appelbaum did some significant research that disproved the landlord lobby's alarmist messages, but this work, like the passionate efforts of tenant activists, was defeated at the polls.

And despite the deep opposition in our region to the oil industry, some ballot initiatives designed to curb it have been defeated, in part because of the hugely disproportionate campaign spending by the oil companies and in part because oil has a grassroots following in the northern reaches of our county.

Most of the time, these defeats have not crushed activist spirit. These campaigns even when lost helped build the activist base—expanding the mailing lists and the volunteer armies for future endeavors. Moreover, most progressive activists are aware from the get-go that electoral activity is a part, but hardly the whole, of a social change strategy.

Mickey and I have always supported electoral strategies as part of an effort for change. Even back in the early days in Ann Arbor, Mickey in particular was active in the local Democratic Party, where we worked hard in behalf of a congressional candidate who opposed the arms race.

The community activism we've been part of has sought to win and preserve majorities in local government. Our arrival here coincided with a demographic shift resulting from the establishment of the university and the defense research/Silicon Beach economy. It's a shift that's reflected in the fact that a once Republican bastion is now strongly Democrat in registration—and this has usually meant liberal victories at every level.

In 1970 our area was represented by conservative Republicans in Congress and the state legislature, and a realtor/banker/developer coalition controlled the city council and the county board. Four decades later, the situation is reversed. The county board is the most difficult government body—since two and a half of its five districts are in the conservative North County. The district that's split north and south contains Isla Vista, which, for decades, has been an important voting bloc in support of environmental and liberal candidates (leading regularly to efforts by the GOP to restrict the student vote in local elections).

It's a lot easier for progressive activists to be heard in a reasonably liberal governmental environment. And Mickey and I have been around and active long enough to be good friends with some of our leading officials. Still, no

FIGURE 13.1. SDS comrades reunite at "the turn of the 1970s," in Santa Barbara, December 31, 1979 (*from left to right*: Leni Wildflower, Honey Williams, Todd Gitlin, Dick, Paul Potter, Mickey, and Al Haber), outside UCSB Conference Center

one, including our friends in office, thinks that electing reasonably progressive folks to office translates directly into policy. And in 1980, the national election results greatly challenged our political expectations.

## LIVING IN THE AGE OF REAGAN

DICK:

Progressive activists were furious with Jimmy Carter by 1980. His economic policies managed to produce scary inflation rates combined with high unemployment. Our friend Stanley (Stan) Sheinbaum, one of the key fundraisers for progressive and liberal Democrat causes and candidates, had become committed to getting rid of Carter, and, eventually, Edward (Ted) Kennedy declared that he would oppose Carter in democratic primaries. Personally, I thought Carter was a man of uncommon decency, and I occasionally would admonish friends that we might regret those who replaced him.

I was a nominal member of the Democratic Socialists of America (DSA). DSA was founded in the seventies by Michael Harrington, who reached out personally to the Port Huron SDS folks to invite us to join up and profusely expressed his regret of the stance he'd taken then. Harrington had broken with others in Max Shachtman's crowd to oppose the Vietnam War. Many of the leading Shachtmanites moved to the right in the sixties, supporting the conservative George Meany's domination of organized labor and endorsing pro-military politicians like Henry Jackson. Harrington moved left during that time, wanting to encourage progressive leadership in the AFL-CIO, opposing the Cold War, and serious about socialism. By the seventies, he was ready to invite veteran ex–Communist Party members like Dorothy Healey to join DSA.

Dorothy had come to be a beloved person in our lives. In the 1940s, she was one of the top leaders of the California Communist Party. Unlike most Party members, she always took an assertive public role as a communist spokesperson, running for public office in Los Angeles and hosting a popular weekly talk show on listener-supported KPFK. Her memoir, as told to Maurice Isserman,[4] shows her to have been a feisty voice while in the Party, challenging slavish obedience to the Soviet line; it is one of the best books I know about what it meant to be a Communist Party activist in the United States. With a few of her comrades, after Khrushchev revealed many of Stalin's crimes, Dorothy spent years trying to reform the Party from within. She finally resigned from it after the Soviet invasion of Czechoslovakia, but remained a visible leader—and mentor—of the broader Left in Los Angeles.

Dorothy had joined the Communist Party in the 1920s when she was about fourteen (she herself was a red diaper baby). She became a dedicated labor organizer in the thirties—a pioneer in efforts to organize California farmworkers. She was physically small—and quite attractive—and wonderfully and charmingly assertive. She embraced Mickey and me, and we always enjoyed the chance to spend time with her. Like for others of her generation, the Party had been her school—she never went to college, but was a voracious reader, always eager to talk about the latest political treatises, which she usually had read before I had tried to. I think she read the *New York Times*, *Los Angeles Times*, and *Wall Street Journal* every day. She had her own opinions—to say the least—but was genuinely eager to hear ours.

I invited Dorothy frequently to come to my classes and submit to intense dialogue with the students. She read my writings on the Left, and I always wanted to get her feedback. Dorothy and some other veteran former Communists had supported a post-sixties effort, led largely by SDS alumni, to create a national New Left organization—the New American Movement (NAM). When Harrington and other Socialists launched what became the DSA, he sought an alliance with NAM—and soon the two groups merged. I was intrigued, to say the least, by the prospect of an organization that would bring old Reds like Dorothy together with very vociferous anti-communist Socialists like Harrington and Irving Howe—along with folks of our generation who had rebelled against both of the Old Left factions they had come out of.

Mickey was encouraged by Harold Meyerson, who was then jokingly described by us as the "LA commissar" of the DSA, to run as a delegate to the 1980 Democratic convention in New York. The DSA supported Kennedy but, more importantly, had the idea that DSA-identified delegates could be elected to form a socialist caucus at the convention. Mickey ran in the Santa Barbara county delegate selection process and was easily elected.

DSA did set up a socialist caucus at the convention, and maybe forty delegates showed up. When we arrived at the caucus, it appeared that sizable media coverage was present. But the cameras and mics turned out to be from European media. The socialist caucus of 1980 didn't get a word of coverage in the U.S. press.

MICKEY:

The DSA position at the convention was in support of Kennedy, believing that he was the more left-leaning of the two candidates. The handful of DSA member-delegates held a press conference, at which the world's left and centrist press was well represented; no U.S. press was there though. . . . Finally, when Carter was about to be nominated, William Wimpisinger, head of the machinists' union, led a "walkout" from the convention. This entailed making our way through the burly members of the New York delegation, who were staunch Carter supporters. They didn't exactly block our way; they just made it a wee bit hard to get past them. After we got out, we were met by reporters, and I was interviewed by Connie Chung, who was then a Los Angeles news anchor.

And I was also invited by Steve Wasserman, then the *Los Angeles Times* op-ed page editor, to send in a report directly from the convention floor, which they published after I submitted it via dictation to a rewrite person (long before e-mail!). They changed only one word from my submission, and they had me paged on the convention floor to get my approval. "*Los Angeles Times* paging Mickey Flacks" was announced at the California

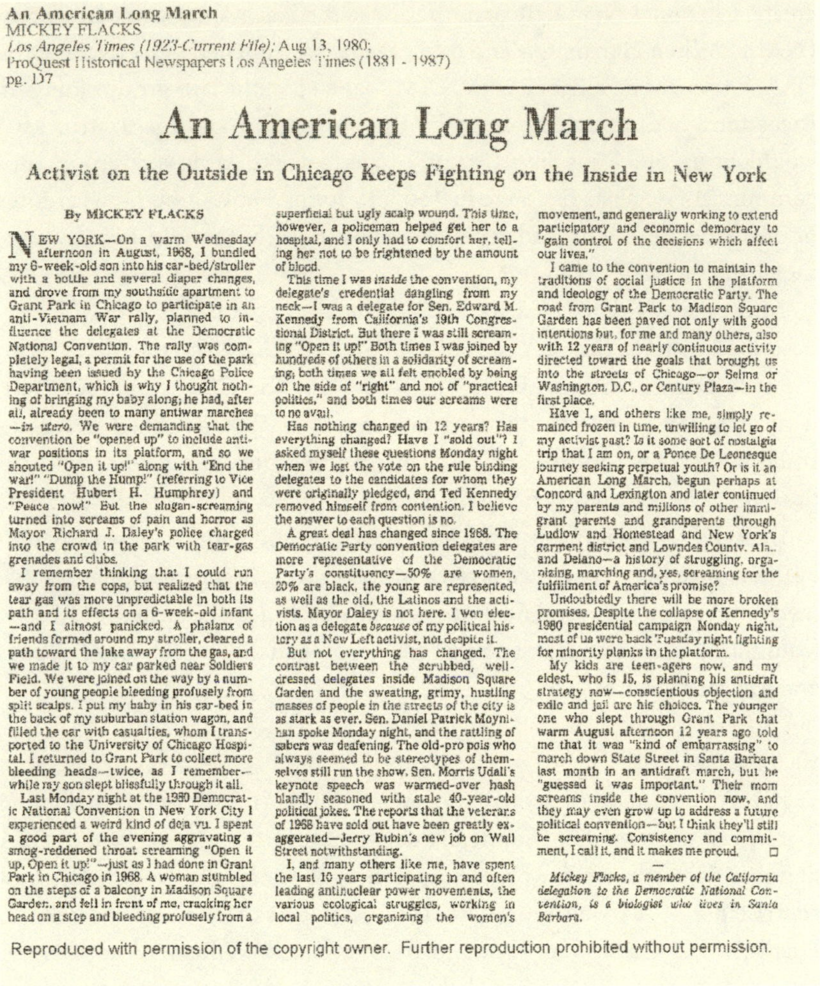

An American Long March
MICKEY FLACKS
Los Angeles Times (1923-Current File); Aug 13, 1980;
ProQuest Historical Newspapers Los Angeles Times (1881 - 1987)
pg. D7

# An American Long March

## Activist on the Outside in Chicago Keeps Fighting on the Inside in New York

### By MICKEY FLACKS

NEW YORK—On a warm Wednesday afternoon in August, 1968, I bundled my 6-week-old son into his car-bed/stroller with a bottle and several diaper changes, and drove from my southside apartment to Grant Park in Chicago to participate in an anti-Vietnam War rally, planned to influence the delegates at the Democratic National Convention. The rally was completely legal, a permit for the use of the park having been issued by the Chicago Police Department, which is why I thought nothing of bringing my baby along; he had, after all, already been to many antiwar marches —in utero. We were demanding that the convention be "opened up" to include antiwar positions in its platform, and so we shouted "Open it up!" along with "End the war!" "Dump the Hump!" (referring to Vice President Hubert H. Humphrey) and "Peace now!" But the slogan-screaming turned into screams of pain and horror as Mayor Richard J. Daley's police charged into the crowd in the park with tear-gas grenades and clubs.

I remember thinking that I could run away from the cops, but realized that the tear gas was more unpredictable in both its path and its effects on a 6-week-old infant —and I almost panicked. A phalanx of friends formed around my stroller, cleared a path toward the lake away from the gas, and we made it to my car parked near Soldiers Field. We were joined on the way by a number of young people bleeding profusely from split scalps. I put my baby in his car-bed in the back of my suburban station wagon, and filled the car with casualties, whom I transported to the University of Chicago Hospital. I returned to Grant Park to collect more bleeding heads—twice, as I remember—while my son slept blissfully through it all.

Last Monday night at the 1980 Democratic National Convention in New York City I experienced a weird kind of deja vu. I spent a good part of the evening aggravating a smog-reddened throat screaming "Open it up, Open it up!"—just as I had done in Grant Park in Chicago in 1968. A woman stumbled on the steps of a balcony in Madison Square Garden, and fell in front of me, cracking her head on a step and bleeding profusely from a superficial but ugly scalp wound. This time, however, a policeman helped get her to a hospital, and I only had to comfort her, telling her not to be frightened by the amount of blood.

This time I was inside the convention, my delegate's credential dangling from my neck—I was a delegate for Sen. Edward M. Kennedy from California's 19th Congressional District. But there I was still screaming "Open it up!" Both times I was joined by hundreds of others in a solidarity of screaming; both times we all felt enobled by being on the side of "right" and not of "practical politics," and both times our screams were to no avail.

Has nothing changed in 12 years? Has everything changed? Have I "sold out"? I asked myself these questions Monday night when we lost the vote on the rule binding delegates to the candidates for whom they were originally pledged, and Ted Kennedy removed himself from contention. I believe the answer to each question is no.

A great deal has changed since 1968. The Democratic Party convention delegates are more representative of the Democratic Party's constituency—50% are women, 20% are black, the young are represented, as well as the old, the Latinos and the activists. Mayor Daley is not here. I won election as a delegate because of my political history as a New Left activist, not despite it.

But not everything has changed. The contrast between the scrubbed, well-cressed delegates inside Madison Square Garden and the sweating, grimy, hustling masses of people in the streets of the city is as stark as ever. Sen. Daniel Patrick Moynihan spoke Monday night, and the rattling of sabers was deafening. The old-pro pols who always seemed to be stereotypes of their selves still run the show. Sen. Morris Udall's keynote speech was warmed-over hash blandly seasoned with stale 40-year-old political jokes. The reports that the veterans of 1968 have sold out have been greatly exaggerated—Jerry Rubin's new job on Wall Street notwithstanding.

I, and many others like me, have spent the last 10 years participating in and often leading antinuclear power movements, in various ecological struggles, working in local politics, organizing the women's movement, and generally working to extend participatory and economic democracy to "gain control of the decisions which affect our lives."

I came to the convention to maintain the traditions of social justice in the platform and ideology of the Democratic Party. The road from Grant Park to Madison Square Garden has been paved not only with good intentions but, for me and many others, also with 12 years of nearly continuous activity directed toward the goals that brought us into the streets of Chicago—or Selma or Washington, D.C., or Century Plaza—in the first place.

Have I, and others like me, simply remained frozen in time, unwilling to let go of my activist past? Is it some sort of nostalgia trip that I am on, or a Ponce De Leonesque journey seeking perpetual youth? Or is it an American Long March, begun perhaps at Concord and Lexington and later continued by my parents and millions of other immigrant parents and grandparents through Ludlow and Homestead and New York's garment district and Lowndes County, Ala., and Delano—a history of struggling, organizing, marching and, yes, screaming for the fulfillment of America's promise?

Undoubtedly there will be more broken promises. Despite the collapse of Kennedy's 1980 presidential campaign Monday night, most of us were back Tuesday night fighting for minority planks in the platform.

My kids are teen-agers now, and my eldest, who is 15, is planning his antidraft strategy now—conscientious objection and exile and jail are his choices. The younger one who slept through Grant Park that warm August afternoon 12 years ago told me that it was "kind of embarrassing" to march down State Street in Santa Barbara last month in an antidraft march, but he "guessed it was important." Their mom screams inside the convention now, and they may even grow up to address a future political convention—but I think they'll still be screaming. Consistency and commitment, I call it, and it makes me proud.

□

*Mickey Flacks, a member of the California delegation to the Democratic National Convention, is a biologist who lives in Santa Barbara.*

FIGURE 13.2. *Los Angeles Times* op-ed, August 1980

delegation. Sitting in front of me was a well-known Los Angeles lawyer/ activist, who seemed to spend most of her time on the floor reading a newspaper. When I responded to my page, her head whipped around to see who was this person who was "famous" enough to be paged by the *Los Angeles Times*? When she saw that it was only me, she went back to her newspaper.

I had another "moment of fame" at the Democratic National Convention. When favorite sons' names were placed in nomination for president, the Northern Californians nominated their wonderful, lefty congressman, Ron Dellums. One by one the favorite sons dropped out—but as time for voting on the nomination approached, Dellums's name was still in. Our delegation's Ted Kennedy whips were determined that whatever number of votes Kennedy came in with would be the number voted on the floor; to that end they asked each delegate how he or she was voting. "Well," I said, "if Dellums doesn't drop out, I have to vote for him." Consternation! They sent for a higher-up Kennedy honcho to come and tell me that Dellums would surely drop out. "Then I'll vote for Teddy," I promised, "but only if Dellums's name is not in nomination. . . ." In a few minutes, they sent for someone from Dellums's office to come to my seat to assure me that he would indeed drop out—they were trying to get the floor to do so. "OK," says I. "When he does, I'll vote for Teddy." And so I did after Dellums's name was dropped. . . . It was, in fact, the only time that I had anything other than an automaton role to play as a delegate.

DICK:

Michael Harrington and DSA advocated a labor-liberal-movement coalition within the Democratic Party that would form a potent Left. But neither Harrington as an individual nor DSA ever pursued a strategy that might bring that idea to fruition. At the Democratic National Convention in New York, in 1980, the most evident expression of the Democratic Left was a town hall rally, featuring well-known movement leaders, each of whom called for a progressive agenda for the party. But no organizing toward that end came from that mostly symbolic gathering.

I'd come to deeply respect Harrington by that time as a brilliant articulator of the possibilities for what he called the "next Left." I was elated by his effort to unify Old and New Left—and his renunciation of his past effort to strangle SDS in its cradle. But I think it's important for young activists now seeking a long-term electoral strategy to realize that, although Harrington advocated a social democratic Democratic Party, he didn't *fail* to make that happen—*he never really tried to lead such a project.* Harrington understood that efforts to create a left-wing third party on a national level led to a dead end and that transforming the national Democratic Party was a necessary goal. Efforts to bring party reform—to democratize it internally and move its politics closer to the labor and civil rights movements—have changed the party over the decades. But the transformative strategy is only now, in the aftermath of the Sanders campaign, getting a real test.

Of course, the Kennedy campaign failed; Carter was renominated; Reagan was elected, not because of a big swing of the electorate in a conservative direction, but because large numbers of white working-class voters in the Midwest (so-called Reagan Democrats) were legitimately discontented with the Carter economic policies—policies that had resulted in both high unemployment and inflation.

I was, in a sense, amused by Reagan's election. After all, as governor, he had talked about me personally; his crack that hiring me as a professor was like hiring a pyromaniac to be a fuse maker in a firecracker factory, I thought at the time, was rather clever, evidence that he was not quite as stupid as some people in the Left seem to think. In any case, it was amusing to think that we now had a president who had uttered my name.

But my amusement masked fear. Reagan's advent, I thought, could usher in a period of serious repression. In Chicago, I had been a victim of an attack that was like the death squad assaults that were happening in various Latin American countries in the late 1970s. Maybe, I thought, with a Reagan White House, a buildup of such death squad activities could happen in the United States.

But to focus on dark fears and paranoiac imaginations was not how we wanted to live. On the contrary, in our own immediate life, the early 1980s were a time of celebration: 1981 marked the fiftieth anniversary of my parents' wedding and, in the same summer, Marc turned thirteen. We decided to create a big family celebration weekend to mark these landmarks. Marc's secular bar mitzvah took place in our backyard on a Saturday; Dave and Mildred's fiftieth wedding anniversary was celebrated the next day. Members of the wider family came from the East, creating a joyful family experience—and, at the same time, both the bar mitzvah and the anniversary party were great community observances.

MICKEY:

Again, I planned a secular "ceremony," led by my brother. We had it on a Saturday evening and invited about one hundred people. (One of our guests was my aunt Rosa, recently arrived from the Soviet Union, to spend her last days in California. This lent a certain degree of authenticity....) Marc agreed to read a new translation that I had done of Sholem Aleichem's "If I Were Rothschild" (which had degenerated into "If I Were a Rich Man" in *Fiddler on the Roof*). In the original, Tevye speaks of using his money to bring about world peace (by bribing the combatants), a far cry from "a staircase just to go up, and another one just to come down" and other examples of conspicuous consumption that are falsely attributed to Tevye in *Fiddler*. Marc also read a bit of "Tevye the Dairyman" and spoke about Sholem

Aleichem and did a saxophone solo. We then had music and dancing and drinking—a lot of partying.

DICK:

By 1981, Mildred and Dave had been living in Santa Barbara for eight years and had become very active themselves, most particularly as leaders in the Gray Panthers. The Gray Panthers was a thriving national organization with at least one hundred very active seniors in our region. These were people, like my parents, who had been political in their younger days, dating from the Depression years—folks who had, back in the day, identified with a wide range of leftisms (their ranks included every kind of socialist, religious liberals, and left-wing Democrats). They had experienced the Red Scare and welcomed the revival of progressive movements in the 1960s. By the 1980s, retired and in their seventies and beyond, they came together across whatever archaic political ideologies might have once separated them. It was an organization that, of course, was interested in senior citizen issues like defending Social Security and Medicare and serving as a kind of watchdog organization with respect to local services for the elderly. But the Gray Panthers in Santa Barbara, and to some extent nationally, were interested in all kinds of issues; they were active troops in election campaigns and fought the good fight on many fronts. Their monthly meetings, which my parents helped organize, were vibrant scenes of debate and resolution passing. There was an added benefit—a ready-at-hand network that could be relied on for mutual support and for caretaking as members aged. Dave soon became an active leader in wider circles of senior citizen advocacy in the county; Mildred loved working as a volunteer in local election campaigns. So, when their fiftieth wedding anniversary was celebrated, a large collection of folks came, including their many tennis partners as well as fellow Panthers.

It was a great pleasure to be able to make these family events occasions for community celebration. Mickey has a talent for making life-cycle celebrations meaningful and special—carefully planning the food and drink to be served as well as the staging of creative rituals. These happenings were important in our personal and family lives, and at the same time, we realized, they helped build the community we wanted to live in and work with.

It was fun to see our sons enter teenage in those years. Both had become public personalities in their own right in their school communities, participating in sports, music, and theater. Santa Barbara high schools may or may not have been very distinguished academically (they were, in fact, pretty good), but they certainly were terrific in the performing arts. Both kids benefited enormously from the chance to engage in performances of many kinds, working with skilled theater and music teachers. Both are talented actors and singers. We actively discouraged them from imagining careers as performers, which we thought would prove more frustrating than rewarding. But sometimes I wistfully feel that we deprived the world of a great brother act, a worthy successor to the Everly Brothers.

We'd deliberately tried to raise our sons so they could connect to the American cultural mainstream more easily than we, red diaper babies, ever could. They both were part of school friendship circles that have lasted through their lives. At the same time, we did create some contradiction and tension for them—making them as aware as we could that our family was part of a tradition of dissent, that it was important to be critical of consumerism (no war toys or sweet cereal allowed!), and that we were Jewish in a gentile world and atheists to boot. Their parents didn't follow most gender roles—Mickey did most of the driving, and for several years, in the 1970s, I did all the cooking so Mickey could keep to a strict weight-watching diet. Marc (most of whose friends came from divorced homes) once wondered why we couldn't be a "normal" family, where the mommy does the housework and the daddy goes to work and drives the car. That was a nice teaching moment.

I guess if we were interviewed in the early 1980s, we would say that we were learning, with some success, how to be committed and public leftists while being respected and integrated into the wider life of the town, both in the neighborhood and in the workplace.

Reagan's election is universally regarded as a sign and a spur to a rightward turn in American political life. But in Santa Barbara, no such turn was discernible. Indeed, the eighties were a time when politics shifted left in our area. Liberal majorities were coming to be regular in city and county elections. Two young politicians came to represent our area in the state legislature—Gary K. Hart and Jack O'Connell—and both achieved considerable power and visibility on the state level, each serving in statewide office. Santa Barbara County was ideologically split—the coastal area is where the leftward trend was well under way, while North County, culturally and politically, resembled the rest of rural, inland California and even the American South. That the Reagans' ranch was located in the mountains above the coast didn't signify that Santa Barbara was Reagan country;

indeed, Jane Fonda's ranch was not far from the Reagans'. If anything, the South Coast was more Fonda land.

In the aftermath of Tom Hayden's senate campaign and as the Campaign for Economic Democracy (CED) got under way, Jane and Tom decided to buy a beautiful place high in the mountains above Santa Barbara, called Laurel Springs Ranch. Perhaps influenced a bit by our stories about our commie camp experiences as red diaper babies, they established a children's summer camp at Laurel Springs (and the place served as well as a small conference center during the year). We had a continuing personal connection with Tom and Jane when they'd show up at the ranch. The camp provided opportunities for children from liberal upper-middle-class families to share a rich experience with kids from farmworker families—experiences that naturally, given Jane's involvement, featured a good deal of creative performance. One could perhaps sum up a lot about the political and cultural wars that were gathering in those years by comparing the Fonda and Reagan Santa Ynez mountain retreats. One was aimed at fostering collective action and doing something for social equality; the other was a kind of movie set for staging scenes of rugged manly individualism on the occasions the Reagans chose to stay there.

Throughout the twentieth century, one resource for liberalism in Santa Barbara has always been the presence of wealthy philanthropists who live in the area full- or part-time. Historically, dating back more than one hundred years, there's been an artsy, bohemian sprinkling in the super-rich enclave of Montecito. These are folks who help support the cultural institutions of the town, making the art museum and the music world more developed than what one would expect to see in a city of under one hundred thousand. Some of these were heirs of eastern wealth who came to California so they could live out their rebellious, artistic, or nonconforming proclivities. And some of these very generously supported environmental preservation and other causes that have enabled the area to stave off the strong pressures for development that constantly threaten its natural beauty and way of life.

By the late 1960s, there was a significant grouping of wealthy liberals with Santa Barbara addresses. Stan and Betty Sheinbaum were key figures in creating a network of progressive philanthropy. Stan had come to the Center for the Study of Democratic Institutions, Robert Hutchins's think tank in Montecito, from an academic career as an economist. At Michigan State, in the fifties, he'd gotten involved with a project in Vietnam that he discovered was a CIA front. He met, courted, and won the heart of Betty Warner (a daughter of a Warner brother), and invested her fortune smartly, and the pair became a local power couple. Stan helped fund *Ramparts* magazine; we'd first met him in the sixties when he came to Chicago on a national tour with an anti-war Green Beret, Don Duncan, whose story *Ramparts* had publicized. In 1966 and 1968, Stan ran for Congress in Santa Barbara on an anti-war program—campaigns that helped foster lasting progressive networks in the region. Betty was a world-class art collector, ran a major local gallery, and made their Montecito mansion a salon where many left-wing political and cultural visitors hobnobbed with the growing local dissident crowd.

The Sheinbaums influenced other wealthy peers to contribute to progressive causes. Maryanne Mott (heir to the General Motors Mott family fortune) has to this day been an important funder of local and national organizations. It was she who provided me with the encouragement and funding to pursue my FBI files early in the 1970s. Kit Tremaine, a New Orleans former beauty queen and heiress, often said that Stan Sheinbaum had made her the "Communist" she turned out to be. Kit was a very generous supporter of many left-wing and culturally avant-garde things in the region—as were the four Peake sisters, who constituted one of the most notable Santa Barbara families of their time.

This tradition of progressive philanthropy was a base for the formation of a new institution in Santa Barbara in the 1980s: the Fund for Santa Barbara. The fund was set up as a kind of United Way for social change, providing seed money and modest grants to all kinds of progressive projects and organizations. The fund dream, successful after a while, was to be able to raise hundreds of thousands of dollars a year, for distribution to a wide range of progressive cultural, political causes, ranging from services for the gay and lesbian communities or Native American youth, to various kinds of political advocacy and environmental innovation. People like Maryanne Mott and Kit Tremaine helped start the fund; today its annual fund-raising banquet and auction attracts nearly one thousand people—including a large coterie of young wealthy donors drawn from the entertainment and IT worlds who've come to have Santa Barbara addresses.

Stories like these depict Santa Barbara as a very particular place—a rich enclave, worlds away from the reality of most communities. This stereotype has a kernel of truth, yet it also misrepresents Santa Barbara. In fact, demographically, the city of Santa Barbara is poorer on average than the state of California as a whole. Its population is one-third Latino. At the same time,

FIGURE 13.3. Who's that with Mickey?! Santa Barbara, 1996

FIGURE 13.4. Celebrating Tom's and Mickey's fiftieth birthdays, January 1990
( *from left to right*: Tom Hayden, Dick, Todd Gitlin, Mickey)

Montecito an unincorporated suburb, is one of the richest enclaves on the planet. Santa Barbara's attractions draw people of means to buy places here, while the university and a growing IT sector provide further population magnets. The resulting inequalities—a very pricey housing market and a relatively low-wage working population—define a lot of the political conflict of the past twenty years.

The region and the state as a whole experienced a political shift in the Reagan years that was markedly to the left. Even Orange County, once the epitome of Nixon and Reagan land, is now majority Democrat. Demographic change—the rise of a huge immigrant population—helps explain this shift. For our region, the 1969 environmental catastrophe and the growth of the university (and the growth in the number of its graduates who've stayed here) are crucial added factors. Even North County is changing politically and demographically, as people who might have been Santa Barbara city residents commute from up there to work where they can't afford to live.

So despite the conventional wisdom that Reagan's election started the movement of America to the right, our own world has shifted left in the same period. Out of the countercultural ferment of the seventies, institutions were established that are now normal features of the landscape.

Meanwhile, established institutions (businesses, schools, churches, city hall, etc.) have changed practices and norms as the sixties generation has taken them over. The cultural changes converge with the politics.

America, it turns out, is too complex to be defined by prevailing ideology or cultural traditions. Moreover, terms like *shift* and *trend* applied to the political mask another part of our experience. History isn't shaped by "trends." What matters is what active people decide to do in the space they inhabit.

# 14 ▸ CONFESSIONS OF A
## TENURED RADICAL

DICK:

At the University of Chicago, my New Left engagement meant that I was isolated intellectually within the sociology department, and ultimately embattled. There were times when I reveled in that situation. I had a good deal of disdain for the dominant culture of the Chicago department, which stood for a brand of sociology that had lost touch—if it ever had much touch—with a great deal of what needed to be understood about society.

My life in Chicago was not bound up with the department. I was much more engaged with my students, both undergraduate and graduate, than with my colleagues. Above all, in our years in Chicago, my primary relationships, both intellectual and social, were the SDS friends who had come to the city when we had, and the wider networks of politically active folk we connected to.

Still, there were times when I wished for a more intellectually and morally congenial academic home. One day, I went up to speak at Northwestern University, in Evanston, and was immensely pleased by the intellectual ferment and interpersonal warmth that seemed to characterize that sociology department. It had become well known as a center for a more diverse and critical sociology than what had come to typify the University of Chicago. In that one day, I felt a sense of easy connection with fellow sociologists that I realized was totally missing from my experience at Chicago.

So, I accepted the offer to come to UCSB—a new department, that looked to Northwestern as a model, deliberately rejecting the definition of sociology that prevailed in Chicago. UCSB's sociology department was making a name for itself by representing cutting-edge tendencies in the field. The very fact that they wanted to give me a tenured position was a sign of their interest in housing critical perspectives. That I was being offered tenure was of course a strong inducement—but I could have had a tenured situation at Chicago. The chance to have a real academic home was a far more important draw.

The Santa Barbara campus was one of the new ones in the University of California system. The first PhD awarded in sociology at UCSB was in 1965. The founding of the UCSB sociology department as a graduate research department is credited to two senior members. Don Cressey, who served as dean during the period of the department's initial construction, was a major figure in criminology, imported to Santa Barbara from UCLA, where he'd helped make a major department there. Dave Gold, a University of Chicago–trained survey researcher was department chair during the found-ing period. One might have thought that Don and Dave, given their own backgrounds and inclinations, would put together a department that exem-plified the sort of "scientific" sociology that had won dominance in the field in the postwar period. Instead, they realized that a new department would make a bigger mark if it challenged the discipline's status quo. Dave hired people whose work irritated him greatly—yet he understood that they would put the department on the map. Leading among these was Aaron Cicourel, along with a group of young ethnomethodologists trained at UCLA, working on deep structures of everyday communication. Cicourel and the "ethnos" were very strong critics of standard sociology.

Bill Chambliss, a pioneer of "radical criminology" was hired, along with Tom Scheff, whose work challenged conventional approaches to "deviance" and mental illness. Harvey Molotch was hired right out of graduate school at Chicago. We'd known Harvey when he was an undergraduate staffer at the *Michigan Daily* working with Tom Hayden, and he'd been in some of my graduate seminars at Chicago. It was Harvey who persuaded us that UCSB was the place to be. And so I accepted the offer, knowing that they wanted me precisely because I was an exponent of what then was being labeled "radical sociology."

By 1970, those in my generation who identified as radical certainly had to think with some clarity and coherence about what we really wanted to accomplish if we were working in academia. By 1970, there were a significant number of people across the country in many disciplines who shared this concern. The organization I had helped to create—New University Conference (NUC)—wasn't altogether helpful in this regard, to my dismay. By the end of the 1960s, its discourse was dominated by what I liked to call "revolutionistic" rhetoric, defining the university as a bourgeois institution. NUC newsletters were filled with calls to either get out of academia or "smash" it.

In any case, in 1968–70, as the Vietnam War escalated, so did the pace of campus mass protest. It was hard to think about the long range. I was largely removed from these debates in NUC in those years—recovering from my wounds and dealing with the troubles at Chicago and the move to California. But once we were settled in Santa Barbara, and I was entering a department very open to new, critical directions, the question of how to be a political radical within the academic arena became urgent.

I had the chance, right at the start, to observe closely an academic situation that proved instructive. Soon after arriving in Santa Barbara, I was a participant in an investigation of academic freedom violations at Simon Fraser University in Vancouver, British Columbia. I'd just been appointed to the newly formed Academic Freedom committee of the American Sociological Association (ASA). The formation of that committee, and my appointment to it, was a sign that the ASA leadership was trying to make some accommodation with the emergent radical mood of the new academic generation.

The first case that committee had to deal with was the situation at Simon Fraser. This was a sociology/anthropology/political science department that was deeply divided and where a number of well-known radical figures had been forced out. I was stunned to learn that those in the department who had done the punishment and who were being charged with academic freedom violations were themselves Marxists of various stripes. The department was racked with factional dispute and personality antagonisms. It appeared that much of the turmoil stemmed from the efforts of various members to create a "radical" department. One major bone of contention was the demands for students to have equal voting powers with the faculty—one of a range of challenges to traditional academic hierarchy based on seniority and professional status.

The ASA subcommittee that visited Simon Fraser University found serious breaches of standards of academic freedom and due process. Various people who had been forced out were accused of significant rule violations without the opportunity to respond to these charges. One wing of the department had allied itself with the much more conservative campus administration in order to get rid of the more radical and flamboyant members. It was a pretty frightful mess.

I'm telling this story but only sketchily—my aim is not to provide an account of the Simon Fraser case (hoping that someone somewhere has tried to keep that historical record). But what happened there was a formative experience for me. I drew a lesson from the situation, which was that efforts to create, within an established university, a utopian department, based on principles that went beyond the established governance frameworks of the institution, or to create an ideologically oriented department— these efforts were bound to end in disaster if one hoped to create lasting institutional change. Another lesson: intellectual identification with Marxism and left politics could go hand in hand with conservative, elitist (and quite dishonorable) treatment of one's colleagues and students

Rather than seeing the university as merely an institution functioning to preserve the established structures of power and privilege, I wanted to take seriously the claims of the university to be a haven for honest discourse and a center for enlightenment, where critical thinking was nurtured and education was a sacred mission. My strategy would be to hold the institution to these claims, even as they were routinely flouted and contradicted in daily practice.

The university's claim to be committed to intellectual pluralism, it seemed to me, was a positive value and so were the principles of academic meritocracy. But I'd learned at Chicago (where lip service to such things was a continuous drone) that the real working of the university emphasized old boy networks, that intellectual narrowness and political bias were often at play. Those contradictions could lead a young idealist to disgust and profound alienation. I thought, however, that the contradictions between professed values and institutional practice might make a space for effective challenge and positive change.

Rather than envisioning a "radical" department, we wanted to make a serious effort to be an intellectually diverse community that was committed to humanistic social relationships and that encouraged the democratic participation of students in department governance.

As a sort of avatar of participatory democracy, I thought a good deal about how the department's structure could be democratized without violating the legally binding rules and practices of the university. It wasn't possible (even if it were theoretically desirable) to have forty-five graduate students have equal voting rights with fifteen faculty. But it was possible (even if almost never practiced) for students to elect representatives who'd have voting rights and voice in department meetings and committees. So we pioneered that sort of representational democracy for students. Ultimately, such practices were adopted across the campus.

One could view this as a pallid compromise of a fulfilled notion of participatory democracy. Yet, the faculty were, after all, the permanent members of the institution, whose future was determined by the decisions being made in these meetings and committees in ways that the students' futures were not. Institutionalizing student voice while preserving faculty power didn't strike me as a compromise (and, in fact, there wasn't student agitation for a more radical plan). Indeed, having students present and vocal at department meetings was a big change; at both Chicago and UCSB, faculty routinely had met behind closed doors. That meetings were now open seemed to me a real democratic reform.

Soon after arriving at UCSB, I witnessed a moment when campus police were called to prevent students from observing an important meeting of the Academic Senate. Only a few years later, undergraduates were represented on all of the Academic Senate committees and were able to speak at general senate meetings. In the years that followed, I insistently advocated that students as well as faculty are legitimate parties to the "shared governance" of the institution.

Shared governance as value and goal has a long history in American academia and particularly at the University of California. For at least a century, the professoriate has fitfully engaged in a sort of class struggle to defend and expand its voice in university policy making. The notion that students ought also to have such voice is even more contested. I've spent a good deal of my energy trying to defend and expand empowerment for both faculty and students on this campus.

One move I made to encourage active student participation was to create and teach courses about the institutional history and operation of higher education in general and UCSB in particular. A freshman course aimed to inspire student interest and competence in institutional participation. An upper-division course brought together student government leaders and other activists for in-depth discussion of key policy issues and some detailed analysis of how policy happens.

I spent about a decade as chair of the Academic Senate Committee on Student Affairs. In that position, I worked closely with student leaders to help facilitate their voice and to open an ongoing space for them to articulate issues and debate administration policy. The committee provided a way for student leadership to gain faculty support as well as advice.

I was gratified when, as I neared retiring, the student government established the Flacks Internship—a paid position designed to foster student participation in campus governance.

It's been an article of my political faith: try, when and how you can, to expand the space for participatory democracy wherever you find yourself. Challenge (with a sense of strategy) authority structures that block or undermine the voice of those who have to live with the consequences of decisions, and insist that elementary protections—free speech rights, due process—be adhered to. In my lexicon, insisting that constitutions, charters, and institutional claims be actually practiced is one way of being "radical," though one might equally acknowledge that it's a stance that's truly conservative.


## RADICAL SOCIOLOGY?

DICK:

In the late 1960s and early 1970s, there was a greatly intensifying critical discourse within sociology. A number of widely circulated books, such as Alvin Gouldner's *The Coming Crisis of Western Sociology*, argued that the post–World War II brand of sociology, once dominant, was reaching a dead end.

One expression of the crisis was the fact that mainstream social science had failed to anticipate the civil rights revolution and the generational revolt of the 1960s. Indeed, a case was made that the theories and methods that defined the mainstream made it unlikely that the discipline could anticipate conflict, movement, and rebellion.

Political sociologists in the 1950s heaped scorn on C. Wright Mills's *The Power Elite*; by the 1970s, his version of political reality turned out to be far more compelling in understanding where America had come and where it was going than the prevailing "polyarchical" models.

Postwar sociology marginalized Marxism, and there were some good reasons for that, since classic nineteenth-century versions of Marxism that emphasized the agency of the working class and the centrality of class struggle were unable to grasp the complexity of conflict and class formation in the American scene. How could you comprehend conflict based on race and gender, on ethnicity and religion, and on age, within a Marxian framework? Moreover, classic Marxism emphasis on economic determination of power relations neglected what Max Weber emphasized—power is an end in itself. Weber understood that established structures of authority might act to defend that authority, whether or not economic interests could be discerned as the heart of the matter. Psychoanalytic insights about the ways in which family relationships and childhood experiences shaped consciousness raised questions about the limits of class consciousness as an explanatory framework. Social science was developed, especially sociology and social psychology, as a debate with nineteenth-century Marxism—a debate that lasted maybe forty years and was very fruitful for social theory.

By 1970, forms of what were called neo-Marxism had emerged in Europe. These involved efforts to synthesize Marx and Freud, to take account of the insights of Weber and other non-Marxist sociologists, to understand how class might operate in advanced capitalist economy, to try to comprehend race and gender as sources of social conflict and social movement. It was turning out that these matters could be comprehended best by making use of Marx's fundamental strategies of theorizing, especially since no other macro-level theoretical framework rivaled Marx's in its capacity to analyze both structure and change. So by 1970, it was time to really integrate Marxism in sociology and much effort and energy was beginning to be devoted to that. Our department in Santa Barbara was at the forefront of this effort in the United States.

Rich Appelbaum, like Harvey Molotch, a University of Chicago PhD, was appointed in 1971 to the UCSB department. Rich was getting immersed in neo-Marxian discourse, and his coming coincided with the interests of a number of graduate students in our program in exploring deeply the critical theorizing emanating from Europe. Somehow the department had resources to invite an intriguing range of pathbreaking visitors, most notably including Jürgen Habermas, who was a world leader in the critical theory movement. Cross-fertilization between the critical theory and ethnometh-odological types was flourishing; young women faculty were arriving with a feminist focus in their work. It was a time—those 1970s years—when creative ferment in sociology was bubbling everywhere and was an ongoing feature of our communal life within the Department of Sociology at Santa Barbara. It was extraordinarily creative to be able to meet and work with people like Habermas, Juliet Mitchell, David Harvey, Dorothy Smith, and others who spent time in our orbit (attracted no doubt by the physical as well as intellectual climate). Personally, it was a pleasure to be, in my thirties, a leader in this departmental community, learning constantly from our discussions and debates about the kind of intellectual work I wanted to do.

There was a second way in which we thought we could implement a more radical vision of sociology. That was to link our research to the needs of the local community. An important instance: Harvey and Rich joined together with community activists to undertake an ambitious and highly influential study of the impacts of population growth on Santa Barbara. That study, which ended up a massive three-volume work, helped define the politics of the community for decades after, because it catalogued the ways in which population growth would undermine, on a number of dimensions, the environment that people in Santa Barbara so cherished. Activists, elected officials, planners, and neighborhood organizations soon were evolving a politics aimed at rational and participatory community development that successfully offset the power of what Harvey termed the "growth machine."

In that same vein, we encouraged graduate students to do studies of the emerging counter-institutional developments in the community. Joyce Rothschild did a case study, which became a landmark, of alternative institutions in Santa Barbara, including the free school, the legal collective, and the alternative newspaper—one of several dissertations examining experiments in workplace democracy based on local community projects. This kind of research was aimed at helping those involved in institution building to understand and take account of problems in the kinds of organizational rules that they were attempting to live by and to document and understand the ways that new consciousness and new social formations were operating.

My graduate research with Ted Newcomb on the persistence of political engagement in the life course of Bennington alumnae began a lifelong interest in understanding how politics and personal life intertwine. . . .

The unifying theme of my intellectual work was to understand "political consciousness"—and particularly the conditions in both personal biography and social circumstance that supported and limited capacities for political engagement. A dynamic group of graduate students were drawn to this interest. In the 1970s, a number of students were coming to the graduate program out of personal histories of activism—and I encouraged them to try, as I was trying, to link their personal experience to their research. We started an ongoing seminar that carried on for decades, focusing on political consciousness and social movements, and this provided a nurturing space for quite a few good projects.

## TROUBLEMAKING?

DICK:

My appointment at UCSB was one of several episodes at the end of the 1960s that gave the sociology department a bad name among the then leaders of the senior faculty on the campus. Whatever their personal political leanings may have been, those leaders feared the state legislature and Governor Reagan and thought that student protest and the counterculture were existential threats to the university. The sociology department, for them, was a hotbed of revolution—and indeed many of the student activists seemed invariably to turn out to be sociology majors. In those early seventies, campus conflict was at fever pitch, and sociology faculty were usually visible in the midst of these happenings.

A good personal example is when, in 1973 I agreed to sponsor a course whose class sessions were to be led by members of the community's newly formed legal collective. Their idea, which I thought smart, was to focus on the legal problems students were encountering: political repression, tenants' rights, drug issues, and the like. There were several young but experienced lawyers who could make the presentations, and they and the paralegals who worked with them helped facilitate student term projects. We developed the course as a version of a long-standing department offering on criminal justice and the community—one of Don Cressey's courses originally, and I cleared with Don the appropriateness of what I wanted to do. The course got written up in the local paper, and a local judge who was teaching his own course in the political science department complained to the dean that radical lawyers were teaching on campus. In the middle of the term,

I was compelled to try to defend the course before a senate committee. Members of the committee expressed the fear that this sort of thing was bringing bad publicity to the campus—another one of sociology's many transgressions of that sort. The committee wasn't interested in the validity of the course, or in Don's defense of it—nor were they embarrassed by the thought of shaping the curriculum around fears of bad publicity. They instead decided to cancel the course midstream, mollifying the students by awarding them A grades. To me, it was an incredible moment of bad faith, and it revealed how scared those faculty were getting at that time and place.

Given incidents like that, and the campus culture they reflected, it was surprising when the administration agreed that I should be made chair of the department in 1975. By then, some of the hysteria of the Reagan years had subsided, as had the turmoil of the Vietnam War period. I told my senior colleagues that I couldn't serve unless promoted to full professor (since at age thirty-seven, I would have been younger than any of the senior faculty). The decision to promote was made.

I came into that role at one of the many times the university's budget was under great strain. So at first glance, it appeared that there was little leeway for further development of the department. But for various reasons, a number of faculty positions in the department were becoming vacant at the time I became chair. That meant that we were able to undertake a pretty extensive program of recruitment of new faculty. I threw myself into that work. Seeing an opportunity to make excellent appointments at a time of considerable stringency in academia at large, I took it on myself to try to identify young faculty prospects. I was especially looking for candidates who combined a capacity for outstanding professional work with evidence of commitment to social change. After a period when the graduate student culture seemed to be rejecting career advancement as a goal, most students, by the mid-seventies, were eager to get the professional skills needed to land jobs. So we looked for people who could make our department an excellent training ground for graduate students, while at the same time doing research and teaching that contributed to democratic possibility.

A good example of someone I was proud to have recruited was William (Bill) Bielby, who was getting his PhD at the University of Wisconsin, Madison, at the time—then the leading research department in sociology. Bill was described by his mentors as the top graduate student at Madison. He was an enormously skillful quantitative sociologist. Unlike stereotypic "quantoids," Bill had a refreshingly relaxed attitude toward the quantitative.

He was not one who fetishized that kind of research—and he was good at translating the technical in ways that avoided intimidating the uninitiated. Bill made it a point of telling me that he had been an SDS member as an undergraduate; of course, that endeared him to me as well (which he may have suspected). Somehow, we were able to persuade him to come to Santa Barbara, along with an equally talented fellow graduate student from Madison, Roger Friedland.

Another appointment that I thought was cool at the time was that of Richard Berk, a young faculty member at Johns Hopkins University, who I had met in meetings of the radical caucus at an ASA convention. Berk was another creative quantitative type, with a strong interest in social policy and evaluation. We were able to make an offer to his new spouse, Sarah Fenstermaker Berk, as well. She was one of the early feminist sociologists of that generation whose work at the time was devoted to empirical study of the household division of labor. We were probably the only department where the Berks could both get jobs.

I was aggressive in efforts to get people I thought were exciting prospects and, it turned out, was pretty skilled at finding resources on campus that might make such appointments possible. We recruited Christopher Jencks when he was probably the most sought-after guy in sociology—because we were able to get the political science department to make an offer to his partner, Jenny Mansbridge, a rising star in political theory and feminist studies. They spent time in Santa Barbara but ended up elsewhere—still, we became warm friends.

Having vacant slots also allowed me to hire, for short-term gigs, some interesting people to teach undergraduate courses. Our friend Derek Shearer, then an up-and-coming lefty journalist, taught some imaginative courses on public policy; the novelist and film critic Clancy Sigal told me that he wanted teaching gigs in California (he was living in Britain at the time), and I hired him a couple of times to teach courses on film and society. Some in the department grumbled about hiring these guys who were hardly sociologists—but most people seemed glad to have them around.

I served as department chair for five years, which was a relatively long term, and enjoyed the opportunity more than I thought I would. Part of the enjoyment was having some resources to work with and to therefore feel a sense of accomplishment about helping the department come into its own.

MICKEY:

At this time, I, as usual, was dieting. Dick volunteered to be the "food per-son" in the household—plan, shop, and make dinner for himself and the kids (while I subsisted on diet shakes). He claimed, after doing it for a while, that after the rigors and structure of the chairman's office, he genuinely enjoyed preparing their evening meal. (The kids had a more tempered reaction.)

DICK:

I also got satisfaction from learning to lead a group of people—faculty and students—in building consensus and in enabling people to feel that we were collectively engaged in solving problems and accommodating one another's values and interests. I ended up feeling quite proud of the job that I had done. I was proud of the department in both professional and moral terms. I also felt satisfaction at having been able to work pretty well with contentious colleagues and with people in the administrative bureaucracy. All the while, I was feeling that I was learning a lot about how an institution like this worked.

My term as chair ended in 1980. As it ended, I was very much in an opti-mistic state of mind. Despite its embattled status in the early years of the decade, the sociology department was thriving, with an interesting and diverse faculty, a considerable number of talented graduate students, and a steadily growing undergraduate enrollment—and all of this, I felt, while ful-filling pretty well my hope that the department would serve democratic, humanistic values in both the content of its work and the quality of its social relations.

Meanwhile, Santa Barbara, a community that, ten years earlier was gov-erned by a largely Republican circle of bankers and realtors, was now responding to the values and policies promoted by a coalition of environ-mental and neighborhood activists determined to make the region a model of good and sustainable planning.

The apocalyptic excitement and dread that marked the beginning of our time in Santa Barbara had passed—and it seemed that an era promising progressive reform had arrived. I was not sorry that this calmer and gentler change of consciousness and emotion was happening.

I'd always felt that if you wanted to use the word *revolution* to apply to the goals of the 1960s New Left, you had to mean that it would be a long revolution—a process of everyday, institutional democratization, of fostering a democratic, egalitarian culture, and of carrying on what European New Leftists had called "a long march through the institutions." By the end of the 1970s, that kind of change seemed to be going on—at least where we were. When I ended my term as chair, I felt a sense of accomplishment and a readiness for the next stage.

## MAKING BOOKS

DICK:

In the five years I served as department chair, I'd had little time to pursue significant intellectual projects. So, when that term ended in 1980, I worked on two significant projects that were eventually books. *Making History: The American Left and the American Mind* was an ambitious effort on my part to try to reinterpret the history of the American Left, having lived through and reflected much about the rise and decline of both the Old Left and the New Left. The ideas I tried to express in that work are a kind of foundation for this book. Its central theses are ideas that both of us have lived by as we've tried to work on how to "make history" and at the same time to "make life." I'll talk about all that in the final chapter.

## BEYOND THE BARRICADES

DICK:

From the days that I had worked with Ted Newcomb on the Bennington study, I've been fascinated with the impact of student culture and the experience of being a student on lifelong values and identities. And that topic, for me, was a piece of a bigger puzzle: how to understand the conditions, personal and social, that sustained and limited people's ongoing engagement in political action.

So in the early 1980s, my friend and graduate student Jack Whalen and I formulated a project that combined my interest in understanding the meaning of the student movement and the Left with my interest in the life-cycle effects of youthful experience. We decided to try to locate people who'd been active in the Isla Vista uprising of 1969 ten years or more after they had left that world. In order to do a kind of controlled long-term study, we focused on a particular group of Isla Vista activists—those who had been indicted on charges related to the burning of the bank. There were seventeen people in the original indictment, and in 1980 we set about trying to locate as many of these as we could and ended up with fifteen people we could visit or reach in some way for in-depth interviewing. As good social scientists, we wanted a control group and set out to match the people we were interviewing in the activist group with a selected sample of people, matched for gender, who had gone to UCSB at the same time but had been living in fraternities and sororities. In addition, Jack found a couple of people who had been present on the steps of the temporary bank when a student, Kevin Moran, was killed by police gunfire. These were people who, like Kevin, had come there to protect the bank from a crowd of protesters who were attacking it on April 15, 1970. Jack tried to interview each of these people in person, though a few were only available for phone or mail interviews. The results of this work became Jack's dissertation; ultimately, he and I co-authored a book called *Beyond the Barricades: The Sixties Generation Grows Up.*[1] The study, I think, was interesting in its own terms, but it took on more particular significance because, at the same time that we were embarking on this project, there was a host of media efforts to claim that the sixties revolutionaries had become conservative. One writer even declared that in the 1960s, those who had burned banks now were bankers themselves. And the movie *The Big Chill*, released in 1983, portrayed a group of former activists as disillusioned, lost and sadly privileged. To me, this depiction was off base; most of the people I knew who had been activists in the 1960s were in some way or other continuing to live out the values they had come to be committed to when they were young. The interviews Jack collected showed that was essentially correct, but the stories people told about their lives were not simply ones of continuing political commitment. The book we wrote is interesting, I think, because, on the one hand, it contradicts the conventional wisdom that comfortably assumes that the idealism of the young turns into the conservatism and cynicism of the older generation. On the other hand, we described intriguing and nuanced complexity in the lives of people who had been activists in the sixties.

The life stories we recorded reinforced what I'd already supposed: the apocalyptic revolutionary fervor of the late 1960s not only turned out to be illusory but, in many cases, proved damaging to sustained political commitment. The more one had believed that a revolution was going to happen, the more one was disillusioned when it turned out that the struggle for democratic fulfillment was going to be a long march without a clear resolution.

Those in our sample of former campus activists who had had a less romantic view of revolutionary possibility were more prepared for the day-by-day political struggles and routines that became necessary in the 1970s and beyond—and more likely to stay engaged.

At the same time, the study documented many of the ways that the sixties generation had experimented culturally and socially in the aftermath of that decade. The people we wrote about, like thousands of others, were building alternative institutions of many kinds. Some had struggled with ways to combine their political identities and professional goals, while others tried to make lives totally embedded in radical movement. There were doctors and professors in the sample as well as people who had joined Marxist-Leninist parties or lived in feminist collectives. You can read the stories that we collected to learn much about the potentials and limitations, the promises and failures, of all kinds of post-sixties experiment. We try to find in these stories ways in which life-cycle demands, and personal opportunities, intertwined with values and circumstances to shape the paths people followed.

When you compare the former activists in our sample with the former fraternity and sorority people, an interesting contrast emerges: The "Greeks," by the time they were in their thirties, had almost all become quite rich. But we detected an almost universal yearning, on their part, to retire early. They were hoping to return to some of the free-spirited life that they had largely postponed, if not abandoned, in order to pursue various kinds of business and professional careers. The activists' sample average income was quite a bit lower—and virtually none had yet had children during the fifteen years between the bank-burning trial and the final contact we had with them. Many were still searching for forms of work and ways of living that were fully satisfying. Some had found a more integrated life, but not one of the fifteen was financially well-off. One woman in the group had become a medical doctor, but she was working in the public sector as a leader in occupational health and safety. The one lawyer was working on employment fairness issues; a journalist was working at a collectively owned newspaper. Some were fulfilled and some expressed a lot of frustration—and all were critics of their choices and circumstances.

In telling the personal stories of a small group of people coming out of the sixties youth revolt, we documented a microcosm of much of the experience of the "sixties generation" in the aftermath. I recommend the book if that is something that interests you!

## RETURN OF THE CAMPUS TROUBLEMAKER

DICK:

In the summer of 1985, I got a call from a friend and faculty colleague in the political science department, Keir Nash. Keir had been elected chair of the UCSB Academic Senate. At the University of California, the Academic Senate is the primary framework for what is called "shared governance"—that is, the right and responsibility of faculty to participate in the governance of the institution. All ladder faculty are members of the senate, led by the chair and a legislative council of representatives. The powers of the senate are considerable when it comes to academic decision making. It's the senate that approves courses and curriculums and that processes the appointment, promotion, and termination of members of the faculty. Legally, the chancellor of the campus, appointed by the board of regents, has final say over all of these decisions, but over a long period of struggle the chancellor and the administration have come, usually but not always, to defer to Academic Senate recommendations in the strictly academic sphere. In short, at the University of California, the faculty have won a strange kind of empowerment. Ultimately, the legal power to make decisions in the university rests with the board of regents—a body composed largely of appointees of the governor (and many of these are big political contributors), who serve for twelve years, as well as a number of ex officio members—the governor and other state officials. The faculty's power is delegated and, in fact, has been overruled. In some sense, the history of the University of California and other major universities is defined by the ongoing struggle between the administration and faculty with respect to decision-making power.

Having won effective control over curriculum and a large measure of control over the hiring, tenuring, and firing of professors, the faculty senate, at places like UCSB, has increasingly sought to force the chancellor to actively consult about budget priorities and resource allocation with key faculty representatives. These are the big shaping policy questions and, typically, chancellors want as much exclusive control over these things as possible.

Chancellor Vernon Cheadle was the leader who had come to the campus in the early 1960s at the time of its initial development as a graduate research institution. He presided over large growth in its enrollments, its staff, and its physical plant and worked with key senior professors to transform what had been a rather sleepy undergraduate college into a significant research university. Cheadle's final years were marked by the student rebellion and his efforts, not always successful, to comprehend, control, and relate to it. He ended his term as a reasonably beloved figure, despite the moments when police had come to the campus and the rebellion seemed overwhelming. It was Cheadle who, for example, negotiated with black and Chicano students to create what became pioneering black studies and Chicano studies programs. Still, when Cheadle retired, in the late 1970s, the campus was struggling with the effort to make it a significant research university, competing with several of the other newly developed campuses in the University of California system for scarce resources..

He was replaced by Robert Huttenback, who had been humanities dean at the California Institute of Technology, in Pasadena. Huttenback was a historian of the British Raj; his style was rather different from Cheadle's. Huttenback was impatient with the machineries of consultation and decision making involving the Academic Senate. He wasn't averse to making decisions without much formal consultation, agreeing to faculty initiatives that were brought to him personally before they passed through the laborious screening and evaluation typical of Academic Senate treatment of new programmatic ideas. For those faculty members who had such new ideas, the Huttenback style was tremendously invigorating. It seemed that you could walk into the chancellor's office and walk out with a few hundred thousand dollars promised to you. Huttenback, of course, was very responsive to science and engineering initiatives, maybe in particular because he had no scientific bones in his body.

It wasn't long before he had quite effectively antagonized the established senate leadership. It was not just personal antagonism but a sense that the chancellor was violating necessary norms of shared governance and rational academic planning. A certain recklessness might be observed, such as when the chancellor seemed to be agreeing to set up and finance a "food and wine institute" under the urging of Julia Child, who had to come live in Santa Barbara and had befriended the chancellor and his wife, Freda. Some of these Huttenback initiatives were amusing and potentially fruitful, but some had darker implications. When Keir Nash came to be chair of the senate, the amusement was beginning to shift toward a justifiable dismay and anger.

Keir called one night to ask if I'd be willing to serve as vice chair of the senate—a position he had the authority to fill on his own. I had no desire to spend time in this way; Keir assured me that it wouldn't be time-consuming, but he needed me, he said, as his "left-wing conscience." That appealed to me, and I agreed to serve, not at all aware of what was brewing.

Soon after I took the post, rumors flew that the chancellor was possibly misusing campus funds. Late evenings, Keir would call me with some new, strange tale implying malfeasance. The chancellor's wife was ordering staff members in the administration to chauffeur her to medical appointments. He was siphoning funds to support his personal research projects—and maybe to refurbish the kitchen in his private residence. (The Huttenbacks insisted on living off campus rather than in the official residence, because they had a teenage daughter who'd be socially isolated if the family lived on campus.)

Several leaders of the Academic Senate began to talk about the need to figure out some way to confront him, but I, and at least one other member of the leadership group, wondered whether, even if the facts were as we were hearing them, he wasn't doing anything different from what chancellors in the University of California system typically did. The chancellors had a large discretionary fund under their control, and that gave a great deal of freedom to allocate money as they saw fit. I thought we could be very embarrassed if Huttenback could show that he was doing what they all did.

Matters came to a head, however, on a strange afternoon: a group of students and others were protesting on some issue, which I no longer can recall, and took it upon themselves to block the exit to the parking lot where the chancellor was preparing to drive out. Rather than back away from the group, the chancellor rolled forward and a protester's foot was caught underneath his tire. The foot in question was not seriously injured, but the fact that the chancellor acted in this fashion was the last straw for the senate leadership, including me. Nine Senate leaders met and came to the conclusion that perhaps Huttenback was beginning to lose his marbles. We drafted what we intended as a private and confidential letter suggesting that the chancellor resign in the face of evidence that we had of misuse of funds. By that time, we had confirmed, among other things, rumors that he had remodeled, at considerable expense, the kitchen of his residence, using university funds (which, if true, would have been illegal). The letter suggested that were these matters to come out, a public scandal that would hurt him and the campus might result, but that if he resigned such a scandal could be averted.

There were a number of other serious complaints that we had about his conduct. For example, he had engaged in a deal with a local businessman and major national Republican political donor, to design a desalinization plant so that the campus could have its own water supply. Funds were allocated to the design, with no prior feasibility study or campus consultation. Huttenback seemed to be promoting a plan intended to evade local environmental constraints. He seemed to think that the water project could get funding from offshore oil company operations—a definite no-no in Santa Barbara political culture. Moreover, making a deal with a major Republican donor turned out to be part of a wider process of ingratiation with the GOP (he had recently hired a leading Republican operative to staff UCSB relations with government, for example). Such moves were peculiar given that the local legislators were leading Democrats whom these Republicans he hired had actively opposed. These activities by the chancellor, just a few weeks before the incident with the car, had provoked the resignation of the executive vice-chancellor, a physicist highly respected by the faculty.

In the same period, the chancellor provoked student anger, disdainfully mocking a student petition with thousands of signatures and trying to bypass and de-legitimize the elected student government when he sought student input at all.

In any event, the letter, signed by seven chairs of Academic Senate committees and the chair and vice chair (me), was almost immediately made public by the chancellor. He was counting, I think, on his friendship with the publisher of the *Santa Barbara News-Press* to present the case from the chancellor's angle rather than from ours. The newspaper quoted him calling the letter signers "the gang of nine" and declaring that we were a group of malcontents whose scholarship was poor and some of whom were Marxists. This story hit the front page while I was out of town for a couple of days doing some speaking gigs in Portland, Oregon. I returned to get the news that Keir Nash had suddenly been hospitalized with life-threatening pneumonia. Naturally, none of the other members of the gang of nine were willing to talk to the press. And so it was left to me, as acting chair of the Academic Senate, to respond to the chancellor's allegations and to try to frame matters in the terms that we, the senate leadership, saw them.

It was also quickly evident that the chancellor had a large number of faculty supporters, given the wide appreciation of his eager willingness to provide resources to some of the top scientists on the campus. What threatened at that point was a situation in which the Academic Senate leadership might be isolated. Even though we knew that the chancellor had committed some gross abuses of office, we might not win the day. I was thrust into a situation I had had no expectation of ever having to deal with.

I have to confess, however, that the challenge of dealing with this matter was quite enticing. I had a possibly naive faith that the questions we had about the chancellor's conduct were valid and couldn't be ignored by the system-wide University of California president, David Gardner, and the system-wide Academic Senate. We saw that our goal had to be to get President Gardner, to whom the chancellor reported, to actively intervene to investigate the allegations. Given the split in the faculty, we were getting some signals from the president's office that Gardner needed clear faculty support before he could readily intervene. We figured out an approach, which ended up being successful: to convene a special meeting of the entire faculty to debate whether to request that the president initiate an investigation into the various allegations about the chancellor—not to consider resolutions of support or opposition to him. That request was supported by both factions of the faculty—an investigation would either clear him or validate the allegations.

Despite the local newspaper's decided tilt in favor of the chancellor, the *Los Angeles Times* began to run a series of front-page stories, day after day, that revealed more and more transgressions on the chancellor's part. There were a lot of whistleblowers in the administration staff, and once an enterprising reporter from the *Times* got involved, he, together with a very creative student reporter on the student newspaper on campus, published a number of revelations, which were rather juicy. The chancellor had remodeled his kitchen not once but twice, at a cost of a quarter of a million dollars in university funds. There were stories about his efforts to illegitimately claim losses to his insurance company due to a theft that had not happened. There were stories of misuse of funds from the UCSB Foundation for his own personal benefit. The *Los Angeles Times* coverage of course defined the issue for a statewide audience.

The president ordered an audit, which eventually showed not only that state funds had been used illegally for the kitchen but that the expenditures for this purpose had been concealed through various book-cooking procedures by top underlings in the administration. In fairness to Huttenback, it was never completely clear whether the cooking of the books was something he had personally understood or whether those underlings who had to do the actual work on his house realized that it might be prudent to pretend that these activities had been conducted on campus, rather than on his off-campus home. In any event, Chancellor Huttenback eventually was forced to resign by University of California president Gardner.

Months later, the district attorney in Santa Barbara County had Huttenback indicted on various felony charges of embezzlement. I was quite surprised at the criminal charges against him; I had thought that removing him
from the chancellorship was a sufficient and necessary way of settling the
matter. Huttenback was eventually convicted of felony charges and as a
result was dismissed from the faculty because he was a convicted felon.
(When he resigned as chancellor, he had continued as a professor in history.) Indeed, Huttenback was one of the very few tenured professors in the
University of California's history to have lost his position.

My instinct at the time—and still—was that the loss of his professorship
was not an appropriate response to his criminal conviction. I think that the
right to a tenured position has to do with academic qualification rather than
extraneous circumstances. I guess my attitude is colored by the experience of the McCarthy years—when my parents, along with hundreds of
other teachers at every level, lost their jobs despite their professional qualifications. There is, of course, the argument that a teacher of the young has
to be an exemplary role model, so felons (like Communists?) should be
disqualified.

I'd much rather have had the university deal with this situation creatively
rather than by a sort of knee-jerk punishment. For example, Huttenback
could have kept his title, based on his professional achievement, but for-
feited his salary (given his abuse of funds). They could even have charged
him to rent an office on campus.

My commitment to the vision of participatory democracy was something I tried to apply to my view of how the university should be run. The
Huttenback affair had meaning to me that went beyond the specific case. I
saw it as an episode in the long struggle in the University of California
and, indeed, in American higher education. The struggle had to do with the
powers of the faculty in the governance of the university. The Huttenback
affair illuminated the ways in which the Academic Senate still had not
achieved real voice in financial and budgetary matters. Chancellors quite
jealously guarded their control over those kinds of decision making and
routinely prevented the Academic Senate from gaining full understanding
or knowledge of the internal budgetary domain. The chancellor's discretionary fund could amount to millions of dollars and was perhaps the worst
example of such a closed decision-making situation. In Huttenback's administration, that closed domain of financial activity benefited a great many faculty people who had been able to appeal directly to the chancellor for

funding without being bureaucratically hamstrung. But that bureaucratic process is what enabled there to be some accountability; it provided the means by which the institution might evaluate claims on its resources in comparison with each other and in light of diverse perspectives. Huttenback's mode of operation reminded me of Chicago ward bosses doling out patronage to those favored by the machine. His demise came when he brazenly resisted being accountable for his decisions, despite evidence of self-dealing.

Huttenback's resignation in the aftermath of many revelations of his self-dealing was in my own mind something of a victory for a more participatory, democratic governance, since it seemed to establish, to a considerable degree, a direct faculty role in decision making about campus resource allocation. That role becomes even more important as budgetary constraints become more evident. How the pain of fiscal crisis within the campus was to be distributed—how to protect vital functions relating to teaching and research in the face of declining budgets—becomes a crucial issue. Academic Senate committees, whose meetings are rarely sites of drama, nevertheless become potentially vital voices in that kind of crisis.


## STUDENT AFFAIRS

DICK:

Another role that I played simultaneously with being vice chair of the Academic Senate was to create and chair a new committee of the senate—the Committee on Student Affairs.

As mass higher education expanded, so did a specialized bureaucracy for dealing with student life. Faculty interest in the extracurricular worlds of students steadily diminished, replaced by a professional coterie of counselors, rule makers, planners, and supervisors, assigned the task of allocating resources and overseeing the undergraduate life space. At UCSB, as at most colleges I guess, student affairs was operating without official liaison or accountability to the Academic Senate.

I'd been interested in student culture and student politics since my work with Ted Newcomb, greatly reinforced by my involvement in the student movement as an activist and as a sociologist. Getting to be a senate leader inspired my interest in enabling the senate to take a role in monitoring and advising the administration of student life.

One important item on my agenda in creating and leading this effort was to explore ways to enable students to become more fully engaged in "shared governance." Huttenback, in his typically cocky, arrogant pose, openly declared his disdain for student government and refused to commit himself to consulting with elected student leaders on various issues, forming his own student advisory council in order to bypass student government. The Committee on Student Affairs, like most senate committees, included student representatives. I helped define it as a space where student leaders could engage with faculty and administrators on key issues. The committee adopted resolutions declaring the official student government as the body legitimately representing student interests in campus governance.

The committee was formed at a time when a number of free speech issues were rather fraught. Huttenback was upset with the campus movement pressing for university divestment from apartheid South Africa. What upset him was the establishment of all-night encampments by masses of student protesters. He pushed through an administrative rule banning sleeping in public on campus. It was a rule that, in practice, was enforced only once—when a campus cop detained a student found dozing with his head down in the library. Our committee helped blunt the chancellor's demands for crackdown.

By the 1980s, minority students were becoming much more assertive in defense of their dignity and rights—in challenging racist expression on campus. Fraternity parties featuring masquerade using stereotypes ("gang-bangers" and "hos") were not infrequent. African American students found derogatory epithets scrawled on their doors. Minority students and their parents were mobilizing to call attention to such behavior.

Student affairs administrators, reflexively, assumed that the way to respond was to move to punish what they tried to define as "hate speech," and, as on many campuses, an effort to create a speech code was undertaken.

Our committee intervened and pressed for an approach that would use these incidents as crucial teaching moments. Disciplinary action seemed a way for the institution to claim that it was taking action—but was not, we argued, fitting, either as a fulfillment of the university's mission or as a method for dealing with racism. We succeeded in helping the student affairs staff to develop programs and procedures that deliberately protected freedom of expression while exposing and educating about issues of race.

The fact that minority students were offended and deeply angered by manifestations of racism did not mean that they wanted simply to see these acts punished. For the most part, they saw that hate speech incidents were symptomatic of deeper and broader problems. It was these that had to be addressed.

In the mid-1980s, as for all of its previous history, UCSB was very much a white campus. One way of coming to grips with the fact that most of the students had very little contact with people of other races and ethnicities and very little knowledge of the history of racial oppression and exclusion was to institute a requirement that all students take at least one course in the ethnic studies departments. The campus Chicano and black studies programs were established in the early 1970s; Asian American studies came a few years later; these programs offered a number of introductory courses that could serve to fulfill an ethnic studies requirement. Minority student demands for this requirement were intense; over several years, these demands were pressed in many ways, including a hunger strike that lasted several days. I was part of the faculty group that sought such a requirement; the Committee on Student Affairs became an important arena for promoting the idea. Faculty resistance to the requirement probably had a number of motives. One argument that seemed plausible was that UCSB students already had a heavy load of required courses and might resent imposition of a new one.

Finally, the requirement was agreed to (incidentally, a reasonably valid poll by the student newspaper prior to the senate vote on the matter showed that the majority of students actually favored this new course requirement).

Despite the tumult surrounding its adoption, the requirement was soon smoothly integrated into the curriculum, no doubt having some of its desired effects on the consciousness of many students. It also had benefit for the departments offering the requisite courses. First of all, the requirement increased student demand for their courses, and that helped these departments make the case that they needed more faculty positions and more resources. The courses taught in once embattled departments accordingly became part of the established and taken-for-granted curriculum at UCSB. Despite stereotypes of such programs as intellectual ghettos, the story at UCSB was quite the reverse. For example, the majority of students who majored in black studies at UCSB were non-black. Black and Chicano studies courses were typically taught, not as expressions of "identity politics," but as portals for understanding American history, culture, and society. Each of the ethnic studies programs, once provided resources, were able to develop flourishing graduate programs and research centers.

It's a striking thing to look back to their early days and realize that the ethnic studies programs, whose members typically thought that the programs would not survive for very long, at UCSB, became fully established elements in the undergraduate curriculum of the campus. Many of their senior faculty members have gone on to play major roles in the campus at large.

Of course, these programs had their share of internal conflict and contention, though probably no more so than many traditional departments experience. Internecine department warfare is not only a theme of academic novels but a disturbing feature of academic life. These battles are fueled, I am sure, by a hunger for drama among a group of folks whose lives are otherwise less than exciting.

I always saw such conflict as a terrible waste of time, energy, and personal well-being. In our sociology department, I did what I could to head off the worst of these. I've always been naive enough to think that there are ways to carry on inevitable intellectual and power struggles without turning them into full-scale warfare or epic family tragedies. There were times when I experienced something like a utopian community of scholars being enacted; more often, the department was like a family, with all the subterranean antipathies, ambivalences, and angst that permeate shared family life.

## STUDENTS' WORLDS

DICK:

I served for a long time as chair of the Committee on Student Affairs—about eight years. It was a campus role that I enjoyed because of my fascination with the student world, a world that I saw, from the time I first worked on the Bennington study, as an important social framework for personal growth and development—with real consequences for the social future.

Our research in the 1950s was about the ways in which student culture shaped its members' values, life orientations, and attitudes. The student world on any campus is constituted by subcultural difference. Subcultural divisions and conflicts in the student body mirror—and transmit—cultural battles in the larger society.

Since the nineteenth century, a culture rooted in privilege, anchored by fraternities and sororities, has been a characteristic of student life. Not infrequently, it's been a framework for preserving smug insulation and power for children of the upper classes. From the beginning of the twentieth century, this subculture of privilege has been challenged by countercultural perspectives. On elite campuses, in particular, "outsiders," including Jewish students in the early years of the previous century and others drawn from working-class background, created a succession of campus countercultures prizing the questioning of authority and privilege, and within which avant-garde art, music, and politics flourished. In the 1960s, the "outsider" culture became dominant in the student world across the country.

By the 1990s, spurred by demographic changes in the state and by affirmative action admissions policies, the student body at UCSB was becoming more diverse. The demographic change coincided with a change in the student climate as we faculty experienced it in the classroom. I was noticing, for example, pretty high absenteeism in my large lecture classes and a certain sense of disconnection. This student disengagement became a topic in collegial conversation. One friend, known for his appealing style as a lecturer, told me that he felt a "fog" in the lecture hall. He wondered whether it was because the age gap between himself and the students had reached a breaking point. Other colleagues, also worried by student disengagement, attributed it to the declining "quality" of the student body. After all, with affirmative action, average student SAT (Scholastic Aptitude Test) scores were declining. Maybe students were less prepared, less academically motivated, because they came from less educated backgrounds?

All this was grist for my mill. First of all, the vague faculty sense of student disengagement needed to be scrutinized in the light of data. Second, my years of research led me to conjecture that student disengagement was connected to student culture. It was time to get back to doing research on student life after years of working on other passions.

That turn was made possible when I began to work with Scott Thomas. Scott asked me to sit on his doctoral committee in the education school because he was doing a study of student culture at Westmont (a locally based Christian college), and the Bennington study was one of the models for the work he wanted to do. When I worked with Ted Newcomb in the 1950s, research on student attitudes and culture was a veritable industry, involving some of the leading figures in social science. After the 1960s, however, studying students fell out of fashion. I was, accordingly, excited to encounter someone like Scott who was interested in studying student culture and who had excellent quantitative skills (which I did not). Soon, we collaboratively undertook an effort to survey students at UCSB—aiming to learn something about the matter of student disengagement. Scott's quantitative skill and his command of current research literature on students created a partnership made in heaven, as far as I was concerned.

Scott made me aware of the fact that student research was now almost entirely being done by institutional researchers embedded in the burgeoning bureaucracy of student affairs and student personnel across higher education. Most of it was driven by institutional needs, rather than, as in my day, by the curiosity of social scientists. One topic, however, that had emerged by the 1990s was the assessment of "student engagement"—efforts to measure how involved students were in academic pursuits and in the life of their campus communities. Much of this assessment was used to compare and rate—one of many sorts of data that colleges were using to compete in the admissions marketplace. Despite such "marketing" uses, we thought the survey instruments that measured engagement could serve our own interests.

We designed a sample survey of the UCSB student population, using questions drawn from national surveys to examine how various forms of engagement and partying might be related to students' backgrounds, life goals, and academic performance. In addition to students' responses to the survey questionnaire, we were able to incorporate data from students' records—data we could then correlate with their responses. That background data included their grades and SAT scores as well as the kinds of demographic information that appears on admissions applications and the like.

The results were fascinatingly clearer than we expected when we started. Essentially, student engagement—in academics, in community service, in civic affairs—was *negatively* correlated with family income and other indicators of relative privilege. And self-reported binge drinking and partying was *positively* correlated with social class measures. At UCSB, kids from wealthy backgrounds spent much less time on their studies and much more time in hedonistic fun than the children of lower-income background. And the poorer students worked jobs as well (on average twenty hours a week); the higher students' family income, the less likely they were to be working—and, naturally enough, the lower their debt. Because SAT scores are so heavily correlated with parents' income, we found that *binge drinking was positively correlated with SAT score*. If we compared white students with students of color, or first-generation immigrant students with "native born," or first-generation college students with those whose parents had college education—we got similar relationships. On average, more advantaged students were less academically and civically engaged that those who came from disadvantaged background.

Conventional wisdom says that advantaged young people with a lot of cultural capital will be more readily engaged academically. It's assumed that financial burdens of disadvantaged students hamper their involvement and that SAT scores predict success in college. Our findings pointed in the opposite direction. I often summed up what we found at UCSB by saying that, if the college persists in recruiting kids on the basis of their SAT scores, it will continue to build up the "party school" culture that has undermined its reputation. If it continues to draw its student body predominantly from the suburbs of Southern California, it will be continuing to degrade the "quality" of its student body.

Scott Thomas and I presented the UCSB research at national student affairs conferences and got a very enthusiastic response. Many people said that our data fit their own experiences. We published pieces on our findings in the *New York Times* Education Supplement and the *Chronicle of Higher Education*, and these got a good deal of circulation.

I had the opportunity to present some of these findings at various campuses of the University of California system to audiences that included many student affairs professionals and institutional researchers. These conversations led me to suggest that surveys like the one we did at UCSB ought to be done for all of the University of California's campuses. The idea was immediately attractive to a couple of key institutional researchers, especially Gregg Thomson, the director of student research at Berkeley. Gregg realized that a partnership between academic researchers like me and institutional research staff could produce a more interesting and fruitful research enterprise than the typical, applied efforts expected of institutional research staff—efforts that were easily ignored and filed away.

Gregg argued that an online survey could be used to solicit participation from the entire student body, rather than relying on small samples traditionally used in survey research. An online survey aimed at more than one hundred thousand students would create a unique database, whose numerical size would permit innumerable finely grained studies. For example, sample surveys on the typical college campus generated only meager data on African American students—their small numbers meant that very few would end up in the usual sample. What Gregg called a "census survey," in which all students were asked to respond, would include data on thousands of minority students.

I found this prospect very enticing, although my training (in the pre-Internet era) made me doubt that online surveying could gain a scientifically valid representation of the student body. In my day, we were taught that face-to-face interviewing of carefully drawn random samples, with intense efforts to induce designated respondents to participate, was the only way to do a scientific survey. A census survey would be much cheaper to do if it could create a respectably representative pool of student respondents

In 2002 the student affairs division in the University of California Office of the President (UCOP) agreed to the creation of what we called the University of California Undergraduate Experience Survey (UCUES). UCUES was established as a partnership between UCOP and the Berkeley-based Center for the Study of Higher Education (CSHE), whose associate director, John Douglass, was a strong supporter of the project (and who'd worked for a time at UCSB, where we'd become friends). I spent a good part of the next five years helping to lead UCUES's development and administration. The original vision was largely fulfilled—biannual surveys, created and administered by campus institutional research staff as well as UCOP and CSHE folks, to which at least twenty-five thousand students across the state system responded. We were creating one of the largest databases on student attitudes and behavior—a database in which students' survey responses were linked to a lot of information about their backgrounds and their academic performance. (Naturally, the confidentiality of these data was fundamental.)

The data we gathered showed, first of all, that academic and civic engagement were not correlated with the SAT but *were* correlated with high school grades; if colleges wanted to recruit an engaged, academically oriented student body, the SAT wasn't a helpful tool. We were able to show empirically that students from disadvantaged backgrounds, who might not score well on the SAT, were more likely to be more academically motivated—and also more committed to making a difference in the community—than many upper-middle-class kids with high test numbers. These findings challenged the usual methods for determining who should be admitted to the university. The research fueled my growing involvement in seeking some fundamental reform of the university's admissions policies.[2]

## REFORMING ADMISSIONS

DICK:

In 1995 the Board of Regents of the University of California abolished affirmative action in admissions. Affirmative action had worked in the following
way: the university was required, by the 1960 master plan for higher education in California, to select students from the top 12.5 percent of the high
school graduates in each year. Such eligible students (by this criterion) were
entitled to be admitted to a University of California campus (but not entitled to the campus of their first choice). To promote racial diversity, each
campus had established methods by which eligible minority students would
be admitted ahead of white students whose test scores might be higher than
theirs—thereby allowing the most competitive campuses a way to recruit
minority students who might not have been admitted to that campus based
on their numbers. In addition, campuses could admit a small percentage of
applicants who weren't "academically eligible" but had special talents—that
is, athletes, actors, musicians, and the like.

The regents, led by Governor Pete Wilson, who was positioning himself
to run for president by exploiting this issue, abolished that affirmative
action policy in July 1995—and their action was reinforced when state voters approved Proposition 209, banning "racial preferences" in state personnel and admissions practice, a measure initiated by conservative African
American regent and Wilson campaign contributor Ward Connerly.

Connerly and Wilson were responding to a decided wave of public anger
over affirmative action. The policy was depicted as enabling the university
to admit less qualified black and Latino students, denying places to more
qualified white and Asian kids. Wilson's presidential hopes never material-
ized, but the popular opposition to affirmative action had won the day, with
the immediate consequence a sharp drop in the number of black students
admitted to University of California campuses and to the professional
schools.

This situation fundamentally conflicted with the university's charter,
which states that the student population ought to reflect the population of
the state. That nineteenth-century requirement provided, to me, a clue
about how admissions policy could be revised to promote equity and diversity while avoiding the outlawed use of "racial preferences." I learned that a
friend and colleague, Rudy Alvarez, of the UCLA sociology department,
had been thinking along similar lines. We co-authored a think piece and

tried to distribute it widely in the university. We suggested that *if eligibility of University of California applicants was determined by their standing within their individual high school rather than their standing in the statewide applicant pool,* this would enable thousands of students, particularly from inner-city and rural high schools, to become eligible. Furthermore, if the university systematically informed the top students in each of the high schools in the state that they were qualified for University of California admissions, this might increase the flow of applications by students of all backgrounds. The segregation by race and ethnicity of secondary schools in California was part of what made the model plausible as a framework to promote diversity. Moreover, Rudy and I learned, a very large percentage of the high schools in California historically sent almost none of their graduates to the university. We suggested that the top 6 percent of each high school graduating class be declared eligible for University of California admissions based on grades alone. Soon after we began circulating this proposal, the University of Texas adopted a similar plan, further reinforcing the plausibility of what we were proposing.

Still, our paper was received rather coldly by the system-wide faculty committee that determined admissions policy. The prospect of admitting numbers of students from academically poor schools was not a pleasant one, especially for science faculty who tended to see even currently qualified students as ill prepared. But faculty opinion quickly shifted when the concept was endorsed by University of California president Dick Atkinson. Atkinson, who was a respected educational psychologist, publicly questioned the university's reliance on the SAT as well.

Inspired by these happenings, I eagerly decided to participate directly in the admissions policy-making bodies at UCSB and system-wide. I became a member of the campus admissions committee and was elected chair, which then led to my representing the campus on the system-wide Board on Admissions and Relations with Schools (BOARS), the faculty body with decisive control over the university's admissions standards and policies. When I joined BOARS, the chair was Michael Brown, who had preceded me as chair of the UCSB admissions committee. Michael was a professor of education at UCSB. He and I shared a passionate interest in changing the system-wide admissions policies in ways that would promote access and diversity while, in our view, strengthening the capacity of the system to admit the most motivated students. Michael's leadership, along with the support from the president's office, propelled BOARS, during my time there, to adopt a number of policies that set the stage for a very significant reworking of University of California admissions. Those changes included reducing the weight of the SAT, adopting a "holistic evaluation" of students so that the full range of students' achievements and hardships could be considered, and, most importantly, making student achievement in their individual high schools the prevailing conception of merit (replacing standardized test scores). Looking back on that work, I can't help but feel pride. It was one of those times in my life where an effort at institutional change really produced some large-scale results. UCSB, in particular, has a considerably transformed student body. It became, in 2015, the first major research university in the United States to be designated as "Hispanic serving"—meaning that more than 25 percent of its undergraduates are Latino.

I think the admissions reforms we helped institute enabled the University of California system to at least maintain the racial diversity that it was beginning to achieve with affirmative action. African American student enrollments have not improved, however, since there are very few predominantly black high schools in the state (so "achievement in the individual high school" doesn't much affect black student enrollments). High-achieving black students in California are likely to get admitted to top-tier private schools (which continue to identify applicants by ethnicity). But I have to confess that Proposition 209 and the debate around affirmative action, even though initiated by self-serving conservative politicians, resulted in a deeper examination within the institution, and maybe even in the wider public, of who the university serves and how to evaluate the readiness for, and the value of, University of California education. At this writing, many University of California campuses, including once lily-white UCSB, are now majority nonwhite. A lot of that is due to the rise of the Asian American population in the past couple of decades, but it also represents the fact that underrepresented minority students have increased their proportion in the student body.

This is particularly true at Santa Barbara, where our early emphasis on the selection of students who were at the top of their high school class as a preference enabled UCSB to be the most receptive to minority students of any of the selective campuses in the system. So I'm proud of this work; but I immediately couple that sense of pride with a strong reminder that the minority makeup of the University of California student body still lags way behind the population of college-age people in the state. Most of the black and Latino children in California do not get to college, and the profound educational inequity my mother struggled against eighty years ago remains a stark reality.

Still, the University of California, among the highly selective public as well as private universities in the United States is probably the most diverse, in terms of both the ethnic and class background of its students. The tremendous damage that austerity has created for public higher education in California is a matter of huge concern, but it's worth taking note that the University of California has become self-critical about its relationship to its constitutional mandate to represent the people of the state. There are many pressures on the university to return to a more elitist model of admissions. One hopes that these pressures can be resisted and that the progress made in the decade before I retired can continue.

Of course, the guarantee of decent education for all children of the state can't be achieved simply by the university. There were times when I was involved in university governance that I found myself questioning the value of this effort, because we were tinkering around the edges or, maybe, rearranging the deck chairs on the *Titanic*. Still, I think now, as I did when I began my academic career, shortly after Port Huron, that these internal struggles within higher education are actually significant in shaping the society's as well as the schools' future.

## THE TRUTH ABOUT TENURED RADICALS

DICK:

For something like a quarter of a century now, right-wing intellectuals have been making an issue of the alleged capture of American universities by "tenured radicals." My own story has to be representative of the situation they claim to decry. If there are tenured radicals, I certainly was one of them—and there's no question that I consciously oriented my research, my teaching, and my role in the university in terms of expressing and advancing my core values.

My agenda was never a secret one. In fact, it was an agenda that I proudly announced.

Like John Dewey, the inventor of the concept of participatory democracy, I believe that education ought to serve a democratic function, that engaged citizenship should be a fundamental goal of the college experience, that democratic learning can be fostered by the curriculum and pedagogical practice—and also by the structure of relationships in the classroom, in the institution, and in the relationship between the institution and the larger society. That was my agenda: to try to carry forward that kind of vision of the uses of the university. That meant challenging the ways in which universities were structured and governed. It meant struggles to expand the horizons of the curriculum. It meant pressing for an inclusive framework of admissions and hiring. It meant protection of academic freedom, so that unpopular perspectives could be voiced and free debate could be possible on the campus—and so that students and faculty who wanted to link themselves to social movement in the wider society would feel the freedom and even encouragement to do that.

Some of the debate stirred by the conservative critique had to do with political advocacy in the classroom. My own practice was shaped by my good fortune to be able to teach courses that bore on the issues of the day and on social movements of past and present. My style was not to appear neutral in these discussions, but to make my own biases clear—and at the same time to insist that the classroom was a free forum for all points of view. Conservative students, for the past couple of decades, have voiced complaints about feeling intimidated or silenced in the liberal atmosphere of the university. My own experience was that it was often peer pressure, as much as, or more than, professorial censure, that led conservative students to feel politically threatened. In the classroom, right-wing argument might be greeted with groans of outrage or derision. So I tried, with some success, to make it possible for conservative students to voice their thoughts and their perspectives in the forums my classes provided.

Just recently, I got an e-mail from a former student. He had graduated ten years before from Santa Barbara, and he reminded me that he was an outspoken conservative Republican student in my classes. He wanted to tell me that he had just been elected mayor of his small city in California. He had gotten back into politics after some years in business. What he wanted to say to me was that my classes had enabled him to find his voice and compelled him to examine and to clarify and sharpen his views. It was the freedom to speak and to debate in these classes that had been a high point of his time in college. This is the kind of message from a former student that any teacher loves to get—but this one was special.

It's often argued that the professionally and pedagogically correct thing for a teacher in a social science class to do is to avoid expressing his or her own political views, striving to represent all perspectives accurately and with balanced objectivity. In my case, it was impossible to conceal my stance. I'm an active participant in the political process in the community. My public history of left-wing activism certainly defines who I am to students. So my approach has been to explain my passions, while putting a clear emphasis on the right of all students to express themselves, actively encouraging such expression, and demanding that all students adhere to the disciplines of logic and empirical evidence. And, of course, it has also been to enable students to understand as fully as possible the logic and the reasons embedded in opposing views. This fusion of political passion and dispassionate analysis seems to work well as a pedagogical approach and as a way of honoring the deep academic traditions of objectivity. For me, objectivity as a teacher and as a scholar resides, not in having no position, but in striving to be open to ideas that contradict one's own and to evidence that does not fit one's preconceptions.

The right-wing critique of the academy is loaded with fabrication and dishonesty. One piece that I most objected to was the constantly reiterated notion that conservatives were being excluded from appointments in the university—as evidenced by the overwhelming proportion of faculty who were registered Democrats. Since party registrations are publicly available, it's easy to do such computations.

There's no question that the percentage of faculty across the campus who are registered Republicans has markedly declined in the past forty years. But the notion that this party registration data was proof of ideological uniformity on the campus or of discrimination against Republicans or conservatives is a delusion. In the first place, the disproportionately Democratic Party affiliation of faculties in the social sciences and humanities has been a fact in higher education at least since World War II. The liberalism of faculty in these disciplines isn't an aftereffect of the 1960s—it was the case for decades before. I think the biggest recent change has been the decline in support for the Republican Party among science faculty. It's hard to imagine how a chemistry department might preferentially hire Democrats rather than Republicans, but not hard to see why scientists are now less drawn to the GOP, given the many ways in which that party has decided to represent the anti-science side of America's culture wars. Never mentioned by conservative critics is the degree to which the Republican Party is inhospitable to the very ways of thinking and the modes of operation of the university (not to mention the propensity of Republicans to attack higher education and research budgets).

A second point, usually ignored by the critics is that Democratic Party registration hardly represents a uniformity of political perspective. A moment's thought makes one realize that registered Democrats range from forms of neo-conservatism and Cold War liberalism to various moderate perspectives on social reform to left-wing pro-labor and progressive perspectives. One could have no Republicans on a faculty in a political science department and still have a very wide range of views on all kinds of social questions as well as on questions about the nature of the university and the issues debated within it.

Our student surveys of recent years produced surprising findings about the ideological makeup of the student body. I would say that in the past ten or fifteen years, student attitudes at the University of California are more to the left than they were in the 1960s on many issues. For example, the proportion of students opposed to the Iraq war (80 percent or so) was higher than in the height of the anti–Vietnam War movement. To some extent, the relative leftism of University of California students has to do with the fact that the *majority of students are now either immigrants or children of immigrant parents.* One political aftereffect of the Pete Wilson years was the branding of the GOP as the anti-immigrant party.

There are some issues that almost totally unite the student body. These include abortion rights and related feminist issues, same-sex marriage and related issues of gay liberation, stem cell research and related issues having to do with science, climate change and other environmental issues, and the legalization of marijuana. Regardless of political identification, students tend to agree on all of these matters—and the identification of the Republican Party and the right wing with opposition to all of these issues has led to large-scale student defections from the Republican allegiances of their parents. Today the proportion of students who identify as extremely conservative is quite miniscule. They are therefore bound to feel uncomfortable, given the consensus of their peers on these matters. The primary influence on student politics does not come from faculty intention to indoctrinate. There certainly are some number of professors in America who are outrageously outspoken—David Horowitz published a book naming the one hundred most dangerous professors (a list I was disappointed not be part of). Most of these are probably as dangerous to the young as was Socrates.

In the late 1960s, a number of us hoped that we could sustain an ongoing organized network within academia identifying with the New Left and social movements. That project, embodied in the New University Conference

(NUC), failed as a structured national organizational force. Instead, an array of radical caucuses in the disciplines and professions, the creation of new disciplines like ethnic studies, gender studies, gay studies, and the like, and a variety of fluid informal networks helped shift the intellectual life in the humanities and social sciences in more critical directions. There is no nationally organized Left in academia—any more than there is in the society at large. Those in the professoriate who identify with the Left have had to adapt themselves to the demands of career, the rules and cultures of institutions, as well as the overarching vicissitudes of daily life and of history. In my own case, my work was sustained, not by national frameworks, but by friendships and mutual supports both locally and in the wider world.

At Port Huron, we began to imagine a different kind of university—a democratic university that could be a resource for societal democratization. Today, when I look at the multicolored stream of students passing by on campus, when I consider the diversity of issues now incorporated into the curriculum, when I think about the ways that colleagues are in fact linking their intellectual work to the needs of communities and movements, I know that some of what we dreamed about fifty years ago has come to pass.

But the new generation of people working in higher education has every reason to be impatient with that observation. They are dealing with budgetary austerities, with the shrinking of opportunity for coherent academic careers and the rise of a sort of academic proletariat, with the corporatization of curriculum and research in many institutions, and with the revival of right-wing attack on the very ideal of democratic higher education. Being a tenured radical at the University of California puts me in a quite advantaged position—not the best angle from which to see and feel the troubles.

For several decades after the 1960s, the left leanings of American academics were accompanied by considerable disengagement from the political world outside the campus. Often, critical theorizing used a vocabulary that seemed willfully cut off from any wider public. Our friend Todd Gitlin, some years ago, bemoaned how "the right marched on Washington and took a great deal of it, while the left was marching on the English department"[3] to dramatize distress over the disengagement of the academic Left from real-world politics.

Still, surprisingly, the academically based debates about race, gender, and sexuality sparked by a rising generation of feminist and racially diverse intellectuals have been reshaping the culture. Ideas and concepts that originated in seemingly ivory-towered academic discourse have had big impact on political practice and collective action. One example from the moment might be the explosion of an esoteric concept like "intersectionality" as a word and a topic. The separations between the worlds of campus and community are deep, and I'm often surprised by a disconnection from political reality that I hear around faculty tables. But I never endorsed Todd Gitlin's sardonic quip. Culture matters a lot—and so do its critics and creators.

And when you add together the students, faculty, and staff, the alumni and the parents, you realize that higher education has begun to reshape politics. The Sanders presidential project dramatized the remarkable consensus for equality and social justice among "millennials." This consensus represents a generational shift toward the left fueled not just by the shared outlooks of an educated class but also by the very precarious future—in both economic and environmental terms—that the young are facing. Accordingly, what happens in the academic and social spaces of the campuses may make more difference than ever.

After my term was over in the admissions policy arena in 2006, I decided to retire from full-time teaching. It was not that I was tired of it, but Mickey and I both wanted some time in our lives for more freedom to travel and to set the terms and pace of our daily lives.

MICKEY:

I kept agitating for him to retire—so we could go to Yellowstone in the wintertime. . . . He did, and we did, and it was absolutely magnificent! No crowds, no oppressive heat, and an opportunity to see, hear, and learn much about the wolf packs in the park, as well as to enjoy the geysers that steam in the cold air, as does the breath from the buffalos wandering about. . . . Highly recommended!

DICK:

My retirement was seen by my dean, Melvin Oliver, by some in the department, and some of my former students as worth making a public occasion. Maybe we could stage something that would contribute to nascent fund-raising efforts to support sociology. Learning of this interest, it occurred to me to suggest convening a conference in which all the speakers would be people whom I had taught or had otherwise had close relationships with in my teaching years who had made contributions to building social movements in the previous forty to fifty years. The result was a two-day "Flacksfest," whose success was due to the efforts of Bill Shay, one of my doctoral

students and research collaborators, and Mickey. Several panels were organized, featuring former students who had become leaders in labor and community organizing, as well as some of the people we'd partnered with
politically in the community. Nothing could have been more validating
than to see one's hopes as a teacher embodied in the experiences and contributions of these people.

Flacksfest began with a banquet, which large numbers of colleagues,
friends, and community people attended. Tom Hayden made the keynote
speech, and other speakers included our congressperson Lois Capps, Chancellor Henry Yang (who helped finance the event), Dean Oliver, and Rose-
Ann DeMoro, head of the California Nurses Association, who made a
special effort to come. RoseAnn had been a graduate student in sociology,
who left the program to become one of the most effective labor leaders of
our time—and who credited her years in our department as formative for
her. The chancellor's participation was particularly moving to me. He
thanked me for being a conscience for him (and gave examples). Quite a
contrast to the way I was officially regarded when I started my career in
Santa Barbara. And Tom Hayden's words reinforced my belief that what we
had been doing all these years was to live out the mandates of Port Huron.

Flacksfest was of course a peak experience for me. It wasn't simply the
number of wonderful things people said about me, which you would rather
have expressed in your presence than at your funeral, but the gratifying
sense that one's own life had interrelated with so many others who were
making a difference in the wider world. There couldn't have been a better
way to bring that stage of my life to a conclusion. And I chose to see the
event not as a finale but as a bridge to the next act in life's drama.

# 15 ▸ PLAYING FOR CHANGE

DICK:

If you were red diaper baby, there is very strong probability that you were raised with folk music as the soundtrack of your growing up. So, from our earliest days, we both had a strong interest in music that expressed social consciousness and embodied our values.

In Camp Wo-Chi-Ca, campers learned labor songs and other anthems of the Left, singing them often in glorious unison, led by counselors with real talent (some of whom had careers in the subsequent popular folk revival). Indeed, if you went to one of the lefty camps (Wo-Chi-Ca, Wyandot, Kinderland, Woodland), singing of such songs was essential to your very being.

It was one of the many things Mickey and I had in common. Mickey had been an active and avid member of the Jewish Young Folksingers, where she had good friends who went on to significant careers in the folk music revival. The group's director was Robert De Cormier, who became a legendary arranger and choral director, working with Harry Belafonte and Peter, Paul and Mary. Indeed, Mary Travis got her start as a member of the Jewish Young Folksingers. Ethel Raim started a short-lived but also legendary a cappella singing group, the Pennywhistlers—seven young women (most of whom were close friends of Mickey's) who mastered the enthralling harmonic singing of Balkan and Eastern European folk traditions (Mickey always says that marrying me and moving to Ann Arbor cost her a chance to be a Pennywhistler). The group lasted only a few years, but made several albums that are still circulating, and helped inspire interest in Balkan folk music and dance, which Raim has spent her life nurturing.

For us, singing folk songs and collecting the growing stream of folk music records was basic to our identity. Back in the 1950s and early 1960s, it was normal for parties in our set to feature group singing. A typical evening might start out with songs that most everyone knew and then evolve into song swapping. The playlist would include folk songs and lefty anthems, but also pop songs and show tunes, accompanied by one or more guitars, simply strummed. Mickey has a great knack for remembering songs and their lyrics (I, for some reason, can almost never remember lyrics even of songs I've been singing all my life). Whenever we're in such group sings, her voice takes the lead.

So folk singing was intrinsic to the daily lives of red diaper babies—a defining feature of the shared, intimate world of family and friendship as we grew up.

Red diaper babies helped initiate a subculture defined by folk music—a scene that became a central part of our teenage years. After World War II, Pete Seeger and his comrades in the People's Songs project in New York City organized what they called "hootenannies." By the time we were old enough, the "hoots" were happening every couple of months, in ramshackle auditoriums like the Pythian Temple on the Upper West Side, attracting a couple of thousand youths to hear old-time banjo pickers from Appalachia and authentic blues guitarists from Mississippi alongside the lefty city folksingers for whom Seeger was a prime model. Seeger was our Elvis, our private Sinatra. After each of these shows, hundreds of kids would throng the stage door, hoping to make a personal connection with the shy, diffident guy who, by then, was pushing forty.

Seeger was at that time totally blacklisted—barred completely from commercial broadcasting and recording. But he made a living on the college circuit, where he cultivated a performance style that emphasized a singing audience and the learning of new songs. A Seeger concert typically involved three-part singing of African rounds, rousing union songs, a bit of pyrotechnic banjo playing, and some beautiful audience harmonies to an uplifting anthem or gospel song.

In the summer, Seeger toured a string of summer camps in the North-east. Whether he planned it or not, these summer camp and college perfor-mances helped build a fan base, not only for himself, but for the music. And that folk song subculture was one of the major seedbeds for the flowering of activism in the early 1960s.

Seeger's blacklisting in the 1950s had shattered his chances to have a major mainstream career. In the late forties, Seeger helped form a folk song quartet, the Weavers. The group included Lee Hays, who in the early 1940s had partnered with Seeger, Woody Guthrie, and others to create the Alma-nac Singers, with the goal of bringing song to the labor movement and other progressive causes, as part of the vast cultural program that emerged in the 1930s from the communist and labor movement Left. That program couldn't be sustained as the Cold War began and the party shriveled. The Weavers' members, besides Hays and Seeger, were two younger performers (who had been counselors at Wo-Chi-Ca), Fred Hellerman and Ronnie Gilbert. Unexpectedly, they caught the attention of major commercial music promoters—and their recordings became big popular hits in the late 1940s and early 1950s. That success in turn caught the attention of the entrepre-neurs of the entertainment industry blacklist—and the Weavers' pop music opportunity rapidly disappeared.

The concert the Weavers presented at Carnegie Hall on Christmas Eve in 1955 was promoted as their comeback—after two years—in defiance of the blacklist. Both Mickey and I (before we had met) were in that audience (I seventeen years old, she fifteen) along with most every other red diaper teenager. Going to Carnegie Hall to hear the Weavers on that Christmas Eve was a way to defy the blacklist—and to assert our collective identity. The very fact that the event was happening at Carnegie Hall signified some-thing important—it was a sign that the Red Scare could be successfully resisted. And, of course, we loved the music and the scene.[1]

You can hear most of the concert on a classic recording put out by what was then a new label—Vanguard. The Weavers' manager, Harold Leventhal, who combined brilliant business savvy with political acumen, had not only wangled a Carnegie Hall booking in the face of the blacklist, but had per-suaded Vanguard to take the risks as well. It was a major hit record (and an influential one in advancing mainstream interest in folk music). There's almost no political reference in the actual content of the performance. Indeed, the most political moment occurs when the Weavers sing the line: "Why can't we have Christmas the whole year around?" The ovation that can be heard greeting that line is a clue to the climate of that time, when speaking aloud a simple desire for peace and human community was considered quite daring. For us, and our tribe, it was a remarkably validating and empowering event.

We set up our household in Ann Arbor at just about the time that LP records were being widely produced. Our prized possession was a jerry-built hi-fi system, consisting of a beautiful (to my eyes) Blaupunkt radio (bought at the Teachers Union discount store) into which we plugged an LP turntable. Our first records were Folkways recordings of Pete Seeger, a hootenanny album, an album of Robert Burns songs by Ewan MacColl (the great Scottish folksinger who had recently married Peggy Seeger), and an album of international folk song by Theodore Bikel and Cynthia Gooding (which we still regard as one of the greatest records ever made). Gooding was a particular find, which we owe to Mickey's oldest friend, Judee Rosenbaum.

Mickey had a cast recording of *Finian's Rainbow*—the pathbreaking Broadway musical with an interracial cast and a plot that involved sharecroppers, racist senators, leprechauns, and a folksinger/organizer named Woody.

Yip Harburg wrote the book and the libretto for *Finian's Rainbow*. Every one of the songs became a classic, and some were explicitly socially conscious: "When the Idle Rich Become the Idle Poor" and "That Great Come-and-Get-It Day." Yip was one of the best of the Broadway lyricists (he wrote the songs for the *Wizard of Oz* as well as quite a few explicit political ditties). Even as teenagers, we both had figured out the class-conscious and socialistic subtexts of the play and its songs. We were both taken with the score; at Camp Kinderland, on a day off, we found ourselves on Mickey's cot, with the *Finian's* record serving as a soundtrack for our making out.

A few years later, we came to be close friends with Yip's son, Ernie. He was probably attracted to us at first because we were these youngsters who knew a lot about his father's work. The times we shared with Yip and his family on Martha's Vineyard and in his Central Park apartment were experiences we much cherished, especially since he enthusiastically appreciated what we told him about trying to make a New Left.

The so-called folk music revival was beginning just when we got married in 1959. That was when the Kingston Trio made mega-hits out of folk songs—a development that provided further proof to us of how capitalism commodified everything. We felt that the crew-cut frat boy style that the Kingston Trio affected—and that was soon imitated and even further cheapened—signified that our particular cultural treasure was being stolen and sold. But the homogenizing side of the folk revival was superseded by the sudden explosion of very talented singing songwriters based in Greenwich Village.

Of these, the most dramatic, of course, was Bob Dylan. We'd heard something about Dylan in Ann Arbor. One day, Bob Ross (our undergraduate friend and student leader at the University of Michigan) mentioned that a fascinating kid had showed up at a party calling himself Bobby Dylan, en route through town to New York. Soon after, a review of Dylan's performance at Gerde's Folk City showed up in the *New York Times*—a piece that instantly established that an amazingly young and creative heir to Woody Guthrie's legacy had arrived in the Village. Instead of commercializing that legacy, Dylan had discovered it for himself and intended to live it and advance it.

I'm always likely to romanticize a cultural or political happening that has the slightest promise of helping remake the world. One of the many ways our relationship is balanced is that Mickey is much more likely to be a skeptic; out of this loving clash, some realistic shared perception might emerge. A good example has to do with Bob Dylan. We were back in the city for Christmas, in 1961, walking through the Village, passing Folk City, where a poster announced that Dylan was on that night. We could look through the plateglass window, and there was this kid in a fisherman's cap sitting on a stool with a guitar, a harmonica strapped around his neck. I remarked that this was the guy Bob Ross had met in Ann Arbor who had just got a rave review in the *Times*. I suggested that maybe we should go in (up to then, our crowd tended to avoid the folk club scene—we were not tourists, after all). Mickey said, "Looks to me like another one of your punk kid folksingers!" So we walked on by—thereby missing the chance to be able to say that we were there when Dylan made his New York debut. But the more of Dylan we heard, the more I followed him with avid amazement. He seemed, in those years, uncannily able to express, in song, a stance toward the world that deeply resonated with our own.

Dylan's first years in New York were very much entwined with our particular subculture. Dylan's girlfriend in those years, Suze Rotolo, was a camper (in the group where Mickey was a counselor) at Camp Kinderland; she's with him in that Greenwich Village photo that adorns the *Freewheelin'* album. Dylan crashed in apartments of some of our close friends, like Sheila Slater, one of Mickey's oldest friends, who always regretted her failure to save the crumpled pages that he had strewn on the floor.

As everyone knows, Dylan was one of a sizable coterie of very young performers who were doing what Guthrie had pioneered—taking traditional song forms, styles, and instruments and making new songs that spoke to the personal and social issues of the time. It was what Pete Seeger and the Almanacs had tried to do in the early 1940s, and what Seeger had sought to encourage in the postwar years. The folk music subculture that we identified with in the 1950s was the seedbed for this new generation, providing both the talent pool and the audience—and the political and moral fervor—for the new song movement. The youth-led civil rights movement, the new young Left and the new young artists were all intertwined and mutually nourishing. And for us red diaper babies, it meant that the esoteric, seemingly private, culture we had grown up with and that had sustained us in our early years, was now entering the mainstream in ways that unexpectedly validated who we were.

The new wave of artists—Joan Baez, Judy Collins, Phil Ochs, Tom Paxton, and others less well known—were, as far as Mickey and I were concerned, singing our songs. Once we got to Chicago, we tried to go to all the concerts (and the University of Chicago was the site for many of these), and I bought all the records they were making.

Many of these performers lent time and energy to the Southern movement. Indeed, most of the music that the 1963 March on Washington featured was performed by the new folkies: Dylan, Baez, and Peter, Paul and Mary (rather than African American performers, except for a rousing moment contributed by Mahalia Jackson). Dylan sang in Mississippi, and many new songs were written in response to the civil rights struggle.

The most politically engaged performer of the Greenwich Village crowd was Phil Ochs. His songs were primarily topical, and he, more than any of the others, was likely to show up at local rallies for a variety of causes, most particularly in opposition to militarism, empire, and war. Ochs sang at the SDS Vietnam march in 1965, doing one of his best satirical songs, "Love Me, I'm a Liberal," which tellingly nails the pretensions of the "white liberal" from the perspective of the young activists of that moment. The much-revered journalist I. F. Stone was on the speaker's platform. Stone was a figure of high integrity and honesty who hardly fit the character Ochs was satirizing—and he made his own telling point. "I'm a liberal," he said, "and so is Senator Gruening" (the Alaska senator who was slated to speak). "And I am pretty sure we'll be in the fight far longer than some of those who call themselves radical today." It was one of many times in those years that generational tensions were dramatically played out.

Ochs performed a stream of songs in those years that articulately expressed our generation's break with authority and conventional politics. Yet, in his heyday, he never reached the iconic, generational spokesman status that Dylan both courted and disdained. Mickey and I had a revealing encounter with Ochs. It was right after he'd given a concert at the University of Chicago's Mandel Hall, attended by at least a thousand. As we walked home, there was Ochs, walking alone on the Midway. We introduced ourselves and told him how much we appreciated the performance. "Thanks," he said. "But Dylan gets to play in Orchestra Hall downtown, while I can only do Mandel." It was a bit of a shock to get a raw taste of his unrequited yearning for fame.

Ten years later, Ochs committed suicide, suffering from depression, dementia, and alcoholism. That death finally made him a legendary figure. At least two biographies and a documentary feature film have told the story—a story dramatic enough for Sean Penn to have seriously contemplated starring in a Phil Ochs biopic.

Certainly, a key to his tragedy was his disappointment in and with the movement. After our encounter with Ochs, we thought about how he was taken for granted, and had reason to feel used, by the movement—and how often people were given to say that Ochs was politically reliable but nowhere as creative as Dylan. At that time, there was little attention paid to how to nourish and support cultural workers in the movement. And Ochs's own difficulty in distinguishing between celebrity and authentic influence was mirrored by the movement audience. Nowadays, forty years after his death, his old songs still have great impact—and are still relevant in the ongoing struggle against the empire that he tried to challenge.

By the end of the 1970s, I had a pretty good collection of music related to social movements, both historical and contemporary, and had been using music in my classes on social movements and related themes. A former UCSB student I'd come to know, the late Corey Dubin, had started to work at KPFK, the Los Angeles Pacifica station. On May Day in 1982, Corey invited me to come down to the station in Los Angeles with a bunch of my labor music records, to do a two-hour live conversation on both the movement and the music. That was of course a really enjoyable experience—being on the radio, to play stuff that I knew something about and to freely talk about music and politics.

Soon after that, Corey called to suggest that I think about starting my own radio show using protest music. Corey was also working at the UCSB campus station, KCSB, as public affairs director. His idea was that I do a series during the summer of 1982.

As soon as I heard the idea I had a jolt of excitement. I realized that I had always wanted to be a disc jockey on the radio, and his idea just immediately connected.

## RADIO DAYS

DICK:

I was excited partly because I was very much a radio person. I must have been about ten when I somehow got permission to have a radio next to my bed, and I often tuned in at night when lights were out and I was supposed to be asleep. We lived a few blocks from Ebbets Field; I could hear the crowd roars at night signifying something major was happening in the night game— I of course would turn on the radio to find out what it was. In those days, boxing was very much a national sport, and I was especially interested in the fortunes of Joe Louis (who, along with Jackie Robinson, was the great sports symbol of racism being overcome). In 1948 Louis was on the decline—and up against Jersey Joe Walcott, who had almost beaten him the year before. I could hear the fight sounds emanating from our upstairs neighbor's radio— so naturally I turned on the fight next to my bed, able to hear the moment when Louis KO'd Walcott and thereby brought his career to a climax.

I think a lot of kids in those years found their radios to be a real source of companionship as well as connection. In high school, I learned all about pop music—past and present—as an addicted fan of *Martin Block and the Make Believe Ballroom* every afternoon. Block played the hit parade, but also deliberately put together fifteen-minute segments featuring bits of the history of swing and pop of the 1930s and 1940s. I was also a fan of Al "Jazzbo" Collins, who broadcast from the Purple Grotto, with a somewhat more sophisticated playlist. I developed an interest in jazz (stimulated by Collins), listening to jazz shows on the radio and devouring jazz history and discographies. Uncle Joey (my father's brother) had a nice collection of 1930s-era jazz 78s, particularly Benny Goodman. I did quite a bit of baby-sitting for Uncle Joey and Aunt Rose, who lived within walking distance. Those evenings, looking after cousins Andy and Hank, gave me the chance to sample Joey's jazz records. And seeing my interest, Joe bought me, for my twelfth birthday, some Goodman LPs. They were among my first long-playing records.

In college, I discovered on late-night radio, the voice of Jean Shepherd. Shepherd would come on after midnight every night and talked for hours, in a virtually nonstop monologue. His voice was a kind of access to the rising new bohemianism in mid-1950s Greenwich Village. At first I thought that I was making a discovery that no one else knew about, imagining, I guess, that I was the only lonely New York kid tuned into the radio in the early morning hours. But one day, Shepherd was invited to speak at Brooklyn College. The room was packed to overflowing. . . .

MICKEY:

A similar event was held at CCNY, with a packed house in the college's largest hall. The following week, a leading politician (a senator, I think) spoke in the same hall to a very sparse crowd. I interpreted this as symbolic of our generation.

DICK:

Jean Shepherd called his audience the "night people," and he began to use his radio show to promote a sort of collective identity. It was the 1950s, so politics as such weren't mentioned, but his subtext was a critique of commercialism and racism and support for ways of being that a decade later would be on the ascendancy among youth.

So when Corey Dubin suggested that I go on the radio, he was striking a major chord in my heart—it a chance not only to publicly explore the political musics I had been collecting but to live out the long-standing love I had for the medium.

The campus radio station at UCSB, KCSB, was not just a college radio station playing alternative music, like many college stations around the country. It was aware of itself as a community radio station with a wide-ranging array of public and cultural affairs programming that was presented not just by students but by older folks, including some faculty members like me. So it made sense from a lot of points of view for me to do this summer experiment. I called the program *Culture of Protest*.

The structure from the start was to build an hour of music around a single theme having to do with social struggle, past and present, or artists who worked in relevant cultural traditions. Though the station has an unusually

FIGURE 15.1. Dick on the radio (KCSB), as shown on local TV news, 1986

rich record library, my operating rule was to use material from my own collection, making it convenient for me to find material and to audition it at home. I thought I'd have enough material for ten to twelve weeks that summer. Spoiler alert: I've been on the air for thirty-five years at this writing.

One of my first programs featured a live appearance by Earl Robinson. Earl is best known for having written the music to the classic labor song "I Dreamed I Saw Joe Hill Last Night"—but in the 1940s, radio performances of his popular "cantatas," "Ballad for Americans," and "The Lonesome Train," made these among the most widely performed contemporary patriotic works. And his "The House I Live In" was a standard song made popular by both Frank Sinatra and Paul Robeson.

Earl had moved to Santa Barbara in the early 1970s; in my childhood, he had lived in Brooklyn after having been blacklisted in the movie business. He was iconic for New York red diaper babies—his songs were at the top of the playlist for kids like us in our formative years. He gave music lessons and organized kids' choruses populated by these red diaper babies (including my sister, Nancy). And Earl was a friend of my parents, who had moved to Santa Barbara at about the same time as he had.

Earl's story was a perfect subject for the July 4 edition of my new show. Here was a guy who had written popular patriotic music and yet was a prime victim of the Hollywood Red purge. That irony was a great subject—as was the fact that he had put a lot of energy into the creation of songs that were inspired tributes to a progressive version of America. And, incidentally, Earl had written a top 40 hit—a song popularized by Three Dog Night called "Black and White," which he'd written (with lyrics by Alan Arkin's father, Dave) to commemorate the Supreme Court decision supporting school integration.

It was natural that summer of 1982 that I would invite him to come on the radio and do a program featuring "Ballad for Americans" and "The House I Live In" to commemorate the Fourth of July.[2]

MICKEY:

In high school, I got 98 percent on the "Regents"—a statewide American history exam, thanks, in large part, to my having memorized "Ballad for Americans," which traces the history of America in a fifteen-minute cantata, the recording of which I played constantly, and then I performed it with the Jewish Young Folksingers chorus led by Robert De Cormier.

DICK:

The July 4 commemoration was the second show of what I imagined as a summer series.

The first four or five shows were taped in advance, with Corey Dubin engineering. At some point midsummer, Corey suggested that I go on live and that I do my own engineering. It was a rather scary prospect, having not only to announce and narrate but also to cue up the records and operate the "board." But it turned out to be thrilling to manage all that. Thirty-five years later, I'm still doing the program, live, ad lib, and self-produced. Regular listeners expect at least one mistake an hour—some technical glitch or miscue—but people diplomatically say that it's an endearing trademark of the program.

What started as a summer series based on my home record library became a significant feature of my life. Almost from the start, I realized that the music I'd collected and the protest songs I knew about were but a small fraction of a vast array of materials. Conventional wisdom assumes that protest music was a sixties phenomenon. I always knew that there was a rich history of social movement–inspired music—that's what my record collection represented. What I hadn't really known in 1982 was that the tradition of political minstrelsy represented by Woody Guthrie and Pete Seeger and carried forward in the 1960s was continuing—that there were quite a number of traveling troubadours, writing new songs, making records, and playing for progressive audiences where they could find them. So, almost from the start, I realized that one purpose of the radio show would be to give these grandchildren of Guthrie some opportunity to be heard. Pretty soon, some of these folks were in touch about the possibilities for getting gigs in Santa Barbara. I didn't want to get too far into the concert-producing business, but I was able to get bookings on campus and in town for some of these. The most regular of these has been Charlie King, who's come to town almost annually for the past three decades. Others who we helped get audiences include Fred Small, the political duo Rebel Voices, David Rovics, and Dave Lippman. Google these names and you can learn about their work.

And these are but a small sampling of artists who have continued the political troubadour tradition, making songs that bring the news of grievance, struggle, and movement, in the style that descends most directly from the example of Guthrie and Seeger.

Globally, the iconic troubadour of our time was Bob Dylan. And soon after *Culture of Protest* was under way, I began to learn that there was at least one Dylan in virtually every country on earth. In Latin America, Victor Jara played that role—and he was part of the continent-wide Nueva Canción (New Song) movement that had its beginnings in Chile in the late 1960s. By the 1980s, musicians throughout Latin America were reviving traditional musical idioms, styles, and instruments and combining these traditional musical expressions with lyrics pertinent to the political—and personal—struggles of contemporary society. A similar sort of fusion was happening across Africa. In Soviet-dominated Eastern Europe and in the USSR, singer-songwriters in the Dylan vein were producing underground cassette tapes that were widely passed around. Wherever collective protest was happening, some sort of musical accompaniment could be heard. My radio show could be an avenue for letting people—especially myself—learn about all this.

It didn't take long for me to learn as well about the ways in which socially conscious music was being created right here in the community. Local activist networks included participants with musical interests and talents; among locals trying to make a livelihood performing were some with political inspiration. Soon people were slipping tapes into my mailbox, and live performance and interviews were not uncommon on the air.

Most important for me was Rob Rosenthal's work. Rob was one of the sociology graduate students with whom I worked closely. Rob had been in a band in his younger years; soon he began to think about how to combine his political/sociological interests with his musical skills. His big idea was inspired by a dramatic episode in labor history: the Seattle General Strike of 1919. Rob and his new life partner, Sunny Banwer, moved to Seattle for a time, and Rob decided with, my enthusiastic support, to write a master's thesis on the strike—particularly focusing on its effects on the community and on the people who'd lived through it. But as that research developed, he added a dimension to the project—to write and produce a rock opera based on the strike. Rob (together with Mike Rawson) ended up writing a couple of dozen songs and formulated a fictional story line. When he and Sunny got back to Santa Barbara, Rob recruited a band of professional musicians in town and self-produced a two-disc album, *Seattle 1919*. It's a superior piece of work, musically and lyrically and, of course, very much a fulfillment of the vision that animates *Culture of Protest*.

Rob and Mike, as his producing partner, did some other political music projects, making two compilations that were released by Folkways Records. Inspired by their work as tenant rights organizers, they collected a set of recordings that reflected tenant struggles past and present, titled *We Gotta Move*. And in the midst of the Reagan years, they reached out to a bunch of political musicians to create an album of anti-Reagan songs.

Rob suggested to me that we co-author a book about music and protest. My own view was that we needed to learn much more than we then knew about the topic—and about the sub-discipline of sociology of music. In the late 1980s, Rob was hired by the sociology department at Wesleyan University. I suggested that, before we tried to do a book, we each start courses at our respective colleges on this theme, thereby forcing ourselves to get immersed in relevant literature and to test out our ideas. Soon we each were teaching a course on music and social movements.

For me, this teaching was an excellent learning opportunity. I required that each student do a class project involving a presentation about some music related to the theme of the course. I may have benefited more than the students, since their presentations gave me the chance to hear and learn about contemporary musical genres that I'd otherwise prefer to avoid—particularly, punk and rap.

Many students did presentations relating to various streams of "DIY" (do-it-yourself). Some were in punk bands, so live performance was a regular feature of the class. This was stuff I could never bring myself to listen to on my own, nor would I dare play it on the air (the station was already well stocked with such programming, and, anyway, my older listeners would certainly turn the program off). I learned a lot about the subcultural formations associated with the music. At the same time, the course influenced quite a few of the punk-oriented kids; many decided right away that Woody Guthrie was the first punk musician—and quite a few of the bands represented in the class became more conscious of political themes. One student was Steve Aoki (now a superstar in the electronic, house, and dance world). Steve formed a band, while he was a student in the class, called This Machine Kills (taking the name from the inscription on Guthrie's guitar—"This machine kills fascists"), and one of their songs is titled "Culture of Protest."

There were of course representatives of hip-hop culture in the array of class presentations over the fifteen years that the class persisted, and, as well, a wide range of feminist performance efforts were displayed. I was never persuaded during all those years that either the esthetic or the political expressions embodied by these forms worked all that well—if one was judging the songs in terms of their potential for fostering social movement. These genres were powerful as expressions of collective identity; indeed, sometimes students in their presentations would point out that the subculture that formed the bands and their audiences was more important than the music itself for raising social consciousness among fans.

My main teaching in the course was rooted in what I call Pete Seeger's project. In those years—from roughly 1992 to 2006—hardly any students, when they entered the class, knew who Seeger was (though many realized they knew some of his songs). Both his biography and his musical work, of course, are wonderful pedagogical resources, bearing on all kinds of issues having to do with culture and politics, the personal and political.

For me, the heart of the Seeger project was his effort to get audiences to actively appreciate and use the power of song. Seeger's concerts were not primarily displays of his own virtuosity. They were moments for collective expression—teaching new songs for mass singing, getting the audience to harmonize, to feel empowered by their collective capacity to make beautiful sound. Contemporary popular music seems to me mostly about the performers and the performance. Even if audiences participate with bodily movement and sometimes sing along, I think it's rare these days to hear

FIGURE 15.2. Dick with Pete Seeger, Vancouver Folk Festival, 1989 (Photo by Leni Wildflower)

songs that can be taken up, learned, and sung by ordinary people. And yet from a social change point of view, songs are the most democratic art form—*a song doesn't require a skilled performer to be reproduced.* Songs have power, fusing ideas and feelings (as Yip Harburg liked to say) as they are taken up, remembered, and sung in everyday life. Plenty of such song making still goes on in the commercial genres called folk, Americana, country, and so forth. And some star performers, as they have tried to make music that would be politically pertinent, have used Seeger as a model. Bruce Springsteen made special homage to him in his *Seeger Sessions* recordings and tour. Tom Morello of Rage Against the Machine has been writing and singing union songs and other acoustically based protest songs in contrast to his punk rock beginnings. It seems that the unadorned creating and singing of songs that can be transmitted and sung by ordinary folk is a constantly recurring cultural practice as social movements reach the point of mass mobilizing.

Rob Rosenthal and I finally wrote the book. It's called *Playing for Change: Music and Musicians in the Service of Social Movements.*[3] It was mostly written by Rob, and a large part of it is based on interviewing he did with a considerable array of working, movement-oriented, musickers (a data-gathering process that lengthened the time it took to finish the book!). It turned out to be something of a how-to manual for those who want to play for change—exploring in detail the sorts of things you need to think about if you want to make a difference as a performer.

These days, I am still getting a lot of satisfaction from putting on the weekly radio show. Doing the program gives me the incentive to keep up with what is being created culturally in relation to social movement (and it allows me to buy recordings and get a tax deduction!). Since I'm no longer teaching courses, the radio show is my main regular opportunity to do a kind of teaching, hoping that there may be a listener, but, even if not, getting some new knowledge for myself each week.

I'm often asked why I don't try to get the show broadcast beyond the local station. I would have to devote much more time and energy to it if I wanted to try to get some kind of national opportunity. A script would have to be written, the production values would have to be far better (professionally engineered). I've always preferred to stay local in most of what I do. Teaching in a classroom is a local activity—and one where you're face-to-face with those with whom you're trying to communicate. I've always said that I measure the value of my teaching by imagining that, each hour, there's one student in the room who might be touched by one idea. I've had a similar aspiration for the radio program—imagining a listener who has a moment of inspiration or pleasure from what's coming over the radio. Nowadays, Internet streaming, in fact, makes it possible to be heard everywhere on the planet—and very recently it's become possible for people to link to past broadcasts as well. I guess I'm hoping that if you read this, you'll give a listen yourself![4]

When Mickey and I were growing up, the music we were immersed in was "ours"—a cultural world that seemed very separate from mainstream taste and values. The Weavers' popularity—and then the 1960s explosion of folk-influenced, politically tinged music—was an exhilarating validation of our once marginalized culture. When Pete Seeger turned ninety, the birthday was celebrated by a huge Madison Square Garden concert, which Mickey and I traveled to—and we paid a good deal of money to get seats right down in front. I guess we felt that it wasn't just Seeger being celebrated: it was our cultural/political identity that was now demonstrably significant in the shaping of American culture.

What that might signify for the future of the society, we have no idea. Maybe the meaning of all this was crystallized by Langston Hughes: "Let America be America again." It's a good statement about what we've always wanted, which we seriously doubted could ever be when we were kids in the McCarthy years and which sometimes seems a little closer to possibility now that we're old (and yet a very dark America certainly looms).

MICKEY:

While I certainly shared with Dick the connection to Pete Seeger, Bob Dylan, et alia, on New Year's Eve, 1999, the turn of the century, I felt the need of a more universal statement of our values. When I was a young adolescent, I remember sitting and trying to imagine what the turn of the century would be like, and would I live to see it; after all, to a kid, sixty years old seems ancient! Also, I liked the notion that I would be "dead on the barricades" by age thirty. . . . So we celebrated that momentous evening at home with some good friends, while the City of Santa Barbara prepared a fireworks display at midnight, which was visible from our upstairs balcony. I pondered what I would choose for our own midnight moment, and I asked Dick to cue up the "Ode to Joy" from Beethoven's Ninth. At the stroke of midnight (Pacific standard time) the glorious sounds burst forth from our home speakers, and I felt that a new century had begun for us in the best possible way. . . .

# 16 ▸ SOME THINGS WE'VE LEARNED ABOUT WHAT'S LEFT

DICK:

The slogan "Think globally, act locally" has defined our style of activism in the nearly half century since we moved to Santa Barbara.

By 1970, those of us at the older edge of the sixties movement were getting beyond youth, figuring out how to live and act in the long term and how to settle in and down. What could be done to advance the "New Left" project beyond its campus base to build a politics relevant to the wider society? One key to an answer: to live and work so as to advance democracy in the workplaces and neighborhoods and community institutions in which we were making our families.

It's a way of doing politics in which one's actions are intimately connected to the actual people who live by your side. But what we do locally, we believe (based on both faith and evidence), is a small piece of a worldwide mosaic of locally based movements and struggles for democracy, justice, and rationality.

A central thread of this book has to do with our effort to figure out how to be politically engaged ("making history") and, at the same time, live lives of love for kith and kin ("making blintzes"). "Acting locally and thinking globally" justifies that balance both as a moral imperative and as an effective strategy for social change.

BUT—"Think globally, act locally" evades some very big questions about power and about the possibilities for change. For if the biggest decisions about the course of history are made by global and national corporate and political elites, how effective can locally based efforts be in moving society in directions these power elites are opposed to?

Our friend Jeremy Brecher argues that the primary strategy for anti-globalization activists resembles the Lilliputians' success in tying down the giant Gulliver. Thousands of Lilliputian communities and grassroots movements render the giant helpless—and make the space and time for a new order to grow and to create a new global order.

What are the chances of this strategy in the face of accelerating climate change, wars that uproot millions, profound dangers to people's access to water and food? The frightful warnings about the impending future that are encoded in every day's news inevitably challenge the relevance of the day-to-day politics we do compared with the scale and speed of threats to human life.

One way of coping is to practice some "denial." Denial, in fact, is a mindset necessary to go on living. Mildred Flacks, my mother, explaining how she lived rather cheerfully with terminal cancer, told me that what you do is get up each day and live that day. This seems good advice for anyone getting old, since all of us are terminal, after all. And it is a fair description also of how we have to act in the political field.

Most of us on the left act politically a good deal of the time because we want to do the right thing—whether or not what we are doing will be practically effective. We act out of conscience—to speak out, to bear witness, to "speak truth to power," to fight the good fight. If we are facing forms of repression and tyranny or mass fear and hysteria or collective complacency, courageous dissent and self-sacrificing protest by saving remnants can save the republic. In America, radicals, despised in their lifetimes, eventually get honored, because, very often, it was they who kept reason and freedom alive in the times that tried souls. So morally based action that appears ineffectual can actually make history in powerful ways.

We've seen this firsthand over our years.

Young communist immigrant agitators like Sonia Hartman, Mickey's mother, experienced a lot of bitter defeat, but they helped pave the way for strong unions and the welfare state. Reds like my parents who refused to cooperate with the McCarthy-era inquisitions lost their jobs—but finally won their cases both legally and in the eyes of history—and thereby widened the meanings of freedom of speech. The weird and isolated pacifists who went to jail rather than be drafted during World War II, or who tried to stop nuclear tests with their own bodies in the 1950s, seemed to have no effect on the military policies they suffered to stop—yet they were prophets of nonviolent resistance that enabled the sixties movements against war, racism, and colonialism.

Gandhi and King and A. J. Muste showed how small groups engaged in moral disobedience can think strategically even as they act out of their hearts. "Nonviolent direct action" describes the way little bands of morally engaged actors can make history without having, or seeking, power over others. It describes forms of action totally opposite to "terrorism" (which also alludes to small bands of people trying to make history). It seems that most of our generation of New Leftists (some of whom at some point had gravitated to or contemplated terrorism in the late 1960s and early 1970s) came eventually to understand the power of nonviolence (after many at one point had dismissed it in favor of "armed struggle").

Now, forms of civil disobedience and nonviolent direct action are powering effective grassroots movements across the globe. The very term *occupied* used by the grassroots movement against Wall Street and corporate power makes that clear. #BlackLivesMatter, the rising struggle of low-wage workers, and anti-fracking and anti–fossil fuel protests—to name just a few of the mass protests addressing national and global issues—are making history by opening gateways to new social direction during the very time we've been writing this.

## THE SOCIALIST DREAM

DICK:

The socialist movement, from its earliest enunciations, envisioned a transformative politics aimed at creating a society in which the working people would be in charge of the economy, exercising political power through genuinely democratic government and economic power through various forms of public (i.e., democratic) control of the organizations that produced and distributed the means of daily life. The socialist movement in nineteenth-century Europe struggled for political rights for disenfranchised workers and created, in countries where workers had some voting rights, political parties that competed in the electoral arena. These parties claimed to represent the working class, in partnership with labor unions.

In the twentieth century, labor and Social Democratic parties got power in many places, and, in most countries, such parties had large popular support whether or not they led governments. But, over the 170 years since Karl Marx and Friedrich Engels wrote the *Communist Manifesto* predicting the empowerment of the working class, these popular Social Democratic parties were never able to replace private control of the economy. Failing that, and largely abandoning or postponing that transformative goal, their programs emphasized expanding the "social wage"—providing society's members with the right to the basic necessities of life, without regard to income.

The Communist parties in Russia and China, in Asia and Eastern Europe also claimed to represent the working class. They took power through various uses of force (most legitimately as in China, Cuba, and Vietnam by leading armies of peasants and workers to take over the state, kick out foreign occupiers, and take full control of the society). The communist-led governments did enact state ownership of the economy. But these states did not represent achievements of worker self-government, and workers were as exploited in these regimes as in capitalist ones. At first, the Soviet and Chinese Communist parties tried to promise that present sufferings would be overcome and the promise of the socialist vision would come to pass. In Eastern Europe, however, such parties went out of business and the Soviet Union disintegrated—to be replaced by weird hybrids of private enterprise, kleptocratic oligarchy, and authoritarianism. In China and Vietnam, the Communist parties consolidated their political control, while promoting all sorts of capitalism. If socialist vision survives anywhere in that world, you won't find it among the "official" Communists.

The argument that socialism was an impossible dream fits the above historical narrative. In SDS, we never made *socialism* our goal. We thought the word carried a lot of negative baggage, especially for Americans—and that using it blocked creative thinking about the kind of society we wanted.

*Participatory democracy* was the term the late Tom Hayden employed and that SDS promoted in the Port Huron Statement.

*Participatory democracy* is an awkward term. It's hard to say, and you couldn't use it in a song or poem. But rightly understood, it encourages thinking about the future society and also about how to remake social institutions in the here and now. All social relations—both macro and micro—should enable everyone to participate in making the decisions that affect them. This idea underlies much of the mass movement of our time. It's the common thread that ties the Lilliputians to each other.

The New Left wanted to revive a transformative social vision, but we understood, for the most part, that the process of "getting from here to there" was probably evolutionary and incremental, that no single scenario could define it, and that the process would be endlessly experimental. We were anarchists as well as Socialists, radical Democrats, and libertarians, wanting to fuse all these radical streams into a new practice for the Left. At the same time, we rejected all ideological labels.

After the 1960s, New Left rejection of established models was confirmed by the course of history. Communist parties collapsed along with the disintegration of the Soviet bloc. In Europe, the established Social Democratic parties, once the political homes of most workers, have been unable, for the most part, to protect past gains. Those gains were deliberately undermined by both neoliberal policy and economic globalization.

The established socialist parties were unable and even uninterested in dealing with the wreckage of working-class-based communities and the precariousness experienced by the rising generation. Right-wing populism provides an avenue of worker resistance, targeting alien others as the main threat. This populism wins an electoral base because of the vacuum left by the decline of the old Social Democratic and Communist parties. But the New Left of the 1960s failed as well to anticipate these times. Fifty plus years after our "New Left" came into being, the times cry out again for another New Left that can counter the appeal of racist authoritarianism with vision, plans, and strategies.

As we finished writing, the primary sign of this next Left was expressed by the Bernie Sanders for President movement in the United States and its aftermath. The Sanders campaign paralleled developments in Europe: new parties in Greece, Spain, and Italy and the grassroots movement to transform the British Labour Party. One new thing about both these European happenings and the Sanders campaign was the astonishing popular support they got for efforts that explicitly aimed at displacing established politicians and speaking to the situation of the young. And, surprisingly, speaking about socialism contributed to that popular surge.

## FEELING THE BERN

DICK:

The Sanders experience is a big deal for us—for our New Left generation. Sanders is one of us, with the difference that, in his college years and after, he continued to identify as a Socialist, even as SDS, and the New Left generally, found the label an intellectual and political burden. Everybody knew that in America you couldn't win elections with that label, even if you felt ideological allegiance to it (which we in the New Left didn't necessarily feel). When Sanders began to win as a Socialist running for mayor, Congress, and the Senate, we said, "Well, of course, in Vermont"—where everyone is an expatriated hippie.

But he ran in the Democratic presidential primary using that label and was unafraid of saying that the campaign was about a "political revolution." Had he won the nomination, he would have had a big struggle with those labels to win the general election, or so says conventional political wisdom. Yet Sanders was one of very few national politicians with majority popular approval.

We need to know a lot more about what *socialism* means nowadays and to whom. It seems that many in the under-forty part of the population, like their peers in Europe, are ready to get past "capitalism." It seems likely that Sanders's acceptance of the socialist label helped make him an authentically different, actually trustworthy, politician. Had he backed away from the label after having declared himself a Socialist for decades, he would have generated a lot of cynicism and wouldn't have appeared much different from dozens of other reasonably liberal senators.

At the same time—and this was brilliant—the program he espoused was an agenda of reforms *that the majority of Americans supported already*. If universal Medicare, free tuition, a $15 minimum wage, massive infrastructure investment, and higher taxation of the super-rich equal socialism, the majority of Americans seemed to want to hear about it.

Equally brilliant was Sanders's strategy of running as a Democrat and continuing to work in the Democratic Party. There were some "Berners" and other lefties who thought that a truly radical electoral strategy would have been to create a new, "non-corporate" party instead of joining a party that is corporate controlled and corrupted, "neoliberal," and, some even say, no different from the GOP. That, for example, seemed to be the message Jill Stein was expressing in her Green Party presidential campaign. It's an argument that says it's evil to vote for the lesser evil, and you'll feel a lot better morally if you vote Green, because you'll be voting for what you really want instead of for half measures and worse. That sort of moralistic "go with your gut" talk has always had appeal to people on the left. Thankfully, Bernie Sanders had a better way.

## HOW WE BECAME DEMOCRATS

DICK:

Our own experience has given us a way to think about this perennial left-wing debate. When we were growing up in New York, we were raised to believe in the American Labor Party. Created in the 1930s by several New York–based unions, the American Labor Party had strong Communist Party support. It was created, however, not as an alternative to the Democratic Party of Franklin D. Roosevelt and the New Deal but as a way for hundreds of thousands of left-wingers in New York to vote for Roosevelt without having to pull the Democratic lever. The New York Democratic Party was the epitome of machine politics. It was the party of Tammany Hall. Ending its local power was necessary for change. The most popular mayor in New York history, Fiorello La Guardia, originally ran as a Republican for Congress—running to the left of the Democrats. New York electoral law, unlike the rules in most other states, permitted independent parties to endorse candidates of other parties. Small parties had to have a certain level of support in statewide races to stay on the ballot, but it was not a high threshold. In 1936 the newly formed American Labor Party garnered hundreds of thousands of votes for FDR and for La Guardia for mayor. So our experience was that a third party could be a useful progressive vehicle, provided it could endorse and help elect the major parties' candidates who were supportive of its platform (rather than taking votes away from such candidates).

The American Labor Party grew for a while and was able to support its own candidates for Congress—especially La Guardia's congressional successor in Spanish Harlem, the charismatic and outspoken Vito Marcantonio (or "Marc," as he was known to his constituents). Marcantonio was a hero to both of us when we were kids.

MICKEY:

In 1952, when Marcantonio ran for mayor of New York, election day was blustery cold. I had agreed to stand near (but greater than one hundred feet from) our neighborhood polling place (my elementary school, Public School 76) to hand out "Marc for mayor" leaflets. My winter coat was a navy-type "pea jacket," made of rough wool, and after a few hours, my neck soon became chapped from the cold wind and the friction of the coat. A neighbor of ours came by and saw bedraggled me. She took pity and told me to come with her for some hot chocolate. "But I have to give out these leaflets!" I protested. "So you'll come back afterward—nobody will blame you . . . ," she assured me. I reluctantly went with her—and returned after about a half hour. That night, before bed, I whispered (to myself): "If there is a God (capitalizing the word in my mind), please let Marc become mayor!" That was the first and last time I uttered something like a prayer. . . . Maybe if he had won, I would have become a rabbi!

DICK:

We named our second son Marc, in his memory.

The potency of independent party politics in New York was enhanced by the fact that the New York City Council was elected by proportional representation. This was based on European parliamentary models: parties were allocated council seats on the basis of their percentage of the popular vote. In our childhood, the American Labor Party had a number of council seats; two council members, Ben Davis from Harlem and Pete Cacchione from Brooklyn, openly represented the Communist Party itself.

Fusion candidacies and proportional representation were mechanisms that enabled third parties to count politically—and to this day, New York state politics is in part shaped by the continuing presence of the Liberal, Conservative, and Working Families parties (the last one a descendant of the American Labor Party). These smaller parties make their own compromises; none are outstandingly principled in their endorsements—but, at least in theory, they provide sizable constituencies with a chance to advance certain issues that the major parties have avoided. In the height of the Cold War, proportional representation was abolished in New York precisely to get rid of the communist councilmembers (despite the fact that they both had substantial followings). And Marcantonio, after serving five terms representing Spanish Harlem in Congress, was defeated by a candidate endorsed by both the Democrats and the Republicans. He outpolled each of these parties but couldn't overcome their combined effect. In the Red Scare climate of the 1950s, the American Labor Party was unable to mount effective statewide candidacies and ultimately lost its ballot position.

In 1948 the American Labor Party in New York linked itself to a national third-party effort. The Progressive Party was called into being by the decision of former vice president Henry A. Wallace to run for president against incumbent and unpopular Harry Truman. Truman, a moderate Missouri senator, was picked by the conservative wing of the Democratic Party to replace Wallace as vice president in 1944 (with many expecting that FDR might not live out the fourth term that he was sure to win). Wallace was given a cabinet post; when Truman took office, he fell under the sway of that side of the American governing class that was against maintaining a postwar continuation of the wartime alliance with Stalin. Soon after the war, Truman was announcing policies hostile to the USSR, including military investment in Greece and Turkey, an American monopoly on the atomic bomb (which Truman had used at Hiroshima and Nagasaki in order to show Stalin our might). Meanwhile, the Red Army occupied Eastern Europe and installed Communist parties to head the new governments in the region. The Cold War was on, and Wallace, in the cabinet, was publicly attacking Truman's policies. He resigned to wage a presidential campaign calling for a U.S.-Soviet peaceful alliance that would accept a Soviet sphere of influence and advocating, among other things, universal health care and a broad civil rights program.

The new party was a magnet for the anti–Cold War Left—with Communists in the forefront. Both Mickey and I were each strongly affected by the Wallace movement, even though we were under ten years old. It was unforgettable to see thousands in my Brooklyn neighborhood pack the streets when Wallace came to speak. Everyone around us was for him! Polls had predicted that he'd get at least 10 percent of the vote. But his candidacy profoundly split the liberal wing of the Democratic Party. Few unions were willing to back him in spite of his pro-labor stance, because of the Red taint he bore and because his candidacy would, if supported, lead to a GOP victory after years of national Democratic domination that had ushered in a period of labor organization not seen before or since. Truman virtually adopted the Wallace domestic program (including national health insurance) and coupled that to a virulently anti-communist attack on him. In the end, Wallace got only 2.5 percent of the national vote. I remember our upstairs neighbor, Mrs. B, coming home to tell Mildred, my mother, in embarrassment that in the booth she couldn't bring herself to pull the lever for Wallace—because, she had realized, it would elect Thomas Dewey (the much disliked Republican).

What Mrs. B told my mother illustrates the basic flaw in the strategy of creating a left-wing national party, given the structure of federal-level balloting. There may well be times and places where, at a local level, running under the banner of a new political force can be a very effective part of a political strategy. But at the presidential level, it's a tremendous waste of energy and sometimes can seem to be a criminal mistake (as when Ralph Nader's campaign drew enough votes in Florida to allow George W. Bush to win the electoral vote and, eventually, undertake the Iraq invasion).

We're convinced that the necessary electoral strategy for the Left is to work systematically to try to transform the Democratic Party. The Democratic Party, at its base, is not simply beholden to corporate interests. It's a decentered, loosely organized thing, whose active supporters are, all over the country, very likely to be hungering for a far-reaching progressive agenda. Many Democratic activists, old as well as young, would, in Europe, be left-wing Social Democrats.

Many opportunities exist at local and state levels to challenge and defeat existing leaderships, to run alternative candidates, to build the grassroots base, and to create arenas for a new vision and program. The party bureaucracy bears a lot of responsibility for the ways that the party has lost its ability to effectively reach white working-class folk, but many of these established leaders would welcome coalition with Sandersistas and a progressive agenda. Sanders showed that campaign money can be raised without depending on wealthy and corporate donors. His campaign energized a grassroots army, and many of these people tried to figure out how to transform the party from the ground up. One of the more hopeful things was the energy, creativity, and effectiveness of this army—despite some rancorous infighting.

This sort of strategy has been advocated by leftists ever since the FDR years. Some people seem to believe that it's a strategy that has failed; but, in fact, it has never been tried as a serious national drive.

Instead, efforts to make the Democratic Party a progressive force have been fragmented. In the thirties and forties, the CIO unions determinedly began to reshape the party in several states and worked, with mixed results, to influence national party platforms and campaigns.

In the aftermath of the sixties, the major progressive social movements worked to gain comparable influence and power within the party, compelling it to promise (if not always deliver) commitment to racial equality and justice, immigrant rights, and feminist, environmentalist, and gay liberation agendas. Successive relatively insurgent candidacies (Jesse Jackson, George McGovern, and Howard Dean) left behind energized individuals who have sought to continue political careers in the party. Party rules have been changed to promote a more diverse leadership and to weaken the power of the old-style entrenched machines.

Still, a concerted strategic effort to make the party genuinely representative of its popular base wasn't tried. Progressives in the past half century have achieved position, shaped the party platform, and built up their caucuses; meanwhile, centrist ideology and wealthy donor preferences have tended to control the party's national identity. Corporate Democrats, influenced by both donors and ideology, are certainly powerful—but hardly invincible.

A new Democratic Party—standing for economic and social democracy—is struggling to be born, in large part because the rising generation won't support what the party has been.

Maybe, someday, a new majority party will come into being—as the result of a major split in the Democratic Party, not because a small number of lefties hoist a flag on the fringe. Working for a real people's party—whether by remaking the Democratic Party or owing to a new party realignment—is a crucial part of a strategy for change. The remaking is the necessary start.

But a new party is not going to solve the dilemmas of political strategy, by any means. We on the left have to face the fact that *no national party anywhere on the planet in all of history has ever been the vehicle for democratic revolution*. All parties, no matter how ideologically perfect they appear, have to compromise in order to gain power. All parties are subject to the bureaucratic self-protectiveness of leaders and professional staff. Any party is going to be internally split, experiencing conflicts fueled by class conflict, moral righteousness, and personal enmities.

Our life experience tells us: be careful what you build, institutionally and organizationally. One of the insights of sociologists is that established organizations routinely drift away from their stated goals and claims. Accordingly, any organization has to be continuously scrutinized, criticized—and, above all, continuously democratized.

Moreover, organizations can become the be-all and end-all of our struggles, seducing us to work for the organization's growth, rather than for real change in the real world. We need to measure the value of our work, not by organizational success, but by whether and how much democracy in the fullest sense is realized in people's everyday experience.

# 17 ▸ TRUMP TIME

MICKEY:

The tragedy of November 2016 happened before we had totally finished this book. I suppose it is incumbent on us, then, to report how his election has influenced our "making history and making life."

I would nominate Donald Trump (or "the Donald") for an award as Organizer of the Year. After standing in a mass of half a million people—of all races, classes, genders, occupations, et cetera—at the Women's March in Los Angeles, and later seeing the millions marching all over the world, I began to consider him for the organizer award. Back in Santa Barbara (where over a thousand people marched), where Bernie Sanders won the primary and Hillary Clinton won 80 percent of the general election vote, hundreds of people were turning out for meetings of a newly formed Progressive Coalition, seeking some work that they could do—all political groupings have grown exponentially. There is a sense of community in opposition and resistance to Trumpism everywhere one goes in town. I have a greater sense of possibilities for measures like rent control to be enacted here than I ever sensed before. After a brief mourning period (for the country as a whole), I have regained energy, optimism, and hope. Perhaps the history outlined in this book, the history of our political lives, will help that hope; it is certainly intended to do so.

DICK:

As we finished drafting our book, Trump had been in office about four months. The results of the 2016 election couldn't have been more contradictory for us. Locally, the most progressive slate of candidates we've ever had were elected at every level, from Congress to the county board. The student community of Isla Vista voted to establish a self-governing district—culminating four decades of efforts to win self-rule. In California, progressive ballot initiatives succeeded. That contrasts with the national situation, where an explicitly authoritarian and racist president was elected with both houses of Congress under the control of his party. This crowd ran with explicit intention to roll back hard-won rights and social protections and to reverse the national effort to deal with the increasingly ominous climate change. For a while, I found it hard to get up in the morning, having to face Trump's America.

All manner of dark scenarios present themselves. The darkest ones recall the way that Hitler and the Nazis seized control in Germany: A trumped-up (no pun intended—yet) terrorist act (the Reichstag fire) justifies draconian laws aimed at the alleged perpetrator network, leading to brutal crackdown. Every act of public resistance spurs expanded repression. A fascist mass movement arises that greatly magnifies the control of the regime. Whether or not Trump personally aims for such a scenario, its possibility can't be denied.

Less draconian scenarios revolve around the "normalization" of the regime: Trump and the Republican Congress partner to enact the GOP program: massive tax cuts for the wealthy, mass roundups of undocumented immigrants, deregulation of the corporations, shredding of the safety net, defunding and disempowering "left" institutions (unions, universities, journalism, cities, public broadcasting, etc.)—and all of this treated, by some of the media at least, as politics as usual. If these policies, including the "infrastructure" plan, generate some economic growth, then Trump could well expand his base of popular support in the 2018 and 2020 elections. Meanwhile, the immigrant deportations, the outbursts of hate assaults, grow.

And yet the very plausibility of these scenarios—and the signs that they are under way—has produced some of the most hopeful democratic happenings in our time. All over the place, at the grassroots, creative initiatives of protest began when the election outcome became clear. The first of these to bear fruit was the post-inaugural Women's March. Initiated outside the national organizational structures of protest, the idea of the march was taken up in every part of the country (and much of the world)—and the result was maybe the largest mass mobilizations in American history. That day helped energize a crescendo of activity—the mobbing of congressional offices and airports, the meeting in towns and neighborhoods everywhere of popular assemblies and roundtables, the flocking of new members and money to the ACLU and Planned Parenthood and all kinds of other progressive organizations, the increase in readerships and audiences for legitimate news, the flourishing, in all the arts, of "woke" expression. Is this the start of a great democratic renaissance—this multi-pronged social upheaval that calls itself the "Resistance"?

As Mickey says, Trump may turn out to be the greatest organizer of collective protest we've ever seen. Rather than pursuing a strategy to expand and solidify his power, he finds, every day, a new way to outrage many and undermine his own legitimacy. More than half the people want to see him gotten rid of as soon as possible—but that would require action by GOP congressional leaders and corporate and national security elites.

Nixon was facing impeachment and forced to resign within two years of his landslide victory. Trump was elected by flukery, and his impeachable offenses are added to on a daily basis, in plain view. Many elite voices seem to want to bring him down.

But we don't place our bets on that scenario. It makes more sense to take heart from the rising "civic engagement" and from the signs that the young folks of America, regardless of race, class, gender, and sexuality, are eager for, and engaging in, social and cultural transformation. No matter what happens around the White House, new energies need to pour into remaking the Democratic Party so that it can, in fact, be a vehicle of social reform, in advancing grassroots organizing for resistance, for progressive electoral success, for community development. Some of the work will be coordinated by national structures and strategies—and much will happen out of locally based creative initiative. That no single plan, party, ideology, or leadership will be able to speak for the "Left" is not a weakness but, more likely, a strength.

Almost every day, I have encounters with young folk with remarkable talent and passion for making change. The New Left generation now taking shape seems far more diverse, far more representative of America, than any previous left-wing generation—and less likely to be hung up by ideologically fueled internecine battles. We're constantly impressed and surprised by how little cynicism we hear.

Along with, and inspired by, the rising activism, there's a desperate need for concerted effort to think and talk and dream about "another possible world."

The Sanders project defined a set of policies, favored in polls by strong majorities, that would, if adopted, allow the United States to catch up to European countries in providing the means for a more civilized daily life in advanced industrial society: health care, advanced education, and child care as guaranteed rights for all regardless of income; some redistribution of the wealth, some limit on the political power of the rich; a fair and rational criminal justice system; and large public investment in necessary collective goods—the means of transportation, the replacement of fossil fuel energy, the physical facilities for schooling and health care, and the restoration and preservation of nature. Sanders called this program "socialistic"—and yet his whole program is theoretically accomplishable while maintaining the "private sector." In fact, his program is necessary if "capitalism" has any possibility of working!

Of course, there is no sign that a significant proportion of the power elite is ready for these reforms. In fact, even at the height of the New Deal, at the depths of the Depression of the 1930s, FDR had only a handful of corporate allies. Achieving any semblance of this program—let alone staving off the global impacts of climate change—will require, as Sanders says, a "political revolution."

What Sanders means by this term is that the current surge of progressive activism is sustained and channeled toward achieving a political democracy— a society where the popular voice shapes priorities and policies.

Such a political revolution and its policy goals, if reasonably accomplished, would be the beginning of the transformations necessary for a better world. The actually existing world is defined by enormous inequality in life chances and power, beset by massive investment in unsustainable means of production, where most people have little or no say in making the rules and decisions that shape their lives. Is another world possible? Not unless there is now more serious attention to the "next system."

At Port Huron, we began to recognize the crucial role that the universities have in shaping the future. Now, more than ever, they provide unique space for the systematic study and debate of next-system questions. Can there be a new student movement that, partnering with professors, can make creative use of that space?

We're pushing toward our eighties. We hope to outlive the Trump time. We love it when people imagine that we have some wisdom based on our years and our experience, and so we try sometimes to seem as if we do. We're excited by our grandkids' occasional interest in our stories. And equally by your interest, if you've actually read this far! In the 1960s, we of the then young generation were all too ready to scorn our elders—so we're very pleased not to be suffering that fate now that we're the elders. A lot of elders turn away themselves, mystified or dismayed by what the young ones do or don't know. Patient conversation across the social divides is better than turning away.

As we say on the radio: "Thanks for listening!"

# 18 ▸ LAST WORDS

MICKEY:

Tom Hayden used to joke that the Flackses see the world's beginning and ending at their own front lawn. In some sense, he was right. In moving to Santa Barbara, we learned about "thinking globally and acting locally." The issues we confront—from big oil off our shores to maintaining a high quality of life for a diverse population and not an enclave of the rich, to becoming "fossil-free by '33" (a local slogan and a goal adopted by the city), to making sure the creeks and the flora and fauna are cared for and preserved, to assuring alternative modes of transportation (biking, walking, mass transit), and to expanding participatory democracy so people have more and more control over the decisions that affect their lives—are certainly global in nature, but they are amenable to local situations. Most importantly, the structure of small-city life allows progressives to have an impact that would be far more difficult to achieve in New York or Chicago or Los Angeles. People in Vermont, where all the cities are small, have learned this lesson well and have perhaps the most progressive state in the union.

We have been instrumental in starting a number of community organizations and have served on countless boards. In 2001 we worked to create a countywide organization that spanned both environmental and social justice concerns, called the Santa Barbara County Action Network (SB*CAN*). We realized some years earlier that we needed paid staff in an organization; we couldn't simply rely on volunteers to attend to the myriad details that keep an organization going. SB*CAN* has raised sufficient funds—mostly from its membership base of several hundred, as well as grants from the small group of progressive millionaires whom we are lucky to have in the Santa Barbara community—to keep itself going and to play an important role testifying before various governmental bodies and recruit folks who are anxious to act in the areas joining environmental and social issues. We have learned, over the years, that most people, even progressives, have lives to lead—they must go to work, care for children, make dinner, do the laundry, recreate a bit—in short, make everyday life. The function of progressive organizations is often to provide paid staff who can research issues, go to hearings, testify before governmental bodies, and provide the logistics needed for mass demonstrations. Social movements, like labor unions, learned that lesson early, and union members were permitted to lead every-day lives while the collective power of their union and its staff influenced both their working conditions and national social policy.

In October 2011, SB*CAN* sponsored "A Roast of the Flackses" (as a fund-raiser). It was repeatedly pointed out how many things seem to have started in our living room—a number of organizations, the local alternative news-paper, SB*CAN* itself, and a number of local candidate campaigns. Little does everybody know that the tradition of "happening in our living room" was because we both wanted to be there and didn't want to pay a babysitter. Of such stuff are social action and politics made. . . .

I always loved the cartoon below that appeared in a long-defunct left-wing magazine, accompanying Dick's piece "Making History vs. Making Life," an early precursor of this volume.[1] To me, it didn't indicate "betrayal of the revolution" (as I suspect the artist intended), but showed the realities of life in "hitherto existing society." Before (and after) we can "make revolu-tion (or history)," we must make life; we've eliminated the "vs."

Our entire life has been lived, we believe, in the spirit that our parents bequeathed us: among Yiddish secularists, "a shenere, besere velt" (a finer and better world); in the New Left, "a participatory democracy where ordi-nary people participate in the decisions that affect their lives." And in the fervent hope that we have passed on some of that to our progeny and the future.

FIGURE 18.1. This cartoon accompanied an earlier item that Dick wrote, a piece called "Making History vs. Making Life: Dilemmas of an American Left."

In some way, I think, it is incumbent on those who dream of a better future to attempt to describe what it might be. "Working-class ownership of the means of production," the traditional Marxian definition of *socialism*, is hardly an inspiration or ideal worth fighting for in today's world. But what would a "finer and better world" resemble? Certainly not the old, bureaucratic, tyrannical USSR; or a Third World country like China (once), Cuba, or Vietnam, with their traditions of corruption, histories of conflict, and repression; or the tepid social democracies of Scandinavia, with their homogenous and tiny populations.

I would like to offer some thoughts on what the future SHOULD look like: its watchwords, I believe, should be "democratic control of just about everything"—from family life to the nation's economic system, "participatory democracy" writ very, very large. Here's a small example from the tiny town of Santa Barbara: some years ago a fire on the town wharf all but destroyed many businesses—restaurants and tourist shops—that rented space from the City of Santa Barbara, which owned the wharf. The city council was to negotiate new leases with some of the old and some of new businesses. Public hearings were held, and among the throngs who packed the council chambers a lively discussion ensued about which kind of business the community wanted/needed. It was decided that this prime real estate should not be rented exclusively to upscale restaurants or shops, but that there should be hamburger joints (not franchises!) as well as trinket shops plus a fine restaurant. The city derives rent from the wharf, as well as a percentage of the profits—but revenue was not the only consideration for the community. Its *needs* were to be met, as were those of tourists and business owners. A future worth fighting for would have all planning decisions made the same way—with wide public participation and consideration of many sets of needs.

In fact, I would like to see cooperative ownership of most of the economy be the norm, the default mode. Entrepreneurs would organize investors, who would each own a share of the business—not simply stocks. Each investor would have one vote to elect a board, which would run the business. Many limited equity housing cooperatives in New York City operate on this model, and it seems to work fine. The only problem in New York is that when the mortgage is paid off, the by-laws of the co-op allow sale of the now highly appreciated property, if agreed to by a majority vote of the residents; for now, too many people can only see dollar signs, but it needn't be that way in the future. In fact, the co-ops that house a large number of "progressives" (often former Communist Party members or red diaper babies) voted to maintain their co-op structure and not realize the profit on their homes. (Another manifestation of their values is that if a resident's income increases, he or she agrees to pay a higher rent—for the self-same apartment!) It isn't a "sharing" sensibility that's required; rather, it's simply a sense of communal and community ownership—as demonstrated by the residents of Santa Barbara, whose city owned the wharf. (By the way, the businesses that were discussed by the public were indeed built on the wharf, along with a fine aquarium—donated by yet another Santa Barbara millionaire!)

What is needed, and is in fact missing from all societies today, is the educational preparation for this degree of popular participation. "Civics" courses should be about much more than voting and knowing how many members of Congress there are; they should teach the ethics and provide the tools of participation. Examples should abound in folks' immediate world, from the structure of corporations (also cooperative) to how decisions get made about who does the dishes at home.

I was motivated to think about this when, soon after we came to California, we were driving along a narrow, twisted road in the Sierra Mountains. We were stuck behind a beer truck, going about twenty miles per hour, and after I overcame my frustration, I began to think about where this truck was going. Eventually, it was going to a little store at a fish camp, which sold, essentially, bait and beer. "Comes the Revolution," I said to Dick, "who's going to make sure that a truck delivers beer way up here? How much beer could it deliver? Not very much, I'll bet." I realized that it had to be more than a few pennies of profit (after deducting for the gas and the driver's time) that accounted for that truck. I surmised that the store was owned by the beer distributor's brother-in-law, but "comes the Revolution," it would be the needs of the fisherfolk that counted.

I don't mean to be facetious or flip about such serious matters, but I do think folks should be thinking, talking, and writing about them in terms that will resonate with ordinary people. It IS possible, I believe, to organize a modern, complex society along these lines.

To give another example: We always feel a little bit guilty about living in Santa Barbara (especially when a summertime weather map shows the Southern California coast as the only place in the country with temperate weather and no tornadoes or hurricanes). A little thought, though, and I realized that not everybody wants to live (or even vacation) in Santa Barbara; some folks like mountains or deserts, or tropical waters, or big cities, or whatever Santa Barbara is not. In our computer age, it should be possible to ascertain everyone's preferences (in the census?) and have the computer arrange for everyone to have their first or second choice. I bet, with the proper weighting, it would come out fine for everyone!

I hope we can resolve, then, to think about a future in (basically) realistic terms that value participatory democracy, liberty, equality, and *mentshlekhkeyt* (the Yiddish word for "human decency"). Can we?

DICK:

There's been a lot of good luck that we've had in making our life together. First of all, we found each other. We shared so much when we met—in the ways we saw the world, in the values we were raised to uphold, in our tastes and interests. We were two kids in 1950s America, who needed each other to affirm who we were as individuals, to make for each other a safe haven in what seemed then a pretty hostile world. We were able to complement each other in really important ways. Mickey was a tomboy, hated conventional

femininity, was assertive, loved to drive cars. Me—I did not feel able to fulfill conventional male expectations—bad at sports, physically awkward,
brains not brawn. When we met, I had not learned to drive. So we meshed
very well, Mickey did the driving and took care of the car; we shared
household chores (except she loved to cook and brought to the marriage a
stack of her mother's recipes including one for blintzes). In Ann Arbor, we
set up a comfortable and very standard apartment, liking the idea of being a
real married couple—and readily being seen by the young people around us
as surrogate parents.

We've been married nearly sixty years, and maybe this shared book provides sufficient evidence that the marriage has worked. It's obvious that
we believe in marriage—for us. It's the only social relationship in our culture
that requires men to put another's needs ahead of their own. A marriage
that works, we have thought, has to be built on that mutual caring, not only
for the other person but for the other's needs, and desires, and, especially
for the male partner, modulating or changing one's own. That's not always
easy, of course—very much subject to negotiation and repair work.

Our sons have taught us the value of divorce! Both have had marriages
and produced children with partners whom they eventually had to leave.
Both have found new and far more fulfilling relationships, despite the continuing pain that such rupture causes. For us, the result is now six grandchildren, whose ages at this writing range from ten months to twenty-five years.
No need to tout the pleasures of grandparenting—but we're having our
share. And the grandkids seem to appreciate us (which is always a source of
puzzlement).

In writing this, we haven't thought it appropriate to try to characterize
our offspring. But the work and lives both Charles Wright and Marc Ajay
have constructed appear to us to be creatively carrying forward the traditions we believe we are part of. If you Google Marc Flacks and Charles
Flacks, you can see some of what they are doing, if you're curious. They
should write their own memoirs!

DICK:

I loved my work as a teacher, which day-to-day of course centered on what
to do in the classroom. Given the chance, as Mickey is wont to point out, I
can talk endlessly, eagerly inspired to tell listeners what they need to know
and think. So, in developing the teaching craft, I worked pretty hard to create courses and pedagogical approaches that would make the classroom a

FIGURE 18.2. At Chuck's wedding, 1988 (Marc, Chuck, Dick, and Mickey). Marc's *"dreadlachs"*—as we called them—vanished after his college graduation

forum rather than a lecture hall. I think that in the 1960s and 1970s, you could draw student followings in sort of a guru fashion—and that was surely gratifying. But in the decades after, I was intrigued to see that a lot of students were pretty eager to hear each other and less likely to expect professorial pontification.

One very validating feature of post-retirement is the frequency with which former undergraduates—many of whom I barely knew—will send messages of appreciation or simply connection. In my case, I think this is because my classes provided occasions for some students to clarify their political perspectives, connect dots, and get some analytic tools for figuring out the world. It's a big reward for a teacher to be told by former students that some of that remains of use for them (even if they likely have reshaped to their own use what they think I said). And, incidentally, Facebook is a rather terrific setup for transmitting the memories and messages.

But the deepest gratifications from teaching resulted from being a mentor—and forming lifelong friendships with students, both undergraduate and graduates. Some of our best and closest friends were once students. I've worked closely with dozens of students on their graduate research and in helping them figure out their professional identity—and, of course, what's gratifying about those relationships is the work they have done. Some of that has been collaborative—in fact, a great deal of what I've written has been the product of research largely done by student partners. My goal as a graduate teacher wasn't, of course, about making disciples— but rather I hoped that I could encourage new generations of academics to fulfill C. Wright Mills's vision of sociology as a tool for sustaining democratic publics (not a domain for esoteric discourse).

I love the fact that some important leaders and organizers in today's social movements were people I'd taught and mentored. I never personally thought I should be credited with what they became—but when they give such credit, I don't mind accepting some. Back in the mid-1960s, I felt a lot of moral pressure to give up my academic path and become an organizer. Mickey—and some of our SDS friends—insisted that I stay on the academic path. Over time I came to feel that one could, as a professor, define oneself as a participant in the training, caring, and feeding of organizers.

Indeed, as Mickey says, one point of this book is to show that the full-time and single-minded organizer/activist identity isn't necessarily the best standard for defining serious political engagement. Social change seems to require such work. But movements defined by the perspective of the most committed activists can risk losing connection with the everyday needs and perspectives of the people to and for whom they claim to be speaking. Our experience tells us that, in the long run, not only do social movements need connection to everyday people, but they need to enable activists to have the chance to make families, and pursue personal interest, and mow the lawn. Those bent on making history without honoring the values embedded in ordinary life become dangerous to living things.

# ACKNOWLEDGMENTS

The idea of this book was generated in Middletown, CT, where we were breakfasting with our friend, Charles Lemert, a sociologist at Wesleyan University, and where our son, Marc, was a junior.

"You two should write a book. Together," said Charles. "About your lives. About politics and everyday lives." He was editor of sociology series for several publishers, and immediately sent us a contract. We never found the time or will to fulfill that contract but the idea kept nagging.

Back in Santa Barbara, our friend, Harvey Molotch, immediately named it: "Making History and Making Blintzes." We all laughed. . . .

Over the years, we thought and talked a little about it, but we were, in fact, too busy making history and everyday life to do any writing. When Dick retired in 2006 (Mickey had already retired in 2002), we began to think seriously about it when we bid successfully at a fundraising auction for a week's stay at a vacation house in Cambria, CA, a beach town, some miles up the coast. We called Don and Kathy Scott, owners of the house, and arranged a time in June 2008 for us to stay for a week. We began the book.

Subsequently, we visited our friends, William and Zelda Gamson, who were living on Martha's Vineyard in a lovely house which they had designed. They had recently built a smaller guest house on their property, and they invited us to stay in the big house during the off-season. We did. Twice. The space and encouragement provided by these friends made this book possible. (We also took some weeks in Hawaii "to write"—which we did. For us, beach communities make great "writer's retreats.")

Early in the writing, we accepted an offer from Marc Rosin, a former student and dear friend who is a professional editor, to do a close read of what we'd drafted. As the writing progressed, various friends would say they couldn't wait to read it. These declarations, whether or not sincere, we seized on, and asked a number of people with editorial experience to review some or all of what we had. We were blessed to have such help from Joan Wallach Scott (who shares some of our childhood history), Peter Dreier (who was particularly generous with feedback), Paul Lauter (a close friend and comrade), Patrick Sheehan (who stood in for the entire millennial generation), and Steve Wasserman (who gave some invaluable guidance on finding a publisher).

Director of Rutgers University Press Micah Kleit's enthusiasm for this project meant that we actually had to deliver it. We hope the result validates the support he and Rutgers have provided.

Among the host of reasons we have for being grateful to our sons is that they have provided us with a wonderful set of grandchildren: Chuck's Maurice and Olivia; Marc's Alison, Marlena, David and Sam. They range in age from two to twenty-five. They provided us with reasons for writing this book, so that they'd be able to see how we understood and refashioned the legacy we received from our parents, passing on, as we say at the Passover seder, *l'dor v'dor*, from generation to generation.

# NOTES

## CHAPTER 1    SONIA HARTMAN

1. Emanuel S. Goldsmith writes that "the Bund viewed its constituents primarily as members of the international proletariat and only secondarily as part of the Jewish populations of their respective countries. . . . The Bund could not, however, remain oblivious to the rising tide of nationalism that was sweeping Europe and attracting more and more of the Jewish masses in the form of Zionism." Emanuel S. Goldsmith, *Modern Yiddish Culture* (New York: Fordham University Press, 1987), p. 80. The Bund eventually embraced the idea of Jewish cultural (as distinct from state-based national) autonomy, distinct from simply a religious community. As it sought to define the concept of extraterritorial national autonomy within the socialist movement, the Bund often encountered hostility on the part of the Russian Social Democratic Party—which it left, and it declared itself an independent party in 1903. It retained its autonomy when it rejoined the Russian Social Democratic Party in 1906, continuing to struggle against both Jewish assimilationist intellectuals like Leon Trotsky and the growing Zionist movement. It saw the future of a liberated Jewry not in Palestine (or some other distant territory—the British offered Uganda!) but in a new revolutionary Russia, one that would recognize the national rights of Russia's minorities. It also played a critical role in the development of Yiddish as a Jewish language, suitable for both home life and revolution. Vladimir Kosovsky (1870–1941), one of the architects of the Bundist program, observed: "The Bund helped develop the Yiddish language, Yiddish literature, the Yiddish school, all the elements of modern Yiddish culture. It proclaimed and strove on behalf of explicit political demands. In short, all of its work was such as to maintain and develop the Jewish nation as a community of culture." Quoted in Goldsmith, *Modern Yiddish Culture*, p. 84. Modern Yiddish, therefore, and Jewish secular identity developed within the context of the Russian revolutionary movement, with the Bund's insisting on both its Jewish and revolutionary identity.

As the new century unfolded and the mass migration of Eastern European Jews to the United States was in full flood, the amalgam of revolutionary socialist ideas (and practice) with Jewish, Yiddish-based, secularism began to take root in the New World. Chaim Zhitlovsky (1865–1943) was the principal theoretician and architect of Jewish socialism, nationalism, and radical secularism in the twentieth century. He held and preached a doctrine that explicitly opposed Zionism as a bourgeois, almost anti-Jewish, movement and sought a future in whatever land Jews found themselves, where Jews would retain their identity as a people, a "nation" defined by its culture (and Yiddish language), and would participate in the international proletarian struggle for socialism. As Jews, Jewish Socialists would look forward to the establishment of an international organization of Jewish workers that would both protect the interests of Jewry and help the nations among which the Jews lived to attain socialism and freedom. In the free socialist community of the future, Jewish culture would flower along with all other cultures. If the world eventually became one nation, and distinct national cultures ceased to exist, Jews, too, would lose their individuality; until then, however, the Jewish cultural nation would continue to exist as an equal among all other nations. "Cosmopolitanism," Zhitlovsky wrote, "has missed the fact that there are many branches of culture which each people expresses in a different national way but which are nevertheless all equally human, all of equal value and can all possess the same degree of truth, justice, beauty and human dignity. For that reason, there is no sense in demanding of any people that it cease to be a people and become 'human.' In all mankind there is no form in which an aspect of culture expresses itself that has more of a right to a people's love than its own national form." Quoted in Goldsmith, *Modern Yiddish Culture*, p.178. Zhitlovsky found that in Jewish cultural heritage—the Bible, the Talmud, rabbinic literature, medieval Jewish philosophy, Hebrew poetry, mysticism, Hasidism, Haskalah (Jewish Enlightenment) literature, and modern Hebrew and Yiddish writing—could be found a basis and relevance for modern struggles. Lack of familiarity with this heritage was proof not of a Jew's humanity, said Zhitlovsky, but of a Jew's ignorance. Zhitlovsky held that abandoning one's own nationality in favor of some universal ideal of "humanity" was to surrender to the chauvinism of a more dominant foreign nationality. "The more human a Jew became, the more Jewish he became"; love of one's own culture was an expression of one's humanity. Quoted in Goldsmith, *Modern Yiddish Culture*, p. 177. By 1930 Zhitlovsky was writing: "Modern Yiddish secular culture is already a colossal oak tree deserving of equal rights with other cultures; it is our national home which binds the entire people together, the intellectuals with the masses in one international unity. And as our ability to withstand assimilation grows, we gather strength with which to fight for the principles of progress, for personal freedom and fulfillment, for cultural enrichment, for social justice and equality, for international brotherhood, equal rights for all nations." Quoted in Goldsmith, *Modern Yiddish Culture*, p. 253.

2.  Todd Gitlin and others have denied the possibility that a national/ethnic identity can contribute to the universalistic identity required of the modern proletariat. Todd Gitlin, *The Twilight of Common Dreams* (New York: Metropolitan Books, 1995). To develop an effective unionism, they argue, the identity of *worker*, shared with other workers, must overwhelm the identity of Jew or Finn or black (or woman); otherwise, Gitlin argues, we are left with the impotent "identity politics" of today's American Left and must fail, thereby, to implement the dream of the Enlightenment. This controversy also arose over a century ago, in the late 1800s in the Russian Pale of Settlement. A growing anti-czarist, socialist movement was influencing young Jews in Vilna, Kovno, Grodno, and Minsk, and socialist study circles were established in the 1870s in which illegal literature was read and discussed. Most of these young Jews who were swept into the revolutionary tide abandoned their ties to Judaism and the Jewish people, truly embracing a "universalist identity." Jewry, they believed, would vanish with the revolution and the new world that would inevitably emerge from it. Goldsmith, *Modern Yiddish Culture*, p. 72. A young student at the Vilna Teachers Seminary, Aaron Samuel Lieberman (1845–1880), was the first Jewish Socialist to conceive the idea of a Jewish wing of the international

socialist movement. In order to communicate with the Jewish masses, however, most of whom did not speak Russian or Polish, the vernacular—Yiddish—was developed as a full-fledged language, with its own literature. Morris Winchevsky (1856–1933) began publishing *Dos Poylisher Yidl* (The [Little] Polish Jew) in London in 1884, which was the first printed socialist newspaper to be issued in Yiddish. In 1893 Arkady Kremer (1865–1935), a Jewish Socialist, published a highly influential pamphlet (in Russian), stressing the importance of "agitation" (rather than simply study groups), mass propaganda integrating political and economic problems in terms that workers could understand. Kremer's seminal pamphlet altered the nature of revolutionary activity throughout Russia, but its immediate objective was, in fact, the justification of socialist activity in the Yiddish language among the Jewish working masses of the Pale. In 1897 representatives met in Vilna to establish the Jewish Labor Bund of Russia and Poland, which was instrumental in the founding of the Russian Social Democratic Party the following year.

3. Chaim Zhitlovsky was an outstanding thinker of the Jewish cultural renaissance in the Yiddish language as it developed in the twentieth century. He was a leading theoretician of Jewish socialism, nationalism, and radical secularism and the principal exponent of Yiddishism in Eastern Europe and the United States. Born in a shtetl near Vitebsk in 1865, he was educated there in the gymnasia, where he encountered the works of Karl Marx and Ferdinand Lassalle. He left school to work among Russian peasants. Eventually, he decided to commit himself to work among Jews, and by 1887 he had settled in Zurich, where he published essays in German on the history and philosophy of socialism. In 1892 he was awarded a doctor of philosophy degree by the University of Bern. His thesis was on medieval Jewish philosophy. He began a career of writing and agitating for Jewish participation as a national, cultural entity in the international proletariat and socialist movement. For him, socialism and nationalism were not contradictory, but he saw socialism as the opportunity for every people to develop its own qualities and talents, with all peoples living in peace and none having any special advantage. The meaning of *internationalism*, as Zhitlovsky understood it, was that all peoples were equal, that none were special or "chosen," and that they had to live as brothers and sisters among themselves. He distinguished between a national identity (like Jews) and a land-based nation that the Zionists were seeking. "As important as its own land may be for the life of a nation, it is no more than a condition, a qualification, an aid to life, but not a part of its being in the world. A nation does not consist of water, earth, hills, valleys, forests and fields. . . . The nation consists rather of living people, with a unique body and soul, with different levels of attainment, with attributes and defects—in whom, even with the best microscope, there cannot be found even one grain of sand and soil, even one atom of land." Quoted in Goldsmith, *Modern Yiddish Culture*, p. 172. In 1906 Zhitlovsky arrived in the United States and found that the Eastern European Jewish immigrants were under the influence of an intelligentsia dominated by assimilationist and cosmopolitan ideas. He set out to combat this situation, calling for a synthesis of international socialism and national culture, of political radicalism and Yiddish culturism. He succeeded in altering the thinking of a section of the immigrant intelligentsia and working class to create a radical, culturally Jewish secularism.

## CHAPTER 3   MILDRED FLACKS

1. My mother is featured in several accounts of the New York Teachers Union, and the school wars of that period. These include: Clarence Taylor, *Reds at the Blackboard: Communism, Civil Rights, and the New York City Teachers Union* (New York: Columbia University Press, 2011); Ruth Jacknow Markowitz, *My Daughter, the Teacher: Jewish Teachers in the New York City Schools* (New Brunswick, NJ: Rutgers University Press, 1993); Ellen I. Broidy, "Enforcing the ABC's of Loyalty: Gender, Subversion and the Politics of Education in the New York City Public Schools, 1948–1954," PhD Dissertation, Department of History, University of California, Irvine, 1997.
2. Taylor, *Reds at the Blackboard.*


## CHAPTER 4   THE HOUSE I LIVED IN

1. Songs of struggle became part of the foundation of our shared identity. In Chapter 15, we explore what music has meant for us.
2. An excellent source about Camp Wo-Chi-Ca is June Levine and Gene Gordon, *Tales of Wo-Chi-Ca: Blacks, Whites and Reds at Camp* (Berkeley, CA: Avon Springs Press, 2002). An academic history of leftwing children's camps is Paul Mishler, *Raising Reds* (New York: Columbia University Press, 1999).


## CHAPTER 5   COMING OF AGE IN THE FIFTIES

1. A website with many photos and ephemera from camps Wo-Chi-Ca and /Wyandot can be found at: www.wo-chi-ca.org.


## CHAPTER 6   STARTING OUT IN THE SIXTIES

1. James Miller, *"Democracy is in the Streets": From Port Huron to the Siege of Chicago* (New York: Simon & Schuster, 1987); see page 125 for quoted reactions by participants at the close of the Port Huron convention. Miller's book provides the most detailed account of that event and of the philosophical and personal contexts for the early SDS. Chapter Nine is devoted to our engagement with SDS.
2. Margaret Mead, *Culture and Commitment: The New Relationships Between the Generations in the 1970s* (New York: Columbia University Press, 1978).
3. Lyrics to the "World Youth Song"
> One great vision unites us
> Though remote be the lands of our birth
> Foes may threaten and smite us
> Still we live to bring peace to the earth!
> All who cherish the vision
> Make the final decision:
> Struggle for justice, peace, and goodwill,
> For friendship throughout the world!

Everywhere the youth are singing freedom's song,
Freedom's song, freedom's song.
We rejoice to show the world that we are strong,
We are strong, we are strong!
We are the youth,
And the world acclaims our song of truth!
Everywhere the youth are singing freedom's song,
Freedom's song, freedom's song!

4. On the fiftieth anniversary of the Port Huron Statement, several academic conferences were convened, and several books were issued derived from their proceedings. See Richard Flacks and Nelson Lichtenstein (eds.), *The Port Huron Statement: Sources and Legacies of the New Left's Founding Manifesto* (Philadelphia: University of Pennsylvania Press, 2015); Howard Brick and Gregory Parker (eds.), *A New Insurgency: The Port Huron Statement and Its Times* (Ann Arbor: Michigan Publishing, 2015). The manifesto itself can be found online at http://www.progressivefox.com/misc_documents/PortHuron Statement.pdf. A host of critical documents from SDS's history are online at: http://www .sds-1960s.org/documents.htm.

## CHAPTER 7    OUR SIXTIES: BLOWIN' IN THE WIND

1. "America and the New Era" was never reprinted. A facsimile of the mimeographed statement can be found at: http://archive.lib.msu.edu/DMC/AmRad/americanewera .pdf.
2. See Daniel Katz, Herbert Kelman, and Richard Flacks, "The National Role: Some Hypotheses about the Relation of Individuals to Nation in America Today," *Peace Research Society (International) Papers* 1 (1964): 113–27.

## CHAPTER 8    OUR SIXTIES: MAKING HISTORY TOGETHER

1. Todd Gitlin and Nanci Hollander, *Uptown: Poor Whites in Chicago* (New York: Harper and Row, 1970).
2. Richard Flacks, "The Liberated Generation: An Exploration of the Roots of Student Protest." *Journal of Social Issues* 23, 3 (1967): 52–75. doi:10.1111/j.1540-4560.1967. tb00586.x.
3. Richard Flacks, Florence Howe, and Paul Lauter, "On the Draft." *New York Review of Books*, April 6, 1967. www.nybooks.com/articles/1967/04/06/on-the-draft.

## CHAPTER 10    OUR SIXTIES: 1968 AND BEYOND

1. Nicolaus' remarks can be found at https://www.colorado.edu/Sociology/gimenez /fatcat.html.
2. See Martin Oppenheim, Martin Murray, and Rhonda Levine, *Radical Sociologists and the Movement: Experiences, Lessons, and Legacies* (Philadelphia: Temple University Press, 1991).

3. The SDS JOIN project is detailed in Todd Gitlin and Nanci Hollander, *Uptown: Poor Whites in Chicago* (New York: Harper and Row, 1970).

4. Janja Lalich, *Bounded Choice: True Believers and Charismatic Cults* (Berkeley: University of California Press, 2004).

## CHAPTER 11    MOVING TO CALIFORNIA

1. Quoted in Los Angeles Times, April 8, 1970. Reagan later claimed he used "bloodbath" as a figure of speech.

2. Louis Lundborg, Future without Shock (New York: W. W. Norton, 1974).

3. Charles Reich, *The Greening of America: How the Youth Revolution Is Trying to Make America Livable* (New York: Random House, 1970); Margaret Mead, *Culture and Commitment: The New Relationships Between the Generations in the 1970s* (New York: Columbia Umiversity Press, 1978, revised edition).

4. Jack Whalen and I produced a book on the Isla Vista rebellion and its effects on participants. See Jack Whalen and Richard Flacks, *Beyond the Barricades: The Liberated Generation Grows Up* (Philadelphia: Temple University Press, 1988). Earlier, in the immediate aftermath of these events, I wrote a short book-length essay that offered a framework—sociological and historical—for understanding the student movement: Richard Flacks, *Youth and Social Change* (Chicago: Markham, 1971).

5. "Summerhill" refers to the famous free school founded by A.S. Neill in the twenties which became iconic in the seventies. Allen Graubard, who moved to Santa Barbara in the late sixties, was a local and national leader of the free school movement. See Allen Graubard, *Free the Children: Radical Reform and the Free School Movement* (New York: Pantheon, 1972).

6. Reagan's quote was widely published in late April 1969, including in the *Santa Barbara News-Press*. A more recent reference can be found in the *Santa Barbara Independent*, May 6, 2006.

## CHAPTER 13    SOCIALISM IN ONE CITY

1. For detailed access to Aperovitz' work, see https://thenextsystem.org/.

2. One of the founders of environmentalism in Santa Barbara has written a detailed memoir of these struggles that provides a readable overview. See Paul Relis, *Out of the Wasteland: Stories from the Environmental Frontier* (Santa Barbara, CA: Community Environmental Council, 2015).

3. John Logan and Harvey Molotch's *Urban Fortunes: The Political Economy of Place, 20th Anniversary Edition* (Berkeley: University of California Press, 2007) is a classic in urban sociology rooted in Molotch's experiences as a participant-observer in Santa Barbara's growth wars.

4. Dorothy Healey and Maurice Isserman, *Dorothy Healey Remembers: A Life in the American Communist Party* (New York: Oxford University Press, 1990).

## CHAPTER 14   CONFESSIONS OF A TENURED RADICAL

1. Jack Whalen and Richard Flacks, *Beyond the Barricades: The Sixties Generation Grows Up* (Philadelphia: Temple University Press, 1989).
2. UCUES continues to this day. For detailed information and archive, see https://www.ucop.edu/institutional-research-academic-planning/services/survey-services/UCUES.html. My work with Scott Thomas on student worlds is summarized in Richard Flacks and Scott L. Thomas, "Outsiders," Student Subcultures, and the Massification of Higher Education." In *Higher Education: Handbook of Theory and Research*, vol. 22, ed. J.C. Smart (Dordrecht: Springer, 2007).
3. The quote is from a radio interview with Ben Wattenberg (http://www.pbs.org/thinktank/transcript235.html) concerning his book: Todd Gitlin, *The Twilight of Common Dreams: Why America Is Wracked by Culture Wars* (New York: Holt, 1991).

## CHAPTER 15   PLAYING FOR CHANGE

1. I wrote an appreciation of Pete Seeger, "Pete Seeger's Project," which was reprinted in Ronald Chen and James Capaldi, *The Pete Seeger Reader* (New York: Oxford University Press, 2014). That volume is an excellent compendium of material by and about Pete Seeger
2. Earl Robinson and Eric Gordon, *Ballad of an American: The Autobiography of Earl Robinson* (Boulder: Scarecrow Press, 1991).
3. Rob Rosenthal and Richard Flacks, *Playing for Change: Music and Musicians in the Service of Social Movements* (Boulder, Colo.: Paradigm Publishers, 2012).
4. There is a Facebook page for the radio show: https://www.facebook.com/CultureOfProtest/.

## CHAPTER 18   LAST WORDS

1. Dick Flacks, "Making History vs. Making Life: Dilemmas of an American Left," *Working Papers for a New Society* 2, no. 2 (Summer 1974): 56–71.

# INDEX

# ABOUT THE AUTHORS

Since this is a memoir, it's ALL about the authors! Some further details:

MICKEY FLACKS is now a white-haired old lady living in a house (built in 1905) in beautiful Santa Barbara. She has worked as a researcher in biology at the University of Michigan and University of California, Santa Barbara; an administrator of survey research projects for the University of Michigan Survey Research Center; as editor of the *Environmental Periodicals Bibliography*; and as a freelance Yiddish translator. She's co-editor (with Mara Vishniac Kohn) of *Children of a Vanished World* (photographs by Roman Vishniac). She could not have imagined, back in 1950, the life she has led. It has been (for the most part) thrilling, intellectually stimulating, emotionally satisfying—mainly because of Dick, the kids and grandkids, as well as all the movements.

DICK FLACKS celebrated his eightieth birthday as this book was going to press. He's been a professor of sociology at the University of California, Santa Barbara since 1969, after teaching at the University of Chicago in the 1960s. Among his books is *Making History: The American Left and the American Mind*. He recently co-edited, with Nelson Lichtenstein, *The Port Huron Statement: Sources and Legacies of the New Left's Founding Manifesto*. His weekly radio program "Culture of Protest" can be heard at kcsb.org.